Sentencing and Punishment

The Quest for Justice

Third Edition

SUSAN EASTON AND CHRISTINE PIPER

OXFORD
UNIVERSITY PRESS

Great Clarendon Street, Oxford, OX2 6DP,
United Kingdom

Oxford University Press is a department of the University of Oxford.
It furthers the University's objective of excellence in research, scholarship,
and education by publishing worldwide. Oxford is a registered trade mark of
Oxford University Press in the UK and in certain other countries

First Edition published 2005
Second Edition published 2008

Impression: 1

British Library Cataloguing in Publication Data
Data available

Library of Congress Cataloging in Publication Data
Data available

ISBN 978-0-19-969353-5

Printed in Great Britain by
Ashford Colour Press Ltd, Gosport, Hampshire

Outline Contents

Part A Sentencing Principles and Policies

Part B Punishing Offenders

Detailed Contents

Part B Punishing Offenders

Preface

Three developments have dominated our updating for the third edition of this text. The first was the result of the change of government in 2010 when the Labour Government was replaced by a Coalition Government with a subsequent loss of of known websites and easily found sources of comparable statistics. The question of access to past policy papers and comparable statistics significantly slowed down the process of research required for this third edition and we would trust that access to, and transparency of, information will soon be restored.

The second development was the public and political debate on sentencing and punishment triggered by the riots which took place in several cities in England in August 2011. This gave a welcome boost to discussion about the justifications for punishment and what counts as a fair and just sentence. However, it also gave rise to misconceptions and, to our mind, injustices when the riot context was given more weight in calculating seriousness than was justified or proportionate in some of the cases reported. Indeed we were prompted to produce our first blogs on the issues that arose.[1]

The third development—the Legal Aid, Sentencing and Punishment of Offenders Bill—was expected but, given that clauses changed in the final months of our editing and that the Bill was not passed before submission of our manuscript, the state of prospective law was still unclear in relation to those aspects to be amended, notably the provisions for dangerous offenders. This is of course a recurring problem with the current plethora of legislation—the Criminal Justice and Immigration Bill was the bête noir for the second edition. However, we have referred to the key provisions in the bill where relevant to our discussion.

The cover of the second edition reproduced Vincent van Gogh's famous picture 'The Round of Prisoners', also known as 'The Prison Courtyard', which shows prisoners walking aimlessly and pointlessly in a circle in the exercise yard at Newgate Prison. The message we wanted to convey was that 'warehousing' offenders without adequate rehabilitation is also pointless as is giving custodial sentences to those for whom a lesser sentence could be justified retributively. The cover of this edition is of a prison hulk and prisoners at work in Woolwich in 1777 and it highlights themes discussed in this book, including the problem of dealing with prison overcrowding at a time of record levels of imprisonment, the provision of constructive activities for prisoners, given the government's commitment to working prisons and the activation of the Prisoners' Earnings Act, and the perennial question of the contribution of prison labour to rehabilitation. We hope, therefore, that the third edition of this book will contribute to the debate on how best to counter the futility of incarcerating an ever larger proportion of the population.

In the last edition we added more material on the impact of sentences on individual offenders and their families. As part of personal mitigation this is still an important issue in relation to the custody threshold and it is also pertinent to prison management especially in relation to older and disabled prisoners and prisoners with young families. We have, therefore, included further discussion on these matters. We have also in the third edition focused in more detail on prisoners' rights, given the recent high profile debates on a prisoner's right to vote, and also on financial penalties because of the relatively new

[1] http://blog.oup.com/2011/08/sentencing-the-rioters/; http://blog.oup.com/2011/09/tough-sentencing/.

approach to calculating fines in the magistrates' courts and because of the increasing use of various fixed penalty notices. In addition, we have expanded our discussion of equality issues in prison to include a broader range of groups. As in the previous editions we have had to make difficult choices as to what to include and what to delete. Much has had to be omitted but we have referred readers in this book and in the Online Resource Centre pages to sources of further information and discussion.

We have taught together for many years a sentencing and penology module to final year Law undergraduates. Because of our different academic backgrounds and research interests we have been fortunate in being able to bring together a variety of approaches to deal with a range of issues—theoretical, philosophical and practical. We strongly believe that penal theory, penal policy and sentencing law should be discussed together and not addressed separately. As in the previous editions, our over-arching concern has been to explore ideas as to what a just system of sentencing and punishment should look like. To talk of a 'quest for justice' may evoke unwanted images from film fantasies such as *The Lord of the Rings: The Return of the King* or *Harry Potter and the Deathly Hallows* but how we make sentencing decisions and how we punish offenders affects real lives, real families and real communities. So we have emphasised the importance of keeping in mind the purpose of punishment and the need to ensure that punishment is just as well as cost-effective.

We began the first edition of this book with the following statement: 'Sentencing and punishment are currently high profile policy issues: proposals for new procedures, criteria and punishments make headline news and generate debate at all levels of public and social life. This policy area is also complex and volatile: legislative change is frequent and recurring, and issues of criminal justice practice and administration are continually in the public domain'. All of these points are still relevant now.

We would like to thank the editorial and production staff at Oxford University Press, particularly Helen Davis, Heather Smyth, Ceri Warner, and Joanna Williams, for their support. We have also benefited from the comments of reviewers and readers of the second edition. Completing this book over Christmas 2011 inevitably meant less time with our families and friends than we would have liked and we appreciate their forbearance. That deadline means that we hope the law is up to date as at 31 December 2011.

Susan Easton
Christine Piper
February 2012

Postscript: 23rd May 2012

We had hoped that by the proof stage of this book in early April the Legal Aid, Sentencing and Punishment of Offenders Bill 2011 would have received the Royal Assent. It had not and so we were able only to amend clause numbers to match those in the Bill published on 21 March 2012. The Bill received Royal Assent on May 1st and so we have been able to provide details of relevant changes made by the Act on the Online Resource Centre. They can be found by following links to the chapters in which we flagged up potential changes.

New to this edition

- Reviews throughout the book the proposed and implemented policies of the Coalition Government
- Takes account of the impact of the relevant sentencing provisions of the Coroners and Justice Act and the Criminal Justice and Immigration Act
- Includes more discussion of prisoners' human rights, especially their voting rights, in the chapter on 'Justice in the Modern Prison'
- Has more focus on the rights and safeguarding of children and young people in the two chapters on youth justice
- Includes more material on contestability and payment by results in relation to community programmes
- Discusses recent and proposed changes in relation to sentencing 'dangerous' offenders
- Discusses the implications of changes in equality law for the experience of imprisonment

Acknowledgements

Grateful acknowledgement is made to all the authors and publishers of copyright material that appears in this book, and in particular to the following for permission to reprint material from the sources indicated:

Extracts from Crown Copyright material are reproduced under Class Licence Number C01P000148 with the permission of the Controller of HMSO and the Queen's Printer for Scotland.

Centre for Crime and Justice Studies for Fig. 2, 'Sources of the mediation movement and their objectives' in T. Marshall, 'Seeking the Whole Justice' in S. Hayman (ed.), *Repairing the Damage: Restorative Justice in Action* (ISTD, 1997).

Council of Europe for 'Breakdown (in percentages) of persons serving CSM or being under probation (STOCK) on 31st December 2009' in Aebi, M., Delgrande, N. and Marguet, Y. (2011) Annual Penal Statistics, SPACE II 2009, Survey on Non-Custodial Sanctions and Measures in the Council of Europe Member Countries, PC-CP (2011) 4, Council of Europe: Table 1.2 . © Council of Europe.

Mennonite Central Committee for Appendix: 'Paradigms of Justice Old and New' in H. Zehr, 'Retributive Justice, Restorative Justice', *New Perspectives in Crime and Justice*, Vol 4 (MCC Office of Crime & Justice, 1985).

NACRO for Chart: 'Sentences under section 91 (1980–2005)' in *Youth Crime Briefing: Grave Crimes, Mode of Trial and Long Term Detention* (NACRO 2007).

National Audit Office for Fig. 1, 'The youth justice system in England and Wales', Fig. 2, 'Proven offences by young people, 2002–03 to 2009–10', and Fig. 4, 'Number of disposals for young offenders by type, 2007–08 to 2009–10' in *The youth justice system in England and Wales, Reducing offending by young people,* Report by the Comptroller and Auditor General, HC 663 Session 2010–2011 (National Audit Office, 2010).

Prison Reform Trust for Fig. 1, 'Total under 18s in custody 2000–1 to 2010–11 against DTO, remand and long sentences 2005–6 to 2010–11', in Allen, R., *Last Resort? Exploring the reduction in child imprisonment 2008–11* (Prison Reform Trust, 2011) and Table 2.1. 'Type of custodial sentence received' in Jacobson, J., Bhardwa, B., Gyateng, T., Hunter, G. and Hough, M. *Punishing disadvantage, a profile of children in custody* (Prison Reform Trust, 2010).

Every effort has been made to trace and contact copyright holders prior to going to press but if notified, the publisher will undertake to rectify any errors or omissions at the earliest opportunity.

Glossary

Key terms included within the Glossary are highlighted in **bold** at the first mention in a chapter to emphasise their importance in this book.

Anchoring point the level at which punishment is set.

Attorney General the principal law officer of the Crown who is responsible for the Crown Prosecution Service.

Autopoiesis a biological term used to refer to a socio-legal theory which analyses communications within systems such as law.

Bifurcation in relation to youth justice denotes a two-pronged policy whereby the majority of offenders are diverted from prosecution and the minority are prosecuted and punished.

Cardinal proportionality non-relative proportionality where the overall level of punishment is addressed.

Cautioning plus a form of cautioning (official warning by the police) which included voluntary participation by the young offender in a preventative programme.

Censure the process of public denunciation and reproof of an offender's criminal behaviour.

Contestability the opening up of the market to new providers of goods and services, for example from the voluntary sector as well as the private sector.

Culpability blameworthiness in relation to criminal wrong-doing.

Deterrence using punishment to deter the general public from offending (general deterrence) or to deter offenders from reoffending (special or individual deterrence).

Discretion the power of the sentencer or other official to make a choice of processes or outcomes available.

Doli incapax a Latin phrase meaning 'incapable of wrong'. Currently this refers to children under 10 years of age in English law.

Felony formerly (until 1967) an offence more serious than a misdemeanour.

Governance different meanings in different contexts. Refers generally to the exercise of power more widely than that covered by the term 'government' but has different meanings in different contexts.

Incapacitation preventing reoffending by removing offenders from society through the death penalty, imprisonment, or other means.

Indictable offence an offence that may be tried on indictment, that is, by jury in the Crown Court. Some indictable offences are triable either way (see below).

Just deserts the term used to refer to punishment calculated in relation to the culpability of the offender. It is an outcome justified on retributivist principles.

Less eligibility the principle developed originally in relation to the Poor Law, that conditions inside prison must be worse than outside prison for the deterrent effect to operate.

Misdemeanour formerly (before 1967) any of the less serious offences.

Moral panic a term used to denote a theory developed to explain the way an incident triggers a generalised and disproportionate public concern about a social issue or penal policy.

New Managerialism using strategies and techniques from the private sector in the management of punishment in the public sector, focusing on the most efficient use of resources, for example, using Key Performance Targets, Key Performance Indicators, and league tables.

New Penology an approach which is concerned with risk management, using actuarial data to predict and manage risk, and which focuses on categories of offenders rather than individuals.

Normalisation in the context of imprisonment, using the same standards in prison which are applied to the lives of offenders in the community as far as possible, within the constraints required by imprisonment, so that prisoners are able to lead as normal lives as possible apart from their loss of liberty.

Ordinal proportionality an amount of punishment which is proportionate to culpability in terms of parity between offenders committing offences of similar gravity, and such that the relative severity of punishment reflects the seriousness-ranking of offences.

Out-sourcing the management technique of tendering part of an organisation's work or services to an external provider.

Paramountcy principle the legal principle that the welfare of the child shall be paramount in the making of decisions about the child's upbringing.

Parsimony principle using the most economical means of punishment, to impose the least severe punishment necessary to achieve the objective of crime reduction.

Populist punitiveness the increased punitiveness of governments to attract public support.

Prisonisation the forms of adaptation of individuals and groups to prison life.

Privatisation the transfer of state functions or services to the private sector.

Protective sentencing sentencing with the aim of reducing the likelihood that the offender will cause harm to the public by offending in the future. The form such public protection takes may be incapacitation through imprisonment.

Prudential disincentive a penalty which is designed to deter an individual from offending.

Quantum the amount of money awarded as compensation or imposed as punishment.

Racism exclusionary practices based on assumptions about racial hierarchies, which see the qualities of social groups as fixed.

Rehabilitative ideal using treatment and training in custody or in the community to rehabilitate individuals so that they can contribute to society.

Restorative justice an approach to crime and disorder which focuses on the restoration of harmony between the victim, the offender, and the community.

Retributivism the theory of punishment which links punishment to the desert of the individual and which matches the severity of the punishment to the seriousness of the crime.

Ring-fencing specifying a proportion of a budget which can be used only for particular purposes.

Summary offences offences that can only be tried before magistrates. Most minor offences are summary offences.

Three strikes laws mandatory minimum sentencing schemes in the United States aimed at repeat offenders where the third sentence mandates 25 years to life in prison.

Utilitarianism a philosophical approach which sees individuals as motivated by the pursuit of pleasure and avoidance of pain and uses this to devise policies which maximise the greatest happiness of the greatest number.

Utilitarian theories of punishment the use of punishment to reduce or prevent crime through deterrence, incapacitation, and rehabilitation.

Table of Statutes

Table of Cases

Table of European Legislation

Table of International Treaties and Conventions

PART A

Sentencing Principles and Policies

1

Influences on penal policy

SUMMARY

This chapter focuses on key questions in penal policy including justice, risk and human rights. It also considers the principal factors which shape the development of penal policy, notably political imperatives, economic influences, and penological and criminological principles, as well as public opinion which has become much more influential since the early 1990s. We also highlight penal policy developments since 1990 to highlight significant trends and problems. We conclude the chapter by focusing on the **governance** of sex offenders.

1.1 Introduction

1.1.1 Our approach

Our approach is to identify what counts as 'justice' in the context of sentencing and punishment, and why. We will therefore examine the ways in which Parliament, judges, and magistrates and criminal justice professionals seek to justify, impose, and implement policies which convey particular answers to these fundamental questions about sentencing and punishment. So we are not concerned only with what 'the law' says about sentencing and punishment, but why the law has developed and whether it can be justified on the philosophical principles underpinning punishment. We are also concerned with what happens when the sentencing outcomes are put into practice: what is the experience of punishment like, what issues do these various penalties raise, do they achieve their intended results?

To understand how the state punishes, we will consider the relevant sentencing law, the policy guidelines, professional guidance, including national standards, and what we know about their implementation. Our interest lies not simply in 'how much' punishment, but also in wider questions about the range and types of punishment. In scrutinising why we punish we will discuss the 'answers' in two ways: first by analysing the political, policy, and pragmatic reasons and second, by focusing on penology—the study of the reasons and justifications underpinning the practice of state punishment. These two questions, the how and why, are linked. The policy reasons or penological justifications for state punishment may determine how the offender is treated. For this reason, we will integrate discussion of policy and theory with analysis of sentencing law or punishment practice.

This chapter will begin this project by reviewing key questions and concepts in penal policy and the major factors which influence its development. Chapter 1 will also look at the emergence of risk-based and rights-based penologies and will explore some of the issues this raises in relation to recent sex offender legislation. A case study exercise is provided at the end of Chapter 1, the aim of which is to encourage reflection on the practical outcomes which flow from adherence to one or other justification. Chapter 1 will look only briefly at penological theories; Chapters 2 and 3 will consider in more detail one of the classical justifications for punishment, **retributivism**, whilst Chapters 4, 5, and 12 will focus on **deterrence**, risk management, and rehabilitation which reflect the other main justification of punishment, namely **utilitarianism**. Chapter 6 will focus on **restorative justice**.

1.1.2 **What is punishment?**

We first need to consider what is meant by punishment. Punishment can be distinguished from other forms of pain or suffering, such as a painful treatment for a medical condition where the harm is not an expression of moral condemnation, and not a response to our misdeeds. Punishment rests on moral reasons, the expression of moral condemnation, in response to rule infringements. Indeed, Feinberg (1994) refers to **censure** or condemnation as the defining feature of punishment. What distinguishes punishment, says Feinberg, is its expressive function: '[P]unishment is a conventional device for the expression of attitudes of resentment and indignation,... Punishment, in short, has a *symbolic significance* largely missing from other kinds of penalties' (Feinberg 1994: 73). So, for example, a penalty in football is not comparable to imprisonment in terms of public reprobation. Punishment is 'a symbolic way of getting back at the criminal, of expressing a kind of vindictive resentment' (ibid: 76). Condemnation or denunciation, he says, conjoins resentment and reprobation.

The criminal law distinguishes between regulating and punitive statutes, often imposing strict liability in the former case. But in practice the line between regulation and punishment may not be so clear-cut, which can cause problems. For example, in the United States there are constitutional safeguards for those facing punishment which are not available if the measure is construed as a regulatory activity. So if a repressive act is defined as non-punitive, then the individual will be in a worse position. Similarly in European Convention jurisprudence there are arguments about what constitutes punishment in relation to Article 7 of the European Convention on Human Rights. In *Gough v Chief Constable of Derbyshire* (2001), for example, the Court held that a football banning order was not a penalty for the purposes of Article 7. Likewise, the European Commission of Human Rights held that the sex offenders' registration scheme did not constitute a penalty in *Ibbotson v UK* (1999). A similar approach was taken by the House of Lords in relation to anti-social behaviour orders (ASBOs) in *R (McCann)* [2003], where their Lordships held that an application for an ASBO was a civil and not a criminal matter as they are designed to prevent behaviour rather than to punish, do not appear on criminal records, and do not immediately entail imprisonment. Similarly, Serious Crime Prevention Orders imposed under the terms of the Serious Crime Act 2007 which may impose prohibitions, restrictions, or other requirements, as civil orders, are deemed not to be punitive and therefore do not breach the prohibition on retrospective punishment in Article 7.

A key feature of punishment is that it rests on a moral foundation, expressing a moral judgement. It is reflective and based on reasons. A further distinguishing feature of punishment is that it stems from an authoritative source, usually the state. Suffering consequent upon misdeeds is not punishment unless those who inflict it have authority over the offender. If we imagine that a murderer chased by the police crashes his car and dies before he can be tried, he has not suffered punishment but escaped it, even if the outcome is more severe than that which might have been afforded by the criminal justice system. A person participating in an illegal cockfight in California died in 2011 when he was stabbed by a rooster with a blade attached to its leg and in a similar incident in India a person had his throat cut by a bladed cockerel. In Indonesia in 2011 a man who went on holiday and left his dogs for 14 days without food or water was eaten by them on his return. We may conceive of this misfortune as 'God's punishment', but we are still conceiving of punishment as derived from a higher power.

Although our focus in this book will be on state punishment, of course punishment may also be informal in so far as it is imposed outside the formal criminal justice system. Informal justice developed as an alternative to state-centred methods of dispute resolution as the parties sought to recapture conflicts from professionals (see Christie 1977, 2010; Abel 1982; Matthews 1988; and Chapter 6). An extreme form of informal justice would be vigilantism, and state punishment is usually seen as a necessary means of avoiding the excesses of unrestrained popular justice, by satisfying the public's demands for punishment.

1.2 Understanding penal policy

1.2.1 Key questions

The question of why some acts are criminalised and not others, and why society deals harshly with some wrong-doing but lightly with others, is much debated in criminology. But when we consider this in relation to penal policy, a fundamental issue is why punishment is seen as an appropriate response to a specific event or mode of behaviour. This entails asking three questions:

- First: what particular response is made and why?
- Second: if the response is penal, which particular penal option is selected?
- Third: what is the particular level of penal response?

These three dimensions of penal policy—what to punish, how to punish, and how much to punish—will shape policy outcomes, and while this book will focus principally on the last two questions, the first is still important as it sets the scene for the latter two elements.

In looking at the first question, we might ask why the response is punitive, rather than taking some other form, such as social assistance or a medical response. The offender might be seen as a wicked person who should be punished, or as a sick person requiring treatment, or as an inadequate individual whose criminality is the result of social deprivation and who needs social welfare support to address that problem, as well as appropriate crime-prevention strategies. So, in some societies, such as the former Soviet Union and modern China and Uzbekistan, political dissidence may be met with a medical response, using incarceration through 'judicial psychiatry' to detain dissidents in psychiatric hospital.[1] Drug therapies such as Ritalin may also be used to control the unruly behaviour of children and these are widely used in the United States and the UK. Experiments on the effect of vitamin supplements have also been conducted on young offenders at Aylesbury Young Offenders' Institution in England, with positive results on behaviour in that the group receiving vitamins committed fewer disciplinary offences than the group given placebos (Gesch *et al.* 2002; see also Benton 2007). The developing science of neurocriminology also draws on research on neurodevelopment to understand and treat anti-social behaviour (Ross and Hilborn 2007). The potential and problems of neuroscience are highlighted by Walsh (2011) in relation to youth justice.

So the punitive response is only one of several possibilities and each response will rest on a particular model of human behaviour. In practice we may find a combination of

[1] http://www.hrw.org/en/news/2005/09/02/uzbekistan-dissident-forced-psychiatric-detention.

policies and strategies, depending on the type of offence and offender and on the political climate. Political pressures may also shift the reaction to crime and disorder from a penal response to a military response. Examples of this approach would be the use of troops to deal with sectarian conflict and disorder in Northern Ireland and in response to strikes in the UK, and of course, in recent years, military responses have dominated the fight by the United States against terrorist-related crime. However, it is conceivable that, in other contexts, pressures on governments might engender a move away from penal and punitive responses to a welfarist response, seeking to address problems in communities by supporting disadvantaged groups and promoting social inclusion. So we may find a variety of strategies depending in part on pressures on governments. In France transformational social therapy has been used to address disorder in the *banlieues*. So when considering the reasons why some harm-generating activities are controlled by criminal law and sanctions, and others are not, economic factors may be significant (see Bowles *et al.* 2008).

Secondly, in terms of the particular type of response made through penal policy, a number of options may be available, from educational programmes, such as driver education or anger management, through to extreme punishments used in other societies, such as amputation, castration and execution. Thirdly, in reviewing penal policy, we should consider the level of response via penal policy, in other words, how long is the sentence of imprisonment, how heavy is the fine, and how firmly is the response enforced.

1.2.2 **Equality, fairness, and justice**

Understanding penal policy also requires a focus on equality and fairness, particularly if some groups are selected for harsher punishment or if apparently neutral policies have differential impact. The concern with equality of impact in the late 1980s and the 1990s focused on disparities in sentencing (see Chapter 10), as well as on direct and indirect discrimination. This was also reflected in changes in the criminal law itself; for example, the Criminal Justice Act (CJA) 1991 made racial motivation an aggravating factor in assaults, and s 95 of the same Act imposed a duty on the Secretary of State to publish information considered expedient to enable those involved in the administration of criminal justice to avoid discriminating against any person on the ground of race, sex, or any other improper ground (see Chapters 10 and 11). The Equality Act 2010 imposes on public bodies, including prisons, a duty to eliminate discrimination and to promote equality, and broadens the range of protected characteristics (see Chapter 11, section 11.1.1).

The principle of equality has also entered penal policy debates on the impact of apparently equal punishments imposed on individuals who are not equal. Examples of potentially unjust punishments would include fines which are unrelated to means, or punishments which impact adversely on people with particular medical conditions, for example those offenders who are mentally disordered (see Chapter 7, section 7.4). Policies may also indirectly discriminate against certain groups, such as women with children, or directly discriminate if there are problems of bias in the imposition of punishment (see Chapters 10 and 11).

Of course the notion of justice is not clear-cut: like 'rights', justice is a slippery concept which has been used by both right and left to embody aspirations and to legitimise policies. Justice was stressed by the Woolf Report (Woolf and Tumim 1991) as one of the key principles which should govern the treatment of prisoners (see Chapter 9). A sense of injustice, it argued, was an important contributory factor in the prison riots of 1990. 'Justice' was also a key strand of New Labour penal policy, expressed in the White Paper *Justice for All* (Home Office 2002c), which said the Government's aim was to 'narrow the justice gap', by which it meant reducing the gap between the number of crimes reported to the police and the number of offenders brought to justice. *Rebalancing the Criminal Justice System in Favour of the Law-Abiding Majority* (Home Office 2006a) stressed that people want to see the system 'delivering justice—with fairer sentencing and fewer occasions when the system seems to let the offender off the hook' (ibid: para 2.2). The Home Office has described its role as 'supporting the efficient and effective delivery of justice' (Home Office 2008: 2). The House of Commons Justice Committee (2010) in its report *Cutting Crime: The Case for Justice Reinvestment* emphasised the value of using 'justice reinvestment' approaches, that is channelling resources on a geographically-targeted basis to reduce the crime which brings people into the criminal justice system. Justice reinvestment was an idea developed in the United States by the George Soros Open Society Institute and refers to the aim of reducing the funds expended on imprisonment and redirecting some of those funds to the communities adversely affected by high levels of incarceration (see also Allen and Stern 2007).

The Coalition Government has also argued for more efficient and effective justice for communities and 'giving communities better information about how justice is delivered, making services more responsive and accountable to the public' (Ministry of Justice 2010a: para 46).

Justice embodies notions of fairness to all members of the community, including victims and offenders, and striking a balance between their competing interests is the cornerstone of current criminal justice policy. But it also assumes a consensus on what constitutes justice, and achieving justice in terms of improving conviction rates, for example, may create injustice for particular individuals or groups. What is construed as fair treatment means different things in different theories of social justice,[2] but its construction also depends on how punishment is rationalised in the different theories of punishment which moral philosophers, penologists, and criminologists have developed, notably the classical theories of retributivism and utilitarianism. By retributivism is meant the approach which links punishment according to the desert or **culpability** of the individual and which matches the severity of the punishment to the seriousness of the crime and the culpability of the offender. By utilitarianism is meant the approach which sees individuals as motivated by the pursuit of pleasure and avoidance of pain and uses this to devise social and penal policies to promote the greatest happiness of the greatest number. Punishment, on this approach, is used to prevent offending and reoffending through deterrence, **incapacitation**, and rehabilitation.

Consequently, determining what constitutes the justice of a particular punishment requires a decision on the theory of punishment to be deployed: just punishment from a retributivist standpoint might seem unjust from a utilitarian perspective and vice versa. As we shall see later, preventive detention may be justifiable if the interests of the wider society are given priority over individual rights but this raises problems for retributivism. Utilitarians and desert theorists also differ on the role that past convictions should play in determining the punishment for a current offence.

The dominant concept of justice may be only one of a number of key factors to consider in identifying the influences on modern penal policies: others might be ideologies, such as laissez-faire liberalism, which is essentially individualistic and construes society as a collection of egoistic individuals in which the state's role in economic and other spheres is minimal, and communitarianism, its opposite, which focuses on interdependence between citizens within the social framework, mutual obligations, trust, and group

[2] For discussions of notions of justice see, for example, the following texts: Campbell (2010) and Rawls (1971) for a liberal concept of justice; for discussion of feminist concepts of justice see Rhode (1989), Heidensohn (2006), and Satz and Reich (2009). For an individualist approach, see Nozick (1974).

loyalty (Etzioni 1993, 2003). Other influences on penal policy which may be significant are political and economic factors and the role of public opinion. So a recurring theme in the following discussions will be the justice and injustice of punishment in the political and economic context in which decisions are made and policies formulated.

1.2.3 **Human rights**

Human rights have implications for both the theory and practice of punishment in justifying specific punishments, in assessing the justice of punishments, and in improving standards in penal institutions. Human rights instruments are, then, a key mechanism for achieving just punishment and rights are themselves an important element of many theories of punishment. For example, natural rights are a significant dimension of retributivist theory, which recognises the right of the offender to be treated with respect as an autonomous human being. Rights have therefore provided a way of criticising the penal system in the UK which has been strongly influenced by utilitarianism, an approach which has been criticised for its failure to acknowledge the rights of the offender and for sacrificing the individual's rights for the wider public interest (see Chapter 4, section 4.4.3). Rights also have implications for issues such as the interviewing and detention of suspects before trial, the treatment of remand prisoners and the granting of bail, the defendant's right to a fair trial, the right to be presumed innocent, the treatment of witnesses, preventive detention, the right to be released when one's sentence is served, and the right not to be subject to unfair or discriminatory treatment. These principles may act as a control on judicial **discretion** and inhibit disparities in sentencing. Rights also extend to victims of crime and help shape policy on their role in the criminal process, on their entitlement to redress. These issues will be considered further in subsequent chapters in relation to the principal justifications of punishment and to sentencing policy and practice.

Rights also have an important function in protecting prisoners from the excessive zeal of their keepers and, if prisoners retain fundamental rights as human beings while serving their sentences, this will help to ensure that they are treated with dignity (Easton 2011a). A system of punishment which respects human rights will have more legitimacy than one which rides roughshod over them, particularly as utilitarian arguments have failed to protect prisoners. Rights are therefore crucial to penal theory and practice and, while rights may be limited when rights are infringed, the state's justifications for doing so need to be interrogated. A rights standpoint is an important critical tool for assessing systems of punishment, providing a check on powerful regimes, and on **populist punitiveness**. The term 'populist punitiveness', coined by Bottoms (1995), refers to the increased punitiveness of governments which they believe will appeal to the public and which has been used to justify increases in sentence severity.

For penal reformers, rights are seen as a way of achieving reform, although not all radical reformers share a commitment to a rights approach. Some Marxist theorists of law, who believe the rule of law may mask social injustice, are suspicious of rights because they are essentially individualist rather than collectivist, abstracting the individual from the historical and social context, and because they fail to deliver substantive justice (Easton 2008a; Boyd 2009).

There are, of course, problems in defining rights in jurisprudence. There is a huge body of literature with disagreement over what rights mean and what they entail, what should be included within their scope, and who possesses them. For Dworkin (1977), the right to equal concern and respect is paramount, while others have broadened their concern to include social rights and positive rights (Marshall 1950; Titmuss 1968; Búrca and de Witte 2005; and Fredman 2008), and some see rights as a means of satisfying human needs (Campbell 1983). But they share a conception of fundamental rights as existing beyond positive law, that is, formal, black letter law in cases and statutes. Rights are entrenched and occupy a privileged position, protecting the individual from the state and protecting the weakest individuals from the majority. For Dworkin (1977, 1986, 2011), rights trump utility and, whilst rights may be limited if they conflict with competing rights, the circumstances in which this may occur are carefully drawn and more narrowly defined than on classical utilitarian models. Rights theorists argue that rights apply to all equally: even the worst offenders, such as war criminals, have procedural rights, for example, to take part in their trial, and, when convicted, to non-degrading punishment. Because rights are universal they have a crucial role to play in the practice of punishment and apply to all offenders and ex-offenders: the mark of a civilised society is to respect the rights of all (see Easton 2009).

Rights have implications across the criminal justice system and at all stages of the criminal justice process, but we will be particularly concerned with the impact of a rights jurisprudence on the experience of custody. Due process and substantive rights have implications for the treatment of prisoners. For example, prisoners can achieve fairer treatment in the context of disciplinary procedures and decision making over issues such as segregation and transfers, but also in terms of substantive rights to food, exercise, and time unlocked (Easton 2011a). The European Convention on Human Rights had a considerable impact in improving prisoners' lives in the UK long before the Human Rights Act 1998 was passed. Following key decisions the UK has had to change secondary legislation, including the Prison Rules as well as Prison Service Orders, to comply with the European Court of Human Rights' judgments and English judges have usually followed the recommendations of the Strasbourg court. These issues will be considered in relation to imprisonment and prison policy in Chapter 9, section 9.6.

It has also meant that human rights compliance has itself become a risk for prison management, involving both organisational risks of intervention in prison management and financial risks for the public as compensation may be paid to prisoners who succeed in establishing rights violations (Whitty 2011; Easton 2011a).

1.3 Key influences

What is seen as an appropriate response to crime—the type and level of response—may reflect political and ideological principles. Ideologies are chains of interrelated ideas, the principles underpinning penal policies. For example, laissez-faire liberal ideology, which was in the ascendant during the Thatcher period, has had an enduring resonance and is reflected in **New Managerialist** approaches to the criminal justice system, including the **privatisation** of prisons and a concern with efficiency and economy of punishment. The role of New Right ideologies has been revived by the Coalition Government with a strong commitment to involvement of the private sector in the delivery of punishment and rehabilitation (Ministry of Justice 2010a, 2011a). In contrast, welfarist ideologies have declined since the 1980s, although New Labour tried to chart a path, or 'Third Way', between them (see Giddens 1998, 2000).

1.3.1 Political imperatives

Debates on law and order and their corollary, crime and punishment, have dominated British politics since the 1970s. Moreover, in a deeper sense the crime question is inherently political in that questions of crime, law, and order raise fundamental questions about the relationship between the state and the citizen, and the problem of how society can be held together, in the face of internal social divisions and the fragmentation of individuals' self-interest,[3] as well as issues regarding how far the state may intervene to protect citizens from each other and from external threats. The political demand for social order has been seen as a key element in increases in incarceration (see de Koster *et al.* 2008). Failure to deal with law and order can be very damaging to governments, as illustrated by the riots in London and other UK cities in the summer of 2011, when the Coalition Government was criticised for its failure to keep the streets safe and for the time taken to restore order.

Simon (2007) has argued that in the United States the war on crime has become a key element of governance, facilitated new forms of governance and generated the growth of legislation to address the problem. Similar processes can be seen in the UK, with a substantial increase in legislation on crime and punishment since the 1990s.

The political dimension raises questions about power, including how much power a government has to implement policy. With a large majority in the House of Commons when it first came to power in 1997, the New Labour administration was in a strong position to enact its legislative programme although it subsequently met opposition from the House of Lords on issues such as fox hunting and jury trial. A weaker government may have to rely on the support of opposition parties or powerful interest groups to gain acceptance for a particular policy. Clearly the current Coalition Government is in a relatively weak position, as the support of the Liberal Democrats was needed by the Conservatives even to form a government. But nonetheless, there is some consensus between the main political parties on law and order policies, and it is unlikely that a party would adopt a 'soft' policy on crime because of the perception that public opinion would be hostile (see section 1.3.3).

This is very clear in the debate over prisoners' right to vote, where both the previous Labour Government and the current Coalition Government have been reluctant to amend the law, and in the Coalition Government's decision to abandon a proposed increase in the sentence discount for a guilty plea because of public hostility to the proposal. When the Government indicated it was considering a reduction of 50 per cent for guilty pleas for offenders in *Breaking the Cycle* (Ministry of Justice 2010a) this met with outrage from the press, the public, and senior judges as well as many Conservative party members, who thought it would be too lenient and undermine public confidence in sentencing. Concern was intensified when the Justice Secretary Kenneth Clarke in a radio interview defended the reduction for rapists, suggesting that some rape cases were more serious than others. The proposal was abandoned in June 2011.

The furore over sentence discounts also highlights the difficulties facing the government when the political need to pursue policies and practices deemed by the public as legitimate conflicts with economic imperatives. Which priority 'wins' may depend on whether the policy would be implemented early or late in the government's term of office. Public opinion is a crucial pressure on the government at election time as parties try to capture floating voters, but may also be a significant force between elections at party conferences and in the constituencies. In the UK, Home Secretaries have been heckled at party conferences if perceived to be weak on law and order, and crime has been a recurring key election issue and highlighted in party manifestos. So political expediency may lead to the decision that it is not worth implementing an unpopular policy even if it saves money or, conversely, a popular policy may be implemented despite imposing huge

[3] This problem lies at the heart of social contract theory: see T. Hobbes' *Leviathan* (1651) and J.-J. Rousseau's *The Social Contract* (1743).

financial costs. An example of the latter would be the strong commitment of successive governments over the past 20 years to prison building and expansionist programmes, which were very expensive, but were intended to show to the public that concerns on crime were being taken seriously.

On the other hand, a government may negotiate these conflicts by trying to formulate policies which appear to protect the public while reducing costs: an example would be risk management which can reduce costs by focusing on those offences posing the highest risk of serious harm to the public. Certainly, since 1990 the key policy aim of public protection has been reflected in a series of measures including the 'longer than commensurate' sentence, the sentence of imprisonment for public protection (IPP), and the establishment of Multi-Agency Public Protection Arrangements (MAPPAs). There is a legal requirement on the police, probation, and prison service in each of the police force areas of England and Wales, to establish arrangements to assess and manage risks posed by sexual and violent offenders, to review and monitor these arrangements, and to publish annual reports.[4]

A government may find it is unable to relinquish a policy because it is so popular. For example, in the United States it may be politically damaging to retreat from the death penalty, when a large majority of the population support it and candidates try to exceed each other in their zealous commitment to it. Governor George Ryan of Illinois waited until he was retiring from office in January 2003 before commuting the death sentence for all 167 prisoners on death row in the state at that time. Yet, whilst the actions of governments can legitimise punitiveness by endorsing punitive policies including the death penalty, support for the penalty correlates with a wide range of variables (Unnever 2010). Local democratic political traditions may also play a key role, as Garland (2010) notes, as the structure of the American polity 'makes it difficult to abolish the death penalty in the face of majority public opinion and deprives governing elites of the opportunity for top-down, countermajoritarian reform' (ibid: 310). The levels of public punitiveness and support for penal expansion in the United States also vary from state to state depending on local and state level institutional structures, as Barker (2009) illustrates in her study of divergent penal policies in California, Washington, and New York. As she argues,

> [T]he apparent link between public participation, punitiveness, and rough justice is not only historically contingent but dependent on specific state structures and patterns of civic engagement, patterns that tend to vary within the United States and across liberal democracies. Public vengeance depends on certain political institutions and collective agency to give it a legal and political expression.
>
> (Barker 2009: 11–12)

The structure of the polity may also be important in the UK as Lacey (2008) has argued: neo-liberal market economies with first-past-the-post systems are more favourable to exclusionary penal policies and expanding prison populations than systems based on proportional representation, and issues of penal policy should be depoliticised to address the problem of prison expansion.

Powerful interest groups may also affect policy regardless of which government is in power, and in the UK the Police Federation and victim movements exert a strong influence, competing with those working with offenders such as NACRO and the Prison Reform Trust. The view that the balance has swung too far in favour of the defendant and away from victims and communities has been strongly expressed in recent policy

[4] See Wood and Kemshall (2007) and Ministry of Justice (2010f) for a review of the workings of these arrangements.

documents (Ministry of Justice 2010a, 2011a). In that context the relative power of groups representing the public may be an important factor in policy initiatives.

One particular policy technique is that of diverting attention by blaming individuals for crime or demonising particular groups such as sex offenders (see section 1.6) in order to defuse hostility to the government over crime and disorder. There are also examples from the recent past of how dysfunctional and anti-social and fatherless families, and youths and truants have been selected as criminogenic categories (see Day Sclater and Piper 2000). Professional failures, for example of social workers and teachers, have also been highlighted for criticism.

1.3.2 **The costs of punishment**

Penal policy can be seen as the result of a negotiation between the desire to sanction a moral code and the problem of limited resources to do so. Economic factors may be much more influential than penological theories and there may be conflicts between the Treasury and the Ministry of Justice over penal policy. The option which may best satisfy the public, namely imprisonment, is also the most expensive in terms of staffing and capital costs. The view that 'prison works', famously expounded by Michael Howard, the former Conservative Home Secretary, is very costly to implement. So a society has to negotiate both the amount of censure and the amount of punishment it can afford to incorporate into its penal policy. Some popular policies have proved massively expensive, as in the case of the '**three strikes**' legislation found in many states in the United States including California and Washington. These are mandatory minimum sentencing schemes aimed at repeat offenders, where the third sentence mandates 25 years to life in prison.

Crime and punishment are costly in financial terms, to individuals who pay increased insurance premiums and to the public whose funds are used to finance law enforcement and punishment. As this is a substantial economic burden, inevitably costs are a significant influence on penal policy. Financial concerns have become increasingly important since the early 1990s, not just because of the ascendancy of New Right ideologies, but because increased punitiveness has been reflected in prison expansion which has led to substantial cost increases. Dobson (2010) has highlighted the heavy reliance of New Labour on the use of custody, the most expensive penal option, and the accompanying economic and social costs.

These economic pressures are even more important now in the current economic climate of recession and cost effectiveness is a crucial consideration in current penal policy. So governments must respond to the public's demand to reduce crime and to make society safe, while reducing economic burdens on the public purse. One way of negotiating this conflict has been to represent community penalties as punitive in order to win public support for them. Value for money, the allocation of scarce resources in the most efficient way, has also become an increasingly important criterion for evaluating penal policy. So we find in the Halliday Report (2001) an emphasis on assessing the costs and benefits of specific measures. Although the origins here are in New Right theory, the quest for economic efficiency was adopted by New Labour and has permeated the public management of a wide range of institutions, and has been intensified by the Coalition Government. All public sector institutions and agencies have to justify their spending by transparent and comparable measurable results. The focus on value for money is a key feature of the New Managerialist approach, reflected in the New Public Management. This approach applies methods from the private sector to the public sector, incorporating a concern with the efficient use of resources, the use of Key Performance Indicators, transparency, a move towards performance-related pay, and a stress on competition and **contestability**, that is opening up the market to new providers of goods and services, and the use of incentives regardless. We refer to this approach in various chapters of the book because it has been applied to the Probation Service, the Police Service, the Prison Service, and the Youth Justice System.

Further measures to cut costs include a policy of privatisation of entire prisons or selected services within prisons or in the context of community punishment, making greater use of voluntary organisations where appropriate, and linking payments to private companies involved in rehabilitation to their results in cutting reoffending (see Chapter 12, section 12.3.5). This expansion of cooperation with the private and voluntary sectors has been described as the New Public Governance (Osborne 2009).

When deciding *what to punish* some offences may be uneconomic to punish, such as minor infringements or minor drugs offences which may exist on the statute book but not be enforced. Other offences, such as counterfeiting of bank notes, may need strong sanctions because they will destabilise the economy. Although the criminal law incorporates a moral code, that is, value judgements about expectations of behaviour, there will always be grey areas, particularly in relation to issues such as sexual behaviour and recreational drug use. In terms of *how to punish*, clearly a community sentence is cheaper than a custodial sentence, and supporters of the death penalty may argue that it is cheaper than life imprisonment, but if the collateral costs of appeals and reviews are included within the calculation, as well as the additional expense of long periods spent on Death Row, the costs per execution will be substantial and may exceed the costs of life imprisonment without parole. For this reason, in the United States several states have recently conducted audits of the costs of seeking execution.

In terms of *how much to punish*, a heavier sentence is more expensive than a lighter sentence, although it may offer more opportunities for rehabilitation which might, in the long term, cut the costs of crime. So when we talk of the 'prison crisis', it is not only a question of physical conditions or overcrowding or disorder, but also a fiscal crisis, with the burden of prison building falling on taxpayers, diverting funds from other essential public services. As it is a labour-intensive mode of punishment, the largest running cost of imprisonment is labour, although prison officers are not very highly paid. The costs of imprisonment have increased substantially since 1990 when the prison population was 45,636, and now stands at over 87,000. The latest available figures for annual cost per prison place are £44,006 overall cost per place and £40,378 overall cost per prisoner (Ministry of Justice 2011d: 68). Whether an increase in prison capacity is still viable in the current economic crisis is questionable and, as Fox and Albertson (2010) argue, more economically efficient alternatives need to be explored.

In addition to running costs, there are capital costs of building prisons and indirect costs, such as welfare support for dependants affected by the imprisonment of the breadwinner, and costs to the national economy with the loss of productive labour and associated revenues. There will also be an impact on the local economy if large numbers of individuals are incarcerated (see Clear 2007).

Research by Grimshaw *et al.* (2010a) for the Centre for Crime and Justice Studies found that by 2010 spending on the prison and probation system in England and Wales had grown by 36 per cent in real terms since 2004. This increase occurred despite major reorganisation designed to cut costs. Spending on the National Offender Management Service, which includes costs of prison and probation, increased in real terms from £3.6 billion in 2004/05 to £4.9 billion in 2008/09. Obviously the increase in the size of the prison population was significant but the costs of building and staffing prisons had also increased. In addition, the economic costs of processing offenders at the earlier stages are significant, as Grimshaw *et al.* (2010b) found in their review of the levels of expenditure in the Crown Court and the magistrates' courts in the period 1999–2009.

1.3.3 **Public opinion**

Public opinion is clearly a key variable in shaping the response to crime and disorder. Indeed, many would argue that public opinion on law and order has been the major influence on penal policy and particularly on levels of punishment since the 1990s. Public opinion may be expressed through electoral choice, public opinion polls, focus groups, or sometimes by direct pressure on sentencers. Judges regularly receive letters from disgruntled members of the public complaining about sentences, mostly because these are seen as too short. Although many members of the public complain that judges and magistrates are out of touch with what the public want, this perception of judges has been challenged by recent empirical research on the judiciary (Darbyshire 2011). Magistrates who undertake the bulk of sentencing see themselves as dispensing popular justice, as representatives of the public, and believe that they should respond to public opinion.

Public opinion can be orchestrated to win support for policies, and public opinion and **moral panics** about particular crimes can be fanned by the media. Since the late 1980s the public mood in Britain has been more favourable to punishment as the main response to criminal behaviour. The Conservative, Labour, and Coalition governments have all responded to and, arguably, encouraged the punitiveness of the public.

Public opinion is important in the sense that, for a criminal justice system to be effective, it must have legitimacy in the eyes of the public but this creates a conflict for professionals in a number of areas of the criminal justice system. Agencies such as the police have to be accountable to the public yet may feel frustrated by the conflicting pressures to control crime while following rules and procedures designed to safeguard civil liberties. This conflict is reflected in efforts to strike a balance between civil liberties and crime control in the Police and Criminal Evidence Act (PACE) 1984, in the Report of the Royal Commission on Criminal Procedure (RCCP 1981) which preceded it, and was recognised by the Royal Commission on Criminal Justice in its Report (RCCJ 1993) and in debates over the impact of the Human Rights Act. It may be difficult to retain public support when the avowed aims of penal institutions and the criminal justice system are not fulfilled, if crime increases, or the defendant is seen to be privileged over the victim, or the system of punishment seems to be ineffective.

The populist punitiveness of governments is problematic because it reinforces the view that crime can be controlled through punishment and leads to problems when harsher punishment does not succeed in controlling crime, as Brownlee notes (1998a). Once a government pursues the punitive route it may find that the public is never satisfied and that the demand for punishment exceeds the supply of punishment. Moreover, by reacting strongly to the perceived public concerns over crime, governments may increase the public's punitiveness. Tonry (2010) argues that the punitiveness of governments can increase the public's fear of crime. He illustrates this with reference to the Blair Government's focus on rebalancing the criminal justice system in favour of the victim and its focus on anti-social behaviour culminating in the introduction of ASBOs. This, Tonry claims, actually increased public concern about antisocial behaviour and undermined confidence in the ability of the criminal justice system to deal with it: '[H]igh levels of fear are at least in part a consequence of the Labour government's unceasing and highly visible preoccupation with crime and antisocial behaviour' (at 403). He points out that in Canada and the United States fear of crime has fallen as crime rates have fallen since 1996, while in England fear of crime has persisted despite similar falls.

In any case, it is arguable that measures to control crime will not work without attacking deeper social causes and hence the problem of social exclusion needs to be addressed (Byrne 2005; Taket *et al.* 2009). This itself may be problematic as the relation between penal policy and social policy is complex. As the welfare state has contracted, the penal system has to some extent taken over its role. There also appears to be a strong positive correlation between punitive penal attitudes and hostility to welfare spending both here and in the United States (Rubin 2011; Garland 2001b; see also the discussion in Chapter 5, section 5.1).

Key concerns for governments are to promote public confidence in the criminal justice system, to stress the need to evaluate the cost effectiveness of different sentences, to achieve more consistency in sentencing, and to introduce stronger punishments for repeat offenders. Section 80 of the Crime and Disorder Act (CDA) 1998 required the Court of Appeal to consider producing sentencing guidelines where there were none, and to review existing guidelines, and this initiative was taken further with the establishment of the Sentencing Advisory Panel and the Sentencing Guidelines Council, now replaced by the Sentencing Council (see Chapter 2). This may lead to conflicts with, and splits within, the judiciary over the desirability of custodial sentences in some cases. Research also suggests that further guidance to magistrates may not be sufficient to reduce continuing variations in sentencing practice (Tarling 2006). This was an issue raised in relation to sentencing following the riots in the summer of 2011 where there was some indication of inconsistency between courts but also some indications of harsher sentences than would normally be given for those involved in the riots and a higher imprisonment rate for offences committed in the context of the riots.

Negotiating public opinion may be particularly hazardous for the government when it is difficult to gauge or identify the public's opinion on issues of crime and punishment (see Roberts and Hough 2005, 2011; Hough and Roberts 2005; Roberts *et al.* 2009). Public opinion cannot be inferred just from the headlines of the popular press, for the media may shape public opinion as well as simply reflect it. Most of our knowledge of public opinion comes from the British Crime Survey (BCS) and similar social scientific research. Identifying attitudes to sentencing may also be problematic in so far as reports of attitudes to sentencing may reflect the methodologies used, as Hutton (2005) has argued. If more information is given in the scenarios presented to respondents, then a more lenient response may be elicited. The BCS research has confirmed a high level of fear of crime in the UK, although this does not necessarily correlate with the actual risk of victimisation. The public also wants strong penalties for violent crimes, but may be willing to accept the decreased use of imprisonment for some crimes and does not object to community punishment for lesser crimes.

Public opinion does impact on legislation but while it may reflect genuinely deeply felt anxieties, it might also be based on inaccurate views and information. Underpinning the apparent public desire for tougher criminal justice policies is a mistaken public belief that offending is on the increase, even though crime fell from 1995 to 2004/5, and crime has continued to decline since then, although less sharply and with some fluctuations. The most recent findings based on the BCS 2010–11 found no statistically significant changes in the number of crimes compared to the previous years (Chaplin *et al.* 2011). Violent crime, including firearm and knife crime fell. There were some exceptions, with small increases in homicides and serious sexual offences and burglary. Since 2009 the BCS has extended its coverage to include crimes against children aged 10–15 and the 2010–11 survey found a higher proportion of violent crimes against this group than against adults.

However, research using data from the BCS suggests that the British public are not necessarily excessively punitive, but are often ill-informed about sentencing and unaware of the increased use of imprisonment in recent years, but once aware of the levels of sentencing, are more willing to accept them (Hough and Roberts 1998; Mattinson and Mirrlees-Black 2000). The public tend to overestimate crime levels, particularly for violent crime and underestimate the severity of the criminal justice system in dealing with crime particularly for serious offences. Yet, whilst they want custodial sentences for persistent offenders, the public do not necessarily support more prison building but are willing to use other forms of punishment including restorative justice. Mattinson and Mirrlees-Black (2000) found that when the respondents were given a sentencing exercise to undertake, they were more lenient than the sentencing guidelines and there was no evidence that being a recent victim increased the punitiveness of their sentencing. Indeed, the victim may prefer redress or compensation (see Kelly and Erez 1997).

A review of data from the 2007–8 BCS, however, found that public confidence in the ability of the criminal justice system to bring offenders to justice and reduce crime had increased in 2007–8 compared to earlier years (Smith 2010). Women were more confident than men and younger people more confident than older people. Those who had been victims of crime in the last year were less confident, as were those who thought there were high levels of anti-social behaviour in their local areas. Data from the 2010–11 BCS found that in terms of perception 60 per cent of people thought crime had risen in the country as a whole, compared to 66 per cent in 2009/10 (Chaplin *et al.* 2011). However the number who thought crime had risen in their local area was only 28 per cent in 2010–11 compared to 55 per cent in 1996. Crime maps giving information on crimes in local area have been available to the public since January 2011. Public confidence in the criminal justice system also increased from 59 per cent in 2009–10 to 61 per cent in 2010–11.

Research on punitive attitudes has found positive correlations with age, gender, and educational achievement, so older people are more likely to be punitive than younger people, men more than women, and those with low levels of education are more punitive than those with higher levels of education. Demker *et al.* (2008) found a correlation between punitiveness and tabloid newspaper consumption in Sweden. Research on possible links between race, religion and fear of crime has found mixed results. However, research on victimisation suggests that differential experience of victimisation does not necessarily increase punitiveness (see King and Maruna 2009). Those who fear crime are more likely to be punitive, but victims of crime are no more punitive than others. Anger has also been found to be a significant predictor of support for punitive penal policies (Johnson 2009). Punitiveness may also reflect what has been described as 'ontological insecurity', that is more general anxieties about social changes and feelings of helplessness (see Giddens 1990; van Marle and Maruna 2010). An Australian study using jurors in actual cases to explore public opinion on sentencing found a contrast between punitiveness in relation to general perceptions of leniency and a more merciful approach in relation to individual cases (Warner and Davis 2012).

A review of Australian and international research on attitudes towards sentencing and punishment, by Gelb (2008) for the Sentencing Advisory Council, found that when the public consider sentencing in the abstract they often believe that sentences are too lenient, but when given further information about the crime or the offender, their level of punitiveness declines considerably. This review of research found that people have little confidence in the courts because they believe sentences are too lenient. But people have little accurate knowledge of crime and the criminal justice system, with the media being the primary source of information on crime and justice issues.

Similar findings have been found in relation to attitudes towards sentencing for murder. In their report, *Public Opinion and Sentencing for Murder: An Empirical Investigation of Public Knowledge and Attitudes in England and Wales*, Mitchell and Roberts (2010) found that public support for a mandatory sentence of life imprisonment for murder is more limited than had previously been supposed. However, the level of public support increased for more serious cases of murder. The respondents also underestimated the amount of time murderers spend in prison before being released on licence. The majority of respondents also believed that the murder rate had remained the same or had increased over the past 10 years when it has actually begun to decline. The Report highlights the need to increase awareness of the public of sentencing to improve public confidence as well as the problems with a mandatory life sentence (see also Mitchell and Roberts 2012).

A key objective of governments is to reduce crime and fear of crime and thereby to promote confidence in the rule of law. But the public's views on sentencing come in part from the media which tends to focus on erratic sentencing rather than dull sensible sentencing, and on grisly violent crimes rather than routine everyday crimes. American and English crime and police television series tend to concentrate primarily on violent crime rather than crimes like 'twocking' (taking a vehicle without the owner's consent) and theft, even though such crimes are numerically far more significant. The press have also highlighted those cases where dangerous offenders have been released without appropriate supervision and have reoffended, which heightens public anxieties.[5] Clearly, the public needs more accurate information on sentencing and the Sentencing Council has the provision of such information as an aim.

In particular, any reductionist policy has to address the issue of communicating to the public the effectiveness of alternatives to custody, the economic and social costs of custody, and also the actual levels of sentencing in cases of serious offences to assuage public concerns and to enhance confidence in the sentencing system. These issues have been addressed in key policy documents including the Carter Report (Carter 2003), the Consultation Paper *Making Sentencing Clearer* (Home Secretary *et al.* 2006), *Rebalancing the Criminal Justice System* (Home Office 2006a), and *Breaking the Cycle* (Ministry of Justice 2010a).

1.3.4 **Policy effects: prison expansion**

The prison population has increased since 1993 for a number of reasons, including the actual number of cases going through the courts and the increase in the custody rate, that is the proportion of the total number sentenced who received a custodial sentence. The number of cases processed was affected by demographic factors, namely an increase in numbers in the crime-prone age groups, and by the impact of drug-related crime. The custody rate in the Crown Court rose in the period 1992–2005, from 44 to 60 per cent (Home Office 2007a: 14) and the average custodial sentence length (ACSL) for adults in the Crown Court increased from 20.8 in 1995 to 25.9 months in 2005 (ibid). Imprisoning offenders who in the past would have received community punishment and giving longer sentences to those who would previously have gone to prison have added to the prison population. There has been an increase in the numbers of prisoners defined as 'serious' and as presenting a risk to the public, and the introduction of the sentence of imprisonment for public

[5] For example, Anthony Rice was convicted of murdering Naomi Bryant in 2005 while released on licence. A subsequent report was very critical of cumulative failings which meant that the risk of harm was not properly assessed or dealt with (HM Inspectorate of Probation 2006a).

protection (IPP), by the Criminal Justice Act (CJA) 2003, both of which have inflated the prison population. Also, some offences now carry longer sentences as a result of changes in sentencing law and guidance. For example, Schedule 28 to the CJA 2003 raised the maximum penalties for drug-related offences, in some cases from 5 to 14 years. In 1995 the prison population passed 50,000 for the first time (Home Office 1996b); by 2002 it had passed the 70,000 total and has continued to increase, with slight fluctuations since then, reaching 85,000 in 2010. On 9 September 2011 the prison population was 86,842 and by the end of the year, on 23 December 2011, it was 87,393. The increase in 2011 was partly attributed to the impact of sentences for participation in the riots which took place in summer 2011. The latest prison population projections for 2017 suggest the highest figure will be 94,800 and the lowest 83,100 (Ministry of Justice 2011h). This higher figure represents a slight decline from the 2010 projections (Ministry of Justice 2010d). The expansion also arose during a period in which more emphasis was placed on retributivism yet, as we shall see in Chapter 3, in some other societies retributivist-based sentencing systems have prevented excessive punishment.

The expansion of the prison population may be affected by legislative changes and increases in crime detection as well as changes in the enforcement of breach proceedings. Probation Officers are now required to start proceedings for breach of a community sentence after a second failure rather than the third specified under the 1995 Standards (see Home Office *et al.* 2000) whilst more offenders are 'recalled to prison for breaking the condition of their licence' (Da Silva *et al.* 2007: 4). Although it is difficult to make firm predictions because there are a number of variables involved, including sentencing guidelines, it seems very unlikely that the current high levels of the prison population will decrease significantly in the near future.

A number of explanations have been given for the increased use of custody in recent years, including the increasing influence of punitive public opinion on penal policy. More weight has been given to persistence and seriousness in offending (see Chapter 3, section 3.2) and more emphasis has been placed on protecting the public from violent and sexual offenders with a corresponding increase in the number of prisoners serving indeterminate sentences. There is also a much wider range of orders, both civil and criminal, breaches of which are punishable by imprisonment and have increased the numbers in custody.

The combination of these factors means that more pressure is exerted on the prison population and that more offenders are returning to prison following a period in the community. The implications of this expansion on the prison regime and the problems generated by overcrowding will be considered in Chapter 9. Already, the expansion has meant that police cells and even court room cells are used to house prisoners when necessary and, a prison ship, *HMP Weare*, was also used for a period from late 1990s until 2005.

The UK now has one of the highest incarceration rates within Western Europe at 155 per 100,000 of population based on August 2011 figures, compared with 87 in Germany and 94 in the Netherlands (International Centre for Prison Studies 2011). This is surprising in so far as the UK has a far wider range of non-custodial options than most other Western European societies. Sentencing levels are also higher in the UK than in some other European societies, as evidenced, for example, by a comparative study of sentencing of burglars in England and Wales and Finland (see Davis *et al.* 2004). Increases in imprisonment rates are often seen as a reflection of public punitiveness but the rates themselves do not give us information on sentence length which may be significant (Frost 2008).

These rising figures for incarceration in the UK were fuelled by increases in both short and long prison sentences in the 1990s but the expansion of custody cannot be attributed solely to sentencers: the sentencing framework within which they operate is potentially more punitive and the Guidance is more prescriptive (see Piper and Easton 2006/7). The implications of these specific changes in sentencing law will be considered in Chapters 3 and 5.

The House of Commons Justice Committee (2010) in the summary of its report *Cutting Crime: The Case for Justice Reinvestment*, referred to the need to address the root causes of expansion rather than simply focusing on providing more prison places. The causes, it said, include 'a toxic cocktail of sensationalised or inaccurate reporting of difficult cases by the media; relatively punitive overall public opinion (compared to much of the EU); a self-defeating over-politicisation of criminal justice policy since the late 1980s, and the responsiveness to all these factors of the sentencing framework and sentencers'. The Commission on English Prisons Today (2009) in its report also argued for a reduction in prison numbers, the closure of some prisons and greater use of community responses as well as more investment in communities.

The problem is how to 'sell' to the public a reductionist policy, that is, one committed to the aim of reducing the use and extent of imprisonment. A modest decarceration programme or expanded use of alternatives needs to take seriously the public's fears of crime and to contest the public view of the courts as 'soft'. To do this the public need accurate information about crime levels and sentencing decisions and policies. For this purpose, Halliday (2001) proposed putting sentencing guidelines online for the public to access and this has now been implemented. The public also have to be convinced that alternatives to custody will be effective and to be aware that the greater use of imprisonment may not substantially affect crime rates. For example, it is estimated that when the crime rate for violent crime fell in the United States in the 1990s, the large increase in incarceration accounted for only 25 per cent of the fall (see Spelman 2000; King, Mauer, and Young 2005). Obviously the relationship between crime and punishment is complex and it may be difficult to isolate the causal effect of an increase in imprisonment.

As we have seen (section 1.3.3), the public may be less punitive than sentencers and the public is also selectively punitive. Roberts *et al.* (2008) report findings from empirical research on public attitudes towards to the sentencing of culpable driving offences resulting in death. With the exception of one offence, they found greater tolerance of current sentencing practice than is commonly supposed. The public tend to underestimate sentences given and when asked to give their own sentence for a particular cases, suggested sentences similar to or more lenient than the Sentencing Advisory Panel's proposals.

Hough *et al.* (2003) argue that it is necessary to widen the awareness of those who sentence as well as the public, particularly in relation to the advantages of using non-custodial penalties, including fines. But changes in sentencing law and practice and changing public attitudes to crime and punishment will not succeed in reducing prison numbers without the political will and commitment to a reductionist policy. The relationship between political and economic factors is therefore complex, fluid, and indeterminate. While they may sometimes bolster each other, they may also conflict.

1.4 The influence of theory on penal law and practice

1.4.1 Principles from criminology and penology

Penological principles also shape the development of penal policies. These principles are the justifications of punishment and include retribution, deterrence, rehabilitation, public protection, and, more recently, the restoration of social harmony, which will be discussed in Chapters 2 to 6 and 12. Together they constitute the store of knowledge regarding what is, theoretically, the best response in dealing with offenders. Because theorists from opposing traditions may agree that punishment is necessary, but differ in their views of what is the best response, the type of punishment may depend on which theory—which purpose of punishment—is implicit or explicit in policy. It may also depend on which philosophical ideas underpin the chosen punishment, for example whether individuals are seen as autonomous or possessing free will, or whether their actions are viewed as determined by the surrounding environment or genetic make-up. Retributivism punishes according to **just deserts**, which assumes a free choice by a rational person who chooses how to act, while a utilitarian approach may use rewards and punishments to channel behaviour into desirable ends and aims to adjust the social context to change the individual's behaviour, using treatments and therapies to rehabilitate the offender. Compared to political and economic factors, the influence of penology and criminology is limited. However, the economic climate may favour the rise of a particular justification of punishment and particular criminological theories may also be appropriated by governments to legitimise a particular policy. For example, 'left realist' criminology, which developed in the 1980s, was used subsequently to legitimise strong law and order policies and to justify increased punitiveness in the interests of public protection. This theory takes crime seriously, while linking crime to class inequality, and focuses on both crime and the social reaction to crime (see Lea and Young 1984). It recognises crime as a serious social problem, in particular for working-class communities, and demands action accordingly. Elements of this approach can be found in the approach to crime and punishment of both Labour and Coalition Governments.

Another perspective which has strongly influenced penal policy since 1990 is the so-called **New Penology**, although it is now over 20 years old. It draws on New Managerialist and actuarial techniques to manage the risk of offending and reoffending, and is now well established as a theory and practice of punishment (see Feeley and Simon 1992; Simon 1998). This approach, also referred to as actuarial justice, uses technology and statistical calculations to enhance the risk management of high-risk groups. Crime is seen as normal, and the best one can hope for is to control crime and risk through actuarial policies and technocratic forms of knowledge, internally generated by the penal system (Feeley and Simon 1992; Simon 1998). This approach focuses on categories of potential and actual offenders rather than on individuals, and on managerial aims rather than rehabilitation of the offender. It can be seen as a reaction to the decline of rehabilitation and to the 'nothing works' pessimism of the 1980s. Risk—the core concept of the New Penology—is no longer calculated on personal knowledge of particular individuals or by in-depth clinical judgements: risk is seen as distributed unevenly across categories of offender (see Chapter 5). Prison would be reserved for the highest risk categories and actuarial justice provides a means of selecting the target population.

The New Penology has been a significant recent influence on penal policy both here and in the United States. It is both an influence on current policy and also itself a policy approach. It is clear that concern with risk management has diffused through the key agencies of the criminal justice system and has been a significant feature of public concern, particularly in relation to dangerous offenders. It has met with some resistance from probation officers at the point of working with clients while being well-established at the central level of policy making and at the Home Office and Ministry of Justice (see Deering 2011). Managing risk in the community and on release from a custodial sentence has been a major challenge for criminal justice professionals and this has been increasingly seen as a joint enterprise involving cooperation between agencies, as we shall see, in relation to sex offenders and dangerous offenders.

1.4.2 **Classical theories of punishment**

The principal justifications of punishment are closely associated with distinct philosophical traditions or schools. Both retributivist and utilitarian theories have a long history. Retributivism was influential in late eighteenth- and early nineteenth-century philosophy, and was revived in the 1970s and 1980s in the UK and the United States (see Chapter 2). It is strongly associated with the German idealist tradition, particularly the work of Kant and Hegel, which focuses on the role of ideas in the construction of reality and sees reality as mediated through consciousness. The rival tradition is utilitarianism, which includes the justifications of deterrence, social protection or incapacitation, and rehabilitation associated with the English philosophers Bentham (1789) and Mill (1861) but also derived from the work of Beccaria (1767).

Retributivist and utilitarian theorists both accept that punishment may be justly inflicted, but differ in their views of what constitutes the justice of a particular punishment. Both seek to limit the use of discretion in sentencing in favour of a more rigorous principled approach and both address the issue of proportionality but from quite different standpoints. Consequently both see a link between punishment and the seriousness of the offence by upholding the idea that custody should be reserved for the most serious offences. However, the utilitarian does so because it is hoped this will prevent the commission in the future of those offences which are most harmful to the public. So it is important to find the optimal level of punishment, to prevent offenders from reoffending, to deter the general public, and to protect the public from future offending by incapacitating individuals who threaten society. So there is scope on this theory for preventive sentencing. However, the aim in devising punishments is to prevent future offending at minimal expense, so utilitarians would not favour excessive or harsh punishment unless there are clear social benefits which result from that punishment. Punishment can also be used to rehabilitate the offender so that he can make a useful contribution within the prison community and on his return to the wider society.

Neither approach can be seen as purely theoretical as each has had a strong impact on penal policy in recent years. What is interesting is that although these theories are strongly opposed to each other in certain key assumptions, in practice they may both be incorporated in the same piece of legislation. The main provisions of the CJA 1991, for example, were based on a version of retributivist philosophy, but parts of that Act and subsequent legislation reflect utilitarian principles. So s 142(1) of the CJA 2003, despite the continuance elsewhere in that Act of retributivist criteria for the use of different levels of sentence (see Chapter 3), imposes a varied—and potentially inconsistent—list of five 'purposes of sentencing' to which the courts must 'have regard': the punishment of offenders, the reduction of crime (including its reduction by deterrence), the reform and rehabilitation of offenders, the protection of the public, and the making of reparation by offenders to persons affected by their offences. Individuals may also hold, for example, strongly retributivist views on violent crimes but take a more utilitarian approach in relation to lesser offences.

On the retributivist approach, just deserts equates to determining a sentence which is proportional to culpability so that offenders receive what they deserve for what they have done. There is no concern with the future effects of the sentence but rather with a just response to wrongdoing. On retributivist theory, justice demands that the perpetrator of the offence suffers punishment, regardless of the effects the individual's suffering may have on himself or others. Justice is served only if the offender is made to suffer. In completing the term of punishment, the offender pays and cancels his debt to society. Chapters 2 and 4 will explore in more detail the foundational writings of the retributivist and utilitarian approaches and the problems they raise, and we have provided at the end of this chapter an exercise which you might wish to do. It makes very clear the difference that the application of principles makes to sentencing outcomes. Next, however, we will focus on just deserts.

1.4.3 The influence of 'just deserts'

One major influence on penal and sentencing policy has been a particular retributivist idea of 'just deserts'. Prior to 1991 its influence was not clear but the CJA 1991 imposed a new constraint on the courts' discretion—that of a presumptive sentencing rationale. In the 1990 White Paper *Crime, Justice and Protecting the Public*, the UK Government had announced its intention to establish 'a new and more coherent statutory framework for sentencing' (Home Office 1990a: para 1.5): 'The aim of the government's proposals is better justice through a more consistent approach to sentencing so that convicted criminals get their "just deserts". The severity of the sentence of the court should be directly related to the seriousness of the offence' (ibid: para 1.6).

A general aim of sentencing on retributivist principles was not, however, invented in 1991. The Streatfeild Committee in 1961 said that 'sentencing used to be a comparatively simple matter. The primary objective was to fix a sentence proportionate to the offender's culpability', the assumption being that practice had diversified with the increased use of rehabilitative, community-based measures so that sentencers could freely choose to sentence on one or more principles. There had emerged a 'tariff system' under which sentencers could use a normal range of sentences and choose what was proportionate to a particular level of offence gravity (see Cross 1981: 167–73) but they could also choose a sentence based on the needs of the offender (see Henham 1995: 221–2).

The significance of the provisions in the CJA 1991 was, then, that they statutorily imposed on judges and magistrates 'just deserts' as the presumptive rationale. The 1991 Act imposed levels of seriousness as 'hurdles' to the use of two of the three main levels of punishment. Consequently, the sentencing decision-making process had to focus first on basic elements of a just deserts approach—the calculation of seriousness and the consideration of a sentence proportionate to it (see Chapter 2). This is not to say that all sentencing provisions in the 1990s were consistent with this rationale, given the existence of the provisions in the 1991 Act justifying custodial sentences on the basis of protecting the public, and the form of cumulative mandatory sentences added by the Crime (Sentences) Act 1997 (see Chapter 2, section 2.3.3) which were explicitly excluded from the just deserts approach (Powers of Criminal Courts (Sentencing) Act 2000, ss 34(b), 79(1)(b), and 127).

This basic question of sentencing rationale—with its long history in classical theory—is still currently high on the policy agenda and the subject of academic critique. In particular the recent changes have raised the fundamental question of 'why punish?'. Justifications are central to sentencing and they are also central to the legitimacy of policy. If sentencing policies are to be justifiable to the electorate they must be capable of being supported by reasons, to justify the actions—or failure to act—of sentencers and the costs of punishment imposed on society. As we have already noted, the CJA 2003 provides five punishment aims to be considered by sentencers. But Dingwall (2008) argues that notions of desert remain very important in modern sentencing law and policy and in the sentencing of adult offenders and may be found in both the CJA 2003 and in the sentencing guidelines.

1.5 Penal policy: conflicts and ambiguities

We have identified a number of key influences on penal policy which we will now consider in relation to the development of penal policy in the UK in the late twentieth and early twenty-first century, and, more specifically, in relation to the governance of sex offenders. Recurring themes are removing inconsistency in sentencing, targeting persistent offending, and improving cooperation between different agencies. There has also been a move towards the aim of a centralised criminal justice system by unifying the separate probation services into a National Probation Service for England and Wales under provisions in the Criminal Justice and Court Services Act 2000, and by conjoining the Prison and Probation Services into the National Offender Management Service in 2004. Further integration is planned by the current Coalition Government.

1.5.1 Policy trends

If we consider the broad shifts in penal policy in England and Wales in the period after the Second World War, we can identify a number of important trends, a major thread being the changing fortunes of the **rehabilitative ideal** with its optimism that the offender could be reformed. As we shall see (Chapter 12), the rehabilitative ideal was reflected in the development of community penalties to operate as alternatives to custody and the treatment approach had gained ascendancy by the 1960s, with a further order, the community service order, introduced in England and Wales in 1972. However, the increase in crime and evidence of recidivism in the 1970s and early 1980s cast doubt on the validity of this approach and its use declined in the 1980s and 1990s (see Chapter 12). Yet, the rehabilitative ideal has in recent years received further support, albeit prompted primarily by pragmatic cost considerations. It survives in the Probation Service and in offending behaviour programmes (see Chapter 12) and has remained a major influence on penal policies in some other European societies, including the Netherlands (see Boone and Moerings 2007).

The 1990s were, nevertheless, marked by an increased use of punishment and incapacitation, with both the Conservative and Labour administrations tending to focus on punishment rather than crime. The endorsement in the CJA 1991 of just deserts as the primary principle of sentencing focused sentencing on proportionate punishment rather than treatment or deterrence *per se*. The increased concern with incapacitation became evident in the electronic monitoring and curfew provisions introduced by the CDA 1998[6] and through prison expansion, whilst a trend of making alternatives to custody more punitive—or at to least appear so—developed. Policies in the 1990s also revealed a continuing acceptance of managerialism, increased concern with safety and justice for victims, and a commitment to speed up the criminal justice process, so as to shorten the period between arrest and trial. The volume of legislation on sentencing and punishment has increased substantially since the late 1990s. The CDA 1998 introduced new penalties for young offenders and new measures such as curfews, anti-social behaviour orders, and sex offender orders, and a wide range of new criminal offences was created by the Sexual Offences Act (SOA) 2003.

We have previously made the point that when the government uses 'punitive rhetoric' to win support it is a double-edged sword: 'tough' penal policies impose substantial

[6] Now consolidated in ss 37 and 38 of the Powers of Criminal Courts (Sentencing) Act 2000; see also CJA 2003, ss 204 and 215.

economic burdens when the government is also under pressure to cut costs. One government technique is to shift the burden for crime prevention to the individual by giving the message that we are all stakeholders in society: the individual and community should take responsibility for safeguarding their homes and property, through better security, neighbourhood watch schemes, by not inviting crime, and by reporting crime.

Since 1990 concern with value for money has, then, loomed large and this has encouraged the introduction of privatisation and New Managerialism within the state sector. On the other hand, there has been much more concern with the rights and needs of the victim, and there have been substantial improvements in the physical conditions and quality of life in prisons (see Chapter 11, section 11.4.2). With the incorporation of the European Convention on Human Rights into UK law in 1998, human rights issues have also assumed increasing significance in prison policy (see Chapter 9, section 9.6).

1.5.2 **Key policy documents 2000–2004**

Since 2000 there have been several major policy documents on sentencing and punishment which provide evidence of the continuing importance in policy of the factors outlined in the previous section. First, the White Paper, *Criminal Justice: The Way Ahead*, published in February 2001, affirmed the Government's commitment to funding another 2,660 prison places and committed an extra £689 million for the Prison Service over the following three years, £21 million of which was to be used to prevent reoffending. The White Paper aimed to reduce both crime and fear of crime, and so also reduce the social and economic costs of crime. It argued that the criminal justice system has to be effective in preventing offending and reoffending and efficient in the way it deals with cases, to be responsive to victims and the community and to dispense justice fairly and efficiently, promoting confidence in the rule of law.

Similarly, the Halliday Report, *Making Punishments Work*, published in July 2001, referred to the need to increase public confidence and reduce crime. It advocated more research on the costs and benefits of particular sentences and proposed a duty on the Secretary of State to disseminate information about the effectiveness of sentencing as well as its costs. The Report argued that the aims of sentencing should cover crime reduction, reparation, and punishment and set out what was needed to achieve these aims: to clarify what is effective, particularly in relation to short sentences, to produce clear guidelines to achieve sentence consistency, and to ensure that previous convictions are reflected in sentence severity. It advocated a statutory Penal Code and guidelines on calculating the seriousness of the offence and recommended closer collaboration between sentencers and other criminal justice agencies to achieve 'seamless sentencing', with the utilitarian aims of informing sentencers about what is available and what works in reducing reoffending. It also recognised the need to improve public confidence in sentencing practice and to involve the public in that process by inviting them to comment on sentencing guidelines and increasing Parliamentary control of sentencing.

Both these policy documents also reflect the rise of actuarial justice, whilst the need to improve public confidence in sentencing was stressed by the Auld Review of the Criminal Courts published in 2001 which included recommendations on sentencing, including advance indication of sentencing for defendants pleading guilty (para 114). It also advocated codification of the law of sentencing (para 198), stressed the need for honesty and simplicity in sentencing (para 199), and advocated practical measures, such as the use of information technology to support judicial sentencing, providing an information service for all judges (para 210).

Research on the public's view of the work of the courts fed into this review. For example, Morgan's research for the Home Office revealed the extent of public ignorance of the role of the lower courts and a resulting lack of public confidence, finding that only 29 per cent of the population thought magistrates were doing a good job (Morgan 2000: 61 and 72). Sanders found that 61 per cent of the population thought magistrates were 'out of touch' (Sanders 2001: 1; see also Morgan 2000: vii). Morgan estimated that in the magistrates' courts 91 per cent of cases were dealt with by lay magistrates and the rest by district judges (formerly stipendiaries) although the public was not aware of that fact (ibid: 2).

In response to the Halliday and Auld Reports the Labour Government issued a White Paper *Justice for All*, which stressed the need to 'rebalance the system in favour of victims, witnesses and communities', to give paramount importance to protecting the public, to restore public confidence in the criminal justice system, and to improve the coherence of the system by closer integration of the police, prosecution, courts, and Probation Service (Home Office 2002c). It proposed to set out the principles of sentencing in legislation and proposed a Sentencing Guidelines Council to formulate consistent guidelines. The White Paper also put forward plans for new sentences: customised community sentences to allow courts to choose between a range of options for individual offenders; custody minus, a new suspended sentence, which would include the same options as the customised community sentence; custody plus, a sentence of up to 12 months which would comprise a maximum of three months' custody, followed by compulsory supervision in the community; and intermittent custody, which would allow offenders to serve their sentence on a part-time basis. A new special sentence for violent/sexual offenders to ensure they remain in custody until their risks are manageable within the community was proposed and also a national strategy for restorative justice.

Justice for All accepted the Auld Report's proposals for a new national Criminal Justice Board responsible for overall delivery of the criminal justice system, an increase in magistrates' sentencing powers to 12 months (not yet implemented) and the abolition of magistrates' powers to commit cases for sentencing to the Crown Court. It aimed to encourage early guilty pleas with a formalisation of plea bargaining, by means of a clearer tariff of sentence discounts and it expressed concern at failures to bring offenders to justice, delays in trial, and the problem of wrongful acquittals (although no evidence was offered in support of the last point). It promised more support for victims, including a Code of Practice and a new Commissioner for victims and witnesses, and said that victims of mentally disordered offenders would be entitled to information about their release.

Many of the proposals in *Criminal Justice: The Way Ahead* and *Justice for All* were enacted in the CJA 2003, a major piece of legislation which incorporated wide-ranging provisions on evidence, procedure, and sentencing, including amending the law on double jeopardy, increasing the time limits for detention under PACE, removing the right to jury trial in complex fraud cases, and reforming the rules on the disclosure of evidence, bad character, and hearsay evidence. The Act introduced a new generic community punishment with a wide range of components (see Chapter 12, section 12.1.2), and the sentence of imprisonment for public protection (IPP). Although provisions for a custody plus penalty which involved costly intensive supervision following custody and intermittent custody were contained in the Act, these measures have since been shelved. The Act also created the Sentencing Guidelines Council (see Chapter 2, section 2.4.3). Because the Act is so massive, with 339 sections, it is possible that only the most controversial clauses were subjected to full scrutiny.

The aim of the CJA 2003, in line with *Justice for All*, was to rebalance the criminal justice system, and this implied increasing the rights of victims, even if this meant fewer rights for defendants. The way this is constructed using a 'zero-sum' view of power, where one side must lose if the other gains, is misleading: increasing the rights of victims does not of itself necessarily mean reducing the rights of defendants. For example, the Youth Justice and Criminal Evidence Act 1999—which seeks to provide greater protection for vulnerable witnesses—also contains complementary provisions to avoid any prejudice to the defendant.

1.5.3 **Policy documents 2004–2009**

Since 2004 the focus on 'rebalancing the criminal justice in favour of the law-abiding majority' and on protecting the public from dangerous offenders and from a range of anti-social behaviours, and particularly from unruly young offenders, has persisted. The policy paper *Rebalancing the Criminal Justice System in Favour of the Law-abiding Majority* (Home Office 2006a) emphasised the need to enhance public confidence in the fairness of the system to law-abiding people and communities, as 80 per cent of the public believed the criminal justice system was fair to the offender but only 36 per cent thought it met the needs of victims (ibid: para 1.20). It recommended a range of measures to assist victims and witnesses and stressed that this rebalancing programme would be supported by stronger enforcement. At the same time it advocated pursuing the use of restorative justice methods and outcomes for juvenile and adult offenders, although most of the initiatives were introduced on an experimental basis (see Chapter 6).

A further key policy initiative in 2005 was the Labour Government's 'Respect Agenda' aimed at combating anti-social behaviour. Supporting families and communities, developing parenting services, improving school attendance, intervening in families, homes, and schools to promote respect, and extending powers to the community to deal with anti-social behaviour and using civil measures were key elements of this Agenda. It also had implications for penal policy, and particularly for youth justice policy, as one element was to improve the way the criminal justice system deals with anti-social behaviour, providing visible and constructive punishment for offenders and improving enforcement (see Chapters 8 and 13).

The consultation paper *Making Sentencing Clearer* (Home Secretary *et al.* 2006) was also intended to be part of the rebalancing process. Its aim was to make sentencing clearer for all parties involved, victims, witnesses and defendants, and to give judges more discretion and flexibility in reducing the sentence discounts for a guilty plea. It also proposed greater use of fines, stronger community sentences as an alternative to custody, and better protection from dangerous offenders through the use of indeterminate sentences.

The Criminal Justice and Immigration Act (CJIA) 2008 amended relevant sections of the CJA 2003, 'clarified' the principles of sentencing for offenders under 18, added further requirements for use with ASBOs, and introduced youth rehabilitation orders which are intended to give more flexibility to the court as the court can incorporate several requirements. It gave sentencers greater discretion, particularly on whether to impose a sentence of imprisonment for public protection (IPP) and extended sentences.

The Coroners and Justice Act 2009 contained provisions setting up the new Sentencing Council for England and Wales with a wide range of duties including the preparation of sentencing guidelines promoting awareness of matters relating to the sentencing of offenders, and assessing the impact of policy and legislative proposals (see Chapter 2, section 2.4.4).

In addition to these specific sentencing initiatives, there have been a number of organisational changes during this period, including the establishment of the National Offender Management Service (NOMS) which was set up in June 2004, following the recommendations of the Carter Report (Carter 2003). NOMS has taken over responsibility for the overall management of offenders. It aims to reduce reoffending by improving the way offenders are managed and by improving family links, education, and skills in both custody and the community. Its major priority is public protection, which has implications for the sharing of information between agencies, regular risk assessments, and reassessments, and effective supervision and closer cooperation between the prisons and probation service in the process of offender management. It also plays a key role in commissioning services from the private, voluntary and community sectors in relation to the punishment, support, and reform of offenders. It is working on ways of improving fine enforcement. The new organisational framework for the provision of probation services was set out in the Offender Management Act 2007 (see Chapter 12, section 12.3.5). Further restructuring and rationalisation of its functions has recently been undertaken, with its geographic structure being replaced by a functional model.

A further major organisational change was the creation of the Ministry of Justice in 2007 which took over responsibility for prisons, probation, and sentencing from the Home Office. The National Offender Management Service and the Prison and Probation Services are now the responsibility of the Secretary of State for Justice and the Ministry of Justice. These changes followed a protracted period of criticism of the Home Office during 2006 and 2007, including the revelation that during the period 1999–2006 over 1,000 foreign national prisoners had been released without being considered for deportation.

The reforms initiated during the last few years of the Labour administration were met with some criticism. The pace of change and the volume of legislation added to the burdens on practitioners working with the criminal justice system. There were also concerns that the balance had swung too far in favour of the state. The increasing range of controls over individuals' movements, in control orders and other civil orders, particularly if based on the prospect of future rather than past offences, has also led to extensive criticisms of the Government (see Liberty 2006, 2007).

1.5.4 ***Breaking the Cycle*: New directions 2010–11**

During the 2010 General Election campaign the need to be tough on crime was stressed by all the main parties. The Labour Party wanted to continue prison expansion, while reducing the number of women and those with mental health problems in prison, and to expedite the transfer of EU prisoners. The Conservatives favoured the abolition of early release and the expansion of prison capacity as necessary, but also a stronger focus on rehabilitation and on the early deportation of foreign national prisoners, with one organisation focusing on rehabilitation. The Liberal Democrats were critical of prison expansion and the failure to reduce reoffending, and favoured greater use of restorative justice and for prisoners to undertake paid work, in order to compensate victims. Obviously the outcome of the Election has muddied these waters further, but the Conservative–Liberal Democrat Coalition Government has in some respects initially appeared to be moving away from traditional Tory values on law and order and punishment.

Following the General Election, the new Coalition Government made clear that it would be placing reform of the delivery of punishment at the forefront of its programme. In May 2010 the Justice Secretary Ken Clarke (2010) announced that he wished to make greater use of community punishments with greater involvement from the voluntary and private sector. He also said that he did not believe that prison expansion had led to a fall in crime. The Green Paper *Breaking the Cycle: Effective Punishment, Rehabilitation and Sentencing of Offenders* published in December 2010 set out the Coalition Government's proposed reforms to the criminal justice system, including sentencing and rehabilitation, and reflected both Liberal Democratic and Conservative criminal justice policies (Ministry of Justice 2010a). The Paper includes specific measures relating to imprisonment, community punishment, sentencing, and policing.

The focus is on effective rehabilitation and the Paper refers to the introduction of new measures to achieve this, and emphasises the importance of the accountability of service providers so that they are paid according to the results they achieve. Payment by results is intended to make providers of rehabilitation services accountable. Providers from all sectors will be given freedom to introduce innovative programmes to achieve results and will be paid according to the outcomes. Much greater use will be made of the private, voluntary, and community sectors, and they will be given more discretion. Six new pilot 'payment by results' projects will be commissioned. It is envisaged that one payment will be made for meeting statutory requirements and ensuring compliance with the sentence. A further payment which depends on the result the provider delivers in reducing re-offending will then be made. The rewards may be given to probation service providers or to the prison, depending on the length of sentence. In addition it is intended that independent providers will enter the market but they may also enter partnerships with public service providers, but at a local level.

The aim of the proposed reforms is to promote competition, increase cost effectiveness and involve local people in these efforts to promotion rehabilitation. The concern is to improve public safety and to reduce both re-offending and the financial burden of imprisonment by breaking the cycle of re-offending. The principles underpinning the Green Paper are public protection, punishing and rehabilitating offenders, transparency and accountability, and decentralisation. The importance of developing a network of community provision is stressed, using education and interventions for drug and alcohol abuse, through probation and the voluntary sector, to deal with offenders with multiple needs. It is also intended to reshape services for offenders with severe forms of personality disorder and that the use of MAPPAs will be continued.

Prisons

The Green Paper acknowledges that a large number of offenders have multiple problems including drug and alcohol problems, housing and employment problems, and few educational qualifications. There will be greater emphasis on work within prison and the aim will be for prisoners to work a normal working week of up to 40 hours. The voluntary, private, and community sectors will be used to develop the 'working prison'. There will also be provision for prisoners to make financial reparation to victims and contribute to the cost of services to victims from their earnings. When prisoners leave prison further support will be given to promote work rather than welfare. The number of IPP prisoners will be reduced and the test for release used by the Parole Board will be reformed. The release targets for current IPP prisoners will also be improved. The number of remand prisoners will be reduced by reforming the Bail Act so that there is no option for remanding in custody defendants who are unlikely to receive a custodial sentence. The Government also plans to cut the number of foreign national prisoners.

Non-custodial options

Outside prison, Community Payback will be made more intensive and should immediately follow the imposition of sentence. More discretion will be given to those who supervise offenders on community orders. Curfew orders will be made tougher and in some cases extended to 16 hours a day and up to one year. It is also intended to pilot a 'payment by results' system for drug recovery in the community. In addition there will be greater emphasis on use and enforcement of fines. The Government will also explore ways in which courts can seize personal property as a disposal in itself. More use will be made of out of court disposals, using community justice. Financial compensation to victims from offenders will be given greater weight. Sentencers will be encouraged to make greater use of compensation orders. Victims will be given more opportunities to give statements to the court so that victim statements are used routinely. It is envisaged that more use will be made of restorative justice. More freedom will be given service providers of rehabilitation programmes with payment by results for those working with persistent offenders (see Chapter 12).

Youth justice

Again, the Green Paper states the Government's intention to place more emphasis on diversion from offending and on reparation to victims, and to give more freedom and flexibility for local bodies. Greater use will be made of parenting orders and of restorative justice. The use of payment by results for youth justice is also being considered to encourage local areas to reduce youth offending. Pilots will be set up to explore how local areas can share in financial savings and risks of custody. The Green Paper also indicated that the functions of the Youth Justice Board would be undertaken directly by the Ministry of Justice, but this proposal has now been reversed.

Sentencing

The aim is to make the sentencing process more transparent and easier for the public to understand and for sentencers to use. Already data on sentencing at individual court level has been made available to the public. More information will be published on sentencing to improve public awareness and understanding. Sentencing law will be simplified so just one sentencing framework applies to all offenders and constraints on sentencers' discretion will be reduced. The process whereby sentencers explain the reason for a particular sentence will be simplified. The IPP sentence will be reviewed. The Green Paper also indicated that the discount for a guilty plea might be increased to 50 per cent but, as noted earlier, this was jettisoned in the face of considerable opposition (see Chapter 3, section 3.3.3).

The Government undertook a consultation on the proposals in the Green Paper and published its response in June 2011, when it reaffirmed the importance of prison as a place of work, the need for prison work to be self-financing and sustainable as far as possible, and the need to make it easier for organisations to work with prisons in providing work (Ministry of Justice 2011a). It intends to implement the Prisoners' Earnings Act and generally to make greater use of financial payback by offenders with a duty on courts to make compensation orders. It also intends to review sentencing for serious sex offenders and violent offenders including replacement of the IPP with a determinate sentencing framework. There will be greater use of restorative justice at all stages and new ways of punishing offenders will be developed, including the use of foreign travel orders.

Many of the proposals in *Breaking the Cycle* and the Government's *Response* were contained in the Legal Aid, Sentencing and Punishment of Offenders Bill introduced to Parliament in June 2011. Part 3 covers sentencing and the punishment of offenders and the provisions include giving courts an express duty to consider making compensation orders where victims have suffered harm or loss; reducing the detailed requirements on courts when they give reasons for a sentence; and allowing courts to suspend sentences of up to two years rather than 12 months. It also introduces new powers to allow curfews to be imposed for more hours in the day and for up to 12 months rather than the current six months and changes the law on bail and remand, aimed at reducing the number of those who are unnecessarily remanded into custody. Under the new 'no real prospect' test, people will be released on bail if they would be unlikely to receive a custodial sentence. In addition the Secretary of State is given new powers to make prison rules about prisoners' employment, pay, and deductions from their pay. The intention of these provisions is that prisoners should make payments which would support victims of crime. It also allows for foreign national prisoners serving indeterminate sentences to be deported when their tariff expires. It also repeals the custody plus and intermittent custody provisions in the CJA 2003.

The Government also announced in July 2011 that the management of an additional eight public sector prisons would be subject to competition with a view to cutting costs and increasing efficiency, and the closure of two smaller prisons. It also set out its competition strategy for offender services which elaborates on the plans for increased involvement of the private and voluntary sectors in the rehabilitation process and the creation of a market in the provision of offender management and rehabilitation (Ministry of Justice 2011e).

It is also clear from recent policy pronouncements that reform of the penal system is likely to remain high on the political agenda and that the pace of change may be increased. Responding to the August 2011 riots the Justice Secretary Ken Clarke (2011) referred to the fact that many of the rioters had previous convictions and observed, 'That is the legacy of a broken penal system—one whose record in preventing reoffending has been straightforwardly dreadful'.

1.5.5 **Current policy criticisms**

The Coalition Government's recognition of the problems with the current system including the problems with the incarceration of offenders with mental health problems and the excessive use of IPP sentences is to be welcomed, as is the need to boost public confidence in community punishment. The Green Paper also recognises the multiple deprivations associated with much of offending and the limitations of prison in addressing these problems. The proposed investment in drug and alcohol abuse and mental health services is also welcome. The Paper is likely to generate discussion on the role of prisons and the question of rehabilitation which is long overdue. However, precisely because of the wide range of factors which affect offending it is difficult to see why improving competition *per se* will provide a panacea for existing problems. Moreover while the aim of the reforms is to cut bureaucracy and centralised control by government, the concern is that regulation and administering the payment by results process will lead to further layers of regulation and control.

The shift away from existing professionals towards a broader range of providers will also need to be carefully monitored as there may be concerns over their expertise and experience. There may also be issues of safety involved for less experienced groups and individuals entering the market. If greater reliance is made on the voluntary sector, they will need sufficient funding to develop their work.

The Government is committed to retaining and using the findings of the new Sentencing Council, which replaced the Sentencing Guidelines Council in 2010, so its role will be crucial in the future developments (see Chapter 2, section 2.4.4). The desire to give more discretion to sentencers may be problematic as discretion in the past has sometimes conflicted with the goal of consistency.

The plans for increasing work in prison may also be problematic. The importance of not undercutting labour outside the prison is acknowledged but if labour is priced at the same level, given the additional costs of setting up and monitoring prison work it is difficult to see how it can compete or offer incentives to private companies to invest. In the United States, where prison work is more developed, there have been concerns over unfair competition as the federal body which employs prisoners sells goods and services to other government departments. There have also been concerns over the exploitation of labour and over whether this could be seen as a new form of penal servitude.

The key question is how far these measures will reduce the prison population. The Secretary of State for Justice has pledged to reduce the prison population by 3,000 within four years and the measures in the Green Paper will assist this process but many would still see this as insufficient to address the problem of penal expansion. This target is also now unlikely to be achieved as the proposed increase in the sentence discount has been dropped.

1.6 The governance of sex offenders: a case study

Some of these issues which we have discussed in relation to the formulation of penal policy will now be considered by focusing on the governance of sex offenders in England and Wales, because this raises concerns about the protection of the public, the impact of populist punitiveness, just deserts, human rights, and the influence of risk management and actuarial justice.

A number of measures aimed at improving the control, detention, and arrest of sex offenders were introduced in the UK in the late 1990s. They included the registration scheme established by the Sex Offenders Act 1997 and sex offender orders created by the CDA 1998, a life sentence for a second serious sexual offence in the Crime (Sentences) Act 1997, and legislation dealing with stalkers in the Protection from Harassment Act 1997. New measures to deal with sex tourism were introduced in Part II of the Sex Offenders Act 1997, as amended by para 4 of Schedule 5 to the Criminal Justice and Court Services Act 2000, and to prevent the improper use of evidence relating to sexual offences in the Sexual Offences (Protected Material) Act 1997. Special measures to assist complainants of sexual offences were introduced by the Youth Justice and Criminal Evidence Act 1999. Monitoring of persons working with children was strengthened by the Protection of Children Act 1999 and the Criminal Justice and Court Services Act 2000 and by the establishment of the Criminal Records Bureau, although there are now plans to limit the vetting scheme and change the system of criminal record checks in the Protection of Freedoms Bill going through Parliament.

In addition, penalties for possession of indecent photographs of children were increased and the regime for inspecting residential homes was improved. Cooperation between agencies to manage the risk posed by sexual and serious offenders in the community was formalised and given a statutory basis in the Criminal Justice and Court Services Act 2000, re-enacted by the CJA 2003. The SOA 2003, changed the law relating to the issue of consent in rape cases, included provisions on sexual offences against children, abuse of a position of trust, abuse of children through prostitution and pornography, and introduced new civil preventive orders designed to protect children. A new offence of possession of extreme pornography was also created by s 63 of the CJIA 2008 (see Easton 2011b).

New measures to control the movements of sex offenders were also introduced in the late 1990s. The Sex Offenders Act 1997 provided for the creation of a register recording all persons convicted of or cautioned for a sexual offence. Part I imposed a requirement for convicted and cautioned sex offenders to notify the police of their name and address and inform them of any changes of residence, including holidays. How long the individual stayed subject to the notification requirements depended on the length of the sentence imposed for the offence. These notification requirements are now found in the SOA 2003.

The CDA 1998 introduced the sex offender order, a civil order which prohibited the offender from engaging in conduct such as loitering near a school. The Chief Officer of Police could apply for an order if a person who is a convicted or cautioned sex offender had acted, since his conviction or caution, in such a way as to give reasonable cause to believe that an order under the section was necessary to protect the public from serious harm. It was not necessary for a particular victim to be identified, nor to prove intent. Once in place the order had effect for a minimum of five years. Once an order was made under s 2 of the CDA 1998, the individual to whom the order applied was also subject to the notification requirements. While the orders were civil restraining orders, if breached offenders incurred penalties of fines and/or imprisonment. The sex offender order was granted on the basis of risk calculations generated by present conduct, so its application was selective in contrast to the Sex Offenders Act 1997. Past convictions were a necessary but not a sufficient condition for granting an order and there had to be an evidential basis for granting an order. The sex offender order has now been replaced by the new sexual offences prevention order (SOPO) in the SOA 2003. The SOPO remains a civil order whose aim is to protect the public from serious sexual harm, although, as before, its breach constitutes a criminal offence, punishable on conviction by a maximum of five years' imprisonment. The order applies to a wide range of sexual offences defined in Schedule 3 to the Act. An application may be made by a Chief Officer of Police and the court must be persuaded that the defendant's behaviour subsequent to the first relevant conviction makes the order necessary 'for the purpose of protecting the public or any particular members of the public from serious sexual harm from the defendant' (s 104(1)(a)). It may prohibit the offender from carrying out any activities described in the order. It will last for a minimum of five years. Once an order is granted the offender becomes subject to the notification requirements of the Sex Offenders Act 1997, which are now included in the SOA 2003. The order also brings the offender within the remit of the Multi Agency Public Protection Panel arrangements. There is a legal requirement on the police, and the probation and prison services, to organise arrangements to assess and manage the risks presented by violent and sexual offenders, to monitor these arrangements, and to furnish annual reports.

The SOA 2003 also introduced foreign travel orders which enable the magistrates' court to restrict the travel of those convicted in the UK or abroad of sexual offences against a child under 16, if the court is satisfied that the defendant's behaviour since the relevant conviction makes this necessary in order to protect children from serious sexual harm from the defendant. The orders may prevent travel to a specified country or travelling to anywhere in the world for a maximum period of six months. Although these are also civil orders, their breach constitutes a criminal offence punishable by a maximum of five years' imprisonment. The Act also introduced a new 'risk of sexual harm order'. This is more extensive, in so far as it is not necessary for the defendant to have been convicted of an offence, but only that on at least two previous occasions, the defendant has engaged in sexually explicit conduct or communication with a child, for example, sending pornographic material to a child over the internet. The order may prohibit the offender from doing anything described in the order which is necessary to protect the child or children from harm from the defendant. The order will be for a minimum of two years but subject to procedures to renew or discharge the order and with a right of appeal. Breaches can be punished by a maximum of five years' imprisonment. Each of the orders in the Act is essentially based on an assessment of the risk of future offending and, as such, raises problems of prediction and justification, which will be discussed further in Chapter 5.

Sex offenders have now been absorbed into the discourse of risk management, and surveillance has extended beyond the prison into ordinary life. Risk assessment is part of this process of transcarceration and the move towards ever greater surveillance and acquisition of knowledge, charted by Foucault (1977) and Beck (1992), has found expression in the new legislation. There is now less public tolerance of sex offenders in the UK, less sympathy for medical models of individual pathology, and greater willingness to see sex offenders as bad rather than mad, to be removed from the community rather than being changed or cured through treatment. The dominant model in therapeutic programmes is the cognitive–behavioural model which accepts that it is more productive to focus on the development of reasoning skills and new ways of thinking, rather than to search for the underlying causes of deviant behaviour, which may be too time-consuming and ultimately unattainable. The issues of risk assessment of sexual offenders, as well as the efficacy of current policies and methods of treatment are assessed by Harrison (2011) who considers the ways of addressing gaps within the system and improving the treatment of serious sexual and violent offenders.

Attempts to categorise levels of risk of sex offenders for the purposes of the registration scheme may be problematic as the criteria for registration are unwieldy and do not distinguish between them in terms of individual risk but, rather, impose a period of registration based on sentence length. The penalties imposed for breaches of sexual offender orders have also been variable (see Shute 2004a). The UK Government's focus on risk management in response to the public's punitiveness, has also raised problems as it has come into conflict with the protection of human rights. For example, the UK courts have already issued a declaration of incompatibility over the imposition of life long notification requirements for offenders sentenced to over 30 months, without any provision for review. In *R (on the application of F and Angus Aubrey Thompson) v Secretary of State for the Home Department* (2010), the Supreme Court has ruled that the absence of a review is disproportionate and breaches Article 8 of the European Convention on Human Rights. The Court ruled that there must be an opportunity for the offender to show that indefinite notification is no longer necessary. In this case one of the appellants had committed the offence as a child. In response to this decision, the Government has drafted a Remedial Order setting out a review mechanism and is awaiting comments on this consultation. It has also undertaken a consultation on strengthening the notification requirements, for example with new provisions for those of no fixed abode.

However, for some sections of the public the measures to control sex offenders currently available are insufficiently punitive and should be supplemented by full disclosure and preventive detention. A limited step towards disclosure was made by setting up public disclosure pilot schemes in 2008 in Hampshire, Warwickshire, Cambridgeshire, and Cleveland police force areas. These schemes permitted parents, guardians, or carers to check with the police if a person with access to their children had convictions for child sex offences. The Child Sex Offender Disclosure Scheme was subsequently extended to all police forces in England and Wales in 2010–11. The One Year Disclosure Pilots were reviewed by Kemshall and Wood (2010) who found a lower number of applications than expected, no evidence of serious breaches of confidentiality, and no changes in compliance of offenders with registration and probation supervision.

The move towards restricting the movement of sex offenders reflects a wider use of civil orders to reinforce the criminal law, while avoiding Article 7 Convention challenges as retrospective penalties. As well as the range of measures directed against sex offenders, we have seen in recent years increased use of anti-social behaviour orders, and s 1 of the Serious Crime Act 2007 has introduced another order, the serious crime prevention order, which is similar in some respects to the SOPO and ASBO, and which aims to exert control over the movements and assets of those involved in serious crime. Although creating civil orders, these provisions create new criminal offences of failing to comply with these orders, which attract criminal penalties. The aim is to protect the public by preventing, restricting, and disrupting involvement in serious crime. In addition, the courts have powers to impose extensive controls on individuals' movements under anti-terrorist legislation.

We also now have youth rehabilitation orders (s 1) and violent offender orders (s 98) in the CJIA 2008. The aim of the violent offender order is to protect the public from serious harm by imposing further restrictions on violent offenders. However, it is likely that if the terms imposed are too restrictive the move towards increasing controls may raise future Convention challenges and arguments over whether they constitute retrospective punishments. Collectively we can see a shift towards controls within the community intended to protect the public by preventing possible future offending which, as we shall see in Chapters 2 and 3, raises problems for retributivism. We also find increasing emphasis on prisoners' rights under the European Convention on Human Rights and Convention challenges being brought in both the domestic courts and the Strasbourg Court (see Chapter 9, section 6).

1.7 Conclusion

1.7.1 Key themes

As we have seen, the state's response to crime formulated in specific penal policies reflects a number of key influences, the relative importance of which may change over time. We have identified the principal developments since 1990 and have also highlighted issues of equality, fairness, and justice which we will discuss in greater detail in subsequent chapters. But here we offer a case study which invites you to think about these influences in relation to a specific penal policy.

1.7.2 Case study: JD

JD, aged 40, has a history of sexual offences against young children over the past 15 years, for which he is currently serving a custodial sentence. His favoured methods of gaining access to children include watching them in the school playground, following them home, approaching children in amusement arcades, and befriending children playing on the seafront.

His last conviction was in 2008 and he is shortly to be released. On his release he plans to move back to his former home town of Brighton where he has many friends and hopes to find employment in the area. He also has a new girlfriend, whom he met on an internet dating site, and hopes to move in with her and her young family. The police are concerned that he remains a threat to young children.

1.7.3 Questions

1. Consider what can be done to protect young children living in the area from this person.

   In answering this question select from the range of measures now available to monitor the movements of offenders released into the community and ways of restricting their movements.

2. Consider the influence of the following factors on the introduction of the raft of new measures to deal with sex offenders in and since the 1990s.
   (a) Political factors.
   (b) Economic factors.
   (c) Public opinion.
   (d) Penological theories.
3. Consider the impact of these new measures on the sex offender released into the community. Do the measures you identify treat the sex offender with humanity and justice? Do they respect the ex-offender's human rights?
4. Are you satisfied that the measures you have discussed are adequate to protect children in the local area? If not, what further measures might be introduced and what problems might they raise?

Guidance on approaching these questions is given in the Online Resource Centre where you will also find references to texts and cases which you might find useful.

2

Structuring sentencing

SUMMARY

A sentencing system in which there were no controls on how the judge or magistrate came to a decision on sentence would not be a principled system and could lead to injustice in individual cases. This chapter examines the ways in which sentencing discretion is constrained, not only through law and guidance but also through the use of a justificatory principle as a constraint. In particular it reviews the development of new forms of sentencing guidance and discusses in detail the importance of a retributivist rationale.

2.1 Introduction

2.1.1 Justice and discretion

Providing a principled structure for sentencing entails constraining the sentencer yet the proper control and exercise of judicial discretion is crucial in the quest for justice in sentencing. Admittedly, what is construed as fair or just depends on changing ideas of social justice and on the theoretical approach which is taken to understanding the notion of punishment itself, but there is a consensus that it would be unjust if an agency or individual could use its power to impose and implement whatever punishment it wished to impose. Justice in sentencing, then, requires at the very least that those individuals who undertake the sentencing of convicted criminals are constrained by a set of principles and by a framework of rules. Further, in a democracy, sentencing may not be perceived as just if those rules and principles are not acceptable to the electorate.

Yet, as Gelsthorpe and Padfield argue, discretion is one of the most contentious concepts in criminal justice:

> Indeed it is the day-to-day discretionary action of police officers, prosecutors, defence lawyers, judges, psychiatrists, prison, probation and immigration officers, among others, which are the 'stuff of justice' and which make for justice or injustice.
>
> (Gelsthorpe and Padfield 2003: 1)

That is why we are focusing on this issue first: the second half of this chapter will concentrate on fundamental principles and how they can be, and are, used to constrain discretion. We will examine in detail the classical retributivist justifications for punishment, with a focus on Kant and Hegel, because those justifications have been, and still are, very important in structuring sentencing discretion. They determine what should be the first, and so most influential, questions that the judge or magistrate addresses in the process leading to a sentencing decision. The notion of 'just deserts', that the punishment is what the offender deserves and that it is proportional to the offence, is the term currently used to sum up a retributivist approach to sentencing and so we will also analyse contemporary thinking on just deserts. In Chapter 3 we will examine in detail the ways, and the extent to which, this approach has been incorporated in English sentencing law.

If we consider discretion to be operating on a continuum from complete to no discretion available to those who must make sentencing decisions in individual cases, it can be argued that outcomes at both ends are unjust. At one extreme, sentencing is unjust because there are no constraints whatsoever on the sentencer, who can then make decisions, if he or she so wishes, based on personal prejudices and whims. Since K. C. Davis published *Discretionary Justice* in 1969 a strand of academic thinking has regarded discretion, as he did, as the major source of injustice and something to be confined and structured (see Hawkins 1992: 16–17). At the other end of the spectrum is the sentencer who has no discretion whatsoever because the rules and principles are so tightly drawn, with all potential factors accounted for, that the sentencer is simply the technician who feeds in the data and reads off the answer, in this case the sentence. This too might be viewed as potentially unjust in that it could not take account of any individual circumstances that had not been foreseen when the rules were drawn up. The logical conclusion is that justice is to be found between the two ends of this discretion spectrum.

One reason why constraints are placed on the sentencer by the state is, then, to respond to the notion that totally unconstrained discretion is inherently unjust: 'In a liberal state, law is to be applied consistently, openly, and dispassionately; rules are regarded as the most appropriate means to these ends. Discretion represents the opposite; it is subjective justice where rules are formal justice' (Hawkins 1992: 150). The expectation is that the rule of law will be upheld because the citizen must have confidence in the law and institutions of the state. 'Discretionary decision-making is condemned as a cavalier disregard for this imperative' and threatens to undermine the 'moral' allegiance of the citizen to the criminal justice system (Salter and Twist 2007).

In democratic states, then, neither the professional nor the lay judge can do just what they might want to do when sentencing. There are rules that, to a greater or lesser extent, guide them in the exercise of their discretion. Having said that, the discretion of the sentencing judge, established in the course of the eighteenth century, has been described as 'the central principle of the English sentencing system' (Thomas 2002: 473) and changes threatening to constrain that discretion still provoke debate as to the right balance between democratic control and judicial independence. For example, the House of Commons Justice Committee revisited the issues when discussing the role of the newly created Sentencing Council (Justice Committee, 2009). Its Report (ibid: para 24) included the statement of the Rt Hon Lord Judge, Lord Chief Justice, that '[t]he point about the judicial discretion is that a judge is trying to do justice in the individual case'[1] and the fear of the Council for HM Circuit Judges that 'executive or legislative encroachment would put the separation of powers at risk undermining the Constitution'.[2] Yet democratic legitimacy requires that Parliament has a role in determining the sentencing framework.

How far rules should constrain the sentencer is, then, a matter of debate. As we shall see in section 2.2, in the UK we have the paradoxical situation where judges and magistrates have, historically, been provided with an increasingly wide choice of available penalties, whilst, at the same time, the trend has been to circumscribe their discretion.[3]

[1] Oral Evidence taken before the Justice Committee on Sentencing Guidelines, 22 January 2008, HC (2007–08) 279-i.

[2] Council of HM Circuit Judges Response to the Sentencing Commission Working Group Consultation, 30 May 2008.

[3] Arguably, the provisions of the Criminal Justice Act (CJA) 2003 aimed at more 'flexible' sentencing indicate some increased discretion: see Chapter 12, section 12.2.2. The Criminal Justice and Immigration Act (CJIA) 2008 also reintroduces some discretion in relation to dangerous offenders.

2.1.2 **Discretion as 'bad'**

This idea that discretion is the opposite of formal justice, arising from debates around the concept of 'the rule of law' (Dicey 1885), has led to a raft of criticisms of a wide discretion for sentencers. One of the most compelling is that it leads to inconsistency of sentencing in which similar cases may not be treated similarly. Indeed, Parliamentary anxiety about the differential treatment of persistent but minor offenders was one of the factors leading to the creation of the Court of Criminal Appeal in 1907 (see Thomas 2002: 474, 484–5).

By the end of the twentieth century a major concern arising from research results was that there appear to be geographic variations in custodial sentencing in England and Wales. For example, in 2000 the custody rate in magistrates' courts varied from 0.8 per cent in Elbes (Lincolnshire) to 23.4 per cent in Luton and South Bedfordshire[4] whilst research on environmental prosecutions in 1999–2003 (primarily on offences relating to pollution and wildlife) also found that the average length of a custodial sentence varied considerably—from two months in Wales to nearly 18 months in the eastern region, with the highest average fine of nearly £5,000 to be found in the London region and the lowest, at under £2,000, in the eastern region and Wales (Dupont and Zakkour 2003: 12, 17). Home Office research on the period 2003 to 2006 also showed that average custodial sentence lengths and the use of life and indeterminate sentences for public protection varied significantly across the 42 Criminal Justice Areas in England and Wales. Again the research found that differences in sentencing practice could not be explained solely in terms of the characteristics of the cases or of the offenders coming before the courts (Mason *et al.* 2007).

The concern is that the exercise of discretion is not being limited to the 'relevant idiosyncrasies' of a case (Feldman 1992: 172–5). Whilst it is not necessarily easy to establish what counts as relevant this must be done or, as Ashworth put it, the notion of disparity 'might be used as a basis for criticising our sentencing system for not treating all red-haired offenders in the same way' (Ashworth 1987: 24). Further, when apparent disparities have been found, the counter argument expressed is that 'no two cases are the same' or that research has not identified the crucial differences. On the other hand, as Hood noted, 'magistrates and judges... place particular value upon their experience in sentencing. Now, if this experience is to be of value, then all cases cannot be unique, they must be comparable in some respects' (1962: 16). Yet whether studies focus on geography, race, gender, or class, whether 'real' disparity is proved, or whether there is only a perception that sentencing is inconsistent, the policy concern is the same—that the legitimacy of the sentencing process may be undermined in the eyes of the public.

What is of particular concern is whether discretion allows 'space' for discrimination—personal or institutional—to occur. Again the focus of research has often been the custodial sentence and, notably, the fact that particular ethnic minorities are over-represented in prison (see Chapter 11). Criminologists have focused on disentangling whether or not this discrepancy is the result of direct or indirect racial discrimination (see Bowling and Phillips 2002: chapter 7; also Chapter 10, section 10.4). Research has also investigated whether personal, class, or gender aspects of the defendant's behaviour influence the sentencer. For example, Hedderman's research suggested that 'women may receive more lenient sentences than men because they are more nervous and act more respectfully and deferentially to the Bench' (1990: 36).

online resource centre

[4] The annually published *Criminal Statistics* web link provides a variety of supplementary tables as well as the national statistics. See the Online Resource Centre.

Wide discretion is also criticised as diminishing the possibility of accurately predicting sentence outcome: sanctions cannot give a clear deterrent message to past or potential offenders, and solicitors and barristers are unable to advise their clients effectively. Further, if judges or magistrates tend to sentence at the top end of what is legally permissible, 'over-sentencing' occurs and resource issues arise. As previously noted, too wide a sentencing discretion has implications for governments wishing to introduce new sentencing policies.

Not all academic analysis has concurred with the idea that discretion is inherently 'bad', that inconsistency is caused by individual behaviour, or that discretion needs to be rule-guided. Writing in the context of prosecutorial discretion in the Health and Safety Inspectorate, Hawkins has argued that '[s]ystems of formal rules, for all their appearance of precision and specificity, work in only imprecise ways. Indeed, precision and consistent practice are not necessarily assisted by the drafting of ever more elaborate schemes of rules' (2002: 424).

In practice, sentencing discretion and resulting sentencing outcomes must be a government concern: the policy imperatives and conflicts outlined in Chapter 1 come into play. The constraints—the techniques and tools by which sentencing discretion is 'structured'—can take many forms. The more obvious ones are the rules relating to the availability and choice of punishments, and to the maximum and minimum amounts of punishment allowed in a particular jurisdiction. They might also be financial or administrative constraints. What has become increasingly important, as we noted in Chapter 1, section 1.4.3, is the constraint of an imposed justificatory principle, a new rationale, and so in sections 2.5 to 2.7 retributivism will be examined in some detail.

2.1.3 **Historical policy trends in structuring sentencing discretion**

We saw in Chapter 1 that there are a variety of complex influences accounting for the changes in penal policy in the 1990s and the early years of the twenty-first century. Here we wish to examine further the longer-term trend towards widening the choice of penalties while narrowing the discretion to choose. This development has not been a steady incremental process but has occurred as periodic responses to particular sets of problems perceived at that time.

Garland argues that 1895–1914 was the crucial period in the history of modern penality, with the number of sanctions almost doubling in this period (1985: 19). Legislation, including the Prison Act 1898, the Probation of Offenders Act 1907, and the Prevention of Crime Act 1908, added probation orders, Borstal training, preventive detention, and detention of those we would now call mentally disordered offenders. The impetus was a general social, economic and political anxiety about the 'underclass' and a belief that a mixture of penal and social welfare reforms could 'solve' the problems (Garland 1985: 244–52)[5] with the aid of the newly emerging sciences in psychology, biology, and social work to classify and treat criminals (ibid: 26–31).

The next period of change was between 1945 and 1973 when two 'bursts' of sentencing legislation took place. The legislation passed immediately after the Second World War and that in the late 1960s and early 1970s evidenced a renewed focus on the offender and the development of rehabilitative and community-based penalties. The Criminal Justice Act of 1948 made the use of fines more widely available and introduced new sentences with a focus on the offender. In 1965 another spate of legislation saw the abolition (for most purposes) of the death penalty, and the addition of suspended prison sentences (Criminal

[5] For a full list of official reports and legislative responses, see Garland (1985: Appendices 1 and 2).

Justice Act 1967), absolute and conditional discharges (Powers of Criminal Courts Act 1973), community service orders, and compensation orders (Criminal Justice Act 1972). The social and political contexts for both these periods were ones of social and economic optimism when there was a strong belief in the power of science, including social work, to solve the problem of crime.

Those contexts contrast with the period 1982–91 when there was a less favourable economic climate and the New Right developed in response. The collectivist and welfarist solutions favoured since the 1940s were increasingly seen as unacceptable and gave way to a focus on legal justice, individual responsibility, and the encouragement of the 'privatisation' of penal provision. For sentencers it meant a greater focus on offender culpability, evidenced in the establishment of 'just deserts' as the main sentencing rationale. It also entailed more punishment for those who were not behaving as responsible citizens, evidenced in increases in maximum terms of imprisonment, the prison building programme, and the greater availability of restrictive conditions for supervision and probation orders. On the other hand, the desire to reduce expenditure on prisons influenced the passing of statutory criteria for the use of custodial penalties, first for minors in the Criminal Justice Acts of 1982 and 1988 and then for all offenders in the Criminal Justice Act (CJA) 1991.

During this period the growing perception that communities were disintegrating, paradoxically, also fed into a policy interest in punishment in and by the community (see Chapter 12) evidenced in the CJA 1991. Further, the emphasis on individual responsibility and economic success, together with the specific problems arising from the enormous profits of crime in relation to drugs, led to new provisions to make it easier for the courts to confiscate the proceeds of crime (see Chapter 6, section 6.2).

The period since 1993 is more difficult to summarise with its new, but sometimes conflicting, strands of policy affecting sentencing discretion. On the one hand, the new penological thinking and the development of the public's punitiveness encouraged 'tougher' sentencing with a reduced discretion in relation to offenders perceived to be dangerous particularly in relation to the new sentences introduced by the Criminal Justice Act (CJA) 2003, until they were amended by the Criminal Justice and Immigration Act (CJIA) 2008 (see Chapters 1 and 5). On the other hand, there has at the same time been a greater focus on community sentences and restorative justice with a corresponding wider range of options for the courts. These different concerns have led to a series of Acts of Parliament which have undermined the coherence of the sentencing approach set up by the 1991 Act. The Criminal Justice Act 1993 apparently allowed more weight to be given to previous offending and the CJA 2003 has consolidated this approach. Several Acts have increased the statutory maxima for custodial sentences for various offences; the Crime (Sentences) Act 1997 introduced automatic life (repealed in 2003) and mandatory minimum custodial sentences, and the Crime and Disorder Act (CDA) 1998 introduced, inter alia, new youth court orders and extended post-custody supervision, and provided new exclusionary penalties.

A long-awaited development was the consolidation of sentencing legislation in the Powers of Criminal Courts (Sentencing) Act (PCCSA) 2000 although most of the sentencing provisions of this Act were quickly superseded. The Criminal Justice and Courts Services Act 2000 changed the terminology for community penalties, but the CJA 2003 subsequently introduced new custodial and community sentences and a revised sentencing framework for their use. The CJA 2003 also established the Sentencing Guidelines Council. The Domestic Violence, Crime and Victims Act 2004 signified the increasing policy emphasis on victims whilst the CJIA 2008, inter alia, included a raft of amendments to provisions for existing orders and offences and introduced youth rehabilitation orders and violent offender orders. The Legal Aid, Sentencing and Punishment of Offenders (LAS&PO) Bill 2011 proposes to significantly alter the sentences for dangerous offenders (see Chapter 5) and make relatively minor changes in relation, for example, to community orders and suspended sentences.[6] However there are no proposed amendments in relation to sentencing guidance.

In the period since 1993, legislation to structure sentencing has evidenced 'traditional' constraints, such as the availability of penalties and restrictions on their use, but also new ways of constraining sentencing discretion, notably statutory 'hurdles' to the imposition of certain penalties. This period has also witnessed very significant developments in relation to the bodies providing guidance to sentencers. These will be considered in sections 2.2 to 2.4.

2.2 'Traditional' constraints

2.2.1 Penalties available to sentencers

Perhaps the most obvious point to make is that judges and magistrates can only impose a penalty which is legally available in the jurisdiction. The current range of penalties contrasts with early sentencing law when there were only three options: 'The penalty for **felony** was death; the penalty for a **misdemeanour** was unlimited imprisonment or an unlimited fine' (Thomas 2002: 473). Even in 1905 the only available penalties for use in England and Wales for offenders aged over 17 were still death, imprisonment, penal servitude, fines, and common law binding-over powers (including supervision by the Police Court Mission after the Probation of Offenders Act 1887). A century later, after the implementation of the CJA 2003, the following penalties were available to the court:

- imprisonment/detention, suspended sentence;
- community orders—with a list of 11 requirements from which the sentencer can choose, including unpaid work, an activity, a curfew, mental health treatment, and drug rehabilitation;[7]
- various ancillary orders including the compensation order;[8]
- fine;
- discharge.

Judges and magistrates are also constrained with respect to the amount of punishment they can order. There are restrictions on the upper 'amount' of sentence that can be legally imposed—the maximum laid down in legislation—whether it be in terms of sentence length for custodial and community penalties or for the amount of a financial penalty. For example, many of the more serious offences, such as domestic burglary, supplying a Class B drug, and racially aggravated criminal damage, carry a statutory maximum of 14 years' imprisonment. These maxima are changed by Parliament in response to public perceptions of seriousness. For example, Schedule 28 to the CJA 2003 raised to 14 years the maximum for other specified drug-related offences.[9]

[6] These will be dealt with in the following chapters as relevant but see also the Online Resource Centre for updates.

[7] There is a twelfth option—an attendance centre requirement for offenders under 25 years of age.

[8] These are dealt with more fully in Chapter 6, section 6.2.

[9] Schedule 26 would have raised the maxima for certain **summary offences**, but was not implemented and repeal is proposed by the Legal Aid, Sentencing and Punishment of Offenders (LAS&PO) Bill 2011.

Taken as a whole, maximum penalties do not necessarily constitute a well-thought-out and coherent system. As a report of the Advisory Council on the Penal System stated 30 years ago, 'on looking into the history of maximum penalties of imprisonment in this country, we discovered that they have grown up largely as a result of historical accident' (1978: para 14). There are also political and pragmatic considerations which over-ride rationality.[10] Neither should the maximum penalty be seen as the 'normal' top end of the sentencing options: the statutory maximum must be used only for the gravest instance of the offence that could occur (*Smith* 1975). Courts established their own 'normal range' of penalties and the new bodies charged with producing guidelines have also largely used this approach (see Chapter 3).

2.2.2 **Rules governing the use of available sentences**

Not all of these penalties are available for all sentencers or for all offenders. There are several different sorts of limit which apply, in addition to the statutory maxima.

Limits on sentencing powers of magistrates' courts

Cases are allocated for trial and sentencing to one or other of the two levels of courts in England and Wales (see, generally, Sanders *et al.* 2010: chapters 9 and 10) and for most offences minors must be allocated to the youth court. The lower courts—the magistrates' and youth courts—are more restricted in their sentencing powers than the Crown Court. So, to use domestic burglary as an example, the magistrates' court cannot impose the maximum sentence of 14 years because the statutory maximum custodial sentence available to the magistrates' court is six months.[11] Magistrates are also subject to a minimum term of five days when imposing a custodial sentence (Magistrates' Courts Act 1980, s 132).

Age categories

Certain penalties may not be available for children and young people or for adults. For example, reparation orders are currently available only for those under 18 years of age (PCCSA 2000, s 73) although reparation may be part of an activity requirement in a community order for any offender (CJA 2003, s 201(2)). There are also extra restrictions on using custodial penalties for minors (see Chapter 13).

2.2.3 **Financial and organisational factors**

There are also important extra-legal factors which influence either the amount of discretion the sentencing courts can exercise or the outcome post-sentencing.

Allocation of resources

In relation to both community and custodial sentences, funding is a major influence on practice. The setting and **ring-fencing** of budgets for the National Probation Service (NPS) and the **out-sourcing** of services affects the content and availability of community

[10] For example, Schedule 25 to the CJA 2003 would have made no longer punishable with imprisonment a long list of offences to be found in statutes covering the period 1824–2000: the LAS&PO Bill 2011 proposes to repeal the schedule.

[11] The CJA 2003, s 154(1) would have raised this maximum to 12 months but the provision was never implemented: the LAS&PO Bill 2011 originally proposed to repeal this section but that was dropped. Note that consecutive terms of imprisonment are allowed by the Magistrates' Courts Act 1980, s 133.

penalties and the custodial experience. This could lead to gender differences in sentencing if, for example, resources did not permit the establishment of community punishment schemes suitable for women, particularly those with young children. It can also lead to a different range of options for sentencers if, for example, a particular Probation Service has not commissioned specific rehabilitation programmes.

Administrative and executive powers

Traditionally the Home Secretary and also bodies such as the Parole Board have had powers which can affect the length of custodial sentences served. In recent years the influence of the European Convention on Human Rights has affected the operation of these powers and proved to be a constraint on their use (see, for example, Chapter 9 in regard to prison procedures and conditions and Chapter 13 for issues relating to minors).

Guidance and training

The guidance from the Sentencing Council and its predecessor bodies will be dealt with in section 2.4, but here we note that the Home Office, in particular, has been involved for some time in developing and circulating guidance generally on policy and professional practice. For example, 30 years ago the Home Office sent a copy of an interim report, *The Length of Prison Sentences,* to every judge and bench of magistrates. The message of that report was that prison should be used as little as possible: '[T]he general rule which we advocate... is to stop at the point where a sentence has been decided upon and consider whether a shorter one would do just as well' (Advisory Council on the Penal System 1977). More recent examples are the National Standards in regard to the aims and best practice of the Probation Service and Youth Justice Services.

It has been accepted since at least the report of the Streatfeild Committee in 1961 that judges require training in the principles and approaches desired by Parliament and laid down in guidance. The Final Report of the Bridges Committee in 1978 had, however, been forced to replace the word 'training' used in the Interim Report with 'studies' because of judicial hostility to what was seen as a threat to judicial independence (see Ashworth 1983). The function of judicial training was for many years undertaken in England and Wales by the Judicial Studies Board (JSB) which after 1985 also had responsibilities for training stipendiary magistrates, now district judges, and had an advisory role in the training of lay magistrates. Since April 2011, when the JSB and Tribunals Judicial Training Group merged, these functions have been carried out by the Judicial College.[12]

Other factors

The background to many of these constraints is the contentious issue of the relationship between public opinion, the media, and sentencing policy. As Chapter 1 pointed out, the nature of the relationship is problematic, given the public's misconceptions about sentencing and the difficulty of researching either public opinion or its influence on those who decide policy or who sentence (see, for example, Roberts *et al.* 2008 in relation to offences involving death by driving, and Hough *et al.* 2009 re sentencing principles). Equally problematic is the potentially influential new constraint, that of the victim's assessment of the seriousness of the offending against him. (For details of the new procedures for gaining the views of victims, see Chapter 6, section 6.4.2.)

[12] See http://www.judiciary.gov.uk/training-support/judicial-college.

2.3 New constraints

2.3.1 The policy context

As we saw in Chapter 1, the policy imperative to reduce the use of custodial sentencing on the grounds of cost was strengthened by the argument in the 1980s that custody does not 'work' in rehabilitating offenders: research suggested that it did not deter or reform, particularly in relation to young offenders (see Chapters 8 and 12). The development of new ideas for what was believed to be more 'effective' punishment in the community provided an opportunity to place restrictions on the use of custody and so force sentencers to divert offenders to other penalties. However, increasingly in the 1990s, the concern of government was to enhance the legitimacy of the sentencing system, if necessary in ways that conflicted with the need to save money. The Halliday Report made this important statement—echoing our discussion about justice and discretion—on the first page of its report:

> At its roots, sentencing contributes to good order in society. It does so by visibly upholding society's norms and standards; dealing appropriately with those who breach them; and enabling the public to have confidence in its outcomes. The public, as a result, can legitimately be expected to uphold and observe the law, and not to take it into their own hands. To achieve this there must be confidence in the justice of the outcomes, as well as in their effectiveness.
>
> (2001: para 1.3)

Policy based on these concerns encouraged a reduction in the use of custody for the 'normal' offender whilst allowing its continued or greater use for particular classes of offender where other policy imperatives, notably the need to restore confidence in the criminal justice system, were deemed politically expedient. Again, this is a bifurcationary, or two-pronged, policy to achieve conflicting policy aims by allocating each aim to different sets of offenders. *Justice for All* referred to these divergent policy aims: 'We have an absolute determination to create a system that meets the needs of society and wins the trust of citizens...' (Home Office 2002c: 13); 'Sentences must be consistent across the country and prison must be reserved for serious, dangerous and seriously persistent offenders and those who have failed to respond to community punishment' (ibid: 17). As Lord Falconer explained, '[I]n other cases, public protection can best be achieved effectively through rigorous community sentences' (Home Office 2002b).

Government concern with public confidence in the criminal justice system has also led to a policy concern with the principles and theories which might be used to justify current practice and proposed changes. The 1970s and 1980s witnessed a reaction against rehabilitative approaches and a renewed focus on seriousness; the 1990s saw the priority given to seriousness diminishing and new ideas about restorative sentencing becoming more influential (see Chapter 6), with discredited ideas about rehabilitation themselves being rehabilitated under a 'what works?' policy focus (see Chapter 12), and concern with risk and public protection (see Chapter 5).

All these ideas gloss over the issue of what enables a judge to decide that a particular instance of offending is 'serious', or that the offender is 'dangerous', or that a particular level and type of punishment is 'right'. The problem of structuring discretion to achieve these policy aims could be seen as one of 'goal ambiguity' (Feldman 1992: 174–6), where the sentencer finds it difficult to decide what should be the starting point for deliberation and which factors of a case should be deemed most relevant and carry most weight in making the sentencing decision. In response there were four developments in the 1990s to help structure sentencing discretion in line with policy aims. These were the incorporation in legislation of new 'hurdles' for the imposition of custodial and community sentences, the introduction of new mandatory sentences, the prioritisation of a sentencing rationale, and the establishment of new bodies to produce guidance on sentencing policy.

2.3.2 **Imposing hurdles**

The CJA 1991 introduced a provision whereby custodial and community sentences could be imposed only if the offence reached a particular level of seriousness so that the statutory hurdle could be surmounted. This technique is not strictly an invention of the 1990s as it had similarities to the first-time offender provision in the PCCA 1973 and provisions for juveniles and young adults in the Criminal Justice Act 1982. That Act had stated that custody could be imposed only if at least one of the following criteria applied: an unwillingness on the part of the offender to respond to non-custodial penalties, that custody was necessary to protect the public, and that the offence was so serious that only custody could be justified. Their policy import was not immediately understood by the judiciary or magistracy (Burney 1985; Reynolds 1985) but Court of Appeal judgments and pressure from the Parliamentary All-Party Penal Affairs Group led to amendments made by the Criminal Justice Act 1988 to strengthen the constraint (Dunbar and Langton 1998: 73–8).

At least partly because of those provisions, the custodial rate for minors had decreased in the 1980s, and that fact was a major influence on the genesis of the CJA 1991 (see Dunbar and Langton 1998: chapter 8). Section 1 borrowed the 'so serious that only' custody could be justified, and the 'only such a sentence would be adequate to protect the public' criteria from the 1982 Act to apply to the imposition of custody for all offenders. Similarly community penalties could only be imposed if they were 'serious enough' for such punishments and a fine had to reflect the seriousness of the offence. These were re-enacted in the PCCSA 2000 (ss 35, 79–80, and 128) and, with minor amendments, in the CJA 2003 (ss 148, 152, and 164). In regard to community sentences for adults and minors, s 10 of the CJIA 2008 inserts a new s 148(5) into the CJA 2003 to give the court discretion not to impose such a sentence even if the hurdle has been surmounted. These provisions will be dealt with in more detail in Chapters 3, 7, and 12.

2.3.3 **Using mandatory sentences**

Parliamentary 'encouragement' of the use of particular penalties by sentencers was not unique to the 1990s (see Tonry 1996: 142–59). In addition to the mandatory sentence of life imprisonment for murder there were already presumptive sentences which sentencers have to impose unless the facts of the case fall within defined exceptions. An example is mandatory disqualification for drunken driving unless 'special reasons' prevail, and mandatory activation of a suspended sentence unless it would be 'unjust to do so'.

However, the passing of ss 1–4 of the Crime (Sentences) Act 1997, re-enacted—with the omission of the original s 1—as ss 109–111 of the PCCSA 2000, signalled the introduction into English sentencing law of a more intrusive tool being used in other jurisdictions, notably the 'three strikes and you're out' legislation of several of the states in the United States. Sections 110–111, in force from 1997 and 1999 respectively, limit judicial discretion when there is repeat offending in regard to specified offences. Section 110 relates to Class A drugs offences (see Drug Trafficking Act 1994) and imposes a minimum sentence of seven years on conviction for a third offence. Section 111 similarly imposes a minimum sentence of three years for a third domestic burglary.[13] More recently the CJA 2003 also inserted s 51A[14] in the Firearms Act 1968 to introduce minimum sentences of five years for various firearms offences[15] and s 29 of the Violent Crime Reduction Act 2006 also imposes a minimum sentence of five years for using someone to mind a weapon.

The 1997 legislation was preceded by a White Paper (Home Office 1996a) and accompanied by ministerial comment, notably Home Secretary Michael Howard's dictum in his speech in October 1993 that 'prison works'. These put forward various policy arguments to support the enacting of these sections, all essentially specific arguments against the existence of a wide sentencing discretion to ensure that sentencing achieves the desired policy ends of protection of the public through containment, deterrence through certainty of punishment, and protection of the public by incorporating discretionary release on criteria of risk.

How mandatory such provisions are in practice, and so how far sentencing discretion is curtailed, depends on how widely drafted is what Ashworth refers to as the 'escape clause'. He argues that in relation to the drug and burglary provisions the escape clause, allowing the courts not to impose the mandatory sentence if 'unjust in all the circumstances', is a wide one; not so the 'exceptional circumstances' of the repealed automatic life sentence provision (1998a: 234–5). The Human Rights Act 1998 proved more effective in significantly reducing the constraint imposed on judges by the latter provision (see the case of *Offen*) which was subsequently repealed.

The sentencing framework for 'dangerous offenders' set up by the CJA 2003 instead introduced a new indeterminate sentence for public protection (IPP) (see Chapter 5, section 5.4.1). The IPP caused even more difficulties for the courts, and led to widespread concern amongst sentencers, campaigning groups, and academics that reduced discretion was causing more injustice to offenders than the provision it replaced. The Government changed the criteria for its imposition by the CJIA 2008—probably because of the resource implications of increased custody—and judicial discretion was reintroduced in this area.

2.3.4 **Criticism: discretion is 'good'**

The use of the tool of mandatory sentences to achieve policy outcomes has been criticised, as noted earlier, on the basis that constraints on the exercise of judicial discretion have gone too far towards the other end of the spectrum. The main arguments are the following:

(a) Reduced discretion results in a decreased possibility that justice can be tailored to the specific circumstances of a case or individual. This might itself lead to injustice.

(b) Research on practice in jurisdictions which have had mandatory sentencing for some time would suggest that its stated utilitarian aims cannot be delivered. Tonry, in a chapter summarising what is known about the effectiveness of mandatory sentences, begins with, 'the greatest gap between knowledge and policy in American sentencing concerns mandatory penalties' (Tonry 1996: 134). The conclusion is

[13] Until repealed, s 109 mandated the imposition of an automatic life sentence on conviction for a second sexual or violent offence as listed in s 109.

[14] As further amended by Violent Crime Reduction Act, s 30.

[15] Or three years' detention if the offender was 16 or 17 years of age when the offence was committed.

that selective incapacitation has little deterrent or protective function in practice (see the discussion in Chapters 4 and 5).

(c) Judges and other legal professionals may seek ways to circumvent mandatory provisions. Discretion elsewhere in the criminal justice process could become the site for increased professional activity to 'negotiate justice' for clients in order that the mandatory sentence might be avoided (Tonry 1996: 148–54). The image used to illustrate this is that of a hose-pipe in which the pressure of water must burst out somewhere if all the 'holes' of discretion are blocked. An example given of this 'hydraulic effect' is plea bargaining: lawyers would negotiate a lower charge in return for a guilty plea to avoid a charge which could lead to a severe mandatory sentence. Judges too might engage in adaptive behaviour and attempt to circumvent sentencing guidelines to avoid doing what they believed would amount to an injustice (Tonry 1996: 150–1, 169–73; see also Ashworth 1998a: 235).

(d) The lack of discretion at the sentencing stage could encourage more 'not guilty' pleas. The accused might consider that more is at stake if the likely penalty is severe and so choose to risk a trial. This would increase the work load of courts and add to the financial cost. Research by the US Sentencing Commission, *Mandatory Minimum Penalties in the Federal Criminal Justice System*, did find significantly higher than normal trial rates where the offence concerned mandatory sentences (Tonry 1996: 150; see also, Henham 1997: 273).

(e) The insertion of specific sentences into an otherwise discretion-based sentencing system will skew the 'tariff' which in practice determines a scale of severity-related punishments.

(f) The lack of discretion may lead to constitutional or human rights violations.

Yet these arguments may have little policy force because there are, as we have seen, political imperatives and symbolic goals which may outweigh the money 'wasted' or even the likelihood of a rights challenge. The new constraint of the mandatory sentence gave a very clear message to the electorate that Parliament would ensure that sentencers were sufficiently tough to protect them. The next two new developments are significantly different.

2.4 New forms of guidance

Discretion is also constrained by various forms of guidance. Traditionally this guidance was purely judicial through Court of Appeal decisions, but since 1998 guidance has been issued by new bodies specifically set up to do so.

2.4.1 Guideline judgments

In the 1970s and 1980s two Lord Chief Justices, Lawton LJ and Lane LJ, had developed more structured guidance through designated appellate judgments referred to as guideline judgments (see Ashworth 1984). Such judgments considered sentencing for a whole category of offences or particular sentencing factors, rather than one individual and individualised case, and gave indications of the 'proper range' of sentences, the interpretation of sentencing legislation, and listed particular factors as legitimately aggravating or mitigating the seriousness of the offending and the level of the punishment. They were also used to endorse a particular principle (possibly with a limited life) such as the 'clang of the prison gates' principle in the early 1980s to justify short prison sentences on first offenders, particularly if of good character, 'who it was thought would be severely affected by any experience of imprisonment, however short' (Henham 1995: 219; see *Upton* 1980). In *Bibi* (1980) the Court of Appeal stated that prison overcrowding should be a relevant sentencing factor in specified situations and this was re-iterated in *Kefford* (2002) by Taylor LJ when he said that 'the courts must accept the realities of the situation' and, where appropriate, they should use community penalties or fines instead of (short) prison sentences.[16]

Another principle established by Court of Appeal guidance in the 1980s is now enshrined in legislation. Enacted as the CJA 1991, s 28(2)(b), now CJA 2003, s 166(3)(b), is the 'totality principle': that the aggregate of consecutive sentences should not be out of proportion to the overall seriousness of the offending and so the court can legitimately mitigate the sentence of a multiple offender (see Henham 1995: 220; Ashworth 2010: 270–7).

Court of Appeal guidance is clearly very limited in scope. Only convicted offenders and, since the Criminal Justice Act 1988, the **Attorney General** can appeal against a sentence. The offender is unlikely to appeal if his penalty is at the lower end of the sentencing portfolio and the Attorney General[17] refers only those cases where it appears 'that the sentencing of a person in a proceeding in the Crown Court has been *unduly lenient*' (s 36(1), emphasis added). Whilst the range of issues and penalties on which the Court commented widened after 1988 the result was still very patchy guidance, given 'the apparent failure of the Court of Appeal to consistently advert to other sentencing decisions in the course of developing sentencing principles' (Henham 1995: 218).[18] Nevertheless, more recent guidance issued by the new sentencing bodies (discussed in sections 2.4.2 to 2.4.4) still refers to particular appellate guidelines where they continue to provide the detailed guidance for a particular offence or principle.[19]

It was further argued specifically in relation to the lower courts that 'there is scant authority to assist magistrates in their sentencing jurisdiction', appellate guidance from the Crown Court being 'generally cursory' and the Divisional Court interfering with outcome only exceptionally (Wasik and Turner 1992: 345). Instead the Magistrates' Association produced its own guidance which posed questions in relation to seriousness, indicated a guideline starting point, and gave examples of potentially relevant mitigating and aggravating factors. These guidelines have since been overseen and published by the new sentencing bodies: the Sentencing Advisory Panel published a new definitive version in 2008, which was updated by the Sentencing Guidelines Council, and is now to be found on the Sentencing Council website. Research would suggest, however, that further guidance to magistrates may not be sufficient to reduce the continuing variations in sentencing practice (Tarling 2006).

[16] See Chapter 3 for examples of offence-based and custody threshold guidance.

[17] See, for information on the role and holders of this post, http://www.nationmaster.com/encyclopedia/Attorney-General-for-England-and-Wales.

[18] For a critique of one early important guideline judgment about sentencing Class A drugs offences, *Aramah* (1983), see Ashworth who argued that it produced a 'needlessly incomplete framework' (1984: 522–3).

[19] See, for example, SGC (2008) *Magistrates' Court Sentencing Guidelines*, Definitive Guideline, updated June 2011 re assault, available online at http://sentencingcouncil.judiciary.gov.uk/docs/Magistrates_Guidelines_including_update_1__2__3_4_web.pdf.

2.4.2 **The Sentencing Advisory Panel**

Given these criticisms of appellate guidance but also aware that the judiciary was protective of its sentencing discretion, the Labour Government introduced a compromise solution in ss 80–81 of the CDA 1998, implemented July 1999. These provisions established a Sentencing Advisory Panel (SAP) with the function of making proposals for new guidelines which the Court of Appeal could issue when a suitable case to do so came before the Court. The SAP's first Chair was Professor Martin Wasik and the Panel's 14 members included Professors of Law (Andrew Ashworth), Ethnic Health (Lord Chan), and Social Policy (Frances Heidensohn), together with members of the judiciary, Crown Prosecution Service, Department for Education and Skills, Parole Board, and Probation Service.

Within the first two years the Panel's advice on the importation of drugs, sentencing racially aggravated offences, and handling stolen goods—backed up by consultation and research—were accepted and incorporated in appellate guidelines. In 2002/03 its advice to the Court of Appeal covered offences involving child pornography, alcohol and tobacco smuggling, rape, and the offence of causing death by dangerous driving (Sentencing Advisory Panel 2003: 1). The obvious value of the reasoned and researched advice given by the SAP, together with an acknowledgement that not all advice could easily and quickly be incorporated in guidelines, led to the establishment of another statutory body—the Sentencing Guidelines Council (SGC) (see section 2.4.3)—to take further the process of providing systematic guidance to the courts.

The role of the SAP then became to advise the SGC and in its first year in the new role it proposed that the SGC should issue guidance on street robbery or mugging, robberies of small businesses, and less sophisticated commercial robberies, published consultation papers on domestic violence and sexual offences, and issued advice on the new sentencing framework introduced by the CJA 2003. The SAP continued to produce useful advice based on research and consultation until its demise in 2010.

2.4.3 **The Sentencing Guidelines Council**

The establishment of the SGC by s 167 of the CJA 2003 was a very significant change in the production of sentencing guidance. Although it had judicial and lay members and was chaired by the Lord Chief Justice it, in effect, took over the Court of Appeal's responsibility for issuing guidelines because of its statutory duty to publish guidelines and consult with the government. Importantly, the Secretary of State could order the Council to review or produce particular guidelines (s 170(2) and (3)) and the Act imposed the aim on the SGC of having regard to 'the need to promote consistency in sentencing' (s 170(5)). This aim had been prioritised by the White Paper preceding the CJA 2003 'to end the unacceptable variations in sentencing' (Home Office 2002c: Executive Summary, 8). Ashworth queried in 2003 whether comprehensive guidance could be produced by the new bodies 'with a part-time panel, an SGC that meets once every few months, and only a modest administrative support' (2003: 9), but the output nevertheless led to criticism from the judiciary that its discretion had been unduly restricted, notably in relation to the discount for a guilty plea, setting the minimum term in a life sentence, and in imposing the indeterminate sentences introduced by the CJA 2003.

The SGC produced consultation papers as well as guidelines, often on the same day as the SAP published its advice on the subject. Its first guideline at the end of 2004 was *Overarching Principles: Seriousness* (Sentencing Guidelines Council 2004a), followed by *New Sentences: Criminal Justice Act 2003* (2004c), whilst those published in its last three years of operation include its definitive guidelines on the reduction in sentence for a guilty plea (2007a), the Sexual Offences Act 2003 (2007c), assault on adults and children (2008a, 2008b), sentencing youths (2009), and corporate manslaughter and health and safety offences which cause death (2010).

The level of compulsion to which the sentencer is subjected is a matter to which we will return. The previous duty is to be found in s 172 of the CJA 2003 which required judges and magistrates to 'have regard' to the guidance issued. In *R v Oosthuizen* (2005) Rose LJ emphasised this duty but quoted the statement of Lord Woolf CJ in *Last* (2005) that 'have regard to' did not mean a guideline had to be followed and also the statement of Judge LJ in *Peters* (2005) that they 'are guidelines: no more, no less': 'It does not necessarily follow that in every case a guideline will be followed'.

2.4.4 **The Sentencing Council**

The Government wished to take further the question of guidance production and the judicial duty to follow it. Lord Carter's *Review of Prisons: Securing the Future: Proposals for the Efficient and Sustainable Use of Custody in England and Wales* (2007) had proposed that a permanent Sentencing Commission should be developed, with judicial leadership. In line with his proposals a working group was set up under the chairmanship of Lord Justice Gage and made up of 15 members including lawyers, academics, judges, and criminal justice professionals. The group received 229 responses to its consultation document (Sentencing Commission Working Group, 2008a), including 203 from the judiciary (Sentencing Commission Working Group, 2008b: 2). The group reported that '[t]here was a widespread belief amongst judicial respondents that a structured sentencing system would mean resources would be prioritised over the justness of an individual sentence' and that '[m]any judges felt that sentencing was "an art not a science" and was not amenable to prescriptive guidelines' (ibid: 3). Many responses were detailed (for example, Hough and Jacobson 2008), some very critical of the kind of sentencing commission to be found in parts of the United States which imposed rigid structures on sentencers.

In the event, the recommendation in its final report (Sentencing Commission Working Group, 2008c)[20] was the creation of an enhanced SGC combining the current SGC and the Sentencing Advisory Panel in one body to be called the 'Sentencing Council'. It also proposed additional duties on the new Council. The Government subsequently published the Coroners and Justice Bill; in response, the House of Commons Justice Committee warned against undue haste in formulating and implementing these proposals (HC 185 Session 2008–9: para 32) and was concerned that there should be more clarity as regards the procedure for Parliamentary scrutiny of new definitive guidelines (ibid: para 33).

Nevertheless, the Coroners and Justice Act received Royal Assent in 2009 and mandated the establishment of a Sentencing Council. This new body for England and Wales began work on 6 April 2010, replacing the SGC and SAP. Its website states that the Council, in accordance with ss 118–136 of the Coroners and Justice Act 2009, will fulfil the following functions:

- prepare sentencing guidelines;
- publish the resource implications in respect of the guidelines it drafts and issues;
- monitor the operation and effect of its sentencing guidelines and draw conclusions;
- prepare a resource assessment to accompany new guidelines;

[20] Now accessible at http://webarchive.nationalarchives.gov.uk/+/http://www.justice.gov.uk/publications/sentencing-commission.htm.

- promote awareness of sentencing and sentencing practice; and
- publish an annual report that includes the effect of sentencing and non sentencing practices.[21]

So far the Council has initiated consultations and research on sentencing for drug offences, burglary, and assault, and has already issued definitive guidelines for those offences (Sentencing Council 2011a, 2011b, 2012).

Departure test

In its final report the Sentencing Commission Working Party dealt at pp 75–6 with what it referred to as the 'departure test' (2008: 25–6) meaning the criterion by which the sentence can justify departing from the duty to implement the relevant guidance. As previously noted, the CJA 2003 required courts to 'have regard to' guidelines but the Working Party proposed a more stringent duty. The Coroners and Justice Act 2009, s 125 replaced the previous provision with the following:

> Every court—
>
> (a) must, in sentencing an offender, follow any sentencing guidelines which are relevant to the offender's case, and
>
> (b) must, in exercising any other function relating to the sentencing of offenders, follow any sentencing guidelines which are relevant to the exercise of the function
>
> unless the court is satisfied that it would be contrary to the interests of justice to do so.

In 1992 the Council of Ministers of the Council of Europe issued Recommendation No. R (92) 17 on 'Consistency of Sentencing' which declared approved principles and suggested techniques for enhancing consistency. Whether these constraints and guidance amount to a principled structuring of sentencing such that there is consistency of sentencing in the UK is not yet clear. However, the duty to explain the sentence in detail and the new mandatory requirement in regard to following guidelines amount to 'significant steps in the direction of transparency' (Ashworth 2010: 372) and can only aid consistency. The work of the Sentencing Council will, therefore, enhance uniformity of sentencing but only if it is not undermined by other changes which might produce the opposite effects. This uncertainty of policy outcome—because of the diverse and sometimes divergent policies being introduced—is an issue which will run through many chapters in this book.

2.5 Retributivist rationales

2.5.1 The concept of the individual and the state

In Chapter 1 we noted the importance of penological principles, particularly retributivist principles, in English sentencing frameworks, notably since the implementation of the CJA 1991 (see Chapter 1, section 1.4.3). It is this imposition of a particular sentencing rationale which is the fourth constraint on sentencing discretion.

On the retributivist theory a wrong action should be met by a sanction appropriate to the action and deserved by the offender, so it is argued that: (i) punishment should be given in response to its being deserved; (ii) the penalty should be appropriate to the wrong action; and (iii) the consequences of punishment are irrelevant. The quest for justice is the underlying rationale of retributivism: justice is satisfied if the guilty are

[21] At http://sentencingcouncil.judiciary.gov.uk/about-us.htm.

punished according to desert and in proportion to the gravity of the offence. An unjust punishment would include an excessive or inappropriate punishment, one which fails to respect the dignity of the offender, and one imposed for external reasons unrelated to desert. Retributivist or desert theory is therefore is arguably more protective of individuals' rights than the utilitarian approach which focuses on deterrence and rehabilitation.

Retributivist philosophy depends on a particular view of human beings. For Kant the model of the individual is of a rational agent for whom law functions as an imperative, not coercively but because the individual recognises that law imposes duties and obligations (Kant 1796). Moreover, the inherent autonomy of each person requires that all individuals, including offenders, should be accorded dignity and treated with respect.

An act which reduces the capacity to act rationally and autonomously would violate human dignity for Kant. Any act which shortens or ends the lives of others is morally wrong, because life has an intrinsic value. Modern examples would be using prisoners, without their consent, to test drugs in order to provide benefits for the population as a whole. For utilitarians such experiments might be justified if they maximise utility; an individual's welfare could be sacrificed if by doing so it maximises the welfare of others. No rational or autonomous creature should be treated as a mere means for the enjoyment or happiness of others. On Kant's theory, we may choose to sacrifice our lives for others, but others should not use our lives or bodies as a means to pursue their goals.

Similarly, Hegel, who was well versed in the philosophical foundations of utilitarianism through the writings of Hume and others, rejected the utilitarian view of the individual as seeking the satisfaction of desires, the pursuit of pleasure and happiness (see Walton 1983; Hinchman 1991). Hegel distinguishes men from animals, who are governed by impulses, desires, and inclinations (Hegel 1832: addition 10). He is critical of those who base their theories of punishment on threats and coercion, because, he says, this 'is to treat a man like a dog instead of with the respect and freedom due to him as a man' (ibid: addition 62). He also rejected the utilitarians' focus on psychological explanations of human behaviour which reduce social processes to the aggregated behaviour of individuals. Instead, Hegel argues strongly for an understanding of the individual through his social relations, and in doing so paved the way for a new approach later to be developed by Marx and Marxist sociologists.

The utilitarian notion of drawing up a balance sheet when deciding on moral choices was seen by Hegel as absurd and self-defeating. Both Kant and Hegel see a good action as one undertaken for its own sake, because it is morally right (see Hinchman 1991), rather than because it offers extrinsic rewards.

Retributivist philosophy also depends on a particular view of the state. In contrast to the social contract theorists, Kant does not see the well-being of a state as lying in the welfare of its citizens or their happiness, but rather '[b]y the well-being of a state is understood, instead, that condition in which its constitution conforms most fully to principles of Right; it is that condition which reason, *by a categorical imperative*, makes it obligatory for us to strive after' (Kant 1796–7: 129). Kant's conception of the relationship between the state and its citizens allows no right to rebellion or revolution; indeed he thinks this would constitute high treason which should be punishable by the death penalty (ibid: 131). He is strongly opposed to the execution of the sovereign even in a defective state; instead, reform should come from the sovereign. Hegel also rejects the conception of the state as a contract. The social contract model does not reach the level of the state as ethical life, but construes it as an instrument for individual pursuits and self-protection. Hegel's own conception of the state is of a higher entity than merely guaranteeing the life and property of its citizens.

These ideas about the nature of the state and the individual are very important in the theories of punishment developed by Kant and Hegel.

2.5.2 **Kantian retributivism**

Punishment is considered by Kant in the context of his analysis of right in *The Metaphysics of Morals* published in 1796–7. 'The *right to punish* is the right a ruler has against a subject to inflict pain upon him because of his having committed a crime' (Kant 1796–7: 140), so the head of state cannot be punished. '*Punishment by a court*... can never be inflicted merely as a means to promote some other good for the criminal himself or for civil society. It must always be inflicted upon him only *because he has committed a crime*. For a man can never be treated merely as a means to the purposes of another' (ibid: 140).

Kant's theory of punishment rests on coherent ethical principles, which recognise the autonomy and rationality of individuals, their capacity to make choices and take responsibility for their actions, and to act on the basis of reason and principles rather than 'passions' and these principles should also be reflected in specific punishments for specific offenders. If justice is sacrificed, for example, by withholding punishment, the quality of life of the community is undermined. For example, the execution of a prisoner might be waived if he agrees to dangerous medical experiments being conducted upon him which might generate knowledge of benefit to the community as a whole. This strategy might be justifiable on utilitarian theory, but would be rejected by retributivists, including Kant, as incompatible with the principle of justice.

The form of punishment and **quantum** of punishment, argues Kant, must be based on the principle of equality, so the 'undeserved evil' the criminal inflicts on the victim is matched by a similar amount on himself. He argues that 'only the *law of retribution* (*ius talionis*)... can specify definitely the quality and the quantity of punishment; all other principles are fluctuating and unsuited for a sentence of pure and strict justice because extraneous considerations are mixed into them' (ibid: 141). To base a decision on whether to punish, how to punish and how much to punish on extraneous considerations, such as which measures are most effective in eliminating crime, cannot generate a just sentence (ibid: 168).

Kant's focus is on the moral foundation of punishment rather than what is useful for society or the criminal justice system. He contrasts his approach—which offers punitive justice grounded in ethics—with mere punitive prudence. Central to punitive justice is the principle of proportionality. The term Kant uses in his discussion of proportionality is *Gleiches mit Gleichem*, usually translated as 'like for like', or measure for measure, which suggests both quantitative and qualitative matching in terms of the amount of pain and type of punishment. He accepts that different types of crime may be difficult to match with the appropriate punishment, but some cases, such as death for murder and castration for rape, may be more clear-cut. Someone who steals should be reduced to the status of a slave through convict or prison labour, he argues, while the person convicted of bestiality should be expelled from civil society because he has shown himself unworthy of membership of it. But the murderer must be executed, says Kant, no other sentence is sufficient to satisfy the demands of justice and a life sentence is inadequate: 'There is no *similarity* between life, however wretched it may be, and death, hence no likeness between the crime and the retribution unless death is judicially carried out upon the wrongdoer, although it must still be freed from any mistreatment that could make the humanity in the person suffering it into something abominable' (ibid: 142).

He gives the example of a civil society, of a people inhabiting an island, who decide to disperse and go their separate ways. In such circumstances, he says, '[T]he last murderer remaining in prison would first have to be executed, so that each has done to him what his deeds deserve…'. If the crimes go unpunished, he argues, the community that withholds punishment will be collaborating in the public violation of justice. Similarly, the right of the sovereign to grant clemency to the criminal by granting lesser punishment or no punishment at all is criticised by Kant, for failure to punish is the greatest wrong against his subjects and should be used only if the wrong is done to himself and to use it would not endanger the security of the people.

Kant sees the death penalty as appropriate for murder, accomplices to murder, and crimes against the state. If a court gave sentenced prisoners a choice between death or convict labour, the man of honour, he says, would choose death while the scoundrel would choose convict labour. For Kant the consequences of punishment are irrelevant: the sole issue is the guilt of the individual. It follows that the innocent person should never be punished, even if it could be shown that to do so would have social benefits. Where punishment is deserved, then the level of punishment should be appropriate to the seriousness of the offence. In focusing solely upon desert Kant is trying to offer a rational and objective standard of punishment which recognises the autonomy of individuals and prevents arbitrariness and bias from influencing outcomes. In this sense his approach may be seen as countering the subjectivity of discretion discussed earlier. It also means that retribution must be imposed by a properly constituted court rather than through private acts of vengeance.

2.5.3 **Hegel: the 'right' to punishment**

Hegel's theory of punishment is found in Part One of *The Philosophy of Right* (Hegel 1832) in his discussion of abstract right, written in 1820 as part of his analysis of the development of the ethical life of the state. Hegel argues that abstract right is the first stage in the development of the concept of freedom and stresses that right is restored by annulling the crime (ibid: para 99). He is critical of the positivist science of law, which sees punishment merely as 'a preventive, a deterrent, a threat, as reformative' rather than focusing on the 'righting of wrong'. Hegel accepts that deterrence and reformation have their place and are worthy of examination particularly when considering modes of punishment, but the key element for Hegel is that those who deserve punishment should receive appropriate punishment. 'The injury [the penalty] which falls on the criminal is not merely *implicitly* just, it is an embodiment of his freedom, his right,… it is also a right *established* within the criminal himself, i.e. in his objectively embodied will, in his action' (ibid: para 100). The reason, says Hegel, is that his action is that of a rational being, the crime is of the 'individual's volition'. In that sense, 'punishment is regarded as containing the criminal's right and hence by being punished he is honoured as a rational being' (ibid: para 100). It follows that '[h]e does not receive this due of honour unless the concept and measure of his punishment are derived from his own act. Still less does he receive it if he is treated either as a harmful animal who has to be made harmless, or with a view to deterring and reforming him' (ibid: para 100).

In Hegel's remarks we find the essence of the retributivist theory of punishment: the presumed rationality of the criminal, the imposition of punishment only if the individual is guilty, the exclusion of social consequences from the prime purpose of punishment and the view that punishment annuls the crime. By punishing the criminal we acknowledge him as a rational individual, rather than treating him like a mad dog, as dangerous and requiring constraint. The criminal, he says, 'gives his consent already by his very act' (ibid: addition 63).

2.5.4 **Punishment as the annulment of crime**

'The annulment of the crime is retribution', says Hegel, and its negation. 'Crime…contains its negation in itself and this negation is manifested as punishment' (ibid: para 101). This might also include an element of reparation, or restoration, as the community is being returned to how it was before crime occurred. Of course, for Hegel, crime is not simply an offence against the individual, but against the law itself, and hence infringement requires a social response in the form of state punishment. Even without an individual victim, crime deserves punishment.

There is a 'necessary connexion between crime and punishment', argues Hegel (ibid: para 101). He acknowledges the absurdity of a literal notion of equality of punishment, of an eye for an eye or a tooth for a tooth, and the problem of what happens if the perpetrator has no teeth, or only one eye, but stresses that the concept of retribution 'has nothing to do with this absurdity' (ibid: para 101). Rather he says, the notion of equality means focusing on the deserts of the criminal. It is hard to see a theft as equal to a fine, but as injuries they are comparable in their value. 'Injustice is done at once if there is one lash too many, or one dollar or one cent, one week in prison or one day, too many or too few' (ibid: para 214).

'The annulling of crime…is principally revenge, which is just in its content in so far as it is retributive' (ibid: para 102). But Hegel's concept of justice is of justice 'freed from subjective interest' (ibid: para 103). Justice demands equal respect for all, including the offender. Hegel, like Kant, argues that punishment must be administered through a proper criminal justice system rather than informally, and applied only to blameworthy individuals in contrast to the arbitrariness of vigilantism. Hegel's concept of punishment applies to a rational ethical state where obedience is based on duty and reason rather than crude coercion. He also notes that harsh punishments are not necessarily unjust. This will depend on the prevailing conditions, and criminal codes will change through time to reflect this. In Hegel's model the individual is implicitly rational, his concept of the state is a form of ethical life.

Desert is the primary justification of punishment for Hegel. However, this does not mean that reformation, reparation and deterrence have no place in a system of punishment. By applying retributivist punishment we may find that a side-effect is reform and education of the criminal. But deterrence from committing future crimes for Hegel is a result of punishment, rather than operating as a threat, or as its prime purpose (see Harvey 1984). The threat of punishment and the sanctions of criminal law do not coerce men into obeying the law; rather criminal law and institutions are a framework within which men become morally good (Nicholson 1982). This would also be consistent with his dynamic model of the development of ethical life, to the point where the state develops sufficiently that individuals understand fully the rational foundation of laws. Moreover, while punishment may have elements of reparation and restitution it cannot be reduced to them, so we cannot conceptualise crimes in the same way as civil offences.

Hegel elucidates the philosophical principles justifying punishment *per se* and the conceptual links between crime and punishment, rather than offering a tariff of particular punishments. So his discussion of the death penalty, for example, is incidental to his theory of punishment rather than offering a specific analysis of its legitimacy and he is not at pains to support or attack it. However, Hegel does accept that the death penalty is appropriate for murder when the only punishment can be the taking away of a second life, but acknowledges that in other types of crime it will be hard to find an equivalent requital (Hegel 1832: addition 64; see also Hetherington 1996; Heyman 1996). The executioner has both a right and a duty to apply the punishment. By the time Hegel was writing, capital punishment had become rarer which, he argues, is appropriate for such an extreme punishment. Hegel argued that campaigns for its abolition were useful because, although they did not succeed, they forced a reconsideration of which crimes should receive this punishment (ibid: addition 63).

2.6 Questions raised by the classical retributivist model

2.6.1 Just punishment or injustice?

The merit of the classical retributivist model is that it seeks to remove arbitrariness and bias from punishment. However, the idea that punishment should and must be imposed regardless of any positive outcomes, simply for the sake of it, could be seen as cruel, pointless, and unjust. Does harming others as an end in itself restore the balance of justice? If the retributivist tempers this by saying that we may sometimes take account of consequences such as deterrence, but desert is the primary justification, then this weakens the basis of the theory. Tonry (1993) argues that proportionality conflicts with parsimony, and the reduction of suffering, because theorists of proportionality will always favour imposing what the offender deserves and treating similar offenders equally, rather than using the most economical means of punishment, imposing the least severe punishment to meet social goals and minimising suffering. Rubin (2003) argues that there is a danger in focusing on retribution as it may be achieved by any means and this opens the door to inhumanity in punishment, in terms of the amount of punishment and the modes of punishment. He contends that in the current climate of punitiveness and penal expansion a focus on rehabilitation rather than retribution is better able to raise standards of decency and humanity in the modern prison and protect the prisoner from abuse, as retributivism gives no guidance on how the offender should be treated within prison.

However, as we shall see, modern retributivists such as von Hirsch argue that proportionality provides a restraint on unlimited punishment and may in practice mean a less severe sentence than demanded by rival theories. The principle has also been used to challenge excessive sentences imposed under three strikes legislation in the United States. It may also have implications for the treatment of prisoners, for example in terms of the penalties imposed on prisoners for offences against prison discipline.

There is also the problem of to whom the debt is paid, whether it is the victim or society as a whole. But how does society as a whole benefit from the suffering of a criminal unless it is through the deterrent effect or the ultimate rehabilitation of the offender? It is therefore hard to avoid referring to consequences and thereby lapse into utilitarianism.

The assumption of individual responsibility and autonomy is also disputed by those moral philosophers and social scientists who see social, psychological, or socio-biological constraints on action as more important than free will. As the human sciences have progressed since the early nineteenth century, it is now recognised that human behaviour is more complex and the development of the individual may be shaped by a range of environmental factors, family dynamics, and other influences.

2.6.2 Equivalence and proportionality

The notion of equivalence, that the punishment should equate with the severity of the crime, is also problematic. Kant advocates a catalogue of qualitative and quantitative punishments, but it may not be so clear-cut and such a system would be difficult to administer in practice. The death penalty for murder might be straightforward but it will be harder with lesser crimes and there may be problems with different types of murder or multiple murders committed by one offender. There may also be problems in relation to the determination of culpability and the appropriate sentence in cases of involuntary manslaughter at the top end of the seriousness scale (Mitchell and Mackay 2011). When we look at sentencing practice, we find a range of mitigating and aggravating factors to consider when deciding the appropriate punishment (see Chapter 3). This is already a very complex process and, if a Kantian model were superimposed, this would mean that there would be insufficient punishments to fit all cases. Feinberg (1994) is critical of those retributivists who try to match the pain exactly to the crime. Apart from the problems of measurement, there are the possible effects on the defendant's innocent family, the problems of comparing blameworthiness, and of dealing with these issues rationally. He argues that it is social disapproval and its expression which should fit the crime rather than the quantity of pain.

A modern example reported by Amnesty International[22] is of a court in Tabuk, Saudi Arabia, which had approached several hospitals to see if it was possible to cut a prisoner's spinal cord in order to carry out the punishment requested by the injured victim who had been paralysed by the offender in the course of the crime. This was widely condemned as torture, inhuman and degrading punishment, and a gross violation of medical ethics. Past forms of 'qualitative proportionality' and retribution used in the Saudi criminal justice system have included eye gouging and tooth extraction. Similarly, in Iran a court sentenced an offender, Majid Movahedi, to blinding with acid drops, after he was convicted of blinding and disfiguring his victim, Ameneh Bahrami, by throwing acid at her, on the principle of strict equivalence in Islamic law. The sentence requested by the victim was due to be carried out in May 2011 in the presence of medical specialists, but the victim in the end pardoned her attacker.

A severe punishment may well affect innocent third parties vicariously as international human rights law has recognised, for example in Article 6(5) of the International Covenant on Civil and Political Rights (ICCPR) which states that sentence of death shall not be carried out upon pregnant women.

Notwithstanding these examples of extreme punishment, it has been argued that proportionality can act as restraint on punishment. Fish (2008) reviews the history of *lex talionis* and argues that it constituted a turning point in the history of punishment in giving justice by punishing in relation to desert and in proportion to the wrong rather than arbitrarily. Moreover, the principle of proportionality offered a restraint on punishment. He claims that proportionality should not be viewed as demanding a literal 'mirror' punishment or as sanctioning state cruelty, but rather as demanding a measured and appropriate level of punishment for the offender's conduct.

Classical retributivism does seem to fit our moral intuitions, that it is intrinsically right that the wrongdoer should suffer, but there may be dangers in relying on intuitions, particularly in the theory and practice of punishment. Human feelings can be capricious and inconsistent as we do forgive some acts but not others. Moreover, the fact that the majority intuitively feel that punishment is appropriate in a particular case would not of itself justify it, as Bagaric (2001) points out.

Walker (1991) is critical of what he sees as fundamental weaknesses of retributivism. He argues that Hegel does not establish why annulment should take the form of a sentence rather than another response and it is not clear why Kant's 'last murderer' should be dealt with punitively rather than in some other way, such as persuading the individual to repent. Retributivism, he argues, does not explain why there should be a

[22] http://www.amnesty.org.au/news/comments/23567, 27 August 2010, accessed on 28 May 2011.

moral obligation to inflict the just desert on the offender. Exact commensurability is unattainable so the best the retributivist can offer is proportionality but this, he says, 'is a ladder with rungs that are both sliding and elastic' (ibid: 138). He also highlights the problems for retributivists in dealing with repentance, remorse, and mercy: it is unclear whether they play a mitigating role in retributivism. Most retributivists exclude them from consideration, but where they do take account of them, this would seem to conflict with the principle of proportionality. (For further discussion of mitigation and mercy see Chapters 7 and 10.)

2.7 Modern retributivism

2.7.1 The revival of desert theory

Given these criticisms of classical retributivism, one might reasonably have expected it to be of historical significance only. For many years, as we shall see in Chapter 4, the other main philosophy of punishment—utilitarianism—was seen as more 'modern' and 'humane'. However, utilitarianism itself was heavily criticised from the 1970s in several jurisdictions. In particular, criticism focused in the United States on the increased use of indeterminate and extended sentences for dangerous offenders, selective incapacitation, and the apparently unrestrained use of state punishment. In the UK and the United States criticism also focused on the 'inequities' and ineffectiveness of rehabilitation, and on wide judicial discretion. Whilst retributivist thinking has always been present in English sentencing, the proponents of such an approach came to believe that a rejigged version was essential if 'justice' as a specific aim of punishment—rather than as the yardstick for judging any penal aim—was to become more influential in practice.

A leading advocate for modern retributivist theory in the 1970s was von Hirsch who argued that fairness and justice should be the key elements of a coherent penal theory. In *Doing Justice* (1976), he maintained that the aim of the penal system should, then, be to 'do justice' rather than to maximise utility. Justice—as in classical retributivism—was defined as giving offenders punishments in proportion to their crimes and, in doing so, recognising them as moral agents possessing autonomy. However, he proposed that penalties should be anchored at a lower level to counter the belief that retributivism leads to harsh sentencing. So, in contrast to the classical retributivists, von Hirsch argued for a maximum incarceration of three years for serious offences and five years for some homicides.

However, theorists have since alerted us to the fact that, depending on the political climate, the adoption of retributivist principles can lead to unintended outcomes. Tonry, for example, has pointed out that 'just deserts' principles do not automatically guarantee the sort of penal system many theorists were hoping for. The pressure for more structuring of what retributivist theorists saw as too wide a judicial discretion, and the focusing only on the offending, can still justify the increased use of higher levels of determinate sentencing. Further, the imposition of rigid guideline systems in the United States are, for Tonry, evidence that 'just deserts has backfired' (Tonry 1996: 13). Yet the 'politicisation' of sentencing and punishment that we discussed in Chapter 1, means, in policy terms, that 'sentencing matters . . . more than ever before' (ibid: 1) and proponents of retributivist justifications have been continually prompted to rethink and refine their theories. For example, Morris and Tonry have re-conceptualised proportionality and parsimony, and von Hirsch has focused on censure. The next sections will look in more detail at some of these principles.

2.7.2 The 'why' of punishment: censure

In *Censure and Sanctions* (1993), von Hirsch describes punishment as the expression of blame—the censure which the criminal deserves. For von Hirsch censure is the prime aim of punishment: 'public reproof' is intended to ensure that the individual recognises his own blameworthiness. If punishment is to achieve this, the degree of censure should be reflected in the severity of punishment and so proportionality is still crucial. A censure-based justification makes sense to most people as in everyday life we make moral judgements about others and blame each other for transgressions. If a person behaves badly—in morally reprehensible ways—others judge him adversely. Censure consists of the expression of that judgement combined with the accompanying sentiment of disapproval. In censuring the individual, we again recognise him as a moral agent, rather than a mere animal, a person capable of choices and worthy of respect, whose dignity is respected. If he were a mere animal, he would not be affected by censure. A dog about to steal another dog's bowl of food will be unmoved by appeals to the moral wrongness of such an act, although he may retreat if met by a growl.

In von Hirsch's reworking of retributivism, censure is addressed not just to the offender but also to the victim and others in society:

1. *The victim*: it acknowledges that the victim's hurt occurred through the fault of the perpetrator.
2. *The perpetrator of the act*: it gives the message that he has harmed someone, he is responsible and society disapproves of what he has done, and that a moral response is expected of him, namely some acknowledgement of his wrong-doing. Even if he is indifferent, he should be made to feel that others do not treat his actions so lightly but it is up to him as a moral agent how he responds.
3. *Third parties*: it gives them a good reason to avoid such conduct, not to avoid the pains of punishment as a utilitarian would argue, but, rather, because they recognise the action as morally wrong.

Censure is given formal expression in the criminal law. Blaming is the central feature of criminal law in contrast to civil law which offers recovery and compensation for losses (see Chapter 6, section 6.2.1). The censure embodied in the sanctions of criminal law conveys that certain types of conduct are wrong and variations in consequences reflect the degree of censure. The moral agent is thus given grounds for avoiding proscribed actions but this appeal to the individual's moral sense of the wrongfulness of the criminal act is backed up by a '**prudential disincentive**'. Censure relies on the individual's sense of moral culpability but, because people are fallible and may be tempted to act badly, they need a further reason to resist that temptation, says von Hirsch, namely a criminal sanction. But this supplements rather than replaces the moral basis of obedience to law. A person who accepts that he should not offend and recognises that he may be tempted can see the sanction as an aid to carry out what he sees as the proper course of conduct. The 'blaming' function has primacy, the prudential disincentive function has only a secondary role, and the level of punishment should not be set too high or fear will displace the moral response. In a recent work, von Hirsch and Ashworth emphasise that the justification of punishment needs to rest primarily on a normative non-consequential retributive theory, namely penal censure, but there is a complementary, albeit secondary, 'preventive' role for punishment, in preventing crime (von Hirsch and Ashworth 2005).

2.7.3 **The mode of punishment: respect for human dignity**

For von Hirsch a degrading or humiliating or intrusive punishment would be unacceptable because the offender must still be recognised as a human being and treated with respect (von Hirsch 1993). So his theory would preclude torture, routine solitary confinement, verbal abuse such as used in boot camps, and degrading rituals. It would also preclude compulsory 'attitudinising', such as forcing the offender to accept views he does not freely choose, for example on the use of drugs, or wearing self-accusing labels which identify him to others as an offender. So modern retributivists have been very critical of harsh penal policies.

Tonry, for example, has castigated politicians for not giving sufficient policy weight to the harmful effects of punishment on people's lives. He refers to the comment made by Trotsky in relation to the suffering that the 1917 Russian Revolution imposed—that omelettes cannot be made without breaking eggs—and argues that 'many of the more cynical recent proponents of harsh crime control policies have apparently decided that elections cannot be won without breaking people' (1996: 194).

For modern retributivists, then, punishment must be administered in ways consistent with human dignity, so compulsory searches of the offender or constant surveillance at home would be inconsistent, although electronic tagging is acceptable. Solitary confinement should be used only if there is an immediate threat to the offender or others. Third parties such as the offender's family should not be affected by a penal sanction any more than is necessary. The rights of offenders' families have been given increasing recognition in international human rights law as illustrated by the European Court of Human Rights' decision in *Dickson v UK* (2007), where a prisoner and his wife succeeded in establishing that the denial of access to artificial insemination breached their right to family life under Article 8 of the Convention.

2.7.4 **The amount of punishment: ordinal proportionality**

Von Hirsch is also hostile to individualised or personalised sentences because of the dangers of caprice and inconsistency. The aim should be to standardise punishment by focusing on objective criteria of the degree of blameworthiness and harm caused by the perpetrator. Looking at how much to punish, we need to focus again on proportionality as von Hirsch's censure-based justification for punishment is necessarily linked to that principle. If punishment conveys blame then it is logical that the quantum of punishment should bear a reasonable relation to the degree of blameworthiness of the individual's conduct. He argues that the proportionality principle fits our intuitions: a child would express a sense of injustice if punished excessively for a minor misdemeanour. So the case for proportionality for von Hirsch rests on three arguments:

1. The severity of the sanction expresses the degree of censure: the harshness of treatment reflects the disapprobation.
2. The state's sanctions against the proscribed conduct should take a punitive form, and impose deprivations in a way that expresses blame or censure.
3. The punitive sanction should reflect the seriousness of the conduct and this is important for fairness and consistency.

The appropriate penalty will be determined by the seriousness of the crime, in terms of the harm caused, that is, the impact on the victim's quality of life and standard of living including economic and non-economic interests, and the extent of the offender's culpability (see also the discussion in Chapter 3, section 3.2.1). The severity of the sanction will be measured by how far it affects the material interests and living standards of the offender.

Von Hirsch discusses the distinction between two types of proportionality, **ordinal** and **cardinal proportionality**. Ordinal or relative proportionality consists of three elements: the first element is parity, which means that persons convicted of crimes of similar gravity should receive punishments of comparable severity. This does not mean that there must be identical punishments for all people who commit particular offences, because of course there may be degrees of culpability, but once they are established, offences of comparable seriousness should receive punishments of the same degree of onerousness. Desert theories encompass some modifications to sentencing for aggravated harms and mitigation to allow for degrees in culpability (von Hirsch 1986; Tonry 1996; von Hirsch and Ashworth 2005) but of course these are still linked to, and proportional to, what the individual deserves for the current offence, rather than reflecting external factors.

The second element is rank-ordering which means that, when people are convicted of crimes of differing gravity, then punishments should be graded. Punishments should be ordered on a penalty scale, so their relative severity reflects the seriousness-ranking of the offence. The third element is spacing. If we imagine three crimes, A, B, and C, and A is considerably more serious than B, but B is only slightly more serious than C, then, says von Hirsch, there should be a larger space between the penalties for A and B, than between B and C. However, as he points out, we could theoretically have a system which satisfies all the requirements of ordinal proportionality, parity, rank-ordering, and spacing, yet is very unfair because it starts with a prison sentence, say of ten years for a minor offence and progresses to torture and death. We need then to look separately at the important issues of cardinal or non-relative proportionality and parsimony.

2.7.5 Cardinal proportionality and reductionist penal policies

Before we can determine the relative punishments for different crimes we need an appropriate **anchoring point** for penalty scales. Von Hirsch challenges the popular view of retributivists as 'bloodthirsty' by arguing that desert theory is capable of finding an anchoring point which may be set relatively low. A huge increase in punishment for a relatively minor offence could be justified on utilitarian grounds if it was effective in eliminating a particular crime. It cannot be justified on retributivist grounds because the degree of punishment exceeds the blameworthiness. Proportionality, then, can constitute a restraint on excessive punishment. Furthermore, some other non-condemnatory measures, for example, a form of civil quarantine for dangerous offenders which could also be justified on utilitarian arguments, would conflict with desert-based retributivist principles. This is because it would be based on future rather than past crimes and would fail to recognise individuals as moral agents with the capacity to choose to avoid future criminal actions.

Consequently, von Hirsch rules out the use of the death penalty as an inhumane and degrading punishment and favours relatively low levels of incarceration, with a longer prison sentence for the most serious and a fine for lesser offences. But von Hirsch argues that a sentence of three years would still constitute a prudential disincentive so that we could reduce levels of punishment without displacing the censuring message. What his theory does not justify is using the state's resources—its penal capacity—as a starting point: this is unprincipled and would lead to differences between states with different capacities.

Von Hirsch favours using the least severe penalty while seeking to impose the appropriate degree of censure. At first sight this might seem akin to the utilitarian notion of parsimony advocated by Bentham and others, which entails using the least severe penalty necessary to deter the criminal, thereby minimising the public costs of punishment. However, the issue for desert theorists is whether desert can be satisfied by setting a lower anchoring point rather than whether costs can be saved (von Hirsch 1986).

Morris (1974) incorporated this idea into a theory of 'limiting retributivism', a hybrid theory, incorporating elements of both retributivism and crime prevention. The argument is that desert can be applied in a parsimonious way because the aims of retributivist theory can be met with a lower anchoring point (von Hirsch 1986). At higher levels of seriousness proportionality prevails, which prevents harsh, excessive, or aggravated punishments which might otherwise be justified on predictive or rehabilitative grounds. But within the parameters set by proportionality the sentencer should be able to impose the least severe sentence consistent with the aims of sentencing. At lower levels there is more scope for flexible parsimonious sentencing.

Against these arguments, utilitarians would say that, if penalties are set too low, the fear of punishment will be undermined. However, as the available research suggests that changing levels of punishment have little effect on crime rates (Cohen 1978; Tarling 1979), then, argues von Hirsch, the arguments against reducing penalty levels are unconvincing and a reductionist policy is at least worth considering. Moreover, the criterion of success for desert theory, he argues, is not whether it reduces crime, but whether the penal response is scaled to the gravity of the crime. It should therefore be able to resist pressures to increase sentences when crime rises or to selectively incapacitate offenders of particular public concern. To help ensure that this occurs in the United States, Tonry has argued that sentencing law and guidance should 'establish a presumption that, within the range of sanctions set out in applicable guidelines, judges should incorporate the least punitive and intrusive appropriate penalties' (1996: 194).

The exercise of scaling a penal response to seriousness raises another difficult issue: should the punishment, or the impact of the punishment on the offender in question, be proportionate to the seriousness of the offending? In the next chapter we will assume the first approach—where a fixed amount of punishment is proportionate to a particular amount of seriousness is imposed. In Chapter 7, we will examine the second approach where just deserts theory operates in relation to the impact of punishment.

2.7.6 **Policy implications**

Von Hirsch acknowledges that his reasoning—that the best way to resist expansionism is to provide a rational way of anchoring penalties and that desert theory is better able to do this than the alternatives of deterrence and incapacitation—may not be politically attractive for governments. If there are public pressures for law and order, policy will include increased penalties, and penal theory on its own will be unable to prevent it. As we have seen, in this chapter and in Chapter 1, this is precisely what has happened in both the UK and the United States since the 1990s when populist punitiveness has prevailed. 'A jurisdiction's traditions in punishment, its politics, and its public's degree of fear of crime and criminals probably will affect leniency or severity more than any choice of sentencing theory' (von Hirsch 1986: 169). However, as Chapter 1 also noted, the financial cost of the growing prison population is also a political issue. As we saw one of the aims in the Coalition Government's Green Paper, *Breaking the Cycle: Effective Punishment, Rehabilitation and Sentencing of Offenders* (Ministry of Justice 2010a), was to reduce the numbers in prison and to provide more effective punishment by focusing on payment by results to providers in the punishment process. While the desire to reduce the numbers in prison has been welcomed by those working within the criminal justice system, there is scepticism whether this is primarily cost-driven rather than based on coherent penological grounds.

Modern retributivism, with its arguments in favour of parsimony and just deserts, may justify fewer and shorter prison sentences and a less expensive penal policy. But it may also improve the conditions of those held in custody. It has been argued by Lippke, for example, that a modern retributivist approach can provide the basis for minimally restrictive and humane imprisonment rather than extreme or harsh conditions of confinement, by providing constraints on punishment. Retributivism, he argues 'sets exacting requirements for liability to punishment and entails substantial constraints on how it is carried out' (Lippke 2007: 265). On this approach the prisoner clearly remains a citizen during his period of incarceration, retaining the fundamental rights of the citizen, including the right to vote, enshrined in human rights law (see Chapter 9, section 9.6). The implications of this will be discussed in further detail in Chapter 9 (see, also, Easton 2011a).

The merit of von Hirsch's principled approach is that it does set limits to punishment in a coherent way. The principle of proportionality can be applied to a range of punishments, offering a way of assessing the burdens of sanctions, and stressing the need for equivalence of penal bite. So, a government with an economic imperative to solve the prison crisis can endorse the application of desert theory to justify increasingly restrictive community penalties as a legitimate punishment which affects the material interests and lifestyle of the offender. Further, a retributivist focus on individual moral culpability buttresses a political ideology stressing the responsibility of the citizen. This focus on the mode of punishment and ordinal proportionality in modern retributivism has been contrasted with the 'vengeful retributivism' of *lex talionis* in which the primary focus is on the harm done to the victim and satisfying the victim by imposing comparable harm on the offender (see Robinson 2008).

Modern retributivism, therefore, seemed to provide a solution to a range of legal, moral, political and economic issues. In England and Wales the response was in the form of the CJA 1991 which, to an extent, has been modified and superseded by more recent legislation. However, the just deserts legacy of that Act is still vitally important in English sentencing, and current law and practice cannot be properly understood without an understanding of the sentencing framework it introduced. Dingwall (2008) argues that the CJA 2003 preserves key concepts of retributivism although it may have reduced the role of desert by requiring sentencers to take into account a range of purposes of sentencing, including punishment, reparation, crime reduction, public protection, and reform and rehabilitation. However, desert still has a key role in the sentencing of adult offenders insofar as the sentence has to be proportionate to the seriousness of the offence and, Dingwall argues, the guidelines provided by the Sentencing Guidelines Council have also retained a central role for desert. There is, however, debate not just as to whether modern retributivist principles are still central to the English sentencing system but also whether that is a good or a bad thing. Chapter 3, therefore, will evaluate the detail of sentencing law, guidance and practice since 1991 with a focus on its retributivist elements.

However, we have not reviewed the increasingly important rights framework within which English law now operates: section 2.8 will remedy that deficit by asking whether rights can be, and have been, used to control sentencing discretion and, in particular, the use of the death penalty in other jurisdictions.

2.8 Rights as a constraint on sentencing

2.8.1 Rights theory

Recent developments in rights theory provide justifications for limiting excessive punishment which are independent of penological thinking although retributivists are usually strongly committed to rights. However, one may find appeals to rights without a commitment to retributivism, notably in civil libertarian critiques of capital punishment. For example, Amnesty International's critique of the death penalty construes the use of the death penalty as ultimately a human rights issue (see section 2.8.2). Rights-based critiques also extend to corporal and custodial forms of punishment. Article 3 of the European Convention, based on Article 5 of the UN Declaration of Human Rights, states that no one should be subjected to torture or to cruel, inhuman or degrading treatment or punishment. Moreover the right is absolute, allowing no derogations in time of war or public emergency. Even when a punishment is deserved and even if a deterrent effect could be established, an extreme punishment would be precluded if it constituted inhuman or degrading treatment. For example, corporal punishment in the Isle of Man was seen as degrading in *Tyrer v UK* (1979–80). Article 3 is relevant to extreme punishments although in practice conditions in prison may have to be quite severe to constitute a breach (see Chapter 9).

While UK lawyers traditionally have been wary of rights, a rights culture is now well established. A rights-based system of punishment will achieve legitimacy for a system of punishment and the use of international standards will be a key restraint on punishment systems and an antidote to discretion. While claims within the UK usually rely on the European Convention, other rights instruments have been invoked worldwide, including the UN Convention against Torture and the International Covenant on Civil and Political Rights. However, this distinction between retributive and rights-based systems should not be exaggerated as the right not to be subjected to a disproportionate punishment is being given more weight in international human rights instruments (see van Zyl Smit and Ashworth 2004).

2.8.2 The death penalty in the United States—a case study

The US Supreme Court has justified the use of the death penalty in retributivist language, as the appropriate penalty for the most serious crimes (Garland 2010: 56). However, a strong retributivist argument for *abolition* of the death penalty is given by Markel (2005) who defends the commutation of all the sentences of prisoners on death row in Illinois by Governor Ryan in 2003. Markel's critique of capital punishment is based on the importance of dignity in punishment, concerns over the reliability and accuracy of the criminal justice system in the face of evidence of errors in the sentencing of death row prisoners, and the problem of arbitrariness in the imposition of the penalty and its implications for equality in sentencing.

From a rights perspective, abolitionists argue that the inalienable right to life is violated by the death penalty, the manner in which the punishment is carried out is inhuman and degrading and shows no respect for human dignity, and the punishment cannot be justified on the grounds of self-defence because it is not undertaken in response to an immediate threat to life.

In the Universal Declaration of Human Rights in 1948 each person has the right to life (Article 3) and no person shall be subject to torture or to cruel, inhuman or degrading treatment or punishment (Article 5). Capital punishment is premeditated killing when other means are available. It is cruel treatment because it is a physical and mental attack on a helpless person. It raises the question whether there is a meaningful difference between, for example, hanging as a form of torture and hanging as a form of execution. Shooting or electrocuting a helpless person would also be seen as torture, so critics argue: it does not make any difference that the state is carrying out that punishment.

UN policy now favours abolition, reflected in Article 6 of the International Covenant on Civil and Political Rights (ICCPR) which protects the right to life. It states that in countries which have not abolished the death penalty, the sentence may be imposed only for the most serious crimes and then not on persons below the age of 18 or on pregnant women, but stresses that nothing in Article 6 shall be invoked to delay or to prevent the abolition of capital punishment, by any state parties to the Covenant. In December 2008 the majority of states in the UN voted in favour of a Resolution calling for a moratorium on the use of the death penalty with a view to abolition and the Resolution had gained more support when reconsidered in November 2010.

International human rights law is becoming more important in the debate, as shown, for example, in *Lagrand* (*Germany v United States*) (2001), *Avena & Other Mexican Nationals (Mexico v United States)* (2004), and *LJR v Australia* (2008) where the treatment of prisoners is reviewed.

On the rights-based argument, the death penalty is wrong even if we can show that it meets a social need such as crime control, prevention of homicides, or providing assistance to efforts to combat drug trafficking. The whole point of the right is that it should not be jettisoned whenever the public interest or welfare seem threatened. Similarly, torture may conceivably be very useful in matters of crime control but this could not justify its use even in the most challenging circumstances, including terrorist attacks, as the European Court of Human Rights emphasised in *A and others v UK* (2009). On the Dworkinian model rights should trump utility and rights have a privileged position, usurping the principles of desert and proportionality (Dworkin 1977, 2011). Rights apply to all and even the worst offenders who have committed terrible crimes retain these rights. So rights have implications for punishment at all levels from the use of non-custodial options, including electronic tagging, to prison and the death penalty (see Chapter 9, section 9.6).

Under the European Convention on Human Rights, Article 2 protects the right to life, but Article 2(1) explicitly states that '[n]o one shall be deprived of his life intentionally save in execution of a sentence of the court, following his conviction from a crime for which the penalty is provided by law'. So here the Convention is not as progressive as the ICCPR. However, in practice European states comply with the spirit of Article 6 of the ICCPR. The Sixth Protocol to the European Convention expresses commitment to abolition and not allowing any executions in the interim period. It has been ratified by all member states of the Council of Europe except Russia while Belarus, which is not a member of the Council of Europe, retains and carries out the penalty and this has constituted a major obstacle to its membership. However, in Russia a moratorium on executions was extended from 2006 to 2010 by the State Duma and in 2009 the Russian Constitutional Court extended it until Russia ratifies the Sixth Protocol, effectively prohibiting its use in peacetime.

Protocol 13 to the Convention adopted by the Committee of Ministers of the Council of Europe in February 2002 abolishes the death penalty in all circumstances including times of war or public emergency. It has now been ratified by most member states and came into force on 1 July 2003. Some of the Convention issues were considered in the case of *Ocalan v Turkey* in 2003. In this case, the leader of the Kurdish Workers Party (PKK) was given a death sentence, later commuted to imprisonment. Here the European Court found that there was a breach of Article 5(4) because Ocalan had been unable to challenge the legality of his detention pre-trial and a breach of Article 6 because he had not been tried by an impartial tribunal. Article 3 was also breached because the death penalty had been imposed following an unfair trial, wrongfully subjecting Ocalan to the fear that he would be executed. The courts also took account of the fact that member states had now rejected the death penalty, in deciding that in this particular case the death sentence amounted to inhuman treatment.

However, the status of the death penalty has arisen in relation to extradition cases to the United States and raises the issue of whether the penalty is a cruel, inhuman, and degrading punishment and therefore prohibited by Article 3. In *Soering v UK* (1989), a case concerning the extradition of a prisoner to the United States to face the death penalty, the Strasbourg Court said the circumstances in which the death penalty was administered could amount to inhuman and degrading treatment, although the death penalty *per se* was not inhuman and degrading. Here the circumstances were that the applicant was likely to be on death row for years and there were also mitigating circumstances in that case. There is now an understanding that defendants will not be extradited to the United States from Europe if they will receive the death penalty but will be dealt with by other means, but this has been criticised for leading to inconsistency. The informal arrangements between the United States and Europe were formalised in 2003 with a new UK–US Extradition Treaty and a separate EU–US Extradition Treaty. Article 7 of the UK–US Treaty states that the executive authority may refuse extradition unless the Requesting State provides an assurance that the death penalty will not be imposed, or if imposed, will not be carried out. But the EU–US Treaty is weaker as it does not make assurances regarding the avoidance of the death penalty mandatory.

The issue has also been considered by the Strasbourg Court in relation to extradition to Iraq. In *Al-Saadoon and Mufdhi v UK* (2010) the Court said that the right under Article 3 of Protocol No 13, the right not to be subjected to the death penalty, ranks as a fundamental right comparable to other rights under the Convention. Since the drafting of the Convention, the passing of Protocols 6 and 13 effectively amounts to a prohibition of the death penalty. This justifies the duty not to expel or extradite a person when he runs a serious risk of receiving the penalty. But the UK government breached Article 3 of Protocol 13 by failing to negotiate to prevent that risk.

Within the United States constitutional rights-based challenges to the penalty have repeatedly been brought under the Eighth Amendment prohibition on cruel and unusual punishment. These led to a temporary moratorium on its use in the 1970s in *Furman v Georgia* (1972), and a narrowing of the application of the penalty to offenders with learning difficulties in *Atkins v Virginia* (2002) and offenders under 18 in *Roper v Simmonds* (2005).

The methods of execution have also been challenged. In *State v Mata* (2008) the Nebraska Supreme Court ruled that the use of the electric chair did violate the constitutional prohibition on cruel and unusual punishment. The evidence showed that electrocution does inflict intense pain and suffering on the prisoner (see also Denver *et al.* 2008; Mills 2009). At that time Nebraska was the only state still using that mode of execution. However in *Baze v Rees* (2008) the majority of the United States Supreme Court decided that the use of the lethal injection does not breach the Eighth Amendment prohibition on cruel and unusual punishment. For capital punishment to be constitutional it must not create or involve a risk of unnecessary or gratuitous suffering and the method of execution used in Kentucky did not create such a risk. This decision paved the way for the resumption of executions as most states had halted executions while awaiting the outcome of this case.

Rights-based arguments have therefore been a key means of challenging extreme punishments and while abolition has not yet been achieved in the United States, the scope of the penalty and the methods of delivery have been changed.

2.9 Conclusions

2.9.1 Are the current frameworks for structuring discretion effective?

This chapter has examined the traditional and the more recent tools for structuring the discretion of those who sentence. In England and Wales the judges have at times resisted the new constraints, on the basis that a wider discretion gives them the power to do justice in individual cases. On the other hand, public and policy pressure has more usually been in favour of constraining judicial independence on the assumption that this would reduce the injustice of inconsistency and achieve particular policy objectives.

Most of these statements and assumptions cannot be tested empirically in any way that will give closure to the debate about sentencing discretion. There is evidence that the provisions of the CJA 1991 did not reduce the use of custody after an initial decrease but what is not clear is why there was an increase from 1993 onwards. Several possible explanations have been suggested: that the amendments made to the Act in 1993 reintroduced discretion in relation to previous offending and associated offences (see Chapter 3), that community penalties lacked legitimacy and were under-resourced, that later legislation provided too many exceptions to the restriction on the use of custody, and that popular and government punitiveness influenced judicial thinking. Some of these factors involve judicial discretion, others do not although the Halliday Report (2001) implicitly blamed the sentencer when arguing that the system was not 'working' in line with policy objectives, that seriousness is not measured 'properly', and that there should be a 'limited' retributivism.

As we have shown in this chapter, the amount and the form of sentencing guidance have changed considerably over the last few years but the results of empirical research as to the practical effect on sentencing of the guidelines are not yet sufficiently clear. The answer may be in the detail and so in Chapter 3 we will examine how the various components of retributivist sentencing have been placed into legislation and how the format and content of guidance is aiming to influence practice.

2.9.2 Sentencing exercise

Imagine that you know no sentencing law and guidance and that you have complete discretion to sentence how you like. What would you do with Arti and Burt in the following scenario?

The following are the agreed facts of your 'case':

Arti, a 20-year-old, and his friend, Burt, aged 17, came back to Arti's family home one evening feeling upset and angry because their twin-sister girlfriends had just ditched them. Arti took his grandad's radio—of great sentimental significance to his grandad because it had been a present from a dying friend—couldn't find the right wavelength and smashed the radio. Burt insulted and swore at Arti's grandad.

Burt and Arti then decided to take the motorbike from the neighbour's yard (without asking him) and, taking turns, drove the motorbike round the town. (Arti had apparently done this twice before.) They then abandoned the motorbike. While they were gone, Arti's grandad had a stroke and died two hours later.

Task:
You should justify an outcome (a 'sentence') separately for Arti and Burt in relation to what each has done. However you should do this twice using the following information and then compare your conclusions.

1. Decide you will punish Arti and Burt in a way which seems to you *what they deserve* for what they have done. State what factors of the case you took into account and decide whether your answer would be any different if you had been aware that insulting or harming grandparents was viewed as *a very* serious matter in their community?
2. Decide *what you think* will be the most *effective* outcome for everyone concerned. State the purpose of your decision and what factors you took into account.

If your answers to 1 and 2 are different that is probably because you were applying different principles or rationales in each one. The first approach asks you to sentence on retributivist principles; the second allows you to choose a utilitarian or even a restorative principle and objective.

online resource centre

See the Online Resource Centre for ideas and further reading around the issues raised by this 'case'.

3

'Just deserts': seriousness and proportionality in sentencing

SUMMARY

Seriousness and proportionality are key concepts in the 'just deserts' approach to sentencing which was endorsed by the Criminal Justice Act 1991. This chapter analyses the extent to which this framework with its retributivist principles has been undermined by subsequent changes in legislation, notably the Criminal Justice Act 2003. It examines, in particular, law and guidance on constructing seriousness and the choice of a commensurate sentence and focuses on examples from custodial sentencing. Finally it discusses criticisms of modern retributivism.

3.1 A retributivist sentencing framework?

As we saw in Chapter 2, the 'just deserts' approach was developed by modern retributivists to address some of the criticisms made of classical versions of retributivism. For England and Wales, it is the Criminal Justice Act (CJA) 1991 which has been viewed as the piece of legislation most infused with a just deserts approach. However, the Halliday Report, when proposing the new framework which was incorporated in the Criminal Justice Act (CJA) 2003, claimed that the just deserts approach had 'failed to take root' in sentencing courts (2001: para 1.34) and it is now argued that the current sentencing framework cannot be viewed as one which acts as a constraint on discretion by mandating a clear 'just deserts' approach. This chapter hopes to address such criticisms.

At the time of writing, the most recent pieces of legislation with sentencing provisions are the Criminal Justice and Immigration Act (CJIA) 2008, the Coroners and Justice Act 2009, and the Legal Aid, Sentencing and Punishment of Offenders (LAS&PO) Bill 2011.[1] However, in so far as they have affected the sentencing framework for adults[2] they have done so by amending the CJA 2003 and so that is still the main source of sentencing law.[3] This chapter will start, then, by summarising the retributivist provisions of the 2003 Act before examining relevant aspects of legislation passed in, and since, 1991 in order to assess the extent to which the just deserts principles underpinning the 1991 Act have—or have not—been diluted.

[1] See the Online Resource Centre for updates.

[2] But see Chapters 8 and 13 for current law regarding minors.

[3] Although the provisions in the Coroners and Justice Act 2009 relating to sentencing guidelines are also relevant: see next section.

3.1.1 **The Criminal Justice Act 2003**

There is no doubt that the calculation of seriousness and of a proportionate sentence is very important in current English sentencing law. Section 143(1) of the CJA 2003 gives guidance on determining the seriousness of an offence which, in effect, summarises the approach of the courts before the 2003 Act: that both the offender's culpability in committing the offence and any harm caused (or intended to be caused) by the offence must be considered as part of the assessment. An indication of the importance of seriousness in the 2003 Act is the fact that one of the earliest guidelines produced by the (then) Sentencing Guidelines Council (SGC) concerned the process of calculating seriousness (Sentencing Guidelines Council 2004a). More recently, Parliament in 2009 mandated the matters to which the Sentencing Council must 'have regard' when producing guidelines: they focus on culpability, harm, and factors which affect the seriousness of the offence.[4]

Further, s 153(2) of the CJA 2003 re-states a longstanding principle that not only should the sentence be proportionate to the level of seriousness but it should also be 'for the shortest term' that is commensurate with seriousness. Both these aspects are features of modern retributivism as are the 'hurdles' for the imposition of custodial and community penalties. Section 152(2) states that '[t]he court must not pass a custodial sentence unless it is of the opinion that the offence, or the combination of the offence and one or more offences associated with it, was so serious that neither a fine nor a community sentence can be justified for the offence'. In practice, how high this hurdle is construed may depend on how low guidance sets the 'anchoring points' (see Chapter 2, section 2.7.5). However, s 166(2) states that s 152(2) 'does not prevent a court . . . from passing a community sentence even though it is of the opinion that the offence, or one or more offences associated with it, was so serious that a community sentence could not normally be justified for the offence'. Sentencers have a discretion, therefore, to take account of mitigation or mental disorder and impose a non-custodial sentence even if the custody threshold is met.

The CJA 2003 also includes, in s 148(1), a statutory criterion for the imposition of a community penalty: the offending must be 'serious enough to warrant such a sentence'. A new sub-section, 148(5),[5] similarly gives the court discretion to take into account any factors which would justify a lesser sentence. However, s 151 allows the court to make a community order even when the offending is not 'serious enough' if on three or more previous occasions when convicted of an offence the offender has received (only) a fine as a penalty, provided that it 'would be in the interests of justice'.[6] Section 151(3) specifies the factors which would have to be considered in making this judgement: the nature of previous convictions, their relevance to the current offence and the time which has elapsed. As we shall see in section 3.2.4, using persistence of offending to justify what would otherwise be a disproportionate sentence does not fit easily into retributivism. However, the CJIA 2008 inserted a new s 150A in the 2003 Act which confines the use of community orders to imprisonable offences, which may limit the effect of this provision.

In section 3.2 we will look at other elements of the current sentencing framework which are predicated on a just deserts approach, notably the determination and application of factors which mitigate and aggravate seriousness. It is true that the generic community order with specified components (see Chapter 12, section 12.2.1)[7] requires the court to assess which requirement is most 'suitable' for the offender. This secondary decision can

[4] Coroners and Justice Act 2009, s 121.

[5] Inserted by the CJIA 2008, s 10 and in force since 14 July 2008.

[6] In force since 30 November 2009, replacing the Powers of Criminal Courts (Sentencing) Act (PCCSA) 2000, s 59, a similarly problematic provision allowing discretion if fines had previously been unpaid.

[7] Introduced by the CJA 2003 to replace the range of community penalties in the PCCSA 2000.

be decided on the basis of aims alien to retributivism, for example, the utilitarian aim of rehabilitation or the restorative aim of reparation, but the restrictions on liberty that the order imposes are retributivist in nature: they must be commensurate with seriousness (s 148(2)).

The fine must also reflect the seriousness of the offending (s 164(2)) and the financial circumstances of the offender can reduce or increase the amount of the fine (s 164(4)).[8] Further, nearly all the guidelines issued by the SGC and the Sentencing Council provide an increasingly structured approach which is concerned almost entirely with determining seriousness and proportionality. The exceptions are in relation to the 'dangerous' offender and to requirements of a reparative nature (which we will deal with in Chapters 5 and 6) but these exceptions prove the rule: the current sentencing framework, despite amendments and additions, is that of just deserts. However, there are aspects of the framework which, arguably, are not as strongly retributivist as those introduced by the CJA 1991. The next section will summarise the original provisions of the CJA 1991 and review the changes made to them.

3.1.2 **Developments 1991–2012**

Crime, Justice and Protecting the Public (see Chapter 1, section 1.4.4) set out the thinking which led to the CJA 1991. It proposed that just deserts should be the primary criterion for sentencing and incorporated in statute for the first time (Home Office 1990a: para 1.6). Elements of the utilitarian concern with social consequences were reflected in the proposed aim of crime reduction (ibid: para 1.7) but deterrence was explicitly criticised as being an unrealistic aim (ibid: para 2.8; see also Chapter 4). Its concept of a bifurcated approach[9]—whereby most offenders are sentenced on the principles of just deserts and parsimony, whilst a minority receive sentences for public protection longer than justified on retributivist principles—still underpins policy.

The Criminal Justice Act 1991

Although the CJA 1991 incorporated retributivist principles it was argued that the Act proceeded towards its objective 'by means of allusion and implication' (Ashworth 2000: 85). Nevertheless, the introduction for the first time of the statutory 'seriousness' thresholds for custodial and community penalties as well as the commensurability principle clearly flagged up the principles of modern retributivism outlined in Chapter 2. More contentiously, those provisions which downgraded the effect of previous convictions and reformed the process of deciding on the amount of a fine could also be viewed as reflecting retributivist principles.

Both the CJA 1991 and the CJA 2003 have been criticised for setting up an unworkable hybrid sentencing framework (see Ashworth 2000: 84; Ashworth and Player 2005; Koffman 2006) but the provisions of the CJA 1991 made clear that the main sentencing decision was to assess just deserts and other considerations, such as rehabilitation, came into play only in the choice of a community sentence. The risk-based sentences were aimed at, and used for, only a minority of offenders[10] and the other exceptions, such as

[8] The Crown Court is specifically empowered by s 163 to fine an offender convicted on indictment instead of, or in addition to, any other penalty.

[9] Note that Ashworth uses 'bifurcated' in a different way and so argues now for a 'trifurcated' system (Ashworth 2010: 421–2).

[10] Although we shall see in Chapter 5 that for a period after 2003 far too many offenders were given an indeterminate sentence because of the mandatory nature of new provisions before they were amended in 2008.

compensation orders and the options for dealing with mentally disordered offenders, are not incompatible with the basic retributivist rationale (see Chapters 6 and 7).

As enacted, then, the CJA 1991 has characteristics which are familiar in current law:

- a presumptive rationale—just deserts—with a focus on a sentence proportionate to the seriousness of the offence in question (not offending history);
- sentences to be treated as punishments which could be theorised in terms of deprivation of liberty (probation previously had not been so theorised);
- statutory hurdles for passing custodial and community sentences so that parsimony in sentencing could be encouraged. In effect it meant the sentencer 'must justify each upward step in the "sentencing pyramid" in accordance with the seriousness of the offence' (Wasik and von Hirsch 1994: 409).

Statutory amendments to the 1991 Act

The provisions of the CJA 1991 were re-enacted in the Powers of Criminal Courts (Sentencing) Act (PCCSA) 2000 but there had already been amendments to the original wording. Three aspects of the CJA 1991 as passed particularly 'upset' influential sections of public and professional opinion (see Worrall 1997: chapter 3): the new system of unit fines, the sentencing focus on the offence in question and only 'one other' associated offence (which reduced the total amount of seriousness to be considered), and the assumed prohibition on sentencers taking past convictions into account when assessing seriousness. The adverse reactions of sentencers to the reduction of their discretion might have been anticipated; the hostility of the tabloid press and the Magistrates' Association to unit fines was more surprising (see Chapter 7, section 7.3). Bowing to such pressure, the Government hastily amended these provisions by ss 65–66 of the Criminal Justice Act (CJA) 1993. Section 18 of the CJA 1991 was replaced by provisions returning the sentencing law for fines to something akin to the pre-1991 situation (see Chapter 7, section 7.3). Nevertheless, a just deserts approach was retained by the new subsection 18(2). 'The amount of the fine fixed by the court shall be such as . . . reflects the seriousness of the offence.' Sections 1 and 2 of the CJA 1991 (relating to custody) and s 6 (relating to community penalties) were also amended, in response to concerns about restrictions on sentencing discretion,[11] to allow the courts to consider 'one or more' associated offences.

The third problem provision, s 29, dealt with those factors which could aggravate the seriousness of the offence in question. The message of the original section was apparently to prohibit sentencers from taking account of previous convictions in assessing seriousness: 'An offence shall not be regarded as more serious' (s 29(1)) because of the persistence of offending. Similarly 'failure to respond' to previous (community) penalties should not increase seriousness. The amendments made to this section by the CJA 1993 made clear the court could take these two factors into account when calculating the seriousness of the offending.[12] The 1993 amendments to s 29—re-enacted as PCCSA 2000, s 151(2)—also added 'offending on bail' as a factor that courts *must* take into account (see Table 3.2). Since then, further mandated aggravating factors have been added: offending

[11] The definition was in s 31 of the CJA 1991, then in the PCCSA 2000, s 161(1), as affirmed in s 305 of the CJA 2003.

[12] Because this issue of persistence has been so important a policy issue in relation to both the CJA 2003 and the CJA 1991, we will discuss it in more detail in section 3.2.4.

that is motivated by religion or race, and where the offender was motivated by or showed hostility based on the sexual orientation or the disability of the victim.[13]

When passed, the criteria for the imposition of community and custodial sentences were intended to be rigid barriers to over-sentencing to help reduce the use of custody as well as ensure consistency of approach. The provisions in the PCCSA 2000 for extending the availability of curfew orders and community punishment orders to 'petty persistent offenders' introduced a degree of flexibility.[14]

In the decade after 1993 other provisions also altered the balance of the sentencing framework. The Crime (Sentences) Act 1997, as we saw in Chapter 2 (section 2.1.3), introduced automatic life and mandatory minimum sentences which could lead to a higher penalty than justified by proportionality. Equally crucial to the maintenance of the just deserts approach was the interpretation of seriousness by sentencers. Despite pressure for a definition to be included in the CJA 1991 this was not done and interpretation was consequently left to the Court of Appeal's Criminal Division and, later, the SGC and Sentencing Council.[15]

We have already noted that the CJIA 2008 made some amendments to the CJA 2003. The most important were those in relation to indeterminate sentences (CJIA 2008, ss 13–19) and they will be dealt with in Chapter 5. The Act also made changes to the disposals for young offenders, notably the introduction of the youth rehabilitation order which will be dealt with in Chapter 8, and minor changes to referral orders (see Chapter 13, section 13.1.2). The LAS&PO Bill 2011 proposes to amend again the sentences for offenders considered to be a risk to the public and to make various more minor amendments to requirements for community orders for adults and minors, and to allow a custodial sentence of up to 24 months to be suspended. None of these changes alters in any significant way the retributivist framework.

3.1.3 **The sentencing framework**

The 1991 Act set up a framework which, though considerably modified, is still recognisable in current law and guidance. To make the evolution of this framework clearer it is useful to view it as one which asks the sentencer a series of crucial questions. These questions are set out in the order they were introduced in the 1991 Act: not the most logical order but the components remain. In Table 3.1 the italics draw attention to the desert-based hurdles to the use of a category of punishment and the underlined words refer to amendments by the CJA 1993. Bold type is used to indicate the three main levels of punishment (custody, community, and financial). The section numbers are given for both the CJA 1991 and their re-enactment in the PCCSA 2000. Where there is a directly comparable provision the section number in the CJA 2003 (as amended, if relevant, by the CJIA 2008) is also given.

[13] By the Crime and Disorder Act 1998, the Anti-Terrorism, Crime and Security Act 2001, and the CJA 2003 respectively, the first two provisions having been re-enacted in the PCCSA 2000, s 153 before all these provisions were consolidated in the CJA 2003. See section 3.2.3.

[14] Section 59(1)–(4), which is no longer in force as regards community penalties.

[15] See, in particular, sections 3.2.1 and 3.3.1.

Table 3.1 The sentencing framework in legislation

Decision Stage	CJA 91 ss	PCCSA ss	CJA 2003 ss	Question	Outcome
1.	1	79	152(1)	Is the offence one that is punishable by custody?	If NO go to 4. If YES go to 2.
2.	**1(2)(a)**	79(2)(a)	152(2)	**Is the offence (+ one or more other/s) *so serious that only* custody[16] is justified?** (But see s 3(1) & (2)).	If NO go to 3. If Yes:
	3(3)(a)	81	156	What information is there about the circumstances of the offence—and the offence or offences associated with it?	and
	2(2)(a)	80(2)(a)	153(2)	What sentence length is 'commensurate with the seriousness of the offence' (or the combination of that offence + one or more associated offences)? (But consider also 5.)	SENTENCE
3.	1(2)(b)	79(2)(b)	224	Is the offence of a violent or sexual nature? (But see s 3(1) & (6).	If NO go to 4. If YES:
	3(3)(a) & (b)	81	229 156(2)(3)	What information is there about the circumstances of the offence, and shall we take into account any information about the offender?	and
	1(2)(b)	79(2)(b)	[225–8[17]]	Would only a custodial sentence be adequate to protect the public from serious harm?	If NO go to 4. If Yes:
	2(2)(b)	80(2)(b		What longer term than one commensurate with the offence seriousness is necessary?	SENTENCE
4.	**6(1)**	35(1)	148(1)	**Is the offence (+ one or more others) *serious enough* to warrant a community sentence?**	If NO go to 5. If Yes:
	6(2)(a)	35(3)(a)	148(2)(a)	What orders are most suitable for the offender?	and
	7(2)	36(1)	156(2)	What information is there about the offender and shall we take it into account?	and
	7(1)	36(2)	156(1)	What information is there about the circumstances of the offence?	and
	6(2)(b)	35(3)(b)	148(2)(b)	What amount of restriction on liberty in the orders are commensurate with the seriousness of the offence (and any others)?	SENTENCE
5. Fines	**18(2)**	See below		**What number of units is commensurate with the seriousness of the offending?** What is the offender's disposable weekly income? Calculate the value of the fine.	SENTENCE

** These provisions are not strictly comparable: see Chapter 5 for a review of dangerous offender provisions in the CJA 2003.
Note: the original s 18 was totally replaced with:
s 18(1) [128(1)] What are the financial circumstances of the offender?
s 18(3) [128(3)] What information is there about the circumstances of the case, including the financial circumstances of the offender? and
s 18(2) [128(2)] What fine 'reflects the seriousness of the offence'?
s 18(5) [128(4)] Should the financial circumstances of the offender increase or reduce the fine?
See Chapter 7, section 7.3 for a discussion of the fines sentencing framework in the CJA 2003, which largely re-enacts previous provisions.

[16] Now 'so serious that neither a fine alone nor a community sentence' can be justified.

[17] These provisions have been significantly altered in 2003 and 2008, with further changes proposed in the LAS&PO Bill 2011. Since 2003 there has been the possibility of an indeterminate, rather than longer than normal, sentence.

3.1.4 Critiques of government policy

Given the criticisms of the sentencing framework by the Coalition Government (see Chapter 1, section 1.5.4) it is worth recalling the case for change put forward by the Halliday Report in 2001:

(1) The 1991 (as amended) sentencing framework has 'a narrow sense of purpose' and is a 'less than complete guide to the selection of the most suitable sentence in an individual case' (para 1.9). Sentencers are not encouraged to consider reparation or crime reduction.

(2) The framework has too much discretion which has led to inconsistency of sentencing: sentencers have insufficient guidance on the measurement of seriousness (para 1.9) and greater clarity is required to aid sentencers (para 1.44).

(3) The framework has 'a muddled approach to persistent offenders' (para 1.11). The research showed that Crown Courts appear to acknowledge the existence in case law of the doctrine of 'progressive loss of mitigation' whilst magistrates' courts are more likely to 'sentence on record' (paras 1.12 and 1.13). The persistence of offending—the issue of criminal history and recidivism as a factor in the process of determining sentence[18]—is one of the Halliday Report's main reasons for advocating change.

(4) Magistrates are frustrated by the lack of suitable sentences to tackle the causes of persistent offending, particularly in a short prison sentence: such a sentence is not a deterrent and, because it is too short for rehabilitation programmes and does not have supervised release, it is not useful for tackling the causes of offending (paras 1.17 and 1.18).

However, the Report was not without its critics. Hudson argued that it offered 'a pick and mix of almost every criminal justice idea of the last few years—public protection through incapacitative incarceration; reparation and restoration; curfews and electronic monitoring; treatments and controls' (Hudson 2001/2: 17) and the fear was that it would undermine the retributive, proportionality principle at the heart of just deserts without providing sufficient new benefits. Baker and Clarkson (2002) also argued that the higher importance attached to risk assessment and rehabilitation in deciding on a sentence could increase disparity.

As we saw in section 3.1.1, the 2003 Act did respond in some way to the Halliday proposals although it left the three-tier approach to sentencing (custody, community, and fines) largely intact and later governments have not found the resources or political will to implement the new short custodial sentences. The major changes since 2003 have been in relation to risk-based and mandatory minimum sentencing (see Chapter 5) and providing more 'effective' programmes for community penalties (see Chapter 12). We argue that, despite these critiques, the basic framework of sentencing is still retributivist, and the following sections of this chapter will focus in more detail on the crucial retributivist elements of the current sentencing framework.

3.1.5 Custodial sentencing

Although we mention financial and community penalties in this chapter, we deal with financial and community penalties in Chapters 7 and 12 respectively whilst the bulk of

[18] For a discussion of the effectiveness of longer prison sentences in relation to deterrence and incapacitative policies see Chapters 4 and 5. See also the articles in Volume 43(4) of the *Howard Journal* (2004) which focus on desistance from offending.

the examples in sections 3.2 and 3.3 of this chapter are taken from custodial sentencing. Before we move to further discussion of just deserts we will, therefore, summarise the current options for sentencers in relation to custody.

The 'standard' custodial sentence—which is the result of an assessment of seriousness and proportionality concluding that the criterion for custody is met—is a determinate sentence: the judge specifies exactly how long it will be. Assuming guidance is followed, that length is subject only to the maximum sentence set in law for each offence and the maximum allowed in a magistrates' or youth court (see Chapter 2).[19] So, for example, the current maximum for domestic burglary is 14 years, whilst the maximum for driving or attempting to drive while unfit is 6 months.

The 2003 Act would have included changes to the courts' powers to impose prison sentences of less than 12 months by introducing new sentences of custody plus, which would have included requirements in a licence period on release, and intermittent custody which would have allowed for specified periods of temporary release until the total has been served. Despite pilots of the latter sentence[20] the new sentences were never implemented and the LAS&PO Bill proposes their repeal.

A re-jigged suspended (custodial) sentence was introduced in the CJA 2003 such that during the period of suspension requirements can be placed on the offender, as in community sentences (see Chapter 12, section 12.1.1). Suspended sentences can be used for any term of imprisonment from 28–51 weeks and must specify a supervision period (for which community requirements are again imposed) and an operational period, each of which must be for a term of six months to two years (s 189). If an offender fails to comply with the requirements, or commits an offence during the operational period, the court is empowered to order the original sentence of imprisonment to take effect.

There is one mandatory life sentence in English law, which is the sentence for an offender found guilty of murder. The judge sets a minimum term—based on the guidance set out in Schedule 21 to the CJA 2003—to be served before the offender can be considered for release. There are also custodial sentences to be used with offenders who are deemed to be a risk such that the public need protection for longer or indeterminate periods. Over the period 1991 to the present there have been many attempts to produce workable, effective, and rights-compliant versions of such special custodial sentencing provisions. For the current law see Chapter 5.

In addition there are the (mandatory) minimum sentences we discussed in the last Chapter in relation to Class A drug trafficking, domestic burglary, certain firearms offences, and the offence of using someone to mind a weapon.

3.2 Calculating seriousness

3.2.1 Culpability and harm

Section 143(1) of the 2003 Act and also subsequent guidelines have increasingly made clear the importance of focusing on the two elements which comprise seriousness: culpability and harm. For example, the *Burglary Offences Definitive Guideline* (Sentencing Council: 2011b), in relation to the offence of aggravated burglary, gives as Step 1 in the

[19] However there is a minimum sentence of five days in a magistrates' court.

[20] See National Probation Service Bulletin (2006) Issue 41, 084/06: *Intermittent Custody: Withdrawal of Authority to Supervise Offenders.*

assessment of seriousness the need to place the facts of the offending in one of the following 3 categories: category 1 which is 'greater harm and higher culpability', category 2 which is 'greater harm and lower culpability or lesser harm and higher culpability', and category 3 which is 'lesser harm and lower culpability'. Lists of factors indicating greater harm or higher culpability are then provided.

However, whilst providing useful, detailed, and necessary guidance, such an approach hides the fact that it is very problematic to make such judgements about culpability and harm or, indeed, to clearly separate culpability from harm. Such an exercise—and the rest of the process of finding a proportionate outcome for the offending in question—entails having answers to the following difficult questions:

(a) What factors can legitimately make something more or less serious? Should previous offending be considered in this process?
(b) How do you decide what sentence is proportionate to any amount of seriousness? In particular where should the anchoring point be and so where, for example, should the custody level be set?
(c) To what extent should the personal circumstances of the offender or his family affect the level of the commensurate punishment imposed and should the state's desire to avoid trial costs or to reduce the trauma of a trial for the victim affect the amount of punishment imposed?

If we focus on the first question, we need to note that there are two very different types of judgement in assessing seriousness. First, there is a normative judgement about wrongfulness. With the exception of murder, different individuals, communities, and nations may have very different ideas about what counts as most or least serious. In the sentencing exercise provided at the end of Chapter 2, for example, our law students might or might not think that the harm done (theft of a motorbike and radio, and verbal insults) was serious, depending on the importance of such in their peer group or country; they might or might not take into account the feelings of and effect on the victim of the offences; and they might or might not feel culpability had been affected by an incident in the offenders' love lives.

Cross, drawing on earlier judicial comments and practice, suggested that four factors affect judicial constructions of seriousness as well as the factor of harm done: wickedness, social disapproval, social danger, and social alarm (1981: 178–82).

(a) *The 'evilness' of the perpetrator.* This focus on degrees of wickedness is perhaps the most difficult, depending as it does on normative judgements and underlying moral codes. In the fragmented modern society there may be little consensus as to what actions are most blameworthy and, further, its focus on the mental state of the offender raises difficult questions as to intention, provocation, malice, and excuses.
(b) *Social disapproval.* This is an equally slippery concept, again depending on society's values. The strength of public denunciation of an offence (within its offence category) is often strongly influenced by the age or sex of the victim: babies or children as victims generally attract more social disapproval and so the offending is construed as more serious. There might also be more social disapproval of an offender if he has committed the offence before.
(c) *Social danger or social alarm.* The clearest example of this factor might now be terrorist-related offences: the degree of extreme social anxiety about global

> terrorism feeds into a heightening of perceptions of the severity of offences such as possession of a firearm or counterfeiting documents. Handling of stolen goods is also seen as very serious because of the danger that the incidence of theft will escalate if those willing to handle stolen goods are inadequately punished. Cross's example of social alarm upgrading seriousness is that of the person illegally entering a residential property—as opposed to commercial property—where the same amount of damage or theft causes a greater alarm.

In providing early guidance on 'seriousness' the SGC approached the issue of culpability by focusing on the 'amount' of intention and identifying four 'levels' for sentencing purposes:

> Where the offender—
>
> (iv) has the *intention* to cause harm, with the highest culpability when an offence is planned. The worse the harm intended, the greater the seriousness.
>
> (v) is *reckless* as to whether harm is caused, that is, where the offender appreciates at least some harm would be caused but proceeds giving no thought to the consequences even though the extent of the risk would be obvious to most people.
>
> (vi) has *knowledge* of the specific risks entailed by his actions even though he does not intend to cause the harm that results.
>
> (vii) is guilty of *negligence*.
>
> (Sentencing Guidelines Council 2004a: para 1.7)

The second element of gravity is the factual judgement on the amount of harm caused by the offending. On the face of it, this is a much easier judgement because 'harm' appears as an objective, value-free concept. Arguably this is so if we are talking about theft, where the offence is the deprivation of an amount of money or property whose value is easy to calculate. But, as we saw with our sentencing problem, the value to the victim may be 'sentimental' because, say, of the giver of the gift stolen, or the offence might be assault where the monetary value to be placed on the injury depends not only on the permanence or otherwise of the harm but also on the context of the victim's life. A scar on the face is, arguably, much more serious if the victim is a model whose living depends on facial perfection, and a jaw injury might take away the pleasure of playing in a brass band, but this raises further questions. Should the loss to a particular individual be part of the calculation of harm or should the offender be punished proportionately to the harm an 'average' victim would have suffered from his offending? How do you put a price, not only on potential loss of earnings, but on the more difficult issue of loss of pleasure, whether caused by the loss of a hobby or of one of the five senses?

One can take a broad interpretation, as did the SGC when referring to the statutory provision as 'widely drafted', so that harm 'encompasses those offences where harm is caused but also those where neither individuals nor the community suffer harm but a risk of harm is present' (Sentencing Guidelines Council 2004a: para 1.8). The Seriousness guideline also provides a list of 'factors indicating a more than usually serious degree of harm' which includes 'multiple victims', 'an especially serious physical or psychological effect on the victim, even if unintended', 'a sustained assault or repeated assaults on the same victim', and offending committed in the presence of friends or relatives (ibid: para 1.23).

Furthermore, the relationship between these two levels of judgement—the normative and the 'factual'—is also problematic: how do you reconcile different amounts of 'wrongfulness' and damage? As the guidance notes:

> Assessing seriousness is a difficult task, particularly where there is an imbalance between culpability and harm:
>
> - sometimes the harm that actually results is greater than the harm intended by the offender;
> - in other circumstances, the offender's culpability may be at a higher level than the harm resulting from the offence.
>
> (ibid: para 1.16)

Some time ago, a survey of residents in Dallas, USA, showed that respondents saw the two dimensions as distinct and that where crimes are perceived as more 'wrong' than harmful, the calculation of seriousness mirrors wrongfulness. Conversely, where crimes are perceived to be more harmful than wrong, harmfulness predominates (Warr 1989). This distinction could be critical as 'many crimes are likely to be evaluated quite differently on the two dimensions' (ibid: 797) and reflect, perhaps, different moral or religious codes (ibid: 819).

Yet these difficult issues are unavoidable in the calculation of proportionality. As noted in Chapter 2's examination of retributivist principles, ordinal proportionality concerns the question of how offences should be punished, relative to each other, on the basis of the seriousness of the offending; cardinal proportionality concerns the choice of the level of severity to anchor the ranked penalties. Empirical research suggests there is some consensus on the seriousness ranking of the most serious crimes, such as murder and rape, but that even in this element of ordinal ranking there was not complete consistency, with, for example, social workers and prison staff ranking actual bodily harm higher than other groups (Cavadino and Wiles 1994: 490–3; see also Rossi *et al.* 1974). There appears to be less agreement about where to 'anchor' the penalty scale: responses to hypothetical cases by practitioners produced statistically significant differences between criminal justice agencies as to the level of seriousness deemed necessary to justify custody (Cavadino and Wiles 1994: 493–8; see, also, for reference to other surveys and interpretation problems, Ashworth 2010: 106–8).

3.2.2 **The process towards a proportionate sentence**

This chapter is focusing on the retributivist concepts of seriousness and proportionality but, whilst a book may proceed chapter by chapter and deal with separate points in turn, sentencing in practice is not like that. The different issues are intertwined and, when faced with a real case, or a problem question, an overall view of the process and possibilities is necessary before decisions can be made about what law and issues are going to be relevant. For this reason, to set the material in this chapter in context, we have provided below a basic checklist. Some of the elements on this list will be dealt with in subsequent chapters and so you are not expected to understand their import at this stage. So, whilst—to a greater or lesser extent—the just deserts approach to sentencing is the 'normal' sentencing framework, steps 1–3 in the checklist relate to the exceptions to that approach and are triggered when the selective incapacitation or extended supervision provisions apply and when the offender is mentally disordered. They will be dealt with elsewhere (see Chapters 5 and 7).

Checklist

In light of the facts of the case in question:

1. Is the offender mentally disordered? Consider the provisions of the Mental Health Act 1983 and any other relevant legislation.
2. Are any of the minimum sentences relevant (particularly PCCSA 2000, ss 110–111, and some firearms offences)? Is the sentence fixed by law (murder)? Are the sentences for public protection applicable (particularly CJA 2003, ss 225–228)?
3. Is the case to be dealt with in terms of proportionality/seriousness/just deserts? What statutory provisions are (most) relevant?
4. What is the statutory maximum penalty? If being dealt with in the magistrates' court, what is the maximum that can be imposed?
5. What is the 'normal range' or 'starting point' for this offence (or category of offence) and what guidelines are there from the Court of Appeal, Sentencing Guidelines Council, or Sentencing Council? If relevant, what do the *Magistrates' Court Sentencing Guidelines* say?
6. Is there an offence-based guideline which provides guidance on levels of culpability and harm in assessing seriousness? Which (other) factors from case law or guidance on mitigation or aggravation are relevant?
7. Which statutory factors must be taken into account to aggravate (or mitigate) severity?
8. Is there any recent guidance which is pertinent to deciding whether the facts of the case fulfil the seriousness criteria for imposing custodial or community penalties?
9. (a) For a fine: should the offender's sentencing record be taken into account?
   (b) For a community sentence: do any facts of the case suggest particular requirements/penalties are appropriate?
   (c) For a custodial sentence: is the sentence length as short as is necessary for the penal purpose?
10. Are there any personal mitigating factors? Should they be taken into account?
11. Is there a sentence discount for a guilty plea? If so, how much?
12. What compensation order should be imposed? If not, why not? Should a victim's surcharge be imposed? Is a confiscation order, or any other ancillary order, relevant?[21]
13. What sentence should be imposed?[22]
14. Are there any other powers that should be exercised for the purpose of protecting the public from harm from the offender?[23]

If we relate the checklist to the discussion in Chapter 2 about ordinal proportionality, we can see that it reminds us to go through the following elements to calculate a proportionate sentence:

[21] Compensation and confiscation orders are dealt with in Chapter 6.

[22] Compensation and other ancillary and preventative orders would usually be decided after sentence but, as we shall see in Chapter 7, a compensation order can be made instead of a fine.

[23] Prevention orders are dealt with in Chapter 5.

(a) Establish the seriousness of the offence *category* on which the offender has admitted guilt or been found guilty. This requires knowledge of the statutory maximum penalty and guidance about the 'normal' range of penalties for that offence.

(b) Establish the seriousness of the offence *in question*. This requires looking at those factors relating to the specific instance of offending under review which make the harm and culpability greater or less than the 'average' in relation to this offence category. It entails assessing whether the facts of the case amount to aggravating or mitigating factors. Aggravating factors, such as breach of trust, the age of the victim, the amount of harm, the social position of the offender, the extent of planning and premeditation, and the offender's criminal record, reflect the ideas previously discussed which account for the fact that guidelines and sentencers consider some aspects of offending as more 'evil' or 'harmful' than others. Mitigating factors relating to the offence, such as provocation or minimal harm caused, similarly decrease seriousness.

Then, having also ascertained or constructed a ranking of punishments in order of severity, the sentencer must choose the punishment which is commensurate to the amount of seriousness calculated for the offence in question.

Finally, the sentencer should consider mitigation relating to the offender. This may be seen as an 'optional extra' but the sentencer, statutory provisions permitting, may take into account those personal circumstances of the offender which are not strictly relevant to offence seriousness but which the court feels justified in taking into account to mitigate the severity of the sentence (see Chapter 7, section 7.1). The discount for a guilty plea might be seen as personal mitigation—if so, this is the exception in that it *must* be given where it applies. It is a pity the same word—'mitigation'—is used at two very different parts in the sentencing model because the potential impact at each part is different.[24]

3.2.3 **Aggravating factors in statute**

Stages 6 and 7 of the checklist relate to aggravating and mitigating factors established either by statute or by guidance and the courts should consider such: s 156(1) of the CJA 2003, replicating previous provisions (see Table 3.1), requires courts, when deciding whether the seriousness of the offence in question merits a community or custodial sentence, to 'take into account all such information as is available to it about the circumstances of the offence... including any aggravating or mitigating factors'. However, Ashworth questions whether all the aggravating factors allowed by legislation and guidance can be theorised in relation to culpability or harm and so fitted into proportionality theory because 'courts have often adopted the terminology of deterrence' (2010: 166; see also Roberts 2008a).

The selection and legitimation of factors which may mitigate or aggravate seriousness are, then, a crucial issue in sentencing. As Lord Bingham CJ noted, 'the seriousness of the offence can vary almost infinitely from case to case', and so 'whether a custodial sentence is required, and if so the length of such sentence, is heavily dependent on the aggravating and mitigating features' (*Brewster*, 1998 at 225–6). A similar approach was taken in *Howells* (1998) and is now taken in the Sentencing Council guidelines.

Statutory aggravations have become increasingly important in the last decade or so and we set out the sections and their history in Table 3.2, which takes the same format as Table 3.1 in section 3.1.3.

[24] We will not be discussing the statutory rules regarding sentencing procedures in this book but see Ashworth (2000: 307–15) and Thomas (2002).

Table 3.2 Statutory mitigation and aggravation of seriousness

Whatever sentencing framework is being used to decide on a sentence the court must consider whether statutory factors apply—either to set a determinate sentence or to set the minimum period of an indeterminate sentence.

CJA 1991	PCCSA	CJA 2003	Question
29(1)–(4)	151	143(2), (3)	Has aggravation of offence seriousness been done where 'allowed'/'suitable'? (*previous convictions, failure to respond to previous sentences,*[25] *whether offence committed on bail*)
N/A	152	144	Can there be a reduction in sentence for a guilty plea? How much?
N/A	153	145	Was there racial or religious aggravation? If so this must increase the seriousness.
N/A	N/A	146	Was there aggravation related to disability or sexual orientation? If so this must increase the seriousness.

Of supreme importance is s 143(2) of the CJA 2003 which replaces the provision enacted in 1993 and mandates aggravation for relevant previous convictions: this will be dealt with separately in the next section. Linked to this is the practice of asking the sentencer to 'take into consideration' offences with which the offender has not been charged (TICs). This practice benefits both the offender and the criminal justice system although there are circumstances when this is not appropriate (see guidance issued by the Crown Prosecution Service[26]).

Offences committed on bail and 'failure to respond'

The amendments made by the CJA 1993 increased seriousness if the offender had failed to respond to previous penalties and if the offence was committed while the offender was on bail (whether or not that bail related to an offence for which the offender was ultimately convicted and imprisoned). 'Failure to respond' was one of the three justifications for imposing custody on young offenders in the Criminal Justice Act 1982. It was not incorporated in the criteria extended to all offenders by the CJA 1991 s 1 and was prohibited as an aggravating factor in the original s 29, but the PCCSA 2000 re-enacted the failure to respond aggravation. In a further twist, the CJA 2003 repealed this provision (Schedule 37, Part 7) but re-enacted aggravation for offences on bail (see Table 3.2).

Racially motivated offences

In 1998 the Crime and Disorder Act (CDA) added motivation by racial hostility as a new statutory aggravation. This had already been established by case law, notably *Craney and Corbett* (1996), and ss 29–32 of the CDA 1998 mandated an increase in offence seriousness for specified offences by increasing the statutory maximum, as well as imposing a duty to increase seriousness in relation to any other offence in s 82. The Sentencing Advisory Panel (SAP) (2000) issued guidance on the amount of sentence enhancement to be imposed and suggested 40–70 per cent for fines, community, and custodial sentences

[25] This is no longer a statutory aggravation.

[26] See http://www.cps.gov.uk/legal/l_to_o/offences_to_be_taken_into_consideration_guidance_(tics)_/index.html see also guidance issued by the Sentencing Council in March 2012.

unless this pushed the sentence over a threshold. In *Kelly and Donnelly* (2001) the Court of Appeal adopted the SAP's list of factors to be used to scale gravity, but rejected formal percentage enhancements (see Ashworth 2010: 160).

Religion, disability, and sexual orientation

The Anti-Terrorism and Security Act 2001 amended the legislation to add 'religiously aggravated offences', now to be found in the CJA 2003, s 145, whilst s 146 of that Act added similar provisions to mandate an increase in sentences for aggravation related to disability or sexual orientation (see Table 3.2).

All these statutory aggravations can be found on the list of 'factors indicating higher culpability' in the guidance on seriousness (Sentencing Guidelines Council 2004a: para 1.22). Note also that the guidance in the CJA 2003 about minimum terms to be served by those convicted of murder gives a starting point of 30 years for murders motivated by race, religion, or sexual orientation (Schedule 21, para 5).

3.2.4 **Persistence as the problem**

Statistics in relation to the national Prolific and Other Priority Offenders (PPO) cohort show that the offence group 'theft' accounted for one-fifth of proven offences by the PPO cohort, that the mean age for offenders in the 2009 PPO cohort was 27 years, and that 97 per cent of the 2009 PPO cohort were male (Home Office 2010). The existence of such a cohort and the availability of statistics is evidence of the current high policy profile of persistence of offending. The issue of whether and how to sentence in relation to persistence is, therefore, a very important but very difficult and long-standing sentencing problem (see Flaherty 2006/7; Roberts, 2008b).

Of the three possible responses—flat-rate sentencing, 'progressive loss of mitigation', and cumulative sentencing—only the first takes no notice of previous record whilst the second and third responses do consider previous offending but conceptualise the importance differently. This reflects the fact that modern retributivists have been divided in their approach to persistence—the relevance of past offending and good character—as a sentencing factor. In utilitarian theory the focus on past offending would be relevant to the calculation of future risks, but in retributivism its role is different.

Von Hirsch allows previous convictions as the only exception to the principle that offences of comparable seriousness should receive a punishment with the same degree of severity (von Hirsch 1986, 1993). If an offence is committed for the first time it might be successfully argued in mitigation that the action is out of character and so there is, in effect, a penalty discount for first offenders, but with each repeated offence this argument will be less plausible. The offender is still being censured for the current act, but censure may be reduced because we acknowledge that it was the first time the person had succumbed to the temptation to act badly and had resisted it before. But while a 'discount' may be appropriate here, von Hirsch emphasises that there must not be a large differential between punishments for first offenders and recidivists: '[A] first offender should receive less punishment than a recidivist, but...this punishment differential should only be a modest one' (1986: 90).

For von Hirsch there would be a limit on how far previous convictions would increase the severity of the sentence and the upper limit would very likely be lower than permitted on utilitarian models (von Hirsch 1986). He acknowledges that past criminal record has implications for desert for the current offence, so he argues for 'primary but not exclusive emphasis on the current offence' (ibid: 78). Other desert theorists, such as Fletcher (1982), would see a focus on previous offending as incompatible with just deserts principles. He argues that previous convictions do not affect desert for the current offence, and should not influence the sentence, as the offender has already been punished for past convictions.

If the offender persists, he would lose what von Hirsch calls his first offender discount and this would be done progressively. However, once that discount had been used up, he would receive the full amount of punishment but no more than this. The alternative of continually increasing punishment for recidivism would lead to the situation where relatively minor offences could incur harsh punishments. The primary concern on von Hirsch's approach is still with the current offence and the size of the differential between the two punishments should be kept 'within proper bounds' (von Hirsch 1986: 91).

However, the efforts of retributivist theory to provide a rational basis for dealing with multiple offences through a 'ceiling' on punishment are criticised by Ryberg (2005) who argues that this approach is both theoretically flawed and unable to provide a practical basis for sentencing.

In cumulative sentencing the sentence increases on each subsequent conviction. If represented graphically, cumulative sentencing is seen as a straight upward line to the 'normal' penalty and beyond to the statutory maximum; progressive loss of mitigation is a line with an upward slope but it then reaches a plateau at the normal ceiling for the offence (Wasik and von Hirsch 1994: 410). Flat-rate sentencing would take no account of previous convictions whatsoever. Figure 3.1 illustrates this in graph form.

The graph assumes:

- the maximum penalty for this offence is 10 years;
- the normal range is five–seven years and the court uses six years as the norm every time;
- previous convictions are all for offences of a similar gravity;

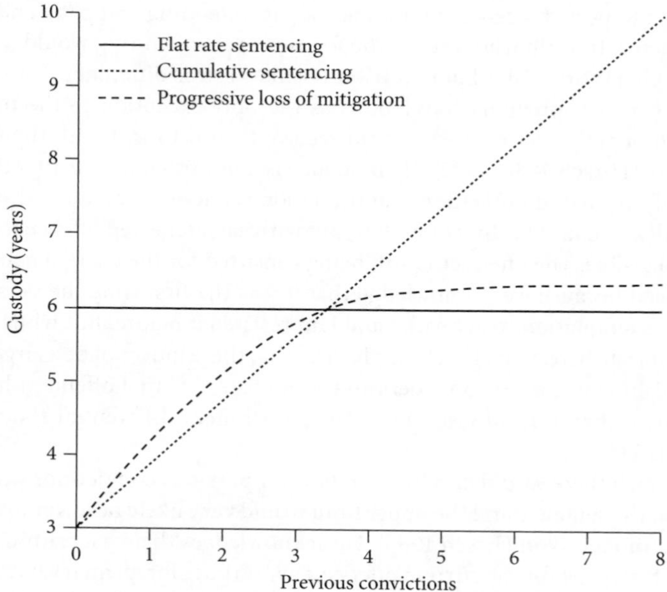

Figure 3.1 Persistence

- the court starts with a three-year sentence for this offence if there are no previous convictions;
- where progressive loss of mitigation operates, the loss for the first offence is greater than for subsequent offences.

Arguably, the progressive loss of mitigation approach was endorsed by the Court of Appeal prior to the CJA 1991 (Wasik and von Hirsch 1994: 411) and *Queen* (1981) was referred to in the White Paper (Home Office 1990a) to justify s 29. As passed, s 29 stated, inter alia, that an offence was not to be regarded as more serious 'by reason of any previous convictions of the offender'. There was some debate as to whether that wording did incorporate the loss of mitigation approach or simply made clear that sentencers could not use previous convictions to aggravate the seriousness in specific cases unless special culpability was disclosed by the record. Wasik and von Hirsch argued for the former, that ss 28(1) and 29(1) together provided the upward 'slope' (by allowable mitigation in s 28) and then the 'plateau' of the progressive loss of mitigation approach (1994: 411). Be that as it may, the CJA 1993 repealed the whole of s 29 and substituted a new section.

The amended subs 29(1) stated: 'In considering the seriousness of any offence, the court may take into account any previous convictions of the offender or any failure of his to respond to previous sentences'. Henham warned that this could 'lead to an increase in cases where individuals are sentenced "on their record" and inevitably a rise in the prison population' (1995: 223). However, Wasik and von Hirsch (1994) argued that this did not give the sentencer 'unfettered discretion' in dealing with previous convictions and, further, that recidivism *per se* does not constitute a 'failure to respond' and so cannot satisfy the second limb for aggravation of offence seriousness. They refer to Hansard, which seems to suggest that the Government wanted only to return to (or make clearer) the pre-1991 approach, not to allow a system of cumulative sentencing (1994: 412–13).

Their arguments do of course raise the question as to whether sentencing practice pre- or post-1991 was the same as the case law suggests. Roberts (2002) cites statistics given in the Halliday Report (2001: Appendix 3, Table 1) which show that the probability of being given a custodial sentence increases in direct relationship to the number of previous convictions. He argues that this suggests there is already 'a robust recidivist premium' in practice and that 'cumulative sentencing is alive and well in England and Wales' (Roberts 2002: 430).[27] Others have argued that these changes in 1993 to the 1991 CJA, taken together, were a 'remarkable *volte face*' in sentencing policy (Henham 1995: 223), and were at least partly responsible for the resumed upward trend in custodial sentencing (Home Office 1994a: 1, see also paras 6–10).

The CJA 2003, in line with the Halliday proposals, enhances the role of past record. Halliday had argued that 'clarification needs to be based on a clear presumption that sentencing severity should increase as a consequence of sufficiently recent and relevant convictions' (2001: para 2.7).[28] The CJA 2003 incorporates this intention in s 143(2):

> In considering the seriousness of an offence... committed by an offender who has one or more previous convictions, the court must treat each previous conviction as an

[27] On a related point, Wasik (2001) pointed to the 'vital importance' of particular previous convictions in relation to the mandatory (minimum) sentences imposed under ss 109–111 of the PCCSA 2000, noting the practical problems caused for practitioners and his concerns that too high a premium is being placed on the accuracy of criminal records.

[28] The Report also considers in some detail various ways of buttressing this presumption, opting for a preferred approach of 'entry points' (2001: paras 2.12–2.20).

> aggravating factor if...the court considers that it can reasonably be so treated having regard, in particular to—
>
> (a) the nature of the offence to which the conviction relates and its relevance to the current offence, and
>
> (b) the time that has elapsed since the conviction.

Section 151 is also relevant. As already noted, it empowers the court to impose a community order on a persistent offender who has previously been fined three or more times but would not otherwise satisfy the criterion for a community sentence.

The effect of s 143 on sentencing practice depends, notwithstanding its mandatory force, on how the courts exercise the discretion not to consider each previous conviction as an aggravating factor. As in case law on this issue, the discretion focuses on the reasonableness of so doing where the nature of the offence may be very different from the current offence, may be relatively trivial, and may have taken place many years previously. There is scope here for sentencers to interpret it in a way which is not significantly different from the progressive loss of mitigation doctrine, and the Halliday Report argued that there should be a 'ceiling' on the effect of previous convictions (2001: para 2.20).

However, detailed guidance would be needed to structure this discretion (ibid: 2.13) as the CJA 2003 does not provide for upper limits (see von Hirsch and Roberts 2004) and the Sentencing Council has not yet issued specific guidance. The first set of figures from the Sentencing Council's *Crown Court Sentencing Survey* shows that '59 per cent of offenders with one to three previous convictions taken into account were sent to immediate custody. This increased to 78 per cent for offenders with 10 or more previous convictions taken into account' (Sentencing Council 2011d). On the face, this appears to be cumulative sentencing and there is no doubt that government policy is to increase the effect of previous convictions on the sentencing decision.

3.2.5 **Guidance on aggravation**

Much more difficult to summarise is the appellate and Sentencing Guidelines Council/ Sentencing Council (SGC/SC) guidance about other factors which should or should not legitimately aggravate seriousness and the extent to which that should be done. In the guideline on seriousness there is a long list—without detail—at para 1.22 of a range of factors which can aggravate (Sentencing Guidelines Council 2004a). There are now a number of detailed offence-based guidelines which include lists of factors and the more recent guidelines divide this exercise into two steps. Referring to s 125(3)–(4) of the Coroners and Justice Act 2009, the recent Assault Guideline, for example, first of all specifies offence ranges—the range of sentences appropriate for each type of offence.

> Within each offence, the Council has specified three categories which reflect varying degrees of seriousness. The offence range is split into *category ranges*—sentences appropriate for each level of seriousness. The Council has also identified a starting point within each category.... Once the starting point is established the court should consider further aggravating and mitigating factors...
>
> (Sentencing Council, 2011a: 2)[29]

The division into a first stage where there are lists of factors indicating greater harm or higher culpability allows for an immediate categorisation into different sentencing ranges

[29] The earlier guideline relating to assaults on children took the previous more narrative approach: see Sentencing Guidelines Council (2008f).

but it is somewhat problematic in the selection of factors for these lists and the subsequent lists of factors increasing or decreasing seriousness. So, for example, in this Assault Guideline the non-statutory factors indicating greater harm in relation to the offence of grievous bodily harm include 'victim is particularly vulnerable because of personal circumstances' (ibid: 4) whilst in Step 2 the location and timing of the offence as well as 'gratuitous degradation of victim' are amongst the aggravating factors (ibid: 5).

For particular offences and offence categories there is also the useful *Guideline Judgments Case Compendium*, first issued by the SGC in 2005 to summarise appellate guidance and updated several times since. It is, however, the growing body of ever more detailed guidance being produced by the Sentencing Council which is most important. This book cannot seek to address aggravating factors comprehensively or in detail. We will simply discuss selected topics which have consistently been upheld as influential, or have been of recent interest.[30]

Breach of trust

The Court of Appeal and now the guidelines have consistently condemned offending which involves a breach of trust, and research suggests that abuse of trust, together with premeditation, are the two factors most likely to tip the balance in favour of a custodial sentence (Flood-Page and Mackie 1998: 11). In 1999 Walker noted that '[a]lmost any sort of dishonesty in breach of trust is regarded as serious enough to justify a custodial sentence' (1999: 53) although this may no longer apply to less serious offending. *Kefford* (2002) reduced the starting point for 'economic crimes' (in that case false accounting) and Flood-Page and Mackie found that in the Crown Court over half of breach of trust theft cases did not result in a custodial sentence because of balancing mitigating factors (1998: 85). However, the current guidelines for the offence of theft in breach of trust (which carries a maximum penalty of seven years) provide starting points ranging from 18 weeks to three years custody for the first three levels of seriousness with a non-custodial range only for the fourth level. Significantly, the criterion for the most serious category is either 'theft of £125,000 or more' *or* 'theft of £20,000 or more in breach of a high degree of trust' and level 2 takes the same approach in prioritising the nature of the breach of trust in relation to the amount taken (Sentencing Guidelines Council 2008d: 11)

The consequences to the victim

The effect of the crime on the victim has gained a higher profile as an aggravating factor. Indeed, legislation has stated that in producing guidelines the Sentencing Council must have regard to several matters including 'the impact of sentencing decisions on victims of offences'.[31] In the context of the (previous) burglary guidelines in *R v McInerney, R v Keating* (2002), Lord Woolf CJ, at the beginning of his *Statement in response to inaccurate comments on the guidelines issued by the Court of Appeal as to the sentencing of domestic burglars* (14 January 2003), noted that the Court had endorsed the principle that 'the consequences to the victim should always be of the greatest significance in determining the appropriate punishment' (para 3).[32] SGC guidelines on seriousness endorse old age or youth, disability, and the nature of a victim's job as potential forms of vulnerability (Sentencing Guidelines Council 2004a: para 1.17) and the vulnerability of the victim is also one that may be linked to abuse of trust in relation to sexual offences with minors.[33]

[30] See Ashworth (2010: 161–8) for a good discussion of various aggravating factors mentioned in guidelines.

[31] Coroners and Justice Act 2009, s 120(11)(c).

[32] See also the *Case Compendium* (SGC 2005: 72).

[33] See *Hubbard* (2002).

The Guideline for sentencing when the offence involves domestic violence also upgraded the focus on the victim. It states that 'offences committed in a domestic context should be regarded as being no less serious than offences committed in a non-domestic context' and then lists various factors arising from the nature of the offender–victim relationship which make the victim more vulnerable and so the offending more serious (Sentencing Guidelines Council 2006: 3–4).

Other forms of vulnerability in the victim have been taken to aggravate. In another reference by the Attorney General (*No 45 of 2000*) reported in 2001, the victim of robbery and false imprisonment was a doctor, seen by the court as a highly vulnerable member of the community when making a house call late at night in unfamiliar surroundings. The judgment stated that courts had a duty to deter the commission of offences against such victims. Such ideas can also be seen in recent guidance. In the Assault Guideline the 'factors increasing seriousness' in relation to the offence of assault occasioning actual bodily harm include the following: on-going effect upon the victim; offence committed against those working in the public sector or providing a service to the public; presence of others including relatives, especially the children or partner of the victim; in domestic violence cases, victim forced to leave their home (Sentencing Council 2011a: 13).

Other factors

There are a number of other factors in addition to the above which are taken as aggravating in relation to a range of offences. Those generally noted[34] are the following: premeditation and planning, a professional or group operation, unnecessary violence, and the seriousness of the harm done. Prevalence might also be added as *Cunningham* (1993) did not rule this out after the implementation of the CJA 1991 and, regrettably, neither did the SGC: 'There may be exceptional local circumstances that arise which may lead a court to decide that prevalence should influence sentencing levels. The pivotal issue in such cases will be the harm being caused to the community' (Sentencing Guidelines Council 2004a: para 1.39).

Two offence categories which raise particular issues about aggravation will be discussed in more detail: causing death by dangerous driving and smuggling.

Causing death by dangerous driving

Causing death by dangerous driving is a particularly difficult offence on which to sentence because the two ingredients of seriousness—the culpability of the offender and the harm done (CJA 2003, s 143(1))—may not point in the same direction. The death—the most serious of harms—was not intended and so the calculation of culpability is relatively low in relation to the total of harm caused. 'Unintended consequences' have in effect downgraded the factor of harm done in relation to this offence and the calculation of seriousness is, rather, made in relation to the dangerousness of, and risk posed by, the offender's driving.

Cooksley and others (2003) incorporated advice from the SAP on sentencing for the offence of causing death by dangerous driving (and also careless driving while under the influence of drink or drugs). As Wasik pointed out in the Preface to the SAP's advice, and as quoted by Lord Woolf CJ in his judgment, '[u]nderstandably, this often leads to calls from the victims' families, and from the wider community, for tough sentencing' (*Cooksley and others* (2003) at para 1). The Court endorsed the view of the SAP that 'briefly

[34] Two sources, apart from appellate guidance, SAP advice, and SGC/SC guidance, are Practice notes by the Lord Chief Justice and the latest version of the *Magistrates' Court Sentencing Guidelines*.

dozing at the wheel' should no longer be viewed as indicating a less serious offence (ibid), and that dangerous driving resulting in death should attract a higher sentence than one that does not, the impact on the family being a matter the courts can legitimately take into account (ibid: para 11). The Court endorsed the 16 aggravating factors suggested by the SAP and listed them (ibid: para 15), before discussing sentence length in four bands: no aggravating circumstances, intermediate culpability, higher culpability, most serious culpability. The lowest starting point would be 12–18 months even on a plea of guilty, the highest six years or more. The aggravating factors likely to place the case in the 8–10 year category might be a combination of multiple deaths, excessive speed, excessive alcohol, and seeking to avoid responsibility (ibid: para 31).

This tougher approach was upheld in *Emery* (2003) where the driver had fallen asleep at the wheel. He had subsequently been diagnosed as suffering from obstructive sleep apnoea, a diagnosis which he contended he had not been told of seven years earlier when he had undergone nose surgery after falling asleep at the wheel of his vehicle on two occasions. Nevertheless, the Court of Appeal endorsed the comments of the trial judge that he had been 'grossly inattentive' of his sleep problems[35] and upheld the sentence of two years' imprisonment.

The consultation guideline on *Causing Death by Driving* (Sentencing Guidelines Council 2008c) listed five factors 'that may be regarded as determinants of offence seriousness': 'awareness of risk, effect of alcohol or drugs, inappropriate speed of vehicle, seriously culpable behaviour of [the] offender and failing to have proper regard to vulnerable road users' (ibid: 4). The definitive guideline published in 2008 states, for example, that the starting points for the offence of causing death by careless or inconsiderate driving should be 15 months' imprisonment, 36 weeks' imprisonment or a community sentence depending on the level of seriousness, and lists appropriate aggravating factors such as 'serious injury to one or more persons in addition to the death(s)' and 'irresponsible behaviour, such as failing to stop or falsely claiming that one of the victims was responsible for the collision' (Sentencing Guidelines Council 2008e).

Smuggling

The SAP issued advice on the fraudulent evasion of excise duty on importing tobacco and alcohol in July 2003. The same month, in *Czyzewski* (2003), the Court of Appeal stated that such an offence is aggravated if a defendant (i) played an organisational role; (ii) made repeated imports particularly after receiving warnings; (iii) was a professional smuggler; (iv) used a legitimate business as a front; (v) abused a position of privilege; (vi) used children or vulnerable adults; (vii) threatened violence; (viii) dealt in goods with an additional health risk because of possible contamination; or (ix) disposed of goods to under-age purchasers. These factors were in line with the SAP's recommendations and a fraud offences guideline—not issued until 2009—noted the *Czyzewski* case as relevant to the aggravating factors listed in regard to revenue fraud against HM Revenue and Customs (Sentencing Guidelines Council 2009a: 28, n 45).

It is worth noting that the aggravating factors of abuse of trust, the vulnerability and suffering of the victim, and premeditation, together with concealment of the body and the use of threats, are now listed in para 10 of Schedule 21 to the CJA 2003 to assist the court in its determination of the minimum term of a mandatory life sentence for murder.

[35] Note that an aggravating factor (g) in *Cooksley* is 'driving while knowingly suffering from a medical condition which significantly impairs the offender's driving skills' (at para 15).

3.2.6 Mitigation of seriousness

The court must also consider mitigating factors relating to the offence when assessing seriousness but has discretion to assign a weight to such factors and to balance them against the weight of aggravating factors. Again, *Overarching Principles: Seriousness* (Sentencing Guidelines Council 2004a) lists appropriate general mitigating factors and offence-based guidelines provide examples of relevant mitigation. As Ashworth points out, however, mitigating factors comprise a 'much more heterogeneous collection' (2005: 160). Some factors amount to the absence of aggravation: less offender culpability, lack of premeditation/impulsiveness, a lone/amateur operation, lack of violence or intimidation, and no previous criminal record. Others focus on the relative lack of harm done. There are also mitigating factors relating to culpability which are in effect criminal defences, not used or not successful in the pre-conviction process but which have a long history as 'excuses' at the sentencing stage. These are necessity, duress, mistake of law, and provocation,[36] to which can be added entrapment,[37] all justified on the grounds that offending with these motivations or in these contexts entails less wickedness (Wasik 1983). More generally, exceptional stress or emotional pressure are potential mitigations of seriousness, as, for example, when someone steals to provide for a dying relative (Ashworth 2000: 140).

Court of Appeal cases and SGC/SC guidelines lay down a wide range of mitigating factors relating to particular offences. For example, the two mitigating factors discussed in the domestic violence guideline are 'positive good character' and provocation (Sentencing Guidelines Council 2006: 5–6), whilst, in relation to fraud offences the specific factors are given as peripheral involvement, behaviour not fraudulent from the outset, and misleading or incomplete advice (Sentencing Guidelines Council 2009a: paras 30–36). The mitigating factors listed in relation to setting the minimum period for murder are to be found in Schedule 21 (para 11) to the CJA 2003 and include an intention to cause serious bodily harm rather than to kill, lack of premeditation, and a belief by the offender that the murder was an act of mercy.

There is little guidance on how to balance mitigating and aggravating factors and so it would be easy for disparity to occur. Further, where the offence is very serious or where the courts wish to give a particular message, notably a deterrent one, mitigating factors relating to the offence or the offender may have little or no effect (Piper 2007). An example could be taken from *Cooksley* (2002), discussed above, where Lord Woolf CJ said: '[I]t is important for the courts to drive home the message as to the dangers that can result from dangerous driving on the road... drivers must know that... no matter what the mitigating circumstances, normally only a custodial sentence will be imposed' (para 11).

3.3 Establishing proportionality

3.3.1 The seriousness thresholds

The CJA 2003 re-enacted the 'so serious that' and 'serious enough' criteria for imposing custodial and community sentences respectively and the SGC published guidance on seriousness in 2004. However, how the appellate courts construed key concepts in the CJA 1991 continues to have an influence on interpretation of the CJA 2003 and so the cases discussed below are not simply of historical interest.

[36] The correlative 'excuse' to the insanity defence will not be dealt with here: the treatment of mentally disordered offenders will be examined in Chapter 7 (section 7.4).

[37] Case law has established this is not a defence in English law: see Ashworth (2000: 140) for cases.

In 1997 Ashworth and von Hirsch wrote an important article entitled 'Recognising Elephants: The Problem of the Custody Threshold'. This intriguing title referred to a test set out by Lawton LJ before the CJA 1991 in relation to the very similar 'so serious that only' hurdle for custody of young offenders in the Criminal Justice Act 1982. The conclusions of the article were based on over 50 reported Court of Appeal cases ruling on the custody criterion in the CJA 1991, the first of which was *Cox* (1993). In that case, Lord Taylor CJ retained Lord Justice Lawton's test of the 'right thinking members of the public' laid down in *Bradbourne* (1985 at 183) whereby a custodial sentence was justified if such right-thinking people, 'knowing all the facts', would 'feel that justice had not been done by the passing of any sentence other than a custodial one'. Lawton, LJ said that he was confident that 'courts can recognise an elephant when they see one, but may not find it necessary to define it'. How the courts were to ascertain the views of these members of the public is a moot point. Ashworth and von Hirsch concluded that this purportedly 'common-sense' test of the 'right-thinking' person was 'conceptually flawed and empirically unsupported' and generally unsatisfactory (1997: 189). It is encouraging to find that Lord Bingham CJ endorsed these criticisms in *Howells and related appeals* (1999 at 53):

> There is no bright line which separates offences which are so serious that only a custodial sentence can be justified from offences which are not so serious as to require the passing of a custodial sentence. But it cannot be said that the 'right-thinking' members of the public test is very helpful, since the sentencing court has no means of ascertaining the views of right-thinking members of the public and inevitably attributes to such right-thinking members its own views. So, when applying this test, the sentencing court is doing little more than reflecting its own opinion whether justice would or would not be done and be seen to be done by the passing of a non-custodial sentence.

The Court of Appeal found itself, however, unable to substitute a new test, deciding it would be 'dangerous and wrong for us to lay down prescriptive rules' (ibid). Its approach, and that of the SGC (2004a), was to focus on the custody/community penalty dividing line, and to specify the mitigating and aggravating factors which would or would not contribute towards tipping the case over the custody seriousness threshold. Lord Bingham CJ first listed five factors for courts 'ordinarily' to take into account: an admission of guilt, self-motivated and proven determination to address the causes of offending if 'fuelled by addiction', youth and immaturity, whether the offender was of previous good character, and whether the offender had previously been sentenced to custody (at 53–4). The Court then dealt separately with *Howells* and each of the other related appeals, discussing these factors and others such as premeditation, the use or threat of violence, the time of day, provocation, and the harm caused. SGC guidance includes these factors in more accessible, simplified lists (2004a).

The case of *Mills* (2002), dealing with offences of dishonesty, also discussed factors that should be considered when the offence is one that often receives a custodial sentence but the circumstances of the particular case reveal mitigating factors. Significantly it stated that, as well as asking whether prison is necessary, 'the sentencing judge also had to take into account the reality of sentencing policy' and, in particular three factors: the inability of the prison service to achieve anything positive in the way of rehabilitation during a short sentence (at 331), the effect on children if a single mother is imprisoned, and, specifically in relation to female prisoners, the fact that she might be allocated to a prison far from her home and children (at 332; also see Chapter 7, section 7.2.5 and Chapter 10, section 10.1.2).

Shortly after the implementation of the 1991 Act the Court of Appeal dealt with another principle in applying the seriousness criteria. In *Cunningham* (1993) the Court was asked to rule on whether deterrence could form part of the calculation of seriousness.

> Section 2(2) of the Act provided that a custodial sentence should be commensurate with the seriousness of the offence or offences for which it is passed. That provision did allow the sentencer to take into account the need for deterrence. The purposes of a custodial sentence were to punish and deter. The phrase 'commensurate with the seriousness of the offence' must mean commensurate with the punishment and deterrence which the offence required... The prevalence of an offence was a legitimate factor in determining the length of a custodial sentence. The seriousness of an offence was clearly affected by how many people it harmed and to what extent.
>
> (Criminal Law Review 1990: 150)

This extraordinary decision, whereby prevalence affected the construction of seriousness in an individual case, reached its goal by eliding a valid general statement about the purposes of punishment with a specific statutory provision designed to ensure that, in individual cases, the commensurate sentence was calculated only in relation to the level of seriousness of the instance of offending in question. Further, it 'proves' its conclusion by the unjustified use of words such as 'must' and 'clearly affected'.[38]

The above cases would suggest that the custody test established by the CJA 1991 was 'easily satisfied' because of its 'broad interpretation' (Thomas 1995: 146–7) and the Seriousness Guideline issued after the 2003 Act specifically notes that 'the clear intention of the threshold test is to reserve prison as a punishment for the most serious offences' (Sentencing Guidelines Council 2004a: 8). However, it too argues that 'it is impossible to determine definitively which features of a particular offence make it serious enough to merit a custodial sentence' and that 'it would not be feasible to provide a form of words or to devise any formula that would provide a general solution to the problem of where the custody threshold lies. Factors vary too widely between offences for this to be done' (ibid: 8, 9).[39] Considerable discretion is left to the sentencer.

3.3.2 **Mitigation relating to the offender**

There is also mitigation relating to the circumstances and character of the offender rather than to the seriousness of the offending. In effect they mitigate sentence once seriousness has been established and s 166(1) of the CJA 2003, reflecting previous practice, states that nothing in the crucial sentencing sections about the criteria for imposing the three levels of sentence 'prevents a court from mitigating an offender's sentence by taking into account any such matters as, in the opinion of the court, are relevant in the mitigation of sentence'. Further, s 166(2) states that the court is not prevented from imposing a community rather than custodial sentence in the light of mitigating circumstances and s 156(2) specifically gives the court discretion to take into account any information about the offender which is before it in deciding the type of community or youth rehabilitation order to impose. The CJIA 2008, s 10 amended s 148 of the CJA 2003 to provide similar judicial discretion in relation to community orders.

[38] For further discussion of judicial thinking about prevalence see Ashworth (2000: 91; 2010: 102–3); for comments regarding prevalence by the SGC, see *Overarching Principles: Seriousness* (2004a: Section F; also note the references in '*Other Factors*' in section 3.2.5).

[39] For a discussion of factors which influenced the custodial decision in the sentencing of domestic violence offenders in New South Wales, Australia, see Ringland and Fitzgerald (2010).

Personal mitigation can be placed into three categories, relating to:

1. The good qualities of the offender.
2. The efficient and fair operation of the criminal justice system.
3. The impact of the sentence on the offender.

The last category of personal mitigation—the adverse or abnormal impact of the sentence on the offender—will not be dealt with here: see Chapter 7. In this chapter we will focus briefly on the first and second categories before dealing in some detail with the guilty plea, a form of personal mitigation justified as a 'reward' for those who help the system.

A 'good' offender

The first category—where the personal characteristics and circumstances of the offender are considered—may not be given effect in sentencing where the offending is of a very serious nature. The offender or his or her lawyer has complete discretion to introduce whichever factors appear relevant; the sentencer has complete discretion to accept or reject that they should reduce the sentence. Where the court does reduce the sentence it can be justified on the basis that the criminal justice system should be administered as mercifully as possible.

The factors which may be considered by sentencers include the following: stress in life at the time of committing the offence (for example, extreme poverty or imminent childbirth), meritorious conduct (for example, making reparation for harm done), leading a law-abiding and stable life since the offence was committed (for example, finding employment or getting married), and the age of the offender (for example, if below 21 or of an advanced age). Moral credit has also sometimes been given for something unconnected with the offence, such as a 'good' war record, donation of a kidney, or starting a youth club (see Walker 1985: 50; see also Ashworth 2010: 182–3) and the effect of the sentence on others, notably children, has sometimes been influential (Walker 1985: 52).[40]

Fair operation of the system

There are other circumstances which can mitigate sentence severity. They can be rationalised either as allowing the criminal justice system to be seen to be administered with as little injustice as possible, or as encouraging cost-efficient and effective criminal justice processes. The discount for a guilty plea is the obvious example of the latter and will be dealt with below. The factor of assisting law enforcement clearly also falls into that category, with the position of informers being a good example. Mitigation—or not—on this basis has a long and varied history and the unfavourable publicity given to the effects of such mitigation in the 'supergrass' cases of the 1970s led to smaller sentence reductions but *Sivan and others* (1988) and *A and B* (1999) confirmed there could be a reduction in sentence where assistance to the police is given before sentence. More recently, *R v P and Blackburn* (2007) has given detailed advice about the approach to sentencing where the assistance to the police relates to provisions in the Serious Organised Crime and Police Act 2005, ss 73–75.

Mitigation relating to 'fairness' includes the approach taken to sentencing co-defendants and to multiple sentences. In relation to the former the sentence may be reduced in order that like cases may be seen to be treated alike. For the latter the court can impose concurrent sentences if the total punishment appears unjust and disproportionate. This 'totality

[40] The influence of the impact of sentence on the offender and the offender's family is examined further in Chapter 7.

principle' is now enshrined in legislation (see Chapter 2, section 2.4.1) and the practice tends to be that consecutive sentences are imposed where the sentences are for unconnected offences,[41] but concurrent sentences where the offences are all part of the same offending incident (Walker 1999: 98–100). The Sentencing Council undertook a resource assessment on totality, TICs, and allocation (Sentencing Council 2011c), and conducted a consultation, and issued guidance in March 2012.[42]

The issue of how to charge and sentence multiple offenders, whether they be offenders whose offending incident gives rise to a variety of charges or whether a prolonged period of offending behaviour produces a long list of similar offences, is, however, much more complicated than this, and the justifications are varied. Ashworth devotes a whole chapter to these issues (2010: chapter 8) and we would refer readers to this.

3.3.3 **Discount for a guilty plea**

Justified as giving credit to the offender for his contribution to the efficiency of the system by reducing the need for a trial with its cost implications and its burdens on witnesses, the discount for a guilty plea can have a substantial effect on the level of sentence and is potentially available for all offenders. Guidance has made clear that 'the sentencer should now address separately the issue of remorse, together with any other mitigating features, before calculating the reduction for the guilty plea after all the matters noted above relating to the assessment of seriousness have been dealt with' (Sentencing Guidelines Council 2007a: para 2.4).

The CJA 2003, s 144 replaced the PCCSA 2000, s 152[43] but the law is the same: where the offender has pleaded guilty the court must take into account the stage in the proceedings at which he indicated his plea of guilt and the circumstances in which it was given.

A particular difficulty has arisen in relation to those who are caught 'red-handed'. *Hussain* (2002) upheld the previous position in case law whereby particular circumstances, such as being caught red-handed, might justify the non-implementation of a discount but stated that some credit by way of discount must always be given if a trial is avoided, especially if there is a vulnerable victim as witness. SGC guidance stated that it is in everyone's interest that those who are guilty of an offence indicate willingness to plead guilty at the earliest opportunity (2004b: Preface) and said that the normal sliding scale applied to those caught red-handed but that '[i]f the not guilty plea was entered and maintained for tactical reasons (such as to retain privileges whilst on remand), a late guilty plea should attract very little, if any, discount' (ibid: 5).

However, the 2004 guidance received criticism in relation to this issue amongst others and a consultation exercise was undertaken by the Sentencing Advisory Panel (SAP), at the request of the SGC, in 2006. The key issues were:

- Does a maximum reduction of one-third properly balance the interests of justice and the encouragement of guilty pleas?
- Should there be an upper limit on the amount of the reduction?
- What further clarification of the 'first reasonable opportunity' for entering a guilty plea is necessary?

41 See CJA 2003, s 155 for powers of magistrates' courts.

42 See http://sentencingcouncil.judiciary.gov.uk/sentencing-guidelines.htm.

43 First enacted as s 48 of the Criminal Justice and Public Order Act 1994 and repealed 4 April 2005.

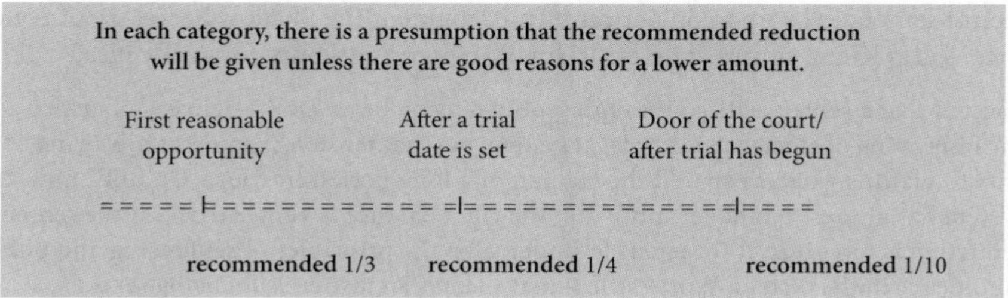

In each category, there is a presumption that the recommended reduction will be given unless there are good reasons for a lower amount.
First reasonable opportunity
After a trial date is set
Door of the court/ after trial has begun
recommended 1/3
recommended 1/4
recommended 1/10

Figure 3.2 A sliding scale

Source: Sentencing Guidelines Council (2007a).

- To what degree, if any, should the fact that the prosecution case is overwhelming influence the level of reduction?

New guidance was issued in July 2007 (Sentencing Guidelines Council 2007a). It confirmed that the level of reduction 'should be a proportion of the total sentence imposed, with the proportion calculated by reference to the circumstances in which the guilty plea was indicated, in particular the stage in the proceedings' and that 'the greatest reduction will be given where the plea was indicated at the "first reasonable opportunity"' (ibid: para 4.1; but note the exception in relation to mandatory minimum sentences for domestic burglary and class A drugs offences: see CJA 2003, s 142(2)). The maximum discount remains at one-third with recommended reductions of one-quarter and one-tenth for pleas given at later stages of the process (see Figure 3.2).

The SGC agreed that some discretion should be introduced where the prosecution case is 'overwhelming' (ibid: para 5.3) but did not accept the recommendation of the SAP to cap the effect of a reduction on very large fines. The guideline specifically noted that where the maximum penalty for the offence is thought to be too low a sentencer cannot remedy perceived defects by refusal of the appropriate discount (ibid: para 5.6).

Annex 1 to the guideline provides further clarification of 'first reasonable opportunity' by listing examples which would count as such depending on the circumstances. So, 'the first reasonable opportunity may be the first time that a defendant appears before the court and has the opportunity to plead guilty' but the court 'may consider that it would be reasonable to have expected an indication of willingness even earlier, perhaps whilst under interview' (ibid: 10).[44]

The general approach of the guideline follows the Magistrates' Association Guidelines before 2003 which suggested a discount of about one-third. However, various research projects and criminal statistics had indicated that reductions in practice varied between 22 per cent and 40 per cent (see Ashworth 2000: 145–7 for references and discussion). Research would also suggest that—at least in the mid-1990s—35 per cent of judges did not consider the stage at which the plea was entered to be of any importance (Henham 1999: 527). Further, whilst discounts appear to be given for custodial and financial penalties, there seemed to be no significant difference in the length of a community service order or a probation order (Flood-Page and Mackie 1998: 92).

The issue of the discount for a guilty plea came to prominence again when the Coalition Government proposed in its Green Paper *Breaking the Cycle* (Ministry of Justice 2010a) to

[44] SGC guidance specifically in regard to sentencing for murder sets a maximum discount of one-sixth.

discount sentences by up to 50 per cent. In Parliament the Shadow Secretary of State for Justice, Sadiq Khan, summed up criticism of so high a discount for guilty plea:

> I accept that a sentence discount represents a tension between the delivery of justice and the improving of efficiency in the legal system, but that tension can potentially bring benefits to victims who are spared the trauma of a long period in court. Up until now, the system has always sought certainty that the right balance is being struck. If the sentence reduction is too great, it threatens to undermine the principles of sentencing and public confidence in the system. Worse still, it may mean that justice is not being served.
>
> (Hansard, 23 May 2011: Column 659)

The Sentencing Council, in its written response to the Green Paper, had also noted that 'in other common law jurisdictions the largest discount on offer is around a third, with some offering up to 35%' and that '[t]he Council has not identified any research to date that indicates that an increase in the level of the discount would be likely to increase the volume of early guilty pleas' (Sentencing Council 2010: 10).

Research sponsored by the Sentencing Council found that '[f]or the general public, there was weak support for higher levels of reductions beyond the current guideline range of up to 33% and a fifth (20%) felt that there should be no reduction at all' (Dawes *et al.* 2011: 4).

The main factor determining whether or not offenders plead guilty was the likelihood of being found guilty at trial. The key 'tipping point' here was when offenders realised that the chances of them being found guilty were greater than being found not guilty. Weight of evidence and advice from solicitors/barristers were pivotal in offenders' assessments of whether they were likely to be found guilty and therefore crucial in determining when a guilty plea was entered (ibid: 5).

The proposal to increase the discount was subsequently not included in the LAS&PO Bill 2011.

3.3.4 **Not a mathematical exercise?**

We have dealt in turn with the most important aspects of the process of determining a proportionate sentence under retributivist principles. At one level this might be seen as a logical process which can be worked through in an entirely objective way and the suggested questions for dealing with the custody threshold in *Overarching Principles: Seriousness* appear unproblematic:

- Has the statutory threshold been passed?
- Is custody unavoidable?
- Can the sentence be suspended, (or be served intermittently)?
- What is the commensurate sentence?

(Sentencing Guidelines Council 2004a: para 1.33)

However, the third update to the *Case Compendium* sounded a cautionary note when summarising the *Martin* case.

> *R v Martin* [2006] EWCA Crim 1035
>
> - The sentencing decision does not represent a mathematical exercise, nor does it result from an arithmetical calculation.
> - It is not the case that each element relevant to the sentencing decision has or should have ascribed to it some notional length of sentence so that, depending on whether the individual ingredient constitutes aggravating or mitigating material, the actual

sentence should increase or reduce in accordance with that figure. The reality is that a sentencer must balance all the circumstances of the case in order to reach an appropriate sentence.

We are well aware that just deserts sentencing leaves many difficult decisions about seriousness and proportionality to the judges and magistrates and that guidance on sentencing levels is not yet comprehensive. That the effect of mitigation can be so crucial in relation to the choice or length of a custodial sentence is an issue we will return to in Chapter 7. The question of whether the difficulties still lie with retributivism itself will be examined next.

3.4 Critiques of modern retributivism

We have reviewed current sentencing practice within a predominantly just deserts framework and summarised the recent changes to that framework and criticisms of them. We will now examine more fundamental criticisms of just deserts as a primary rationale.

Criticism of retributivism has come from all shades of the political and theoretical spectrum and so we will, in this section, consider the current penological debates and also the critiques from Marxist perspectives.

3.4.1 The limits of just deserts

The approach of modern retributivism, based substantially on the work of von Hirsch, does not satisfy all critics of retributivism or resolve all the problems with the retributivist approach. In particular, there remains the issue of the extent to which proportionality as the primary purpose of sentencing should take priority over other factors in 'exceptional' cases. For example, should effectiveness and efficiency, or public safety, take priority over individual rights as in the case of dangerous offenders who need to be quarantined, or, with certain 'abhorrent' crimes, is it sufficient simply to apportion blame, when it appears difficult to find a commensurate sentence? Perhaps the greatest difficulty in practice is how to find a mechanism and a consensus to calculate seriousness, to rank offences, mitigations, and aggravations, and to rank penalties in such a way that the key element of proportionality is clear and justly operationalised. However, the attempt to achieve clarity by producing accurate theoretical models of ordinal and cardinal proportionality could result in as many types of punishment as there are offenders, with different degrees of culpability, which would be impossible to administer.

As we have seen, the present system has been criticised for its complexity and incoherence. The problem that emerges is that, even if we take full account of desert and proportionality, we can still end up with some cases of lesser offences receiving much harsher sentences than serious offenders with mitigation, which would have implications for the legitimacy of the system and public support. So it may be better, as Bagaric (2001) argues, to have fixed penalties (see Chapter 7, section 7.3.4), but this raises the sort of questions about the inflexibility of grid-type sentencing that prompted Tonry to rethink retributivism.

These difficulties with the key issue of proportionality in desert theory have prompted new thinking. Braithwaite and Pettit (1990) have developed an alternative theory, grounded in restorative justice (see Chapter 6, section 6.1.2). They distinguish their own model, which advocates instrumental shaming, from the penal censure of retributivism, because they seek to separate shaming from the degree of severity of sanctions. They also advocate reducing the level of punishment until the point at which crime starts to increase. Censure for them is essentially stigmatising and may be achieved by a variety of means, including adverse publicity.

Another major issue is whether it is ever possible to make the justification for a retributivist approach sufficiently clear and logical for both popular understanding and political legitimacy. For example, it has been argued that von Hirsch's modified form of retributivism may be hard to justify without lapsing into consequentialism, which is a utilitarian rather than retributivist notion. So von Hirsch, Bagaric (2001) argues, never establishes why his censuring account of punishment is morally justifiable. Yet there are good consequentialist reasons to support von Hirsch's theory, such as his recognition of the secondary role of deterrence and the positive functions of blaming, and the beneficial social consequences of the acknowledgement of harm done to the victim which satisfies the victim and may prevent vigilantism. As Bagaric observes, there is no point in blaming the offender if there are no beneficial effects. Showing the third party that an action is wrong may ultimately prevent offending, another good consequence.

Retributivism has also been criticised more generally as a conservative and repressive theory which can too easily lend legitimacy to punitive penal policies. The main elements of that critique are that the theory, by focusing only on desert, fails to acknowledge the implications of poverty and social inequality for offending behaviour, and that it is most strongly associated with reactionary regimes around the world—whether based on religious or secular principles—and is repressive in the sense of generating an escalation of punishment. Rubin (2003), for example, argues that embedding retribution within the Model Penal Code of the American Law Institute would have an adverse effect, leading to longer sentences. But each of these assumptions is problematic and is not a valid basis for jettisoning just deserts.

First, there is no automatic association between right-wing regimes and retributivism. As von Hirsch and Ashworth (2005) emphasise, if we look around the world we find the most progressive regimes in Scandinavia have used proportionality and desert as principles of punishment rather than incapacitation or rehabilitation. In contrast the Stalinist penal regime, one of the most repressive in history, was based on an extreme form of 'social efficiency' rather than desert. But we find in Sweden there is a presumption against custody unless the offence is serious. Past convictions have a very small role there, being limited to the past three or four years. However, there has been increasing pressure in recent years to expand this role as the Swedish public has become more punitive, seeing sentences as too lenient (see Demker *et al.* 2008; Asp 2010).

Second, a concern with desert and proportionality may limit excessive punishment in its rejection of exemplary sentences and selective incapacitation. Although it is true, as von Hirsch acknowledges, that incarceration increased in some states in the United States, such as California, which adopted a just deserts model in the mid-70s, closer examination shows that the prison population was already increasing before the model was adopted. Furthermore, proportionality was not used in making the decision to impose custody, but only in determining the length of the sentence. Moreover the impact of penal justifications is also shaped by local political structures and conditions as Barker (2009) demonstrates and in California the impact of populism on penal sanctioning was a key variable in penal expansion.

Yet, as von Hirsch notes (1986), the Minnesota sentencing guidelines of the late 1970s and early 1980s, which were based on a modified desert principle, did lead to consistent sentencing. At the time they prevented the expansion of the prison population because they imprisoned those convicted of the most serious crimes, but imprisoned fewer convicted of lesser crimes, and were subject to safeguards to limit the size of the prison population. Moreover, as he points out, the Sentencing Commission in Minnesota did take account of prison capacity when drawing up the sentencing guidelines. Minnesota still has a lower imprisonment rate than states such as Texas and Nevada whose sentencing guidelines give less weight to desert. It has also been argued by Lippke (2007) that retributivism, by limiting punishment to those who have committed serious harms to others, and not sentencing simply to satisfy public opinion, can be an effective constraint on increased punitiveness. Furthermore, he argues, a penal system which recognises and does not crush offenders' capacities to lead autonomous lives will result in a more humane form of imprisonment. As we saw in Chapter 2, section 2.8, limiting excessive punishment can also be achieved by an appeal to human rights.

Criticism of retributivism has also come from radical approaches which have challenged desert theory for not addressing the underlying social problems of inequality, poverty, and injustice, which may be linked to offending.[45]

3.4.2 **Radical critiques of retributivism**

Marxist critiques of retributivist theory, for example, have used social scientific research to show the problems with individualist models and the links between marginalisation and criminality. This is a valid criticism but it raises the question whether it is the task of any penal theory to undertake the gargantuan task of solving problems of social inequality: certainly rival theories of punishment from utilitarian traditions or from restorative justice do not do so. But at the least one can say that desert theory is not antithetical to progressive social policies, as evidenced by those European jurisdictions—such as Sweden and Finland—which have primarily desert-based sentencing systems and progressive welfare and social programmes.

Radical critiques also raise the issue of whether we should focus on the social disadvantage of offenders when imposing punishments, and treat disadvantage as a mitigating factor. On desert theory the individual is still culpable even if this culpability is reduced by extreme poverty or economic distress. In any case most crime falls far short of necessity in the sense used in the criminal law[46] and recent studies of wealth and poverty in the UK have focused on inequality and relative deprivation rather than absolute poverty (see Dorling *et al.* 2007). Even if deprivation is a factor in the circumstances surrounding the offence, this does not mean proportionality is no longer relevant, although reducing a sentence for a particular offender on social grounds would be unfair on the retributivist model. Moreover, if social and economic factors are given precedence over issues of desert, this may work to the disadvantage of economically and socially deprived offenders; for example, social and economic factors are already included in OASys (the Offender Assessment System), to predict the risks posed by offenders and to make decisions on their release and management.

Furthermore, one could argue that poor or disadvantaged offenders may be more strongly protected by desert theory than by rival theories. As von Hirsch (1993) argues, there is more scope for raising such issues in desert theory and poorer offenders would be better protected by lowering the anchoring points for penalties than by looking at individual disadvantage, which might encourage the disadvantaged offender to be seen as a

[45] Some of these problems in relation to social exclusion will be considered in Chapters 7, 10, and 11.

[46] *Dudley & Stephens* (1884) 14 QBD 273. While Kant accepts the non-criminality of homicide from necessity and gives the example of the person who, in order to save his own life in a shipwreck, pushes another person, whose life is equally in danger, off a plank on which he has saved himself, this is far removed from the kinds of choice relevant to discussions of 'everyday' crime (Kant 1796–7). See also von Hirsch and Ashworth (2005).

higher risk, although this argument is unlikely to satisfy those who want compensation for disadvantage.

The problems which arise in taking account of the impact of punishment in an unequal society are further considered in Chapters 7 and 10, whilst the issues of inequality and discrimination will be considered in Chapter 12 in relation to the experience of imprisonment.

Marx himself says little on punishment and does not offer a theory or justification of punishment but, rather, is concerned to contextualise punishment in its social, economic, and historical context. He did write a short article on 'Capital Punishment' (Marx 1853) where he argued that it would be 'very difficult, if not altogether impossible, to establish any principle upon which the justice or expediency of capital punishment could be founded' while Engels says that how to punish criminals is a topic he leaves to his readers (Engels 1843). The implication of Marx's analysis for modern critiques of the death penalty are discussed by Bohm (2008). However, Marx is more sympathetic to retributivism than to **utilitarian theories of punishment**. He is critical of the view that punishment may be ameliorating or intimidating, because of the absence of proof of the effectiveness of punishment in preventing crime, and he does praise Kant's and Hegel's theory of punishment because it recognises human dignity and the rights of the person punished, treats the individual as 'a free and self-determined being', and focuses on rights and autonomy. But he argues that the retributivists' reification of free will fails to take account of the impact of social and economic pressures on the individual (Marx 1853)[47] and that German idealism abstracts the individual from society. What the idealists see as universal features of all societies are products of a specific mode of production and limited to specific strata. Given the incidence and recurrence of crime in nineteenth-century society, effort should be addressed to dealing with the underlying social system which generates crime, rather than focusing attention on refining systems of punishment.

Marx's relationship to retributivism is considered by Murphy (1973) who argues that, while Marx sees retributivism as the most defensible theory of punishment, the conditions in modern society render the theory inapplicable in most modern societies and rob those societies of their moral right to punish. The picture of individuals exercising free will and of autonomy and rationality fits uneasily with the reality of the alienation of modern capitalist society, which is crime-ridden, where individuals act out of greed and self-interest, and society is marked by an absence of reciprocity, in contrast to the Hegelian State where there is a genuine community and where the rules are internalised. In our society, says Murphy, it is hard to see how the socially deprived benefit from membership or to construe individuals as acting freely when responding to severe social deprivation, but these issues are overlooked by the classical retributivists. Murphy cites the work of the Marxist criminologist Willem Bonger (1916) who links crime and deprivation.

Murphy argues that, if society were reconstructed to meet the Marxian ideal of a society where all individuals participate in relations of mutuality, then it would fit the retributivist model because there would be genuine autonomy of all individuals and in that case retributivist punishment would be justifiable, although, in any case, in such a society crime would be likely to decrease.[48]

[47] A similar argument is advanced by Marx and Engels in their critique of the Young Hegelians in *The Holy Family* (1845).

[48] The relationship between justice and the mode of production may itself be problematic within Marxian theory. See Wood (1972, 2004), McBride (1975), and Easton (2008a). But Marx argues in *The Holy Family* that in communism, 'under *humane* conditions punishment will *really* be nothing but the sentence passed by the culprit on himself' (1845: 179) which is closer to the Hegelian ethical idea.

The implications of social deprivation for retributivism will also be considered in the context of a discussion of equality of impact and impact mitigation in Chapter 10.

3.4.3 Modern Marxian critiques

Modern Marxists have been more concerned with processes of criminalisation than with punishment, although humanist Marxist social historians, including Thompson (1977) and Hay *et al.* (1975) have considered the historical development of modes of punishment, the legitimacy of punishment, the significance of the notion of the rule of law as an ideal and ideology, and the role of law in maintaining the hegemony of the ruling class. Critical legal scholars have subjected key concepts of liberal legalism, including rights and equality, to a rigorous critique. An historical materialist approach to punishment means understanding punishment historically, changing through time and varying with each mode of production. On classical Marxist theory the specific form which punishment takes will reflect underlying economic conditions, and the needs of the dominant class. In early capitalism, as the demand for labour increased in the new factory mode of production, imprisonment displaced capital punishment. Punishment does not simply reflect desert as on a retributivist model but punishment is a means of social control. Punishment is also used to discipline the working class, in so far as conditions in prison are made worse than the poorest conditions in the labour market outside, to inculcate work discipline through the experience of imprisonment and, historically, to provide a source of labour through transportation to the United States, replacing slave labour after the abolition of slavery (see Rusche and Kirchheimer 1939). Rusche and Kirchheimer see the declining use of imprisonment in the early twentieth century as reflecting the shift towards disciplining the work force within the production process, as new processes such as the assembly line developed. Structuralist Marxists such as Althussser (1971) consider the role of the penal system as part of the repressive state apparatus but also emphasise the ideological functions of law.

Using historical materialist methods, we can see that the levels and forms of punishment vary according to economic conditions in the sense that when labour is scarce, punishment is less severe and when labour is oversupplied, punishment is harsher. So in times of full employment, such as the 1960s, we see a liberalisation of punishment, a concern with reform and rehabilitation, and loss of support for capital punishment here and in the United States. But in times of recession punishment becomes harsher and incarceration rates increase and at the level of consciousness fear of crime supplants fears of economic decline.

Recent economic analysis, for example the work of Loic Wacquant (2001a, 2001b, 2007, 2008a), has focused on the role of the prison as a way of absorbing surplus labour as changes in the forces of production have reduced demand for unskilled labour, while the marginalisation and demoralisation of the 'lumpenproletariat' has contributed to rising crime. Wacquant argues: 'What the state needs to fight is not the symptom, *criminal insecurity*, but the cause of urban disorder: namely, the *social insecurity* that the state itself has spawned by becoming the diligent handmaiden to the despotism of the market' (Wacquant 2008a: 118). Recent work in the political economy of punishment has also focused on the criminalisation of migrants. De Giorgi (2010) examines the use of incarceration as a strategy in the war against unauthorised migration in the context of a de-regulated neo-liberal economy.

How useful are Marxian and critical approaches to punishment? Classical Marxism has been criticised for its economic reductionism and failure to offer concrete proposals for penal reform. Modern critical approaches have been criticised for their failure to generate radical changes in the penal system or criminal justice system generally. Even those modern theorists sympathetic to sociological models of punishment, such as Garland and Murphy, find Marxian theory of limited value in giving guidance to modern penal institutions and policies and, as we have argued, this was not a project of interest to Marx himself. But the value of the model is to highlight the inherent problems facing crime reductionist policies which fail to take account of underlying social and economic conditions which are criminogenic. It also offers an alternative to liberal conceptions of state punishment. Although Hudson dismisses Marxism as a form of modernism whose time has gone, many of Marx's concepts, such as alienation, are still relevant to postmodern debates on crime and social exclusion (see Easton 2008b).

Placing punishment in its social, historical, and political context is part of Marx's legacy and is reflected in modern sociological perspectives on punishment. For example, Garland (1991) has considered the impact of economic and social factors on contemporary sentencing and, while cautious regarding monolithic explanations of complex behaviour, he appreciates that Marxian analyses transcend a narrow approach to penal theory and practice. There has also been some interest in developing communitarian approaches to punishment and to criminal justice which recognise the primacy of social relations (see Lacey 2003).

3.5 Conclusions

3.5.1 The importance of seriousness

Policy debates in the last decade have been dominated by legislation and proposed changes in relation to the offender deemed to be a serious risk to the public and also in relation to the effectiveness of community punishment. However, in law and in practice it is the issues of seriousness, proportionality, and just deserts principles which are the bread and butter of those who sentence and the determinants of outcome for most offenders. Sentencing guidelines are making this process ever more technical and detailed but clearly within a retributivist framework. The riots in England in the summer of 2011 also revealed popular support for ensuring offenders received their just deserts as an aim of punishment, albeit that some calls were for a sentence which might be viewed as disproportionate. However, those riots also led to a focus on deterrence, a utilitarian aim, which we will consider in the next chapter.

We would also point out that issues regarding the victim, reparation, rehabilitation, and control are grafted on to this retributivist framework and we do not ignore the fact that another framework—for the dangerous—runs alongside it. In Chapters 5, 6, and 12 we will focus on these other issues.

3.5.2 Case study

This sentencing exercise is about Tess who was arrested, charged, and pleaded guilty to fraud by false representation under s 2 of the Fraud Act 2006, for which the maximum penalty is 10 years' imprisonment. The facts of the case, on which the Crown Court Judge must pass sentence, are as follows:

Tess, a 21-year-old undergraduate, has been working part-time for the last two years as a care assistant at a Residential Home for the Elderly. In this capacity she persuaded six elderly residents to hand over £60 each to her, ostensibly to pay into a Christmas fund. This they all did one morning as arranged and she told them she would collect another instalment the following month. Tess used the money to pay her rent as she had large debts and could not rely on her father whose his business had just collapsed. She was seriously depressed and was attending counselling sessions.[49]

Tess's deception was discovered before the next instalment was due because one of the residents from whom she had obtained money asked the Matron about the Christmas fund. Tess did not at first plead guilty, fearful that she would never obtain employment on graduating and believing the elderly residents were too ill and mentally confused to give evidence. In the event, a change of medication dramatically improved the physical and mental health of one of them. Consequently, Tess, changed her plea to guilty before the trial.

In between the offending and trial, Tess graduated and was left a legacy of £3,000 by an aunt. After paying her debts she has £150 left. She was given a reprimand[50] at the age of 14 for shoplifting (under the Theft Act 1968, s 1) and had one previous conviction, at the age of 16, for burglary of a dwelling under s 9 of the Theft Act 1968, for which she received a referral order. (She was not given detention in a young offender institution because of mitigation in relation to the death of her mother and a subsequent depressive illness.)

1. Sentence Tess, explaining and justifying your chosen sentencing framework and particular sentence.
2. Decide whether your sentence would be different if:
   (a) Tess had no previous convictions.
   (b) Tess defrauded the residents because they were all South Asians.
   (c) The current offence was committed whilst Tess was on bail awaiting trial for a drug offence—a charge of which she was subsequently acquitted.
   (d) Tess's current offence was burglary in a dwelling, not fraud.

You might find helpful the checklist provided in section 3.2.2 and also the relevant guidelines:

Sentencing Council (2011b) *Burglary Offences: Definitive Guideline*, London, Sentencing Council.

Sentencing Guidelines Council (2009a) *Sentencing for Fraud, Statutory Offences: Definitive Guideline*, London, SGC.

The Online Resource Centre will provide further guidance.

online resource centre

[49] You are not expected to use the provisions of the Mental Health Act 1983 in this exercise: these possibilities will not be dealt with until Chapter 7, section 7.4.

[50] Reprimands and warnings replaced police cautions for minors: see Chapter 8, section 8.3.3. The court might view this as a previous conviction.

4

Utility and deterrence

SUMMARY

In this chapter we examine an approach which focuses on the consequences or outcomes of sentencing and punishment. The origins of this approach in the work of Beccaria and Bentham, and its modern expression in the work of writers such as Wilson and Kennedy will be discussed. We will focus here on the specific outcome of deterrence, considering whether punishment is effective in reducing offending, reviewing the available research and the problems which arise in establishing a deterrent effect. We will also consider some of the difficulties with this justification for punishment.

4.1 A focus on outcome

4.1.1 **Recent trends**

When the *Magistrates' Court Sentencing Guidelines* were revised in relation to knife crime the accompanying note issued by the (then) Sentencing Guidelines Council[1] drew attention to the comments made by Sir Igor Judge (President, QBD) in the *Povey* (2008) appeal:

> Offences of this kind, carrying an offensive weapon or knife, have recently escalated. They are reaching epidemic proportions.... For the time being, whatever other considerations may arise in the individual case, sentencing courts must have in the forefront of their thinking that the sentences for this type of offence should focus on the reduction of crime, including its reduction by deterrence, and the protection of the public.
>
> (*Povey* at para 4)

This case had not overruled the previous guideline case, *Celaire and Poulton* (2003), but had stated: 'Conditions now are much more grave than they were five and a half years ago and the guidance given in *Celaire and Poulton* should be applied with the current grave situation as we have endeavoured to explain it' (ibid: para 5). What was therefore justifying treating and punishing such offences as more serious than before was a focus on prevalence of the offending but also deterrence and protection of the public. In other words the outcome of punishment was seen to be as much of a factor as providing just deserts.

Such judicial comments are comparatively rare although the riots in England in the summer of 2011 led to a renewed focus on deterrence by the public and the judiciary. The issue was whether and to what extent the context of offending should influence sentencing levels in terms of both retribution and deterrence. Whilst some sentences led to

[1] See http://sentencingcouncil.judiciary.gov.uk/docs/sentencing_guidelines_knife_crime.pdf.

successful appeals[2] others did not and, in the appeals heard in *R v Blackshaw and others* (2011), Lord Judge, Lord Chief Justice, endorsed deterrence as a justification:

> There is an overwhelming obligation on sentencing courts to do what they can to ensure the protection of the public... This is an imperative. It is not, of course, possible now, after the events, for the courts to protect the neighbourhoods which were ravaged in the riots or the people who were injured or suffered damage. Nevertheless, the imposition of severe sentences, intended to provide both punishment and deterrence, must follow... They must be punished accordingly, and the sentences should be designed to deter others from similar criminal activity.'
>
> (*R v Blackshaw* at para 4)

To justify sentencing in terms of outcome in this way clearly contrasts with the retributivist, 'just deserts', sentencing framework, discussed in Chapters 2 and 3, which is not primarily concerned with outcome or the consequences of the sentencing decision other than that of ensuring that justice has been done. Only when we discussed the *Cunningham* (1993) case did we note reasoning similar to that in the *Povey* case where prevalence justified a sentence which was, in effect, a deterrent one.

In policy documents, however, deterrence has often been claimed as an aim, together with wider aims of reducing offending. In 2001 *Criminal Justice: The Way Ahead* argued that an effective, well-run criminal justice system must be, inter alia, 'effective at preventing offending and reoffending' (Home Office 2001a: para 4).[3] More specifically, that White Paper gave priority to the aims of reduction of offending and reparation to the victim: sentencing will be 'based on the offender not just the offence', and will pay 'more attention to sentence outcomes such as crime reduction and reparation' (ibid: para 2.66).[4] The Halliday Report also made clear that, of the sentencing goals identified, 'reform and rehabilitation' (rather than incapacitation or deterrence: see 2001: paras 1.58–1.68) were their favoured methods of achieving crime reduction (ibid: para 1.69). One result of these proposals was the inclusion in the Criminal Justice Act (CJA) 2003 of new, but never implemented and now set to be repealed,[5] prison sentences of custody plus and intermittent custody with community supervision components to put the released or 'intermittent' prisoner through offending reduction programmes. The CJA 2003 also rejigged not only community sentences but also suspended custodial sentences and increased the supervision component of longer custodial sentences, both with provision for offending reduction programmes. These will all be examined further in Chapter 12.

Making Sentencing Clearer (Home Secretary *et al.* 2006) also made very clear that the Government's sentencing aims were outcome focused: 'The proposals in this document are... designed to ensure that the public are better protected from dangerous offenders and that resources are targeted at the offenders who pose the most significant risks' (ibid: Foreword). Some changes made by the Criminal Justice and Immigration Act 2008 also might be seen to increase the focus on outcome of sentence. Arguably, the following provisions have a utilitarian element: sections 1 (youth rehabilitation order), 9 (sentencing aims for young offenders), 39 (youth default orders which will enable a court to impose an unpaid work requirement, curfew requirement or attendance centre requirement on

[2] See, for example, Bowcott (2011).

[3] These characteristics relate to the criminal justice system as a whole but Part 2 of the document makes it clear they also relate specifically to the sentencing stage.

[4] Reparation and responding to the needs of victims constitute an approach that is already being implemented with young offenders but which cannot easily be 'pigeon-holed', and so we will examine separately its implications in Chapter 6 when we focus on restorative justice.

[5] The Legal Aid, Sentencing and Punishment of Offenders Bill 2011 proposes to repeal them.

a young offender in lieu of an unpaid fine), and 98 (violent offender orders). For example, by s 102(1) the court can include in a violent offender order, prohibitions, restrictions or conditions preventing the offender:

(a) from going to any specified premises or any other specified place (whether at all, or at or between any specified time or times);
(b) from attending any specified event;
(c) from having any, or any specified description of, contact with any specified individual.

This reveals a focus on incapacitation and regulation rather than a (purely) proportionate and retributivist response. The new orders aimed at minors also reveal a utilitarian focus on rehabilitative and restorative aims.

The Halliday Report (2001) acknowledged but side-stepped the philosophical confusion caused by this imposition of outcome-based aims on a just deserts sentencing framework. It simply stated that '[o]pinions differ as to whether punishment is a goal in its own right or is, rather, a means of achieving the other two goals' (2001: paras 1.4 and 1.5). Neither did the Criminal Justice Act 2003 clarify the situation, rather the reverse, when it specified five purposes of sentencing in s 142(1)(a):

(a) the punishment of offenders;
(b) the reduction of crime (including its reduction by deterrence);
(c) the reform and rehabilitation of offenders;
(d) the protection of the public; and
(e) the making of reparation by offenders to persons affected by their offences.

Whilst the first purpose is retributivist and the fifth restorative, the remaining three are utilitarian. Yet, theoretically speaking, if the justification is utilitarian, the issue of proportionality should either be downgraded or ignored; if the justification is retributivist, the sentence should be calculated solely on the basis of proportionality. The 'solution' introduced by the CJA 1991 was that there could be a 'secondary' focus on outcome. So, whilst the primary sentencing decision concerns just deserts, the specified amount of retributively imposed punishment could be used to achieve outcomes other than that of a sense of justice achieved through the application of retributivist principles. The CJA 2003, however, increased the focus on this second set of aims and so reinforced the utilitarian aspect of sentencing and punishment.

4.1.2 **Deterrence as a sentencing aim**

Aiming to reduce offending by deterring offenders or others from committing crimes in the future is only one outcome-based sentencing aim and, as we have seen, it is not one to which recent sentencing policy documents have generally given priority. However, there is a widespread assumption that the resulting punishment *will* deter the convicted offender from reoffending, or potential offenders from offending and, as we have noted, cases such as *Cunningham* (1993) and *Povey* (2008) are evidence that deterrence as an aim of punishment is still in the minds of sentencers. As Ashworth points out, deterrence continues to be given as a reason for sentencing in particular types of crime, notably drug importation, counterfeiting goods and passport offences (2010: 102). The 'exemplary sentence', where the penalty is arguably higher than a strictly proportionate sentence, is also justified in terms of general deterrence and, notably in relation to robbery or 'mugging', this rationale has been a long-standing sentencing feature (ibid: 82). Whilst *Cunningham* did not endorse exemplary sentences in individual cases, it did uphold 'prevalence' of offending—albeit only if it creates a climate of fear—as a valid factor in sentencing (at 448), a factor 'clearly linked to general deterrent reasoning' (Ashworth 2000: 92). Guidance from the Sentencing Guidelines Council (SGC) also allows prevalence to be taken into account in exceptional circumstances if justified in terms of greater harm caused (2004a: para 1.39). However, in *R v Oosthuizen* (2005), where the judge at first instance had decided to impose a deterrent sentence owing to the prevalence of robbery of handbags in the area because '[w]omen in Guildford were entitled to feel safe on the streets in broad daylight' (at para 9), the Court of Appeal stated that the deterrent element in a sentence must be supported by statistics about prevalence: '[E]ven a judge with experience of that area should not assume that prevalence was more marked in that area than nationally' (at para 16). In *R v Hussain (Mohammed)* (2005), a custodial sentence of three years and seven months was given to Hussain for stealing postal votes: the aim of the sentence was to deter electoral fraud.

So we see deterrence linked with punishment and even with proportionality in a retributivist system of sentencing. This is evident in the phrase 'retribution and deterrence' or 'punishment and deterrence' used, commonly, by official guidance and by the courts in relation to the 'tariff' or minimum period of a mandatory or discretionary life sentence (see Chapter 5) or of detention during Her Majesty's pleasure for minors (see Chapter 13). For example, in the House of Lords, in *R v Lichniak, R v Pyrah* (2001), Lord Hutton noted that the young person is not detained indefinitely 'but rather is only detained for the tariff period sufficient to satisfy the requirements of retribution and deterrence in the circumstances of the particular case' (at para 29).[6] Mr Justice Silber also used the same phrase—'retribution and general deterrence'—in relation to the minimum term to be served in *Gareth Wealleans* (2008 at para 10).

The inclusion of 'deterrence' in this phrase is usually not explained. In advice from the Sentencing Advisory Panel (SAP 2002) on minimum terms[7] in murder cases, for example, 'retribution and deterrence' was used in the introductory pages. However, the detailed justification for the proposed minimum terms was (only) in terms of seriousness (ibid: para 15 (*et seq*)) and there was no discussion as to what would deter others: the 'public' are mentioned only in terms of risk to the public and of public confidence that the murderer is sufficiently punished.

Deterrence is then the taken-for-granted outcome of punishment and one which causes concern only if it is believed that a sentence would not be sufficiently tough to deter. So whilst it is currently neither a priority aim in sentencing law and policy, nor—at the level of individual deterrence—a current factor in the delivery of punishment, deterrence is an outcome which is still of significance in judicial and policy thinking and one to which the public has great attachment. As we shall see, the theory and the delivery of deterrence are much more complicated than political and media pronouncements would suggest. Deterrence is also only one form of punishment outcome which can be justified on utilitarian grounds.

Other beneficial consequences of punishment would include incapacitation of the offender to protect the public and rehabilitation of the offender and we will deal with these

[6] Unless there are 'elements of dangerousness and risk' to justify longer detention (*Stafford v United Kingdom*, Application No 46295/99, 28 May 2002 at para 87): see Chapter 5.

[7] The SAP suggested that 'tariff' should be replaced with 'minimum term' for the sake of clarity (2002: para 2).

desired outcomes in Chapters 5 and 12 respectively. First, we will examine utilitarian theory before returning to a focus on deterrence.

4.1.3 **Utilitarianism: good or bad?**

Utilitarian philosophies of punishment have received a mixed response. Their apparent advantage over retributivist justifications is that they aim to reform or deter or prevent reoffending and by focusing on costs and benefits, that is, the consequences of punishment. They seem to offer the prospect of a more efficient use of punitive resources. Further, a utilitarian theory of punishment has for long been associated with reform of punishment, for example, in the work of its earliest 'modern' proponents, Beccaria and Bentham, in the eighteenth and early nineteenth centuries. Bentham argued penal institutions should be assessed against the yardstick of utility: if an institution fails to meet its stated purpose, then reforms are necessary. In the nineteenth and early twentieth centuries, utility was a major theoretical tool used to implement and defend reforms in the United States, the UK, and Europe. It focused public policy on the concrete effects of the penal system and considered the implications for human suffering and the broader social aims of deterrence, rehabilitation, and social protection.

On the other hand, utilitarian philosophies, or reductivist philosophies as they are sometimes called because they aim to reduce offending, may justify harsher sentences than retributivist theory. For example, it may be seen as in the public good to give some offenders very harsh punishments to deter others, or long prison sentences to incapacitate them and so severely restrict their capacity to reoffend. Such sentences may undermine individual rights and appear unjust, as the needs of the state or the community are given more importance than the severity of the offending in question, when the sentencing decision is made.

4.2 Utilitarian justifications

4.2.1 **Classical principles**

Utilitarian theories have their origins in the classical criminology of Beccaria and Bentham. Beccaria's *On Crimes and Punishments*, first published in English in 1767, was one of the first utilitarian theories of punishment and a key influence on Bentham. Like Bentham, Beccaria sees individuals as motivated by the pursuit of pleasure and the avoidance of pain and uses utility as a basis of social criticism. Laws should be assessed, he argues, 'from the point of view of whether they conduce to the greatest happiness shared among the greater number' (1767: 7). He saw the retributivism of his time as pointless, arbitrary and excessively harsh. For Beccaria the aim of punishment is to prevent offenders from committing new harms and to deter others from doing so, rather than to punish just for the sake of it:

> [T]he purpose of punishment is not that of tormenting or afflicting any sentient creature, nor of undoing a crime already committed... The purpose, therefore, is nothing other than to prevent the offender from doing fresh harm to his fellows and to deter others from doing likewise... [P]unishments and the means adopted for inflicting them should, consistent with proportionality, be so selected as to make the most efficacious and lasting impression on the minds of men with the least torment to the body of the condemned.
>
> (ibid: 31)

Beccaria includes the key utilitarian notions of deterrence and the optimal level of punishment, the minimum pain necessary to achieve the aims, but also refers to proportionality. Punishment should be enacted as swiftly as possible, and fit the nature of the crime, so non-violent thefts, for example, should be met with fines, violent thefts with a combination of corporal punishment and penal servitude, and social parasites should be banished.

He was also one of the first to focus on the importance of certainty rather than severity: 'The certainty of even a mild punishment will make a bigger impression than the fear of a more awful one which is united to a hope of not being punished at all' (ibid: 63). If punishment is too severe, the offender may seek to evade it by committing further crime (ibid: 64). It is essential, he argues, that punishment 'should be public, speedy, necessary, the minimum possible in the given circumstances, proportionate to the crime, and determined by the law' (ibid: 113), rather than imposed through acts of vigilantism. The level of punishment should be as much as is necessary to prevent harm to society, to protect the public from the offences committed by individuals. Beccaria thought that, as society progressed, the severity of punishment would diminish. He was also very critical of the death penalty, and saw it as wasteful, of questionable deterrent value, and denying the community the person's future potential contributions.

It is, however, Bentham, whose work has become synonymous with utilitarianism. Although the principle of utility had already been used by Beccaria, Hutcheson, and Priestley, Bentham is seen as the source of modern utilitarianism and a key voice of the English enlightenment. His work on *The Rationale of Punishment*, published in English in 1830, is seen as a major contribution to nineteenth-century debates on penal reform, but in fact was written much earlier, in the 1770s.

4.2.2 **Bentham's approach**

Bentham's *Introduction to the Principles of Morals and Legislation*, first published in 1789, aimed to promote the public interest and happiness through the use of reason. His philosophical approach is quite distinct from retributivism and expresses his aim to introduce rationality into all stages of the criminal justice system. For Bentham utility is the arbiter of law and morals. The principle of utility is 'that principle which approves or disapproves of every action whatsoever, according to the tendency which it appears to have to augment or diminish the happiness of the party whose interest is in question' (Bentham 1789: 12). Utility means the minimisation of pain and suffering and the maximisation of pleasure. 'Nature has placed mankind under the governance of two sovereign masters, *pain and pleasure*' (ibid: 11, emphasis in the original).

Utility is maximised when the result adds up to the greatest happiness of the greatest number. Bentham devised a felicific calculus, and argued that how we assess acts, choices, and ways of behaving is to calculate whether the sum of pleasures exceeds the pain. In calculating the costs and benefits we measure a number of factors: the intensity of pain and pleasure; its duration; the certainty or uncertainty of benefits accruing; the propinquity or nearness of the ensuing pleasure, that is, how quickly the pleasure will be generated; its fecundity, whether it will generate further pleasures or pain; its purity, whether or not it is likely to be followed by its opposite, pain or pleasure, whether it is unmixed with painful consequences; and its extent, that is, the number of people affected by it.

By using these criteria, we can see if the sum total of pleasures outweighs the costs. Bentham says that the quest for pleasure and the avoidance of pain is the key to understanding human behaviour. We can build social policies on this assumption and use rewards and punishment to channel behaviour to maximise the greatest happiness of the greatest number.

Like all utilitarianism, Bentham's theory is consequentialist: the only matter for the evaluation of laws and policies is consequences in terms of the pain and pleasure resulting from the event, policy, or state of affairs. A good policy maximises the happiness of the majority, and utilitarianism is essentially a majoritarian approach.

When this theory is applied to punishment, then punishment is justified only by the good consequences which will result from it, so suffering should never be imposed unless it will prevent greater suffering, because all suffering is intrinsically bad as it causes pain: 'But all punishment is mischief: all punishment in itself is evil. Upon the principle of utility, if it ought at all to be admitted, it ought only to be admitted in as far as it promises to exclude some greater evil' (ibid: 158). Punishment should not be inflicted just because someone has done something wrong because that, considered on its own, will only increase the total amount of human suffering. But if by inflicting it we can prevent greater suffering, either by preventing the offender from doing further harm, or by deterring others from doing the same thing, it is not only morally justified but morally necessary.

Punishment for Bentham cannot be justified merely as an act of retribution but only by the fact that the harm done by punishing the offender is outweighed by the benefits. Given that punishment is a 'cost-expense' in terms of the suffering of the incarcerated and the cost to society of keeping them in prison, the aim should be to maximise income, that is the deterrent effect, at the least possible expense, using a cost–benefit model. Punishment should not be inflicted if it is groundless, inefficacious, unprofitable, or needless, argues Bentham. Some cases may turn out to be too unprofitable to punish at all because costs outweigh benefits, for example, trivial offences or victimless crimes, where the evil of punishment outweighs that of the original offence.

The aim of punishment is to prevent offences, to prevent worse offences, to minimise the 'mischief', and to prevent the mischief as cheaply as possible, to achieve the object with least possible expense (ibid: 165). Punishment may also satisfy the injured party and public concerns.

4.2.3 **Frugality in punishment**

Bentham argues that we should calculate the optimum level of punishment and, if effective deterrence could be achieved by a lesser sentence than on utilitarian principles, it is a useless and needless expense to impose a higher sentence. Bentham was critical of the excessive and arbitrary punishments of his time, including the death penalty which was often used for relatively minor offences. He wanted an external standard against which sentencing decisions might be judged, so ideally two sentencers armed with the same knowledge of the facts of a particular case would reach the same decision on the type and level of punishment.

For Bentham, punishment is not justified on the ground of being good for the individual as the individual can have no interest in being punished at all. Instead, what justifies punishment is what is good for society, sacrificing a few individuals for the greater good of others. Punishment deters others from engaging in certain acts, promotes the public good, and promotes greater happiness. The 'happiness' of the person punished is considered alongside that of others but if it is necessary to ensure the happiness of the majority, his happiness may be sacrificed.

Bentham is committed to the principle of frugality, or what we would now call parsimony, to use the most economical means of punishment, to impose the least severe punishment to meet the social objective. Frugality is achieved where no superfluous pain is imposed on the person punished. The amount of punishment should not be less than needed to outweigh the profit of the offence. If it is too little it will be inefficacious, if too much it will be needless. The optimal level of punishment will depend on the circumstances. Generally the greater the mischief of the offence, says Bentham, then the greater is the expense which it may be worth incurring in the administration of punishment and punishment should be adjusted so that a person would favour a lesser rather than a greater offence.

This means that there should normally be gradations in severity of punishment to match the seriousness of the offence. Bentham says that there should be upper and lower limits on punishment to guide judges. So, there is room for proportionality in his theory of punishment because penalties will normally be linked to the gravity of the crime. However, proportionality is deployed on a basis quite different to retributivism, as it is determined by the need to deter the offender, rather than being based on desert, and is linked to crime prevention. Bentham argues that greater deterrence will be achieved by increasing the penalty as much as is necessary to prevent future crimes, rather than reflecting the degree of censure or blame. But deviations from the principle of proportionality, such as exemplary sentences, for example, may be justified in the public interest.

We should consider whether a less expensive means of punishment could achieve the same purpose and whether it is profitable to punish at all. In deciding on a mode of punishment we should take account of the aims, the principal ones being example, reformation, disablement, or what we would now call incapacitation, and compensation. However, Bentham acknowledges that achieving disablement may run counter to frugality, for example, when a disabled offender could still benefit others through future actions.

Bentham favours imprisonment because it is able to achieve fine gradations and in the 1780s he designed a model prison completely based on utilitarian principles. Capital punishment in contrast is the most unfrugal method of punishment, he argued, as well as raising the problem of irreversibility in cases of error. Bentham's point is well made as 139 prisoners on death row in the United States have been exonerated since 1973 (Council of Europe, Parliamentary Assembly 2011: 12).

For Bentham, the system of law and punishment should be designed so that when people seem to follow their interests, they are led to do those things which result in the greatest happiness of the greatest number. Prolonged punishment of an infirm individual who is unlikely to reoffend, or to threaten society, would be hard to justify, while on a retributivist model, the offender's advancing years or state of health at the time of sentencing would be irrelevant; what is important is his culpability at the time of committing the offence. Bentham is usually seen as an act-utilitarian, in so far as he focuses on the immediate consequences of a particular course of action, and this is contrasted with rule-utilitarianism, in which one considers the effect of generalising that particular course of action as a general rule and then considering the consequences of such a rule.[8]

Utilitarians may favour leniency in applying the principle of parsimony, accepting in some cases a punishment which is less severe than retributivists favour, depending on the particular circumstances. Retributivists, on the other hand, favour the punishment that is appropriate, which may entail severity. But for the utilitarian it depends on the consequences and empirical facts of the particular case. So there may be situations where the utilitarian might demand a harsher punishment than a retributivist would contemplate, punishing disproportionately to the offence to achieve a positive outcome, for example, to allay public concerns. Utilitarians might also recommend punishment where a

[8] For further discussion of rule and act utilitarianism, see Mill (1861) and Smart and Williams (1973).

retributivist would say there should be none at all, as in the extreme case of punishing the innocent. It is for this reason that many find the utilitarian approach unacceptable.

4.2.4 **Contemporary utilitarianism**

Bentham's work has been a major influence on modern utilitarianism. Modern writers in this approach would include Wilson (1985), Andenaes (1974), van den Haag (1981), and Kennedy (2009). These theorists are primarily concerned with deterrence and incapacitation rather than rehabilitation. In contemporary utilitarianism the consequences which justify punishment are:

1. General deterrence, that is deterring the general public from doing the act punished.
2. Special deterrence, that is, deterring the person being punished.
3. Incapacitation, that is, protecting the public by removing a dangerous person from society so he or she is unable to re-offend. This has been an increasingly important element of penal policy in recent years. It recognises that prison may not work in deterring offenders but it aims to protect society, by giving the public a temporary break from a persistent offender, or by removing dangerous offenders from society until they are no longer a threat, or if necessary, incarcerating them permanently.
4. Rehabilitation, where a period in custody, or of supervision within the community, is used to rehabilitate an offender, so that in the future the person can contribute to society.

Although each of these consequences may be construed as utilitarian, they may conflict with each other. For example, as Simon (1995) observes, indeterminate sentencing, which is usually associated with a rehabilitative model, makes it harder for an individual to make rational calculations of the costs and benefits of criminal activities, while determinate sentences have been criticised for undermining both rehabilitation and incapacitation, because sentences cannot be individualised. So rehabilitation has been criticised by those who favour incapacitation and deterrence as well as from the retributivist standpoint.

Utilitarianism is also associated with the use of predictive sentencing to control crime in contrast to retributivism which focuses on punishment for past crimes. In modern sentencing practice utilitarianism favours sentencing tailored to the individual while retributivists support sentencing according to a tariff. Utilitarians use scientific knowledge to target resources effectively and counter limitless penal expansion whilst retributivists argue that a desert-based theory which reserves prison for the most serious crimes, limits expansionism more effectively (see von Hirsch 1986). Moreover, utilitarianism may generate penal expansion through exemplary and predictive sentences, the most expensive penal option, although a strict application of the principle of parsimony should in some cases provide a brake on expansionism.

Utilitarianism has flourished in modern penal policy and practice because it focuses on future effects and seems more appropriate to the rational planning essential to a complex modern society. Utilitarianism, in effect if not name, is found in the Halliday Report (2001) and in the White Paper, *Criminal Justice: The Way Ahead* (Home Office, 2001a). Similarly in *Rebalancing the Criminal Justice System in Favour of the Law-Abiding Majority* (Home Office 2006a) the utilitarian approach is paramount; the key aims are cutting crime, reducing reoffending, and protecting the public. The stress is on meeting the needs of whole communities and giving more weight to the needs of the majority, including victims, and less to the offender, to protect the public from crime and to make the criminal justice system more efficient. Utilitarian considerations also underpin the current focus on the anti-social behaviour of deviant individuals and families which threatens the peaceful habitation of the majority.[9]

More attention is now being given to the risks of reoffending and measures to reduce reoffending. *Criminal Justice: The Way Ahead* (Home Office 2001a) further argued that sentencing should take more account of crime reduction, by considering the outcomes of sentences and what works for particular groups of offenders. It also emphasised that prisons need to focus more on preventing reoffending, such as preparing for work outside, as well as 'punishing'. The Labour Government considered that the CJA 2003 had begun the process of putting more 'effective' sentencing and punishment in place but the 2006 White Paper made clear that more work was needed to deal with prolific offenders including drug users (Home Secretary *et al.* 2006: para 1.19).

Utilitarianism also strongly underpins the Coalition Government's criminal justice policy, which is shaped by cost–benefit concerns. The Green Paper *Breaking the Cycle* (Ministry of Justice 2010a) focuses on competition, promoting work opportunities and work discipline in prison, making prisons more cost effective by using prisoners to contribute to prison services, and ensuring prisoners are in work rather than dependent on welfare when they leave custody, and reducing the financial burdens on the state. It also refers to the Government's aims of reducing the costs of foreign national prisoners and cutting the number of remand prisoners, and increasing investment in drug, health, and alcohol services as part of the drive to cut reoffending. It also focuses on payment by results and giving sentencers greater discretion. Breaking the cycle of reoffending is the central aim and providers of rehabilitation services will be paid by the results they achieve in reducing reoffending. Pilots have already been initiated. So 10 per cent of the contract price with SERCO for the running of HMP Doncaster will be returned to the Government if SERCO does not reduce the reoffending of its offenders on release by 5 percentage points (Ministry of Justice 2011a: 7). Maximising value for money underpins the proposed reforms.

Similarly, in the United States the financial costs of prison expansion have led to greater attention on the effectiveness and efficiency of punishment, instead of focusing simply on retribution which has been seen as contributing to that expansion. As Steen and Bandy argue (2007) these costs issues have encouraged increasing attention to the need to be 'smart on crime' and to target resources effectively, and this can stimulate penal reform.

4.2.5 **Collateral issues**

We will concentrate, for the rest of this chapter, on the particular issues raised by deterrence. Incapacitation will be considered in Chapter 5 when we also focus on the discourse of risk and danger in penal policy because incapacitation—either in terms of custody or using electronic means to control the activities of offenders in the community—has been the main tool for responding to the new concerns. Rehabilitation will be discussed in Chapter 12 when we focus on punishment in the community, as it is the Probation Service which will be at the forefront of offence-and drug-focused programmes to reduce reoffending. Offending behaviour programmes in custodial establishments will be considered in Chapter 9.

[9] See also Chapter 8, section 8.4.4 for a discussion of the use of anti-social behaviour orders.

4.3 **Deterrence**

4.3.1 **Key concepts**

Penal institutions may combine individual and general deterrence: if conditions are harsh in prison it will deter the individual offender from reoffending and also warn those outside prison of the costs of committing a crime. For general deterrence to work, then, the public need to be aware of the probability of punishment, so perceptual deterrence must be enhanced. Bentham advocated using the principle of **less eligibility**, whereby the conditions in prison must be worse than outside prison for the deterrent effect to operate on the individual or the general public.

Whether punishment does have a deterrent effect has been subject to debate and raises questions about how a deterrent effect may be measured or ascertained. Even if we accept the desirability in principle of using a particular mode of punishment or level of punishment to reduce crime rates, in practice we may have insufficient knowledge to ensure the success of a policy designed to deter. We also need to distinguish between primary deterrence, when a deterrent effect results from a punishment imposed on conduct previously unpunished, and marginal deterrence, changes in deterrence which result from an alteration in the level of punishment for actions already punishable. Most modern policy debates have been centred on increasing levels of punishment, rather than creating new criminal offences. Although the research so far has been most promising in linking effective deterrence to the certainty of punishment rather than the severity of punishment (see section 4.3.2), policy debates in the UK and the United States, as we saw in Chapter 1, have tended to focus on increasing the severity of punishment as a significant element of populist punitiveness.

So, even when there is a lack of evidence of a deterrent effect for a particular punishment and even when the economic costs are very high, it may be retained for political reasons, to satisfy public demands for high levels of punishment. For example, the 'three strikes' laws in California have imposed significant financial burdens, as they have contributed to the swelling prison population, yet there is no compelling evidence of a deterrent effect. But it has not yet proved possible to amend or repeal these laws (see Domanick 2004; Barker 2009). The death penalty also imposes substantial economic burdens in California and other retentionist states, but retains the support of the public, many of whom believe in its deterrent effect.

Deterrence theory was popular in the late 1970s and early 1980s in the work of writers such as J. Q. Wilson (1985) and E. van den Haag (1981) who argue that crime may be reduced through punishment. More recently the use of deterrence has been defended by Kennedy (2009) who focuses on deterrence as a process involving communication of risk of arrest and punishment to offenders.

On this approach, issues of desert are displaced to the outer limits of setting punishment scales. The emphasis in modern utilitarianism has been primarily on special deterrence rather than general deterrence, although the latter is still important.

So Wilson is committed to the use of punishment to deter as well as to selectively incapacitate, and to using preventive detention when appropriate, strategies which would normally be prohibited on a retributivist model. In *Thinking about Crime*, he argued that deterrence does work in reducing crime and that it does so not simply by removing offenders from society (Wilson 1985). Wilson claims that there is sufficient evidence to justify the claim that the crime rate is influenced by the costs of crime and that we could reduce the crime rate by increasing the certainty of criminal sanctions. In terms of criminal justice policy, then, we should try to enhance the benefits of compliance while increasing the costs of crime. In assessing deterrence, argues Wilson, we need to calculate the amount of crime which can be prevented by increasing the certainty, or the severity of punishments. He gives the example of Ehrlich's work on the death penalty, which calculated that for every murderer executed, eight murders were prevented (Ehrlich 1975).

For Wilson, crime is a rational enterprise and like other activities, shaped by rewards and penalties and, he argues, criminals make similar calculations to ordinary citizens: 'People are governed in their daily lives by rewards and penalties of every sort... To assert that "deterrence doesn't work" is tantamount to either denying the plainest facts of everyday life or claiming that would-be criminals are utterly different from the rest of us' (1985: 121). Even if criminals have a weaker conscience than others, they still take account of the costs and gains of crime and make rational choices. Deterrence theory is useful because it seems to fit our intuitions and because we act in ways consistent with it in everyday life, that is, we do engage in cost–benefit calculations. Research suggests that the certainty of sanctions is a major influence on this calculation.

4.3.2 **The certainty of punishment**

Despite methodological problems in devising appropriate experiments, there are some indications that the crime rate is influenced by the costs of crime, if detection, imprisonment, and punishment are certain. Wilson cites the work of Wolpin (1978), who examined changes in crime rates and changes in the chances of being arrested, convicted, and punished in the period 1894–1967 and found that 'changes in the probability of being punished seemed to cause changes in the crime rate' (Wilson 1985: 123).[10] Another example often cited is the experiment of Sherman and Berk (1983) in Minneapolis using different police strategies to deal with domestic violence. Those who were arrested were less likely to be reported to the police for subsequent assault than those receiving counselling or sent out of the house to calm down. Increasing police attention and intervention in domestic violence incidents in Killingbeck, West Yorkshire, in 1997 also led to a substantial reduction of re-offending (Hanmer *et al.* 1999).

There is evidence to suggest that, when certainty is removed, the crime rate increases.[11] An example often cited is the Melbourne police strike in 1923, when mobs poured into the city and looting lasted for two days before order was restored. In Egypt in the spring of 2011, during the period of the uprising when the police force was weakened, crime increased. The initial absence of a strong police presence on the streets was also seen as a significant element in the continuing disorder in UK cities in the summer of 2011. In Britain, when the breathalyser was first introduced, there was a decline in road accident casualties (Ross 1973). If fear of detection does reduce crime, then an increased police presence may be more useful than increasing the severity of sentencing.

Kennedy (2009) cites the example of the successful elimination of overt drug markets in a US city, 'High Point', in North Carolina, where dealers were carefully identified and information on their activities accrued to a point where an arrest warrant could be issued. At that point dealers were called to a meeting and advised that if they continued they would be arrested, so the consequences were made very clear. Attention was also focused

[10] However, Wilson acknowledges that it may be difficult to draw a sharp distinction between rehabilitation and special deterrence, as both involve inducements and negative sanctions for non-compliance with therapy and both involve restrictions and coercion.

[11] For further discussion of the significance of certainty, see Blumstein *et al.* (1978), Beyleveld (1980), and Ross (1992).

on strengthening community norms against dealing. The strategy succeeded, as the drugs market vanished and the nature of the community changed. Moreover displacement of those activities did not occur. As he observes: '[I]t is what matters to offenders... that matters in deterrence. It means that if offenders do not know about the sanctions they face, those sanctions cannot matter' (ibid: 182).

Wilson argues that evidence suggests that 'changes in the probability of being punished can lead to changes in behaviour' (Wilson 1985: 137). Even in crimes undertaken under the sway of emotions, rational calculations occur. He gives the example of the fact that the arrival of a police officer will often end a fight and that costs are still calculated at times of heightened emotions, so in a pub brawl one is likely to avoid hitting the toughest opponent, while arguing couples will avoid throwing the best china. Similarly, Kennedy (2009) points out that even psychopaths will avoid killing in front of the police and drunk drivers will drive more cautiously if they see a police car.

Wilson argues that we need to see people's deterrability as lying on a continuum. Some people have strong internal restraints on their behaviour and may also think how much they have to lose by being caught, but others may have few internal controls yet fear external constraints of imprisonment. Some have little fear and few internal constraints, others may wish to commit crimes because of their status within a criminal subculture. Some individuals, he argues, mostly young males, will lack strong internalised restraints on misconduct and greatly value a quick reward. Others may conform not simply because of the fear of formal sanctions, but because of the belief that crime is morally wrong, while others will commit crime regardless of the risk, and others are 'only dimly aware that there are any risks' (Wilson 1985: 252). For some informal sanctions such as the stigma of a criminal conviction and the shame of the criminal prosecution may be sufficient.

The results of some UK surveys reflect this complexity. A *Youth Lifestyles Survey* conducted in 1998–9 asked 12–30 year olds what would stop them committing a number of crimes. Almost half (45–47 per cent) of respondents said they would not commit any of the specified offences because 'it was wrong'.[12] On the other hand, in a MORI *Youth Survey* in 2000, 45 per cent said that the main deterrent would be 'worry about how parents react', 45 per cent also said that 'fear of being caught' would have the biggest effect. The 2004 survey, perhaps not surprisingly, found that '[y]oung people who commit the most offences are the least likely to think being caught will stop them from offending' (Youth Justice Board 2004a: 41).[13] Clearly the options open to respondents in their replies are crucial here but, just as important, we need to know more about the social context in which offending occurs and the impact of other influences on decision making before we can adequately assess the research findings.

The issue of certainty of detection has been considered in the context of the use of closed-circuit TV cameras (CCTV) to deter crime, but the results have been variable. Gill and Spriggs (2005) conducted a study of the impact of cameras across 13 sites but found a decline in crime in only one case, which could be attributed to their presence, namely vehicle crime in a car park. A review of the impact of CCTV by Welsh and Farrington also found that CCTV reduced crime only to a small degree, but was most effective in car parks (Welsh and Farrington 2002). However, cameras may, of course, still have value in providing evidence of crime, and technological tools are being increasingly used to deter car and other crime (see Lyon 2006). For example, the DVLA has developed a set of initiatives to deter car crime including a range of vehicle identity checks.[14] Research on

[12] Details can be found at http://www.esds.ac.uk/findingData/snDescription.asp?sn=4345.

[13] See, for links to MORI Youth Surveys, http://www.yjb.gov.uk/publications/Scripts/prodView.asp?idProduct=187&eP.

[14] See http://www.direct.gov.uk/en/Motoring/VehicleCrime/index.htm.

offenders suggests that they are unconcerned about cameras, but those who have been caught through cameras see them as more of a threat. Civil libertarians have argued that the case for CCTV surveillance as a crime detection strategy has not yet been made out and have highlighted the dangers of breaches of the right to privacy and the need for greater regulation (see Crossman 2007). Furthermore the use of surveillance technologies may also reflect political and social processes rather than the extent of the threat. As Coleman and McCahill (2010) note, far more effort and expense is expended on surveillance relating to benefit fraud than tax evasion, although the latter incurs greater economic losses to the public purse.

Deterrence theory has been criticised by those who reject the underlying rational choice approach to crime, while others argue that the empirical research is not encouraging, that crime rates and recidivism have increased despite deterrent sentencing, while some question the methodology used to 'prove' a deterrent effect.[15] Critics of deterrent penalties usually point to the high rate of recidivism as evidence of their failure to deter.

Walker (1991) argues that scepticism over deterrence is due to exaggerated interpretations of the empirical evidence. Instead of saying 'nothing works', we can say that deterrence may be intermittent and that some people may be temporarily undeterrable. Certainly the association of crime rates with the length of imprisonment is weak. Much of the research on deterrence is on the deterrent effect of the death penalty on homicides, but less is known on other offences, although homicide may be comparable to serious assaults. A person who is minded to consider the consequences before committing violence, is more likely to focus on *whether* he is likely to go to prison rather than how long.

Von Hirsch *et al.* (1999) reviewed research on deterrence from the 1970s to the late 1990s and found that the research shows that deterrence does work and that recent studies continue to support the thesis that the certainty of punishment can affect decisions to offend. Increasing certainty of punishment, they conclude, can increase marginal deterrence. Changes in sentencing policies may also affect how a crime is committed rather than whether to commit it; for example, the decision to expedite a burglary to avoid staying at the crime scene. In the research drawn from England, the United States, and Western Europe, we do find a negative correlation between certainty of punishment and crime rates. The National Academy of Sciences Research Study (Blumstein *et al.* 1978) drew attention to the methodological problems of proving the effects of either incapacitation or deterrence on crime rates, but did find that deterrent sanctions influenced some individuals.

4.3.3 **The severity and celerity of punishment**

However, the evidence is much less convincing for a link between the *severity* of punishment, that is, how stringently the person is punished once caught, whether a custodial sentence is imposed and its duration, and crime rates (von Hirsch *et al.* 1999). For example, recent research in New South Wales, Australia by Weatherburn and Moffatt (2011) of the specific deterrent effect of high fines on drink-driving offenders found no significant deterrent effect from higher fines. This was despite substantial variation in the fines imposed in the study sample by magistrates.

Furthermore, although perceptions of severity are important, changes in severity levels will be less visible and immediate than a stronger police presence and perceptions may not match the reality of sentencing. What evidence there is suggests that the length of imprisonment is less important than the certainty of imprisonment and increasing

[15] See, for example, Robinson and Darley's critical review (Robinson and Darley 2004).

sentence length will not produce corresponding gains in deterrence. In the United States, we find falls in crime rates in states with and without harsher sentences.

The celerity of punishment also needs to be considered, that is, how quickly the punishment is delivered. Beccaria (1767) argued that punishment should be enacted as swiftly as possible to strengthen the association between the ideas of crime and punishment and that delay would weaken the link between the two ideas. Bentham also argued that in calculating the consequences of an action the proximity of the punishment to the offence would be considered and weighed against the immediacy of the profit of the offence (Bentham 1789: 169). So, if the individual receives immediate gratification from the offence, this may well be more significant than the prospect of a distant punishment.

However, the celerity of punishment has been under-researched, compared to certainty, although it has been discussed in relation to capital punishment where there can be considerable lapses of time before the punishment is carried out and in relation to penalties for drink-driving (see Ross 1992). But informing drug dealers that they would be arrested and punished on a specific date in the near future was effective in the High Point study (see Kennedy 2009). The delays in delivering the punishment have been seen by supporters of the death penalty as weakening its deterrent value. Jeffrey (1965) argues that it should be enacted immediately to be an effective deterrent. However, Bailey (1980) found no evidence that the speed of executions was significant.

4.3.4 **The mode of punishment**

The role played by the actual nature of the penalty is less clear: although there are some positive examples. Replacing parking fines with wheel clamps in central London did lead to a substantial decline in illegal parking (see Walker 1991). We also know that disqualifications are more feared by drivers than fines. So the nature of the penalty may be a consideration (see also section 4.4.1).

Reconviction rates have been used as a measure of the effectiveness of different types of punishment in deterring and/or rehabilitating offenders and research on reoffending is regularly conducted by the Home Office. A study of England and Wales in 1972 referred to by Walker (1991) found that reconviction rates for imprisoned offenders were better than for those with suspended sentences, which suggests that the experience of prison deters more than a mere threat. However, more recent studies have found little difference between prison and community punishments.

Kershaw *et al.* studied the reconviction rates of offenders sentenced or discharged from prison in 1995. They found that 58 per cent of all sentenced prisoners discharged in 1995 were reconvicted of a standard list offence within two years (Kershaw *et al.* 1999). Standard list means all **indictable offences** and some of the more serious summary offences, such as indecent assault, child neglect, and assault on police officers, but it excludes most summary motoring offences. For offenders commencing community penalties, that is, the then community service orders, probation orders, and combination orders in 1995, the reconviction rate was 56 per cent. So after taking into account all possible relevant factors, in this study there was no significant discernible difference between custodial and community penalties. The results of similar comparisons suggest little real difference in reconviction rates for earlier years: 44 per cent of offenders given a conditional discharge and 43 per cent of offenders fined for a standard list offence in 1995 were reconvicted for another such offence within two years, and there were lower rates for fines and discharges than for community penalties.

A study published by the Home Office in December 2005 supplied information on reoffending by adults, defined as over 18 (Cuppleditch and Evans 2005). The reoffending rate of adults increased from 57.6 per cent in 2000 to 58.5 per cent in 2002. For the purposes of this research reoffending means that the offender committed an offence within the two-year follow-up period and was convicted in court. The figures relate to those released from prison and those who commenced community penalties in the first quarter of 2002. A follow-up study was conducted in March 2007 for the Home Office by Cunliffe and Shepherd (2007). This showed that for 2004 the reoffending rate was 55.5 per cent. As not all of those who reoffend may be caught or convicted and some may reoffend beyond the two-year period, then these figures may be under-estimates of the true reoffending rate.

An analysis of the reconviction of prisoners based on a longitudinal survey, *Surveying Prisoner Crime Reduction* was published in 2010 (Ministry of Justice 2010b). Data from the study on reoffending rates for adults discharged from custody or who started a court order under probation supervision between January and March and who were reconvicted at court within one year, showed a reconviction rate of 40.1 per cent (Ministry of Justice 2010b). The reoffending rate for juveniles who received a reprimand or warning, left custody, or started a court order, was 37.3 per cent. A comparison was made of short custodial sentences (less than 12 months) and court order commencements under probation supervision. This found that the latter were more effective than short custodial sentences in reducing one year reoffending rates. Completion of a cognitive behavioural programme *Enhanced Thinking Skills* also reduced the one year reconviction rate.

4.3.5 **The type of offender**

A number of factors affect the propensity to reoffend including age, sex, and previous criminal history. Some studies of recidivism have found that men are more likely to be reconvicted than women, teenagers are more likely to be reconvicted than older offenders (although in the longer term recidivism does decline with age), those with the greatest number of previous convictions are more likely to be reconvicted in future, and the unemployed are also more likely to be reconvicted than the employed (see Kershaw *et al.* 1999). Reoffending rates also vary with the type of offences.

In Kershaw's study for the Home Office, burglars had much higher reconviction rates than sex offenders. Prisoners serving sentences for burglary, theft and handling were most likely to be reconvicted within two years (Kershaw *et al.* 1999). The rates were 77 per cent for burglary and 69 per cent for theft and handling. The lowest rates, calculated as the percentage reconvicted within two years, were 18 per cent for sexual offences, 29 per cent for fraud and forgery, and 33 per cent for drug offences. Most of the prisoners were not reconvicted for the same offence, although they were more likely to be convicted if originally convicted for burglary or theft. The reconviction rate was higher for young male offenders than for adult males. Those originally convicted for homicide and released on licence have lower reconviction rates than other offenders, which has implications for the debate concerning the alleged uniquely deterrent effect of the death penalty. Although reconviction rates for women were lower than those for men in the 1990s, in 2002 reconviction rates for women in England and Wales reached the same level as those for men (Home Office 2003f). Older offenders tend to have lower reconviction rates than younger offenders; reconviction rates are lower for those serving longer sentences. The greater the number of previous convictions the higher were the reconviction rates. So past criminal history is the most influential variable for prediction of any future offending, although controlling samples to take account of prior probabilities of reconviction may be difficult.

Of course we cannot know for sure whether some individuals did not reoffend or reoffended but simply did not get caught. We also cannot infer a causal connection from a correlation without further analysis of the intervening variables. However, given the contemporary concern with risk management, an actuarial approach to criminal justice could take these statistics at face value, without a full understanding of the underlying factors, and could concentrate resources on those offenders perceived to be most at risk of reoffending (see Chapter 5).

Gender is also an issue to consider although gender differences in relation to deterrence have been under-researched. However, Corbett and Caramlau (2006) studied the deterrent effect of speed cameras and found significant differences between men and women on issues of driver safety: women drove more safely than men, were more safety-conscious, and more positive regarding the value of speed cameras than men. Male drivers in the study were more likely to have been 'flashed' by cameras at least twice and were more likely to view them as a money-raising exercise than as a genuine contribution to road safety. Differences were also found between older and younger drivers with the former being more safety-aware.

The *Surveying Prisoner Crime Reduction* survey (Ministry of Justice 2010b) considered prisoners' early life experiences, accommodation, education and employment, substance use, and mental health needs. Data based on the sample of prisoners studied found that reconviction rates were higher for prisoners who reported seeing violence in the home as a child, and for those who had been expelled or excluded from school. Higher reconviction rates within one year were seen for 79 per cent of offenders who were homeless before entering custody. The survey confirmed that prisoners were less likely than the general population to have worked before entering custody and more likely to have been homeless. Of the sample, 81 per cent reported using drugs before entering prison. The highest reconviction rates were found in the sample for those who were poly-drug users in the four weeks before entering custody, that is, using Class A drugs with Class B and/or Class C drugs. Juveniles receiving a reprimand or warning had a higher proven offending rate than adult offenders receiving a caution. Seventeen per cent of offenders said that they had been treated or counselled for a mental health or emotional problem in the year before their imprisonment.

Deterrence theorists assume that people's attitude to lawbreaking is rational and calculating, that we obey the law to avoid the pain of punishment, but there may be a moral obligation independent of the fear of consequences, as retributivists would argue. Many of us think it is wrong to steal irrespective of the penalty and this element has received little attention within deterrence theory. Moreover, rationality may not be universal and the development of reasoning skills is an important feature of offending behaviour programmes which use cognitive-behavioural models which suggests that rationality can be developed. Cognitive behavioural programmes have been used with some success with sex offenders (see Moster *et al.* 2008). We also do not know if offenders will favour short-term benefits against longer-term costs.

4.3.6 **Methodological problems in proving deterrence: interpreting the evidence**

The difficulty is how to test the deterrent effects of punishment. It may be unclear whether individuals were deterred by the unpleasant experience of a penalty, reformed because they now believe it is wrong to offend, or were rehabilitated by being given useful employment. It is also unclear whether we should measure the deterrent effect of imprisonment simply by looking at those who have already been punished and returned to society, or the population as a whole who may be tempted to commit a crime, that is, general deterrence. Those who have already committed a crime have shown themselves to be less deterrable than the rest of the population, because they have already risked punishment by committing the crime. Moreover desistance from crime may be uneven—some may commit further offences less frequently, others may commit less serious offences—so desistance takes place gradually rather than abruptly but this makes it harder to measure (see Kazemian *et al.* 2009; Shapland and Bottoms 2011). It may also be affected by wider structural changes which require social policy responses (see Farrall *et al.* 2010). Moreover as Walker (1991) notes, many studies measure the objective probability of conviction, when it is the subjective probability which is the most important influence on behaviour as a low estimate of risk is usually associated with high frequency of offending and vice versa. So potential offenders may consider whether they are likely to get caught and the possible consequences.

The methodology is also crucial in determining the correct time scale if we try to ascertain the likelihood of future offending, or view offending retrospectively. If there is a long delay then the initial response to a change in sentencing levels may no longer operate and if there is a short delay, then it may be too early to consider whether the individual has been fully deterred. The deterrent effect of a change in punishment may also decline over time, a process known as deterrence decay, as perceptions of apprehension change, for example if individuals think they might have miscalculated the chances of being caught or over-estimated the rigour of enforcement. Furthermore, studies of deterrence do not always distinguish sufficiently clearly between the issues of certainty and severity.

If we consider general deterrence, we find that some societies with harsh systems of punishment, such as the United States, also have high crime rates which are used to justify the high incarceration rates (see Garland 2001a). When crime rates do fall it may be hard to link this with the degree of severity of punishment, but the fact of being punished may be more important than the precise level of punishment. Moreover, when we look at these statistics, we face the problem of isolating the precise causal effect of punishment from the numerous intervening variables and of distinguishing deterrent and incapacitating effects. If we find an increase in punishment severity and a fall in crime rates we could not immediately infer a causal relationship. We need to know whether the changes actually led potential offenders to refrain from crime, and clearly many factors may influence the final crime figures.

Official statistics are notoriously inaccurate as a true measure of crime; for example, figures on prison populations may be an inaccurate measure of criminal activity if not all offenders are caught and punished, and of course if this is well known it may undermine the deterrent effect of punishment. Prison numbers may fluctuate as a result of sentencing policies and guidelines as well as the range of factors considered in Chapter 1.

Even if the crime rate fell following an increase in punishment we cannot be sure that this resulted from the punishment rather than from the numerous other factors which affect crime. If we find a group for whom a particular punishment does have a deterrent effect, it may be hard to generalise. Moreover, sanctions may affect behaviour without necessarily deterring; for example, sanctions against drugs use or arms dealing may lead users and arms dealers to become more secretive rather than giving up their habit, or curtailing their trade.

Statistics do not take account of local variations in law enforcement and local applications of sentencing policies. This is a particular problem in the United States, where variations between states may be obscured by aggregated statistics, but there have also been concerns in the UK. In her comparative study of California, Washington, and New York, Barker (2009) also shows that key differences in local political institutions and democratic traditions shape penal and social policies. Similarly, Garland examines the implications of local democratic traditions for the survival of the death penalty as 'it continues to be driven by local politics and populist politicians' (Garland 2010: 33). As he observes, 'In America... all politics are local and democracy can kill' (ibid: 310). Because power is devolved to the local level and individual politicians are accountable to the local populace, there is much more scope for majority public opinion to prevail on this issue.

Most of the comparative work has been undertaken on England and the United States but we also need to know more about other similar European societies. What we do know of other European countries, such as the Netherlands, suggests that a reductionist policy does not necessarily lead to a sudden increase in crime rates. We also need to control for other significant variables which might affect crime rates. If crime rates fall as the quantum of punishment increases, we cannot infer a causal effect, we need to know whether the increase affected the behaviour of offenders or whether other factors were operating. To ascertain this, it would be useful to compare the effects of two similar laws in two jurisdictions, one with sanctions attached to it which are strongly enforced, and one without such sanctions or enforcement, to measure the effect. It might be difficult to find a government willing to suspend sanctions. But even if we find a difference, this might be attributed to other factors, such as cultural factors or strong religious sanctions.

The problem for utilitarian theory is to calculate the optimum level of punishment. If punishment is increased over time it may have diminishing returns, if individuals do not believe it will apply to them, or think that they will not be caught. If an increase in punishment produces an immediate response in terms of crime reduction, this may not be sustained in the long term. So a punitive policy may prove uneconomic on the principle of parsimony, regardless of the issues of unfairness which would trouble retributivists. An increase in sentencing levels across the whole range of crimes may also weaken the gap between serious and less serious offences. An increase in punishment at the lower end of the scale may be unnecessary if it is excessive for those who would have been deterred by a lesser punishment and are unlikely to commit offences in any case. On the other hand, an increase at the higher end may have little effect on those strongly committed to criminal activity or with long criminal careers. Some of these issues have been addressed in relation to the death penalty.

4.3.7 **The death penalty**

In the UK the death penalty has not been available as a sentence since 1965. However, we are including a brief discussion here because research on whether the death penalty for murder has a unique deterrent effect has been an important element of the debate on deterrence. Empirical research in the 1950s and 1960s in the UK and other jurisdictions challenged its unique deterrent effect and brought into question the underlying assumptions of deterrence theory. However, deterrence theory revived in the late 1970s and Ehrlich's work on the deterrent effect of capital punishment contributed to this revival (Ehrlich 1975). While it might be argued that the offence of homicide raises specific issues which make it hard to generalise research findings to many other offences, murder is not so dissimilar to other serious offences against the person.

Many defenders of the death penalty still argue that the death penalty has a uniquely deterrent effect in preventing future crime, particularly homicides and drug trafficking offences, thereby promoting public welfare, although evidence of this is inconclusive. Sarat (1976) argues that, if the public were fully informed about the absence of a unique deterrent effect, their attitudes would change. But public support for the penalty also may be based on retributivist grounds and on the belief that no other penalty can match the enormity of the crime or communicate public anxieties over law and order so powerfully.

The debate on deterrence has produced much empirical work, often conflicting in its findings, and which is beset by difficult methodological problems, some of which have been discussed in this chapter. The body of work has been reviewed periodically and the empirical research suggests that the death penalty does not have a unique capacity to deter.

The Royal Commission on Capital Punishment's Report (1953) found that the evidence available at that time did not support the claim that abolition of capital punishment would lead to an increase in homicide rates, or that its reintroduction after abolition would lead to a fall in homicide rates. Reviews of research in the 1980s (Zimring and Hawkins 1986) and the 1990s (Bailey and Peterson 1997, 2003) also found no conclusive proof to support the claim that it had a greater deterrent effect than life imprisonment. There was no clear link established between the penalty and changes in crime rates. Given that the death penalty is given relatively rarely and the sentence is not always carried out, its deterrent potential may be limited. The US Supreme Court has also justified the penalty principally on retributivist grounds as an appropriate punishment and an expression of public censure for the most heinous crimes rather than because of its deterrent effect.

We can find abolitionist societies, such as Canada, where the homicide rate fell after the death penalty was abolished, in contrast to the UK where the homicide rate increased in the 1960s following abolition. However, the increase in the homicide rate was smaller than the increase for other violent offences which were not affected by abolition.

In the United States we can find variations in crime rates in states with and without the death penalty, which suggest that other variables may influence crime and homicide rates. Murder rates are lower in non-death penalty states than in states with the penalty and this gap has increased over the past 10 years. In societies which have used the death penalty to control drug trafficking, such as Malaysia, drug trafficking has continued despite these penalties, which has led some to argue that measures such as surveillance, crop elimination in supplier states, and building up local economies may have more success in controlling the supply of drugs. Hood and Hoyle (2008) also conclude from their review of the evidence that it has not provided scientific proof that executions have a greater deterrent effect than life imprisonment and any future conclusive proof is unlikely to be forthcoming.

There are several reasons why it is difficult to sustain the argument for the unique deterrent effect. First, the causes of crime are complex and punishment is only one factor in crime control and may be swamped by other factors which affect offending. It is difficult to draw any meaningful inferences from the figures from longitudinal studies before and after abolition, because of the difficulties of isolating the causal effect of abolition. But even if a correlation were found between the death penalty and high or low crime rates, this would not of itself establish a causal link. Donohue and Wolfers reviewed the available statistical evidence on the United States and found that 'the death penalty... is applied so rarely that the number of homicides it can plausibly have caused or deterred cannot be reliably disentangled from the large year to year changes in the homicide rate caused by other factors' (Donohue and Wolfers 2006: 791). Prisoners who are given capital sentences may find their sentence reversed through exoneration or through the appellate process so the executions are carried out relatively rarely. As Hood and Hoyle point out: 'Even restricting the calculation to those murders that are statutorily "death-eligible" the probability of being sentenced to death is only about 1 in 10 and of being executed between 0.6 and 1.25 per 100' (2010: 323).

Societies moving towards abolition may use the penalty less frequently in the years leading up to abolition because of changing attitudes, which may make it difficult to accurately test the deterrence thesis. There is also the problem of determining the appropriate time span for comparison. The Royal Commission found some examples where societies experienced an increase in crime rates for a short period following abolition, but there was no long-term increase in crime. Cross-cultural comparative studies are difficult as one may be comparing societies with quite different cultures, legal systems, criminal procedures, and social problems.

Second, if many homicides are committed under the sway of emotions, or psychological disturbances, or in a state of panic, or under the influence of alcohol or drugs, it is unlikely that offenders weigh up the consequences of their action and consider the outcome in a rational way. It may well be that many murderers do not make a meaningful decision to kill at all, initially, let alone weigh up the penalties if caught. Of course some homicides are premeditated but even those who do calculate rationally may find the prospect of a long prison sentence as frightening as a quick death. Project criminals, that is, professional robbers who commit well-planned and organised crimes purely for financial gain, may be more calculating, but may still think the risk worth taking as they are unlikely to get caught precisely because the crime is highly planned. Examples of project crimes would be the Great Train Robbery in 1963 and the Heathrow Brinks-Mat Robbery in 1983. Moreover, the certain and self-inflicted death of the perpetrator may already be an essential element of the *modus operandi* of some crimes, as in the case of the modern suicide bomber.

The Royal Commission did find an American case where a man drove his wife across the state line before killing her because there was no death penalty there, but not all homicides will be so calculating. In the case of premeditated terrorist or political crimes, the perpetrators may not be deterred if their motives are altruistic rather than individualistic. Thirdly, murderers as a group have relatively low rates of reoffending compared to other offenders, and good parole records. This might be used to support the claim that prison has a sufficient deterrent effect, or simply indicate that the nature of the crime is such that it is unlikely to be repeated. A study in New York of the period 1930–61 found that of 63 first-degree murderers released on parole, only one committed another crime (see Stanton 1969). Similar results have been found for other states and in later studies (see Marquart *et al.* 1989; Bedau 1997).

What we can say is that the death penalty may have a stronger deterrent effect than other methods of punishment on *some* people, but a negligible effect on others. Imprisonment may be sufficient to deter some potential murderers, but not others. Given that it is difficult to establish the uniquely deterrent effect, and in the absence of conclusive evidence, the utilitarian principle of parsimony would suggest that it would be better to use more humane methods of punishment if they can achieve the desired deterrent effect in a less painful way. However, the fact that the deterrent effects are inconclusive may not defeat the case for the death penalty. For example, van den Haag (1985) argues that, even if the deterrent effects of the penalty are uncertain and inconclusive, it is still better to risk the lives of convicted murderers than to risk the lives of innocent people who might be possible future victims. When outcomes are uncertain he argues, future victims should be given more weight in our calculations than convicted murderers. Moreover the penalty may also be defended on retributivist grounds. However, those who oppose the penalty on human rights grounds, who see it as inhuman and degrading punishment, are unlikely to be persuaded by any evidence of its deterrent effect (see Council of Europe, Parliamentary Assembly 2011).

4.4 Problems with the theory and practice of utilitarianism

4.4.1 Does deterrence work?

In view of these problems and the available empirical research, we cannot say that deterrence never works, but we can say that punishment may deter fewer offenders and potential offenders than we would like. Prison deters some offenders, provided that they are in deterrable states of mind. At the other end of the penalty scale, there is also some limited evidence that deterrence operates. Research in the 1980s on 'regulatory offences'—where there is a breach of a regulation, generally an omission rather than a deliberate act of commission—such as road fund licence evasion or not declaring excess duty-free goods, suggested that people were deterred by having to go to court and receiving adverse publicity rather than by the size of the fine (Orton and Vennard 1988: 168). The exception was TV licence evasion where 40 per cent of respondents regarded the size of the fine as a deterrent (ibid). However, the researchers pointed out that respondents gave their answers within the context of 'mostly mistaken' ideas about the likelihood of being caught and the maximum level of fine (ibid: 175–6).

In the context of custody, the 'pains' of imprisonment may affect different offenders differently. In a study of the subjective experiences of adolescent male offenders in Germany sent to prison for the first time, Windzio found that there was a deterrent effect from the deprivation of contact with people outside the prison, but this did not affect those without strong bonds, so prisoners will experience prison in different ways. He also found no deterrent effect from the fear of other prisoners, but rather he found that 'the higher the fear of other inmates, the higher the rate of recidivism' (Windzio 2006: 341).

For deterrence to work, it is not essential that all individuals conform to Bentham's model of economic rationality, calmly calculating costs and benefits using the felicific calculus. The question is whether deterrence operates to a sufficient extent, to influence enough people to make a difference to crime levels and make a deterrence-based policy justifiable. Some individuals may be acting under the impulse of emotions or mind-changing substances or may simply have so little to lose that an increase in certainty or severity of punishment would have little effect. Von Hirsch (1999: 36) cites Farrington's (1997) work to show that impulsivity is a key characteristic of persistent offenders which raises problems when using deterrent strategies in such cases.

One problem is that increasing levels of punishment and drawing more individuals into the punitive net may have the effect of normalising punishment so that it is less stigmatising. Within criminal subcultures the experience of surviving harsh punishment may itself be a source of status within the group and imprisonment may become more tolerable over time as the individual develops adaptive strategies. This is discussed, for example, in Clemmer's work on the process of '**prisonisation**' which examines how different groups adapt to imprisonment (Clemmer 1940) and also in more recent studies by Toch (1976) and Gravett (2003).

Explaining why punishment fails to deter in some cases may mean we need to look at the social context of offending, drawing on the symbolic interactionist approach in criminology, to focus on the effects of labelling and the changing self-image. Moreover, incarceration may itself provide increased illegitimate opportunities to commit crimes, both inside prison and on release, in enabling offenders to make contact with each other. Punishment is only one factor in reoffending. Research using data from OASys, the Offender Assessment System, shows that offenders have on average four problems or 'criminogenic needs' which may contribute to their offending: for example, accommodation, unemployment, substance misuse, and low levels of educational achievement (see Harper and Chitty 2005). Many offenders have poor basic skills which contribute to their poor employment histories and these are the issues which need to be addressed in rehabilitation programmes in custody and in the community.

In testing the effects of specific policies we need to know whether potential offenders were aware of those changes, whether the changes affected their behaviour, and if so, what they perceived as possible outcomes and the significance of being punished within their social groups. Perceptual deterrence is under-researched but what we do know is people's awareness of sentencing may be misinformed and unrealistic, as illustrated by the discussion of the British Crime Survey research in Chapter 1, section 1.3.3. If the public underestimate levels of punishment or the certainty of punishment, then the deterrent effect of a change in policy will be weakened, so perceptual deterrence is crucial. Improving the public's understanding of sentencing policy and practice is an important feature of current penal policy and this may not only reduce the fear of crime, but also communicate the risks of committing crime to potential offenders. Most research on perceptions so far has been on whether fear of punishment will affect the decision to offend, rather than on whether a specific change in severity, certainty, or celerity of punishment will affect decision making. Perceptions of severity and celerity should therefore also be considered at the subjective level.

Kennedy (2009) argues that the risk of detection in many cases is very low and offenders are aware of this, but deterrence can be effective if attention is focused on selected offenders and groups, and if messages are clearly communicated because 'a risk that is not known cannot deter' (ibid: 27).

4.4.2 **Theoretical difficulties**

Criticism has also been levelled at the underlying principles governing utilitarianism as well as the specific problems raised by the utilitarian theory of punishment. The problem with a deterrence-based approach is that increasing severity of punishment imposes substantial economic costs, but also social costs, increasing the social exclusion of offenders. Moreover, an indiscriminate increase in levels of punishment may weaken the gap between less and more serious crimes and undermine the incentive to commit less serious crimes. A deterrence policy may itself be a high-risk policy if it imposes social costs without the benefits of crime reduction. Using the utilitarian calculus, we need to consider whether to focus attention on crimes which affect large numbers of people such as property crimes; or crimes which affect fewer people but cause more damage, such as crimes of violence; or whether to focus on crimes where risks are widely distributed; or where they are concentrated. We also need to decide who to include in the calculation: just victims of crime or also those whose lives may be affected by fear of crime. So refining sentencing policy will require these calculations and the problem, as we have seen, is that we may not have the necessary information to formulate an effective policy, on utilitarian criteria, regardless of the issues it raises for retributivism.

Punishing the innocent

A strong objection to this theory is that it potentially allows for punishment of the innocent if circumstances warrant it. As a majoritarian approach, utilitarianism accepts that the individual may be sacrificed for the benefit of others, in sharp contrast to the Kantian view that people should be treated as ends in themselves. For example, it is possible that punishing innocent third parties, such as relatives of the offender, could achieve greater deterrence than punishing the specific offender. Some regimes have done this: in Stalinist Russia the Criminal Code created the offence of being a relative of the enemy of the people, and a principle of collective family responsibility and punishment for the transgressions of individual family members is in operation now in North Korea. It was also reported in 2003 that a utility company in Vladivostok planned to confiscate the family pets of those who did not pay their electricity bills. Yet our moral intuitions tell us that the punishment of the innocent is morally wrong and inappropriate to a legal system which tries to do justice.

According to Bagaric (2001), a modern supporter of utilitarianism, the reason utilitarianism lost favour was because it seems unable to confine punishment to wrongdoers and punishment of the innocent is inconsistent with the concern for individual rights. But Bagaric argues that punishment of the innocent is no worse than many other measures we condone in extreme situations. If society is faced with desperate circumstances then it may have to sacrifice individuals for the good of the whole. In any case retributivists have to accept that punishment of the innocent is a possibility, as any system of punishment is open to error. While the risk of error could be substantially reduced by improvements in criminal procedure, for example, by a corroboration requirement for confessions, it would not necessarily be eliminated.

Punishing the guilty: the problem of proportionality

Utilitarianism also raises problems even if punishment is confined to the guilty because it does not take sufficient account of proportionality, yet this is a fundamental principle of systems of law in France and Germany, European Union law, and the European Convention on Human Rights: the punishment should be proportionate to the crime and the remedy should be proportionate to the mischief. In the United States the Supreme Court will hold grossly disproportionate sanctions invalid under the Eighth Amendment, the constitutional prohibition on cruel and unusual punishment.

But while there is room within utilitarian theory for proportionality, it may be jettisoned when the public interest demands. Bagaric (2001) argues that proportionality is the best way of dealing with the issue of severity of punishment and sanctions should be commensurate to the offence. A disproportionate sentence undermines the criminal justice system and leads to social disorder, while proportionality improves the consistency and fairness of the sentencing process. But unlike retributivism, the proportionality principle is not absolute. However, Bagaric argues, we should retreat from proportionality only when necessary to pursue a more pressing utilitarian objective of punishment.

Ethical problems

Once proportionality is rejected in favour of utility, there may be consequences which are ethically unacceptable. Nothing is ruled out *a priori* on a strong utilitarian approach if it maximises happiness and public welfare. If we find that those with longer criminal histories are more likely to commit future offences, then a risk-based strategy could allow this to determine the length of sentence and extended sentences might be justified on grounds of incapacitation or enhanced deterrence.

For most retributivists the sentence should be based on the current offence and the risk of reoffending is irrelevant to the sentence given as we saw in Chapter 3. Even those, such as von Hirsch, who accept that first offenders should be treated less severely than recidivists, would still argue that primary emphasis should be given to the current offence and that any differential between first offenders and recidivists should be kept as low as possible. In practice most modern sentencing systems have far too wide disparities and premiums are not necessarily effective. Kazemian's review of the available evidence suggests that 'extended sentences for repeat offenders may, under certain circumstances, lead to crime reductions in the short term, but such policies are less likely to impact recidivism rates in the long term' (Kazemian 2010: 242).

For retributivism, as we have seen, desert is always the prime determinant of the severity of punishment for different offences. Once any minor deviation is allowed, it opens the door to larger deviations. As von Hirsch says: '[I]n practice, it may be quite difficult to permit only small deviations from desert parity, while holding the line at larger deviations.

The operation is like inviting the hungry Doberman to share in the family picnic, but only one bite' (1986: 163).

However, Bagaric does reject additional weighting of past convictions because it violates the principle of proportionality and effectively punishes the offender twice for the same offence. Instead he favours fixed penalties. Bagaric (2001) also argues from a utilitarian standpoint that suspended sentences should be abolished because they involve no pain for the offender. He favours using sanctions such as the denial of work and education, even if this incurs welfare costs, as they will still be cheaper than imprisonment.

A further difficulty is that it is not clear whose interests policy makers should be concerned with, those living now or in the future, whether short-term or long-term effects should take priority and how conflicts between them should be resolved. This is important for penal policy in deciding whether to pursue an expansionist prison policy or to focus on the underlying causes of crime where the benefits may take longer to reap.

The concept of the individual

Difficulties also arise with utilitarianism as a theory of human behaviour. No coherent account is given of the disinterested individual, although Bentham does accept that they exist; indeed he sees himself as one, trying to make social life better for others, but altruistic individuals are still seen as deriving pleasure from helping others. The assumption that people are governed by self-interest is clearly a crude generalisation. To dismiss altruistic individuals as pleasure seeking does not do justice to them. Moreover, given that most criminal activities are undertaken in the context of group activities, whether gangs or subcultures, or criminal networks, any intervention needs to take account of group dynamics (see Kennedy 2009).

Bentham's model seems to reduce humans to 'cheerful robots', or to what Marcuse would describe as a 'one-dimensional man', when other motivations may supersede the pursuit of pleasure and it is hard to find a place for perfectionist aspirations within this model (Marcuse 2002). His assertion that pushpin, a precursor of bingo, is equal to poetry in his *Rationale of Reward* (1825) would be seen as philistine by perfectionists who would distinguish higher and lower pleasures, particularly when formulating public policy and funding allocations. It is also difficult to apply his felicific calculus if there is a 'subjective' element and one person's pleasure is another's pain, or to talk meaningfully of calculations in the moral sphere. However, one might defend Bentham's model of the self-interested individual governed by the quest for pleasure and avoidance of pain, by saying it fits *enough* people to make policies based on it workable, even if there are some exceptional individuals who cannot be accounted for within the theory. In the case of Aristophanes' *Lysistrata*, the example given by Kennedy (2009), the eponymous heroine is motivated by altruistic wishes to end the Peloponnesian War, and yet successfully uses the threat of withdrawal of the women of Sparta to deter the men from continuing warfare.

4.4.3 **Rights versus utility**

The role of rights in the utilitarian model is also problematic. Bentham (1843) in his discussion of the French Revolution himself dismisses rights as mischievous nonsense and there is no room in his approach for non-legal rights. On the contrary he is extremely sceptical regarding their value in resolving difficult ethical, social and political problems because, he argues, rights cannot be construed apart from positive law (see Schofield 2007). Even if we could identify fundamental rights, sooner or later rights conflict, and when that happens we have to weigh up conflicting interests and fall back on utility. It is this potential for rights violations which underpins the liberal critique of utilitarianism. But for liberal critics such as Dworkin (1977, 2011), rights should trump utility.

Yet utilitarianism, as Bagaric (2001) argues, is not necessarily antagonistic to rights. There is room for rights within utilitarian ethics as the recognition of rights promotes utility. An example here would be Mill's argument in *On Liberty* (1859) that the right to free speech leads to the truth, and may add to the happiness of the community. But for the utilitarians rights have no independent life of their own. Utilitarianism can also resolve clashes between rights, by considering the consequences when rights conflict, thereby providing a rational way of deciding between competing rights claims in such cases.

4.5 Conclusions

4.5.1 Alternative approaches

Utilitarianism, as we have seen, offers more scope for individualised sentencing while retributivism favours a 'tariff' approach. But are these the only possibilities? Given the inherent problems with both retributivism and utility, several writers have tried to combine the two.

Braithwaite and Pettit (1990) have formulated a consequentialist theory of justice which seeks to retain the future-oriented approach of utility and the use of calculations, but which treats individuals as persons rather than as means to ends and which focuses on autonomy and choice. But they are critical of proportionality, the linking of the sentence to the gravity of the offence. They refer to dominion rather than utility, by which they mean the individual's ability to exercise choice over how he or she lives. This would act as a restraint on sentencing because a very severe sentence would not enhance an individual's sense of control over his life. In sentencing, calculations could be made considering how much loss of dominion was caused by crime and fear of crime and how much a particular level of punishment would reduce the dominion of the person punished. The aim would be to find an optimum level which gives least loss of dominion. They also argue for a decremental strategy which reduces the levels of punishment until the point crime starts to increase.

Von Hirsch is critical of their approach and says that it would be even harder to devise a scale of punishments on this approach than on traditional utilitarianism. Moreover, on their theory preventive detention could be justified because the extended sentence would protect the dominion of potential victims. But this may open the door to the intensification of punishment if the protection of victims' dominion warrants it, especially if fear of crime is also taken into account.

These are issues which will be discussed further in Chapters 5 and 6.

4.5.2 Problem scenario

To clarify the differences between the utilitarian approach considered in this chapter and the retributivist approach discussed in Chapters 2 and 3, you may wish to reflect on the following scenario. Guidance on tackling this question is given in the Online Resource Centre.

online resource centre

Consider the following problem:

80-year-old former Ku Klux Klansman Edgar Ray Killen was tried for three counts of murder in June 2005. The charges related to his involvement in the killing in 1964 of three civil rights activists in Mississippi, who were in the area assisting in the registration of black voters. The victims were taken from their car by a mob and shot dead and their bodies concealed. During the trial Killen appeared frail; he was on oxygen and in a wheelchair having broken two legs in a logging accident. He was convicted of manslaughter and sentenced to 60 years, the maximum term (20 years for each death). This was upheld on appeal in 2007 and he is now in prison.

On the facts of this case, do you think the decision to commence proceedings against Mr Killen in 2005 was correct? Give reasons for your answer.

5

Risk and danger

SUMMARY

This chapter reviews the current policy focus on the 'dangerous' offender and the aim of protecting the public from the risk posed by an offender's reoffending. It discusses developments in relation to a 'culture of control' and examines the utilitarian justifications for selective incapacitation of offenders, or groups of offenders, believed to be dangerous. The chapter examines the changes in sentencing law, focusing on particular types of penalty and order, and the provisions for control of dangerous prisoners through discretionary release procedures.

5.1 Managing criminality

5.1.1 A culture of control

The second edition of this book reproduced on its cover van Gogh's painting, *The Round of Prisoners* in which a circle of prisoners are moving around a prison courtyard. Referring to this painting, Rivera Beiras argued that, a century later, 'this human contingent can form another "round", another circular view: such a number could go twice round the world' (Rivera Beiras 2005: 167). His aim was to illuminate worldwide trends towards new punitive rationalities which have resulted in a greater use of incapacitation through imprisonment as part of an overarching strategy to minimise risks (ibid: 174–5).

In this chapter we focus on such incapacitation which is another utilitarian tool but one which uses the temporary removal or, in those jurisdictions with the death penalty, the permanent removal of an offender from public life. The purpose is not just deserts but, rather, the management of risk by preventing an offender from reoffending, or at least by confining his offending behaviour within the walls of the prison. In particular, it examines the increasing use for 'dangerous' offenders of indeterminate sentences which require evidence of rehabilitation before release.[1]

Many would see incapacitation as a key aim of punishment at the present time, at least for certain categories of offender. For them, even if there is no prospect of reform or deterrence of offenders, at least they can be contained. If this is the only justification, prison becomes simply warehousing. Recent penal policies have included provisions for 'selective incapacitation', whereby selected offenders or those convicted of particular offences can be given custodial terms which could not be justified on retributivist principles. The development of such policies is rooted in ideas about crime control, about who counts as a 'dangerous' offender, and new techniques for the management of risk. Garland (2001b)

[1] We leave until Chapter 12 an examination of the policy aim to lower reoffending rates of convicted offenders by tailoring community punishments and post-custody licence periods to individual offenders.

referred to these ideas collectively as a 'culture of control', a culture which is underpinned by new criminologies—new perspectives on crime and criminality—which had developed by the end of the twentieth century.

Garland places these criminologies into two categories: criminologies of 'everyday life' and criminologies of 'the other' (2001b: 182–5). Whilst both view crime as 'a normal, routine, commonplace aspect of modern society' they have very different conceptions of 'the criminal' and of responses to criminality (ibid: 15). From the perspective of the criminology of everyday life criminals are normal and rational, and can be deterred or diverted by systematic and pragmatic techniques. These might include situational crime prevention, that is, the reduction of opportunities for crime by removing security weaknesses or coordinating transport and housing systems. Garland characterises this approach as 'amoral and technological' (ibid: 183). It does not deal in values so it 'sits easily' with policies on the one hand that would exclude certain groups of people—if that would reduce crime—or, on the other hand, that would transfer increased crime prevention resources to the most vulnerable—if they are the targets for criminality (ibid).

The criminology of the other, by contrast, focuses on values and seeks to assert absolute moral standards. The very 'normality' of crime is a catastrophe and one to be combated by the imposition of order and authority. Furthermore, from this perspective, some criminals are decidedly not 'normal' but are, rather, evil or wicked. They are, then, dangerous, different from us and, being 'other', can be dealt with in ways, such as very long or indeterminate prison sentences or community exclusion orders, which we might not otherwise endorse (ibid: 184).

Crucially, both these criminologies view the offender in ways which are very different from the 'social criminologies' dominant in the mid-twentieth century (see Garland 2001b: chapter 2). In the context of enhanced notions of risk, 'the resulting sense of insecurity has led us to embrace habits and policies that would have seemed unthinkably repressive thirty years ago' (Owen 2007: 4) and which differ from the perspectives of classical utilitarianism which underpinned the more 'welfare'-orientated approach of non-custodial sentencing at that time. Indeed, Beckett and Western (2001) argue that states with social welfare are negatively associated with incarceration, and Rivera Beiras documents the trend towards 'the punitive management of poverty, the thoroughgoing flexibilization of markets, more and more criminalization for dissenters and the "rolling back" of state-provided welfare' (2005: 180). This reflects a shift towards a more exclusionary and punitive approach to the regulation of social marginality and is evidence of the view that it is pointless to expect to find the underlying causes of crime, or to search for social or political explanations of crime, if the individual is responsible for crime. So, in the United States, states with large minority populations, particularly those with larger black populations, spend less on welfare and have higher rates of incarceration.[2]

Because the new criminologies conceptualise the offender differently from previous perspectives, they justify different responses. In what is referred to as a 'post-modern penality', the individual is, it is argued, increasingly invisible. He is submerged in the actuarial, group-based approach of the so-called New Penology to which we referred in Chapter 1[3] and, in the new penality, a 'superordinate goal' for punishment—a specified consequence—is absent (Feeley and Simon 1992: 459). This is not to say that outcomes are unimportant, but that, within this approach, the search for, and adherence to, general

[2] Rehabilitationism, however, has survived the challenges of the past 30 years to emerge in a new form: see Chapter 12.

[3] Mauer has argued that this is also due to the increase in determinate, retributively based sentencing: see Mauer 2001: 12.

justifying aims and consequences are no longer of great importance. However, the new criminologies have refocused thinking on the particular outcome of deterrence, and also buttress the incapacitative policies which this chapter will explore.

The movement to this more 'economic' approach to punishment is evidenced by the increasing importance of a managerial discourse in the criminal justice system and also by the pervasiveness of managerial concepts and aims such as effectiveness, key performance targets, quality audit, systems management, out-sourcing, and value for money (see Chapter 1).

> Managerialism—with its portable, multi-purpose techniques for accountability and evaluation and its 'can-do' private sector values—has flowed into the vacuum created when the more substantive, more positive content of the old social approach lost credibility. The crime control field—from crime prevention work and policing to the prison regimes and the practice of parole—has become saturated with technologies of audit, fiscal control, measured performance, and cost–benefit evaluation. The old language of social causation has been displaced by a new lexicon (of 'risk factors', 'incentive structures', 'supply and demand', 'stocks and flows', 'crime costing' and 'penalty pricing') that translates economic forms of calculation into the criminological field.
>
> (Garland 2001b: 188–9)

Garland suggests that thinking about crime in this way probably occurred first in those parts of the private sector that wished to reduce their losses caused through crime (ibid: 189–200) but, if we focus on one element of the managerial discourse, that of risk management, we can contextualise it more widely within 'the risk society'. This is the term which some theorists have coined to symbolise the apparent increasing preoccupation with risk—at the level not only of the economic but also of the personal and political—by the end of the twentieth century.

5.1.2 **Notions of risk**

In Chapters 2 and 3 on retributivism and just deserts sentencing there was little reference to risk assessments or sentencing influenced by calculations of risk to public safety. It is true that sentencers must work within statutory maxima and offence categories that Parliament has imposed in response to particular perceptions of risk and danger: the sex offender legislation is one example of this, the Dangerous Dogs Act 1991 another. Just deserts sentencing, however, should not include an assessment of risk because it looks to the past rather than the future. So those provisions which entail an assessment of the offender's potential to reoffend and to harm members of the public, inevitably sit uneasily alongside the sort of sentencing examined in Chapter 3, where the focus is (only) the seriousness of the offences already committed.

The end of the twentieth century saw a focus on the 'risk society', seen as one where the management of insecurity—of potential and unknown harms—had become the dominant theme (see, for example, Beck 1992; Giddens 1990; Vail *et al.* 1999). As Giddens noted, 'The idea of a "risk society" might suggest a world which has become more hazardous, but this is not necessarily so. Rather it is a society increasingly preoccupied with the future (and also with safety) which generates the notion of risk' (Giddens 1999: 3). Because scientific and expert knowledge cannot ensure certain and predictable outcomes when applied to individuals, generalised prescriptions regarding risk of harm have been developed so that decisions which reduce societal anxiety can still be made. In relation to children and young people, their 'scarcity' and irreplaceability have put a much higher premium on risk management (see Farrington 2007; James and James 2008; Piper 2008).

In relation to offenders, the high political and economic costs of failing to protect the public from dangerous people (see Chapter 1) have similarly imposed such a premium.

There are three implications of these trends to which we wish to draw attention. First, the attempts to manage crime and risk of crime are not confined to sentencing. Indeed, the criminal justice system itself is only one part of a government's crime reduction and risk management strategy. Paradoxically, sentencing has gained a greater political importance at a time when its practical effect is diminishing. Statistics which show how marginal sentencing is in terms of the ability to punish all those who commit offences underline the importance for governments of spreading crime prevention much more widely across policy areas. Much crime is neither reported nor recorded: only about 3 per cent of crimes are proceeded with, and a large proportion result in a caution.[4] Indeed the numbers proceeding to prosecution fell again—by 4.4 per cent—in the year ending June 2011 (Ministry of Justice 2011n: Table Q1.1).

Consequently, 'a whole new infrastructure has been assembled at the local level that addresses crime and disorder in a different manner' (Garland 2001b: 16) with programmes, initiatives, and partnerships such as Safer Cities, Neighbourhood Watch, the New Deal for Communities, and Multi-Agency Public Protection Arrangements (MAPPAs).[5] These are all geared towards strengthening communities and are oriented towards a new set of objectives, 'prevention, security, harm-reduction, loss-reduction, fear-reduction', that are very different from traditional criminal justice goals (ibid: 17). What we have then is a network of community 'empowering', crime-prevention partnerships which utilise managerial techniques to produce the most cost-effective ways of managing risk and of targeting resources (ibid: 19). The second implication of the trend towards the cultural pre-eminence of a managerialist and technological, risk-management culture is that it justifies a selective response to offending. Further, its emphasis on cost effectiveness can cut across 'justice' issues whilst Hebenton and Seddon (2009) argue that 'precautionary logic' is refiguring the institutions of law and science in the management of sexual and violent offenders. The use of risk-management tools, it is argued, has reduced professional discretion to decide suitable and individualised responses (see Chapter 12).

Third, these developments led to the evolution in the 1990s in the UK of a sentencing policy which treats what was until recently a very small minority of offenders as dangerous, Garland's 'other', and from which the public needs protection. Such offenders are so 'risky' that a quite different sentencing framework is legitimate for dealing with them and it is legitimised on the basis that it will prevent harm to people in the future and yet harm is itself a problematic concept (see Baker 2010). How important is this focus on risk and preventive sentencing? We have made frequent reference to Garland's influential book, *The Culture of Control*. He began that text with the following statement:

> We quickly grow used to the way things are...On both sides of the Atlantic, mandatory sentences, victims' rights, community notification laws, private policing, 'law and order' politics, and an emphatic belief that 'prison works', have become common place points in the crime control landscape...
>
> (Garland 2001b: 1)

[4] For a discussion of the difficulties of gaining information about crime including from official statistics, see Maguire (2002); for a discussion of the decline in the numbers of cases proceeding to prosecution, see Ashworth (2004: section 3).

[5] See Nash and Williams (2008: chapter 4) for a discussion of MAPPAs and also the National Offender Management Service (NOMS) in relation to serious repeat offenders.

Not only have we grown used to the increase in crime but we have also, he argues, accepted harsher punishments for those selected so that 'the most prominent measures of crime control policy are increasingly orientated towards punitive segregation and expressive justice' (2001b: 17). What has been justified is the development of means of exclusion such as the curfew and exclusion requirements in community orders and on early release which stipulate times and places that are 'out of bounds' and also the range of civil orders introduced by the Sexual Offences Act 2003, including the foreign travel orders, which aim to control the dangerous with the threat of a penal sanction for non-compliance. Such prevention orders are reviewed in section 5.5.1.

Other analysts have endorsed this shift in the penal culture of Western punishment in the 1990s. Pratt explains this as a move from an era of the 'civilising' of punishment with the focus on seriousness that had characterised two centuries of penal policy (1998: 506). With new cultural notions of risk, such developments are not only acceptable but, at least in the tabloid press at the beginning of the twenty-first century, are welcomed and encouraged. This has been described as 'a new culture of intolerance' (Pratt 2000: 47).

On the other hand, some commentators contend that these developments are not as novel as they are portrayed and even Garland makes the point that nothing in the penal system has actually been replaced. His argument is, rather, that their repositioning has been crucial in changing the penal culture. Brown similarly argues, in the context of nineteenth-century colonial history, that current more punitive policies can be 'interpreted within a framework of *recursions* within penal modernity, rather than signalling an end or fundamental transformation of the modern state' (2002: 403). More recently, Donoghue (2010) has provided an alternative analysis of responses to antisocial behaviour.

Further, the focus on the dangerous offender is not a totally new development: 'Like the poor the dangerous have always been with us' (Freiberg 2000: 51). Nevertheless, the categories of those who are perceived as dangerous have changed over time (Dingwall 1998; Pratt 1996; see section 5.1.3). More significantly, the Criminal Justice Act (CJA) 2003 used for the first time the heading 'Dangerous Offenders' and the term 'dangerousness'. Those terms were found in commentary and reports in the past, but not in sentencing legislation until 2003. Further, the numbers of those sentenced as 'dangerous' increased significantly after the implementation of that legislation.

5.1.3 **The dangerous offender**

Risk, and the designation of individuals as dangerous, are not inventions of the twentieth or twenty-first centuries. Many examples of groups being designated as risks to the social order can be found in the nineteenth century (Pratt 2000: 36) and legislation was part of a mix of protective measures being taken by the state at the end of the nineteenth century against various 'evils' such as unemployment, crime, and poverty—a form of early state risk management (ibid: 38). At one level, then, 'the dangerous' are those groups which represent social dangers which are historically contingent, shaped by the result of ideas and events from a specific time and place. Such groups are not confined to the population of (convicted) offenders.

Even in relation to the offending population, it is by no means self-evident what we mean by dangerous offenders. The fact that different ideas, different constructions of dangerousness, have developed historically and internationally would suggest that the concept of dangerousness is constructed for political, professional and judicial purposes. As the Floud Committee, which focused in detail on dangerousness, noted: 'Dangerousness is not an objective concept. Dangers are unacceptable risks' (see Floud 1982). This transfers the quest for a definition of dangerousness to the risk discourse and rephrases the analysis into a designation of those people and crimes seen as unacceptable risks.

These two levels are linked. The development of policy has been from a concentration in the early nineteenth century on 'dangerous classes' to the current emphasis on dangerous offenders, or groups of offenders such as sex offenders (Pratt 2000: 36–8). Nevertheless, current dangerousness laws 'have the potential to remove an increasingly broad range of the socially undesirable' (ibid: 47) in that they target those who are often already socially excluded.

However, the focus on the individual offender reveals another development—the pathologisation of the dangerous offender. Mason and Mercer (1999) draw on Foucault's analysis of six serious cases during the period 1799–1835 to examine the medicalisation of the offender. That development construed dangerous offenders as mentally ill and brought into question the border between sanity and insanity. This can lead to problematic responses in regard to both the dangerous offender and those with mental health problems (see section 5.4.5 and Chapter 7, section 7.4). As Greig notes, in relation to her analysis of a high-profile Australian case, 'When the fluidity of madness is superimposed onto the notion of badness, it elicits an intuitive sense of fear among observers' (Greig 2002: 11).

Most preventive sentencing measures are aimed at the offender who is mentally 'normal': there are clear and separate provisions for those who fit within the legally defined category of the mentally disordered. Yet the normal offender is affected by those social ideas which fuse mental abnormality and offending because all offenders can then be seen as in some way irrational and a threat. Consequently, the social fear they engender can be reduced by the imposition of indefinite and disproportionate custodial sentences. So, as we saw in relation to sex offenders in Chapter 1, when perceptions of such offenders as ill have become less powerful, they have been replaced by perceptions of them as evil (Simon 1998). Both constructions of the dangerous are, then, of the 'abnormal' and legitimise the continuous surveillance of offenders even when they are released on licence.

5.2 Incapacitation and public protection

5.2.1 Assessing the utilitarian justification

Incapacitation as a means of crime reduction is a strong strand in current penal policy in the UK and the United States. It gathered support in the early 1980s and was a key element of the penal policy of the Reagan administrations in the United States. It has also been used in the UK since the early 1990s and is reflected in the tendency towards longer sentences as well as in some non-custodial penalties. For example, the disqualification of drivers for motoring offences is a form of precautionary, incapacitative sentencing. The controls on the movements of sex offenders discussed in Chapter 1 are also intended to reduce the opportunities to reoffend.

Incapacitation is a utilitarian approach because its aim is to maximise happiness and to protect the interests of the majority of society by restraining and removing dangerous offenders. For persistent offenders who are not dangerous, prison removes offenders from the community for a temporary period even if it does not succeed in deterring them.

Incapacitation is not necessarily incompatible with the justification of rehabilitation, as incapacitation could be combined with programmes intended to reform the individual. So in the UK we find a strong commitment to offending behaviour programmes designed to rehabilitate offenders, as well as acceptance of **protective sentencing**. Offenders may, therefore, be incapacitated while recognising that there is no prospect of reform.

On the utilitarian model, society should be protected for as long as possible from persistent and dangerous offenders, so the individual's liberty is sacrificed for the greater good of society. Whilst the most effective form of incapacitation is the death penalty, imprisonment is seen as the best method in abolitionist jurisdictions. However, there is still the risk of prisoners escaping, there may be opportunities to commit a wide range of crimes in prison, and offending may be resumed upon release, so incapacitation will not solve long-term problems of crime. Because incapacitation is an expensive penal policy, a shift towards the use of prisons as warehouses may mean that reduced funding will be available for costly treatment programmes within the prison. There is also the problem that when offenders are incarcerated, others will move into their territory and replace them, for example in relation to drug dealing, as there is not a finite pool of offenders.

There is also the question of whether prison does incapacitate effectively if it ultimately leads to higher offending rates than non-custodial sentences because of factors such as the stigmatising effects of prison, the difficulty in obtaining employment on release, the effects of prison dehumanisation on the offender, and the opportunities to learn from other offenders. As we saw in Chapters 1 and 4, there is a high level of reoffending in the UK and the relationship between imprisonment and crime levels is a complex question, not least because of the problems of isolating the effects of imprisonment from other criminogenic forces. But even if we could establish that imprisoning more offenders and increasing sentence length leads to a reduction in crime, we would need to assess the economic burdens because we know that incapacitative measures, such as the 'three strikes' laws in the United States, for example, are very expensive and that the indeterminate sentence for public protection introduced by the CJA 2003 contributed to the prison overcrowding problem in England and Wales (Piper and Easton 2006/7). By the end of December 2009 6,034 offenders had been given IPP (imprisonment for public protection) sentences (see section 5.4.3) and there were 5,828 IPP prisoners in custody in January 2010, of whom over 2,500 were detained beyond their tariff (Jacobson and Hough 2010: 9). In their review of the operation of the IPP sentence Jacobson and Hough highlight the social and economic costs, as these prisoners have a very low release rate. This is attributed to a range of factors including delays in obtaining parole board hearings, the problem of access to offending behaviour programmes which are a crucial step towards demonstrating reduced risk, the problem for prisoners of proving that they are no longer dangerous, and the increased tendency towards risk-aversion in decision-making by the Parole Board (ibid). The Coalition Government has indicated that it is reviewing the sentencing of serious violent and sexual offenders (Ministry of Justice 2011a: 10) and provisions to replace the IPP sentence are contained in the Legal Aid, Sentencing and Punishment of Offenders (LAS&PO) Bill 2011: see section 5.4.1.

One reason why the Coalition Government is looking to cut the number of prison places is because of the financial burden this represents. If one could ensure that crime rates would fall by expanding the use of imprisonment, there would be political advantages for governments in implementing such a policy, despite the economic costs, but that would require evidence that removing offenders from society would result in a substantial reduction in the crime rate. Yet available research from the UK and the United States suggests that even a substantial increase in the use of custody would achieve only a small cut in the crime rate, the reason being that punishment is only one factor linked to criminality (see Tarling 1993; Spelman 2000; King, Mauer, and Young 2005). The Carter Report (Carter 2003) calculated that only a 5 per cent reduction in crime in the UK in the period from 1997 to 2003 resulted from the higher custodial rates in that period. So using incapacitation as a crime reduction strategy is therefore an extremely expensive option and may not be cost effective if large numbers must be incarcerated to produce a small effect on crime rates.

There are a number of reasons for the relative ineffectiveness of incapacitation. First, punishment is only one factor which may influence crime rates and it may be swamped by other factors. Second, the impact of punishment on crime will be limited if only a small number of offenders come before the court and receive custodial sentences, which raises the question of whether it is better to invest resources in policing than in punishment. Third, as with deterrence, it is difficult to isolate the causal effects of incapacitation and an expanding prison population, on the overall crime rate. Moreover there is an inherent tendency for incapacitation to be an expansionist policy, for if mistakes are made in predicting high-risk offenders, then the public's response may well be to demand that the range of offenders/offences within the net is broadened. Governments may be reluctant to resist pressures for more incarceration and so be unable to abandon incapacitation as a strategy (see Chapter 1).

In the light of these problems, the tendency in recent years has been to focus on the incapacitation of those particular offenders or groups of offenders who are most at risk of reoffending. From a utilitarian standpoint it is better to target resources on the most prolific offenders and reserve prison for those most likely to reoffend, which would also reduce the overall costs of imprisonment at a time when those costs have increased. So, following the scepticism over deterrence in the late 1970s and 1980s, and particularly in view of the critique of methodological problems, more specific studies have been undertaken to identify the offenders most at risk of reoffending.

5.2.2 **Selective and categorial incapacitation**

We also need to distinguish different forms of incapacitation. Selective incapacitation means incapacitating particular individuals who may be at high risk of reoffending, and here a variety of factors may be identified including employment history and drug use. Categorial incapacitation focuses on incapacitating those who commit specific categories of crime, offences which carry a high risk of reoffending such as burglary. Both selective and categorial incapacitation are forms of predictive sentencing.

Selective incapacitation is attractive to policy-makers and governments as it offers the possibility of reducing crime by incarcerating the most crime-prone offenders, but it may also serve to contain the size of the prison population, allowing precious resources to be used most effectively against those offenders. So it is not surprising that it is popular with governments. To calculate the risks of reoffending various indices have been used, such as data on crimes, or the individual's record, employment, or social circumstances.

However, selective incapacitation could be seen as unethical as it may mean that an offender is given a higher sentence than the offender deserves if he or she is deemed to be at risk and because it denies autonomy to the individual and sacrifices the principle of proportionality for the goal of public protection. It presumes the individual will follow a particular course of action in the future and punishes that person accordingly for a choice not yet made: we do not know that the individual would have reoffended, especially if he or she is a first-time offender. For both reasons it conflicts with retributivist principles. Such policies also raise the issue of who should shoulder the risk of harm: potential future victims or the offender who may receive a longer sentence than he or she deserves.

Moreover, we are still a long way from certainty in our predictions of future offending. Research studies usually are based on convicted offenders rather than the wider population of offenders which includes unconvicted and potential offenders. If we over-estimate the risk, there is the danger of incarcerating unnecessarily. However, the public is more concerned that the risk will be under-estimated, exposing them to the release of dangerous offenders into the community. If selective incapacitation of dangerous offenders is introduced but the policy fails to detain all dangerous offenders, then there will be an increase in public demands to broaden the categories of risk. While risk-management techniques are becoming more sophisticated, they may still be insufficiently precise to provide a basis for fair and just penal policies and respect for the rights of offenders. The ability to predict risk accurately may be over-estimated and this may mean extended and unjustified periods of detention. So as the focus on human rights has become more important, this may come into conflict with the emphasis on risk-management (Whitty 2011).

But is selective incapacitation inherently unfair? We know from the available research that those with a criminal history are more likely to offend in the future than those who have never committed an offence. A person subjected to a protective sentence, that is detained on the basis that he likely to constitute a threat to the public, is not presumptively innocent but has committed exactly the type of offence for which he is being detained and future detention or control may be justified on utilitarian grounds. However it is hard to justify on desert theory, as we saw in Chapter 3, as the primary focus in retributivism is on the current offence rather than past or future offences and very limited weight is given to past offences. Moreover, because the offender possesses agency and autonomy, it is possible he will not reoffend. In any case, as von Hirsch (1986) points out, a predictive index would include factors such as drug use, age, and employment and may also use self-reports of offending behaviour, factors which would be irrelevant to retributivist sentencing.

Because of these problems, many prefer categorial incapacitation in which an entire class of offenders will be incarcerated to prevent reoffending. This meets the objection of unfairness raised against selective incapacitation. It satisfies the principle of equality, in so far as it treats all burglars alike, although we still cannot know for certain that everyone in the class, or indeed if any of them, would have reoffended.

However, we do know that recidivism rates vary between offences. For example, murderers have low recidivism rates and robbers higher rates, so we could in theory maximise crime prevention by giving longer sentences to those with the highest potential for reoffending. Von Hirsch (1986) does find categorial incapacitation is more compatible with desert theory than selective incapacitation, provided the sentence is linked to blameworthiness and proportionality. But while it satisfies the retributivist demand for parity between offenders committing the same crime, it does not give parity with other serious crimes. Even if we operate within broad desert limits on sentencing, we are still treating offenders as a class differently, on the basis of the offence, compared to other serious offenders. It is also problematic for rank ordering if one offence is taken out of the ordering and still does not tell us where to anchor the scale, so it does not address the issue of cardinal proportionality.

An attempt to converge past and future crimes in crime prevention strategies will undermine the principles of fairness and proportionality. Von Hirsch is sceptical regarding the attempt of Morris and Miller (1985) to converge prediction and retributivism by using prediction within broad limits governed by desert, so the punishment extended by dangerousness would not go beyond that justified as a deserved punishment independent of the prediction. As he says, this still begs the question of the reliability of evidence underpinning claims of dangerousness as well as the moral objection that it is 'unjust to give unequal punishments—and thereby unequal amounts of condemnation—to offenders whose conduct is equally reprehensible' (von Hirsch 1986: 141).

5.2.3 **Mass imprisonment in the United States**

An extreme example of the use of incapacitation as a penal policy is to be found in the United States where the imprisonment rate, that is the numbers in custody as a proportion of the general population, has increased substantially since 1972 and is much higher than in European, and particularly Scandinavian, countries. For much of the twentieth century the imprisonment rate in the United States was around 110 per 100,000. In 1972, the rate had decreased to 93 per 100,000 of the population but since then it has increased substantially, to 452 per 100,000 by 1999 and 743 by 2009. Indeed, the 1990s saw a doubling of the prison population until there were over 2,000,000 in prison by 2001, a shift Zimring (2001) characterises as being from 'lock them up' to 'throw away the key'. There are currently over 2 million people in US prisons or jails, of whom nearly 900,000 are African American males. The expansion of imprisonment in the United States has been marked by the presence of young black males from urban areas. One in eight of black males in their twenties is in prison. As Mauer observes, 'If current trends continue, 1 of every 3 African American males born today can expect to go to prison in his lifetime, as can 1 of every 6 Latino males, compared to 1 in 17 White males' (Mauer 2011: 88S).

This has had a number of social effects, including the disenfranchisement of a section of the population, an increase in the number of single-parent families headed by women in those communities, and the alienation of those groups affected. The result has been the overlaying of penal exclusion on racial and economic exclusion, so deepening social divisions. The economic costs are also substantial.

This shift towards 'mass imprisonment' and the increase in the number of black defendants has been attributed to a combination of factors, including the rise of determinate and mandatory sentences and also the war on drugs which included much harsher penalties for crack cocaine than powder cocaine, with the same sentence for 5 grams of crack cocaine and 500 grams of power cocaine, and for offences committed in school zone districts. African American defendants constitute the majority of crack cocaine offenders, while white and Hispanic defendants dominate powder cocaine offenders. Curry and Corral-Camacho (2008) found that young minority males in their sample of drug offenders in Texas suffered a heavier penalty at the point of sentencing. The new Fair Sentencing Act 2010 passed by Congress aims to reduce this disparate impact. As young black Americans are more likely to live in densely populated urban areas rather than suburbia they are also more likely to commit offences within these school zones. Tonry (2009) argues that key factors in shaping harsh penal policies in the United States have included race, religion, and libertarianism and its constitutional structure.

The 1990s were also marked by increasing inequality in the United States, as the gap between the middle class and black working class widened. Arguably, it is easier to punish those with whom there is little contact outside the courtroom. The three strikes laws have also narrowed the gap between serious and non-serious offences, so undermining the retributivist sentencing framework. Moreover, the constitutionality of the three strikes laws was upheld in *Ewing v California* (2003) where a 25-year sentence imposed for a minor theft was held not to infringe the test of gross disproportionality (see the discussion in van Zyl Smit and Ashworth 2004). Garland argues that the persistence of capital punishment is also a significant factor as 'the availability of the death penalty permits very lengthy sentences of imprisonment, even life imprisonment without parole, to appear comparatively humane, thereby contributing to the nation's extraordinary rates of imprisonment' (Garland 2010: 312).

However, these incapacitative policies are now harder to sustain given the fiscal crisis in the United States. As the prison population has expanded, this has led to increased pressure on the system which makes overcrowding inevitable. This problem has been acute in California where we find a conflict between pragmatism to keep costs down and populist demands for high levels of punishment (see Barker 2009). The courts have also become more activist in demanding improvements in prison conditions which may only be achievable through reductions in overcrowding. By December 2009 the prison population of the United States exceeded 2.3 million compared to 1.2 million in 1990, but it fell to just over 2.2 million by December 2010. In *Coleman v Schwarzenegger/Plata v Schwarzenegger* (2009) the California District Court ordered the state to reduce prison overcrowding within two years and this was upheld by the US Supreme Court in *Plata v Brown* (2011). The case focused on the implications of overcrowding for mental and physical health as the overcrowded and squalid conditions undermined the ability to provide appropriate medical care. As Simon argues, the case highlighted the fact that prisoners 'are now placed *at risk* by the prison system, rather than the source *of risks* that it prevents from circulating' (Simon 2011: 253). It is also a significant turning point, he argues, in recognising the humanity of prisoners.

As a utilitarian measure, incapacitation has to be linked to social benefits which outweigh social and economic costs but this is difficult to demonstrate in relation to mass imprisonment. However, policy makers and politicians may be reluctant to jettison incapacitative policies despite costs, because of the rise in populist punitiveness and public anxiety over crime, particularly dangerous offenders, and the emergence of crime and punishment as a key political issue. For example, Proposition 66, a measure to limit three strikes laws in California to new violent and serious offences, was defeated by a public vote in 2004 (Barker 2009).

5.3 Sentencing on risk of harm

5.3.1 The history of protective sentencing

Whilst the development of protective sentencing did not begin in the twentieth century, the more recent forms of sentencing have been more draconian in application and extent. The early provisions for preventive detention at the beginning of the last century were aimed at persistent offenders, 'habitual' or professional criminals, seen as a danger, not because of the seriousness of their offending but because of their propensity to engage in criminality as a way of life. Such behaviour not only threatened in particular the propertied classes but was evidence of a continued refusal to conform. So, for example, the Prevention of Crime Act 1908 was passed in England and Wales, the Habitual Criminals Act 1906 in New Zealand, and the Crimes Act in 1914 in Australia. In England and Wales the 1908 Act provided for post-sentence preventive detention of 5–10 years, replaced by a sentence of preventive detention for 5–14 years by the Criminal Justice Act 1948. That in turn was replaced by the extended sentence in the Criminal Justice Act 1967 (Powers of Criminal Courts Act 1973), which was a custodial sentence with a much longer period of rehabilitative probation, aimed at the persistent more serious offender who was a risk to society. This sentence was abolished in the Criminal Justice Act (CJA) 1991 (see Dingwall 1998; Scottish Executive 1999: Chapter 4) and replaced by the 'longer than commensurate' sentence discussed at section 5.3.2.

Yet what is clear from research on the operation of these earlier provisions in England and Wales and other jurisdictions is how little they were used (Dingwall 1998: 179; Freiberg 2000; Walker 1999: 62). Explanations have been in terms of judicial adherence to retributivist principles, suspicion of expert evidence, judicial concern at encroachment on sentencing discretion, or because of more widely held ethical, constitutional, or human rights concerns. These reasons have ensured that, for almost a century, preventive measures generally remained as exceptions to a 'normal' sentencing approach and were used, in practice, for only a minority of offenders. In contrast, recent developments, as noted in relation to the IPP sentence, have affected more offenders and have had a significant impact on prison resources.

So which offenders are now perceived as the most 'dangerous' to the public? The longstanding legislative concern with sexual and violent offenders continued as the focus of the newer sentences—additional incapacitation, mandatory minimum sentences, and custodial sentences with extended licence periods—introduced or amended by legislation in and since 1991. However, the legislation has also added drug traffickers, domestic burglars, and those possessing firearms to the list of the dangerous.

The crucial issues for discussion in section 5.4 relate to the new protective sentencing framework introduced by the CJA 2003, which included a separate chapter in Part 12 dedicated to 'Dangerous Offenders'. Sections 225–228 provide sentences of 'life imprisonment', 'imprisonment for public protection' (with comparable forms of detention for offences committed by those under 18 years of age: see Chapter 13), and an extended sentence (for under- and over-18-year-olds). These provisions have been subject to criticism and amendment since 2003 but are still the current three forms of preventive sentences (although the IPP sentence is under threat: see section 5.4.1). It should be noted also that the persistent offender is again viewed as a social danger: in the CJA 2003, the repetition of offences may be part of the 'proof' of risk in some of the provisions, and is a mandatory aggravation in relation to all provisions (see Chapter 3, section 3.2.4).

To summarise, contrary to the then Government's statement that the CJA 2003 introduced for the first time 'a distinction between dangerous and non-dangerous offenders as a basis of custodial sentencing' (Home Secretary *et al.* 2006: para 1.10; see also Piper and Easton 2006/7), governments have tried various ways over the years to implement an aim of incapacitating selectively those considered at the time to be dangerous. Methods include the extension of a prison sentence beyond what is proportionate, an extension to the licence period after imprisonment and/or the imposition of incapacitating conditions on the licence period, and the imposition of indeterminate sentences where the release date depends on assessment of risk. We will discuss recent examples of these methods in the following sections.

5.3.2 **Longer than commensurate sentences**

The first new protective sentence in the more recent past was the 'longer than commensurate' or LTC sentence, introduced by the CJA 1991[6] which enabled sentencers to impose longer determinate custodial sentences on those convicted of sexual or violent offences than were proportionate to seriousness. This amounted, in effect, to selective (additional) incapacitation. The range of violent and sexual offences to which these provisions related was relatively narrow, reflecting the continuing policy aim to reduce custody for most offenders whilst allowing for (longer) custodial sentences for a very small minority of dangerous offenders (see von Hirsch and Ashworth 1996). The sentence could be used if 'only such a sentence would be adequate to protect the public from serious harm from [the offender]' and in such cases the sentence was 'for such longer term (not exceeding that

[6] Later consolidated in ss 79(2)(b) and 80(2)(b) of the Powers of Criminal Courts (Sentencing) Act (PCCSA) 2000 and repealed by the CJA 2003, Schedule 37, Part 7.

maximum) as in the opinion of the court is necessary to protect the public from serious harm[7] from the offender'. 'Serious' harm had already been interpreted by the courts in *Birch* (1989)[8] when Mustill LJ stated that the court 'is required to assess not the seriousness of the risk that the defendant will re-offend, but the risk that if he does so the public will suffer serious harm... the potential harm must be serious, and a high possibility of a recurrence of minor offences will no longer be sufficient'.

However, this left several key issues to be interpreted by the courts, notably the crucial question of the likelihood of reoffending and also the question of whether the calculation of risk could be based solely on a history of previous similar convictions or whether a clinical diagnosis of dangerousness was required (Clarkson 1997: 287). However, the most difficult issue for the sentencer was intrinsic to this method of achieving selective incapacitation—the calculation of the 'additional element' to be added to a proportionate sentence. Until *Chapman* (2000), cases often, but by no means always, supported the statement in *Crow and Pennington* (1994) that there should be a 'reasonable relationship with the seriousness level' and that the enhancement could be up to 50 per cent (see also *M (James Samuel)* (2003)) though Clarkson (1997: 289) found an average enhancement of 73.5 per cent in cases in the period 1993 to 1997. In *Chapman* (2000) the Court argued that there was no necessary ratio between the punishment—justified on retributivist principles—and the protective parts of the sentence.

In some respects this latter reasoning was logical: if an offender is a serious risk, but does not meet the criteria for a life sentence, a few more years of public protection (see *Szczerba* 2002) may appear ineffective in relation to a lifetime of offending. With relatively short periods of extra incapacitation, especially when early release is taken into account (see section 5.5.3), LTC sentencing in practice was not, perhaps, based on the rationale—protection of the public—which justified the sentence (Clarkson 1997: 285; see, also, Walker 1999; Freiberg 2000).

The new sentence also raised an issue which was to become increasingly important—whether it was rights compliant. *R (Giles) v Parole Board* (2004) tested the legality under Article 5(4)[9] of the European Convention on Human Rights (ECHR) of implementing the extra period of custody without an independent review once the punitive element had been served. The Court of Appeal and then the House of Lords refused to treat such a sentence as similar to a discretionary life sentence (see sections 5.3.4 and 5.4.4) and stated that the whole sentence was pervaded by a punitive element and so not to be treated as having two parts.

Not surprisingly, therefore, it was argued that Parliament and the Court of Appeal were at cross purposes (Dingwall 1998), that rights issues had not been given adequate appellate consideration, and that, in any case, the preventive LTC sentences were being used only sparingly by the judiciary.[10] Clearly this 'additional custodial element' approach was not effective and the CJA 2003 discontinued the LTC sentence.

[7] The Act noted that 'harm' covers 'death or serious personal injury, whether physical or psychological, which would be occasioned by future violent or sexual offences committed by the offender' (PCCSA 2000, s 161(4)).

[8] In relation to s 41 of the Mental Health Act 1983.

[9] 'Everyone who is deprived of his liberty by arrest or detention shall be entitled to take proceedings by which the lawfulness of his detention shall be decided speedily by a court and his release ordered if the detention is not lawful.'

[10] Flood-Page and Mackie (1998) found in 1995–6 that only 3 per cent of custodial sentences for violence and 6 per cent for sexual offences were given LTC sentences.

5.3.3 Mandatory (minimum) sentences

The second set of new sentences introduced in the 1990s used a different method for selectively incapacitating repeat offenders. They specified particular minimum sentences the courts had to impose in relation to particular offences but they were also problematic because they severely restricted judicial discretion and because they also raised rights issues. Until 1997, only one mandatory penalty was in existence for use by English courts—that of life imprisonment for murder. That was deemed, in *Lichniak* (2001), not to contravene either Article 3 or 5 of the ECHR[11] but the judiciary, in this and other jurisdictions,[12] has resisted the imposition of other mandatory provisions (see Chapter 2). Indeed, there is some intermittent pressure for repealing the mandatory sentencing for murder (see Mitchell and Roberts 2012).

The new sentences, added by ss 1–4 of the Crime (Sentences) Act (CSA) 1997 and re-enacted in ss 109–11 of the Powers of Criminal Courts (Sentencing) Act (PCCSA) 2000, were mandatory in relation to specified forms of reoffending. Parliament specified those offences where custody had to be imposed, possibly where it would not otherwise have been imposed or where a shorter term might have been imposed, and ensured that where these provisions apply they take precedence over the just deserts sentencing framework. The first of these provisions provided what became known as an 'automatic' life sentence on conviction for a second offence when both offences were in the list provided specifically for the purpose of the provision, whilst the second and third provisions, now in ss 110–111, mandate a minimum sentence for a third specified offence. A problematic element of such mandatory provisions is the inclusion of a 'get-out' clause: the 'exceptional circumstances' of s 109 and the 'unjust to do so' provisions in ss 110–111 which can be used to justify a departure from the rule.

The sentences in ss 110–11 of the PCCSA 2000 remain in force: the court must impose a minimum sentence of seven years on the third conviction for a Class A drug trafficking offence and three years on a third domestic burglary conviction.[13] Ashworth argued for the relative unimportance of these provisions, given that most third-time offenders would receive seven years in relation to drug trafficking, and that few burglars had been sentenced under s 111 (Ashworth 2002b: 1096). However, whilst the number of third-time burglars sentenced under this provision was only six in 2001, the number rose to 13 in 2003, 46 in 2004 and 89 in 2005 (Home Office 2007c: Table 2.6). Figures given to Parliament in September 2011 show that many third-time burglars do not get an immediate custodial sentence, although 778 did, but it is not clear from Crispin Blunt's answer whether those sentences were for three years or more (see Table 5.1).[14]

Further mandatory sentences have been introduced since 2000. Sections 287 and 292 of the CJA 2003 amended the Firearms Act 1968 and the Firearms (Northern Ireland) Order 1981, respectively, to provide for a mandatory minimum sentence of five years' imprisonment for those aged 18 or over in England and Wales (21 or over in Scotland

[11] The judgment in *Offen No. 2* (2001) was distinguishable because that dealt with cases less serious than murder. Note however that the (English) Privy Council has jurisdiction over territories where the death penalty still pertains. See, for example, Bailin (2002) for rulings on death penalty cases in the Eastern Caribbean.

[12] See, for example, van Zyl Smit (2000) in relation to similar sentences introduced in South Africa in 1997.

[13] For examples of cases where the mandatory minimum custodial sentence was not imposed because it was 'unjust in all the circumstances' see *Hoare* (2004) and *Gibson* (2004); see also guidance on this matter in *McInerney and Keating* (2002).

[14] Available at http://www.publications.parliament.uk/pa/cm201011/cmhansrd/cm110907/text/110907w0001.htm.

Table 5.1 Sentencing on a third burglary conviction

All offenders	2006	2007	2008	2009	2010
Absolute discharge	—	1	—	—	—
Conditional discharge	3	2	6	4	5
Fine	1	2	1	—	—
Community sentences	34	38	38	34	52
Fully suspended	23	36	51	38	37
Immediate custody	434	500	620	692	778
Other	3	14	22	21	29
All offenders	498	593	738	789	901

Source: Hansard, 7 September 2011 Col 630W.

and N. Ireland) convicted of possessing a prohibited firearm.[15] For those aged 16–17 in England and Wales (16–20 in Scotland and Northern Ireland) the mandatory minimum is three years. Section 29 of the Violent Crime Reduction Act 2006 added a mandatory minimum five-year sentence for using someone to mind a weapon and the Provisions in the LAS&PO Bill 2011 would insert a new s 139AA in the Criminal Justice Act 1988 (offence of threatening with article with blade or point or offensive weapon on school premises or in a public place) to make a minimum six-month sentence mandatory for an offender over 18 years of age convicted of this offence unless 'unjust to do so'.[16]

5.3.4 **Discretionary, 'automatic', and s 225 life sentences**

The discretionary life sentence, a common law penalty, is available where the statutory maximum (not mandatory) penalty for an offence is life imprisonment: it cannot be used unless a life sentence is legally available (*Hodgson* 1996). Further, this sentence is 'not to be treated as a sentence to be passed for the most serious manifestation of each offence' (Ashworth 2000: 189–90). Until the new protective sentences, notably the life sentence in the CJA 2003, imposed criteria for the imposition of life sentences for offences to be found in Schedule 15 to the Act,[17] the life sentence for all offences was governed only by the criteria laid down some time ago in *Hodgson* (1967). As the Bar Council noted, only the relatively few offences not on that list but which carry the life sentence as their maximum penalty, for example Class A drugs trafficking, are, presumably, subject solely to the *Hodgson* criteria (Bar Council 2006; section 3B) which required the offending to be grave, the offender to be suffering from mental instability and the offender assessed as posing a risk to the public for some (unforeseeable) time.

In *Wilkinson* (1983) Lord Lane CJ had noted that the discretionary life sentence should be used only in 'the most exceptional circumstances' and Smith's research, which examined 50 Appeal Court judgments over a 10-year period, found that such sentences were most commonly imposed in respect of rape convictions (23 cases) and manslaughter (12 cases) (Smith 1998). In *Chapman* (2000) the Court stated that it might not require an offence whose seriousness was proportionate to at least five years' imprisonment, if the

[15] Firearms Act 1968, s 51A as amended by the CJA 2003. The Firearms (Sentencing) (Transitory Provisions) Order 2007, SI 2007/1324 was introduced as a response to an appellate decision about the illegality under the Act of the sentence for those aged 16 and 17.

[16] Clause 143(2) of the Bill.

[17] There is also now a Schedule 15A and a proposed Schedule 15B—see section 5.4.

prediction was of very serious future harm, although *Kehoe* (2009) upheld the importance of reserving this sentence for particularly grave offences.[18] *McNee, Gunn and Russell* (2008) clarified that mental instability might not always be a requirement and that the authorities do not require, as a matter of uniform practice, medical evidence to establish good grounds for considering that the offender is likely to be a continuing danger for an indeterminate time in the future.[19]

The 'discretionary' life sentence is now governed—until proposed legislation is implemented[20]—in relation to the offences listed in Schedule 15 to the CJA 2003 by the criteria in s 225, provided that the offender has been assessed as dangerous under s 229. The criteria are that the offence is punishable by life imprisonment and that 'the court considers that the seriousness of the offence...is such as to justify the imposition of a sentence of imprisonment for life' (s 225(2)). However if all those conditions are met the court 'must' impose a life sentence (ibid). Nevertheless, now that the assessment of dangerousness is not constrained by presumptions, these conditions allow the court considerable discretion in establishing both seriousness and dangerousness.

Automatic life sentence

The introduction of what became known as the 'automatic life sentence' in 1997 heralded an apparently different approach to imposing a life sentence but it was very problematic[21] and its history provides lessons for current policy development. It was a mandatory sentence of life imprisonment for a second serious violent or sexual offence: both offences had to be on the list provided. Because the provision inevitably caught people whose convictions were separated by a considerable period of time or whose offence was not of the most serious, the early appeals (notably *Kelly* (1999); *Offen No 1* (2001)) focused on the interpretation of 'exceptional circumstances' and confirmed that this covered only circumstances that were very unusual, special, and extremely uncommon. After the implementation of the Human Rights Act 1998, Offen's further appeal, *Offen No 2* (2001), was successful: the lack of any unacceptable risk of future harm from the offender was taken to constitute 'exceptional circumstances'. The importance of rights jurisprudence in these cases cannot be over-estimated. In Matthew Offen's case, a history of psychiatric illness in childhood, and the fact that he had committed the 'amateurish' robbery in carpet slippers, that he admitted the offence to his friends immediately afterwards, and that the money was quickly recovered, had not been construed as exceptional circumstances in *Offen No 1* (2000). Similarly in Ian Turner's case, a gap of 30 years between the commission of the two relevant offences had not amounted to exceptional circumstances but, when the Criminal Cases Review Commission brought the case back to the Appeal Court after *Offen No 2*, the imposition of the automatic life sentence was overturned because Turner presented no risk to the public (*Turner* (2001)).[22] So *Offen* established that the justifying focus of any form of preventive sentence had to be on risk of future harm to the public.[23]

When imposing life sentences the court must specify the part of the sentence—the minimum term—which is to be served for the purposes of punishment and deterrence. This should equate to one-half to two-thirds of what would have been the appropriate determinate sentence. As discussed in section 5.5.3, the determination and the consequences of the minimum term are very important.

[18] For further discussion of recent cases on life imprisonment see Ashworth (2010: 229–231).

[19] For further discussion of the issue of mental instability see the second edition of this book at pp 155–6.

[20] See the Online Resource Centre for updates.

[21] In 2002, 44 offenders were given automatic life sentences under s 109 (Home Office 2003g: Table 4G).

[22] See also *Stark* (2002), *Watkins* (2002).

[23] See *Baff* (2003), and *Wallace* (2001).

The criteria introduced by the CJA 2003 for the life sentence and for the sentence of imprisonment for public protection (IPP), whose effect is almost identical to life imprisonment, have again prompted a focus on the 'discretionary' life sentence not least because of its resource issues. For some time England and Wales—with over 70 offences providing a life sentence option—has had the highest lifer population out of all the 45 countries of the Council of Europe (Prison Reform Trust 2004a) and official estimates suggest that—had the law not been changed—the number of offenders on the IPP sentence by 2012 would have amounted to a third of the current prison population (see, for example, Carter Report 2007: 7; The Howard League for Penal Reform 2007). We deal with the IPP sentence in section 5.4.

5.3.5 **Extended sentences**

Henham's research revealed a judicial preference for the extended sentence provided in s 85 of the PCCSA 2000 over the LTC sentence that was then available (Henham 2001: 707). The precursor of this extended sentence was in s 44 of the CJA 1991, which empowered the courts to make an order extending the period of release on licence in regard to sexual offences (then for sexual and violent offences, ss 58–62 of the Crime and Disorder Act (CDA) 1998). As consolidated, s 85 of the PCCSA 2000 allowed an extension to be added to commensurate or LTC sentences if the normal period of licence was inadequate for the purpose of rehabilitation and crime prevention.

The CJA 2003 provided a new extended sentence with similar effects. As passed s 227 required the courts to impose an extended sentence on an offender over 18 years if the offender was deemed 'dangerous' under s 229, if the offence was one of those specified in Schedule 15 to the Act and it was not a 'serious' offence as defined in the Act. *Lang* (2005) gave guidance on the use of extended sentences as first enacted, emphasising that the custodial term must be a proportionate one and that the **parsimony principle** applies (ibid: para 12).

However, after extensive criticism, s 15 of the Criminal Justice and Immigration Act (CJIA) 2008 amended s 227 of the CJA 2003 such that the court now has a power rather than a duty to impose an extended sentence, to be exercised only where either of two conditions is met: the immediate offence must attract an 'appropriate custodial period' of at least four years; or the offender has on a previous occasion been convicted of one of the 23 offences listed in Schedule 15A for England and Wales, with separate lists for Scotland and Northern Ireland.

The extension period of the current extended sentence must not exceed five years for a specified violent offence or eight years for a specified sexual offence. The whole must not exceed the maximum allowed for the offence (ss 227 and 228 for adults and minors respectively).

5.4 Problematic court orders

5.4.1 **Proposals for change**

In July 2011 the Coalition Government announced that it would introduce legislation to amend the framework of protective sentencing set up by the CJA 2003. It said that the current sentences led to inconsistency and were not sufficiently protective in relation to the more offenders. It said it would achieve its objectives by:

- Abolishing IPPs, so that more dangerous offenders can be given straightforward life sentences by judges.

- Introducing a 'two strikes' policy so that a mandatory life sentence will be given to anyone convicted of a second serious sexual or violent crime. Making it the only time a mandatory life sentence must be given, other than for murder.
- Creating a new 'extended sentence' for criminals convicted of serious sexual or violent offences, which will mean they cannot be released from prison until they have served at least two-thirds of their sentence (by comparison to the normal halfway point) and for the most serious offenders only then if the Parole Board agrees it.
- Coupling this with long licence periods for these offenders, so that when they are released from prison they will be monitored for long periods and returned to prison if necessary. This will be an extra five years for violent offenders and eight years for sexual offenders.

(Ministry of Justice 2011f: 2)[24]

The LAS&PO Bill 2011, clause 124 would abolish the IPP and extended sentences currently in ss 225 and 227 of the CJA 2003 and clause 123 would introduce a new sentence—a life sentence for a second listed offence (by inserting a new s 224A in the CJA 2003). The two offences will be from a new Schedule 15B and the offence must merit a sentence of imprisonment for 10 years or more. To qualify for the mandatory life sentence the offender must have been given a life sentence or a determinate sentence of at least 10 years for the previous listed offence.[25] A new s 226A would introduce a new extended sentence in relation to the new Schedule 15A. This new schedule (to be found in Schedule 18 to the LAS&PO Bill) lists a total of 48 offences.

And so we are back to a two strikes provision, albeit with somewhat different criteria[26] which should ensure it is used for the most dangerous offenders. The abolition of the IPP is to be welcomed, as it made more likely the use of indeterminate sentences notwithstanding the fact that the amendments to the CJA 2003 criteria gave back considerable discretion to the judiciary (see next section). It would appear from the document extracted (Ministry of Justice 2011f) that the IPP is seen as too lenient for those who could be given a life sentence. The latest Explanatory Notes to the Bill (7 November 2011) shed no light on this. The report on the LAS&PO Bill by the Human Rights Joint Committee (2011) approves of the repeal but asks that there be legislation to deal with the many prisoners already sentenced disproportionately to an IPP sentence. Given that, even if passed, these provisions will not be implemented immediately, we will discuss in the following sections the current CJA 2003 framework and the 2008 amendments to it (implemented in 2009).

5.4.2 **The approach of the Criminal Justice Act 2003**

It may be helpful to summarise at this stage the approach of the protective sentencing framework set up in 2003 for use with offenders convicted of offences in Schedule 15 to the Act. That Schedule provides a considerable list of specified offences—a total of 153, including 65 specified violent offences in Part I. The current life, IPP, and extended sentences can be imposed only in relation to the 'specified' offences listed in the Schedule but there is an important sub-group of specified offences called, confusingly, 'serious offences'. These are defined as specified offences punishable by imprisonment for life or by a determinate sentence of at least 10 years. All specified offences count as a 'relevant'

[24] Originally available at http://www.justice.gov.uk/publications/bills-and-acts/bills/legal-aid-and-sentencing-bill.htm.

[25] Or an extended sentence under the new provision of at least 10 years.

[26] You might at this stage wish to go back and recall the reasons why the automatic life sentence was abolished.

offence for these provisions (s 229(4)). Both life sentences and IPP sentences apply to persons over 18 and only where 'dangerousness is established: in other words, that 'the court is of the opinion that there is a significant risk to members of the public of serious harm occasioned by the commission by him of further specified offences' (s 225(1)(b)). The life sentences and IPP sentences are both indeterminate sentences, the Act specifically stating that the court should specify a tariff period when imposing the new IPP sentence (s 225(4)). Schedule 18 to the Act also amended s 31 of the CSA 1997 to include reference to the new sentence (see section 5.5.3).

These provisions, as passed in 2003, in effect provided mandatory sentences. If the criteria were met, the court 'must' impose the relevant sentence of imprisonment or an extended sentence. The choice of sentence depended on whether or not the 'specified' offence was also a 'serious' offence. The life sentences and the IPP sentences in s 225 are applicable only to those offenders who have been convicted of offences defined as 'serious offences'; the extended sentences were also applicable only to specified offences which were not also serious offences as defined in the CJA 2003.

Difficulties arose in relation to two parts of the new framework which have led to legislative change: the assessment of dangerousness and the mandatory nature of the criteria for imposing the IPP sentence. We will deal with the latter first and then move on to dangerousness.

5.4.3 **The IPP sentence**

The IPP sentence is an indeterminate sentence, in effect a life sentence although with different provisions for release. As originally enacted, providing the dangerousness and 'serious' offence criteria were met, and if only one of the requirements for the imposition of a life sentence (whether legally available and whether the offending was sufficiently serious) could be met, the court was mandated to impose an IPP sentence.

This lack of judicial discretion led to the imposition of IPP sentences in relation to less serious trigger offences which would not have led to an indeterminate sentence before 2003. As the Carter Report noted:

> The fact that an IPP must be given, no matter how serious or otherwise the trigger offence, has led to substantial numbers of IPPs with short tariffs.... The Review and NOMS have jointly developed proposals that will mean that the trigger offence must reach a reasonable seriousness threshold. They will allow sentencers much greater discretion about when to give an IPP; those who do merit an IPP will continue to get one.
>
> (Carter Report 2007: Annex E)

The CJIA 2008, s 13 reintroduced more discretion by amending s 225 of the CJA 2003 such that 'may' was substituted for 'must' in relation to the imposition of an IPP: the court is given a power rather than a duty. Further, this power can now be employed only if the offender has met one of the following conditions in a new subsection 3:

> (3A) The condition in this subsection is that, at the time when the offence was committed, the offender had been convicted of an offence specified in Schedule 15A [This is a new schedule to the CJA 2003 listing 'very serious' offences.]
>
> (3B) The condition in this subsection is that the notional minimum term is at least two years.

This 'seriousness' threshold in subsection 3B set at two years minimum custodial time—which applies to the extended sentence as well as the IPP sentence—means that it should be used only for those who would receive at least a four-year determinate sentence. The threshold in subsection 3A is such that Parliament has decided which offences are most serious for this purpose. This means that the court has the discretion to decide that an extended sentence might be more appropriate for an offender deemed to be a risk.

5.4.4 **Assessing dangerousness**

The assessment of dangerousness caused as many if not more difficulties than the mandatory aspect of the life, IPP, and extended sentences in their original wording. The assessment of the offenders' dangerousness is crucial because none of the protective orders are otherwise available. Section 229, headed 'the assessment of dangerousness', gives guidance in relation to the assessment of risk. It does not provide a definition and as enacted in 2003 was, in effect, a presumption which was reversed for different offenders. So, if the offender had no previous 'relevant' conviction (see section 5.4.3) or was under 18 years of age, the court had to take account of all information about the offence and could consider information about the offender, and any pattern of behaviour of which the offences form a part, in making a judgement.

For adult offenders, however, if the current conviction had been preceded by a previous conviction for a relevant, that is specified, offence then 'the court must assume there is such a risk', unless the court considers it 'unreasonable' to so conclude (s 229(3)). This is clearly akin to the automatic life sentence which it replaced and which is discussed in section 5.3.4. The new provisions were drafted specifically to avoid the human rights issue to which *Offen No 2* (2001) drew attention although, as Ashworth noted, the provisions appear to have been based 'on a policy of going as far as possible to minimize or otherwise avoid these rights' (2004: section 5(i)).

Not surprisingly the presumption of dangerousness led to appeals, the first of which was *Lang* (2005). Paragraphs 15–19 in the *Lang* judgment dealt with the assessment of dangerousness. Referring to these sections as 'labyrinthine', Rose LJ stated that '[i]n our judgement, when sections 229 and 224 are read together, unless the information about offences, pattern of behaviour and the offender... show a significant risk of serious harm... from further offences, it will usually be unreasonable to conclude that the assumption exists' (ibid: para 15). Extensive guidance was then given on the factors to be borne in mind in assessing whether there is a significant risk, including the statement that '[i]f the foreseen specified offence is not serious there will be comparatively few cases in which a risk of serious harm will properly be regarded as serious' (ibid: para 17). The Court also made the following forceful comment: 'It cannot have been Parliament's intention, in a statute dealing with the liberty of the subject, to require the imposition of indeterminate sentences for the commission of relatively minor offences' (ibid). It could be argued, then, that the tenor of *Lang* was towards a restrictive interpretation of the new provisions and helped to downgrade the presumption of dangerousness after convictions for two specified offences.

However, *Lang* left considerable discretion in the application of statutory criteria and the somewhat divergent judgments in the cases of *Folkes, McGrady,* and *Thomas* in 2006 led to the following observation:

> The source of the problem is the ill-conceived legislation which deprives courts of discretion in deciding when to use the dangerous offender sentences and when not to do so—it is unlikely in the extreme that any of the offenders in these three cases would have received a sentence of life imprisonment or a longer than commensurate sentence under the earlier legislation.
>
> (Thomas 2007: 172)

In September 2007 the SGC issued guidance which dealt with the assessment of dangerousness in Part 6. It made clear, citing *Lang*, that there are two parts to the 'serious risk' test:

- there must be a significant risk of the offender committing further specified offences (whether serious or not), and
- there must be a significant risk of serious harm to members of the public being caused by such offences.

(Sentencing Guidelines Council 2007b: para 6.1.2)

It further noted that '[t]he court is guided, but not bound, by the assessment of dangerousness in a pre-sentence report' (ibid: para 6.1.4). Again citing *Lang*, it states, 'Usually it would be unreasonable to assume that the offender is a dangerous offender if, but for the assumption of dangerousness, the offender would not be found to be a dangerous offender' (ibid: 6.2.4).

Citing *Johnson* (2006 at 21), the guideline specifically stated that '[t]he existence (or non-existence) of previous convictions does not determine whether an offender is a dangerous offender: an offender with no previous convictions may be a dangerous offender, whilst an offender with previous convictions may not' (ibid: para 6.4.3.1).

Given the criticism, the CJIA 2008, s 17 amended s 229 of the CJA 2001 to remove the two-strikes presumption of dangerousness. The relevant part of s 129 now reads as follows:

(2) The court in making the assessment referred to in subsection (1)(b)—

(a) must take into account all such information as is available to it about the nature and circumstances of the offence,

(aa) may take into account all such information as is available to it about the nature and circumstances of any other offences of which the offender has been convicted by a court anywhere in the world,

(b) may take into account any information which is before it about any pattern of behaviour of which any of the offences mentioned in paragraph (a) or (aa) forms part, and

(c) may take into account any information about the offender which is before it.

The Lord Chief Justice in a case heard shortly after the amendments were enacted made the following comment:

> It is worthy of immediate notice that the statutory assumption of dangerousness in section 229(3) has disappeared. No court will mourn its departure. Its judgment of dangerousness can now be made untrammeled by artificial constraints. That said, the sentencing option of imprisonment for public protection in the appropriate case remains an important sentencing alternative available to the court.
>
> (*Att-Gen's Reference No. 55 of 2008, R v C & other* (2008) para 6)

The removal of the presumption of risk has not reduced the difficulties in assessing risk, however. The CJA 2003 states that:

> The court must obtain a pre-sentence report before deciding that the offender is a dangerous offender unless, in the circumstances of the case, the court considers that such a report is unnecessary (s 156(3) and (4)). Where the offender is under 18, the court cannot conclude that a pre-sentence report is unnecessary unless there are one or more previous pre-sentence reports, the most recent of which is in writing and is before the court (s 156(5)).
>
> (Sentencing Guidelines Council 2008g: 15)

Although *Lang* established that the court is guided but not bound by reports (2005: 17(ii)), there is a reliance on the pre-sentence report prepared by the Probation Service which will have used the OASys (Offender Assessment System) actuarially based tool for assessing the offender's level of risk of reoffending (see NPS 2003; Home Office 2005a). Guidance states that there are three groups of factors that are relevant in the assessment of whether there is a significant risk of the offender committing further specified offences:

- the nature and circumstances of the current offence and the offender's 'offending' history…including whether the offending demonstrates any pattern,
- the offender's social and economic circumstances including accommodation, employability, education, associations, relationships and drug or alcohol abuse, and
- the offender's thinking, emotional state and attitude towards offending and supervision.

(Sentencing Guidelines Council 2008g: para 6.3.1)

There are no easy decisions here. The guidance makes clear that '[t]he existence (or non-existence) of previous convictions does not determine whether an offender is a dangerous offender; an offender with no previous convictions may be a dangerous offender, whilst an offender with previous convictions may not' (ibid: para 6.3.3). Preventive sentencing will always produce moral as well as practical dilemmas when the future must be predicted for sentencing purposes.

5.4.5 **Controlling the dangerous mentally disordered offender**

Policy in mental health as well as crime is 'permeated by perceptions and attributions of risk': mentally disordered offenders who also fall into the current constructions of 'dangerous for sentencing purposes' are then particularly likely to be perceived as 'an unquantifiable danger' (Peay 2002: 747). This is despite the fact that 'most mentally disordered offenders are neither seriously ill nor dangerous' (Burney and Pearson 1995: 292) and evidence from the United States suggests that major mental disorder accounts for up to 3 per cent of violence (see Bowden 1996; Peay 2002: 772–3). Indeed, research suggests that a diagnosis of schizophrenia is associated with lower rates of violence than a diagnosis of depression (see Peay 2007: 513). What is true is that more prisoners have mental health problems than the rest of the population (see Chapter 9, section 9.2.1) and the implications of this are considered in Chapter 7 (section 7.4; see also Chapter 10 in relation to women prisoners).

Those offenders who can be categorised as 'mentally disordered' under s 1 of the Mental Health Act (MHA) 1983 and who meet the necessary criteria can be given various therapeutic disposals. Those provisions allow, when the conviction is for an offence punishable by imprisonment, for the imposition of a hospital order with restriction order under s 41 of the MHA 1983 if a Crown Court considers such an order necessary 'for the protection of the public from serious harm' (see Chapter 7, section 7.4.2). Section 41(1) lists the factors the court must consider in assessing dangerousness and the effect of adding a restriction order is that the offender cannot be released without the consent of the Secretary of State or a Mental Health Tribunal.[27] A person serving a custodial sentence may be transferred to a hospital under s 47 of the Act and a restriction direction can be added. Arguably, such an open-ended order may appear more punitive than a determinate prison sentence. The

[27] Section 40 of the Mental Health Act 2007 removed the power of the Crown Court to make restriction orders under MHA 1983, s 41 for a limited period.

court which imposes a prison sentence on a mentally disordered offender may also add a direction for immediate admission to hospital, subject to restrictions (a hospital and limitation direction under s 45A of the MHA 1983).

The hospital order leads to compulsory admission to a psychiatric institution or unit in a general hospital. These treatment sites are categorised in terms of degrees of security. The highest security hospitals, previously called special hospitals, are at Ashworth, Broadmoor, and Rampton, although patients subject to a restriction order, and others, may also be treated in regional secure units, NHS psychiatric in-patient acute units, or independent hospitals. The number of restricted patients at the end of 2006 was given as 3,601, making it the highest figure for the last decade (Ministry of Justice 2007c; for an analysis of earlier statistics, see Howard and Christophersen 2003) although Table 5.2 (Ministry of Justice 2010e: Table 1, p 3) gives differently calculated figures which show a continuing rising trend.

The focus on danger and security has led, it is argued, to inappropriate 'custodial' measures in secure units and hospitals. For example, the proposals of the Tilt Report (Tilt *et al.* 2000), which examined the issue of security, have been criticised by psychiatrists. 'The emphasis throughout the report on the more tangible aspects of security such as high walls and better locks, and the virtual absence of consideration of the less overt contribution of relational security, fits in with the official preoccupation with "dangerousness" in recent years' (Exworthy and Gunn 2003). Again, the tension between the focus on risk and on treatment is apparent.[28]

If, on the other hand, the use of non-punitive therapeutic disposals is to be promoted for the dangerous but mentally disordered offender, then there are clear difficulties with the current sentencing framework. Section 166 of the CJA 2003 makes clear that courts are not required to pass custodial sentences (where they would otherwise have done) on offenders who are mentally disordered. It does not say they cannot pass custodial sentences and a judge may not be able to impose a hospital order because of the lack of a suitable hospital place. The discretionary life sentence (see section 5.3.4) is also seen as an option (where available as a sentence on conviction) for the dangerous and mentally disordered offender who cannot be fitted into the criteria of the MHA 1983.

Table 5.2 Restricted patients detained in hospital by sex

England and Wales 31 December											Number of patients
Sex	1998	1999	2000	2001	2002	2003	2004	2005 (1)	2006 (1)	2007 (1)	2008 (1)
Male	2,430	2,515	2,536	2,636	2,631	2,720	2,886	2,984	3,159	3,448	3,460
Female	319	327	322	333	358	398	396	411	442	458	477
All patients	2,749	2,842	2,858	2,969	2,989	3,118	3,282	3,395	3,601	3,906	3,937

(1) Figures for 2005, 2006, 2007 and 2008 were derived from a manual matching procedure.

Source: Ministry of Justice 2010e: Table 1.

[28] See Prins (2005), an update of a text first published in 1980, which provides an interdisciplinary approach to the issues raised.

One particular group of the mentally disordered, for whom the provisions of the MHA 1983 have been seen as inadequate by legislators, are offenders suffering from a 'psychopathic disorder' as defined in the original s 1 of the MHA 1983 but amended by the Mental Health Act (MHA) 2007. 'Appropriate medical treatment' must be available for the offender (MHA 1983, s 37(2)(a)(i)) but that is problematic in that such disorders are generally believed to be resistant to treatment and the psychiatric report may not offer the court the reassurance it legally needs.

This difficulty fed into government initiatives for other means to deal with dangerous people with severe personality disorder, notably the DSPD (dangerous and severe personality disorder) Programme (see Department of Health/Home Office 2000; Impalox Group 2007) which became 'a prime focus for service development and legislative provision' in the last decade (see Peay 2007: 518), despite concerns that the programme and associated publicity could 'further demonise this group' (ibid: 519; see also, Seddon 2008) and that forensic psychiatrists found no medical basis for the categorisation as DSPD (see Davies 2010). A recent summary of research studies found favourable outcomes, but wide variations in practice (Ramsay 2011, see also Trebilcock and Weaver (2011a, 2011b). There have been proposals for such persons to be detained indefinitely, until they are no longer a risk to the public, even if they have not committed a crime and regardless of whether there is any effective treatment.

Following the Richardson Report and a Green Paper in 1999, and the White Paper of 2000, a Draft Mental Health Bill was published in June 2002.[29] It proposed a new compulsory treatment order which would be available for those considered a risk to the public but who could not currently be sectioned under the MHA 1983, but the Draft Bill was strongly criticised by a range of professionals on the grounds, inter alia, that the proposed reforms would divert resources from other people with mental health problems, that the treatment proposed was unclear, that civil liberties might be infringed and innocent people detained compulsorily, and that such provisions would increase the stigma of mental illness. In the event, s 32 of the MHA 2007 introduces a community treatment order (CTO) available for a person who had previously been detained in hospital, provided that—inter alia—it 'is necessary for his health or safety or for the protection of other persons that he should receive such treatment' (new s 17A inserted in the MHA 1983).[30]

The justice of new forms of civil detention for the dangerous offender has also been considered by penologists. For example, von Hirsch (1986) acknowledges that in the case of a dangerous physical illness we might accept medical quarantine to protect others but this would be very exceptional and used only if such a strategy proved to be effective in containing disease and provided that the person is not stigmatised. But incapacitation of dangerous or persistent offenders is far removed from this situation. While it might be acceptable if it were an effective strategy, it is difficult to justify if it does not work. In connection with its use in criminal justice, distinguishing between offenders who have committed the same offences is also problematic, as it shifts the focus away from the blameworthiness of the present conduct.

The courts are not required by statutory provisions to impose custody in relation to the mentally disordered and that message was reinforced by the amendments to s 37 of the MHA 1983, which inserted a new subsection 1A. The law now states that, in the case of an offence coming under the otherwise mandatory provisions of s 51A(2) of the Firearms Act 1968, ss 110(2) or 111(2) of the PCCSA 2000, or ss 225–228 of the CJA 2003, 'nothing

[29] See http://www.dh.gov.uk/PolicyAndGuidance/HealthAndSocialCareTopics/mentalhealth/fs/en.

[30] The Mental Health (Care and Treatment) (Scotland) Act 2003, Part 7 introduced new compulsory treatment orders for Scotland, in force since October 2005.

in those provisions shall prevent a court from making an order . . . for the admission of the offender to a hospital'.

5.5 Post-custody and other provisions

5.5.1 Prevention orders

There are several so-called preventive orders, some of which, notably the risk of sexual harm order (see Chapter 1, section 1.6), the violent offender order, and also the serious crime prevention orders (imposed under the terms of the Serious Crime Act 2007, Part 1), can be made by a court without a charge having been brought for an offence at that time. There are other ancillary orders which can be theorised as reparative or as ensuring just deserts are not undermined by profiting from an offence and these will be discussed in Chapter 6 (section 6.2) whilst others may be added to the punishment or be imposed by a civil court. Examples here would include anti-social behaviour orders and parenting orders (see Chapter 8, section 8.4.4 for their use with those under 18 years of age) as well as banning orders (Football Spectators Act 1989, s 14A; Violent Crime Reduction Act 2006, s 1).[31]

All these additional and free-standing orders of an injunctive nature have contributed to the control of anti-social and nuisance behaviour as well as that deemed dangerous. As Ashworth notes, many of these ancillary orders raise serious human rights concerns and often fudge the line between a penalty and prevention (2010: 359–60, 362). Ashworth also points out that breach of such orders is common and penalties for breach may be severe (ibid: 369). These orders, therefore, raise serious issues but space precludes discussion of them all and we will deal with two only, those which relate to offenders deemed most dangerous.[32]

Sexual offences prevention orders

As we noted in Chapter 1 (section 1.6) sexual offences prevention orders were introduced by the Sexual Offences Act (SOA) 2003 to replace the order in s 5 of the SOA 1997. Section 104(1)(b) of the SOA 2003 empowers the court to make such an order if it is 'satisfied' that it is necessary to do so for the purpose of protecting the public from serious sexual harm' whilst s 106 notes that the harm can be physical or psychological. In *Richards* (2006) the court noted that the order was not dependent on a conviction or any particular sentence so that it could be imposed even if an extended sentence under the CJA 2003 (s 227) was not required.

Violent offender orders

The CJIA 2008 makes provision for violent offender orders (Part 9) whereby magistrates' courts are empowered to make orders, on application from a Chief Officer of Police (s 100), of at least two years' duration (s 98). The orders impose restrictions on the offender for the purpose of protecting the public from the risk of serious violent physical or psychological harm caused by the offender committing one or more 'specified offences' (s 98(1) and (2)).

[31] Clauses 72–73 of the LAS&PO Bill 2011 also propose further restrictions in relation to curfews and foreign travel requirements in criminal orders.

[32] Ashworth (2010: 359–70) provides a very useful summary of all the ancillary orders and the reader is directed to that.

For the purpose of these new orders, a specified offence is (only) one of the following (s 98(3)):

(a) manslaughter;

(b) an offence under section 4 of the Offences against the Person Act 1861 (c. 100) (soliciting murder);

(c) an offence under section 18 of that Act (wounding with intent to cause grievous bodily harm);

(d) an offence under section 20 of that Act (malicious wounding);

(e) attempting to commit murder or conspiracy to commit murder; or

(f) a relevant service offence.

The order may be imposed on an offender aged 18 or over who has a conviction for a specified offence (as defined in s 98(3)) and been given a prison sentence of at least 12 months. It can also be imposed on an offender found not guilty by reason of insanity, or who has been 'found to be under a disability and to have done the act charged in respect of a specified offence', and been given a hospital or supervision order (s 99).

The CJIA 2008 also contains provisions for imposing violent offender orders on offenders found guilty in countries other than England and Wales of relevant offences. The magistrates' court must decide that offender has 'acted in such a way as to make it necessary to make a violent offender order for the purpose of protecting the public from the risk of serious violent harm' (s 101(3)). The order does not come into force until a custodial sentence or its licence period (or that of a hospital order or a supervision order) has come to an end (s 101(4) and (5)).

5.5.2 **The justifications for early release**

For an offender the exact date of release from a custodial sentence is clearly very important but early release has also been of importance to the management of prisons and also in controlling and rehabilitating offenders on release.[33] Despite regular bouts of public and government criticism that prisoners are not serving the whole of the prison sentence early release has continued: it is too important a management tool.

The earliest form of early release was the 'ticket of leave' system, awarded for good behaviour to offenders subject to transportation and so aimed at maintaining good order and discipline in prison. This is a response to the difficulty of operating suitable sanctions for what might be termed anti-social behaviour in a custodial setting. This was later replaced by forms of remission—in which time is remitted or taken off for good behaviour in prison. However, the introduction of parole—early release on licence—had a different aim, that of providing an opportunity to control and/or rehabilitate offenders on their release from prison. Custodial time is traded in for the opportunity to either re-integrate the offender more successfully back into the community or put conditions on the offender and allow the possibility of recall to prison for the purpose of public protection. The terms of the release determine whether the non-custodial period operates as a continuation of punishment in any meaningful sense in the community.

Release from custody before the period of custody specified has been fully served provides, then, another example of the co-existence in English law, albeit uneasy, of retributivist and utilitarian principles and also of the co-existence of more than one utilitarian objective.

[33] We examine aspects of early release in Chapter 12 in relation to the post-custody community supervision.

Early release from a custodial sentence has always been viewed as problematic. With a just deserts-based system of sentencing, early release, especially where discretionary, can be seen as a process which upsets all the fine-tuning of calculations of proportionality. Further, there are problems in relation to the legitimacy of the criminal justice system, given the frequently expressed view of the public that prisoners do not 'really' serve their sentences and that, therefore, the system is too lenient. In response a Conservative Government in the 1990s said it wished to establish 'honesty in sentencing' (Home Office 1996a) and enacted, in the Crime (Sentences) Act 1997, Chapter 1 of Part II, a new approach. This would have entailed no automatic early release and a subsequent change in sentencing practice to take this into account. The subsequent Labour Government repealed Chapter 1 and criticism has continued, with further proposals for change. The provisions for custodial sentences in the CJA 2003, whilst aiming at more effective intervention to reduce the risk of reoffending, also attempt to address the issue of dishonesty by introducing a clear scheme of custodial penalties with specified supervision post-release.

Not all early release schemes can be justified in relation to prison discipline or benefits of supervised release, however: significant changes in early release provisions have, on two occasions, been the result of a need to reduce the prison population quickly. In 1940, when manpower was needed for the armed forces at a critical stage in the Second World War, the standard period of remission was increased from one-sixth to one-third; in 1987, at the height of a prison overcrowding crisis, the period was increased from one-third to one-half for offenders serving sentences of less than 12 months. The introduction of the Home Detention Curfew (HDC) Scheme in 1999 for earlier release of prisoners, with the use of electronic tagging, can also be seen in the same context as can the 'end of custody licence' introduced in June 2007, which allows release up to a maximum of 18 days early for prisoners serving terms of four weeks to four years.

Before the implementation of the CJA 1991 any discretionary release through the Parole Board established by the Criminal Justice Act 1967 was essentially granted to 'good' prisoners and required a prisoner to acknowledge their guilt. Release was then seen as another way of encouraging and rewarding good behaviour. As a consequence, whilst about 80 per cent of those serving sentences of less than two years received earlier release under licence the possibly more dangerous or criminally minded had to serve their sentence until the period at which their remission began. They were therefore released directly into the community without supervision, so that, in practice, the 'worst' offenders were not controlled, supervised, or reformed on release. Further, it was seen by offenders as an unfair system and one that led to prolonged prisoner stress.

Finally, an increasingly important rights discourse meant that the discretionary elements of decision making would come under greater criticism. Because of these problems, the government set up the Carlisle Committee whose Report (1988) led to proposals in the 1990 White Paper (Home Office 1990a) that short sentences should no longer be subject to discretionary release but 'dangerous and uncooperative prisoners who might need the full sentence to protect the public' would continue to be subject to discretionary early release (ibid: para 6.10). The 1991 Act also made all release conditional in the sense that the offender is liable to be returned to custody on reoffending.

5.5.3 **Fixed and discretionary release**

Fixed-term prisoners

The law now is that prisoners are released at the half-way stage of their sentence but that does not mean the whole scheme is wonderfully simple, because there are offenders still in prison who are subject to previous legislation or subject to the exceptions. As Padfield notes:

> English rules on early release from prison are a nightmare to understand. Not only have the rules been dramatically and regularly changed...but under each regime different rules apply to different 'categories' of offenders: short-term, long-term, indeterminate, determinate, and so on. In addition, there are difficulties in calculating release dates due to the complex and changing rules on consecutive sentences and the effects of pre-trial remands.
>
> (Padfield 2007: 255)

The law is now to be found in the CJA 2003 as amended by the CJIA 2008 but the scheme set up by the CJA 1991 for determinate sentences had three principles which are still relevant: that all parts of the sentence should have some punitive meaning, that supervision post-release should be for the purpose of public protection, and that decisions on release should be based solely on an assessment of risk factors (Ashworth 2000: 255–7).

The current framework is simpler than that in the 1991 Act. The 1991 scheme had different frameworks for 'long-term' (four + years) and 'short-term' (under four years) prisoners. For short-term prisoners half the sentence was served. For those on sentences of more than a year, early release was made subject to supervision and recall, but those on sentences of less than a year were not subject to supervision by the Probation Service on release. For 'long-term' prisoners release was on licence and set at two-thirds of the sentence and discretionary release had not been entirely abolished.[34]

The CJA 1991 scheme remained essentially the same until replaced by Chapter 6 of Part 12 of the CJA 2003 (see Gullick 2004). Section 26 of the CJIA 2008 brought prisoners serving four years or more who were convicted before 2005 into the general scheme so that they too are released at the half-way stage. Prisoners serving sentences for the equivalent armed services offences are also released at this point but those convicted of sexual or violent offences specified in Schedule 15 to the 2003 Act are exceptions to the scheme.

However, one change proposed by the CJA 2003—for offenders receiving sentences of 51 weeks or less—has not been implemented because 'custody plus' sentences have not been implemented. If such sentences had been implemented no offender receiving one would have been released without moving on to probation supervision. Since this has not been implemented, those serving a sentence of less than 12 months are still released at the half-way stage but are not then under supervision by the Probation Service.[35]

In contrast, as previously noted, all determinate sentences of 12 months or more (except for the extended sentences introduced by ss 227–228 of the CJA 2003) are subject to a duty to release on licence at the half-way stage of the sentence (s 244). This first half of the sentence is the 'requisite custodial period' which has to be served and the second half is the licence period. Since the implementation of the CJA 2003, the court has been empowered to recommend conditions which should be included in the licence (s 238; see also Sentencing Guidelines Council 2004c: 18–19). This is not a duty and does not mean the recommendations will necessarily form part of the punishment: the Secretary of State must simply 'have regard to' the recommendations. Section 239 continues the role of the Parole Board in decision making in relation to life prisoners under Chapter 2 Part 2 of the Crime (Sentences) Act (CSA) 1997.

[34] Section 35 gave the Parole Board the power to recommend the release of a long-term prisoner after half of the sentence has been served if 'safe' to do so.

[35] The LAS&PO Bill proposes amendments—see Online Resource Centre for updates.

There remains the power to release on licence any fixed-term prisoner (except on an extended sentence) before the mandatory release date. Section 246 allows this to occur up to 135 days before that date, providing the requisite custodial period is at least six weeks, that the offender has served at least four weeks of his sentence and at least one-half of the custodial period.[36] The possibility of release on an HDC before the date of automatic release, available previously only for prisoners serving less than four years, is now a possible outcome for all prisoners (CJA 2003, s 246). Those serving less than four years might also be eligible for the end-of-custody licence scheme which could mean release 18 days early. Particular rules for extended-sentence prisoners are to be found in s 247.

Indeterminate sentences

Indeterminate sentences have long raised issues about the use of executive, as opposed to judicial, authority to determine the release date. More recently they have raised rights issues, and several of the more recent changes in case law and statute have been the result of cases brought in relation to rights in the ECHR, particularly Articles 3, 5, 7, and 14.

The law on release from discretionary life sentences, and (as amended by Schedule 18 to the CJA 2003) sentences of imprisonment (or detention for minors) for public protection (IPP sentences), remains that established in the CSA 1997 and Practice Directions from the Lord Chief Justice. For all life sentences, the judge must now set, and explain in court, what used to be called the 'tariff' part of the sentence. Since the *Practice Statement* (*Crime, Life Sentences*) (2002) Lord Woolf CJ, following advice from the Sentencing Advisory Panel, mandated the use of 'minimum term' to specify the part of the custodial sentence which must be served before discretionary release can be considered. For discretionary life sentences this is normally calculated as half of the determinate sentence that would have been passed 'for punishment and deterrence', commensurate with seriousness (PCCSA 2000, s 82A(3)).

However, Lord Carter's Review of Prisons: *Securing the Future: Proposals for the Efficient and Sustainable Use of Custody in England and Wales* (2007) stated that one of the drivers of the current increase in prisoner numbers is the 'greater awareness of risk, and greater political prominence of public protection' (2007: 5), of which one consequence is that the Parole Board rate for discretionary conditional releases had reduced from a peak of 52 per cent of 7,297 cases considered in 2004/5 to 36 per cent of 6,923 cases considered in 2006/7 (ibid: 12). The Sentencing Commission Working Group also noted that '[t]he Parole Board is more risk averse than hitherto... The rate of release on parole decreased from 21.6% in 2004/05 to 14% in 2007/08 for lifer releases' (2008c: para 2.7). On the other hand, as we have noted, there are policy imperatives which encourage early release.

Discretionary release for murderers

For life imprisonment for murder (a sentence 'fixed by law') previous practice was for the trial judge to decide on the minimum term to be recommended to the Lord Chief Justice after the trial. He in turn conferred with the Home Secretary who made the final decision. In *R (Anderson) v Secretary of State for the Home Department* (2002) the House of Lords ruled that this procedure contravened Article 6 of the ECHR and the CJA 2003 introduced provisions to rectify this. Section 269 of the CJA 2003 requires the trial judge to specify the minimum term in open court.

The Supreme Court and Lord Woolf CJ have been greatly exercised with the question of the minimum term for murder, the starting point for decision making about release. The *Practice Statement* (*Crime, Life Sentences*) (2002) gave extensive guidance, a major

[36] For other exceptions, see CJA 2003, s 246(4).

influence being the Practice Statement on the minimum term for juveniles convicted of murder issued after the European Court of Human Rights upheld the Article 6 claims of *Venables and Thompson* (2000) (see also Valier 2003 and Padfield 2002). A revised Practice Direction (*Practice Direction* (*Crime: Mandatory Life Sentences*)) was issued in May 2004 to give guidance in relation to the statutory provisions on setting the minimum term contained in Schedule 21 to the CJA 2003. The 2002 Practice Statement set the minimum term at two levels for murder: a 'normal' starting point of 12 years and a 'higher' starting point of 15–16 (comparable to 24- and 32-year sentences respectively); the CJA 2003 gives starting points (and indicative criteria) of 'whole life', 30 years, or 12 years, and the Practice Direction of May 2004 gives guidance on these categories.

Successful applications to the European Court of Human Rights (see *Thynne, Gunnell and Wilson* (1991); *Hussain v United Kingdom* (1996)) established that all life sentence prisoners have the right to challenge the grounds for continued detention after the minimum period has expired (Article 5(4)). A panel of the Parole Board meets at the prison where the offender is located and the prisoner is entitled to Legal Aid at the hearing. It is also now established that continued detention contravenes Article 5 of the ECHR if it is not justifiable on the grounds of public protection. The case of *Stafford* (2002) concerned an offender who had been released on life licence in 1979, after spending 12 years in prison for murder. He was detained again in 1989–90 following a breach in his licence conditions but was again released on licence. In 1994, when Stafford was convicted of fraud the Home Secretary revoked his life licence for the murder conviction and so, when he became eligible for release from his custodial sentence for fraud the Home Secretary refused to order his release, on the grounds of risk of future non-violent offending. The House of Lords in 1999 decided that the Home Secretary had properly used his discretion and Stafford appealed to the European Court of Human Rights. That Court held that, once the punishment for fraud was completed, no medical or other evidence of risk of future violent offending had been put forward to justify continued detention for murder. Article 5(1) requires a sufficient causal connection between the original offence and the risk of reoffending; Article 5(4) requires that detention after the expiry of the minimum period in custody can be justified only on the grounds of risk of reoffending associated with the original sentence.[37]

For life-sentence prisoners the licence remains in force until the offender's death and many contain specified conditions (CSA 1997, s 31). Section 31A inserted by the CJA 2003 in regard to prisoners serving IPP sentences means that the Parole Board may order that the licence ceases to have effect at the end of the 'qualifying period' provided the offender is no longer deemed a risk to the public. The qualifying period in this instance is ten years (of release on licence). *R v Costello* (2010) (see Update to *SGC Guideline Judgments Case Compendium* 2010) has provided detailed guidance sentencing in relation to an offence committed on licence where the offender had been administratively recalled to prison following breach of that licence, noting the different rules regarding offences committed before or after 4 April 2005.

All these provisions have resource implications. The protective sentences potentially provide longer sentences for more offenders. The early-release provisions reduce the time spent in custody for many offenders, but the new provisions for licence and conditions in licences increase the cost of community supervision. They also enhance the role of the Probation Service in protective sentencing (see Chapter 12). As we have seen, there are also several important rights issues raised by discretionary life, extended and other

[37] For further discussion on these issues see Amos (2004); Shute (2004b).

indeterminate protective sentences. Many cases are currently before the courts and they may effect a change in law and practice. Further, this section has been able to review only some of the issues: see the Online Resource Centre for further developments.

5.6 Conclusions

5.6.1 Critique of current policy

We have already examined the criticisms of incapacitative policies from the perspective of retributivist theory (see section 5.2). There are also specific critiques of the provisions in the CJA 2003, notably that 'the concept of risk is becoming more and more woolly for sentencing purposes' (Carlen 2002), that there are gender dimensions to risk (Hannah-Moffat and O'Malley 2007) and that incapacitation is now part of a 'smorgasbord' of sentencing aims to which the CJA 2003 returns the sentencing framework (von Hirsch and Roberts 2004). At one level these are contradictory critiques—that sentencing on risk is increasing or that it is now simply one of several approaches, including the increasingly important aim of rehabilitation.

However, we have noted the use of a new form of rehabilitation (see also Chapter 12) aimed at increasing desistance from reoffending and we have also referred to the increased use of controlled periods of supervision on release from prison for the same purpose. Public protection—whether via incapacitation or risk management in the community—is the common thread and the public justification for these and a wider range of policies and legislative provisions. What is also apparent is that, whilst the new dangerousness provisions in the CJA 2003 are confined to specific sexual and violent offences, the list in Schedule 15, and the proposed Schedule 15B, is long. Further, 'three strikes' provisions in relation to domestic burglary and drug trafficking remain, and the enhanced role of previous convictions in the calculation of seriousness will increase the sentences imposed on all but first-time offenders.

All these changes suggest that the scope of the class of potential 'risky' offenders is now very wide indeed and Ashworth comments that the concentration on the record of the offender is 'objectionable' because 'the offence is then used as a mere peg on which to hang allegedly preventive (and sometimes severe) measures' (2010: 238). Further, because protective policies are linked to subjective feelings of danger and insecurity, they can justify a dangerous conversion of punitiveness into public protection (Ashworth 2004: section 4) and a legitimation of provisions that pay little more than lip service to rights considerations. Even if such policies increase public confidence and decrease feelings of social insecurity, they are not justified on that basis because the power of politicians and the media could, instead, 'be used to highlight the declining crime rate, the role of alcohol and drugs, the importance of prevention and detection rather than harsh sentences, and other realities' (ibid: conclusions).

Not only from a retributivist but also from a human rights perspective, disproportionate sentences of the kind that have emerged from the protective provisions—at least before the amendment of the IPP criteria—raise serious moral, constitutional, and practical problems (see van Zyl Smit and Ashworth 2004) but which rarely surface in public discussion and media comment. Even if we accept that a measure of (extra) detention for purposes of public protection is justifiable, the crucial question is, given our knowledge of the difficulties of accurate prediction of risk and of the limited effectiveness of extra incapacitation, 'how much inaccuracy and individual injustice can be justified in the public good?'

5.6.2 **Discussion questions**

- Review the ethical and moral issues raised in this chapter by the practice of sentencing for public protection.
- Review the justifications from penal theory for a policy of selective or categorial incapacitation.
- Read the passage below which summarises the results of a Home Office Research Study.

Then answer the following question:

How much inaccuracy of prediction of risk can be justified on the grounds of public good?

> A study of reconviction rates years after their release from long determinate prison sentences among serious sex offenders who were classified as high risk by the Parole Board, found the proportion reconvicted of another sexual offence during both follow-up periods was under 10 per cent, but those who were reconvicted had committed very serious offences (Hood *et al.* 2002). The figures varied according to the type of victim. None of those imprisoned for an offence against a child in their own family unit was reconvicted of a sexual or serious violent crime. Just over one-quarter of those imprisoned for a sexual offence against a child outside the family were reconvicted of another sexual offence and nearly one-third were imprisoned for a sexual or violent crime. Of those imprisoned for an offence against an adult, one in 13 was reconvicted of an offence against an adult and one in seven was imprisoned for a sexual or violent offence within six years of release from prison. All the offenders who were reconvicted of a further sexual offence within the four-year follow-up period, and all but one followed up for six years, had been identified as high risk or dangerous by at least one member of the Parole Board. Where no member of the Parole Board panel had identified a sex offender as high risk, only one was reconvicted of a sexual offence after six years.

5.6.3 **Case scenario**

Read the following case scenario and then sentence Jack as suggested.

Jack and Jill lived together. Jill stopped loving Jack and left him. Jack was very angry and broke into Jill's hairdressing salon and trashed it, causing £25K worth of damage. He was arrested, pleaded guilty and was convicted at the Crown Court, under s 9 of the Theft Act, of burglary in a non-dwelling for which the maximum penalty is 10 years' imprisonment. The relevant Sentencing Council Guideline (2011b) states that the 'starting point' for the highest level of seriousness is two years with a range from 12 months to five years.

- First, sentence Jack under the normal retributivist framework.
- Then sentence again with the knowledge that s 9 of the Theft Act is a 'specified offence' for the purposes of s 224 of the Criminal Justice Act (CJA) 2003 when the intention was to cause unlawful damage in the building in question and that Jack had, some years ago, been convicted of assaulting a former girlfriend. Do those facts make any difference to your sentence? Why?

Guidance is given on the Online Resource Centre.

You may also wish to look now at the sentencing exercise at the end of Chapter 7. This also raises issues around sentencing on risk of future harm.

6

Making amends

SUMMARY

This chapter reviews the various ways in which the sentencing system is able to mandate or encourage offenders to make amends for the harm they have caused by offending. Some of these developments have aimed to ensure the offender does not profit from crime and pays financial compensation to the victim. More recent developments focus on restorative justice approaches. This chapter will, therefore, examine these very different strands of policy and the penal justifications which underpin them, as well as locating them within the current policy emphasis on victims and their rights.

6.1 Towards a restorative justice policy[1]

6.1.1 A different approach?

> We are proposing using restorative justice interventions at each stage of the justice system. Most responses to the consultation welcomed our emphasis on greater use of restorative justice.
>
> (Ministry of Justice 2011a: para 28)

This quote is taken from the Coalition Government's response to *Breaking the Cycle* (Ministry of Justice 2010a) which proposed to increase the range and availability of restorative justice approaches across the criminal justice system. This is the latest in a long line of policy papers and pronouncements which support restorative justice in place of (purely) retributivist or utilitarian approaches to delivering justice. There is, then, cross-party support for restorative justice and it is always publicly lauded but it has not yet, as we shall see, had a transformative effect on the criminal justice system, although there has been some progress. This chapter will, therefore, address this apparent paradox, reviewing the roots and ideas of restorative justice, examining those aspects of the sentencing system which can be seen as restorative and assessing the difficulties halting the progress of restorative justice.

Words and phrases which indicate the emergence of a new concept of 'penal' justice have been appearing in the literature of sentencing and punishment over the past four decades. Words such as making good or making amends, compensation, community, reconciliation, restoration, reintegration, and reparation have not usually been associated

[1] We have entitled this chapter 'Making amends' but are aware that this term has been used to describe one particular model of restorative justice (see von Hirsch *et al.* 2003). However, we use it in its most general sense.

with punishment[2] and have not featured in our reviews of retributivist and utilitarian justifications. These ideas constitute a third paradigm—that of restorative justice.

Whilst all potentially benefit from successful utilitarian strategies, and all may benefit from an enhanced sense of justice through retributivist sentencing, the victim and the community are largely bystanders in these accounts. In restorative justice, the victim and community take centre stage with the offender in the context of new ideas about responding to offending.

However, this chapter is not solely concerned with new ways of encouraging a just response to offending but also with longer-standing means of making amends. Confiscation and compensation have become increasingly important in sentencing but their origins are earlier, and their development was not part of an articulated restorative justice agenda. This chapter, therefore, has sections which are united under the aim of making amends but which are not necessarily conceptually and theoretically coherent. We have decided to deal with the 'old' and 'new' forms of reparation and restoration here because there are links and issues of 'fit' which the courts and professionals are being forced to address. Nevertheless, it is reparation and restorative justice which, by the early twenty-first century, were 'receiving more concentrated attention than ever before from both criminologists and policy makers' (McEvoy *et al.* 2002: 469; see also Weitekamp and Kerner 2002). The European Forum for Victim–Offender Mediation and Restorative Justice was established in 2000,[3] the Restorative Justice Consortium (now Council) in the UK published its *General Principles for Restorative Justice* in 2002,[4] the UK Government published a Consultation Paper on its restorative justice strategy in 2003 (Home Office 2003a), the Domestic Violence, Crime and Victims Act was passed in 2004, and also in 2004 the Government published *Compensation and Support for Victims of Crime* (Home Office 2004a).

Since then, there has been an increased academic interest in restorative justice, evidenced by a plethora of books on restorative justice (see, for example, Aertsen *et al.* 2006; Bottoms and Roberts 2010; Braithwaite 2003; Christie 2007; Hall 2010; Miers 2004; Johnstone 2011; Murphy and Harris 2007; Roche 2003; Shapland *et al.* 2008, 2011; Sherman *et al.* 2007b; Strang 2003, 2007; von Hirsch *et al.* 2005; Woolford and Ratner 2007). However, it is difficult to find as much evidence of practical changes, as Strang notes when reviewing developments in several jurisdictions:

> There is no shortage of writings on restorative justice. Indeed, it seems sometimes that there is more energy put into writing about it than actually doing it. While restorative justice as a justice practice attracts oodles of advocates and scholars and much commentary about its supposed unstoppable spread, there has not actually been very much extensively institutionalized in its most recent manifestation.
>
> (Strang 2007: 204)

The same impression is given by Baroness Miller's comment in a Parliamentary debate on restorative justice in November 2007: 'There was a moment when the Government seemed very keen on restorative justice. Back in 2003, the then Home Secretary, David Blunkett, spent some time talking about it'.[5] A written answer given to Parliament earlier in 2007 suggests one reason why, except in relation to children and young people, despite the continuing high policy profile and academic interest, there is less activity 'on the

[2] You may wish at this stage to complete the first exercise in section 6.5.2.

[3] See http://www.euforumrj.org.

[4] See the Restorative Justice Council website at http://www.restorativejustice.org.uk for information on the organisation and its publications.

[5] Hansard HL 26 November 2007, Col 1101.

ground': 'The Government's strategy is to encourage, but not require, the use of adult restorative justice whilst building the evidence base to establish the impact of its use, particularly in relation to reoffending' (*Official Report*, 14 June 2007; col. WA277). It is clear from *Breaking the Cycle* that the Coalition Government hopes that its proposals have implications for the reduction of re-offending (Ministry of Justice 2010a: para 79). Governments have, then, been concerned not to spend much money on restorative justice unless and until there are proven cost benefits in terms of reduction of reoffending rates. However, as we shall see in the next section, reparative and restorative measures are important in sentencing and punishment because of the coming together of a number of influences and motivations, notably to increase victim satisfaction, but not all of these motivations are consistent with each other.

6.1.2 **Restorative justice**

> Restorative justice has many routes that cannot be easily separated. It emerged as a 'movement' espoused by a relatively small but energetic group of activists, academics, non-governmental organisations and policy entrepreneurs.
>
> (McLaughlin *et al.* 2003: 2)

One important strand in the early movement was that which originated in religious communities who gave priority to the reduction of conflict and the promotion of harmony. This is not surprising as many of the world religions promote restorative justice as an implicit part of their ideas. More specifically, the Mennonite sect in the United States and the Quakers in the UK, for example, were influential in bringing restorative justice ideas to the forefront of debate. Because the principles of restorative justice are more intangible perhaps than those of, say, utilitarianism, proponents may reveal a sort of missionary zeal. The comment made by a restorative justice coordinator that 'you do need a certain amount of evangelical fervour to promote the use of Restorative Justice not only to the public, but also to colleagues and managers in the agencies that make up the criminal justice system' (Jones 2003: 9) endorses the acceptance by proponents of restorative justice in its wider forms that they must persuade others into a quite different way of thinking about crime, conflict, and justice. What is being encouraged is not a new form of punishment but something to replace punishment, a form of penal intervention which does not carry the same connotations as punishment. One of the most influential early writers on restorative justice, Howard Zehr, wrote:

> We define crime as an offence against the State. We define justice as the establishment of blame and the imposition of pain under the guidance of right rules.
>
> I think it is essential to remember that this definition of crime and justice, as commonsensical as it may seem, is only one paradigm, only one possible way of looking at crime and at justice. We have been so dominated by our assumptions that we often assume it is the only way, or at least the only right way, to approach the issue.
>
> It is not. It is not the only possible model or paradigm of justice—not logically, not historically.
>
> (Zehr 1985: 4)

In this article Zehr used words associated with 'restorative justice' such as restitution, atonement, community, victim, accountability, victim involvement in outcome, reintegrative shaming, repairing damage, and problem solving—words which signify concepts underpinning a different paradigm (see Table 6.1).

Table 6.1 Paradigms of justice old and new

Old Paradigm: Retributive Justice	New Paradigm: Restorative Justice
1. Crime defined as violation of the state	1. Crime defined as violation of one person by another
2. Focus on establishing blame, on guilt, on past (did he/she do it?)	2. Focus on problem solving, on liabilities and obligations, on future (what should be done?)
3. Adversarial relationships and process normative	3. Dialogue and negotiation normative
4. Imposition of pain to punish and deter/prevent	4. Restitution as a means of restoring both parties; reconciliation/restoration as goal
5. Justice defined by intent and by process: right rules	5. Justice defined as right relationships: judged by the outcome
6. Interpersonal, conflictual nature of crime obscured, repressed; conflict seen as individual vs. state	6. Crime recognised as interpersonal conflict; value of conflict recognised
7. One social injury replaced by another	7. Focus on repair of social injury
8. Community on sideline, represented abstractly by state	8. Community as facilitator in restorative process
9. Encouragement of competitive, individualistic values	9. Encouragement of mutuality
10. Action directed from state to offender: – victim ignored – offender passive	10. Victim and offender roles recognised in both problem and solution: – victim rights/needs recognised – offender encouraged to take responsibility
11. Offender accountability defined as taking punishment	11. Offender accountability defined as understanding impact of action and helping decide how to make things right
12. Offence defined in purely legal terms, devoid of moral, social, economic, political dimensions	12. Offence understood in whole context—moral, social, economic, political
13. 'Debt' owed to state and society in the abstract	13. Debt/liability to victim recognised
14. Response focused on offender's past behaviour	14. Response focused on harmful consequences of offender's behaviour
15. Stigma of crime unremovable	15. Stigma of crime removable through restorative action
16. No encouragement for repentance and forgiveness	16. Possibilities for repentance and forgiveness
17. Dependence upon proxy professionals	17. Direct involvement by participant

Source: Zehr (1985).

Restorative justice as a new paradigm not only looks for different responses to crime but locates crime in a different context altogether; not the criminal justice system but the whole range of social and interpersonal conflicts and disputes. That wider approach to conflict management not only renders problematic traditional notions of crime but also means that restorative justice proponents have encouraged the use of those alternative dispute resolution (ADR) techniques that have been pioneered by the ADR and mediation movements. Restorative justice shares values of community and individual responsibility and empowerment with the ADR movement (see Mulcahy 2000). Conversely, therefore, some sections of the new 'dispute-processing industry' which has developed in the last 30 years have incorporated and promoted restorative justice principles and techniques in their professional practice (see Kennedy 1990; Olson and Dzur 2004).

An influence on both 'movements' was evidence from historical and anthropological studies to show that the distinction between the civil and the criminal is not universal, and that disputes (including those which might otherwise be categorised as crimes) have been settled in various ways at different times and in different places.[6] Given that restorative justice is primarily concerned with repairing damage done and restoring harmony, the role of the victim is very important in theory and practice, whether the victim be perceived as an individual or a community. Braithwaite, a leading criminologist and influential exponent of restorative justice, notes that it has two important dimensions.[7] The first is the issue of process—how decisions should be made by all those involved in the harm or offending done, and the second dimension is that of values—values signified by those concepts such as reintegration and respect that we have already noted (Braithwaite 2003: 7–14).

So, in relation to process, restorative justice advocates that the victim and/or community as well as the offender should be involved in decision making, so that techniques such as mediation become very important in this process. In relation to values this means that, in the mediation of outcome, the values of reintegration and forgiveness take precedence over notions such as punishment and retribution. For this to happen, the victim or a representative of the community must be involved in the process and also, as relevant, in the outcomes. An outcome may include an apology to the victim or it may include some form of practical reparation to the victim or to the community. This emphasis on values sat easily with the Labour Government's Third Way or communitarian ideologies: the four core values outlined by Le Grand (1998), for example, were community, opportunity, responsibility, and accountability. The emphasis in relation to restorative justice is particularly on encouraging the offender to own a sense of responsibility for what he or she has done and to be motivated, therefore, to put things right.

This does not mean that the objectives of restorative justice are in practice necessarily different from those of the traditional criminal justice system. The restorative aim of reintegrating the offender into the community entails preventing the offender from reoffending, a traditional aim of the criminal justice system. Nor is a desire to be cost-effective and to 'do justice' excluded from thinking in restorative justice. However, the concept of justice is different and the criteria for cost-effectiveness will relate not only to the narrow objectives of the criminal justice system, but may well relate to community 'health' as well as to victim satisfaction and offender reformation.

Although restorative justice is concerned with reparation and reconciliation it still involves denunciation. Censure within a restorative context can record a wrong done but is thought to be less damaging than harsh retribution. 'Reintegrative' shaming of the

[6] See, for example, Roberts (1979); Sayles (1950: chapters 11 and 14); Stein (1984: chapter 5).

[7] For a review of two of Braithwaite's books (2002, 2000) see Sanders (2003).

offender may be effective in deterring him (or her) from future criminality and allow for the offender's reintegration into society on the basis that if the offender is simply stigmatised he will be alienated and less likely to change his behaviour (Braithwaite 1989; Richards 1998).[8] So, crime prevention and deterrence may be achieved in ways other than harsh punishment, as, for example through continuous reparation, and victims may want redress for harms suffered rather than punishment. Restorative justice recognises the autonomy of the offender and victim and some proponents argue that there should be a right for victims to meet offenders and a right for offenders to offer reparation and contribute something back to victims and society (see Wright 1996).[9]

Supporters of restorative justice, in common with the ADR movement, subscribe to one or other of two fundamentally different aims: that of establishing a totally new system of justice/dispute settlement to replace the traditional systems of justice, and that of establishing new techniques and principles to graft onto the old. The remainder of this chapter will examine developments in the UK to see which of these objectives is being pursued.

6.1.3 **Current policy in the UK**

'Rebalancing' the criminal justice system has been a governmental policy aim since the *Justice for All* White Paper of 2002 (see Chapter 1, section 1.5.2) and, as Walklate comments, 'It is taken as axiomatic that such rebalancing means placing the victim at the centre of the criminal justice system and its operations' (2011: 330). Victims, then, have a very high priority in the 'messages' that the Ministry of Justice and the Home Office wish to convey. The latest Green Paper—*Breaking the Cycle*—is littered with references to the victim and to proposals that will improve the outcomes for victims (Ministry of Justice 2010a: see, for example, paras 75–81). Much older examples can be found: *A New Deal for Victims and Witnesses: A National Strategy to Deliver Improved Services* stated that 'the government... wants to do everything it can to make sure victims and witnesses are treated with respect... supporting victims and witnesses is a worthwhile end in itself. It is also fundamental if justice is to be achieved' (Home Office 2003d: Foreword). A year later a Government website, billed as 'the number one online information resource for the crime reduction community', gave the following message:

> The government aims to maximise the use of restorative justice in the criminal justice system (CJS) as it works well at both addressing the needs of the victim and in reducing offending.
>
> Evidence suggests that restorative justice can help to deliver key objectives across the CJS: improving victim satisfaction, reducing crime and re-offending, delivering justice effectively and building public confidence.[10]

The instrumentalist thinking behind these policy priorities was made evident in *Justice for All* which proposed to 'rebalance' and put victims and witnesses at the 'heart' of the criminal justice system (Home Office 2002a: para 0.22) so as to reduce crime and secure more convictions (see Jackson 2003: 311; for recent discussion see Reeves and Dunn 2010; Shapland *et al.* 2011). Similarly, the *Restorative Justice* Consultation Paper stated: 'We also

[8] However, Braithwaite's comment is based on research on white-collar offenders and so might be more likely to work for young first offenders from law-abiding regimes than with sophisticated criminals in large cities (Walker 1991: 48).

online resource centre

[9] For further reading on restorative justice see the Online Resource Centre.

[10] This was previously available at http://www.crimereduction.gov.uk: in a section entitled 'Working with Offenders' available on the website in early 2004.

want a system that encourages responsibility, so that offenders face up to what they've done, and make amends. And we want the wider community to be involved in finding positive solutions to crime and anti-social behaviour' (Home Office 2003a).

Most recently, *Breaking the Cycle* makes clear in the following statement that Government policy is still to increase the range and availability of restorative justice approaches: 'While it is a well established concept in youth justice, restorative justice for adults is sometimes viewed as an afterthought to sentencing. We are looking at how we might change this so that in appropriate cases restorative justice is a fundamental part of the sentencing process' (Ministry of Justice 2010a: para 79). The Paper sets out three strategies:

> Firstly, this is likely to involve using restorative approaches as a better alternative to formal criminal justice action for low level offenders... Secondly, in instances where a court case is likely to lead to a fine or community sentence, we will explore how it could best be used at the charging stage. Here, restoration would be delivered as part of an out-of-court disposal, for example as a condition attached to a conditional caution.... Thirdly, restorative conferences carried out pre-sentence for offenders who admit guilt and who agree to participate, could be reported to the court with the victim's consent as part of pre-sentence reports. They could therefore inform the court's decision about the type or severity of sentence handed down. In some cases, and for some offences, sentencing could be deferred pending successful completion of actions agreed.
>
> (Ministry of Justice 2010a: paras 79–81)

All of these strategies have, as we shall see, been piloted some decades ago or been used with young offenders yet are still being presented as relatively novel. Similar policy proposals and developments can be found in relation to Northern Ireland (see Dignan and Lowey 2000). A number of proposals were put into effect under the Justice (Northern Ireland) Act 2002, notably family group conferencing (O'Mahoney 2004), and the Northern Ireland Office published a *Protocol for Community-based Restorative Justice Scheme* (Northern Ireland Office 2007). In Scotland, too, criminal justice policy has given a high priority to victims. A *Scottish Strategy for Victims* was published in 2001 with an accompanying *Action Plan* (Scottish Executive 2001). The strategy has three 'pillars', echoing English policy objectives: provision of practical and emotional support, information to victims, and greater participation in the criminal justice system. The Scottish Executive also published a Paper (2002a) to explain how the Scottish criminal justice system complies with the Articles in the EU Framework Decision on the Standing of Victims in Criminal Proceedings.

This European Framework was implemented in 2002–6.[11] Article 2 states that '[e]ach Member State shall ensure that victims have a real and appropriate role in its criminal legal system' and that States 'recognise the rights and legitimate interests of victims with particular reference to criminal proceedings'. Against this backdrop of the Council of Europe's concern to ensure minimum standards for treatment of victims across the EU, the UK's policy objectives raises several questions. Clearly a link is being made between victims and the effectiveness of witnesses, but another explanation given by Jackson was that concern for victims was linked 'to the logic of Labour's philosophy that tackling crime effectively' also depends upon 'reviving the spirit of the community and empowering individuals' (Jackson 2003: 311–12). These tensions prompt the question as to whether victim involvement in the criminal justice process is being used as a means to an end of restorative measures to impact on reoffending, a means to improve the victim's health

[11] L 082: adopted by the European Council 2001; for details, see: http://europa.eu.

and happiness, or a means to increase public confidence in the criminal justice system. However, Sanders sounded a note of caution:

> This is often framed in terms of a zero-sum game: what's good for suspects and defendants (less punitiveness, more welfare) is bad for victims and vice versa. Thus increasingly authoritarian penal measures, in the UK for example over the last 10 years, are often justified by government claims to be putting victims 'at the centre' of penal policy... Advocates of Restorative Justice (RJ) describe this apparently win–lose situation as actually a lose–lose situation.
>
> (Sanders 2003: 161)

On the other hand, McEvoy and colleagues have suggested that restorative justice appeals to governments 'because it offers the possibility of taking crime seriously without ever-increasing repression and exclusion' (McEvoy *et al.* 2002: 469) and because it appears as a solution to the perceived need underpinning the proposals of the Royal Commission on Criminal Justice (1993) almost two decades ago, to 'balance' the interests of offenders, state, and victims when formulating criminal justice policy (see Ashworth 1998b: 30–40).

Community

'Community,' although not a newcomer, is now much more prominent in the rhetoric of restorative justice. Community Payback—part of a community penalty (see Chapter 12)—and the piloting of the community impact statement are evidence of the new focus. The latter covers a specific time period and area and aims to illustrate the concerns and priorities of that community regarding crime and anti-social behaviour. The statements are compiled by the police in the form of a witness statement.[12] The statement can be used in conjunction with out of court disposals, such as conditional cautions, as well as at the sentencing stage after a successful prosecution. Whilst this development may well have advantages it would also appear to be a response to the difficulty of implementing restorative justice in regard to particular victims or where there is no clear victim.

The crucial question is whether the possibilities and prospects offered by restorative justice can be delivered in practice. One of the side headings in a Working Paper on the use of restorative justice published by the Commission on English Prisons Today—'The Current State of Play: all talk and no action'—suggests insufficient progress in the first decade of the twenty-first century (Hoyle 2008: 2). The paper was particularly critical of the way that the use of restorative justice in reprimands and warnings for young offenders appeared to have decreased rather than increased. In all settings the best intentions of those committed to restorative justice interventions struggle against limited resources and incompatible organisational goals (ibid: 8). Crawford's statement that restorative justice initiatives in quantitative terms 'remain at the margins of criminal justice' in systems across Europe, North America, and Australasia (2000: 29) is, therefore, still valid although the body of research is now more useful in terms of quantity and quality and there are also signs that there is now an 'industry' of training for the delivery of restorative justice.

'Restorative Solutions' is, for example, a not-for-profit company 'working in partnership with a number of agencies, organisations and other charities in order to develop a capacity to deliver restorative interventions'.[13] September 2011 saw the launch of a Restorative

[12] See http://www.justice.gov.uk/guidance/youth-justice/working-with-victims/restorative-justice/community-impact-statements.htm.

[13] http://www.restorativesolutions.org.uk.

Justice Register of qualified restorative justice practitioners, funded by the Ministry of Justice and the Restorative Justice Council.[14] Subsequently, Crispin Blunt MP, writing to Local Criminal Justice Boards, Community Safety Partnerships, National Offender Management Service Senior Managers, Youth Offending Teams, and local authorities, to offer funding for training, stated he was convinced that '[r]estorative justice is most effective when it is locally driven and therefore responsive to tackling crime and disorder in the local area'.[15] There is also a BTEC qualification in restorative justice.[16] It is, therefore, possible that the time is now ripe for restorative justice to move from the margins.

However, this chapter is also concerned with earlier measures that encouraged or mandated reparation by offenders without necessarily referring to, or being based in, restorative justice. They were, rather, added to the traditional range of disposals justifiable on retributive or utilitarian principles and their presence raised conceptual difficulties. Because, chronologically, they were developed first and reveal other origins for reparative sentencing, we will deal with them first.

6.2 Confiscation and compensation

6.2.1 The historical context: 'traditional' remedies for loss and harm

As we have noted, it would be wrong to think of reparation and restorative justice as totally new concepts. Within modern times, in the English legal system generally—as opposed to the criminal justice system in particular—the place of reparation has been in the civil courts. There have always been substantive laws and procedures by which civil liability can, potentially, be established and a remedy awarded to the 'victim'. Those remedies are contained within particular branches of law such as contract and tort and the remedies take the form of damages—financial restitution—or injunctions, ordered by the court or negotiated in the shadow of the law. However, the norms—the jurisprudence—and the aims of civil and criminal law have traditionally been very different. Whereas the civil law gives remedies, the criminal law aims to punish (whether for retributivist reasons or utilitarian ends) the person who commits one of those 'wrongs' which have been specifically designated as a criminal offence, an offence which is against the public good. So criminal law is activated by the state; the civil law can be activated only by an individual wronged.

In Chapter 1 (section 1.2.1) we focused on the justifications for designating certain actions as ones for which the response must or could be punitive and we contrasted that with possible social welfare, medical, or even military, responses to deviant action. In this chapter, we are not focusing on these particular alternative responses to deviancy but on alternative outcomes for those who have committed offences and for the person wronged. In a country with a traditional criminal justice system, such as the UK, if an action is specified as an offence and dealt with accordingly, the victim's remedy is to see the offender punished by the state. This may be exactly what the 'victim' wants, money not being able, in the victim's mind, to compensate for the wrong done. If that is so, it is a considerable advantage to the victim that the resources of the state are available to apprehend and punish the wrongdoer. On the other hand this may not be what the victim wants.

[14] See http://www.restorativejustice.org.uk.

[15] Parliamentary Under Secretary of State for Justice, letter of 14 December 2011.

[16] Advanced Award in Practitioner Training for Restorative Approaches: see http://www.cspacademy.ac.uk/Community-Restorative-Justice-Academy.htm.

Certainly, increasing evidence of the ineffectiveness and unfairness of the system of civil remedies for harm was one factor feeding into the pressure for change. The attractiveness for the wronged individual of using the civil justice system to achieve compensation or reparation decreased as evidence of the 'roulette' character of civil justice accumulated through the work of radical lawyers and socio-legal researchers in the 1960s and 1970s. To use that system the individual must successfully pass through a series of hoops: the circumstances of the wrong done must fit the legal criteria and it must be possible to pinpoint a named individual as causing the wrong; the claim against the perpetrator must be accompanied by evidence and proof which may be hard for the wronged individual to obtain; the perpetrator must be available but may be in prison, dead, or untraceable; perpetrators must have enough money to pay the damages and must not avoid attempts to make them pay; the person wronged must have the psychological or financial resources to take court action (see, for example, Genn 1988, 1999).

6.2.2 **Influences on policy**

As well as these internal, and increasingly visible, deficiencies in the civil system, external factors contributed to the pressure for alternatives. A new factor coming into play was the focus on victims.

The victim

In the 1980s, Stockdale and Devlin, both Crown Court judges, quoted a Canadian writer, J. W. Mohr, noting that his comment now applied to England: 'There has been a development, even if ever so slow, to shift from principles of punishment, deterrence and rehabilitation to the principle of undoing the harm done by means such as restitution, compensation and community service'.[17] They write of a 'growing concern about the victim' which has 'coincided with increasing disenchantment with the traditional theories of punishment' and their ability to ensure the volume of crime decreases (Stockdale and Devlin 1987: 36). Further, they argue, 'Whatever doubts one may entertain about other aims of punishment, nobody doubts the justice of aiding the victim' (ibid: 37).

This points to some of the new measures being introduced in the criminal justice system at that time by which a person wronged by offending behaviour could gain a remedy for loss. The passage also points to the importance of the victim focus in the legitimation of new approaches in sentencing policy. Such a focus appears as a self-evident 'good': to argue against helping victims is akin to arguing against peace. This raises the question why victim-based policies became so important at that particular time.

The contexts are the changes in governance to which we referred in Chapter 5 when rising crime rates and changing economic climates led to a view that the crime problem could not be solved but only managed (Walklate 2004: 29; see also Garland 2001b). In that transformation, not only have the public voice and interest groups become more influential, but the victim has been 'politicised' (Walklate 2004: 30–2). Consequently, the powerful idea that the state had 'stolen' the 'wrong' (that is, the offence) from the victim (Christie 1977), allowing the victim to feel excluded, powerless, neglected, and uncompensated was, paradoxically, a politically useful one. It prompted self-evident and positive remedies: helping victims to 'cope' with the effects of crime is a welcome policy initiative to a 'less than confident State', tackling rising crime rates which appear impervious to policy initiatives (Rock 2002: 9).

[17] Stockdale and Devlin (1987) citing Grosman, B. (ed), *New Directions in Sentencing* (1980: 26).

By 1997 the authors of a book on victims of crime could begin by stating, 'in less than 20 years, there has been a revolution in the criminal justice system. Each criminal case involves more than the government versus the defendant. There is another party with a burning interest' (Davis *et al.* 1997: vii). The interests and feelings of victims 'are now routinely invoked in support of measures of punitive segregation' and the 'symbolic figure of the victim has taken on a life of its own', argued Garland (2001b: 11; see also section 6.4).

Yet the development of the academic study of victims—victimology—within criminology was problematic, the early victimology being regarded as 'this dismal science' (Burney 2003: 405), the 'lunatic fringe' of criminology (Rock 2002: 3). 'Until the late 1970s, victims were almost wholly neglected in criminology and criminal justice' (Rock 2002: 1), all the four main theoretical approaches to crime and deviance that Rock outlines having no 'place' for victims (ibid). A positivist victimology, the earliest strand, does date back to the middle of the twentieth century with the work of criminologists such as von Hentig and Mendelsohn but this early strand focused upon the responsibility of the victim for a criminal event occurring, a 'blame the victim' approach which hardly improved the plight of victims.[18]

Sanders argues that it was the growing interest in the effects of crime on victims—particularly victims of rape, domestic violence, and race hate crimes—and in victim involvement in the criminal justice system which re-invigorated victimology in the 1980s (2002: 198, n 2) rather than the other way round. Consequently, the campaigning of the feminist and anti-racist movements were influential in the development of a new strand of victimology in the 1980s. However, it is fair to admit, as have Maguire and Shapland, that the reasons for the growth of interest in victims of crime across the world in the last two decades of the twentieth century 'are not totally clear' (1997: 212).

Additional factors

The focus on victims did not, of itself, challenge retributivist-based sentencing. Indeed, the focus on 'just deserts' in sentencing encouraged a focus on restitution for victims. If the punishment must be proportionate to culpability then any profit from offending must be taken into account and, in that process, returned to the offender as goods or compensation. Linked to this development was a very specific influence which stemmed from the increasingly large scale of drug trafficking in the 1980s. Because of the vast sums of money such trafficking involved, with extremely high profits for the criminal, the previously neglected issues of 'the profits of crime' became more important. Confiscation and compensation were prioritised in the Drug Trafficking Offences Act (DTOA) 1986 which specifically targeted drug-related crimes and profits and which became the forerunner of more general provisions, in particular Part VI of the Criminal Justice Act (CJA) 1993. More recently the concern with terrorist activities and the 'laundering' of money for such purposes has given a further impetus to confiscation provisions. Similar legislative developments have happened in other European jurisdictions and in the United States in relation to organised crime generally. They were driven by a sense of justice and of proportionality but were supported, and given examples of implementation, by those campaigning for a new and restorative approach more generally (Richards 1998: chapter 5).

The consolidation of retributivist sentencing was a factor that encouraged those critical of that development to look to other penal philosophies. As we saw in Chapters 2 and 3, in the 1980s in many jurisdictions, and after 1991 in the UK, there was a clear trend in sentencing based more consistently and comprehensively on just deserts principles.

[18] See Davis *et al.* (2003: 2–5) for a review of the strengths and weaknesses of the three perspectives in victimology which developed in the second half of the twentieth century.

This trend did not attract universal approval and was opposed by a body of thinking which desired an outcome-focused approach. Utilitarian theories of rehabilitation and reform were relatively unpersuasive in the 1980s, and proponents of restorative justice consequently tailored their arguments to appeal to this philosophical 'gap'. For example, Richards specifically reviewed the arguments made against classical justifications for punishment and argued instead for restorative justice (1998: chapter 4). Restorative justice was also an impetus for ADR more generally (see Table 6.2).

This range of separate developments since the 1960s has encouraged the development of the policies we have reviewed. The result appears to be three sets of policy aims:

- to ensure the return to the victim, or seizure by the state, of the 'fruits of crime';
- to make greater use of techniques of mediation and reparation in sentencing and in punishment with, more recently, a focus on the involvement of the 'community';
- to focus on the needs and, if appropriate, the involvement of the victim in the processes of prosecution, sentencing and punishment.

Table 6.2 Sources of the mediation movement and their objectives

Source	Objective
1 Access to justice	Involvement of citizens more directly in crime resolution; bring legal institutions closer to the people
2 Victim movement	Satisfaction of victims' needs, both material and emotional
3 Abolitionism	Liberation from state domination and bureaucracy, and specifically the eradication of prisons
4 Decentralisation and local community control	Create community fora and institutions for dealing with own conflicts and misdemeanours
5 Participatory justice	Involvement of citizens in crime resolution in order to make use of community resources
6 Social work professions	Reduction in misbehaviour by (a) encouraging social responsibility in offenders, (b) involving their families and other community supports, and (c) reducing the stigma of prosecution
7 Some legal professionals and various 'liberal' pressure groups	Find more effective means of dealing with crime which are also more humanitarian and less reliant on punishment
8 Caseload and resource crisis in criminal justice	Find less costly and de-escalatory methods of dealing with crime
9 Privatisation	Reduction in state responsibility in favour of market forces
10 Conflict resolution movement	Apply constructive conflict resolution techniques and problem-solving approach in favour of more lasting resolutions
11 Restorative justice	Synthesis of several of the above, notably 2–7 and 10

Source: Marshall (1997).

This latter aim is both an independent strand and one which feeds into the previous two strands. Nevertheless the development of new forms of confiscation and compensation to victims 'should not be seen as being associated with a broader victims' movement' (Davies *et al.* 2003: 20) and some of the developments to be discussed in the following section were not in essence the result of restorative justifications for punishment. They were, rather, changes in response to pressures within a largely retributivist framework. It is not surprising that these provisions were introduced before some of the other sentencing changes in relation to victims of offending because they can more easily fit into traditional sentencing frameworks.[19]

6.2.3 **The 'fruits of crime': restitution, forfeiture, and confiscation**

Section 28 of the Theft Act 1968 gave the court the power to order the restitution, the handing back, of stolen goods (or their equivalent) to the victim. This power is now in s 148 of the Powers of Criminal Courts (Sentencing) Act (PCCSA) 2000 but courts rarely make such orders (see Ashworth 2010: 361). The Powers of Criminal Courts Act (PCCA) 1973 originally gave the courts very limited powers of forfeiture of property connected with the offence (s 43) but the amendments made by the Criminal Justice Act (CJA) 1988 extended the courts' powers to any offence, whether indictable or summary, and whether punishable or not by custody (by s 69). Section 143 of the PCCSA 2000 now provides the court with the power to impose a deprivation order in relation any property used in committing an offence if seized at the time of arrest or summons. This would include a car if relevant.

Courts also have a duty to confiscate any proceeds. The DTOA 1986 first imposed this requirement specifically in relation to the growing drug trafficking problem. As previously noted, the CJA 1988, Part VI extended it to the benefits of property obtained in relation to (that is, as a result of or in connection with the commission of) any indictable offence.[20] In 1993 the DTOA 1986 was amended introducing detailed practical provisions to make confiscation easier for the courts to impose and some provisions were re-enacted in the Drug Trafficking Act 1994.[21] The civil standard of proof is to be used to address the practical difficulty for the court of finding and proving what was gained in the commission of the offence. The CJA 1988 was also amended to give more compensation order situations (CJA 1993, ss 27–8) and the Terrorism Act 2002 increased powers in relation to forfeiture orders. Cases have tested the rights compliance of these provisions, *Welch* (1995) finding that confiscation orders are to be considered as a penalty, and so retrospective implementation is in breach of Article 7 of the European Convention on Human Rights.[22] The court commented that the order, following conviction, caused a detriment to the offender, and the aims of crime prevention and reparation are consistent with a punitive purpose.

[19] Nevertheless Stockdale and Devlin pointed to a 'dilemma facing the courts' even in regard to these provisions. They noted the reluctance of the police and the courts to be involved in processes that have the appearance of allowing defendants to 'buy their way out of trouble' by offering or being able to make restitution or pay compensation (1987: 37).

[20] This provision also relates to a summary offence if it is joined with an indictable offence and with a high-value benefit.

[21] This Act and the provisions in the Criminal Justice Act 1988 are still in force in relation to offending before 2003.

[22] The House of Lords has since considered the potential impact of ECHR Article 6 and Article 1 of the First Schedule on the confiscation provisions in s 72AA of the CJA 1988 in *Rezvi* (2002), finding them to be reasonable and proportionate responses to a public interest.

The Proceeds of Crime Act (PCA) 2002,[23] 'designed to make the recovery of unlawfully held assets more effective' (Home Office 2002d), consolidated some existing powers and added new powers to ascertain the whereabouts of proceeds of crime.[24] It is 'extensive and detailed' (Ashworth 2010: 363) and requires the Crown Court—providing the second condition is also met—to make a confiscation order against the offender in relation to any offence if (first condition) the offender was convicted, or committed for sentence, at the Crown Court (s 6(1) and (2)) or if the prosecutor asked the magistrates' court to commit the convicted offender to the Crown Court with a view to a confiscation order being considered (s 70). The second condition is that the prosecutor or the Director of Public Prosecutions asks the court to proceed under s 6 or the court believes it is appropriate to do so (s 6(3)). The court is then instructed to decide 'whether the defendant has a criminal lifestyle' (s 6(4)(a)). If he (or she) has, the court must decide whether he has benefited from his 'general criminal conduct'; if not it must decide 'whether he has benefited from his particular criminal conduct' (s 6(4)(b) and (c)).[25] If the court decides that the offender has benefited from either, it must decide the recoverable amount and make a confiscation order (s 6(5)). Only if the victim is engaged in civil proceedings against the offender does this duty become a power (s 6(6)).

The property which may be confiscated is defined as 'all property wherever situated' and includes money, all forms of real or personal property, and 'things in action and other intangible or incorporeal property' (s 84). Confiscation orders can take precedence over fines, forfeiture, and deprivation orders (s 13), but otherwise do not influence sentencing so can be combined with other penalties. There are no limits on the sum to be confiscated provided it does not exceed 'the defendant's benefit from the conduct concerned' (s 7(1)). Sections 13(5) and (6) of the PCA 2002 also impose a duty on the court to order that monies obtained from the sale of confiscated property should be used to pay part or all of a compensation order if the defendant would not otherwise have sufficient means.

The context for the PCA 2002 is wider than sentencing alone: the concern is with the use of proceeds of crime and illegal laundering of money for terrorist and other organised international crime. Part VII of the Act (which deals with money laundering) imposes much wider—and potentially draconian—duties on the 'regulated sector', which includes practising solicitors: professional advisers must disclose information to help detect money launderers and so ultimately assist the criminal justice system and further the possibility of making confiscation orders.[26] Failure to disclose information obtained in situations not covered by the narrowly defined 'privileged circumstances' (s 330(10)) can amount to an offence (s 331), punishable by a maximum penalty of five years (s 334(2)). If any person is involved in dealings in relation to 'criminal property' (see ss 327–329) the maximum penalty is 14 years (s 334(1)). The thinking is that, 'if you find the hoard you can catch the criminal. That, put simply, is the purpose of Part VII of the Proceeds of Crime Act 2002' (Brasse 2003: 492).

The Serious Organised Crime and Police Act 2005 introduced further relevant measures. Section 97 extends the powers in Part 2 of the 2002 Act to magistrates' courts, with a limit of £10,000 on any confiscation order, whilst s 98 inserted a new s 245A in the 2002

[23] Schedule 12 to the PCA 2002 repealed Part VI of the CJA 1988.

[24] The Halliday Report (2001) dealt only briefly with compensation orders: see para 6.18. For an interesting article on the tax evasion provisions see Alldridge and Mumford (2005).

[25] 'Criminal lifestyle' is defined at s 75 and 'criminal conduct' at s 76.

[26] An implication of the confiscation order for family lawyers is to be found in *CPS v Grimes* (2003) (see *Family Law* 2003: 635). A spouse of an offender needs to be an equitable owner or have a divorce pending; otherwise the matrimonial home could be included in the proceeds that are confiscated from the offender. See also *X v X* (2005) (re confiscation order against husband—case note in *Family Law* 2005: 543–4).

Act such that the enforcement authority can apply to the court for freezing orders as well as recovery orders. Further, ss 95–96 deal with international obligations in respect of forfeiture and freezing of property. In particular the provisions respond to the Council Framework Decision 2003/577/JHA of 22 July 2003 on the execution in the European Union of orders freezing property or evidence.

Nevertheless, there will be benefits to victims where compensation results from confiscation, and where s 72 of the PCA 2002 is used. This provision empowers a court to award compensation without a conviction in two circumstances providing there has been 'serious default' by members of specified bodies such as the police force or the Crown Prosecution Service (s 72). The circumstances are that either a criminal investigation was initiated but did not result in criminal proceedings, or criminal proceedings did not result in a conviction.

Research—based on data held on the central Joint Asset Recovery Database (JARD) and on a sample of 155 confiscation order cases—found that, although the amount of criminal proceeds recovered had increased, there was 'a striking overall reduction between the value of criminal benefit initially assessed by Financial Investigators (FIs) and the amount eventually recovered—a total reduction of around 95 per cent' (Bullock *et al.* 2009: 1).[27]

6.2.4 **Compensation to the victim**

In *Breaking the Cycle* the Government announced its intention to encourage the use of compensation orders but such orders have been available to the courts since the 1970s and successive governments have attempted to increase their use. However an older attempt to find a direct remedy for the victim's loss in the face of offending took two forms in relation to the development of state compensation, and we will deal with that first.

Compensation by the state

Compensation paid to the victim by the state was set up in the 1960s—earlier than the statutory scheme for criminal compensation orders. The Criminal Injuries Compensation Board (CICB), established in 1964, technically as a voluntary scheme created by administrative fiat, was the first such scheme to be set up in Europe. This scheme is separate from sentencing and does not require an offender to be successfully prosecuted and sentenced, although a sentencing court will take into account any compensation paid by the CICB and vice versa so that a victim cannot be compensated twice. Not until 1988 was the scheme given a statutory basis by ss 108–117 of the CJA 1988, with the relevant definitions in ss 109–112 (replaced by the Criminal Injuries Compensation Act 1995).

Nevertheless, the scheme set up in 1964 was highly significant because it meant that the state had accepted responsibility for harm done to citizens through offending. The state very rarely accepts such responsibility and, as Harris noted, 'it is testimony to the political power of the victim lobby that the 1980s should have seen such unquestioning support for this position when the emphasis in other areas of social life was on self-help and personal responsibility' (1992: 60). The European Convention on the Compensation of Victims of Violent Crime was enacted in 1983 to recognise the duty of states to compensate victims if other sources were not available. Such schemes may also be seen as a symbolic act by governments to show concern for victims (see Miers 1990) but they have significant disadvantages for governments because of their high initial cost and the relative inability of governments to control take-up (Maguire and Shapland 1997: 217).

[27] For research on enforcement see Bullock 2010.

In the UK, as in some other jurisdictions where schemes are relatively long-standing, there has been a policy of restricting access to such compensation. In England and Wales and Scotland, for example, the 1964 scheme was originally a very wide-ranging scheme 'providing compensation to any victim of violent crime (or person assaulted in the course of preventing crime) of any nationality who was victimised or injured in Britain' (ibid). Because of the increasing cost of the scheme the Criminal Injuries Compensation Act 1995 introduced an 'enhanced tariff' approach based on types of injury rather than individualised consideration of harm and damage. There has also been a tendency in such schemes to define the kinds of victims that are seen as deserving by states and so, for example, awards may be reduced or refused if victims are not believed to be truly blameless. Maguire and Shapland argue that 'victims see it (quite correctly) as a judgement by the State on the worth of their claim and their status as victim' (1997: 218).[28]

Victims' surcharge

A more recent development has been the establishment of a Victims' Fund in England and Wales with money coming 'principally from imposing a surcharge on offenders and from resources released from changes to the Criminal Injuries Compensation Scheme' (Home Office 2004a: 4). The reason given for establishing the Fund was that the existing schemes did not deliver a good enough deal to victims whose offender was not convicted so the resulting monies would be ring-fenced to fund victim support organisations and schemes. The Domestic Violence, Crime and Victims Act 2004 inserted a new s 161A in the Criminal Justice Act (CJA) 2003 requiring a court to impose a surcharge when dealing with an offender for one or more offences although, if the court wishes to impose a compensation order and the offender has insufficient means to pay both, the court may reduce the surcharge accordingly, 'if necessary to nil'.

The CJA (Surcharge) Order 2007[29] fixed the maximum amount of the surcharge at £15. The amount to be charged depends on the offence(s) committed, the means and age of the offender and how the offender is being dealt with, including whether he is being fined (s 161B(2)). This surcharge came into operation on 1 April 2007 and does not apply to fixed-penalty notices. For administrative reasons the surcharge is currently only imposed on fines: according to Crispin Blunt it raised £10.5 million in 2010–11 but 'This figure excludes deductions taken under the Prisoners' Earnings Act 1996[30] from which we estimate that revenue in the first 12 months, beginning in September 2011, will be up to £1 million'.[31] In this connection there is debate as to whether pay rates for prisoners should be increased so that they are better able to compensate victims. There is also pressure for the surcharge to be used to help fund payment of compensation and a compensation fund is proposed in the Legal Aid, Sentencing and Punishment of Offenders (LAS&PO) Bill 2011.[32]

Compensation orders

The LAS&PO Bill 2011 proposes to make it compulsory for all sentencers to impose a compensation order although, as will be noted, this is in effect the current law. However,

[28] It is worth noting that in Northern Ireland the compensation scheme had to be revised in the light of the particular problems presented by victims of terrorist violence: Criminal Injuries Compensation (Northern Ireland) Order 2002, SI 2002/796.

[29] SI 2007/707.

[30] This Act, which allows deductions for the benefit of victims, did not come into force until September 2011. Previous governments had decided it would be too costly to administer but it was brought into effect by the Coalition Government, the measure having been in the Conservative Party Manifesto.

[31] In a written answer: see Hansard HC Deb, 13 October 2011, c512W 13 October 2011. For a fuller explanation of the figures see the Minister's answer to a question in Hansard HC Deb, 24 October 2011, c56W.

[32] See Online Resource Centre for updates.

the statutory change is to be welcomed if it does indeed lead to an increase in the numbers of orders made, because such orders have a somewhat disappointing history. Currently about 40 per cent of the compensation is paid in the year when it is imposed but, because of the poor payment record, the amounts outstanding are now between £120 million and £150 million.[33] The Chairman of the Magistrates' Association has expressed concern that 'many victims still have to wait a long time for compensation to be paid, this can only cause extra anxiety and difficulty with no closure. We urgently want to see steps taken to collect outstanding compensation orders and ask the Government to again consider setting up a victim compensation fund so that victims can be paid the full amount of compensation immediately' (John Fassenfelt: Statement 21 November 2011).[34]

Compensation orders imposed on individual offenders at the sentencing stage stem from the Report in 1970 of the Advisory Council on the Penal System: *Reparation by the Offender* which led to the Criminal Justice Act 1972 (re-enacted as PCCA 1973, ss 35–38). These provisions gave criminal courts a power and duty to consider making a compensation order at the sentencing stage in relation to a conviction or to offences taken into consideration. The power could only be exercised if the offence had caused personal injury, or loss or damage to a victim, but did not cover compensation to relatives in cases of murder. The Report of the Hodgson Committee (1984), *The Profits of Crime and Their Recovery*, resulted in a statutory power to award compensation to relatives for murder (except car death) (CJA 1988, ss 104–105) whilst the Criminal Justice Act 1982 amended s 35 of the 1973 Act so that a compensation order could be a 'stand-alone' order, in other words it could count as the punishment. The legislation to make provision for compensation orders in Scotland was somewhat later (Criminal Justice (Scotland) Act 1980 Part IV), coming into force in 1981.

The legislation applicable to England and Wales[35] was re-enacted in the PCCSA 2000, ss 130–134,[36] which give the court discretion to impose a compensation order, but if the court does not impose an order when there is an identifiable victim it must give reasons (s 130(3)). Further provisions are that:

- the maximum award in magistrates' courts is £5,000 but there is no limit in the Crown Court (s 131(1) and (2));
- a compensation order can be instead of any other disposal or punishment: PCCSA 2000, s 130(1), except in relation to those mandatory sentences found in recent legislation: s 130(2).[37] The compensation order can take priority over a fine and be the sole punishment but this is rare: Moxon *et al.* (1992) found that 94 per cent of compensation orders had been accompanied by another penalty.

Compensation orders, which may be ordered for damages such as pain and suffering as well as for material loss, would seem to be an ideal response to the problem of victims' difficulties in gaining damages through the civil courts in relation to offences. However, compensation orders raise practical and theoretical difficulties. One problem, as noted, has been the under-use of legislation. Moxon *et al.* (1992: 6) found that, after the 1988 CJA amendments to encourage their use, the award of compensation orders had risen to

[33] According to Helen Goodman MP, Public Bill Committee, Legal Aid, Sentencing and Punishment of Offenders Bill, Session 2010–2, Hansard col 576 15 September, available at http://www.publications.parliament.uk/pa/cm201011/cmpublic/legalaid/110915/am/110915s01.htm#11091556000107.

[34] Available via http://www.magistrates-association.org.uk.

[35] See PCCSA 2000, s 167 for the extent of the provisions of the Act.

[36] As amended by the CJA 2003: Schedule 32 para 117. Sections 137–138 of the PCCSA 2000 deal with compensation orders to be paid by a parent or guardian where the offender is under 18 years of age.

[37] See Chapter 5, sections 5.3.3 and 5.4.1.

(only) 17 per cent of Crown Court cases in 1989 (as compared with 11 per cent before the Act) and to 39 per cent (from 31 per cent) of cases surveyed in magistrates' courts (1992: 10).[38] Figures for indictable offences in 1996 also revealed only occasional use for more serious offences: 19 per cent in magistrates' courts (half in relation to offences of violence and criminal damage), with 8 per cent in Crown Courts (Wasik *et al.* 1999: 662). Scottish research based on data collected 1989–92 found even lower use: 4.6 per cent of persons with charges proved (Hamilton and Wisniewski 1996), a figure which had risen to only 5 per cent in 2001.[39] For England and Wales the situation has not improved overall: 'The trends are broadly downwards for indictable offences and upwards for summary offences' (Ashworth 2010: 326).

Some sentencers may still have difficulties in assessing the amount of a compensation order and also in using an order as part of the 'punishment' repertoire (Maguire and Shapland 1997: 220). Further, the ability to impose a compensation order on an offender being sentenced to custody is limited by the level of prisoners' earnings. The first tier of courts is guided by *Magistrates' Court Guidelines* (now issued by the Sentencing Council). The 1997 version of the *Guidelines* incorporated examples of suitable amounts for various injuries, based on the Home Office Circular of 1993 (see Wasik *et al.* 1999) and the 2003 *Guidelines* increased the amount. Current examples of suggested starting points (from Sentencing Guidelines Council 2008h: 166) are: £1,000 for a fractured little finger, £1,750 for loss of a front tooth, and £3,800 for a laparotomy (6–8 inch stomach scar). Research suggests that small amounts are often ordered and one reason may be that offenders are often not able to pay the full amount. The amount they can pay is assessed in line with assessment for imposing fines. So, whilst case law—and now guidance—allows compensation to be paid in instalments and stresses that there can be some hardship to the offender in paying, there is still a limit to what can be paid and that limit may be less than is due to the victim. (See Chapter 7, section 7.3 for comparable provisions for fines.) If an offender is imprisoned he may have no way of providing—for a long time—the means to pay a compensation order, a fact taken into account in *Sullivan* (2003) where the court stated that '[a] compensation order should not be made if it would subject the offender on release from prison to a financial burden he might not be able to meet without committing further crime'.

A related difficulty, to which we have already referred, clearly concerned Scarman LJ when compensation orders became available: 'compensation orders were not introduced into our law to enable the convicted to buy themselves out of the penalties of crime' (*Inwood* (1974)). So, in line with this thinking, the voluntary repayment to the victim in advance of the trial is normally accepted as a mitigating factor, but the court would require evidence that the offender feels genuine remorse. There have also been instances where the offender has misled the court into believing he had the means to pay a compensation order (and so perhaps avoid a stiffer sentence) when he did not. In *Dando* (1996) the court stated that in those circumstances the offender must pay the compensation or serve a period in prison in default.

All these difficulties[40] arise from the uneasy mix of aims arising from the awarding of what is comparable to a civil order for damages in a sentencing court, where punishment is expected. The *Magistrates Court Sentencing Guidelines* also point up the difficulty of satisfying everyone: 'Compensation should benefit, not inflict further harm on, the victim. Any financial recompense from the offender may cause distress. A victim may or may not want

[38] See Newburn (1988) for earlier Home Office research on the use of compensation orders.

[39] See http://www.scotland.gov.uk/Publications/2010/01/28095318/3.

[40] See Ashworth (2010: 322–7) for further discussion.

compensation from the offender and assumptions should not be made either way' (Sentencing Guidelines Council 2008h: 165). The compensation order ought to be a pragmatic compromise which satisfies judge and victim, but so far it has not always proved to be so.

6.3 Reparation and restorative justice

6.3.1 Mediation and reparation in the 1980s

It was the 1980s which witnessed the development of victim–offender mediation schemes as a result of a burgeoning interest in restorative justice (RJ) and in alternative dispute resolution (ADR). Experimental projects were funded by the state or charitable bodies but they were 'supply led' and had a different rationale from that of both forms of compensation reviewed here. The latter are based on the idea that the state should retain some responsibility for reimbursing the victim of crime, directly or via the sentencing courts. Victim–offender mediation, on the other hand, depends on an idea that offending is a harm which is primarily a matter between individuals, and that the two main people, the victim and offender, should have responsibility for the outcome. The experimental schemes developed in the 1980s therefore took from restorative justice the principle that reparation and apologising to the victim are very important, whereas they took from the ADR movement the idea that the agreement should be voluntarily negotiated and imposed. More recently the involvement of and benefit to the community have been seen as important, particularly in relation to unpaid work by the offender through Community Payback schemes.

The early schemes were implemented in the UK at three different points in the criminal justice system: at the pre-prosecution stage as part of diversion of young offenders from prosecution, at the stage between conviction and sentence, and also as part of punishment itself. These three stages for restorative justice are very similar to those proposed in *Breaking the Cycle* (Ministry of Justice 2010a). In the 1980s the pre-prosecution schemes were possibly of the highest profile and the Exeter scheme set up in 1979 was typical in that minors who had previously been cautioned might be offered some form of what became known as '**cautioning plus**', in which reparation and mediation were a part. Davis *et al.* (1988; see also Blagg 1985; Davis 1992) found that such schemes very rarely gave the victim any practical remedy for harm done, the reparation being in terms of apologies and other symbolic offers of help. Victims sometimes felt under pressure to take part in these schemes of mediation although evaluation of court-based schemes in South Yorkshire showed that participating victims found it rewarding to help young offenders change their attitudes (Smith *et al.* 1988).

Reparation inserted between conviction and sentence can be seen as reparation which gives the offender the possibility of providing himself with mitigation because a report on the outcome of victim–offender mediation is given to the court before sentencing. In the 1980s four such experimental schemes were funded by the Home Office. However, Young found that this link between mitigation and reparation appeared to be 'unpalatable to both victims and offenders' (Young 1989: 464) and he criticised the scheme for allowing the offender little choice as to whether his sentencing would be deferred, which meant victims doubted the voluntariness of the offender's involvement. The inducements to attend mediation were generally seen as counter-productive because 'altruism and contrition is called into question' (Davis 1992: 140) and so two-thirds of the offenders felt that even if they were genuine in their desire to mediate, the victim would still think that they were lying.

The third stage in which reparation was inserted into sentencing and punishment in the 1980s was as part of punishment itself. Such schemes for use with offenders in custody were developed in North America and were referred to as victim offender reconciliation programmes (VORPs: see Umbreit 1994 in Smith and Hillenbrand 1997: 250). In the UK these schemes were pioneered within the youth justice estate, notably at Rochester Youth Custody Centre, the Mount Prison in Hertfordshire, and HMP Long Lartin (Liebmann 2000: 1) and usually entailed group meetings of victims and offenders, not the offender meeting his particular victim.

Research results for these and the other schemes noted were mixed or critical. 'The current attempts to promote reparation in this country are half-baked' wrote Davis and colleagues (1988: 128) and, by the 1990s, the schemes were described as 'bit players' (Shapland 2003: 211; see also Stewart 1998; Table 6.1). So by the early 1990s, one commentator wrote, 'It is now fair to say that, within government circles, mediation and reparation schemes constitute something of a "dead" subject' (Davis 1992: vii). Nevertheless, the professionals involved in these schemes communicated a 'broad consensus that room should be found within the criminal justice process for some kind of reparation or reconciliation' (Smith *et al.* 1988: 378) and the Home Office publicly gave support (ibid: 378–9). Why then were these schemes generally seen as unsuccessful and what light does that shed on current policy proposals?

One possible reason is that 'restorative justice' was rarely used to describe these schemes with many supporters of mediation and reparation viewing them simply as process tools for different end products. Proponents of a wider vision of restorative justice argued that restorative justice principles would locate such experiments differently: 'crime is unimportant... it is just part of a wider problem' (Marshall 1992). Perhaps more importantly, the experiments were also relatively small, time-limited under threat of withdrawal of funding, and scattered across the country. Further, the schemes were 'stand-alone' schemes (Dignan and Lowey 2000: 45[41]) in the sense that there was no specific statutory provision authorising their development and they could have only a limited impact on mainstream practice. Surprisingly, however, the prediction of one very critical researcher that 'the vision that they largely failed to realise will endure, and... the shortcomings of our criminal justice system are so profound that further attempts will be made' (Davis 1992: 1) has apparently been fulfilled. The politicisation of law and order in and since the 1990s has produced a greater willingness on the part of the government to look seriously at any alternatives, including restorative justice. The most recent analysis of research findings from current schemes summarises the situation as follows:

> Restorative justice has made significant progress in recent years and now plays an increasingly important role in and alongside the criminal justice systems of a number of countries in different parts of the world. In many cases, however, successes and failures, strengths and weaknesses have not been evaluated sufficiently systematically and comprehensively, and it has been difficult to gain an accurate picture of its implementation and the lessons to be drawn from this.
>
> (Shapland *et al.* 2011: summary)

We will first examine progress in relation to restorative justice with young offenders.

[41] See http://www.nio.gov.uk for this report to the Northern Ireland Office.

6.3.2 **Restorative justice for young offenders**

Restorative justice has been given greater priority and more resources in relation to youth justice for some time[42] because politically it is less risky and because developing rehabilitative projects is more urgent. Restorative justice projects for young offenders have included victim–offender mediation (between the offender and the victim or a representative of the community), victim awareness programmes, reparation (symbolic in the form of an apology or as a practical piece of work), and family group conferences (FGCs).[43] The Crime and Disorder Act (CDA) 1998, consequently, had a substantial component directed at children and young people (see Piper 1999), and the Youth Justice and Criminal Evidence Act 1999 gave statutory backing for the first time to restorative justice processes in youth justice. The Government presented this reform package as moving the system 'away from exclusionary punitive justice and towards an inclusionary restorative justice capable of recognising the social context in which crime occurs' (Muncie 2000: 14).

Out-of-court options

Chapter 8 (section 8.3.4) reviews the use of restorative processes in relation to reprimands, warnings and the youth conditional caution (YCC). The scheme of reprimands and warnings for first- and second-time offenders, introduced by the CDA 1998, includes referral to a Youth Offending Team (YOT) on a 'final' warning. Victim–offender mediation and an apology or reparation to the victim or community can be part of the programme devised to reduce the likelihood of the young person reoffending. A youth restorative disposal (YRD), piloted 2008–9,[44] gives 'specially trained police officers and police community support officers on-the-spot discretion to hold to account young people who have committed certain minor offences'. It can be used only for a first offence, both the victim and harmer have to agree to participate, it involves a meeting between the victim and offender, an apology and possibly additional action 'to right the wrong caused', and is recorded locally but not nationally. The youth offending team is involved with the police in setting the conditions which can include restorative measures. Evaluation of the scheme showed the average age of the young person receiving a YRD was 13–14, 59 per cent were male (but with big variations between police forces), and shoplifting (52 per cent), assault (22 per cent), and criminal damage (19 per cent) were the main offences dealt with but, again, there were considerable differences between areas (Youth Justice Board 2011c: 3). As another recent report noted, 'restorative justice approaches are now often used as a bespoke out-of-court response to low-level offending where the police and victim agree that an informal resolution would provide the most appropriate outcome for all concerned'. The report added that with young offenders such approaches 'can provide an opportunity for the offender to understand the consequences of their conduct, make reparation and avoid the criminalisation associated with a formal criminal justice outcome' (Office for Criminal Justice Reform 2010: para 4.17).

[42] Harris, for example, notes that 'the UK system, though not devoid of restitutive creativity, has expended much of it on juvenile work' (1992: 62).

[43] For a discussion of FGCs in relation to youth justice in the 1990s see Jackson (1999).

[44] See http://www.justice.gov.uk/guidance/youth-justice/courts-and-orders/disposals/youth-restorative-disposal-pilot-scheme.htm.

Court orders

Reparative components have also been added to court orders for young offenders. The PCCSA 2000 (ss 73–75)[45] provides for reparation orders and action plan orders, although the latter order is now available only for offenders whose offence was committed before 30 November 2009. If imposing a reparation order the court may order the young offender to repair any damage to the victim's property, remove any graffiti from buildings that belong to the public, or take part in 'mediation' with the victim. It usually takes 24 hours to complete a reparation order, spread over a number of days within a three-month period.[46] The reparation order can stand alone and the reparation can be directed at the community or the victim. The CJA 2003 continues the status of the reparation order as a penalty that is not a community order (see Chapter 13). Youth rehabilitation orders (YROs) can also include a requirement that the young offender engage in reparation but the restrictions on liberty imposed by both YROs and reparation orders must be commensurate with offence seriousness (CJA 2003, s 148(3)(b)). This is in line with Recommendation No R (99) 19 of the United Nations Congress on Crime Prevention and the Treatment of Offenders which was adopted by the Committee of Ministers of the Council of Europe on Mediation in Penal Matters: 'The proportionality requirement means that there should be correspondence between the burden on the offender and the seriousness of the offence'. This contrasts with a purely utilitarian approach where a desired outcome could justify a burden heavier than that determined by seriousness.

The Youth Justice and Criminal Evidence Act 1999 Part I introduced the referral order as the presumptive sentence for first-time offenders in the youth court. Referral is to a young offender panel where a 'programme of behaviour' is agreed which can include reparation (see Chapter 8; also Ball 2000: 211–22). YOTs are also encouraged to use restorative processes in the delivery of all intervention programmes (Home Office/Youth Justice Board 2002: para 10.15) which are part of the warning scheme and must use the YJB's Asset assessment tool to determine the young offender's risk profile 'and thereby the intensity and duration of the programme' (ibid: paras 10.11–10.14; see Chapter 13). Similarly referral orders should lead to some reparative component and, in the eleven areas in which referral orders were piloted and researched, the most common compulsory element (in 40 per cent of all contracts) was some form of reparative activity. The most common form of reparation was community reparation (42 per cent), followed by a written apology (38 per cent), with direct reparation to the victim or payment of compensation counting for 7 per cent (Newburn *et al.* 2002: viii–ix). The introduction of the YRO and the Scaled Approach programme (see Chapter 13: section 13.2.1) led to revised National Standards and also revised referral order guidance following the amendments made by the Criminal Justice and Immigration Act 2008 (see Youth Justice Board 2008; also see Chapter 13: section 13.1.2).

Conferencing

Family group conferences (FGCs) and restorative conferencing were promoted in consultation documents of the Labour Government—*Respect and Responsibility* (Home Office 2003b), *Every Child Matters* (DfES 2003), and *Youth Justice—The Next Steps* (Home Office 2003c)—and an extensive literature has been produced in the last decade or so. It is argued that the process of using referral orders 'draws elements from family group conferences

[45] Originally enacted in the CDA 1998, ss 61–64 and 69–79.

[46] For further details see http://www.direct.gov.uk/en/YoungPeople/CrimeAndJustice/Typesofsentences youngpeoplecanget/DG_10028367.

and children's hearings in Scotland' (Ball 2000: 217),[47] whilst the meetings at which the new warnings (and sometimes reprimands) are given should if possible be organised as restorative group conferences.

Different versions of family group conferencing were pioneered in New Zealand and Australia, where there are now statutory bases for their use. In New Zealand the first scheme was set up in 1989 where the impetus for development was the concern expressed by a working party about the 'cultural appropriateness' for the Maori people of the principles of family law derived from a colonial system of justice (King 1997a: 134–5). This concern about the loss of indigenous systems of justice with restorative principles was also expressed in Canada and Australia: see Tauri and Morris (2003: 45).

In the UK, however, there was no such impetus and the early schemes were ad hoc initiatives (Gelsthorpe and Morris 2002: 245; see also Dignan and Marsh 2001) but the context for their use is now as part of statutory orders and processes, directed by extensive guidance.[48] Restorative cautioning or conferencing, developed as local initiatives by police forces in the 1990s (Hoyle *et al.* 2002: 7), is now encouraged as part of the process of giving, inter alia, warnings.[49] Such processes are being encouraged to bring home to young offenders what they have done and so help reduce the likelihood of reoffending. Earlier guidance to the police and YOTs on the final warning scheme stated: 'A restorative approach can make final warnings more meaningful and effective...Research into the delivery of final warnings shows that the use of restorative processes reduces offending...and can be of benefit to victims' (Home Office/Youth Justice Board 2002: para 9.22).[50]

Restorative justice has also been seen as a way of promoting both the welfare and the rights of children and young people. Allen (1996), for example, suggests that taking part in restorative justice initiatives helps restore personal respect and encourages the taking of responsibility, avoids stigmatisation, and promotes reintegration in the community. Likewise, *No More Excuses* (Home Office 1997: 31–2) summed up restorative justice principles as the '3Rs' of restoration, reintegration, and responsibility. However, NACRO has questioned the commitment of the providers of restorative justice projects to the third 'R' of 'reintegration' (NACRO 2003e)—a sign that it might be proving easier to incorporate individual responsibility or restoration—the making of amends—into the criminal justice system than the much wider aim of providing support and guidance to reintegrate a young person into social and economic structures that will decrease exclusion and offending.

The stated benefits of restorative approaches, in helping offenders to understand and regret the effects of their offending, are benefits, research would suggest, that can be delivered only if restorative procedures are done well (Hoyle *et al.* 2002; Holdaway *et al.* 2001: 39). Professional assumptions and biases can undermine the tenets of restorative justice, as can any abuse of process such as the administering of final warnings without a clear admission of guilt. The use of a 'script'—'doing' the techniques—is not effective without a proper understanding of the underlying principles. Dignan makes a similar point that experience has shown that it is 'the dialogue which accompanies the face-to-face meeting with victims and offenders which provides the transformative experience for both parties' (1999: 54). Wilcox *et al.* (2004) compared the reconviction rates of offenders

[47] For children's hearings see Chapter 8 (section 8.2); for discussion see Young (1997).

[48] See, for example, the YJB's *Key Elements of Effective Practice: Restorative Justice, Guidance.*

[49] See, for example, Standard 7 of the YJB's *National Standards for Youth Justice* (B420), available at http://yjbpublications.justice.gov.uk/Scripts/prodView.asp?idproduct=466&eP.

[50] Holdaway and Desborough found that 31 per cent of their sample reoffended within a year (2004: 5).

experiencing traditional cautions with those experiencing restorative cautioning in their Thames Valley Police study but were unable to establish whether restorative cautioning made an impact on 'resanctioning' rates or the seriousness and frequency of subsequent offending. (The study used the word 'resanction' to cover cautions, final warnings and reprimands, and convictions.)

Evaluation of 30 funded projects including final warnings found that the majority of parents and young offenders[51] expressed positive views about the projects, but also suggested that it is difficult to ensure satisfactory meetings with a victim present:

> Despite their benefits, very few Final Warnings were restorative conferences. The overwhelming majority of warnings, 80%, were of the standard type. 16% were restorative warnings and just 4% were restorative conferences. Very few victims were present when a Final Warning was delivered.
>
> (Holdaway and Desborough 2004: 6–7)

More recent research on restorative justice within referral orders comes to similar conclusions:

> Restorative approaches are resource-hungry and should be reserved for cases where the time and resource input gives a good chance of success, rather than a default position for all first disposals.... The key issue... is the inherent tension in directly involving victims in youth offender panels in the English youth justice system. The conclusion is that this process is frequently not working, and can potentially cause more harm than good for the very few victims who are actually prepared to become involved in the process. Given the attitude of many young offenders, and their own particular needs and difficulties, we should be questioning the benefit of encouraging victims to attend youth offender panels.
>
> (Newbury 2011: 263)

There are other obstacles to the success of restorative justice initiatives. Restorative justice is difficult to use in the juvenile secure estate because of the high numbers of young people in custody placed away from their home area where their victims and families live (Youth Justice Board 2004b: summary). Another problem in evaluating obstacles is the fact that it is difficult to make generalisations because of the differing conceptions of restorative justice and the different methods of delivery (Miers 2004: 30).[52] Recent research on Australian schemes with young offenders also draws attention to the difficulties of researching restorative justice in context, asking in particular for more detailed data on the offending histories, offence types and offence seriousness of juveniles referred by police to restorative justice processes (Richards 2010).[53]

6.3.3 **Punishment and payback**

The first chapter of *Breaking the Cycle* is entitled 'Punishment and Payback' and outlines, inter alia the Government's plans to ensure offenders 'will make greater financial reparation to the victim and the taxpayer' and also to use community sentences for 'making

[51] See, also, Hine (2007) for the findings of research to assess young people's perspectives on final warnings.

[52] Miers had evaluated seven schemes conducted for the Home Office in 1999–2000, five dealing with young offenders.

[53] See also Sherman, Strang, and Woods (2010) Recidivism patterns in the Canberra Reintegrative Shaming Experiments (RISE). Canberra (available at http://www.aic.gov.au/criminal_justice_system/rjustice/rise/recidivism.aspx).

them pay back to society and the taxpayer'. This is a continuation of emphases already seen in the CJA 2003 but with a greater focus on making amends to the community, either through unpaid work or through payment into the criminal justice system to benefit the taxpayer.

A conditional caution was introduced for adults by s 22 of the CJA 2003[54] and the generic community order for adults allows for specified requirements which could include unpaid work[55] or restorative meetings (see Chapter 12). Section 201(2) of the CJA 2003 gives details of the 'activity requirement' which 'may consist of or include activities whose purpose is that of reparation, such as activities involving contact between offenders and persons affected by their offences'. The aggregate number of days for any activity cannot exceed 60. Similar requirements can be specified in a licence for prisoners serving the community part of a custodial sentence or for the requirements that can be specified in a suspended sentence order (s 182). As we have seen, both the Labour and Coalition Governments have implemented initiatives to develop work with agencies in the voluntary and local government sectors, and have communicated with key stakeholders to develop training and accreditation policies. Another development is that the mediation and reparation 'as mitigation' schemes piloted in the 1980s have, in effect, been resurrected (see section 6.5.1). The Halliday Report proposed that there be an interim review order: which would be, in effect, a deferment of sentencing for a period of no more than six months (as is currently possible) but with the power for the court to ask for an undertaking from the offender to enable the offender 'to tap into reparation and restorative justice schemes, where they exist, at the pre-sentence stage' (2001: para 6.20). 'The activities carried out and the progress shown would act as a mitigating factor in any subsequent sentence passed' (ibid: 44). The CJA 2003 (s 278 and Schedule 23) introduced this procedure so that ss 1 and 2 of the PCCSA 2000 now read:

> (1) The Crown Court or a magistrates' court may defer passing sentence on an offender for the purpose of enabling the court, or any other court to which it falls to deal with him, to have regard in dealing with him to—
>
> (a) his conduct after conviction (including, where appropriate, the making by him of reparation for his offence); or
>
> (b) any change in his circumstances;

One might question the potential effectiveness of this proposal, however, given the criticisms of the earlier schemes we have already noted.[56] Nevertheless, *Breaking the Cycle* proposed that 'restorative conferences carried out pre-sentence for offenders who admit guilt and who agree to participate, could be reported to the court with the victim's consent as part of pre-sentence reports. They could therefore inform the court's decision about the type or severity of sentence handed down. In some cases, and for some offences, sentencing could be deferred pending successful completion of actions agreed' (Ministry of Justice 2010a: para 81). There appears, however, to be no further legislation in the pipeline. Finally, Appendix 5 of the Halliday Report summarised research regarding, inter

[54] This is in effect a development of the reprimands and warnings system which was already been in operation for minors.

[55] See *Working to Make Amends* which is the report of an inspection of a scheme of enhanced community punishment and unpaid work under the previous sentencing options (HM Inspectorate of Probation 2006b).

[56] Edwards (2006) examined two cases where the Court of Appeal had taken into account—as mitigation—the offender's engagement in a restorative justice programme in prison but these appear to be isolated reported cases.

alia, practitioner support for restorative justice, with support ranging from 34 per cent (judges) to 73 per cent (probation officers).[57] It would be interesting to know whether support is now greater.

6.4 Victim involvement and victims' rights

6.4.1 What role for victims?

The review by the Victims' Champion for the Ministry of Justice of the treatment of victims and witnesses highlighted the following statement in its report: 'A great deal of positive work has been done to improve the support available for victims and witnesses but there is still a disparity between policy and reality for victims' (Payne 2009: 4). This conclusion highlights two issues we will go on to address: that the role of victims is often conflated with that of witnesses whose help is required for the sake of the system and, secondly, that despite an increasingly public and persistent policy support for victims, the practice is often different.

If we approach the issues historically, it is possible to see the role of victims in criminal justice policy in England and Wales changing in three stages: 1960–75—the period associated with the development of compensation; 1975–80—the period associated with the development of specific schemes to support victims; and the period from the 1980s onwards when victim support was institutionalised and a greater involvement of victims in the criminal justice process was demanded (Newburn 1995). The focus on victims in the last two decades has had two very different aspects: one could be called a victims' welfare approach, as evidenced by the Victim Support movement, whilst the other approach is to give victims a status to influence outcome.

The needs of victims were strongly emphasised in *Criminal Justice: The Way Ahead* (Home Office 2001a). Since October 2001 victims have been able to submit a personal statement to the court setting out the effects of the crime on them and their lives. A new Code of Practice for the Victims of Crime became law in April 2006; a document issued under s 32 of the Domestic Violence, Crime and Victims Act 2004 gives the victim of crime the 'right' ('is entitled') to a minimum standard of service; and there is now a Victim's Commissioner.[58]

Apart from the victim's interests in any reparative components of sentencing and punishment, current criminal justice policy, to summarise, covers the following disparate elements:

- victim support initiatives;
- facilities for, and communication with, victims during the criminal process;
- the Victim's Charter 1996 (reviewed 2001–2) and replaced by a Code of Practice in 2006;
- victim personal statements.

This list could be seen as one that progresses from the least problematic to the most problematic aspects of victim-focused policies. The victim supportive initiatives are essentially those where victims are contacted after they have reported an offence to the police and are given counselling and any practical help which is required in order to cope with the aftermath of the offending. Secondly, facilities being provided for victims and communication

[57] See Halliday 2001: Figure 11 and paras 86–89.

[58] See http://www.justice.gov.uk/about/vc.

with them in the course of the progress of the case may also be seen as relatively unproblematic, although not when it overlaps with the issue of support to victims in order to give evidence. That raises issues as to whether the support and possible coaching of victims is unfair to the accused and, more generally, raises the possibility of a conflict between the rights of victims and of defendants and offenders (Fenwick 1997).[59]

It is doubtful that the Victim's Code of Practice (previously the Charter) is a rights-based document, notwithstanding the original subtitle, 'A statement of the rights of victims of crime'. Fenwick argued that the Charter appeared to be 'a response to certain international declarations on victims' rights, including the UN Declaration of the Basic Principles of Justice for the Victim of Crime and Abuse of Power', adopted by the General Assembly of the UN in 1985 (1997: 317). However, in 1996 the subtitle was changed 'to the much less ambitious, but more accurate "A statement of service standards for victims of crime"' (Williams 1999: 387). Since 2006 the Ombudsman has had a statutory duty to respond to complaints by victims of crime in relation to obligations under the Code.[60]

It would appear that the Code can be located within a managerialist discourse where objectives are formulated and standards are set for citizens to be able to complain if necessary. By framing rights in terms of consumerist principles, it 'provides a mechanism for putting added pressure on the public agencies to be more cost efficient and productive' (Williams 1999: 388). However, it may marginalise the more radical, anti-racist, and pro-feminist victim support groups (ibid: 388–9).

6.4.2 **The victim personal statement scheme (VPSS)**

In some jurisdictions the victim has an influential say in sentencing, either by giving a victim impact statement or by being able to decide the penalty. Such schemes, variously called in the past and in other jurisdictions victim impact statements (VIS), victim opinion statements (VOS), or, as now in England and Wales, victim personal statements (VPS), are of great importance because they give victims a limited opportunity to give their views to the court about the impact of the offending on them. A family impact statement is also being piloted (see Chapter 10: section 10.1.2; Department for Constitutional Affairs 2006; Roberts and Manikis 2011). The scheme applies only to offences of murder or manslaughter charged on or after 24 April 2006.[61]

The Government noted, in *Breaking the Cycle*, that there has been 'widespread confusion about whether the personal statement is there to help courts understand the impact of a crime, to help relevant agencies assess victims' needs, or to give victims a chance to express themselves. These purposes do not necessarily conflict, but lack of clarity over the role of the Victim Personal Statement has caused confusion for victims, courts and practitioners' (Ministry of Justice 2010a: 21).

What is seen as particularly problematic is whether a VPS could unduly influence a sentencing decision or be viewed as amounting to a procedural right to be involved in sentencing. For example, in its *Response to Breaking the Cycle: Effective Punishment, Rehabilitation and Sentencing of Offenders* the Judiciary of England and Wales stated that

[59] See, also, JUSTICE 1998: 5.

[60] See http://www.ombudsman.org.uk/make-a-complaint/how-to-complain/the-victims-code-how-to-complain.

[61] See *A Protocol Issued by the President of the Queen's Bench Division Setting Out the Procedure to Be Followed in The Victims' Advocate Pilot Areas*: accessed at http://www.judiciary.gov.uk/docs/victims_advocate_protocol_030506.pdf.

'[t]he court can of course take the VPS into account but must not be bound by it'.[62] The victim personal statement is, then, a far cry from the situation in those states where the victim's family can decide whether the death penalty should be imposed: instead it is seen by its supporters as a desirable form of victim participation in criminal justice.

When such proposals were first mooted for the UK, it was argued that 'the right to submit a VIS may be high in profile but low in improving genuine respect for victims. We should hesitate and reconsider before going further in this direction' (Ashworth 1993: 509). The issues raised were the question of sentencing for unseen results of offending behaviour on the victim, the preservation of defendants' rights, and the difficulty of raising expectations in the minds of victims which cannot be met (ibid: 505–7). Sanders *et al.* also noted that 'a firm theoretical basis for victim participation in adversarial systems has yet to be mapped out' (2001: 448).[63]

In England and Wales the VPS is now produced by the police in consultation with the victim/witness and can be updated at particular stages of the process. Participation is optional for victims and in recent research only half (55 per cent) of all victims who recalled having been offered a VPS had completed one (Roberts and Manikis 2011: 3). In a Practice Statement the Lord Chief Justice also made clear that the extra information it provides about the consequences to the victim will simply be added to all the factors taken into account in sentencing; the opinions of the victim about the sentence are not relevant.[64] Victims appear to think so too: 'Of all respondents who reported having submitted a VPS, less than half (39 per cent) held the view that the statement had been fully taken into account' (Roberts and Manikis 2011: 3).

Recent research has shown that concerns that victims will be more punitive than the judge or the public appear to be misplaced. Dawes *et al.* note that '[w]hile a key criticism of sentencing among the public was that it did not always result in justice for the victim, some victims and witnesses actually tended to be relatively satisfied with the sentences handed down' (2011: section 2.2). They also found that, while the public associated long sentences with justice being done, victims often gave more consideration to utilitarian objectives such as changing the behaviour of the offender: 'I think that's the most important thing [to rehabilitate offender]. I don't think we are here to revenge anybody' (Victim: quoted on p 14).

What is not clear, however, is why victims are given this role in sentencing. Edwards reviews four possible justifications, arguing that none has achieved prominence in the UK (2001: 44–5). One rationale is that the making of a VIS is therapeutic but this is not universal in practice; nor can the VPSS ensure that the criminal justice system operates more efficiently, nor that sentencing outcomes are improved, nor that it will contribute towards establishing a more participatory and rights-based system. 'It is perhaps unrealistic though to expect sentencing procedures themselves to do too much, such as delivering real psychological benefits to victims' (Edwards 2001: 51).

[62] See http://www.judiciary.gov.uk/Resources/JCO/Documents/Consultations/judicial-response-green-paper-breaking-the-cycle.pdf.

[63] This article also reviews the arguments of Erez (1999).

[64] *R v Perks* (2001). However, one of the two exceptions to this is '[w]here the victim's forgiveness or unwillingness to press charges provide evidence that his or her psychological or mental suffering must be very much less than would normally be the case'. See, also, the SGC *Case Compendium*, section on 'Victim's Wishes' and also Edwards (2002).

6.4.3 The role of the Probation Service

The Probation Service has a major role to play in many of the restorative justice initiatives. Probation officers may be the responsible officers for young people aged 16–17 who are given reparation orders, they have to liaise with victims of serious sexual or violent offences in those cases where the offender is sentenced to more than 12 months' imprisonment, and must in those cases distribute the 'Release of Prisoners leaflet for victims'. They are responsible for reparative components of a community penalty and also for any reparative elements of the conditional cautions for youths and adults. Traditionally, however, the focus of the work of the Probation Service has been with offenders and there is some evidence that the Service finds the focus on both the victim and the offender difficult (Wargent 2002) and problematic to translate into practice (Crawford and Enterkin 2001: 708; see also Chapter 12, section 12.3).

A thematic inspection report by HM Inspectorate of Probation focused on the victim perspective in 2000 (Home Office 2000b). In the Foreword the Chief Inspector of Probation noted that he was 'encouraged by the finding that the service has taken a constructive approach implementing the contact service to victims, placing their concerns and safety first... There is ample evidence of cooperation with other agencies which is essential in some cases to secure the protection of victims'. A subsequent inspection found that most of the nine areas inspected had improved their performance on victim contact work, but that there had been a variable take-up rate with three areas achieving a face-to-face meeting in only 50 per cent of cases (Home Office 2003e).

There is also potential conflict for the Probation Service between the aims of punishment and reparation which surfaced in the 1990s. Masters argued that 'the Probation Service would be best to adopt a relational ethos in all their current work' (1997: 243), and Duff (2003) subsequently applied to probation work his ideas on sentencing and punishment as 'communicative penance' within a restorative framework. For him and, he would argue, for the Probation Service, the 'supposed opposition' between restorative and retributive punishment, which he notes 'has become a commonplace amongst theorists', is not a problem (ibid: 195, n 3).[65]

6.5 Tensions in policy, theory, and practice

6.5.1 Critiques

This chapter has reviewed the diverse developments in policy, sentencing law, and practice which in some way try to 'make amends' to the victim, or to society more generally, for harm done or loss suffered through criminal behaviour. In most of these initiatives, and particularly more recently, the victim and restorative justice principles have played key roles. This has raised questions as to the policy imperatives behind these developments and their likely consequences. It has also highlighted the question raised in relation to the Probation Service as to whether and how 'making amends' in its various forms can be inserted into the current criminal justice system and sentencing. This is not simply a practical issue but also one of how practice is justified in principle and theory. The difficulties in drawing conclusions to these issues are compounded by the lack of clear and coherent links between the different aspects of policies to make amends. Difficulties in assessing the benefits of restorative justice also stem from similar deficiencies in linking the different victim roles. As we have seen, and as Miers summarises it, the victim

[65] See also the contributions to the volume by von Hirsch *et al.* (2003).

is cast as supplier of information, beneficiary of compensation and other benefits, and partner in crime prevention (2004: 23). Victims are consumers on the one hand and, given the values of restorative justice, are also participants (ibid: 24). Victims will not automatically benefit from the initiatives promoted on their behalf. Strang drew lessons from research on failed conferences to list the conditions which must be right if restorative practice is to be beneficial (Strang 2003; see also Tickell and Akester 2004: 24–7) and more recent research (Sherman *et al.* 2007b) also focuses on the detail of delivery and targeting.

Restorative justice tools and processes can be fitted more easily and effectively into some aspects of the process of sentencing and punishment process than into others. However, that still begs the question as to whether this can be justified as an 'add-on' to systems underpinned by retributivist or utilitarian justifications or whether the tools and processes can be used effectively to 'restore harmony' only within a system underpinned by restorative justice. We argue elsewhere that retributivist principles should continue to limit punishment and that restorative justice should remain as a useful addition (Piper and Easton 2012). However, we are aware that there are strong arguments for opposing views.

It is not yet clear that restorative justice principles have infused all projects and the approaches of the professionals involved or that the specified outcomes can be delivered for most offenders and victims. As we have seen, research into restorative justice within the delivery of referral orders raised the concern that neither victims nor young offenders were well served. However, in relation to adult offenders, the fourth report of restorative justice research begun in 2001, conducted by Cambridge University and funded by the U.K. Home Office (comparing approximately 400 adult cases in which offenders attended restorative justice conferences to approximately 400 adult cases in which they did not) found that restorative justice conferences decreased reoffending by an average of 27 per cent. Victims participating in the conferences found the experience helpful and positive. In addition, the report found conferences to be much more cost-effective than conventional justice processes (Shapland *et al.* 2008).

Earlier research by Miers had concluded that research in 1999–2000 (Miers *et al.* 2001) offered 'no conclusive support' for the view that restorative justice is more likely to lead to mutually satisfactory outcomes than standard criminal justice responses (2004: 32). He also noted that the mixed findings confirm a 'generally held view among both victims and offenders that such interventions are, at least at the time, "better" than the conventional alternatives' (ibid). Further, the review by Sherman, Strang, and colleagues of research on schemes in the UK was also generally positive but they make some important points: 'The most important conclusion is that *RJ works differently on different kinds of people*. It can work very well as a general policy, if a growing body of evidence on "what works for whom" can become the basis for specifying when and when not to use it' (2007b: 8) and, surprisingly perhaps, '*RJ seems to reduce crime more effectively with more, rather than less, serious crimes*' (ibid; italics in the original).[66]

Shapland *et al.* in their longer term research also concluded that 'overall, the findings suggest that victims and offenders participating in the three restorative justice schemes were very happy with how the schemes operated and with their experiences of restorative justice' and that, although victims had different expectations, most of their expectations were met (2007a: 46). However, they note that 'particularly if [the scheme] is set within a framework provided by criminal justice, participants need to know whether the offender

[66] For further analysis see Christie (2007); Murphy and Harris (2007); Woolford and Ratner (2007).

has tried to complete elements of the outcome agreement and what happened at sentence (if the meeting was pre-sentence). The continuing failures of criminal justice personnel to notify victims of the outcome of cases do not help in this' (ibid: 48).

What is often overlooked in policy discussion, though now well documented, is that in practice the categories of victim and offender are often not separate ones. Many people are both victims and offenders.[67] Indeed, official statistics make clear that high crime areas are also areas with high rates of victimisation. Further, the criminal justice system, and particularly its custodial establishments, has its own potential to victimise the offender (see Chapters 9 and 11). Developing policy through separate categories is unhelpful. As with young offenders (see Chapters 8 and 13), it can lead to distorted images of victims and offenders, and may not provide the best basis for policy development.

Not surprisingly, then, the material covered in this chapter reveals more tensions, ambiguities, and complexities than any other chapter in this volume. Restorative justice has also generated more vivid prose than most topics:

> So restorative justice at the moment is an adventure of research and development, where the research is proving tremendously encouraging in some ways, discouraging in others. As we use empirical experience to repair this leaky ship at sea, we should be careful about being too sure about a plan for the voyage.
>
> (Braithwaite 2003: 4)

As noted, critique has been developed on two levels, the practical and the theoretical: does restorative justice 'work', and are policy and practice conceptually coherent? The two levels are linked in the sense that a focus on practice and 'effectiveness' necessitates establishing the criteria for evaluation: those depend on aims, and they in turn depend on the theoretical frame and the conceptual values that underpin practice. Morris and Maxwell rephrase the research questions into 'are the values underpinning the particular model chosen ... restorative?' and 'what are the consequences of adopting restorative justice processes compared with those associated with the continued existence of retributive or conventional criminal justice processes?' (2001: 267).[68]

However recent governments have focused much more narrowly on a utilitarian aim for restorative justice—does it reduce re-offending? The fourth report of Shapland and her colleagues (2008), using data from their three schemes for adult offenders, focused on this issue and concluded (though with caveats): 'Summed over all three restorative justice schemes, those offenders who participated in restorative justice committed statistically significantly *fewer* offences (in terms of reconvictions) in the subsequent two years than offenders in the control group' (ibid: 66). However, '[w]hen considering the restorative justice schemes summed together in terms of *severity of reconviction* there were no significant differences between the restorative justice and the control groups' (ibid: 67 emphasis in original). They also found that one scheme saved money if all the costs of reconviction were taken into account, others did not (ibid) but that '[t]here were no statistically significant results pointing towards any criminogenic effects of restorative justice (making people worse) in any scheme' (ibid).

There are, then, now good detailed reviews of the research on restorative justice programmes which summarise findings about different outcome measures and

[67] For a review of research and theory about the inter-relationship, and also research about the 'victimisation' of offenders on probation, see Farrall and Maltby (2003).

[68] However as Harris notes, even this approach assumes a consensus that may not exist on the core values of restorative justice (Harris 1998).

different models of victim–offender meetings or FGCs, which compare the results of using or not using statutory frameworks and mandatory referrals, and which focus on the influence of factors specific to particular jurisdictions and cultural contexts. All emphasise that it is not possible to generalise—and many produce findings that are not statistically significant—but there are examples of well-run projects with clear principles which achieve restorative outcomes. Within the confines of this chapter it is impossible to do justice to these reviews where the detail and the caveats are so crucial. What is clear is that 'restorative justice... has now become embraced by the countries of the United Nations as a preferred option for the future resolution of disputes' (Morris and Maxwell 2001: 277) and that recent and current governments in the UK fully support it.

What is less clear is how far such preferences are influenced by evocations of a, perhaps fictional, past time when communities could resolve disputes in such ways (ibid), or are grasped as a desperate attempt to address what is perceived as an ever-escalating crime problem. Consequently, the restorative justice movement now faces the same problems as those faced by the family mediation movement nearly two decades ago. Is it better for the restorative justice movement to keep control of their principles—such as voluntary participation and of outcomes which are not necessarily those of the formal justice system—at the expense of expansion or even survival, or to accept government money and monitoring, and work within a system with different values in order to prove the worth of restorative justice used more widely?

In previous editions of this text we expressed concern that training might not be keeping up with demand for restorative justice practitioners. We referred to the comment of Tickell and Akester that '[a]nger, resentment and hostility will not automatically wither away in the face of good intentions' (2004: 25) and to the example of bad practice given by Roche which entailed a 12-year-old boy agreeing in a restorative conference to the proposal of his mother and the store manager that he wear outside the shop a T-shirt announcing 'I am a thief' (2003: 1). It is difficult to distinguish this from the increasing use of degrading and punitive 'shaming penalties' which can provoke vigilantism (ibid: 18). We have already noted however that the issue of training and registration is now being addressed and we welcome this.

Over 20 years ago von Hirsch wrote: '[I]t is unfair, once the institution of punishment is in place, to shift in an eclectic fashion between condemnatory and non-condemnatory responses: to mediate when the parties are prepared to talk to one another, but punish otherwise' (1986: 36). This focuses us also on the viability of restorative justice and victim-focused policies within a traditional criminal justice system (Shapland *et al.* 2007b; see also von Hirsch *et al.* 2003; Blad *et al.* 2012) Some commentators are concerned, on the other hand, not with the difference between restorative justice and the traditional criminal justice system, but that restorative justice has a 'correctional ethos' embedded within it (Hutchinson 2006: 450). It is not therefore seen as inconsistent with penal developments focusing on preventive and retributivist aims but the concern is that it can have marginalising and repressive tendencies (Hine 2007; Hutchinson 2006). There is also potential gender discrimination in relation to restorative justice programmes which has so far received little attention. For example, case studies of victim–offender conferences in the *Restorative Justice* Consultation Paper (Home Office 2003a) suggest that such meetings might have a disparate impact on boys and girls: the reference by a participant in one case study to 'a broken little girl' is of concern (see Piper 2006: 178–9).

Whether all these fears materialise, and whether the tensions prove easy or difficult to resolve still remains to be seen.

6.5.2 **Discussion exercises**

Reparation

Do the following colour association test:

- *without* taking time to think in any conscious or considered way
- decide what colour you think of when focusing on the word 'reparation'.

If you completed this exercise when you first started reading this chapter you may wish to note whether your ideas have changed. If you are doing this for the first time you might wish to consider what parts of the chapter most influenced your response.

This may seem to be a rather odd way of reflecting on the issues dealt with in this chapter. Our intention is to help you appreciate the complexity of the concept of reparation within criminal justice and the ambiguities inherent in the different ways of encouraging or mandating the offender to make amends. At the Online Resource Centre you will find some comments on responses to this exercise.

Most of the associations suggested by the chosen colours are part of the complex mix of motivations and concepts that underpins the range of reparative and restorative options currently available in the criminal justice process. Understandings of reparation do indeed range from an account-balancing process, akin to a financial 'eye-for-an-eye' approach, to a visionary and, possibly, idealistic paradigm about social harmony and personal reintegration. Not surprisingly, questions such as 'what is reparation?' or 'what does restorative justice mean?' have no easy answer. As we have seen, it is difficult to isolate one perspective or one influence which has been the major determinant on the development of options to 'make amends' for the harm done to property, people, and relationships. For further reading on these issues see the Online Resource Centre.

Sentencing exercise

Ade, a student aged 20, worked on Saturdays in the local newsagents until the proprietor—Mr B—cut down on part-time staff. Because she knew about a dodgy window catch she broke into the shop one night and took several boxes of crisps and chocolate. She sold these to a local youth club for £50 (having been asked to get new supplies), saying that she had lost the till receipt. At the local magistrates' court she was found guilty of burglary. She has no previous convictions.

- Would your answer be different if Ade had worked in an electronics factory and had stolen goods worth £5,000?
- Are there options which include restorative justice that the police and CPS could have used instead of prosecution?

Decide which outcome is appropriate for Ade. You might refer to the sentencing checklist in Chapter 3 (section 3.2.2) and consider, in particular, any restorative options. The Online Resource Centre discusses possible approaches.

7

Mitigating the sentence?

SUMMARY

This chapter examines the issue of the impact of a sentence on the offender and uses financial penalties and policy regarding mentally disordered offenders as case studies. The discussion considers the role of mitigation in retributivist and utilitarian sentencing and, therefore, focuses on whether personal factors should be taken into account in deciding on the appropriate sentence. In particular, it reviews arguments on reduced culpability where there are economic and medical factors which might make (commensurate) penal outcomes unjust.

7.1 Justifying impact as a sentencing factor

7.1.1 Personal mitigation

In Chapter 3 we examined the factors that could mitigate the seriousness of the offending in question and also reviewed the personal factors about the offender which might be taken into account to mitigate the severity of a proportionate sentence (see Chapter 3, section 3.3.2). Such mitigation has always been highly contentious but there is now research which indicates that it plays a crucial role in the sentencing decision (Jacobson and Hough 2007). The researchers summarise their key findings as follows:

- personal mitigation takes many forms, relating to: the offender's past; the offender's circumstances at the time of the offence; the offender's response to the offence and prosecution; and the offender's present and future
- personal mitigation plays an important part in the sentencing decision; it can be the decisive factor in choosing a community penalty in preference to imprisonment
- judges cited at least some factor of personal mitigation as relevant to sentencing in almost half of the 162 cases observed in the study
- in just under a third of the 127 cases where the judge made the role of mitigation explicit, personal mitigation was a major—usually the major—factor which pulled the sentence back from immediate custody
- in a just over a quarter of the 127 cases, mitigation including personal factors resulted in a shorter custodial sentence.

(Jacobson and Hough 2007: vii)

Other research in England and Wales indicates, in particular, how important mitigation is on the 'in/out' line: in those 'cusp cases' where the seriousness of the offending lies on the community/custodial sentence boundary (Hough *et al.* 2003) whilst Scottish research suggests that the criminal history of the offender is very influential in such cases (Tombs

2004) with the result that a relatively minor offence could lead to custody as a 'last resort' (Tombs and Jagger 2006). The implication is that there needs to be a greater awareness of the importance of personal mitigation if more 'cusp cases' are to be moved down the penalty ladder. Lovegrove suggests that the public also needs more detailed information about mitigating factors in the context of real cases. His research in Victoria, Australia used actual cases and judges and the responses of the participants to sentencing decisions showed a much greater propensity to approve of mitigating factors and the application of mercy than has been found in more generalised surveys of public opinion (Lovegrove 2011). He concludes that 'the current trend to harsher sentencing by way of less personal mitigation appears seriously misplaced' (ibid: 55).

As we noted in Chapter 3, however, there is very little guidance on personal mitigation although, as Jacobson and Hough point out, 'personal mitigation casts into sharp focus some fundamental issues about sentencing principles and judicial discretion' (2007: 1) and yet they note that 'few of our respondents made explicit the connection between particular sentencing rationales and particular forms of mitigation' (ibid: 39). Indeed one of their respondents, a judge, who described sentencing as 'terrifying because it's a very subjective exercise', commented that 'when the offender comes into court, and you have that first long, hard look at him, you can see so much in that first split second' (ibid: 48). As Jacobson and Hough conclude, 'a descriptive account of the role of mitigation then poses a set of normative questions about the acceptability of current sentencing practice' (ibid: 61). There is no Sentencing Council guidance on personal mitigation as such but the recent guidance on assault offences has listed 'Factors reducing seriousness or affecting personal mitigation' at Step 2 (starting point and category range) of the seriousness assessment process (after the offence category has been determined: see Chapter 3). For the offence of common assault for example, this includes the following: remorse, good character and/or exemplary conduct, serious medical conditions requiring urgent, intensive or long-term treatment, mental disorder or learning disability, where not linked to the commission of the offence, sole or primary carer for dependent relatives (Sentencing Council 2011a: 25). This development is helpful although—in terms of evaluating the justification—it is a pity that the issue of (further) mitigation of seriousness and personal mitigation are placed in the same list.

Considerations of space preclude a detailed discussion of all forms of personal mitigation but, instead, we will focus on a particular form, that relating to the impact of punishment on the offender (for example, being a carer in the assault guideline), because this ties in with our discussions of the prison experience and of sentencing rationales. Therefore, in this chapter we will review arguments in favour of placing more emphasis on impact mitigation although the approach of the courts to other personal mitigation is very similar to their response in the impact cases we will discuss later.[1] We will be focusing in some detail on the approach of the courts to physical disability, employment, old age, illness, vulnerability in prison, and family circumstances as well as using financial penalties and the court's approach to mentally disordered offenders to illuminate some of the issues. This is clearly a selective discussion of the many aspects of justice and fairness raised by the question of sentence impact. Limitations of space necessitated the choice of issues on which to focus; personal interest and current policy concerns combined, importantly, with the availability of research and analysis, influenced our selection. Further, other issues, notably race and gender, are addressed in Chapters 9–11. Where we may have neglected issues, this is not to say they are of any less importance. We will take up the theme of mitigation and personal circumstances in Chapter 10 where we review

[1] In the second edition of this text (at p 10) we used the following case as an example: *Robinson* (1993).

socio-economic factors associated with offending as well as related personal factors, such as family issues, which are more difficult to theorise as coming within penal, rather than social, policy. Chapter 11 will then examine the difficulties posed for the Prison Service by the fact that particular types of prisoner and categories of problem are over-represented in the prison population.

7.1.2 Equal impact

So far in our analysis of sentencing and punishment, we have looked only tangentially at the question of the impact of a particular punishment on an individual offender. We have reviewed research on the impact on offenders generally of deterrent and incapacitative sentencing (in Chapters 4 and 5) and we will deal with the general effect of rehabilitative penalties in Chapter 12. In Chapter 6 we also focused on the increasing use of confiscation orders so that the punishment is not negated by the offender benefiting from offending (section 6.2.2).

This low priority for the issue of sentence impact is reflective of the fact that, whilst current policy focuses on the offender and what will deter or reform him most effectively, 'just deserts' is still the dominant sentencing principle and, consequently, what Shapland (1981: 55) categorised as 'future personal circumstances' present particular difficulties for retributivist theory. Not only that, this is also an issue where public opinion is a policy factor.[2] The public apparently needs to 'see' equality of treatment for similarly serious offences: an outcome that 'looks' too lenient or too severe in comparison to known cases generates a sense of injustice and undermines the legitimacy of the sentencing system. This approach to equality in sentencing appears to assume that the offender is not a variable in this calculation: the impact of the punishment is the same for all offenders, or any differential impact is irrelevant. Yet it is possible to argue that a retributivist approach to sentencing does not depend on an end product of a fixed amount of punishment for a particular amount of seriousness. It can also operate in terms of a proportionate amount of punishment impact where, in effect, the 'quality' of the experience is taken into account, rather than simply the quantity. This form of equal treatment means that punishments for the same offence may look different and so, whilst the offender and the sentencer may believe that a fairer proportionality has been achieved by a focus on impact, the process may lack legitimacy, particularly to those without knowledge of the individual offender concerned.

If it were accepted that the aim of retributivist sentencing was a just amount of impact for a particular offender, or class of offenders, then the focus of attention would shift to the selection and justification of factors in the life and health of an offender that should be allowed to influence the sentencer in determining impact. These factors could be personal or they could be structural, that is, relating to general social and economic factors. In sentencing policy (but only to a certain extent in the eyes of the public, as we will see in relation to unit fines), the financial means of the offender has been a legitimate factor to take into account—and the courts routinely do so—in the calculation of financial penalties.[3] Apart from fines, the exercise of sentencing discretion has usually focused on the impact of custodial rather than community penalties. Even here, the courts only reluctantly take into account the health and family circumstances of the offender (see section 7.2).

There are also utilitarian arguments for taking impact into account. For the utilitarian, the assessment of what Bentham referred to as 'the several circumstances influencing

[2] For a general discussion of the importance of public opinion see Chapter 1, section 1.3.3.

[3] With the exception of fixed penalties: see section 7.3.4.

sensibility' (Bentham 1789: 169) and the calculation of the 'pain' of punishment, are aimed at assessing the likely effectiveness of punishment. So Bentham was concerned with the issue of impact in relation to sentence outcome: '[A] punishment which is the same in name will not always either really produce, or even so much as appear to others to produce, in two different persons the same degree of pain' (ibid). Therefore, in determining the quantity of punishment, he argues, we should take account of 'the several circumstances influencing sensibility' (ibid). Bentham specifies 32 circumstances influencing sensibility, including health and strength, firmness of mind, strength of intellectual powers, moral biases, sympathetic biases, insanity, sex, age, rank, education, and social status (ibid: 52).

Whilst such an extensive list could not be put into operation, more recent commentators have focused on the issue of 'sentence feasibility', the likelihood that an offender will be able to undertake the proposed sentence effectively. The utilitarian is also frugal: the amount of punishment should be the least possible and the most cost effective for the purpose. Therefore, if an effective outcome is unlikely, this would justify reducing the use and amount of imprisonment, or not imposing particular community penalties, if it were the case that, for example, the very old or very ill were not capable of responding to rehabilitation programmes or were not in a position to reoffend. So Carlen, noting that many offenders have disadvantaged backgrounds in relation to housing, employment and income, comments that 'their probation officers might rightly calculate that, given the tensions and frustration already existing in their homes, the clients would be unlikely to complete any [community] order involving home calls, curfews or house arrest' (1989: 22). Further, lack of substitute carers for their children might preclude parents from being offered a community service programme, as might lack of public transport to some community schemes (ibid). Carlen also comments that 'it might be unrealistic to expect emotionally and mentally damaged recidivist clients to complete a punitive... order' (ibid).

There is a further issue regarding the distribution and impact of punishment which is beyond the scope of this book, a problem which Lacey has called 'the problem of uniformity of application': 'should each and every dispositionally responsible offender be detected, convicted and punished?' (1998: 404). Like cases are not treated alike if only a small proportion of offenders are detected, arrested, prosecuted, and sentenced. There is no punishment impact on the 97 per cent of offenders who do not proceed to sentence. Pettit and Braithwaite have used this as a justification for the differential treatment of offenders on conviction under their republican theory of criminal justice: '[A] concern with the material differences between how we punish convicted offenders is not as well motivated as it might be if we were able to identify and indict most offenders' (1998: 330).

The fact that so few offenders proceed to the sentencing court raises political issues concerning the allocation of resources and the minimum levels of policing, prosecutions, and punishment necessary to accord the system legitimacy. It also leads to questions about priorities in crime detection, processing, and punishment: it is not just a matter of the level of resources but the targeting, say, of crimes more or less likely to be committed by the socially disadvantaged. It may also be linked to our focus on ethnic minorities in Chapter 10, section 10.4, if **racism** plays a part in any of these decisions.

7.1.3 **Disproportionate punishment?**

Given these arguments in favour of taking impact into account in order to construct an 'equal' sentence or an effective one, it is possible to isolate instances where punishment could be seen as disproportionate and so the sentencing for such punishment as unjust. In particular, 'full-time' deprivation of liberty can exacerbate or impose suffering stemming from personal circumstances or characteristics, whilst the Prison Service has a limited capacity to treat inmates differentially (see Chapter 11). Those who are very young, ill, old, or disabled, and those who have family members who depend on them, may suffer greater physical and psychological harm from a lack of freedom than do other inmates. In addition, those whose offending attracts the most social denunciation, notably those who sexually assault or murder children, also face a high risk of ostracism or harm from their fellow prisoners.

For all these types of offender, their vulnerability is likely to make the punishment disproportionately worse for them. As Tonry has observed:

> In subjective terms... two years' imprisonment in a single setting will have very different meanings to different offenders who have committed the same crime. Two years' imprisonment in a maximum security prison may be a rite of passage for a Los Angeles gang member. For an attractive, effeminate twenty-year old, it may mean the terror of repeated sexual victimization. For a forty-year-old head of household, it may mean the loss of a job and a home and a family. For an unhealthy seventy-five-year old, it may mean a death sentence.
>
> (Tonry 1996: 19)

Later in this chapter we will focus on two particularly problematic issues: how to impose 'fair' fines and how to deal justly with mentally disordered offenders. Financial penalties make discrepancies of impact much clearer whilst the problematic status of the offender who has been deemed sufficiently mentally 'well' to plead or to be found guilty but is sufficiently mentally ill to come within the relevant provisions of the Mental Health Act (MHA) 1983 is self-evident. The MHA 1983 allows the sentencing court to treat the offender as one whom Parliament has decided need not be punished after conviction but the rationale for this exception is not entirely clear. Because these offenders have been held to be criminally liable a penal response which is proportionate to culpability is theoretically justifiable and is still open to the courts. We return to the choice of therapeutic or punitive disposals—and the impact issues that choice raises—in section 7.4.

One possible justification for special provisions—and for similar personal mitigation where the offender does not fall within the MHA 1983—is that the offender may be treated unfairly if the sentencing outcome is equal to that of a mentally 'normal' offender: the impact of a particular punishment may be greater for such an offender. Further, the offender may be less receptive, because of mental health problems, to the intended utilitarian effect of punishment, whether that be deterrence or rehabilitation. Peay (2002: 746) has referred to the need for a 'capacity-based intervention' (for all offenders) so that therapeutic, crime reduction and reparative measures can be tailored to the individual capacity—abilities and vulnerabilities—of the offender. Without taking into account mental health issues, the retributivist punishment may be too severe—the quantum may be unjustifiable—and the utilitarian or restorative purposes may be frustrated and pointless.

There are, of course, valid arguments against admitting impact as a mitigating factor (Easton 2008c) and we shall examine them in more detail in Chapter 10. To summarise, such mitigation may not satisfy the requirements of retribution and denunciation and may entail a loss of deterrent effect as some classes of offender might feel they can offend with impunity because they would not have to pay much or would not be sent to prison for long. It can also be argued that it is not unjust to ignore mitigating factors: the offender whose particular circumstances are dire should know that any punishment will have more serious impact. This equates to a 'you should have thought of this before you offended' approach to offenders for whom punishment will impact particularly harshly on family, health, or social and employment status.

7.2 Impact as mitigation in practice

7.2.1 The approach of the courts

In practice the defence may argue that the particular impact of the sentence on the offender should be treated as a mitigating factor and sentencers, from magistrates up to the Court of Appeal, have accepted such arguments from time to time.[4] Some guidelines have also included an offender impact factor in the assessment of seriousness. For example, in the causing death by driving guideline, 'Injury to the offender may be a mitigating factor when the offender has suffered very serious injuries' and 'Where one or more of the victims was in a close personal or family relationship with the offender, this may be a mitigating factor' (Sentencing Guidelines Council 2008c: 5). However, as noted in Chapter 3, there is no duty on the sentencer to take impact into account, or for mitigation to have any precedence over factors relating to seriousness and the causing death by driving guideline specifically notes that 'the degree to which the relationship influences the sentence should be linked to offender culpability in relation to the commission of the offence; mitigation for this reason is likely to have less effect where the culpability of the driver is particularly high' (ibid).

Further, if impact operates as a mitigating factor it can only lead to a reduction in sentence, it cannot operate to increase a sentence to allow for greater equality of impact across the board. Within a retributivist approach to mitigation, 'character', including the propensity—or not—to offend, should not be taken into account as mitigation of sentence.

Arguably, the Court of Appeal has tried 'to bring some order to an area of law which may appear as chaotic as some of the lives under review' (Piper 2007: 142). However, case law suggests that the first concern of judges—in line with the effect of the guideline quoted—is not to downgrade a message about seriousness. So, if the court is dealing with what it considers to be serious offending, the court is anxious not to reduce the potential deterrent effects or the amount of censure by reducing a sentence. Therefore, if the circumstances of the offending are relatively less serious the courts are more likely to take into account mitigation based on impact.

If, when impact factors are taken into account, the courts explicitly justify their approach then the reduction in sentence is generally explained as an exceptional act of mercy. For example, the following statement made by Lord Lane CJ almost two decades ago in *Attorney-General's Reference (No. 4 of 1989)* (1989) was endorsed more recently by Sir Igor Judge when declining to increase the sentence on an 81-year-old sex offender: 'Leniency is not in itself a vice. That mercy should season justice is a proposition as soundly based in law as it is in literature' (*Attorney-General's Reference No. 73 of 2006* (2006)). If so, however, the courts are, arguably, mean with mercy and this approach has also led to two unhelpful outcomes: there is no clear or clearly articulated justification for taking impact mitigation into account and, in the current sentencing climate with higher levels of seriousness accorded to particular offences and factors, it is now less likely

[4] See, for example, Shapland (1981) for research on the process of, and speeches in, mitigation; Walker (1999: 100–3) on the 'exceptional circumstances' justifications for suspending a prison sentence; Jacobson and Hough for their recent research in relation to the influence of physical illness and employment issues on sentencing in the Crown Court (2007: 36–7).

that mitigation based on impact will influence sentencing. The inclusion of impact-based factors in sentencing guidelines may prompt a more principled approach.[5]

7.2.2 **The offender: vulnerability and age**

The Court of Appeal has been faced with the issue of added impact of punishment stemming from the personal vulnerability of a prisoner, whether stemming from old age, youth, or the expected 'dangers' of prison life. When being of an advanced age is allowed as mitigation, the justification is on grounds of physical infirmity and also of shorter life expectancy. In *Varden* (1981), for example, the offender—a man of 71, who had unlawful sex with a 13-year-old child with severe learning difficulties—would inevitably be spending his sentence under Rule 45 (of Prison Rules 1999, formerly R.43) in a vulnerable prisoner unit where a prisoner is segregated for his own protection. His age and likely segregation were taken into account as mitigating factors and he was given a reduced sentence but other cases at that time held that the impact of Rule 45 was not relevant and *Parker* (1996) took the same approach. The Court of Appeal said that it was not relevant to sentencing that an offender found it exceptionally hard to adjust to prison life, an approach also taken in *Nall-Cain* where a sentence of five years imposed on Lord Brocket was upheld because 'a defendant's treatment by other inmates is not generally a factor to which this court can have proper regard' (1998 at 150, *per* Rose LJ).

The overriding importance of offence gravity is also evident in a decision on the minimum term to be served by an elderly prisoner on an indeterminate sentence. *Bata* (2006) was an unsuccessful application for a reduction in his 10-year minimum term (previously notified by the Secretary of State) by an 80-year-old prisoner who had been sentenced to life for murder imposed for shooting a person on his neighbouring allotment at close range. The judge believed that the 10-year minimum already incorporated a considerable reduction for old age and illness, given the seriousness of the circumstances of the offending.

The effect of the increasing number of long determinate and indeterminate sentences, together with this cautious approach to reducing the sentence of a serious offender on account of old age, has had an effect on the composition of the prison population which ought, perhaps, to be further taken into account by sentencers. There are now more prisoners serving life sentences than in the early 1990s and more prisoners serving indeterminate sentences for public protection. Older prisoners are also more likely than younger prisoners to be serving longer sentences because of the type of offences committed. They may experience particular problems if they are held far from home as this will make it hard for them to maintain family ties if their visitors are also older. They may also be more likely to suffer health problems associated with longevity.

Prisoners aged 50 or over constituted 9 per cent of sentenced male prisoners and 6 per cent of sentenced female prisoners in 2006 (Ministry of Justice 2007a: 77) whilst on 31 March 2010 there were 605 prisoners aged over 70 (Prison Reform Trust (2010). Prisoners in the 'over 60 years old' category also had the largest percentage increase (149 per cent) in the decade 1996–2006 ((Ministry of Justice 2007a: 96). The number of older women prisoners has also increased (see Wahidin 2004) and Lord Phillips, then Lord Chief Justice, warned that in 30 years' time the prisons would be full of geriatric lifers (Phillips 2007). Steiner (2003) drew attention to the formal system for dealing with the early release of seriously ill and elderly prisoners introduced in France in 2003 but a Report in 2008 was critical of the fact that there is still no national strategy for older prisoners in England and Wales (HM Chief Inspector of Prisons 2008).

[5] See Ashworth (2010: 190–1) for further discussion of 'mercy'.

Of course there are also issues around age and vulnerability in relation to younger offenders. In Chapter 8 we examine the justifications for treating children who offend differently and in Chapter 13 we examine the use of custodial penalties for children and young people, where it is acknowledged that youth is a factor to be taken into account. We have already noted that old age may be accepted as mitigation: the offender has not much time left and there is a common notion that time 'goes more quickly' the older a person is. When youth is taken into consideration it rests on the notions of reduced culpability and also loss of precious 'developmental time'. There is also research based on offenders 'doing time' which has shown that for young prisoners time passes slowly, and examines the various techniques and strategies that may be used to make time go more quickly (Cope 2003).[6]

Cases would suggest that the courts consider 'youth', as with other impact mitigation, of little significance if the offending is very serious. In *Attorney-General's Reference (Nos 21 and 22 of 2004)* (2004), for example, where the offenders were aged 17 and 19, the court stated that, for such types of offending (robbery late at night on public transport as part of group), a custodial sentence must be imposed 'save in the most exceptional cases, such exceptions arising, for example, by reasons of extreme youth'. No distinction was made between the two offenders on grounds of age and no reduction was given for age. Similarly, the fact that an 18-year-old had a mental age of 10-and-a-half had little influence on the decision in a case involving a series of offences with very serious aggravating factors: '[The] youth and low intelligence of the second offender, provide no explanation and only modest mitigation' (*Attorney General's Reference (Nos 39, 40 and 41 of 2005)* [2005] at 26, *per* Holland J). The riots in several towns in England in the summer of 2011 also led to publicity for many cases of 'tough' sentencing which appeared to take little account of (young) age.[7]

For reasons of space, we have neglected the age category of 18–20-year-old offenders in this book. They were ignored by the reforms of the Crime and Disorder Act 1998 which apply to those under 18, and '[i]mproved regimes for the under 18s have thrown into sharp relief the poor treatment of 18–20-year-olds', as revealed in reports of the Chief Inspector of Prisons (Lyon 2003: 28) and a briefing by the Prison Reform Trust (2007a). A recent unannounced inspection of a prison which includes a young offender institution found higher rates of victimisation and self-harm among the 18–20-year-olds (HM Chief Inspector of Prisons 2011b: 27–8) suggesting there is still much room for improvement. This is an important issue and one which deserves a much higher profile than is possible within the constraints of this book.

7.2.3 **Illness and disability as mitigation**

There are also issues for sentencers raised by the resource difficulties faced in relation to the growing numbers of the ill and disabled in prison, partly caused by the increase in the size of the prison population and also the increase in older prisoners. A recent report found that 15 per cent of prisoners reported having a disability (HM Inspectorate of Prisons 2009a). Prisons have a duty not to discriminate against prisoners on the grounds of disability under the Equality Act 2010 (and formerly under the Disability Discrimination Act 2005), so the issue of accessibility to resources and treatment is important. Research has been undertaken on this particular group (see Crawley and Sparks 2005, 2008) and the Commission for Equality and Human Rights, which has

[6] See also Chapter 4 and the texts by Clemmer (1940) and Toch (1976) on 'survival' techniques used by prisoners generally.

[7] See, for example, Piper (2011).

taken over the role of the Disability Rights Commission, must enforce duties under the Equality Act 2010. A report by the Chief Inspector of Prisons found that women with disabilities were particularly critical of a range of services, including healthcare (HM Chief Inspector of Prisons 2008: 28).

However, the guideline judgment given in *Bernard* (1997) makes clear that a medical condition that might in the future affect life expectancy does not preclude a prison sentence (see Ashworth and Player 1998: 256–61). Cases before and after *Bernard* suggest, however, that a high risk of (earlier) death because of prison conditions and facilities may be accepted by the court as excessive impact of punishment which merits a reduction in sentence. In *Green and Leatherbarrow* (1992), for example, Green had sickle cell anaemia and Leatherbarrow had chronic emphysema. Green's sentence had been fixed at 18 months (and would have been five years if the illness had not been taken into account).[8] The Court of Appeal suspended 14 months of the 18-month sentence so he could be released immediately because of the risk of sudden death if there were no immediate access to suitable medical facilities.[9] Leatherbarrow's 15-month sentence had not taken the illness into account; on appeal, eight months of the sentence were suspended to allow immediate release.

However, the Court's approach in *Avis, Thomas, Torrington, Marques and Goldsmith* (1997) shows what is perhaps a more common stance. This case was a guideline judgment for firearms offences where, in relation to some of the appellants, old age and illness were submitted as mitigating factors, but the Court argued that the aggravating factors outweighed the mitigation. It is, therefore, relatively rare for the Court of Appeal to find it appropriate to downgrade a message about seriousness by taking into account factors impacting on the prison experience. Courts might, however, refer cases to the Home Secretary for the exercise of the royal prerogative.[10]

A case involving a disabled prisoner makes clear that the courts will only apply 'mercy' when, as in equity, the claimant has clean hands. Where the court believes that the offender has 'traded' on his disability then it is unlikely any reduction in sentence will be given. Indeed, the facts might aggravate seriousness as in *Kesler* (2005) where Ouseley J, having noted that '[h]e used to give the impression of innocent behaviour by going out with his dog to collect the drugs, and because of his disability had a stick, but it was hollowed out so that he could keep his drugs in it' (at 8), concluded as follows, '[i]t is plain that he has been using his health as a means of obtaining sympathy and of deception and he has already gained from his previous sentences such benefit as could possibly be accorded to him for those matters' (at 14).

7.2.4 **Loss of employment**

The same balancing approach has been taken in relation to expected loss of employment resulting from conviction or imprisonment. In *Hubbard* (2002), a case concerning abuse of trust in relation to a sexual offence, the Court of Appeal upheld a two-year sentence, apparently not taking into account the devastating personal consequences for the teacher. Generally, where the offence is serious the loss of employment is not given any weight. Where the offence is less serious and where job loss is accompanied by other mitigation (*Dockerill* (1988), *O'Hara* (2004)), it may be taken into account. Loss of employment is

[8] For further discussion on these issues, see Ashworth (2000: 153–5).

[9] See Dyson and Boswell (2006) for information about the medical context for *Green*.

[10] See, for example, *Moore* (1990) and *Stark* (1992), both HIV/AIDS cases.

also more likely to be taken into account if it impacts on third parties, whether they are family members or employees of the offender's business.

However, research provides 'some evidence that a defendant's steady job, or involvement in studies or vocational training, can be a mitigating factor' (Jacobson and Hough 2007: 37). In one case the 23-year-old offender was in the process of completing entry to the Marines and 'the judge stressed that the offence deserved custody but passed a community sentence—stating that a custodial sentence would prevent him "taking a course in your life that could do all of us some good"' (ibid).

There is, however, an ambivalence here which is reflected in public opinion. As Tonry has pointed out:

> The relevance of employment to sentencing varies with circumstances. Most people believe it is irrelevant that a wealthy securities law violator will, if imprisoned, lose his or her job... People have widely divergent views on whether a lower-middle-class head of household's job loss, if imprisoned, is relevant... From the perspective that employed defendants are often middle-class, and more likely than unemployed defendants to be white, concern about racial and class disparities may make job loss appear irrelevant.
>
> (1996: 22–3)

There is also the point made earlier that 'although it seems reasonable to view the loss of a job as a quasi-fine, taking prospective job loss into account unintentionally discriminates against the unemployed who are unfortunate enough to have no job to lose!' (Levi 1989: 432).

Even if loss of employment is not a mitigation issue, employment status may well affect the choice of sentence. Research some time ago by Crow and Simon (1987), based on six magistrates' courts, examined unemployment rates and sentencing statistics in 1974–84, controlling for courts with above- and below-average custody rates and with un/employment categories found that for the unemployed the movement could be up or down the scale of penalties. Further, Crow and Simon concluded that the effect of employment status on sentence was statistically small. However, the small differences stemming from employment status could have a 'ratchet' effect in relation to sentencing on a subsequent conviction whilst research in the early 1990s concluded that 'the sentencing of unemployed offenders differs considerably from the sentencing of those in employment' (Home Office 1994a: para 17). It found that 69 per cent of all adult male offenders sentenced to indictable offences in one study period were unemployed at the time they were sentenced and noted that some offenders lost their jobs following arrest (ibid: para 15).

Unemployment is another dimension of the financial circumstances of the offender which are considered in relation to the issue of compensation orders (see Chapter 6). But the clearest impact of wealth and poverty is in relation to fines, which we will deal with in section 7.3.

7.2.5 **Separation from children**

The case of *Mills* (2002), also discussed in Chapter 3, does seem to allow as mitigation the particular impact, if the offender is a mother, of being allocated to a prison far from her home and children.[11] This can be theorised as causing a disproportionate impact of punishment because the sorrow at loss of contact with your child is greater for the main caregiver, usually the mother, and because a female prisoner is likely to be further away from

[11] For a review of judicial thinking in the 1960s on the social consequences of conviction and the use of mitigation, see Martin and Webster (1971).

home than a male prisoner and so the visits will be less frequent (see Chapter 11, section 11.3.2). There is, also, a growing concern about the separation of fathers from their children, perhaps as a spin-off from the high profile given to fathers' groups campaigning for more contact with their children on separation and divorce (see Watson and Rice 2004). Both these circumstances, to a greater or lesser extent, could be included in the calculation of proportionate impact because the extra suffering, particularly for mothers, is now well documented (see, for example, Codd 2004, 2008; also Chapter 10, section 10.1.2).

The never implemented intermittent custody order (see Chapter 3, section 3.1.5), despite potential drawbacks for women, might have provided a means of imposing custody which does not totally disrupt care-giving relationships. When such an order was suggested in a Green Paper issued as long ago as 1984,[12] the explicit aim was to reduce the disruption of family ties and loss of employment which may result from continuous custody, and the intention in 2003 was also to 'maintain jobs, family ties or education, all of which have been shown to play a part in reducing reoffending'.[13]

We would also note before we move on to discussing fines that the range of protected characteristics under anti-discrimination law has broadened under the Equality Act 2010. As a consequence prisons have a duty not to discriminate against prisoners on the basis of age, disability, and other grounds, as well as a duty to promote equality and to test policies for equality impact. These issues will be discussed further in Chapter 11.

7.3 Equality of impact: a focus on fines

7.3.1 Fines as punishment

Fines might appear to be the easiest and most appropriate punishment to fix proportionately, there being available a very detailed money tariff. It might, therefore, also be thought to be easy to implement the policy imperative of encouraging the use of non-custodial sentences, including fines, to reduce the use of custodial penalties. However, with fines the issue of (in)equality of impact is more visible than in relation to other penalties. Further, there are very problematic categories of offenders in applying fines, notably the very poor (especially those dependent on state benefits), the unemployed, and the very rich.

A fine is a presumptive sentence in the sense that it can be imposed without passing a seriousness hurdle as is the case with custodial and community penalties (see Chapter 3). A fine can be used when the statutory criteria do not apply, so it is suitable for offences which are not at the top end of the seriousness scale. However, a fine can be added to other penalties (Criminal Justice Act (CJA) 2003, s 163) and can be imposed in magistrates' and Crown Courts. The maximum fine for a summary or either-way offence in a magistrates' court has been £5,000 since 2002[14] but the Legal Aid, Sentencing and Punishment of Offenders (LAS&PO) Bill 2011 proposes to remove this maximum.[15] In its *Equality Impact Assessment* of this measure the Government stated its belief 'that removing the upper limit represents a proportionate response so that proportionate fines can be imposed on wealthy or corporate offenders and organisations' (Ministry of Justice 2011j: 1–2). Further, it states: 'Seriousness is the main factor in deciding any sentence, but taking account of the income of the offender as well ensures that a fine poses

[12] *Intermittent Custody*, Cmnd 9281, London, HMSO.

[13] Explanatory Notes to the Criminal Justice Act 2003.

[14] Although higher fines are possible for certain specified offences.

[15] Clause 86. In Scotland the maximum has been £1,000 since 10 December 2007.

an equal burden for a particular level of seriousness regardless of income' (ibid: 3). There is no maximum in the Crown Court. Fines were set at five levels by s 37 of the Criminal Justice Act 1982 and, as amended in 1991, the levels are as follows: Level 1 £200, Level 2 £500, Level 3 £1,000, Level 4 £2,500, and Level 5 £5,000, The LAS&PO Bill[16] proposes to give the Secretary of State the power to substitute higher sums for those currently in Levels 1–4.

Fines should, then, operate as a useful penalty and in numerical terms they have done so: in 1995, 75 per cent of all those dealt with by the courts were fined (Brownlee 1998b: 137). However, this had dropped to 69 per cent by 2002; in 2009 it was 67.3 per cent, and in 2010 it was 65.5 per cent (Ministry of Justice 2011k: 7).[17] Figure 7.1 shows the trends in the numbers of offenders fined in 1989–2009 (see also Ministry of Justice: 2011m: Table Q5.4).

Furthermore, the use of financial penalties in the Crown Court decreased by 46 per cent over the period 1995–2006 (Carter 2007: 7) whilst the use of fines for indictable offences generally also decreased from 27 per cent in 1999 to 17 per cent in 2009.[18] On the other hand, the use of custodial and community sentences increased in 1995–2006 (Carter 2003: 3; Tarling 2006: 29–31) and the proportion of community sentences remained stable from 2007 (Ministry of Justice 2011k: 8) although recent statistics suggest the increased use of community sentences may have stalled[19] whilst fines continue to decrease in use (see Table 7.1). The restriction on the use of community orders such that only those convicted of imprisonable offences can be subject to such an order, might encourage more use of financial penalties (see Chapter 3, section 3.1.1).

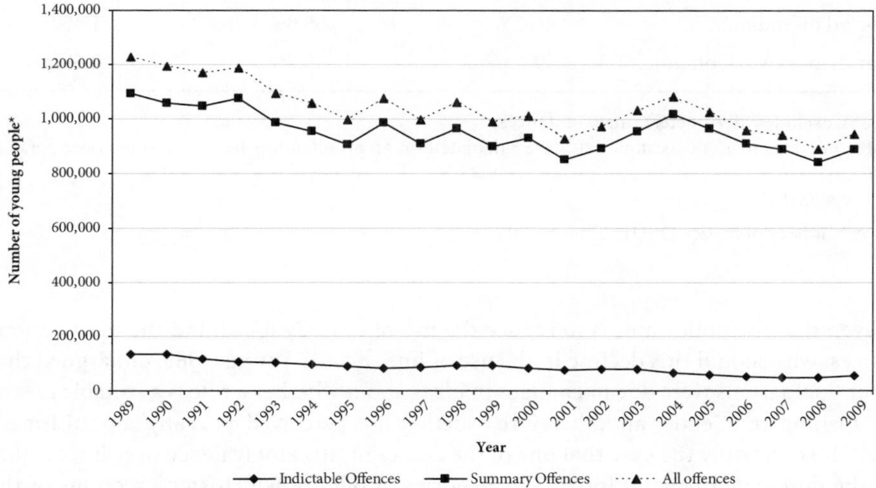

Figure 7.1 Number of all offenders who received a fine 1989–2009

Source: Ministry of Justice (2010a: Evidence Report, Figure 3.5).

* Error in original. This should read 'Number of all offenders'.

[16] See the Online Resource Centre for updates.

[17] Although annual statistics collated three months later give a figure of 68.4 per cent for adults for the 12 months ending March 2011.

[18] See http://sentencingcouncil.judiciary.gov.uk/facts/facts-and-figures.htm.

[19] However this is almost certainly because of the decrease in the use of community sentences for offenders under 18 years of age; the rate for adults is very slightly higher: see Ministry of Justice (2011m: 42).

Table 7.1 Offenders sentenced by principal sentence, 12 months ending June 2010 to 12 months ending June 2011, and percentage change

	12 months ending June 2010	12 months ending June 2011^(P)	Percentage change^(P)
Total offenders sentenced	1,389,421	1,335,460	-3.9%
Total persons sentenced	1,381,186	1,327,928	-3.9%
Immediate custody	99,550	101,976	2.4%
Suspended sentence	46,456	48,729	4.9%
Community sentence	188,401	183,203	-2.8%
Fines	927,363	872,150	-6.0%
Other disposals	127,651	129,402	1.4%
Average custodial sentence length (months)^(1)	13.8	14.1	2.0%
Percentage of those sentenced^(2)			**Percentage point change**
Immediate custody (persons)	7.2%	7.7%	0.5%
Suspended sentence (persons)	3.4%	3.7%	0.3%
Community sentence (persons)	13.6%	13.8%	0.2%
Fines (all offenders)	66.7%	65.3%	-1.4%
Other disposals (all offenders)	9.2%	9.7%	0.5%

(1) ACSL excludes life/indeterminate sentences
(2) May not sum to 100% as some rates are calculated on an all offenders basis and some on a persons basis
(P) Provisional

Source: Ministry of Justice (2011n: Table Q1.2).

Given that the policy aim is to reduce the use of custody for all but the most serious offences, why should this decline in the use of fines occur? Young (1989: 46) argued that earlier fluctuations were due to changes in ideas about whether a fine is a suitable means of punishing an offender and, therefore, whether it is perceived as 'really' a punishment or not. It is certainly the case that one of the causes of this ambivalence over fines is that it is the designated penalty for those categories of offence which some sections of the population do not regard as 'really' criminal. Parking offences and regulatory offences like those in relation to TV licences might come into this category. More controversially, other motoring offences such as speeding, and health and safety infractions, might also be included (see Corbett 2000; Carter 2003). Where citizens do not regard an offence as really criminal, they do not perceive the outcome as a punishment but rationalise it instead as a tax—a morally neutral nuisance which is the occasional result of choosing not to obey what are deemed as non-criminal regulations. The problem is that such thinking then influences the conceptualisation of financial penalties for 'real' crimes.[20]

[20] See O'Malley (2009) for an extended discussion of issues.

In relation to property offences there is the added difficulty that 'the value of the punishment must not be less in any case than what is sufficient to outweigh that of the profit of the crime' (Bentham 1789: 166). From a utilitarian perspective, the fine or other punishment, taken together with any compensation and confiscation orders, must be sufficient to make committing the crime unprofitable, otherwise there is no deterrent effect. From a retributivist perspective, as we have seen, commensurability would also be undermined by disregarding the profits of crime.

The difficulty which arises, then, is this: what amount of financial punishment is proportionate to the level of seriousness established by the court? This question cannot be answered without considering two fundamental questions: how does a fine operate as a punishment and how should the level of fine be correlated to seriousness and culpability?

Money and punishment have very different connotations and are underpinned by very different cultural values. So there are 'shock horror' media stories about cases where even the large fine imposed has not been seen as a punishment sufficient to reflect the seriousness of the offending in question. There is a strong popular feeling that there are particular harms, notably crimes of violence and sexual offences, that are not 'compensatable' by a financial penalty. Whilst a fine, then, may legally be sufficient and proportionate to gravity, morally it may not be accepted by the public as enough punishment.

So, a major problem hindering the use of fines in the UK, and also in the United States (see Tonry 1996: 124–7), is its ambivalent position as a punishment. However, there is a related problem regarding the quantum of punishment. Fines punish the offender by depriving him of whatever consumables or non-working time would have been purchased with the money 'lost' through the payment of the fine. The problem with this approach is that the amount of deprivation or loss is affected by how much disposable income the individual retains, or how much impact the fine has on the person's financial circumstances. It could be theorised as the deprivation of the amount of time, 'liberty', required to earn enough to replenish personal savings. As Tonry points out, this is possible: some European states and some states in the United States have a more positive attitude to fines as punishment. For example, in the Netherlands a fine is legally presumed to be the preferred penalty for every crime and reasons need to be given for rebutting this presumption (Tonry 1996: 124).

7.3.2 **Units of financial deprivation**

Two approaches are possible for correlating seriousness with an amount of money:

- to have a fixed fine for each amount of seriousness (for example, by fixing a certain sum of money as the fine for each offence and with specified factors to take the amount above or below the starting point)
- to have a unit of financial deprivation correlated with each unit of seriousness (that is, the penalty is fixed at a particular percentage of the offender's financial resources for a specified level of seriousness).

The outcome in terms of an amount of money will often be very different. Let us take the scenario of a £2,000 fine which is considered adequate punishment for a specified serious offence. The sentencer and the public may be happy with that amount and justice may be perceived to have been done. But students with an income of £8,000 are left below the breadline, whereas those on £80,000 may not be unduly concerned. If, instead of 'visible' equality of justice, we decide to aim at equality of impact then either the fine imposed on the student need be only £200 or, instead, £20,000 on the high earner, so that both 'suffer' an equal impact on their lives in terms of deprivation of goods that can no longer be purchased. However, the £200 fine might appear to the media as proof that the student had 'got away with it'. On the other hand, a £20,000 fine would seem to be a very large amount of money to a person who is not used to the state depriving him of resources, and who feels the fine is disproportionate and unjust in comparison with the student's fine.

These ambivalences are illustrated by two earlier reported cases. In *Markwick* (1953) a wealthy man was fined £500—a large amount then—for stealing in breach of trust but on appeal the Court increased the sentence to two months' imprisonment, justified on the ground that imposing a high fine instead of custody 'would give prisoners of means an opportunity of buying themselves out of being sent to prison'. On the other hand, in *Fairbairn* (1980), where a fine of £7,500 and a custodial sentence were imposed to reflect both the gravity of the offence and the ability to pay of an offender who owned two houses, the fine was reduced on appeal to £1,000 on the grounds that any higher sum was disproportionate because only £700 had been stolen.

Day fines

The approach of English sentencing law and practice until 1991 was to use a fixed amount of fine which could be reduced by the court if the offender was unable to pay. At the end of the 1980s, however, the government pursued the idea of 'day fines' which were already being used in parts of the United States and in Scandinavia. These were called day fines because what the offender earns in a day became the basis for assessments of the total fine. In England such a scheme was successfully piloted (see Gibson 1990), though referred to as 'unit fines', and was implemented across the country for magistrates' courts by means of s 18 of the Criminal Justice Act 1991.

In the original s 18, seriousness was designated by a number of units from 1–50. The fine was then determined by multiplying the number of units by an amount of money calculated on the basis of the offender's disposable income. Problems arose where the offender refused to submit details of his financial circumstances to the court for assessing this sum. The legislation provided for this by allowing the courts to take the highest figure where no information was forthcoming. The instances where this happened were highly publicised in sections of the media and brought disrepute on the system.

Nevertheless, this does not explain why the original s 18 was replaced so quickly in 1993 by what has been referred to as 'perhaps the most astonishing and unjustified *volte-face* in the history of the English Criminal Justice System' (Cavadino and Dignan 2002: 128). It is true that the scheme rolled out was more draconian than the scheme piloted but the assessment problems could have been overcome, and the education of the public on the principle of equal impact could have been attempted. At the time a lay magistrate suggested that the sense of outrage was fuelled by better-off members of society who were dismayed that '[f]ailing to comply with a traffic sign, going through a light on red or parking on a zig-zag was previously worth the price of a meal out for two; now it can cost as much as taking the family to Florida' (Block 1993: 308). The embattled Conservative Government did not wish to alienate public opinion further[21] and a new s 18 was inserted by s 65 of the Criminal Justice Act 1993 and largely re-enacted in the Powers of Criminal Courts (Sentencing) Act (PCCSA) 2000 (s 128).

This in effect returned the situation to what it had been before 1991 with one difference: the court could raise as well as lower the amount of the fine in taking the offender's means into account. This legal framework is now in ss 162–165 of the CJA 2003. Research would

[21] See Brownlee (1998b: 146) for the role of the Magistrates' Association.

suggest that magistrates returned to imposing lower than proportionate-to-impact fines on the employed (Brownlee 1998b: 147) but in 2003 it looked as if unit fines were to be re-introduced. The Carter Report proposed that fines should replace the 30 per cent of current community orders imposed on low-risk offenders (2003: 27) and that 'day fines' should be introduced. There was no mention of the ill-fated unit fines system although the report did propose, perhaps with the English experience in mind, that minor offences should be excluded to 'avoid excessive fines for very low level crimes' (ibid). The Government promised to explore the issue (Home Office 2004b: Annex para 35)[22] and a study at that time of two large city-centre magistrates' courts suggested support for a new system (Moore 2003a). The Management of Offenders and Sentencing Bill 2005 did indeed propose to amend s 164 of the CJA 2003 so that fines would be fixed by reference to daily disposable income but the Bill fell when Parliament was prorogued for the General Election[23] and subsequent legislation has not included such a provision.

Changing thinking

However, there have been significant changes in relation to the impact of fines. First, guidance for use by magistrates is now much more impact-focused. The introduction to the 'The Approach to the Assessment of Fines' section of the 2008 *Magistrates' Courts Sentencing Guidelines* states: 'The aim is for the fine to have an equal impact on offenders with different financial circumstances; it should be a hardship but should not force the offender below a reasonable "subsistence" level' (Sentencing Guidelines Council 2008h: 148). The current approach is to place the offending in question within a band—normally one of three bands—depending on seriousness; then financial liability is fixed according to the individual's means (see Table 7.2). 'Where an offender's only source of income is state benefit... the relevant weekly income is deemed to be £100' (Sentencing Guidelines Council 2008h: 148). Two further bands are provided which apply where the offence has passed the threshold for a community order (Band D) or a custodial sentence (Band E) but the court decides that it need not impose such a sentence and that a financial penalty is appropriate. Band D is 250 per cent of the relevant weekly income and Band E is 400 per cent (Sentencing Guidelines Council 2008h: 151).

In other words fines in the magistrates' court are no longer fixed as a set amount which is taken up or down. This is clearly a development to be welcomed although there remains the

Table 7.2 Fine bands

For the purpose of the offence guidelines, a fine is based on one of three bands (A, B or C). The selection of the relevant fine band, and the position of the individual offence within that band, is determined by the seriousness of the offence.

	Starting point	**Range**
Fine Band A	50% of relevant weekly income	25–75% of relevant weekly income
Fine Band B	100% of relevant weekly income	75–125% of relevant weekly income
Fine Band C	150% of relevant weekly income	125–175% of relevant weekly income

Source: *Magistrates' Court Sentencing Guidelines* 2008 (Sentencing Guidelines Council 2008h: 148).

[22] See http://webarchive.nationalarchives.gov.uk/+/http://www.homeoffice.gov.uk/documents/reducing-crime-changing-lives?view=Binary.

[23] The Queen's Speech of 17 May 2005 stated that the Bill would be reintroduced but it was not.

problem raised in relation to unit fines that the impact approach 'is best suited for defendants with regular, measurable (and legal) income flow' (Greene 1998: 269) and this clearly does not apply to all offenders. A report on day fines by the Sentencing Commission for Scotland (2006) which concluded that there was no 'compelling case to change the existing system governing the imposition of fines in this country', did so because, they argued, day fines could not be introduced until there was a 'simple, reliable and cost-effective method of obtaining information on offenders' income' in Scotland (ibid: Foreword by the Rt Hon Lord Macfadyen). This has also been an issue in England and Wales.

The second significant development is the recent focus on sentencing for serious crime by commercial firms and the resulting guidance on fines to be imposed on companies convicted under the Corporate Manslaughter and Corporate Homicide Act 2007 has led to the setting of fines at a high level.[24] The guideline states that for corporate manslaughter 'The appropriate fine will seldom be less than £500,000 and may be measured in millions of pounds' (Sentencing Guidelines Council 2010: para 24). It may be that this will influence thinking about the use of fines. Indeed, in its 2010–11 report the Health and Safety Executive reported that duty holders found guilty of health and safety offences prosecuted by them received fines totalling £18.6 million, giving average penalties on conviction of £35,938 per case (Health and Safety Executive 2011: 10).

However, there will also need to be further training of those who impose the majority of fines. Research undertaken in 2006 in the magistrates' courts of England and Wales to assess the extent to which magistrates were using new structured sentencing guidance for fines found that, whilst all participants were using the guidance to reach a decision, many panels 'subsequently chose to change their minds' (Raine and Dunstan 2009: 29). The researchers explain that, where the guidance generated very low fines 'the concerns were about the justice process failing to ensure "just deserts" and appropriate punishment and fears of giving the wrong message to both the offender and the wider public' (ibid: 32) whilst in relation to high fines for less serious offences but where the offender had the means to pay the concern was that the outcome was based too heavily on equity and not enough on proportionality (ibid). The thinking in early cases that we noted at the beginning of this section would appear to continue.

7.3.3 **Default and enforcement**

Fines become payable as soon as imposed but guidance has established that payment can be by instalments. These should not normally be spread over more than 12 months, concern being that a long repayment period allows the poorer offender to be fined to an amount that has more impact than the same amount imposed on an offender who can afford to pay it immediately. 'It is generally recognised that the maximum weekly payment by a person in receipt of state benefit should rarely exceed £5' (Sentencing Guidelines Council 2008h: 152). *Olliver* (1989) allowed the period to be, exceptionally, 24 months and that is the period allowed for payment of fines which are imposed in the exceptional bands D and E (ibid). Despite these provisions many offenders do not pay any or all of their fine. The full payment rate for fines was only 62 per cent in 1999–2000, dropping to 55 per cent in 2002–3. Table 7.3 gives statistics since 2003–4 and shows an overall but not steady improvement in the rate of payment. There has also been a gradual increase in full

[24] Concern is evidenced by the title of a recent article: 'Death knell for companies? High fines anticipated for corporate manslaughter after first conviction' NLJ (*New Jaw Journal*) Vol 161, Issue 7454, 25 February 2011.

Table 7.3 Enforcement of financial penalties 2003–4 to 2010–11

Financial year	New amount owed [(1)] (£)	Paid [(2)] (£)	Payment rate [(3)] (%)	Payment rate excluding administrative cancellations [(4)] (%)
2003–04	366,653,329.16	212,785,348.05	74	—
2004–05	351,746,801.62	221,505,558.19	80	—
2005–06	368,923,934.48	233,332,326.01	83	81
2006–07	364,298,841.54	244,555,539.82	92	80
2007–08	376,569,882.06	256,117,662.65	95	82
2008–09	393,121,638.79	246,519,704.18	85	71
2009–10	406,660,591.18	259,241,082.01	86	74
2010[(5)]	312,719,840.11	213,916,998.74	92	80

[(1)] New amount owed is the sum of amounts imposed in the courts plus net transferred amounts [(2)] The amount paid is monies received by the courts against any outstanding fine irrespective of age and will not necessarily be for fine amounts imposed in the same period. [(3)] The payment rate is calculated by dividing the amount paid to HMCTS over a financial year by the new amount owed less the value of fines legally and net administratively cancelled for the same period. [(4)] The payment rate excluding administratively cancelled is only available from 2005 only. Prior to that the data are not comparable due to changes in the way the payment rate was calculated. The payment rate excluding administratively cancelled is calculated by dividing the amount paid to HMCTS over a financial year by the new amount owed less the value of fines legally cancelled for the same period. [(5)] April to December only.

Source: Hansard (21 June 2011).[25]

payment of FPNs in England and Wales from 77 per cent in 1997 to 87 per cent in 2003 (Ministry of Justice 2007d: para 5.14 and Tables 5.4 and 5.5), settling around 89 per cent in 2006–9 (Povey *et al* 2011: Table 3d, 62).[26]

The Labour Government had considered the problem of fine default to be a major reason why fines were not used more extensively. Consequently the Courts Act 2003 amended parts of previous legislation to provide a new framework for fine enforcement and a Unified Courts Agency was created in 2005, with a phased implementation of a new National Enforcement Service from April 2007.[27]

Section 82 of the Magistrates' Courts Act 1980 provides the criteria for imposing custody on fine default. Sections 79–118 provide other process options and powers for reviewing and enforcing fines. Home Office research in the mid-1990s found that, despite Best Practice Guidelines issued in 1992 and 1996, there was no one standard practice—attachment of earnings or deduction from benefit, distress warrants,[28] reviews, warrants for arrest—by which fines were enforced (Whittacker and Mackie 1997: 5). Half of the defaulters in the sample had more than one outstanding fine whilst four out of five defaulters owed less than £500 (ibid: 15). The main reasons defaulters gave for their fine arrears were that there had been a (detrimental) change in their financial circumstances since the

[25] Accessed at http://www.publications.parliament.uk/pa/cm201011/cmhansrd/cm110621/text/110621w0002.htm.

[26] Hansard HC 16 April 2007, Column 9W.

[27] See Einat (2004) for a review of research on enforcement in other jurisdictions.

[28] For a discussion of the use of distress warrants, see Moore (2003b).

fine was imposed and/or that they had other financial commitments and debts. Women defaulters were typically in very restricted financial circumstances with 81 per cent having dependent children and only 11 per cent were in employment, whilst 22 per cent of male defaulters were unemployed (ibid: 13–14). Moore found that in some cases it simply might not be possible for magistrates to implement the principle that a fine should have detrimental impact but not cause significant financial hardship (Moore 2003a: 23–5).

The Report of the Select Committee on Public Accounts found that, of a total of £397 million of fines imposed in 2001–2, around 59 per cent were collected, but £58 million were written off (largely because the offender could not be traced), and £90 million of fines were cancelled because of successful appeals or a significant change of circumstances (2002: para 2). There were wide variations in the collection rate and the Report pointed to ineffective administration and a failure to prioritise the issue. Until the early 1990s immediate or suspended prison sentences were the main response to fine default but reliance on this sanction then decreased (see Brownlee 1998b: 148–9 for references), and research found that magistrates acknowledged that fines were likely to impact disproportionately on offenders with limited means and that fines now often 'seemed like the imposition of "debt" rather than punishment' (Mackie *et al* 2003: 28; see also Raine *et al.* 2004).

The Crime (Sentences) Act 1997 extended the availability of non-custodial penalties for fine default and s 300 of the CJA 2003 empowers magistrates to impose a 'default order' whereby the offender must comply with an unpaid work, curfew (which may include electronic monitoring), or attendance centre[29] requirement. Section 301 allows the magistrates' court to disqualify the defaulter from driving for a period of up to 12 months.

Attention has also turned to improving collection of fines. Under the Fines Collection (Amendment) Regulations 2004[30] the (then) Department for Constitutional Affairs piloted a range of new fine-collection measures including a new type of attachment of earnings order.[31] The Criminal Justice and Immigration Act (CJIA) 2008 amended[32] Schedule 5, Part 3 of the Courts Act 2003, such that, on request to the Secretary of State, the staff of Her Majesty's Courts Service (HMCS) can gain access to benefit records held by the Department for Work and Pensions (DWP) for the purpose of fine enforcement. The Courts Act 2003, Schedule 6 also made provision for people to work off the outstanding financial penalty by undertaking unpaid work. Referred to as Fine Payment Work (FPW) this was piloted in seven areas between 2004 and 2009. The court made a work order which stated the amount of the fine and, using a statutory conversion rate (£6 per hour), the hours of work to be completed. (See Rix *et al.* 2010 for the research report.)

The difficulty is that, while some offenders are in the 'won't pay' category, others 'can't pay': their non-payment is not necessarily wilful. Even research evidence that people pay fines at the last minute—when threatened with an imminent custodial order—does not prove they could have paid all along. It is also explained by the generosity of friends who offer financial help only when that threat is likely to be implemented (Morris and Gelsthorpe 1990: 842). Where offenders have genuine difficulties in paying even small fines, for example many of the single mothers fined for non-payment of their TV licence, 'enforcement, be it deductions from benefits that are already inadequate, seizure and sale of family possessions, or especially imprisonment, that is not mitigated by positive intervention and assistance in other areas of life can only serve to reinforce existing patterns of social inequality in the criminal justice system' (Brownlee 1998b: 151).

29 For age 16–24 year olds: inserted by CJIA 2008, s 40.

30 Attachment of earnings: SI 2004/1407, pursuant to the Courts Act 2003, Schedule 5.

31 See http://www.paypershop.com/news-cat/courtak.html.

32 Section 41 inserted new paras 9A–9C.

7.3.4 Fixed and regulatory penalties

There are fixed penalties for some offences, notably for many motoring offences,[33] but the range has widened to include, for example, environmental offences. Table 7.4 lists those statistics collected by the Home Office but excludes those collected by other bodies, notably the Ministry of Justice and Local Authorities, and the enforcement notices issued by the Health and Safety Executive.[34]

These notices have been described as a compromise between the principle of equal impact and administrative efficiency (Ashworth 2000: 211); the level of fine does not vary according to the offender's means and the assumption is that the level is set sufficiently low for it not to cause injustice.

There are also so-called 'regulatory offences', often 'newer' offences regulated by bodies other than the police, which deal with issues of, for example, fair trading, consumer protection, vehicle licensing, and health and safety. We looked briefly at the deterrent effect of such fines in Chapter 4 (section 4.4.1) in relation to regulatory offences generally, and particularly TV or road fund licence evasion. There are also PNDs (penalty notices for disorder)—the so-called 'on the spot' fines issued by the police—currently set at £50 or £80, which were introduced by ss 1–11 of the Criminal Justice and Police Act 2001 and implemented across England and Wales by April 2004.

O'Malley has recently critiqued this trend as depersonalising the individual: 'New forms of "simulated" justice and policing are emerging at the convergence of telemetric regulation with two linked trends: the monetization of justice and the development of risk-based technologies of governance. A definitive example is the traffic fine' (O'Malley 2010: 795).

We are also concerned that official statistics suggest that the number of crimes handled directly by the police through cautions and fixed-penalty fines now exceeds those dealt with by convictions in courts although the totals may no longer be rising. The Ministry of Justice statistics for out-of-court disposals (including PNDs) 2010–11 give a total of 448,526 which compares with 1,336,494 convictions for the same period (see Table 7.5) and there were 13.4 per cent fewer PNDs issued in the 12 months ending June 2011 than in the 12 months ending June 2010 and 38 per cent fewer than the peak in the 12 months ending June 2007 (Ministry of Justice 2011n; see also Table 7.5).

However, these figures should be set in the context of lower totals for convictions and other out-of-court disposals and also of changes in police and prosecution targets 2008–10 (ibid). Further, these statistics do not include all the other fixed penalties because collection of statistics on the other penalties is the responsibility of the Home Office. On the latest figures other FPNs issued by the police appear to have peaked in 2003–4 (Povey *et al.* 2011: Figure 3a, see also 61–62). For example, the number of FPNs for motoring offences issued by the police (including traffic wardens) in 2009 was 2.1 million, down 9 per cent on 2008. Speed limit offences comprised 54 per cent of all FPNs issued in 2009 and, as well as fixed penalty notices, the police issued 27,000 written warnings for motoring offences and 78,000 Vehicle Defect Rectification Scheme (VDRS) notices in 2009 (ibid: 99).

These exceptions to the range of variable fines for standard criminal offences, which were the focus of the discussion in section 7.3.2, raise several issues. In relation to fixed penalties the difficulty is again the setting of the financial amount. If it is too high it may be unfair on offenders of limited means and it might also increase evasion of payment. If it is too low it might not act as a deterrent and be treated simply as a (small) tax to be paid

[33] Fixed penalty notices (FPNs) were introduced in the 1950s for parking offences.

[34] See for annual statistics: http://www.hse.gov.uk/statistics/index.htm.

Table 7.4 Fixed penalty notices by offence type, 2000–2009

Numbers (thousands)										England and Wales	
Offence group	Offence type	2000[1]	2001[1]	2002[1]	2003	2004	2005	2006	2007	2008	2009
4(pt)	Careless driving offences (excluding use of handheld mobile phone while driving)	32.2	34.7	32.7	34.9	16.7	12.6	8.9	7.0	2.8	3.4
4(pt)	Use of handheld mobile phone while driving[1]	..	..	..	1.9	74.0	126.6	166.8	122.1	115.9	125.5
7,9,10	Licence, insurance[2] and record-keeping offences	49.5	50.3	49.6	67.6	70.0	80.3	88.7	100.8	99.7	86.1
13,15	Vehicle test and condition offences	10.5	9.3	7.9	10.2	12.7	16.5	21.8	35.6	56.8	69.3
16	Speed limit offences	941.7	1,151.1	1,407.3	1,894.8	1,924.4	1,979.9	1,828.5	1,473.8	1,247.0	1,136.0
17-19	Neglect of traffic signs and directions and of pedestrian rights	183.4	175.1	176.9	227.0	219.6	208.6	208.5	203.8	200.1	183.0
20	Obstruction, waiting and parking offences	1,595.4	1,325.0	1,165.0	1,044.3	882.5	573.4	496.3	446.8	331.8	264.1
21,22	Lighting and noise offences	23.0	19.9	20.7	20.1	23.2	19.4	18.9	19.0	20.4	20.9
23,24	Other offences[3]	3.9	3.2	3.1	3.7	4.9	5.2	3.9	3.8	4.7	5.8
25(pt)	Miscellaneous motoring offences (excluding seat belt offences)	3.5	5.1	7.9	6.8	4.9	6.7	5.4	3.6	3.7	5.2
25(pt)	Seat belt offences	155.3	144.4	126.4	145.6	201.8	234.6	226.2	220.1	227.0	203.4
Total		2,998.2	2,918.0	2,997.4	3,456.7	3,434.7	3,263.9	3,073.8	2,636.6	2,310.0	2,102.7

1. Introduced as a specific offence as from 1 December 2003.
2. As from June 2003, the offence of having no insurance was added to the road traffic fixed penalty offence system.
3. Includes load offences and offences peculiar to motor cycles.

Source: Povey *et al.* (2011: 61, Table 3).

Table 7.5 Activity in the Criminal Justice System, 12 months ending June 2010 to 12 months ending June 2011

	12 months ending June 2010	12 months ending June 2011(P)	Percentage change
Out of court disposals	499,770	448,526	-10.3%
Cannabis warnings(p)	86,362	80,537	-6.7%
Penalty notices for disorder	152,895	132,434	-13.4%
Cautions	260,513	235,555	-9.6%
Defendants proceeded against	1,682,303	1,607,832	-4.4%
Indictable offences	425,903	429,259	0.8%
Summary offences	1,256,400	1,178,573	-6.2%
Defendants convicted	1,391,646	1,336,494	-4.0%
Indictable offences	337,015	348,204	3.3%
Summary offences	1,054,631	988,290	-6.3%
Prison receptions(A)	92,053	90,032	-2.2%
Probation starts(B)	182,504	180,075	-1.3%

(A) Receptions for offenders given a custodial sentence (figures include fine defaulters).
(B) Offenders starting Community Order or Suspended Sentence Order supervision by the Probation Service.
(P) Provisional
Source: Ministry of Justice (2011n: Table Q1.1).

for the advantage gained by the illegal action. In relation to regulatory penalties, and in relation to white collar crime generally, the issue has been whether those subject to such sentencing are treated too leniently: that the level of fines for such offenders is then unfair to other criminals treated more harshly.

Fining companies and organisations—where community or custodial sentences may not be an option—has been a particular problem for many years.[35] Croall found that few offenders were imprisoned for business regulatory offences and that fines were relatively low for offences under safety and public health legislation (1992: 111) although offences of fraud and tax evasion were given a broader range of punishments including custody. Croall concluded that 'the broad distinction between crimes against and crimes in the course of capitalism appears to have some substance' (ibid: 112; see also Sanders 1985). Cook came to similar conclusions in relation to the differential treatment of those defrauding the Inland Revenue by evading tax, and those defrauding the Department of Social Security by claiming benefits to which they are not entitled (1989; see also Levi and Pithouse 2000).

There is a further issue raised by a report published in 2008. This is that the trend towards pre-court summary justice for a range of offences may not be being used fairly and effectively and that this trend remains outside of the official inspection regime (Morgan 2008). The report warns that there is 'an accountability deficit' and calls for a 'thoroughgoing' review of the use and impact of summary powers.

[35] See Ashworth 2010: 335–7 for further discussion.

7.4 The treatment of mentally disordered offenders

In Chapter 5 (section 5.4.2) we briefly examined the sentencing provisions in relation to those offenders who are deemed to be both dangerous and mentally disordered.[36] Here our concern is with the issue of impact and just punishment in relation to all offenders who are, or could be, categorised as mentally disordered.

7.4.1 The extent of the problem

Our starting point is the fact that there are higher rates of mental health problems in the prison population than in the wider population, with a higher incidence of neuroses, psychoses, personality disorders, drug dependency, and histories of abuse (see, for example, Burney and Pearson 1995: 292–4). Research studies in the 1990s found that 37 per cent of male and 56 per cent of female sentenced prisoners had psychiatric disorders, with an incidence in the remand population of 63 per cent, and 5–10 per cent suffering from psychosis (see Peay 2002: 761, 772–5). A major study of over 1,000 prisoners, for example, found that 7 per cent of male sentenced prisoners and 14 per cent of female sentenced prisoners had a psychotic disorder (Singleton *et al.* 1998). The number of prisoners transferred to hospital because they suffered from mental health problems which were too serious to be treated within prison increased in 2002–6 (HM Prison Service 2007: 33).

A report on the treatment of male prisoners with mental health problems, *Troubled Inside: Responding to the Mental Health Needs of Men in Prison* (Rickford and Edgar 2005), published by the Prison Reform Trust, reviews the treatment of such offenders and highlights the problems prisons face in managing mental health problems and the damaging effects of imprisonment on those suffering from mental illness prior to entering prison. It was highly critical of the use of prisons to warehouse those with mental health problems instead of diverting them from prison and recommended improvements in policy and practice to improve their treatment (see also Seddon 2006; Peay 2007). A review by HM Inspectorate of Prisons, *The Mental Health of Prisoners: A Thematic Review of the Care and Support of Prisoners with Mental Health Needs* (2007), was also critical of the use of drugs rather than counselling etc. in dealing with prisoners' mental health problems.

In 2009, the Department of Health published *Lord Bradley's review of people with mental health problems or learning disabilities in the criminal justice system.* The first two paragraphs of the Introduction to the Executive Summary make the following points:

1. Evidence suggests that there are now more people with mental health problems in prison than ever before. While public protection remains the priority, there is a growing consensus that prison may not always be the right environment for those with severe mental illness. Custody can exacerbate mental ill health, heighten vulnerability and increase the risk of self-harm and suicide.
2. The policy of 'diversion' for people with mental health problems or learning disabilities has been supported by Government since as far back as 1990. But the lack of a nationally guided approach has meant that implementation has been inconsistent.

(Department of Health 2009a)

There appear to be particular problems in relation to offenders serving an indeterminate IPP (imprisonment for public protection) sentence (see Chapter 5). 'IPP prisoners 'appear

[36] For further discussion of these issues, see Baker (1993).

to suffer from significantly higher rates of mental health problems than other prisoners' with more than half of IPP prisoners having 'emotional wellbeing' problems compared to 4 in 10 lifers and 3 in 10 of the general prison population (Jacobson and Hough 2010: 15–16). This research also showed a low rate of release (approximately 4 per cent) of prisoners from the IPP sentence after they had served the minimum term and one of the reasons was that 'many of those serving IPP sentences are refused places on programmes on various grounds including limited intellectual capacity or mental illness'—and attendance at a programme was compulsory before assessment.

These statistics and research findings have fuelled demands for improvements in healthcare provision not only to meet the mental health care needs of prisoners, but also to divert offenders from prosecution to voluntary mental health services where appropriate, or, at the sentencing stage, to treatment under the MHA 1983 (as amended by the Mental Health Act (MHA) 2007). As the Report *Snakes and Ladders: Mental Health and Criminal Justice* (O'Shea *et al.* 2003), published by the 'Revolving Door' charity, points out, many people with mental health problems are caught in a cycle of crisis, crime, and mental illness, in which they are repeatedly in contact with the police and often detained in prison.[37] The prevalence of mental health problems within the prison population also has implications for the experience of imprisonment and can add to the demands made on the Prison Service when it is already overstretched by the numbers entering prison. This issue will be considered in chapter 11 (section 11.4.4) in relation to women prisoners and their health needs.

The treatment of mental health problems in prison was also an issue considered by Lord Keith in his inquiry into the murder of Zahid Mubarek by his cellmate, who suffered from a personality disorder (Keith 2006). The Mubarek Report noted that, because of insufficient appropriate resources, such prisoners could be shuttled between healthcare centres and the segregation unit or left with other prisoners.

Given the high incidence of mental illness in the prison population and the lack of resources to deal with prisoners with mental health problems, these problems may be exacerbated. Although some prisoners find their health improves in prison, with a more settled routine, proper meals, and denial of access to drugs and alcohol, those with pre-existing mental health problems may find them exacerbated by imprisonment, which could have severe consequences for their fellow prisoners as well as themselves. Until recently a prisoner with personality disorder could be transferred to a secure hospital only if his or her condition was treatable. This has now been replaced with a new 'appropriate medical treatment' test by s 4 of the MHA 2007 (see section 7.4.3).

The Mubarek Report recommended a comprehensive review of the quality of care given to prisoners with mental health problems. The National Institute for Mental Health in England (NIMHE) has been commissioned to implement a comprehensive national prison mental health programme to improve the quality of mental health services for offenders. Since the death of Zahid Mubarek there has been more training in mental health awareness for officers and the commissioning of healthcare services has been transferred to Primary Care Trusts.

The studies noted, which are evidence of the higher level of 'non-dangerous' mental illness and disorder amongst the prison population than in the population as a whole, prompt the question as to why this should be so. Possible explanations are that the mentally disordered are more inept and visible offenders, that they are repeat petty offenders, or that the 'gatekeepers' who make the decisions in the criminal justice system have stereotypical views. For example, Cummins (2006) examines the role—in this outcome—of

[37] See, for a review of this report, Bui (2004).

police powers and the appropriate adult at the questioning stage of police investigation. However, it may be that there is currently simply a lack of adequate mental health services to diagnose offenders early in the process.[38]

7.4.2 **A policy of diversion**

The Home Office Circular 66/1990 (*Provision for Mentally Disordered Offenders*), provided guidance on how to deal with mentally disordered offending, stating that there should not be a prosecution unless it was required by the public interest. Health service options should be used, rather than penal options with a focus on diversion of such offenders from the penal system (see Laing 1999). The Reed Report also proposed that mentally disordered offenders should, 'wherever appropriate, receive care and treatment from health and personal social services' (Department of Health and Home Office 1992: para 2.1). However, this policy has not been implemented unproblematically. As we noted in Chapter 5, there is a common perception of the mentally disordered as prone to act in dangerous and anti-social ways, with a corresponding reluctance to promote therapeutic disposals which are not under the control of the penal system.[39] From time to time such concerns are fuelled by publicity about murder cases where the defendant has been involved with mental health services.

These concerns reflect an underlying ambivalence in policy and practice, a tension between treatment and public protection aims. Further, a policy of diversion requires resources to identify and provide services and treatment for the criminal with mental health problems, but this is not a use of scarce resources which attracts widespread public support. A decade after the clear policy was laid down, 'the impact of Circular 66/90 and its underlying themes [had] been leavened by a series of risk-infused policy developments' (Peay 2002: 748). The proposals contained in three documents published at the end of the 1990s reveal these often conflicting underlying principles of public protection, treatment, non-discrimination and equal human rights (see Ashworth 2000: 342–3; Peay 2002: 748). The Richardson Report (Department of Health 1999) focused on civil powers, upheld principles of patient autonomy and equal treatment for the physically and mentally ill, and gave priority to treatment over punishment for mentally disordered offenders. The Consultation Paper (Department of Health 1999), on the other hand, was concerned with public protection and risk assessment, whilst the Home Office (1999a) paper on dangerous people with severe personality disorder presaged a concern with finding ways to detain such people without their having committed an offence. The subsequent White Paper on high-risk patients (Department of Health/Home Office 2000) and the draft Mental Health Bills of 2002 and 2004 (see Chapter 5, section 5.2) reflected, together with other developments, 'a growing desire to maintain penal control over mentally disordered offenders' (Peay 2002: 749).

This policy trend persists another decade later. The Bradley report pointed out—again—that '[t]he first step to the effective management of offenders is the existence of good early identification and assessment of problems, which can inform how and where they are most appropriately treated' (Department of Health 2009a: Executive Summary para 80). The Report also encouraged the greater use of the mental health requirement in a community sentence, rather than custody, for offenders with mental health problems

[38] For a systematic review of the international literature on the *Epidemiology of Mentally Disordered Offenders* see the Centre for Reviews and Dissemination (1999).

[39] See Prins (2005)—an update of a text first published in 1980—which provides a useful interdisciplinary approach to the issues.

(ibid: para 38) and, to that end, recommended more research on its operation and the making of service level agreements between Her Majesty's Court Service, the NHS and the Probation Service. Although the report stresses that screening for mental health problems should take place early in the criminal justice process, it also recommends that there should be better screening at reception into prison (ibid: para 43).

The House of Commons Justice Committee welcomed Lord Bradley's preventive approach on economic grounds, stating that '[t]here is a very strong financial case for investing substantial resources in more preventative work with: former offenders; those with drug and alcohol problems; people with mental ill-health; and young people on the outskirts of the criminal justice system or who have been in custody' (2010: para 127) and that, in relation to mentally disordered offenders, there is 'strong evidence that swift action in this area, in particular to broaden access to diversion and liaison schemes and to secure hospital treatment, could yield short, medium and long-term reductions in the prison population and result in cost savings to the public purse, as well as provide more humane approaches to managing offenders with mental ill-health' (ibid: para 158).

The Government's response to that report included the following statement:

> We also agree that less serious offenders can often be better dealt with in the community, and that in some cases we must do more to divert from custody those for whom a criminal sentence may not be the most appropriate response to their offending behaviour.... Implementation of the Bradley review is still in its early stages, and we are placing an emphasis on those system reforms—for example, better commissioning and the widespread introduction of liaison and diversion services—that will help ensure better access to community based treatment.
>
> (Ministry of Justice 2010f: 3–4)

The Government also pointed out that 'publication of the Health and Criminal Justice Delivery Plan, *Improving Health, Supporting Justice*, on 17 November 2009 set out agreed cross-departmental actions aimed at improving access by offenders to mental health, alcohol and other NHS treatment services' (ibid: 27).

7.4.3 **Treatment under the Mental Health Act 1983**

Statutory definitions are very important in sentencing (possibly) mentally disordered offenders: they will determine the 'label' and the options for the defendant. The legislative history of current provisions can be found in the criticisms of the Mental Health Act 1959 by the Butler Committee and a DHSS Review in the 1970s. The legislative framework set up by the resulting MHA 1983 remains largely unchanged. The MHA 2007, ss 1–3 (categories of mental disorder), 4–6 (appropriate treatment test), 7 (definition of medical treatment) and 8 (fundamental principles) have been in force since 3 November 2008. These provisions have amended ss 1 and 37 of the MHA 1983 so that previous criteria and definitions no longer apply.

Before the amendments made by the MHA 2007, s 1(2) defined mental disorder as 'mental illness, arrested or incomplete development of mind, psychopathic disorder and any disorder or disability of mind' and 'psychopathic disorder' was defined as 'persistent disorder or disability of mind... which results in abnormally aggressive or seriously irresponsible behaviour': a definition which did not 'absolve itself of a tautological association with behaviour likely to be criminalized' (Peay 2002: 753). There was a further categorisation into major and minor forms of mental disorder (see Peay 2002: 753) and also a 'treatability' criterion. These provisions caused difficulties.

The following are the main changes relevant to sentencing as summarised in the Government's Explanatory Notes:

> *Definition of mental disorder*: The Act changes the way the 1983 Act defines mental disorder, so that a single definition applies throughout the Act, and abolishes references to categories of disorder. These amendments complement the changes to the criteria for detention. Section 1, therefore, amends the wording of the definition of mental disorder in the 1983 Act from 'mental illness, arrested or incomplete development of mind, psychopathic disorder and any other disorder or disability of mind' to 'any disorder or disability of the mind'.
>
> *Criteria for detention*: It introduces a new 'appropriate medical treatment' test which will apply to all the longer-term powers of detention. As a result, it will not be possible for patients to be compulsorily detained or their detention continued unless medical treatment which is appropriate to the patient's mental disorder and all other circumstances of the case is available to that patient. At the same time, the so-called 'treatability test' will be abolished. Because of the removal of categories of disorder by s 1, the appropriate medical treatment test applies equally to all mental disorders.

The relevant orders for the sentencing court are to be found in Part III of the MHA 1983. Section 37 allows the court to order that the offender be admitted to hospital, provided the receiving hospital agrees—s 37(4), or be placed under the guardianship of the local social services department.[40] The conditions include that the offence of which the offender has been convicted is an imprisonable offence and the court believes an order under s 37 is the most suitable method of dealing with the offender. Evidence from two doctors is necessary to establish that the offender is suffering from one of the forms of mental disorder and that detention for treatment in hospital is appropriate. Transfer from prison to hospital by order of the Home Secretary is possible under s 47, and Crown Courts may impose a s 45A order (see section 7.4.4), both on similar criteria to those in s 37.

The effect of a hospital order is as outlined in the following information provided by the charity MIND:

> Most section 37 hospital orders are initially for six months... At the end of that period, you have the right to apply to the Mental Health Tribunal. Your responsible clinician (RC) has the right to discharge you at any time, as do the hospital managers, but the RC can also renew the section at the end of the first six months, again at the end of a second period of six months, and at yearly intervals thereafter. If your section is renewed, you can apply to the Mental Health Tribunal for discharge.[41]

The Mental Health Tribunal (formerly the Mental Health Review Tribunal) is now part of the First-tier-Tribunal, Health, Education and Social Care Chamber. The Justice website gives the following information about its role:

> The Tribunal is an independent judicial body that operates under the provisions of the Mental Health Act 1983 (as amended by the Mental Health Act 2007). Our main purpose is to review the cases of patients detained under the Mental Health Act and to direct the discharge of any patients where the statutory criteria for detention are not met... Tribunal hearings are normally held in private and take place in the hospital where the patient is or used to be detained or a convenient community unit.[42]

[40] Guardianship orders are rarely used.

[41] See http://www.mind.org.uk/help/rights_and_legislation/mind_rights_guide_5_mental_health_and_the_courts.

[42] See http://www.justice.gov.uk/guidance/courts-and-tribunals/tribunals/mental-health/index.htm. This website is not as informative as that of the former MHRT: see the second edition of this book at p 233.

If the Crown Court believes that further restrictions should be placed on release from hospital it may also make a restriction order 'where necessary for the protection of the public from serious harm' (MHA 1983, s 41; see Chapter 5). A magistrates' court may refer a case to the Crown Court for consideration of this order. MHA 2007, s 40 also amends s 41 of the 1983 Act, removing the power of the Crown Court to make restriction orders for a limited period. The court cannot make such an order unless at least one of the two doctors recommending a hospital order gave evidence orally. Where a restriction order is in force the Responsible Clinician needs the permission of the Ministry of Justice or the Mental Health Tribunal to discharge an offender. At the end of the custodial term (now the 'release' date under s 294 of the CJA 2003) of a prison sentence the restriction order ceases to have effect and provisions similar to those of the hospital order apply.[43]

7.4.4 Penal disposals

The previous section briefly outlined the main possibilities for treating an offender as mentally disordered rather than as requiring punishment. There are in addition two 'mixed' orders where a penal disposal is given but it includes treatment. First, a probation or supervision order with a psychiatric treatment condition had been available since the Criminal Justice Act 1948. The PCCSA 2000, Schedules 2, 3, and 6, re-enacted the criteria and requirements in relation to community rehabilitation orders and s 207 of the CJA 2003 provided, instead, for the imposition of a similar mental health treatment requirement in the new community order (and also a suspended sentence order). Such a requirement under s 207 is 'with a view to the improvement of the offender's mental condition', and the treatment can be as a resident or non-resident patient in a care home or hospital, or under the direction of a medical practitioner or psychologist. A doctor must certify that the offender's condition 'may be susceptible to treatment' but does not warrant a hospital or guardianship order.

Secondly, the Crime (Sentences) Act 1997 inserted a new s 45A into the MHA 1983 to provide the courts with hospital and limitation directions. If the offender is suffering from a psychopathic disorder and the court, having considered a hospital order, decides to impose a custodial sentence, it can, nevertheless, direct that the offender be admitted immediately to hospital (with similar further criteria as for hospital orders). If the offender does not respond to treatment (or, possibly, recovers), he is then transferred to prison. This order is, arguably, an unjustifiable compromise between treatment and punishment. It is a clear example of the response by government and the courts to public fears that a mentally disordered offender will 'escape' punishment and control.

Such sentences do, however, provide treatment. As Peay notes, while 'some restriction orders are imposed unnecessarily... most disordered offenders do not receive a therapeutic "hospital order" disposal, even though their culpability may be mitigated, if not absolved, by their mental state' (2002: 755). One possible reason why those suffering from mental health problems are not treated as such at the sentencing stage is that they are not diagnosed early enough to be diverted from the penal system; another is that not all such offenders may 'fit' the MHA 1983 criteria, notably the availability of hospital care (see Genders 2003). A third explanation lies in the widespread ambivalence over the offender's culpability and just deserts, reflecting much deeper concerns regarding the origins of 'evil' in the 'normal' offender.

[43] See http://www.mind.org.uk/help/rights_and_legislation/mind_rights_guide_5_mental_health_and_the_courts.

As a result of these conflicting imperatives and ideas, the sentencing framework allows the sentencer to choose or reject the penal options even when the MHA 1983 criteria are met. Section 166(5) of the CJA 2003 empowers the court to disregard provisions which would otherwise mandate the passing of particular sentences when the offender is mentally disordered. Section 157(1) mandates the court to obtain a medical report before passing a custodial sentence on an offender who 'is or appears to be mentally disordered', although that requirement does not apply if, 'in the circumstances of the case', the court feels that it is unnecessary. Further, before passing such a sentence the court must consider any information about the offender's mental condition and assess 'the likely effect of such a sentence on that condition and on any treatment which may be available for it' (s 157(3)).

If the court decides that it cannot or will not use MHA 1983 options, it could choose penal disposals ranging from 'non-punitive' discharges and bind-overs, through fines, community penalties, and imprisonment. In the case of the latter, a determinate and proportionate sentence may be passed or, where available, a discretionary life sentence. Where a relatively long sentence is passed there may be time and opportunity for therapeutic treatment to be given in prison, but there can be no guarantee of this and, paradoxically, the encouragement of shorter sentences may preclude the possibility of such treatment.[44]

This area of sentencing law and practice is complex and difficult and we have been able only to outline the possibilities and problems. What is clear is that, despite advances in diversion schemes and the standard of mental health care in prisons, our treatment of the mentally disordered offender is still a prime example of unprincipled compromise in relation to issues of sentence impact and effectiveness, as well as offender culpability. It is also an area where a propensity to label as a homogeneous category what is in practice a diverse group of people with diverse needs makes any assessment of sentence impact in individual cases very difficult.

7.5 Review

7.5.1 Conclusions

This chapter has covered a very wide range of issues in relation to the impact of punishment. It has inevitably revealed competing claims for what should count as justice. As we saw in Chapter 6, one of the strengths of restorative justice is that it allows for 'tailor-made' agreed outcomes: 'Diversity and flexibility are crucial in dealing with individual circumstances. There is no definitive model and "one size" is never likely to fit all' (Tickell and Akester 2002: 102). A similar comment could be made about punishment imposed on utilitarian or retributivist principles, if no account whatsoever is taken of structural disadvantage, institutionalised discrimination, or severe personal difficulties. On the other hand, individualised sentencing, as we have seen, can also lead to inequalities of treatment which may be unjust, in the same way as restorative conference outcomes may be punitive and heedless of rights.

In the remaining chapters of this book we will revisit some of these themes in relation to the punishment of minors in Chapter 8, and when focusing on community penalties in Chapter 12. The issue of the differential impact of custodial penalties on adults will be

[44] There is a similar concern in relation to the amount of time required for rehabilitation programmes to be effective: see Chapter 12.

examined in more detail in Chapter 11. There we will focus specifically on the experiences of ethnic minorities and women, asking whether justice requires difference or equality in the treatment of prisoners with different needs and backgrounds.

7.5.2 **Case study**

We have seen that there is no clear approach to taking account of the impact of the financial, medical, and social factors that we have examined. That is not surprising, given that the questions raised by the issue of impact relate to the fundamental principles and assumptions underlying the criminal justice system and what justice might mean.

We have provided a sentencing exercise which draws on the material in Chapter 5 as well as on the themes discussed in this chapter. It brings together difficult questions relating to proportionality, dangerousness, and personal mitigation. Further help is available in approaching this exercise at the Online Resource Centre.

Facts of the case:

Zack is 38 years old and has suffered from mild schizophrenia for almost 20 years. Three years ago he spent a month in hospital for psychiatric treatment to establish a new medication regime. His condition has since been stable and he works as a labourer. He has always lived with his mother who is now elderly and infirm and depends on him for her shopping and laundry.

When doing building work over a period of time in a family home Zack made friends with Yasmin, the 7-year-old daughter of the family, and persuaded her to let him take several photos of her, in particular poses, when she was undressing. He told her to keep the 'photo shoot' as their little secret but Yasmin was excited, thinking she could become a model when she grew up, so she told her parents about the photos. They contacted the police and the photos were found on the computer in Zack's house. The computer provided evidence that he had copied the photos to three friends.

Zack pleaded guilty at the magistrates' court to a charge of taking and distributing indecent photographs of a child (s 1 of the Protection of Children Act 1978). The maximum penalty for this offence on indictment is 10 years and it is a specified offence listed in Schedule 15, para 99 to the Criminal Justice Act 2003 (and also listed in the new Schedule 15B which would be inserted by the Legal Aid, Sentencing and Punishment of Offenders Bill). The photos were referred to COPINE (Combating Paedophile Information Networks in Europe) which graded the images as being of the lowest category of severity. Zack has two previous convictions (for being drunk and disorderly and for theft in breach of trust) for which he received a fine and a short custodial sentence respectively.

You are Zack's solicitor. Explain to him what options are open to the magistrates' court at the sentencing hearing (including referral to the Crown Court for sentencing) and what the judge is most likely to decide.

Would your answer be any different if he was at the time of conviction still attending regular out-patient appointments at the local hospital's mental health unit?

You might wish to consult the following:

Sentencing Guidelines Council (2007) *Sexual Offences Act 2003, Definitive Guideline*

Sentencing Guidelines Council (2008, updated 2011) *Magistrates' Courts Sentencing Guidelines, Definitive Guideline* 74–5.

8

Treating children differently

SUMMARY

This chapter focuses on the ways in which, and the extent to which, the state deals differently with children and young people under 18 years of age who commit criminal offences. It discusses what is known about the offending of children and young people, reviews the ways in which the treatment of minors who offend has been theorised and examines the policies developed over the last century to divert minors from prosecution. It, therefore, reviews the history and use of cautioning, reprimands, warnings and the new youth conditional caution, and summarises the key elements of the youth justice system set up by the Crime and Disorder Act (CDA) 1998. However, it also examines the development of responses to anti-social behaviour, the role of civil orders and contracts, and the images of 'youth' which underpin such policies.

8.1 Introduction

8.1.1 A separate system

Article 40 of the United Nations Convention on the Rights of the Child (UNCRC), declares that:

> States Parties shall seek to promote the establishment of laws, procedures, authorities and institutions *specifically applicable* to children alleged as, accused of, or recognised as having infringed the penal law, and, in particular:...
>
> (b) Wherever appropriate and desirable, measures for dealing with such children *without resorting to judicial proceedings*, providing that human rights and legal safeguards are respected.
>
> (para 3: emphasis added)

In effect Article 40 lays down principles of separate or different treatment for children—defined in the UNCRC as being under 18 years of age—and endorses diversion away from the criminal justice system However, whilst the UNCRC was adopted by the UN as recently as 1989 and was ratified by the UK in 1991,[1] the idea and practice of having a separate system for dealing with children who offend is, as we shall see, much older. The nature of the systems for adults and minors has varied over time, as has the degree of 'separateness', but the distance, conceptually and spatially, from the adult criminal justice system, has been the essential attribute of the juvenile, now youth, justice system from

[1] Although with reservations (now withdrawn) about the care of young offenders (article 37(c)) and young refugees (article 22). For a critical review of the UNCRC, see Fortin (2009: 36–55); also see Williams (2007).

its inception over a century ago. The long-standing policy aim of ensuring that formal processes are child-friendly and that, where possible, formal criminal proceedings are avoided stems from our ideas about children and their development, and our fears for their 'contamination' by adult offenders.[2]

The legislation which set up the first courts specifically for juveniles in the UK endorsed the idea that young offenders are 'children in trouble' rather than 'evil'. In the terminology of the nineteenth century, they could be 'saved' from a life of crime because 'kindness could nip crime in the bud' (Harris and Webb 1987: 15). Statutory provisions to set up the earlier industrial and reformatory schools[3] were also based on those ideas, although we might dispute whether treatment was kind by later standards.

By the early twentieth century, new branches of knowledge as to why children offend had led to the belief that the 'deprived', those we would now refer to as 'children in need', and the 'depraved', now children and young people who offend, are not necessarily separate categories and, though treated separately from adults, should not necessarily be treated separately from each other. That consensus of opinion did not survive into the twenty-first century. Referring to the Children Act 1948 and the committee which made the proposals enshrined in that Act, Cretney made the following observation:

> The belief (…held in the Home Office well before World War II) that 'whether a young child commits an offence, goes out on the loose, or is just unruly or naughty is purely fortuitous'[4] only began to be seriously questioned in the 1970s.[5] Those responsible for the formation of policy over those years would view with disbelief the apparent consensus of the nineties on the need for a punitive approach to young delinquents.[6] It is in this respect that the philosophy of the 1948 legislation has been most dramatically overturned: for the Curtis Committee the emphasis was not to be on what a child had done in the past but on what the child's needs were at present.
>
> (Cretney 1998: 459)

Others have also expressed concern: according to Weijers and Duff 'the last few decades…have witnessed remarkable changes in views both of juvenile offenders and of the proper role of the state…A century after its foundation, the future of the juvenile system is very much in doubt' (2002: 1). This chapter will review past and present developments to assess whether these fears are founded in relation to youth justice developments in England and Wales. We will focus on what research tells us about children who offend in section 8.1.3 and in section 8.4 we will examine further our ideas about children who offend: we need to appreciate how important are our ideas and fears about children, families, morality and social stability in order to understand developments in youth justice. How we 'visualise' children has implications for how we decide what counts as justice for them when they offend or what outcomes appear legitimate and justifiable. In this regard we also focus on the development of contractually based options as well as civil orders

[2] For a historical review of juvenile justice policy in the United States see Zimring (2005).

[3] For a discussion of the Industrial School Acts 1857–1880 and the Youthful Offenders Act 1854, see Pinchbeck and Hewitt (1973: chapter 16).

[4] *Seebohm Report* (1968), para 188 (n 293 in Cretney 1998).

[5] Cretney's footnote (n 294) includes the following comment: 'The Children and Young Persons Act 1933 did make a clear distinction between prosecution and protection measures, and the anomalies to which this was thought to give rise were analysed by the Ingleby *Committee on Children and Young Persons* (1960) Cmnd. 1191, which (inter alia) recommended amendments to the "care and protection" provisions of Children and Young Persons Act 1933, s.61'.

[6] In n 295 Cretney notes at this point that courts must still heed the welfare principle in the 1933 Act (see section 8.1.4).

to address anti-social behaviour. Human rights are also important in relation to youth justice and we will examine issues of compliance with rights conventions in Chapter 13 (section 13.4.1).

This chapter needs to look further, therefore, than the substance of sentencing principles and policies covered in earlier chapters. It must acknowledge the relevance of policy areas other than youth justice because public concerns about wider social issues have also led to a policy focus on the child who offends (see Koffman 2008; Piper 2008: chapter 3; Welshman 2007). For all these reasons, this chapter reviews more than sentencing law and policies. This chapter examines why prosecution and sentencing are not necessarily the next stages after offending has been admitted by minors, and reviews the alternatives that have developed in both the criminal and civil justice systems.

8.1.2 **Offending by minors**

Another difficulty when seeking to understand developments in this area of law and policy is that media and political debate is not always conducted in the context of what we know about the extent of offending by minors. Often the assumption that offending is on the increase is used to promote particular responses. This is understandable in that different sets of data may suggest conflicting trends.[7] Life history interviews, self-report studies, and victimisation surveys in various jurisdictions confirm that 'actual' offending rates are higher than official statistics would suggest. The 1998 MORI survey of 11–16-year-olds reported in the 1999 Annual Report of the new Youth Justice Board found that only 70 per cent of children could say with certainty that they had not committed an offence in the previous 15 months (see NACRO 2000c: 1) and the Audit Commission noted that 'between 1999 and 2003, the rate of self-reported offending by young people remained constant at one in four' (2004: 3).[8] However, the MORI Youth Survey in 2008 (Youth Justice Board 2009a: 5) showed that the overall proportion of young people reporting that they had committed an offence in the previous 12 months had declined compared with previous surveys.

Self-report methods have their limitations, however (Graham and Bowling 1995: 8–10), and there are different messages from official statistics and self-report studies about the issue of 'growing out' of crime: the reduction in offending after the age of 20 may be due to engagement in less visible offending as well as reduced frequency of offending (ibid: 30). The higher visibility of offending by young people may also account for public perceptions of the danger from young criminals. Research in 2008–9 showed, for example, that 30 per cent of people perceived teenagers hanging around to be a problem in their local area (Parfrement-Hopkins and Hall 2009).

However, there is some consensus that there were large increases in recorded crime for adults and juveniles from the 1930s to the 1970s, but that the rate of increase of recorded crime in England and Wales slowed down in the 1980s and fell after the mid-1990s (Gelsthorpe 2002: 47; see also NACRO[9] 2000c: 1 and Scottish Executive 2002b). The British Crime Survey data then suggests that offending fell until 2004–5 and remained relatively stable in 2005–8 (see NACRO 2010: 1); recorded crime data suggests a slight rise

[7] See, for example, Graham and Bowling 1995: 1.

[8] Based on an annual school survey by MORI of children aged 11–16 (Audit Commission 2004: 8–9); self-reported offending by excluded pupils was also constant but at almost two in three pupils (ibid).

[9] The crime reduction charity, formerly the National Association for the Care and Resettlement of Offenders.

with a peak in 2006 and declining levels in 2007–10 (National Audit Office (NAO) 2010a: see Figure 8.1).

It was estimated that 11 per cent of all known offenders were between 10 and 17 years of age in 1997 (Mattinson and Mirrlees-Black 2000: 11), 12 per cent in 2005 (NACRO 2007c: 2), and 17 per cent in 2009 (National Audit Office 2010a: 11)[10] However as NACRO has pointed out, it is adults aged 21 and above who are responsible for more than three-quarters of offences (2007c: 2). When we wrote the second edition of this text there was some consensus that the long-term trend up until 2003 of a decline in recorded crime committed by those aged 17 and under had not continued into 2007, but the decline has in fact continued: the recent National Audit Office report asserted that there had been a 25 per cent fall between 2002–03 and 2009–10 (2010a: 11). The latest Statistics Bulletin from the Youth Justice Board and the Ministry of Justice also notes that '[t]here were 198,449 proven offences committed by young people aged 10–17 which resulted in a disposal in 2009/10. This is a decrease of 19% from 2008/09 and 33% from 2006/07' (2011b: 2–3).

The 'peak' ages for offending are thought to be in the age group 15–20, with different peaks for males and females, and for different offences (Farrington 2002: 426; Graham and Bowling 1995: chapters 2 and 3; Flood-Page *et al.* 2000: 10): in 2005 statistics for recorded indictable offences suggested a peak age of 17 for males and 15 for females (see NACRO 2007c: 2). 'Overall, girls still appear to be involved in offending in general for a shorter period, to commit fewer offences than boys and, on the whole, to commit less serious offences' (Youth Justice Board 2009b: 19). The majority of crime committed by boys and girls is not serious offending but is property-based. 'In most categories fewer offences were committed in 2009–10 than in 2002–03, with the biggest falls in motoring offences, vehicle theft and theft and handling' (National Audit Office 2010a: 11). However, violence against the person is now the second largest group of proven offences: theft and violent offences accounted for over 40 per cent of proven offences in 2009–10 (ibid: 2).

Commentators were puzzled by the fact that the number of children receiving a reprimand, final warning, or conviction for an indictable offence increased by 19 per cent in the period 2003–6 although the number was still lower than the equivalent figure for 1992 (NACRO 2008: 2). It was suggested that this increase was the result of target-led police practices (NACRO 2008) and this would appear to be so (NACRO 2010: 3).

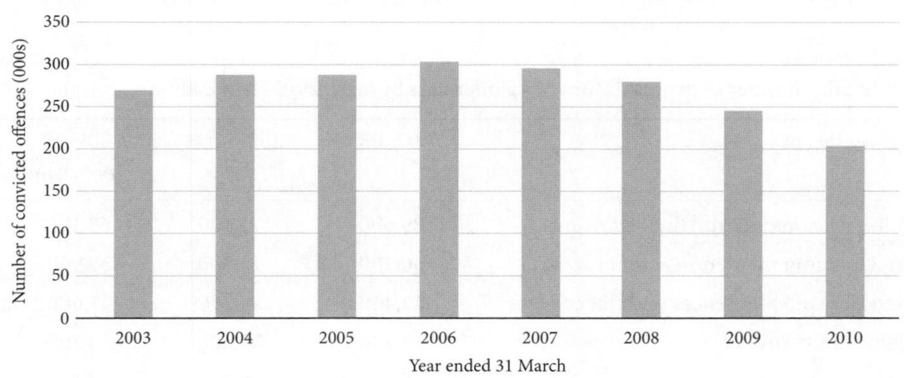

Figure 8.1 Proven offences by young people, 2002–3 to 2009–10
Source: National Audit Office (2010a: 12, Figure 2).

[10] Based on unpublished analysis of Police National Computer data for NAO by the Ministry of Justice (November 2010): ibid fn 2.

There has been particular concern about young people who commit the most serious of offences but there is no clear upward trend as assumed: the number of 10–17-year-olds sentenced to some form of detention for life did increase from 11 in 1996 to 28 in 2005 but a total of 29 was reached in 1999 and only 11 in 2003 (Home Office 2007a: Table 2.7). In September 2011 official prison statistics showed that 4 per cent of 12–17 year olds in custody or secure accommodation were on indeterminate sentences whilst 28 per cent were on determinate sentences of less than a year and 20 per cent were being held on remand (Berman 2011: 4). Overall, however, the recent figures (using Youth Justice Board data) show not only a decline in the use of custody for young offenders but also reduced numbers of other court imposed orders and police reprimands and warnings (see Table 8.1).

What we know about the incidence of offending by children and young people is, then, contested and does not prove that offending is on the increase, either in total or in severity, despite the fact that the public continues to believe that it is. One research study found that almost two-thirds of respondents (63 per cent) thought that crime had increased over the previous 12 months, with 30 per cent believing that it had risen a lot (Patterson and Thorpe 2006: 34; see also NACRO 2007c: 1 and NACRO 2010: 2). However, it is still a valid cause for concern because it cannot be in the longer-term interests of young people to allow them to persist in offending without providing support and appropriate help: only a few people pursue a 'successful' career in crime.

8.1.3 The offenders: who and why?

The factors associated with offending suggest that young offenders are marginalised young people, often with a range of problems which require medical, social work, or educational responses. Those who offend might, therefore, be classed as in need of protection. Goldson argues, for example, that 'it is well established that the social circumstances of children in trouble, "young offenders", are invariably scarred by complex configurations and multiple interrelated forms of disadvantage' (Goldson 1999: 3, also 2000b; see also: Barry 2005; Fortin 2009: 682–3 and references therein). For example, there is research evidence of the abusive background of a large proportion of 12–14-year-olds eligible for what are now detention and training orders (Crowley 1998), of those sentenced for murder and very 'grave crimes' (Boswell 1991) and of persistent young offenders (Hagell and Newburn

Table 8.1 Number of disposals for young offenders by type, 2007–8 to 2009–10

Disposal type	2007–08	2008–09	2009–10 (provisional)
Police reprimands and final warnings	89,600	75,100	63,100
First tier court sentences with orders	50,700	45,200	39,900
First tier court sentences without orders	22,400	19,200	17,600
Community orders	41,200	38,500	30,200
Custody	6,900	6,700	5,100
Total	210,700	184,800	155,800

Notes
1 Columns may not add up due to roundings.
2 First Tier sentences are defined by the Youth Justice Board as less serious than Community Orders.
Source: National Audit Office (2010a: 15, Figure 4).

1994). The vast literature on the childhood risk factors which correlate with offending by young people tells the same story (see, for example, Beinart *et al.* 2002; Farrington 2007; Youth Justice Board 2001) as does recent information provided for MPs about prisoners which notes the following:

> 47% of male sentenced prisoners and 50% of female sentenced prisoners had run away from home as a child. This compares to 10% of the general population.
>
> Over 25% of prisoners had been taken into care as a child compared to 2% of the population.
>
> (Berman 2011: 16)[11]

That document also notes that '35% had a family member that had actually been in prison' (ibid) although recent longitudinal research using data sets from 1946 to 1981 found no significant relationship between parental imprisonment and offspring offending in Holland and, in England, a relationship was found for sons only and that parental imprisonment only significantly predicted sons' offending when it happened after the sons' seventh birthday (Besemer *et al.* 2011).

These correlations between harm done to children in childhood and their offending persist into adulthood, so it might be argued that children should not be treated as a special case but the idea that responsibility and culpability should be mitigated has more force in its application to children and young people. They do not have the capability and independence to rise above their circumstances and, further, propensities to offend can more easily be 'treated' when the offender is young. Deciding outcomes on retributivist or restorative principles requires, then, a better understanding of the stages by which children acquire the ability to be given, and benefit from, an appropriate level of responsibility (see Weijers 2002: 139–42).

The riots in England in August 2011 have led to research into the reasons why young people took part. The project commissioned by the Cabinet Office used notions of 'nudge'—factors which facilitate involvement—and 'tug'—factors which inhibited involvement. Table 8.2 summarises the factors they discovered: it emphasises the complexity of motivations for offending, the interrelationship with situational factors and the impossibility of finding easy answers as to why young people offend.[12]

Official statistics of arrests rebutted the prevalent notion, for example, that the riots were the result of gang culture: 'Overall 13 per cent of arrestees (417) were reported to be affiliated to a gang. Outside London, the majority of forces identified fewer than ten per cent of all arrestees as gang members' (Home Office 2011a: 18). Correlations between offending and particular life circumstances are certainly not the whole picture but the Home Office report included the following which bears out the links between offending and forms of deprivation:

> The findings from these analyses reveal those appearing before the courts tended to be from more deprived circumstances than the wider comparable populations in England:
>
> - Thirty-five per cent of adult defendants were claiming out-of-work benefits, compared to 12 per cent of the working age population;
> - Forty-two per cent of young people brought before the courts were in receipt of free school meals during their time at school, compared to 16 per cent of pupils in maintained secondary schools; and

[11] Available at www.parliament.uk/briefing-papers/SN04334.pdf based on research published in 2002.

[12] See also Bowen *et al.* (2008a and b) in relation to anti-social and other problem behaviours in children.

- Sixty-four per cent of those young people (for whom matched data was available) lived in one of the 20 most deprived areas in the country—only three per cent lived in one of the 20 least deprived areas.[13]

(Home Office 2011a: 20)

Table 8.2 Factors affecting decision-making of young people

	Facilitators	Inhibitors
Situational	*Group processes*: Feeling disinhibited and swept along by the power of the group, seeing others 'get away with it', feeling anonymous	*Group processes*: Actively thinking toward future goals and not focussing on the 'here and now' (see also individual factors)
	Peer pressure: Friends getting involved	*Peer pressure*: Friends not involved
	Information: Seeing it on the TV, getting texts/Facebook/BBM messages	*Information*: Didn't get any messages, not watching TV
	Circumstances: Not otherwise occupied, it was nearby/easy to get to	*Circumstances*: More difficult to get to (further away, no buses)
	Presence of authority figure: No adult telling them not to, everybody was doing it and nobody seemed to be getting caught	*Presence of authority figure*: Parents, relatives or youth workers telling them not to
Individual	*Previous criminal activity*: Easy to get involved, 'This is what they do round here'	*Previous criminal activity*: Been caught once, know the risks
	Attitudes towards authority: Cynicism/ anger towards politicians, authority, negative experience of the police	*Attitudes towards authority*: No negative experience of the police
	Prospects: Poor job prospects, low income, limited hope for the future, 'Nothing to lose'	*Prospects*: In work or expectations of work, aspirations – a lot to lose
Family or Community	*Family attitudes*: Relatives not disapproving	*Family attitudes*: Disapproving, 'Not brought up like that'
	Community: Attachment to a community with a culture of low-level criminality	*Community*: Attachment to a community with pro-social values/culture (including religious communities)
Societal	*Belonging*: Little sense of ownership or stake in society	*Belonging*: Sense of 'ownership' or stake in society
	Poverty and materialism: Desire for material goods, but no means to pay for them	

Source: Morrell *et al.* (2011: 34, Table 4.1).

[13] Available at http://www.cabinetoffice.gov.uk/sites/default/files/resources/The%20August%20Riots%20in%20England%20(pdf,%201mb).pdf.

8.1.4 **The welfare principle**

Section 44 of the Children and Young Persons Act 1933 established that courts must 'have regard to' the welfare of the child:[14] an important mandatory requirement to ensure that children have been given at least a modicum of 'special' treatment when appearing in a court and, particularly, when appearing in a Youth or Crown Court. Further, under s 10(4) and (5) of the Children Act 2004 a youth offending team (YOT) is identified as one of the authorities which is a 'relevant partner of a children's services authority in England' and therefore under a duty to co-operate with the authority in making relevant arrangements. By s 10(2), authorities must make arrangements:

> ... with a view to improving the well-being of children ... so far as relating to—
>
> (a) physical and mental health and emotional well-being;
>
> (b) protection from harm and neglect;
>
> (c) education, training and recreation;
>
> (d) the contribution made by them to society;
>
> (e) social and economic well-being.

Section 11(2) of the 2004 Act also makes clear that a YOT is one of the bodies which must make arrangements for ensuring that they and any partner agencies discharge their functions 'having regard to the need to safeguard and promote the welfare of children'.

However, 'to have regard to' both the longstanding and the more recent duties constitutes a weak welfare principle in comparison with the **paramountcy principle** in s 1 of the Children Act 1989. That duty—placed on courts in the family justice system dealing with the upbringing of children—means that the child's welfare must be the determining factor in the court's decision. However, this duty does not apply to decisions about guilt or sentence in the criminal jurisdiction. The duty to 'have regard to' means that, providing consideration has been given to the interests of the child or young person, magistrates' and Crown Courts can legally give precedence to other interests such as the need to protect the public and to prevent reoffending. There is, admittedly, some overlap between the family and youth justice jurisdictions. Offending may be a factor in care proceedings which are governed by the paramountcy principle, but such offending is relevant only in so far as it is evidence that the child is at risk of suffering significant harm (Children Act 1989, s 31).

The case of *R (on the application of the Howard League for Penal Reform) v Secretary of State for the Home Department* (2002) did establish that the duties of the local authority to children in need or at risk (Children Act 1989, ss 17 and 47) do not end at the door of a prison service establishment (para 136 *per* Munby J). However, the paramountcy principle is not thereby incorporated into decision making in the youth justice system or the Prison Service, whilst s 37(1) of the CDA 1998 established a potentially conflicting aim by declaring the prevention of offending as the 'principal aim' of the youth justice system in England and Wales. The Criminal Justice and Immigration Act (CJIA) 2008 would have stated that '[t]he court must have regard primarily to the principal aim of the youth justice system' but that clause was dropped after opposition to such a downgrading of the welfare principle and the final version is a fudged position.

[14] As did the Prosecution of Offences Act 1985 in relation to the Crown Prosecution Service (CPS).

A new s 142A in the Criminal Justice Act 2003, inserted by s 9(1) of the CJIA 2008, reads as follows:

(2) The court must have regard to–

(a) the principal aim of the youth justice system (which is to prevent offending (or re-offending) by persons aged under 18: see section 37(1) of the Crime and Disorder Act 1998),

(b) in accordance with section 44 of the Children and Young Persons Act 1933, the welfare of the offender, and

(c) the purposes of sentencing mentioned in subsection (3).

We can see the same dual aims evident in the Justice (Northern Ireland) Act 2002. The principal aim of the youth justice system 'is to protect the public by preventing offending by children' but the relevant persons 'must also have regard to the welfare of children affected by the exercise of their functions... with a view to furthering their personal, social and educational development' (ss 53(1) and (3)).

8.1.5 **Conceptualising welfare and justice**

The terms 'welfare' and 'justice' need some explanation in the juvenile justice context. We will concentrate on the period since the 1950s, simply noting that in the first half of the twentieth century the separateness of the juvenile court had been consolidated[15] and social work approaches developed.

The shorthand terms of welfare and justice have been used to indicate whether the *main* focus of policy and practice is the child's needs or the child's offending, and whether the constraining principle is the child's best interests—widely interpreted—or the young offender's rights to due process and an outcome which accords with his or her 'just deserts'. Consequently, the justice approach is characterised as involving 'informed and transparent decisions' in courts, and with an end product of punishment 'portrayed as rational, consistent and determinate' (Scraton and Haydon 2002: 311). The welfare approach is, instead, associated with interventionist measures of care, protection and rehabilitation, which have drawn on knowledge from medicine and criminology since the early twentieth century. To quote Shaw, Lord Advocate in 1908, 'many high-minded men and women,... have been working upon this subject, and of recent years one is glad to note a large development of scientific knowledge. All these facts... made out a case for this Bill'.[16]

The welfare approach is, consequently, associated with decision making by professionals trained in social work or the 'psy-sciences', exercising their discretion to determine what is in the child's best interests. From the justice perspective, this approach is criticised for 'leaving children to the discretionary, permissive powers of professionals' (Scraton and Haydon 2002: 311) and for being based on philosophically unsound principles. According to Asquith, '[I]t is not possible to identify criteria which can either be employed to explain delinquent behaviour or to inform the measures to which children are subjected in their "best interests"' (2002: 276). Some proponents of children's rights would argue that 'only in a system in which children are punished for what they have done

[15] For example, the Children and Young Persons Act 1933 made it a requirement that there should be an hour's interval between sittings of the adult and juvenile courts. The CDA 1998, ss 47–48 repealed this requirement and also amended Schedule 2, para 15 to the 1933 Act to allow a stipendiary magistrate (now District Judge) to sit alone in a youth court.

[16] Speaking in the debate on the Children Act 1908: Hansard, 1908, Vol 186, cols 1 251–2.

can their rights be best protected' (ibid), an echo of the debate referred to in Chapters 1 (section 1.2.3) and 4 (section 4.4.3) on whether rights are more protected under a retributivist system than a utilitarian one.

On the other hand, the justice approach is criticised on the same ground as modern retributivism: it is unable to deliver substantive justice because it cannot take sufficient account of social mitigation (Scraton and Haydon 2002: 315; see also Chapter 10). 'Critics, therefore, posit the notion of a "'just' criminal justice system within an unjust society" as a contradiction in terms' (Morris and Giller 1987: 246, referring to Bottoms 1985: 110) and this is one of the 'five main areas of attack' on the justice model which Morris and Giller summarise (1987: 246).

What this review suggests is that perceptions of justice for minors who offend are in large part determined by a choice of one of two overarching principles to determine outcome: the welfare of the child or due process rights. But it is more complex than this. What counts as justice also depends on changing ideas about the most important factors for promoting the welfare of the child and about changing conceptions of the child as a rights holder. Ideas about children and childhood are relevant as are the debates charted so far on justifications for the punishment of adults.

The justice approach—to a greater or lesser extent in different decades for different age groups—has incorporated a retributivist ethos of personal culpability (see Morris and Giller 1987: 247–8). The 'welfare' approach is more clearly a utilitarian approach as its justification lies in the intended outcome of improvements in the minor's development and well-being. So, in the Scottish Children's Hearings system for young offenders, established as a welfare approach, 'the anticipated consequences of the different available disposals are the overriding criteria in all decisions made on behalf of children' (Adler 1985: 77).

In practice, of course, even if it is possible to delineate theoretically 'welfare' and 'justice' approaches in the history of juvenile justice in England and Wales, there has always been an uneasy integration of both elements. Sections 102–103 of the Children Act 1908 established that, to protect the child, there should be separate places of detention for the under-17s but these were still penal establishments. Further, as previously noted, the long-standing duty to have regard to the child's welfare contrasts with the just deserts-based criterion of seriousness for imposing sentences of detention on young offenders (now s 148 of the Criminal Justice Act 2003) and may conflict with the narrower aim of preventing offending.

Writing in 1985, Clarke argued that it was already 'ill conceived' to see juvenile justice as the site for 'justice v welfare', arguing that social work had contributed to, rather than replaced, punitive juvenile justice (Clarke 2002: 284, 287). Developments based on restorative justice principles are also difficult to fit into the existing theoretical frameworks: a decade ago Gelsthorpe and Morris asked whether restorative justice amounts to 'the last vestiges of welfare' (2002: 238) and Vaughan noted how the new aim of prevention is justified both as a welfare measure and a retributivist focus on offending (2000: 355). More recently prevention has been justified in economic terms and in benefits to the community, not the offender: 'Preventing crime by young people is one of the most cost effective ways to provide long term benefit for communities' (Ministry of Justice 2010a: para 230). Further, crime control perspectives cut across and deconstruct such labels and the distinction between welfare and justice also does not adequately elucidate the place of rights in current youth policy and practice.

Hazell, in a comparative examination of 'system models and key principles' analyses several variations on the basic welfare and justice models, giving examples of typologies whereby England and Wales are classified as 'Neocorrectionalist' (Cavadino and Dignan 2006: 2001) or 'Corporatist' (Winterdyk 2002 and 2005) (Hazell 2008: 25–6).

One way forward is to abandon the assumptions that welfare and justice are signified by particular places or particular types of professional and to apply an approach developed by Teubner and Luhman to focus on how law, as a system of communication, 'thinks' about the people with whom it deals. What results are 'semantic artifacts', 'not real flesh and blood people...They are mere constructs' (Teubner 1989: 741) and this means that law constructs children as victims, offenders, witnesses, and so forth for different purposes. These constructs are not necessarily consistent with each other or with constructs from social work or medicine. This approach[17] sheds light on the difficulties of inter-agency cooperation: failure results not only from the lack of workable and effective means of communication but also because of quite different ways of thinking. From this perspective, Law has a particular difficulty if the 'truths' of other systems do not 'fit' law's ways of thinking which happened in those periods when social and psychological science constructed the courts as 'bad' for children who offend. The encouragement of out-of-court police-based outcomes can then be seen as a coping strategy, but also as a response to retain authority in dealing with offenders through the traditional criminal court system (King and Piper 1995: 103–12).

The next sections therefore will briefly review the history of juvenile justice in the UK, in the light of these different perspectives, noting a different development in Scotland, and summarising the policies of **bifurcation** and diversion which emerged.

However, during the Labour Governments new discourses emerged in relation to the 'respect' and inclusion policy agendas, which cut across concepts of welfare and justice and made problematic the boundaries, not only between the juvenile and adult justice systems but also between social and penal policy relevant to children and young people. We will deal with these later in this chapter.

8.2 Developments in diversion

8.2.1 Diverging approaches

The Children Act 1908 established a juvenile court for the whole of the, then, United Kingdom of Great Britain and Ireland and, except in Scotland, the name and role of the court lasted for almost a century. The 1960s proved to be the watershed in the way young offenders were dealt with in different parts of the UK. Commentators present the debates in that decade as 'the heyday of youth justice welfarism' (Muncie and Hughes 2002: 7) but by the end of that decade the two strands of welfare and justice had become more distinct. Perhaps even more importantly, juvenile justice had become 'politicised' (Pitts 1988): broadly speaking, the Left aligned with the 'welfare' approach to juvenile justice and the Right with the 'justice' approach, although this is an over-simplification (Harris and Webb 1987: 24, 26). Two White Papers setting out reforms for England and Wales (*The Child, the Family and the Young Offender* 1965 and *Children in Trouble* 1968) and for Scotland (the Kilbrandon Report 1964) received polarised responses in the different jurisdictions but the opposition was much stronger in England and Wales (Harris and Webb 1987: 26–9). The result was that policy in England and Wales diverged from that in Scotland.

The compromise scheme introduced by the Children and Young Persons Act (CYPA) 1969 for England and Wales retained juvenile courts but gave Social Services Departments

[17] Based on the theory of **autopoiesis**.

a bigger role, ended detention in the criminal system, and lowered the age of criminal responsibility.

However, several key sections were not implemented and, in effect, there occurred, as in the United States, a 'back to justice' swing (Asquith 2002: 276) despite the increased role for social workers. In comparison, for Scotland, the Social Work (Scotland) Act 1968 produced a clearer change. Issues of guilt (determined if necessary by the courts) were separated from issues of child welfare, with a network of Children's Panels to oversee assessment, treatment, and reappraisal by social workers with outcomes such as care, supervision, and residential orders. Scotland, then, developed a decision-making forum with a 'welfare' approach whilst England, Wales and Northern Ireland retained a 'justice'-based juvenile court, albeit one able to draw on, if it so wished, a wider range of 'welfare' intermediate treatment options.

There were, however, some differences in relation to Northern Ireland. The Children and Young Persons Act (Northern Ireland) 1968 continued the mixed care and crime jurisdiction of the juvenile court as in England and Wales but until 1995 the most common form of custodial sentence was the semi-determinate training school order and, in practice, juvenile offenders spent 'longer in custody than their counterparts in England and Wales' (O'Mahoney and Deazley 2000: 56) and so the criticisms made of the 1960s version of welfare in England and Wales were, consequently, made of 'justice' practice in Northern Ireland in the 1990s (ibid: 57–8).

There are, in any case, no agreed ways to incorporate 'welfare' into practice. In France in the 1980s, for example, the juvenile court judge, the *juge des enfants*, most commonly interviewed the juvenile in the judge's office on court premises, usually with the minor's parents (Hackler and Garapon 1986: 7), and focused on the child and family functioning (King and Piper 1995: 113). Courts are, however, only part of the story of juvenile justice.

8.2.2 **Diversion before the 1990s**

The development of diversion of children and young people from the criminal justice system stems from the period after the Second World War when there was a large measure of consensus that policy should move towards treating children who offend in terms of their welfare and that diversion was in their best interests.

Diversion became part, however, of the policy development of 'bifurcation'. In the case of juvenile justice, bifurcation referred to the policy of diverting most young offenders from prosecution whilst a smaller number of serious offenders are processed through the criminal justice system and punished (Bottoms 1985). This policy means that, as with adult sentencing, the higher-profile serious cases can be seen to be treated in a 'tough justice' fashion whilst the rest can be diverted, either *from* the system or *to* preventive measures. The practice of diversion is not part of sentencing as such but the starting point is the same—a 'finding' that an offence has been committed—and records of reprimands, warnings, and youth conditional cautions (see section 8.3.3) are made available to the courts on subsequent convictions. For these reasons we are examining diversion in some detail.

In the UK the main policy tool for diverting young offenders from the criminal justice system in the second half of the twentieth century was cautioning, first tried with young offenders after the First World War but discouraged by the Moloney Report (1927). Policy initiatives after the Second World War (see Home Office 1951) led to the establishment of juvenile liaison schemes in England and Wales by the end of the 1960s and an official policy of encouraging diversion began to develop. A Home Office Circular in 1978 stated that first offenders should be cautioned for all but serious offences and that subsequent offences could also result in a caution if the offence was trivial and not committed a short time after the previous offence. Subsequent circulars did not have an overt aim to increase cautioning, but that was probably the aim implicit in the 1985 and 1990 circulars urging more uniformity of police practice (Wilkinson and Evans 1990: 166).[18] The first and second editions of the *Code for Crown Prosecutors* (CPS 1988, 1991)[19] gave a similar message by stating that the factor of 'youth' could 'properly lead' to a caution instead of prosecution and that prosecution might actually increase the likelihood of reoffending:

> The stigma of conviction can cause irreparable harm to the future prospects of a young adult, and careful consideration should be given to the possibility of dealing with him or her by means of a caution.
>
> (CPS 1988: Code, para 8(iii))

> It is a long standing statutory requirement that the Courts shall have regard to the welfare of the juvenile... There may be positive advantages for the individual and for society, in using prosecution as a last resort and in general there is in the case of juvenile offenders a much stronger presumption in favour of methods of disposal which fall short of prosecution unless the seriousness of the offence or other exceptional circumstances dictate otherwise. The objective should be to divert juveniles from court wherever possible. Prosecution should always be regarded as a severe step.
>
> (CPS 1991: Code, paras 20–21)

The Government endorsed this approach:

> Minimum intervention is a key concept in work with juvenile offenders.... Most juveniles commit offences during their adolescence... and most grow out of it. It is of central importance that our response to delinquent acts does not serve to drive a wayward youngster into becoming a career criminal.
>
> (in Britton *et al.* 1988: 26)

This approach led to the establishment of various inter-agency bodies to make the 'diversion' decisions (see Rutter and Giller 1983: 20) although the source of their authority to make cautioning decisions remained with the police.[20] As a result, fewer children and young people were prosecuted[21] and the use of cautioning vastly increased for juvenile offenders in the 1970s and 1980s (Ball 1995; Goldson 1999, 2000a).[22] Cautioning also proved to be a useful peg on which to hang preventive initiatives in the form of 'cautioning plus' under which a caution was accompanied by the minor's voluntary involvement in some activity intended to reduce the likelihood of reoffending and set up by local authority Social Services Departments and the police (see Marshall 1985).

[18] Similarly in Northern Ireland, from 1975 the police operated a specialist Juvenile Justice Liaison Scheme for 10–16-year-olds (O'Mahoney and Deazley 2000: 36–7).

[19] The Code gives guidance to the Crown Prosecution Service (CPS) in making a decision whether or not to prosecute any suspect above the age of criminal responsibility. It is issued by the Director of Public Prosecutions under s 10 of the Prosecution of Offences Act 1985.

[20] See *Chief Constable of Kent and Another ex p L* (1991).

[21] For example, between 1980 and 1988 the numbers of children sentenced by the courts for indictable offences fell by over 58 per cent (NACRO 1989: 50).

[22] The proportion of juveniles cautioned rather than prosecuted rose from a quarter to nearly a half in the period 1968–73 and to nearly 60 per cent by 1983 (NACRO 1985: 6). By 1994 figures for 10–16-year-old males showed a national rate of 78 per cent with police force area rates ranging from 93 per cent in Suffolk to 63 per cent in Durham.

The other 'half' of the bifurcated policy for responding to offending by minors is the use of sentencing and punishment through the courts (see Chapter 13) and there is some evidence that diversion encourages the belief that minors who are prosecuted are the 'hardened criminals' towards whom the courts can justifiably be tough.[23] The policy of bifurcation has continued in a modified form (see section 8.3) and this concern remains.

However, by the 1990s the juvenile justice system had proved that it was not immune to the increasing influence of a managerialist discourse with its emphasis on 'corporatism' and 'systems management': 'if we are to succeed in effectively managing the problem of juvenile offending, then it must be effectively organised' (Locke 1988: 1). Better management—albeit with an aim of limiting the use of punishment and promoting diversion—became an end in itself[24] and, whilst the aim might be welfarist, the decision-making was often offence-focused (King and Piper 1995: 122–5) and it was economic considerations which helped drive social work cooperation with the police (Pitts 1992a).

There was another specific 'scientific' impetus for diversion—the development of labelling theory (see Lemert 1967) which proposed the idea that most children will 'grow out of' offending if they do not receive and internalise the label of 'criminal'. The White Paper *Children in Trouble* had endorsed this view (Home Office 1968),[25] as had the Black Committee (1979) in Northern Ireland and a Consultation Paper in 1988 which stated that 'even a short period of custody is quite likely to confirm them as criminals...They see themselves labelled as criminals and behave accordingly' (Home Office 1988a: paras 2.17–2.19). Further, statistical monitoring has consistently showed that cautioning of 10–17-year-olds is at least as successful as other outcomes in reducing reoffending.

Perhaps most crucially, cautioning, even if accompanied by preventive intervention, proved to be much cheaper than prosecution followed by either detention in the penal system or care in the child protection system (Pitts 1992a: 175–6). Partnerships to provide preventive projects also allowed useful experimentation in ways of reducing offending (see NACRO 1986).

Arguably, however, these professional ideas and policy advantages allowed the focus to shift from the causes of offending to the managerialist agenda in which juvenile justice could be reconceptualised as a 'delinquency management service' (Muncie 1999: 149–50; see also McLaughlin *et al.* 2001: 308). Fears were expressed that the 'New' Penology and actuarially based decision making (see Chapter 1) was 'colonising' juvenile justice (Kempf-Leonard and Peterson 2000: 88). Practice also showed that measures designed with one aim may lead to quite different outcomes.[26] However, policy attitudes to diversion and to the use of custody changed (again) in the 1990s.

8.2.3 **Changing ideas**

The Home Office Circular and National Standards issued in 1994 (Home Office 1994b) and the revised *Code* for the CPS (CPS 1994) can perhaps be viewed as early evidence of a sea change in thinking about young offenders which 'threatened with reversal' the practice of diversion (Evans 1994: 566). The Circular on cautioning no longer referred to young offenders as those who should normally be diverted from prosecution (Home Office 1994b: Note 3A) and it appeared to amend the policy of multiple cautioning (ibid: para 8;

[23] For example, in the period 1965–77 more minors were given 'custodial' orders: see Pitts 1992a: 174.

[24] See Cavadino and Dignan (2002: 292–8) for a discussion of systems management.

[25] 'It is probably a minority of children who grow up without ever behaving in ways which may be contrary to the law. Frequently such behaviour is no more than an incident in the pattern of a child's normal development' (Home Office 1968: 3–4).

[26] See the second edition of this book at pp 253–4.

see also NACRO 1993). Similarly, the revised CPS *Code*, issued two months later,[27] indicated a tougher approach. According to the Home Secretary when he introduced the new *Code*, 'from now on your first chance is your last chance. Criminals should know that they will be punished' (Michael Howard, quoted in Ball 1995: 198). The 1994 CPS *Code* amalgamated and amended sections from previous Codes to dilute the message about diversion to be found in earlier versions:

> Crown Prosecutors must consider the interests of a youth when deciding whether it is in the public interest to prosecute. The stigma of a conviction can cause very serious harm to the prospects of a youth offender or a young adult. Young offenders can sometimes be dealt with without going to court. But Crown Prosecutors should not avoid prosecuting simply because of the defendant's age. The seriousness of the offence or the offender's past behaviour may make prosecution necessary.
>
> (CPS 1994: para 6.8)

In the further revised CPS *Code* issued six years later the removal of the second and third sentences of the quoted paragraph weakened the presumption further. Instead, it stated, 'Crown Prosecutors should not avoid prosecuting simply because of the defendant's age. The seriousness of the offence or the youth's past behaviour is very important' (CPS 2000: para 6.9). What we have here is a much starker focus and a trend evidenced by statistics showing that the percentage of those cautioned (out of the total of those cautioned or convicted) fell from 70 per cent in 1992 to 58 per cent in 1999 (NACRO 2001a; see also, for later statistics, Audit Commission 2004: 33–4).

These developments were an unpleasant and unexpected shock to youth justice professionals. It would appear there were two—sometimes conflicting—imperatives forcing change: the need to reduce government expenditure and the political need for the government to be seen to be 'doing something' at a time of declining confidence in the criminal justice system generally and the youth justice system in particular. The economic case for reform was put forward by the Audit Commission (1996, 1998) in its reports entitled *Misspent Youth* which gave a clear and damning account of the cost of processing time in relation to outcome and were immensely influential (Audit Commission 1996: 24–5, 33). The 1996 report argued that custodial sentences were ineffective because 90 per cent of young males aged 14–16 sentenced to custody for up to one year were reconvicted within two years (ibid: 42; see also Audit Commission 1998: 31–6).

Another finding, that there was an almost equal probability of reoffending after prosecution and after the third caution and that on the fourth caution the probability of reoffending was greater than after prosecution, was also very influential (Audit Commission 1996: 23). The Audit Commission's reports were criticised as revealing an inadequate understanding of youth crime and the criminal justice process (Jones 2001; Downes 2001/2: 9; Gelsthorpe 2002: 55) but the political climate was such that the evidence in the reports was capable of supporting a tougher approach. As one commentator put it, there was, in effect, 'a Dutch auction of who could seem to be most tough in relation to young people' (Littlechild 1997: 80). The murder of James Bulger by two 10-year-old children, Robert Thompson and Jon Venables, also played a major part in refocusing law and order rhetoric about young offenders. As Scraton and Haydon argue, it was 'an exceptional tragedy conveniently exploited' to construct a 'crisis' (2002: 314) using the rhetoric of a moral panic, a theoretical concept developed in the 1960s and 1970s with the pioneering studies

[27] The Attorney General's policy intention was 'that the public interest factors *in favour of* prosecution [are] brought out more clearly': see Hansard HC, 14 December 1993, Vol 234 col 1049, italics added: see Piper (2001: 34).

of Jock Young and Stan Cohen to help explain the 'amplification' of deviance (McRobbie and Thornton 2002: 69). Similar analyses were done in relation to the Bulger episode (see, for example, Diduck 1999; Hay 1995; King 1997b).

The developing policy focus on increasing control of young offenders was not confined to youth justice concerns. The Youth Service, because of resource difficulties, sought funding elsewhere and, consequently, became subject to new priorities which included crime prevention and a focus on young people 'at risk' of offending (Piper 2001: 32–3). As we will see in section 8.4, there was also an influential discourse around anti-social behaviour.

There were other influences: Gelsthorpe and Morris (1999: 211) isolated the eight interrelated strands of just deserts, managerialism, actuarial justice, 'community', restorative justice, 'public voice', active citizenship, and populist punitiveness. These influences are discussed elsewhere in this volume but, in relation to minors, the result was, arguably, 'a return of unbridled "authoritarian populism" in juvenile justice' (Newburn 1996: 69). In section 8.4 we will examine the ideas about children which have underpinned and justified youth justice policy since the mid-1990s but first we will consider the new administrative system set up to implement policies of early intervention, offender responsibility, and restorative justice for young offenders, which were introduced in the CDA 1998.

8.3 The 'new' youth justice system

8.3.1 No more excuses

It may seem odd that we have entitled this section as 'The "new" youth justice system' when that system has now been in operation for well over a decade. However we focus on 'new' for two reasons. First it is to stress that even when established there was critique as to whether the system was in fact 'new' or simply 're-packaged', given the earlier focus on creating the more systematic approach that we have referred to. Secondly it was new in that the 1998 administrative and diversionary framework was a statutory one for the first time. That system has not been changed in any fundamental way since it was introduced.

In 1997 the in-coming Labour Government issued a White Paper whose title, *No More Excuses: A New Approach to Tackling Youth Crime in England and Wales* (Home Office 1997), indicated a more interventionist response to offending which would hold children and young people to account and implement those elements of New Labour's 'Third Way' policies which encouraged and assumed responsibility in young people. The Preface stated that the Government aimed to 'nip offending in the bud' because 'today's young offenders can too easily become tomorrow's hardened criminals', whilst the Introduction argued that 'allowing young people to drift into a life of crime undermines their welfare and denies them the opportunity to develop into fully contributing members of society'. It proposed reprimands and warnings to replace cautions and argued for the earlier use of prosecution. It thereby undermined the premises of labelling theory and appeared to presage a more interventionist and less diversionary approach (see Goldson 2000a).

No More Excuses also extolled the benefits of restorative justice, pointing out that its proposals for reform built on the principles underlying concepts of restorative justice—restoration, reintegration, and responsibility (Home Office 1997: para 9.21). It argued that 'reparation can be a valuable way of making young offenders face the consequences of their actions and see the harm they have caused' (ibid: para 4.13) and proposed victim–offender mediation as part of final warnings (ibid: para 5.1.5). However, as pointed out in Chapter 6 (section 6.3), government enthusiasm for such approaches in the late 1990s was an intriguing development, given that schemes set up in the 1980s had generally not survived as anything other than localised, small-scale projects (Shapland 2003: n 14). It would appear that the high policy profile being given to the victims of crime, the growing strength of the restorative justice lobby, and the political need to be seen to be doing something different about young offenders, gave reparation and mediation a new lease of life.

8.3.2 The age of criminal responsibility

The responsibility of the youth justice system in England and Wales is for children and young people from the age of 10 until their eighteenth birthday. Debate as to when and to what extent a minor can distinguish right from wrong is a long-standing one: in 1852–3, a Select Committee of Parliament heard conflicting evidence on the issue with opinions setting the age of capability between 10 and 16 (May 2002: 109). In fact the age of criminal responsibility was not raised to 8 until 1933 and then 10 in 1963. The CYPA 1969 had intended to raise the age from 10 to 14 but this was never implemented and was repealed in 1998. This means we have very divergent tests of competence in criminal and family law (see Keating 2007: 187 *et seq*).

The White Paper of 1997 made clear its intention to remove the presumption that children aged over 10 and under 14 years of age are **doli incapax** so that all children over 10 would be liable to prosecution. It argued that 'presuming that children of this age [10–14] generally do not know the difference between naughtiness and serious wrongdoing... is contrary to common sense' (Home Office 1997: para 4.4). What such 'common-sense' thinking ignores is that emotional maturity, and the understanding which comes with more experience of life, are prerequisites of understanding not just the 'fact' of wrongdoing but also its impact and, in particular, the very notions of death as permanent and injury as 'un-mendable' are acquired with age.

> A defendant not old enough to legally buy a hamster can be tried... as though the level of psychological sophistication required to look after a domesticated rodent is worthy of a longer period of development than to understand the moral responsibility inherent in the commission of a serious criminal act.
>
> (Brooks 2011)

However, in line with the White Paper proposals, s 34 of the CDA 1998 abolished the presumption that children aged 10–13 are not capable of being held criminally responsible. Consequently, there is now no presumption to rebut in order for children under 14 (but over 10) to be processed through the youth justice system if they offend. This reform has been much criticised (see Ball 2004: 174–5; Bandalli 1998). The Beijing Rules (see Chapter 13) state that the age of criminal responsibility should 'not be fixed at too low an age level' (rule 4.1) and the UN Committee on the Rights of the Child asked the UK in 1995 to give 'serious consideration' to raising the age of criminal responsibility (Committee on the Rights of the Child 1995: para 36). England, Wales, and Northern Ireland[28] now have the lowest ages in Europe (see Howard League 2008: 6–7), with the age being set, for example, at 18 in Luxembourg and 16 in Spain and Portugal.[29]

[28] The Republic of Ireland and Scotland both raised their minimum age from seven to 12 in 2006 and 2011 respectively.

[29] In Germany the age of criminal responsibility has been 14 since the Youth Court Act of 1923, with the equivalent of a rebuttable presumption for 14–18-year-olds: see Crofts 2002.

Not surprisingly, in 2002 the UN Committee was more critical (Committee on the Rights of the Child 2002: para 59) given the lack of a positive response and the negative change of abolishing the presumption of *doli incapax*. Before the submission of a further UK Report the Committee on the Rights of the Child issued its General Comment 10 which asserted that 'it can be concluded that a minimum age of criminal responsibility below the age of 12 years is considered by the Committee not to be internationally acceptable' (2007: para 32). Therefore, when the UK Government submitted its consolidated third and fourth report to the UN Committee on the Rights of the Child in 2007 without altering the age of 10 years the report received a critical response and a recommendation to raise the age (Committee on the Rights of the Child 2008: para 78).[30] There have been no moves to do so.

8.3.3 **A national system**

The CDA 1998 set up a national and local administrative framework for the youth justice system in England and Wales. It might be seen as a further development of the managerialist approach to youth justice that was developed in the 1980s. Section 38 imposed duties on each local authority, police authority, probation committee, and health authority to provide—or cooperate in providing—youth justice services, and s 38(4) lists 10 functions for these services. It required that youth offending teams (YOTs) with a specified inter-agency composition be set up in each local authority (LA) area (s 39), and mandated the formulation and implementation of a youth justice plan (s 40). These provisions, and the further requirements for agencies to cooperate mandated by the Children Act 2004, have brought better 'joined up' thinking and responses (see Figure 8.2) although there is still room for progress.

Further, the Act set up a national Youth Justice Board (YJB) for England and Wales to monitor the youth justice system and to advise the Secretary of State (s 41). The status of that body was under threat after the Coalition Government came to power in 2010 but opposition appears to have ensured the Youth Justice Board's continuance as before.

As presaged by the White Paper (Home Office 1997: paras 2.3–2.6), s 37(1) of the CDA 1998 introduced for the first time in legislation in the UK an aim for the new youth justice system—to prevent offending. Bottoms (2002) has characterised it as 'explicitly correctionalist', suggesting something different from welfare or justice, and we have already noted that the welfare principle is now only one of a list of matters of which the court must have regard (see section 8.1.4).

The youth offending team (YOT) is now one of the seven partners of the children's services authority listed in s 10(4) of the Children Act 2004. All of these partners 'must co-operate with the authority in the making of arrangements' as specified, 'with a view to improving the well-being of children' in relation to the five outcomes for children which are also specified in s 10. The guidance to the Children Act 2004 noted that YOTs would have 'an important role to play' in the work of Children's Trusts in planning and delivering services relevant to existing statutory duties (HM Government 2005: para 1.16). However, the Coalition Government withdrew statutory children's trust guidance[31] and Children's Trust Boards are no longer required to produce a statutory Children and Young People's Plan.[32] Nevertheless cooperation must still continue.

[30] Which can be accessed at http://www2.ohchr.org/english/bodies/crc/docs/AdvanceVersions/CRC.C.GBR.CO.4.pdf.

[31] 31 October 2010: see http://www.education.gov.uk/childrenandyoungpeople/healthandwellbeing/a00202982/anewapproachfor-childrenstrustboards.

[32] Ibid.

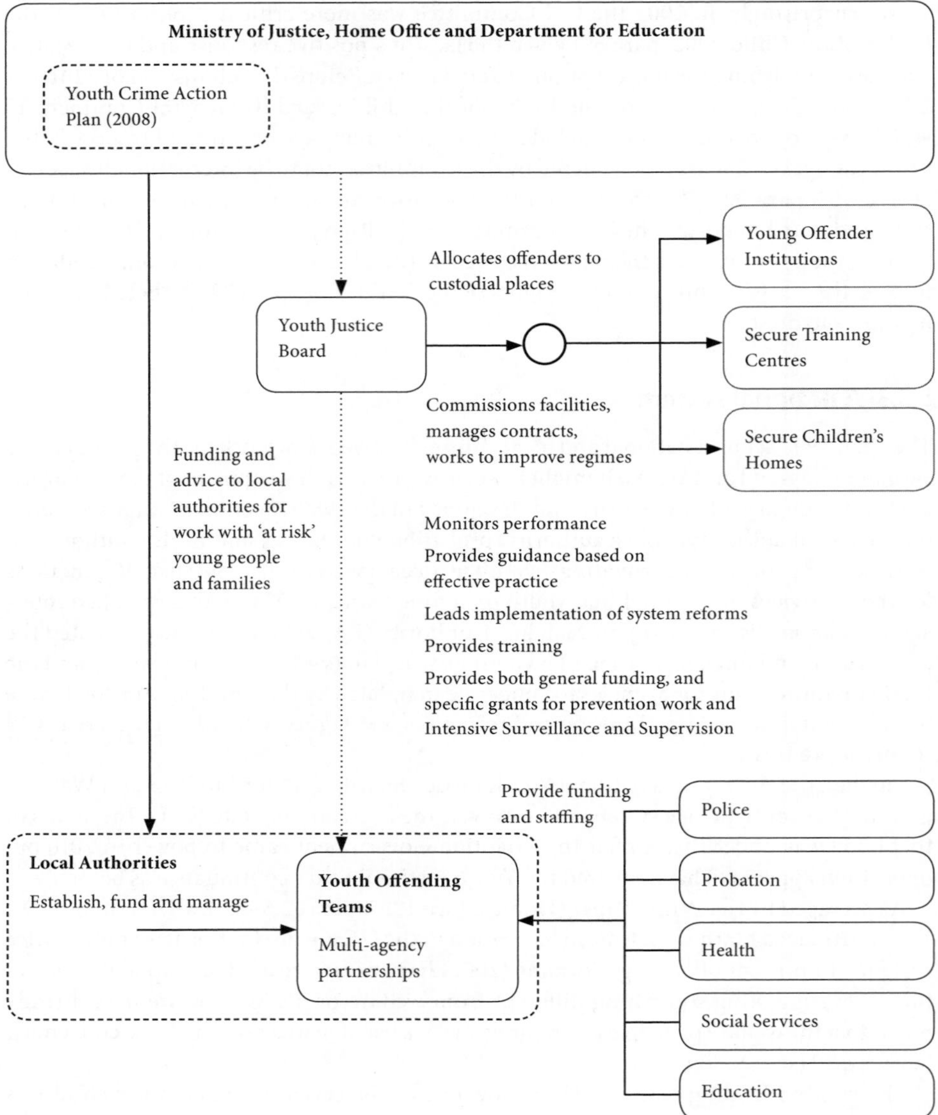

Figure 8.2 The youth justice system in England and Wales

Notes:

1 The Ministry of Justice was the main departmental sponsor of the Youth Justice Board and shared sponsorship for a time with the Department for Children, Schools and Families, now the Department for Education.

2 The three departments jointly introduced the Youth Crime Action Plan and provided funding through it to Local Authorities.

3 The Board has a joint strategy for youth offending in place with the Welsh Assembly Government which reflects the different situation in Wales.

Source: National Audit Office (2010a: Figure 1).

8.3.4 **Reprimands, warnings, and the youth conditional caution**

Sections 65–66 of the CDA 1998 introduced a new pre-court system of reprimands and warnings to replace cautions. Like cautions they are the responsibility of the police but, unlike cautions, they do not require the consent of the minor. They were presented in the White Paper as part of the Government's 'Effective Intervention in the Community' proposals (Home Office 1997: paras 5.12–5.15), with the aim of earlier intervention in the life of the young offender and a reduction in the use of repeat cautions. The reprimand is, in effect, the first caution although a young offender can be moved directly to a warning if the offence is serious (s 65(4)). Normally, the first warning is the only warning although a second may be given if there has been at least a two-year gap since the first (s 65(3)(b)).[33] A warning can be cited as a conviction (s 66(5)(b)).

Guidance emphasises that seriousness of offending will be a very important factor in the decision whether or not to reprimand, warn, or prosecute and that the police should use the Gravity Factor System devised by ACPO (the Association of Chief Police Officers). This gives all offences a score of 1–4 and the guidance states that a score of 4 should always lead to a charge with a 3 leading to a warning (for a first offence) or a charge (Home Office/Youth Justice Board 2002: paras 4.21–4.25).

The *Durham* (2005) case, which concerned a young person who had not been told that a final warning for indecent assault involved a registration requirement as a sex offender, raised rights issues about the final warning. In that case the House of Lords concluded that reprimands and warning do not constitute punishment and that informed consent is not required of children and young people in connection with the use of these provisions. Koffman and Dingwall (2007) have argued that juveniles are in fact being diverted, not from punishment, but to a different form of punishment and, therefore, see the decision in this case as contentious.

The policy of the Youth Justice Board is that the warning should, if possible, be given at a restorative conference (Home Office/Youth Justice Board 2002: 16; see also Chapter 6, section 6.3.2; Fox *et al.* 2006). The warning is then accompanied by referral to a YOT for assessment, and there is a presumption that the young offender will engage in a rehabilitation programme (s 66(2)). The preventive measures are generally offence-focused. There can be a 'prior assessment', completed by a member of the YOT using the Asset assessment tool,[34] before the police make a decision, to explore whether the offender will engage effectively with a rehabilitation programme as well as to suggest the content of it (Giller 2000). A matrix was provided to help YOTs decide the appropriate levels of intervention. This, for example, equates low Asset assessment scores with a low risk of offending and 1–4 hours of intervention whilst a score of over 20 requires 10 hours of intervention (Home Office/Youth Justice Board 2002: para 10.14). Sanctions are also available: 'unreasonable non-compliance with the intervention programme could be cited in any future criminal proceedings' (ibid: para 10.6).

The principles of early intervention and offender accountability—consistently evident in Government policy since *No More Excuses* (Home Office 1997)—are seen as crucial to the effectiveness of reprimands and warnings in reducing reoffending. As *Youth Justice—The Next Steps* noted of reprimands and warnings: 'Young offenders who admit their offence can be dealt with up to twice without going to court, but in a structured way that ensures that they face up to their behaviour. Most Final Warnings are supported by

[33] Research suggested that not all those operating the new scheme were clear about the details of the new legal framework: sometimes several reprimands were given, for example (Audit Commission 2004: 17).

[34] We have concerns about the use of the Asset tool: see Chapter 13, section 13.2.1.

intervention programmes, and if the young person offends again they go straight to court' (Home Office 2003c: para 4). The findings of early research suggested that the interventions accompanying final warnings had led to significant improvements in some of the 13 aspects of the lives of the young offenders which had been assessed but not in others and suggested the introduction of 'a more tailored approach that uses resources in a more targeted way' (Audit Commission 2004: 19).

The CJIA 2008 (ss 48–50 and Schedule 9) introduced a new pre-court disposal—the youth conditional caution (YCC) for use with 10–17-year-olds. This provision came into force early in 2009 but implementation has been phased. It has been piloted since early 2010 with 16–17 year olds in a small number of areas. A young person who had previously been given a reprimand and/or warning is eligible for a YCC—providing the offence is admitted and that the offence is listed in Annex A to the guidance[35]—although those existing two options could be bypassed. They are not available after a YCC has been given. Guidance has been issued to the CPS, Police and youth offending teams by the Director of Public Prosecutions and this notes:

> The decision to administer a Youth Conditional Caution will bring about the suspension of the prosecution while the youth is given an opportunity to comply with the conditions. Where the conditions are complied with, the prosecution should not proceed. However, where there is no reasonable excuse for any non-compliance, the prosecution for the original offence should go ahead as if the Youth Conditional Caution had not been administered.[36]

The Youth Justice Board website states that:

> YOTs will be responsible for the following subject to approval and oversight by the CPS:
>
> - assessing cases
> - recommending conditions
> - supervising young people on YCCs, including delivering conditions
> - monitoring compliance.[37]

8.4 Discipline and responsibility

8.4.1 Constructions of childhood and adolescence

This review reveals that the youth justice system is 'a strange blend of authoritarianism and liberalism—indeed it is permeated with contradictions and tensions' (Fortin 2003: 547). There is now evidence of a policy rhetoric which is punitive and more controlling and it is reflected in images of children which currently underpin youth justice and even family policy. In contrast to the ideas about childhood that helped ensure the establishment of juvenile courts a century ago, we now hold, it is argued, 'extraordinarily narrow views' about children and offending (Fortin 2003: 556) which are reflected in changing nomenclature. The juvenile court is now the youth court and, as we have seen, the CPS *Code* reveals, in successive versions, minors being transformed from 'juveniles' and 'young offenders' through 'youth offenders' to, simply, 'youths' (Piper 2001). There is a valid case for changing from 'juveniles'—it had acquired pejorative overtones—but

[35] See *The Director's Guidance On Youth Conditional Cautions* (2010) at http://www.cps.gov.uk/publications/directors_guidance/youth_conditional_cautions.html. [36] Ibid.

[37] Available at http://www.justice.gov.uk/guidance/youth-justice/courts-and-orders/disposals/youth-conditional-caution-pilot-scheme.htm.

'youth' as a replacement is also problematic. As Garland has noted, 'penal laws and institutions...are framed in language and sign systems which embody specific cultural meanings, distinctions and sentiments and which must be interpreted and understood (1990: 198). At present, the cultural meanings constructed around 'youth' are often negative, with its image of an older (male) person and, arguably, 'youths hanging about' have become 'the universal symbol of disorder and, increasingly, menace' (Burney 2002: 473). The images and tabloid reporting of the riots in England in the summer of 2011 have only added to the pejorative undertones of 'youth'.

Such changes in thinking are important because how we conceptualise 'a child' (Jenks 1996: 51) and what we believe distinguishes a child from an adult (Archard 1993: 20) help determine what is appropriate treatment of children. Referring to minors as youths, we would argue, has facilitated the introduction of criminal justice policies for minors which are at odds with former ideas about the offending child as one who is 'in trouble' and in need of help (Vaughan 2000; Piper 2001). If 'youth' draws on disparate ideas ranging from the 'dangerous' to the 'nearly adult', it conveys the connotation of a person who can legitimately be disciplined, be accorded culpability from a young age and be held to account. He or she can then be expected to take part in the processes of mediation and reparation which assume responsibility in the participants (see Chapter 6). He or she can also be expected to participate in intensive community programmes designed to prevent reoffending which have potentially severe penalties for non-compliance (see Chapters 12 and 13), and can legitimately be punished more harshly for persistence. Scraton and Haydon have criticised this development: '[I]t imposes surveillance disguised as prevention, subservience disguised as discipline and punishment disguised as correction' (Scraton and Haydon 2002: 315).

What has been called the 're-moralisation' agenda further legitimises a focus on discipline and responsibility and so we focus on this next.

8.4.2 **'Re-moralisation'**

In the 1990s an influential moral discourse explained the perceived increased lawlessness of the young as being the result of their not having been taught right from wrong, an approach which was part of a wider project to 're-moralise' the family. The context was a growing belief that 'profound changes in the economic, technological, and social make up of western societies' had undermined social cohesion and increased social and personal insecurity (Junger-Tas 2002: 40). This was of concern because a liberal state is dangerously dependent on its members internalising norms of self-control and citizenship. Analysts who use the theoretical framework developed by Michel Foucault (see, for example, Foucault 1977; Donzelot 1980; Rose 1987, 1990) have focused on this issue of social discipline and have examined ways in which techniques of control have been deployed historically through the workhouse, the factory and the prison, for example. Most importantly they have focused on the family as a site for forms of 'gentle' social control. What is now seen as problematic is whether the family, this traditional main 'tool' for the inculcation of morality, still has the ability and the authority to act as 'a place of socialisation of the young' (Junger-Tas 1994: 18).

Building on Progress: Families stated that the family is a 'fundamental building block of society' (PMSU 2007: 10) and the Labour Governments developed policies to support and 'encourage' parents. The clear message of policy documents was, however, that the help offered to parents to improve their parenting *should* be accepted: parents were being made more accountable (see Reece 2005). Hollingsworth's review of mechanisms introduced to encourage parental responsibility in the youth justice context focuses on a 'matrix of powers' to 'instil' parental responsibility: the liability of parents in relation to fines and parental compensation orders, the power of the courts to bind parents over,[38] the introduction and increasing scope of parenting orders, and the sanctions for non-compliance (2007). These civil orders for parents can also accompany civil orders imposed on their children and can be imposed where children have been playing truant from school.

Such approaches have continued under the Coalition Government.[39] The DirectGov website states: 'Perhaps the most important thing to remember is that a young person's parents are the first and most important role models they will have in their life. If a child's parents set good examples of behaviour and respect others then they are much more likely to do the same'.[40] After the riots Prime Minister David Cameron focused on the moral issues: 'Tragically, we... saw people who were just drawn into it, who passed the broken shop window and popped in and nicked a telly. That is a sign of moral collapse, of failing to recognise the difference between right and wrong'.[41] So parents and children are both part of the re-moralisation project to prevent offending now and in the future.

This is not a new concern. Institutions such as schools, reformatories, and the armed forces have in the past been used as norm-imposing substitutes for family or religion, and it would appear that research on young offenders 'habitually produces results that point to the adverse effects of certain features of family life' (Day Sclater and Piper 2000: 138).[42] Not surprisingly, then, the 'parenting theme' has always been dominant in policy debates about criminality. Debate focuses on the correlation between offending and family disruption, and includes a particular concern that boys are not receiving discipline and support from (non-residential) fathers. Research which found, for example, that boys not living with their mothers were most likely to become persistent offenders, would suggest the situation is more complex (Haas *et al.* 2004).

The 'solution' to these contemporary concerns, although they stem from a complex set of structural and demographic changes, has been presented as a simple one: a 'normative project' to re-impose 'traditional' duties on families. None of this proves that there is a decline in moral authority or parental discipline but these attitudes have 'seductive appeal': they feed into a belief 'that the process of change and modernity has gone too far' (Pearson 2002: 45–6) and they have legitimised those provisions previously noted relating to the parents of offenders to be found in and since the CJA 1991. They reflect the belief that the family is crucial in teaching children to act responsibly and refrain from offending and so, if parents do not act responsibly in this way, they themselves must be 'trained' (see Koffman 2008). A policy concern to involve fathers is evident here, given that research on the pilots for parenting orders revealed that over 80 per cent of the parents involved were female, whilst 80 per cent of the children and young people involved were male.[43]

[38] CJA 1991, ss 57–58 and Criminal Justice and Public Order Act 1994 Schedule 9 para 50. In 1994 the Law Commission had recommended abolition of binding-over (Law Comm No 222) but in a 1998 consultation paper (*Bind Overs: A Power for the 21st Century*, Cm 3908) the Home Office instead proposed changes to allow binding-over to be used with more effectiveness and clarity.

[39] Indeed a Private Members' Bill, 'to make provision for a mechanism to hold individuals to account for any criminal sanctions imposed upon young people for whom those individuals hold parental responsibility' had its first reading in December 2011 (http://services.parliament.uk/bills/2010–12/youngoffenders parentalresponsibility.html).

[40] http://www.direct.gov.uk/en/Parents/CrimeAndYoungOffenders/DG_4003031,accessed 11 December 2011.

[41] 'Rioters need tough love, says David Cameron', BBC News, 2 September 2011, accessed at http://www.bbc.co.uk/news/uk-politics-14760686 on 11 December 2011.

[42] For a summary of such research, see Audit Commission (1996: 60–6); see also Farrington (2002).

[43] There are gender issues here and concerns about domestic violence and child abuse: see Piper (2006).

The focus on the family to ensure the young are adequately socialised has another implication if it is believed that the task of moralisation cannot safely be left to the family alone. 'The only norm enforcing system that remains in force and has the pretension to fill the void is the criminal and juvenile justice system' (Junger-Tas 2002: 40). From this perspective, an increase in the scope of, and sanctions available to, the youth justice system is both necessary and legitimate. Further, it has legitimised the range of civil orders to control both parents and children which focus on anti-social behaviour rather than offending but are increasingly being seen as part of the repertoire of youth justice. It also legitimised an extension of these controlling measures as part of the 'Respect' agenda.

8.4.3 **The Respect agenda**

In the 1990s the Audit Commission had flagged up the difficulties for the police in dealing with what they referred to as 'juvenile nuisance', the subject of 10–20 per cent of calls to the police (1996: 13) and a Labour Party policy document talked of 'a rising tide of disorder which is blighting our streets, parks, town and city centres and neighbourhoods' (Straw 1996: 1). This influential new discourse around anti-social behaviour and community safety reflected a sense of social insecurity which was utilised by politicians to legitimise the introduction of new statutory responses to the behaviour of children and young people, notably new civil orders—anti-social behaviour orders (ASBOs) for children of 10 years old and above (see Cracknell 2000),[44] child safety orders for children under 10 years old (see Hayes and Williams 1999; Piper 1999), and parenting orders. Their introduction by the CDA 1998 led Muncie to conclude that 'now it is not so much neglect and delinquency that are conflated, but misbehaviour and crime' (1999: 170). They are not strictly within the remit of this criminal justice text but until quite recently they appeared on the Youth Justice Board's website[45] under the heading 'Sentences, Orders and Agreements' and we will discuss them further in the next section.

The same rhetoric was used in *Respect and Responsibility—Taking a Stand against Anti-social Behaviour*, which argued that anti-social behaviour 'creates an atmosphere in which more serious crime takes hold... It blights people's lives, undermines the fabric of society and holds back regeneration' (Home Office 2003b). That Paper proposed further civil penalties to be imposed on children and their parents for anti-social behaviour via housing and education law. It urged that 'all organisations in any local area need to follow a consistent principle—that the protection of the local community must come first' (Home Office 2003b: para 2.51).

To implement and promote such changes the Government developed a Respect campaign, run by the Respect Unit based in the Home Office and then by a Youth Taskforce based in the, then, Department for Children, Families and Schools.[46] With the advent of the Coalition Government in 2010 that department and its remit changed but by that time a series of government papers had endorsed negative images of young people which have continued.

For example, *Youth Matters* (DfES 2005) proposed measures to give all youngsters equal access to opportunities to allow them to be fully 'included' young people but the

[44] Although the early guidance showed that the original intention was to avoid their use for the under-18s: see Burney (2002: 473). For a Home Office-commissioned review of the use of ASBOs see Campbell (2002).

[45] The Youth Justice Board website was subsumed under the 'Justice' website after the Coalition Government took power.

[46] The new Department with responsibility for implementing *The Children's Plan: Building Brighter Futures* (DCFS 2007).

following policy statement in the Preface shows the approach: 'It is wrong that young people who do not respect the opportunities they are given, by committing crimes or behaving anti-socially, should benefit from the same opportunities as the law-abiding majority. So we will put appropriate measures in place to ensure they do not' (ibid: 1). A new Respect Action Plan issued in 2006 by the Home Office stated that 'respect cannot be learned, purchased or acquired, it can only be earned' (Respect Task Force 2006: 30) and focused on enforcement and changes to ASBOs (see also Home Office 2006c). *Tools and Powers to Tackle Anti-social Behaviour* (Respect Task Force 2007) summarised the results of research by the Task Force into the use of parenting contracts and acceptable anti-social behaviour contracts and agreements as well as anti-social behaviour and parenting orders.[47] What these developments illustrate is that non-criminal deviance, anti-social behaviour, began to be dealt with in ways which blur the boundaries of the criminal and civil systems and law. This has been viewed as an indicator of a trend noted in other jurisdictions towards the use of 'criminalisation' as a state response where structural factors such as poverty and educational disadvantage ought rather to be addressed (Boyle and Lipman 2002; see also Chapter 10). What we are seeing, to quote a Barnardo's Report, *Children in Trouble*, is 'a tendency to criminalise children unnecessarily and at younger ages, and a corresponding tendency to treat them as adults too soon' (Monaghan *et al.* 2003: 6).

8.4.4 **Civil orders**

The new civil orders and similar contracts and agreements constitute new tools but they have an ambivalent role: they are an alternative court based method of responding to anti-social and criminal behaviour through the civil justice system and they are also seen as a method of delaying the 'criminalisation' of children. In practice these developments have drawn more children and young people within the ambit of state surveillance and, as we shall see, may hasten entry into the criminal justice system.

Further, there are other concerns because of the context for these new initiatives. Cleland and Tisdall (2005) have noted that the traditional 'triangle of relationships between the state, parents and children' should be replaced with a square, because of a fourth 'side' which is now very important—the community—but, they go on to argue, the values represented by that fourth element are 'profoundly worrying' because they encourage punitive treatment of children engaging in anti-social behaviour (ibid: 413; see also Chapter 12, section 12.1.3 for a discussion of 'community'). There are also rights issues raised by these developments.

Anti-social behaviour orders

Anti-social behaviour orders (ASBOs) and child safety orders were the first new orders introduced in 1998. The common criterion is that the child or adult has acted 'in a manner that caused or was likely to cause harassment, alarm or distress' to one or more persons outside the family (CDA 1998, ss 1(1) (a) and 12(3)(c)). The ASBO must last for not less than two years whilst the maximum period for a child safety order is three months (exceptionally 12 months). ASBOs can be awarded by magistrates in their civil jurisdiction or, with the implementation of the provisions in the Police Reform Act 2002 (and the Criminal Procedure (Scotland) Act 1995), can be imposed by the criminal courts against individuals convicted of a criminal offence. These orders are sometimes referred to as CRASBOs. The number of such orders now exceeds the numbers imposed as a result of

[47] For critique, see McDonald 2006, especially 196–8.

'stand-alone' applications under s 1 of the CDA 1998. If applications for ASBOs are made under s 1 in the magistrates' courts and the person on whom the order is being sought is under 18, then the magistrates should be ones who are also youth court magistrates (*Practice Direction on the Composition of Benches* 2006). Child safety orders, on the other hand, are a little-used family jurisdiction supervision order.

The Anti-Social Behaviour Act (ASBA) 2003 incorporated the proposals in *Respect and Responsibility* (Home Office 2003b) by widening the scope and use of ASBOs (s 85). Sections 85–86 of the Act increase the range of the 'relevant authorities' who can apply for an ASBO to include county councils and Housing Action Trusts as well as the local authority with housing responsibility, the police and registered social landlords. The ASBA 2003 also introduced a presumption that a parenting order will be made with an ASBO (s 85, amending the CDA 1998, s 9), whilst the CJA 2003 (s 322 amending the CDA 1998, s 1) added the presumption that an ISO (individual support order) would be made alongside an ASBO for the under 18s. The Criminal Justice and Immigration Act 2008, s 124 now makes this a requirement. The ISO adds a positive requirement 'in the interests of preventing any repetition of the kind of behaviour which led to the making of the anti-social behaviour order'—as opposed to the negative requirement of the ASBO—and can be imposed for a period up to six months.

Further, Part 2 of the ASBA 2003 amends housing legislation to allow landlords to make applications to the court on the basis of anti-social behaviour by the tenant. If successful, such applications have serious implications for security of tenure and residence, implications which extend to the tenant's children, whether or not they have been involved in the anti-social behaviour.

The ASBA 2003 also provided the police with controversial new powers to disperse groups in 'designated areas' and to remove from that area individuals who do not live there. These powers relate to all ages but, in addition, there is the power to return home an under-16-year-old (ss 30–36) but this power was challenged in *R (W) v Commissioner of Police of the Metropolis and Another* (2005) which held that s 30(6) did not give the police the power to use reasonable force to return a child home (see Hollingsworth 2006).

The Government had originally expressed its unwillingness to use ASBOs with juveniles, explaining that they were aimed at adults, but then stated that they would be used only for those over 12, before reducing the lower age to 10 (see Burney 2005: 97–8). The result was that, by the end of 2004, 52 per cent of orders had been given to 10–17-year-olds. Statistics also suggest that there is 'injustice by geography' in that some areas impose considerably more orders than others and research done for the Youth Justice Board (2006a) found that a disproportionate number of the sample—22 per cent—were from black and minority ethnic groups. It is local authorities and the police who apply for ASBOs but some commentators have pointed to the role of the judiciary in their increasing use. Donoghue stated that 'it is the judiciary who primarily define their legitimacy, their purpose and scope, and their function in law' (Donoghue 2007: 428) and Bateman accused magistrates of giving insufficient attention to the legal requirement to impose an order only if it is 'necessary', assuming—wrongly—that alternatives have been tried already (Bateman 2007: 313–20). Further, in the *McCann* (2003) case in relation to Article 6 of the European Convention on Human Rights (ECHR)—the right to a fair trial and the issue of the standard of proof—the Court of Appeal decided, albeit not unanimously, that 'these restrictions are imposed for preventative reasons not punishment' (*per* Lord Hope). In Scotland, however, there is no curfew or 'naming and shaming' available for use with under-18s (see NACRO 2007a: 7; see also MacDonald and Telford (2007) for a discussion of the use of ASBOs in Scotland).

ASBOs can include various constraining requirements. Donoghue maintains that 'the potential for ASBOs on conviction to be issued inappropriately by the courts is clear: not only is there no statutory requirement for proof of prior inter-agency consultation, but there is also the possibility that the order will contain inappropriate conditions' (2007: 426). The Youth Justice Board research includes the following findings:

> Geographical 'exclusions' and 'non-association' with anti-social peers were regarded on all sides as the most problematic prohibitions in terms of compliance. Young people and their parents/carers reported that being prohibited from associating with friends in familiar local territories resulted in a serious—and in some cases counter-productive—restriction of normal daily activities. The qualitative data confirmed that the majority of breach cases centred on failure to comply with these types of prohibition.
>
> (Youth Justice Board 2006a: 8)

ASBOs are ineffective if the number of breaches of prohibitions is an indicator of failure: the Audit Office found that over half of those in their sample group—46 per cent of whom were under 18—breached their order, and a third did so on two or more occasions (Home Office 2006c: paras 5b and 5h of the Executive Summary). A breach is dealt with by the criminal courts and, because breaches have provided the sentencing courts with a growing body of work for the courts, the Sentencing Advisory Panel (SAP) issued advice on the sentencing of young offenders for breach (2007: para 78ff).

There is another issue raised by the practice of ASBOs and that is the issue of the 'naming and shaming' of those given orders, which may be seen as an element of what Cobb describes as the incremental reduction in anonymity rights for minors over the last decade (Cobb 2007: 360–1). Yet *Stanley v Metropolitan Police* (2004) did not declare the publicity practices to be in breach of Article 8(1) of the ECHR (see Burney 2005: 96–7; see also Taylor 2006), although the practice of 'aggressive publication of ASBOs, through, for instance, the door-step distribution of leaflets containing the names and addresses of children subject to ASBOs' has been criticised by a Commissioner on Human Rights (Gil-Robles 2005: 37; see also Donoghue 2007: 420–1). The Judicial Studies Board justifies the procedure because 'it is in the community interest that any order will be enforced in order to protect the community. Unless the nuisance is extremely localised, enforcement of the order will normally depend upon the general public being aware of the order and of the identity of the person against whom it is made' (undated: section 3.6). The Children and Young Person's Act 1933, s 39, as amended by the Youth Justice and Criminal Evidence Act 1999, gives the court a discretion to forbid identification in any civil or criminal proceedings, but the courts have justified over-riding the child's anonymity under this provision by taking account of the deterrent effect of publicity on the young defendant. Brown LJ argued in *Winchester Crown Court* (2000) that 'these deterrents are proper objectives for the court to seek' because the effect is beneficial in reducing the young person's offending (at para 13).

However, the Coalition Government proposes to replace the ASBO with a Crime Prevention Injunction (see Home Office 2011b). Whether this will affect attitudes and use is yet to be seen.[48]

Parenting orders

Parenting orders, available since 2000, are triggered if the child or young person is subject to a range of orders,[49] is convicted of a criminal offence, or fails to comply with a school

[48] For recent critique see Crawford 2009; Mackenzie *et al.* 2010; Waiton 2008.

[49] A child safety order, an anti-social behaviour order, and a sex offender order (now sexual offences prevention order), these orders being created, respectively, by ss 11, 1, and 2 of the CDA 1998.

attendance order.[50] They were introduced by the CDA 1998 (ss 8–11) and can last up to 12 months. Particular requirements can be added if the court considers it to be desirable to prevent further anti-social behaviour or offending. Parents must also attend, for a concurrent period not exceeding three months and not more than once a week, parenting classes or counselling as determined by the responsible officer.[51] However, in *R (M) v Inner London Crown Court* (2003) the court concluded that a parenting order did not breach either Articles 6 or 8 of the ECHR because it deemed a parenting order not to be disproportionate, given the pressing social need to address the problems created by juvenile crime and the early research on such orders.[52]

The ASBA 2003 also widened the scope of parenting orders (ss 18, 20–24, 26–29), and included detailed provisions in relation to parenting contracts (ss 19 and 25). The latter were developed as voluntary agreements between youth offending teams and parents of children referred to them but s 27 of the Act mandates the court, when deciding whether to make a parenting order under s 26,

> to take into account (amongst other things)—
> (a) any refusal by the parent to enter into a parenting contract under section 25 in respect of the child or young person, or
> (b) if the parent has entered into such a parenting contract, any failure by the parent to comply with the requirements specified in the contract.

A professionally developed tool is thereby brought within the scrutiny of the court and so given a quasi-legal status in that there are ramifications for non-participation or non-compliance. Further, the Act extends the use of parenting orders in cases of exclusion from school (s 20) and allows for a penalty notice, in effect an 'on the spot' fine, to be served on a parent who could otherwise be convicted of an offence under s 444 of the Education Act 1996 on account of the child's irregular attendance at school (s 23). By s 18(3), parenting orders made in these circumstances or any other situation may include attendance at a residential course as part of the requirement to attend a guidance programme.

A recent statement on the 'Justice' website suggests that parenting 'support' will be more, not less interventionist:

> The Youth Justice Policy Unit and the YJB have developed a 'good practice in parenting' guidance DVD for dissemination to youth offending teams…This will detail the importance of using a more assertive approach to engaging parents and providing strong parenting support using the three step approach (voluntary, contract and order) and give advice on the practical use and benefits of the Parenting Order.[53]

Parental compensation orders

The parental compensation order (PCO) was introduced by the Serious and Organised Crime and Police Act 2005 (s 144 and Schedule 10) which inserted ss 13A–13E into the CDA 1998. Pilots for the orders commenced in 2006. A magistrates' court may make a PCO on application from a local authority when it is satisfied that the child (who must be under 10) has taken, or caused loss of or damage to property in the course of committing

[50] Under the Education Act 1996, ss 443–444: CDA 1998, s 8(1)(d).

[51] The Anti-Social Behaviour Act 2003 amended s 8 so that the parenting class or counselling requirement is discretionary if the specified parent/s has already attended a programme. The 'responsible officer' is defined in the CJA 2003, s 197.

[52] In fact the order was quashed in this case because the magistrates' decision to impose the order in relation to a neighbour dispute was seen as irrational: see [2003] Fam Law 477–8.

[53] http://www.justice.gov.uk/guidance/youth-justice/courts-and-orders/disposals/parenting-order.htm.

an act which, 'if he had been aged 10 or over, would have constituted an offence; or acting in a manner that caused or was likely to cause harassment, alarm or distress to one or more persons not of the same household as himself; and that it would be desirable to make the order in the interests of preventing a repetition of the behaviour in question'. The Government believed the orders would encourage parents and their children to understand their responsibilities and to take responsibility for behaviour.[54]

Conclusion

In this section we have reviewed a diverse range of orders which affect parents, and indeed the whole family, of children who engage in criminal and anti-social behaviour. Some of them would appear to be disproportionate to the behaviour which triggers them and would appear to punish family members who might have little influence on the actions of other family members. They evidence a grey area in policy which has been driven by ideology and media interest, and they may not achieve their aims. Rather, they may create further problems for parents and their children. They also conflict with retributivist principles in so far as they may impose 'punishment' on third parties (see Chapter 2, section 2.5).

8.5 Conclusions

8.5.1 Stability and change

There is a difficulty in trying to assess trends in current youth justice policy and practice. The policies of the previous Labour Government had been critiqued and were being re-thought (see for example, Carrabine 2010; Home Office *et al.* 2008; Silvestri 2011; Solomon and Garside 2008) and the policy of the current Coalition Government is far from clear. In its Green Paper, *Breaking the Cycle*, the Government has set out the agenda for its section on youth justice as its proposals on how to:

- prevent more young people from offending and divert them from entering into a life of crime, including by simplifying out-of-court disposals;
- protect the public and ensure that more is done to make young offenders pay back to their victims and communities;
- ensure the effective use of sentencing for young offenders;
- incentivise local partners to reduce youth offending and re-offending using payment by results models; and
- develop more effective governance by abolishing the Youth Justice Board and increasing freedoms and flexibilities for local areas.

(Ministry of Justice 2010a: 67)

In regard to preventing offending it stated that it would:

- encourage Youth Offending Teams to improve the quality of work with parents including through greater use of parenting orders where parents will not face up to their responsibilities;
- simplify out-of-court disposals; and
- increase the use of restorative justice.

(Ministry of Justice 2010a: 67)

[54] Tony McNulty MP, the Minister for Policing, Security and Community Safety, Hansard, HC 20 July 2006, Cols 44–45WS.

The statement that '[i]ntervening early in the lives of children at risk and their families, before behaviour becomes entrenched, can present our best chance to break the cycle of crime' is to be welcomed (ibid: para 230)[55] as is the acceptance of the need for 'a local, joined up approach to address the multiple disadvantages that many young offenders have and the chaotic lifestyles that many lead' (ibid: para 232). The issue, of course, is in the detail of implementation which is not as yet documented.[56]

Part A of this book has examined sentencing principles and policies, mainly with reference to adult offenders but, of course, much of the discussion in previous chapters is also relevant to those under 18 years of age. Rights are as relevant for young offenders as for adults and determination of their sentence and punishment should also be governed by the proportionality principle. Chapter 6, when focusing on restorative justice, referred mainly to schemes for young offenders (section 6.3.2) because the youth justice system is where restorative policies are currently most important. Further, whilst the justifications for the punishment of minors have often been located within different theoretical frameworks, retributivism and utilitarianism have underpinned those frameworks.

This review of current developments in youth justice, together with the analyses in Chapters 5 and 6, suggests a complex picture of policy concern with the lives, as well as the offending, of young people and their victims and not one which can any longer be categorised simply as welfare or justice. Even the earlier diversionary schemes operated with legal constructs such as 'offence', 'seriousness', and 'culpability', rather than with child welfare science constructs such as 'emotional and physical development' or 'needs' (King and Piper 1995: 115–25) and what we know of current diversion schemes, notably the provision in official guidance of offence-based and gravity-score criteria for reprimand, warning, or prosecution decisions, would suggest this is still so. Whilst more evidence has emerged since the first and second editions of this book it is still difficult to draw clear conclusions about what is happening in youth justice practice.

These developments in out-of-court processing have also legitimised the lack of any substantial change to youth courts: they continue to be used basically like adult sentencing courts. Indeed, arguably, the raising of the upper age limit of the youth court and the changes made by legislation in and since 1998 have further aligned the adult and youth courts. The requirement that there be an hour's interval between sittings of the adult and youth court (now repealed) was originally enacted to strengthen the provisions, to ensure that the young offender was never likely to come into contact with the adult criminal who might encourage him in criminality. We might deride the 'medical' analogies behind the earlier provisions, but the issue is a serious one: that one more element of separate and different treatment has disappeared.

However, as Muncie comments, 'The 'new' never replaces the old. In the twenty-first century discourse of protection, restoration, punishment, responsibility, rehabilitation, welfare, retribution, diversion, human rights and so on exist alongside each other in some perpetually uneasy and contradictory manner' (Muncie 2004: 249; see also Muncie 2006; Cobb 2007: 369). Many of the provisions enshrined in legislation passed in 1994–2003 were developed in the 1980s, often as ad hoc local initiatives, using powers and resources available to the Police and Probation Services and Social Work Departments. *No More Excuses* (Home Office 1997) also echoed a much earlier document in its use of the courts to order preventive programmes: in 1927 an official report had concluded that the practice

[55] See, for a discussion of early intervention, Piper (2008).

[56] See also the policy adopted by the Liberal Democrat party spring conference 2011 available at http://www.libdems.org.uk/policy_motions_detail.aspx?title=Motion_carried_with_amendment%3A_Taking_Responsibility_(Youth_Justice_Policy_Paper)&pPK=d95143d8-3b9d-4eb6-92e4-b55653fe5a5d.

of cautioning to divert from court was 'objectionable' because it was 'usurping the functions of the tribunal' (Moloney Report 1927: 22) and the court was perceived as the site for assessment (see Pratt 1986: 214–19). The Ingleby Report had also argued that trivial offences are 'often only a symptom of an underlying condition requiring early and specialised treatment that was revealed only when the child came before the court' (1960: 51). To go back further, the split custody and community penalty, introduced in 1994 for the 12–14 age group and then enshrined in the detention and training order, has echoes of the Borstal approach developed at the beginning of the twentieth century.

In section 8.2 we reviewed policy reasons for supporting diversion in the 1970s and 1980s and there is clearly continuity between those factors and the policy imperatives in the early twenty-first century, notably the need to legitimise the system by reducing offending, and by locating initiatives within—or in proximity to—the legal process. There are further continuities in the policy desire to reduce expenditure by diversion from custody and also to reduce recidivism through pre-court interventions.

Whether the re-packaging of 'old' products has incorporated lessons from the past is debatable (see Downes 2001/2: 8). There is the related concern that there is little acknowledgement of the disadvantages of pre-court processing. Cautioning was not without its critics in the 1970s and 1980s, particularly in relation to the issue of whether there was 'injustice by geography' or whether discriminatory decision making was taking place, which research suggested there might be (Ditchfield 1976; Farrington and Bennet 1981; Landau 1981). Commentators were particularly concerned about 'net widening' and an 'inflationary spiral' (Pratt 1986: 212). Where the current diversionary systems differ from those of the 1970s and 1980s is in their apparent lack of acknowledgement of the potential dangers of 'heavier' intervention in lives of young people, and, arguably, in the downgrading of the importance of social work skills in favour of risk-based assessments and narrowly focused preventive programmes. It is a pity that these historical insights into the positive and negative factors to be found in the practice of diversion and pre-court intervention were disregarded in the development of the 'new' youth justice system because similar criticisms have developed more recently: see, for example, Field (2007); Hine (2007); Koffman and Dingwall (2007).

History also suggests, however, that we cannot assume that the effective lowering of the age of criminal responsibility, by abolishing the presumption of *doli incapax*, heralds a more punitive policy. There are jurisdictions with a low age of criminal responsibility but with infrequent use of criminal processes for children as, for example, in Scotland, where the age was still eight until 2011 (when s 52 of the Criminal Justice and Licensing (Scotland) Act 2010 raised the age to 12). Conversely, a youth justice policy which aims to make young people more accountable does not necessarily require a lower age: the Canadian Youth Criminal Justice Act 1999 left the age of criminal responsibility at 12 (Junger-Tas 2002: 33). What matters is how the possibility of prosecution is used. This chapter suggests that there is a punitive strand in current youth justice policy and we will look more closely at that policy element in Chapter 13.

8.5.2 **Discussion questions**

This chapter has touched on many related issues: the linked webpage gives suggestions for further reading on several topics. You may also wish to consider the following questions before consulting the Online Resource Centre for guidance.

1. Do you think that the benefits of the current system of reprimands and warnings, together with the new option of conditional cautions, 'outweigh' the disadvantages?

2. What lessons are to be learnt, if any, from an examination of past policies and practices?
3. How important a part of policy and practice is restorative justice in the youth justice system? [Before you answer this question you may wish to re-read Chapter 6, especially section 6.3.]

PART B
Punishing Offenders

9
Justice in the modern prison

SUMMARY

In this chapter we will focus on the treatment of adult prisoners, examining a number of aspects of prison life as well as considering the aims of imprisonment. Key developments since 1990 will be considered including the Woolf Report (Woolf and Tumim 1991), managerialism and privatisation and the impact of the Human Rights Act (HRA) 1998, to assess whether the just treatment of prisoners has been achieved. While substantial improvements in prison regimes have been made since the early 1990s, there has also been considerable pressure on them from the expanding prison population. The problem of reconciling respect for the rights of prisoners with the administrative needs of the prison system and the deterrent function of prison will be highlighted. The potential to limit prison expansion in the current political climate will also be considered. The impact of imprisonment on specific groups of prisoners will be reviewed in Chapter 11. The treatment of young offenders given a custodial order will be considered in Chapter 13.

9.1 Introduction

9.1.1 Justice behind prison doors

Throughout the book we have been exploring the notion of a just punishment with reference to a range of theoretical traditions, as well as its implications for sentencing law and policy, and for particular groups of offenders such as young people. However, justice extends beyond the prison door and we have seen the subjection of prison regimes to increasing judicial scrutiny by the domestic courts and the European Court of Human Rights. The quest for justice in imprisonment was a key theme of the Woolf Inquiry in 1991, many of whose recommendations have shaped the modern prison system. As the Woolf Report emphasised: 'The system of justice which has put a person in prison cannot end at the prison doors. It must accompany the prisoner into the prison, his cell and to all aspects of his life in prison' (Woolf and Tumim 1991: para 14.19). Lord Woolf stressed that this was not simply a matter of the formal judicial processes governing prison life or providing physical conditions which are non-degrading but rather that 'prisoners as well as staff, must feel the system is itself fair and just' (ibid: para 14.20).

Fairness and justice are crucial because prisoners are especially vulnerable to arbitrary treatment because of their isolation and the fact that they are in prison 24 hours a day, dependent on the prison organisation for every need, and also shielded from the wider society. Given that they are 'invisible' and marginalised, then protection for prisoners, whether through a system of formal rights or principles of fairness, is essential. Their rights should be infringed no more than is necessary to safeguard the security of staff, other prisoners, and the public outside the prison. Respecting rights emphasises the common heritage of prisoners and ordinary citizens and contributes to the process of **normalisation**, bringing conditions inside prison closer to those outside, contributing to a sense of justice and recognising that prisoners remain citizens during their period of incarceration. This has been stressed by prison reformers and by those responsible for the oversight of prisons including the Chief Inspector of Prisons.

The treatment of prisoners is linked to the justifications of punishment. From the standpoint of retributivist theory the offender as an autonomous individual should be treated with respect and the punishment consists purely in the deprivation of liberty. The offender should not be subjected to degrading or inhuman treatment during the period of incarceration. So this approach may give more weight to prisoners' rights and the treatment of prisoners as citizens. On utilitarian theory, the pains of imprisonment should not be imposed without positive outcomes, so the effects of imprisonment in reducing reoffending must be assessed. The positive effects could include its deterrent and incapacitative functions but also its potential rehabilitative function. Modern rehabilitationists argue that prisoners have a right to rehabilitation, the right to services and activities which enable them to address the problems which lead to their offending (see Chapter 12, section 12.4.4). The state has a duty to provide them with an environment which facilitates their rehabilitation. This may also mean provision of sufficient opportunities to attend relevant courses. This is especially important if release decisions are based on assessments which require information based on completion of relevant offending behaviour courses.

9.1.2 **The aims of imprisonment**

The aims of imprisonment have been much debated by penologists, prison reformers, and governments. The formal and 'official' aims of the prison system in the UK have been set out in statements of purpose issued by the Prison Service and the Ministry of Justice, are embodied in the Prison Rules, and reflect the justifications of punishment discussed in Chapters 2, 3, 4, and 5. However, there is no consensus amongst commentators on which of these aims should be given priority or the extent to which they have been realised in practice. The Woolf Report argued that prisoners should be treated with humanity and justice, by striking a balance between security, control, and justice, and that the need for justice should not be swamped by concerns with control and security (Woolf and Tumim 1991: para 1.148). Many critics argue that prisons are now merely warehouses as they struggle to cope with rising numbers of inmates. The focus on security has been strengthened, particularly over the use of drugs and mobile phones in prison. Concerns over the punitiveness of the public, as we saw in Chapter 1, have also created a climate in which penal expansion and penal austerity can flourish. However, as we shall see, this has been counterbalanced, and to some extent restrained, by the increasing emphasis on rights.

The Prison Service has described its objectives as holding prisoners securely, reducing the risk of re-offending, and providing safe and well-ordered establishments in which prisoners are treated humanely, decently, and lawfully. Its duty is to look after prisoners with humanity and to help prisoners lead law-abiding and useful lives in custody and on release. The 'decency' agenda introduced in 1999, 'caring for and treating with respect everybody in the Service's care', which has implications for suicide, accommodation, assaults, equal treatment, and participation in constructive activities, has focused attention on the prisoner's right to be treated fairly and respectfully (HM Prison Service 2007: 26).

In 2004 the Prison Service became part of the National Offender Management Service (NOMS), following the recommendations of the Carter Review of Correctional Services,

Managing Offenders, Reducing Crime (Carter 2003), and in 2007 NOMS became part of the new Ministry of Justice. NOMS as an organisation is much larger than the Prison Service, and is responsible for offender management in both prison and the community. It aims to manage prison capacity while ensuring that the required standards on decency and safety are met and control in prisons in maintained.

The National Offender Management Service in its statement of purpose says that its role is 'to commission and provide offender management services in the community and in custody ensuring best value for money from public resources. We work to protect the public and reduce reoffending by delivering the punishment and orders of the courts, and supporting rehabilitation by helping offenders to reform their lives' (NOMS 2011: 4). It emphasises that its values include treating offenders with decency and respect, taking full account of public protection when assessing risk, using resources in the most effective way, delivering value for money for the taxpayer, and incorporating equality and diversity in all its activities (NOMS 2011: 15). The problem of course is maintaining standards of decency in the face of expanding prison capacity.

Prison Rule (PR) 3 (formerly PR 1) states that the purpose of the training and treatment of convicted prisoners shall be to encourage and assist them to lead a good and useful life. The reference to treatment here suggests that the reports of the death of the rehabilitative ideal are somewhat exaggerated. Preventing reoffending is still a key rationale governing education and training provision in modern prison regimes. The problem has been putting PR 3 into practice in the context of rising numbers, increasing financial costs of imprisonment and in the face of public punitiveness, as we saw in Chapter 1. Moreover, the focus on treatment in the past has been used to justify indeterminate and extended sentences (see Chapter 5). Prison reformers have argued that the prisoners should not be subject to treatment coercively, that they should be subject to the minimum levels of security necessary to protect the public, and that as far as possible the same standards which apply to ordinary citizens in the wider society should be applied to offenders. It is now well established that prisoners retain their rights guaranteed by the European Convention on Human Rights (ECHR) while in prison, and although these rights may be limited by the needs of the prison and the interest of the public, any infringements must be proportionate (see section 9.6). Although prison reform may be limited by potential conflicts with populist punitiveness and the less eligibility principle, this principle is itself being eroded by the increasing role of external standards in prison governance, in the form of international human rights instruments.

9.1.3 **The impact of managerialism**

The delivery of offender management is governed by performance testing using Key Performance Indicator Targets. These have been criticised as being more concerned with cost cutting than quality of life, but they have included targets regarding access to purposeful activities, overcrowding, and time unlocked, as well as cost per place and escapes. The stress is on quantifiable measures, such as the number of escapes, assaults, and completion of offending behaviour programmes. The impact of managerialism also means devolved budgets for criminal justice agencies.

The Key Performance Indicator Targets (KPITs) for the period 2010–11 included: reducing reoffending; public protection, defined in terms of the number of escapes; safety and decency in custody, which covers assaults and overcrowding; offender management and interventions, which includes mandatory drug testing; and pathways to reducing reoffending, which includes numbers finding employment and settled accommodation on release. All of these were maintained or improved.

The managerialism governing offender management reflects a wider shift towards managerialism in the criminal justice system and public services as a whole, including the police and court services, which originated in New Right theory of the Thatcher era but which was retained during the Blair and Brown Labour administrations, and has been given a new lease of life by the Coalition Government.

Criminal justice agencies, including NOMS, publish Corporate Plans, setting out Key Performance Indicator Targets and performance is reviewed and reported annually. Performance tables are also used to assess the relative performance of individual prisons.

The focus over the past 20 years has increasingly been on cost effectiveness, limiting spending, improving efficiency, and maintaining security and safety, including controlling drug use. However, improved levels of literacy and numeracy, or basic skills, have also been included as targets.

What counts as a target may change, so some of the key yardsticks for prison conditions, such as time unlocked and time in purposeful activity, are no longer included in the calculations, although these issues are reviewed by the Prison Inspectorate which carries out regular inspections and publishes Thematic Reviews on specific areas of concern or on particular groups of prisoners. Moreover, some of these targets, such as those on overcrowding, are arguably pitched too low and are unenforceable. The focus now on offender management means that there should be a continuous plan for offenders in the community and in custody to manage their individual sentences.

A new system of commissioning was introduced following the reorganisation of offender management, intended to improve the efficiency and effectiveness of service provision (see also Chapter 12, section 12.3.5). The focus has increasingly been on competition or **contestability** in which providers of services compete for contracts, and this will be developed further in relation to rehabilitation programmes.

Changes relating to prison governance were introduced by the Offender Management Act 2007, including new provisions on powers of search and detention in contracted-out prisons (ss 16, 17), new offences relating to prison security (ss 21–24), and the removal of the requirement to appoint a medical officer (s 25), a post incorporating managerial and clinical responsibilities. The change reflects the fact that clinical duties are now performed by externally contracted GPs from the NHS and managerial responsibilities are no longer part of the medical officer's role.

The Act reflected some of the proposals in *Improving Prison and Probation Services: Public Value Partnerships* (Home Office 2006b) which set out the Labour Government's plans to extend contestability, and partnerships with the private and voluntary sectors, and also ways of challenging underperforming prisons and Probation Boards. The Carter Review of Prisons in 2007 also envisaged further development of contestability and the need to ensure cost effectiveness in the supply and functioning of prisons (Carter 2007).

Greater use of the private and voluntary sectors is also now envisaged in the provision of rehabilitation programmes as made clear in the Green Paper, *Breaking the Cycle* (Ministry of Justice 2010a), with payments linked to results.

9.2 The prison population

9.2.1 The composition of the prison population

Information on prison life and the prison population may be obtained from official statistics, reports from the Home Office and Ministry of Justice, and reviews and reports from the Prison Inspectorate. There are relatively few qualitative studies, not least because of the problem of access to prisons and the transience of the population. The need for security and the smooth running of the prison also makes ethnographic research difficult. However, research has been undertaken by the Home Office and for the Chief Inspector of Prisons and by campaigning groups such as the Howard League for Penal Reform, NACRO, and the Prison Reform Trust (PRT) which has focused on particular problems and particular groups of prisoners, and has highlighted the importance of humane regimes. We also have information from government-sponsored reviews, such as the Wedderburn Report and the Corston Report on Women Prisoners, as well as from the Mubarek Inquiry (see Chapter 11) and from independent researchers. An independent commission on prisons, the Commission on English Prisons Today, published its first report *Do Better Do Less* in 2009, which advocated a reduction in the size of the prison population, closing some prisons, replacing short prison sentences with community-based measures, dismantling of NOMS, and decentralising the prison service (Commission on English Prisons Today 2009). The Commission aims to promote public and academic debates on imprisonment and examines the issues which have led to the rise in the prison population.

Although prisoners may come from a wide range of social groups and classes, a profile of the typical prisoner can be compiled from Home Office data and research studies. These indicate that the typical prisoner is likely to be young, male, economically and socially deprived, or socially excluded, and a persistent property offender, experiencing problems with accommodation, and with finding employment, or if in work in an unskilled occupation, from an inner-city area, of low educational achievement, and with past experience of being in care. Social exclusion is the most striking characteristic of the prison population.[1]

According to the Social Exclusion Unit (2002), prisoners are 13 times more likely to have been in care than the general population, 13 times more likely to have been unemployed, and 10 times more likely to have been an habitual truant. It is estimated that one-third of prisoners suffered from housing problems before entering prison and a similar number face housing problems on release. Moreover, prisoners may lose their housing as a direct result of imprisonment. A large number of prisoners are unemployed before going into prison and of course many will lose their jobs through imprisonment. This is important as homelessness and unemployment are also significant factors associated with reoffending.

Similar results were found in prisoners sampled for a longitudinal survey, *Surveying Prisoner Crime Reduction*, which considers prisoners' early life experiences, accommodation, education and employment, substance use, and mental health needs (Ministry of Justice 2010b). The survey confirmed that prisoners were less likely than the general population to have worked before entering custody and more likely to have been homeless and had higher rates of mental health and emotional problems. Reoffending rates were also higher for those who had been excluded from school or who had prior experience of drug use.

The prison population is also still overwhelmingly male as we can see from Figure 9.1. The proportion of female prisoners varied between 3 per cent and 4 per cent of the total prison population during most of the 1990s but by 2004 had reached 6 per cent and since then has fluctuated between 5 and 6 per cent. It is clear that men commit more offences than women but also commit more offences of violence than women. Theft and handling are the most common offences for women given custodial sentences.

[1] For further discussion of social exclusion see: Young (1999); Byrne (2005); Pantazis *et al.* (2006); Dorling *et al.* (2007).

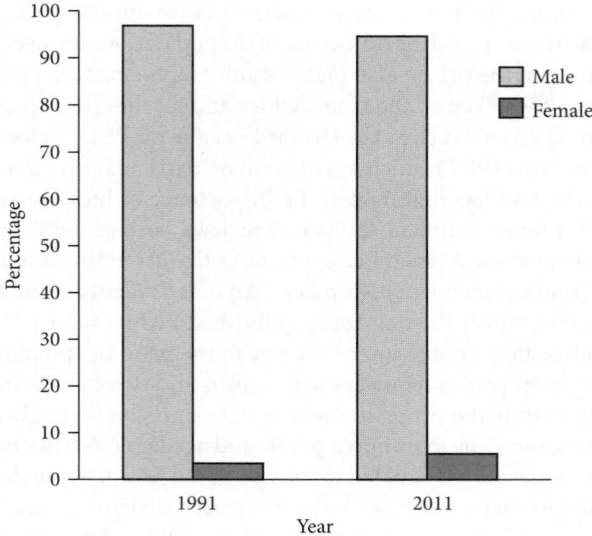

Figure 9.1 Composition of prison population by gender

However, drugs offences are also becoming more significant accounting for an increasing number of male and female prisoners and, of course, many property offences may be drug-related.

The demographic structure of the prison population is changing as far as age is concerned. Like the population at large, the prison population is ageing and the number of elderly prisoners has increased significantly since 1995, although this may also reflect the increase in sentence length (Howse 2003). The number of older sentenced prisoners, aged over 60, increased by 128 per cent from 2000 to 2010 and raised issues regarding appropriate provision for this group (Prison Reform Trust 2011a: 47). Ill-health may be a particular issue for older prisoners (Department of Health 2009b). However, there are still relatively large numbers of young adult prisoners in the 18–20 age group; there were 8,317 on 30 September 2011 (ibid: 45). Members of this group are more likely than adult prisoners to experience mental health problems and are at higher risk of suicide. The number of children and young people aged under 18 in custody has been falling, from over 3,000 in 2007–8 to 1,890 in April 2011 (Youth Justice Board 2011a). The problems young offenders face in custody will be considered in Chapter 13.

Although some prisoners have gained degrees while in prison, the majority of prisoners have no formal qualifications on entering prison. Over half of male adult prisoners and over two-thirds of female adult prisoners have no educational qualifications. Over one-half of the prison population have low levels of numeracy and literacy; one-third of prisoners were habitual truants while at school, whilst one-third of female sentenced prisoners and nearly one-half of male sentenced prisoners were excluded from school (Prison Reform Trust 2011a:). These figures are much higher than for the general population. For this reason, there is increasing emphasis on acquiring basic work and literacy and numeracy skills while in custody. It is also estimated that 20–30 per cent of prisoners have learning disabilities which will affect their ability to cope with imprisonment (see Talbot 2007, 2008; Talbot and Riley 2007; Loucks 2007; HM Inspectorate of Prisons 2009a). Information on these disabilities will not necessarily be available to staff on arrival at prison and they may not always be identified while in prison. It is also estimated that there are also from 15 to 25 per cent of prisoners with physical disabilities, depending on whether self-reported data is used.

A high number of prisoners will have been drug users before admission. The number of prisoners imprisoned for drugs offences and drugs-related crime has increased and drug use will frequently be resumed on release from prison. The rates for drug problems and mental health problems are higher within the prison population than the general population (Department of Health 2011; Dudeck *et al.* 2011). This increases the demands on prisons in dealing with problems raised by these prisoners. There may also be problems in identifying mental health problems, as the Bradley Report observed (Department of Health 2009a). Moreover, mental health problems may develop for the first time inside prison. In the *Surveying Prisoner Crime Reduction* study 17 per cent of offenders had been treated or received advice on mental health or emotional problems in the year preceding their imprisonment (Ministry of Justice 2010b). Over half of prisoners interviewed in this study had dependent children on entering custody. It is estimated that 160,000 children now have a parent in prison (Prison Reform Trust 2011a: 28), and 27 per cent of prisoners have experience of being in care as a child compared to 2 per cent of the general population (ibid). The impact of imprisonment on prisoners' families is wide reaching and the problems facing prisoners' families have been charted by Codd (Codd 2008).

Offenders are more likely than non-offenders to be unemployed before entering prison (Ministry of Justice 2010b). Moreover, if unemployed they may be less likely to receive a fine or suspended sentence and more likely to receive a custodial sentence or community penalty and if they subsequently experience further unemployment, then reoffending may be more likely (see Chapter 10). The link between unemployment and imprisonment is complex but employment status will also have implications for bail, as being in regular employment will increase the chances of being given bail, as will having stable accommodation. Remand prisoners made up 14.6 per cent of the prison population in 2011.

Just under 26 per cent of prisoners are from minority ethnic groups with 21,878 such prisoners in 2010, which is clearly disproportionate to the numbers in the population as a whole (Ministry of Justice 2011c). The implications of this for issues of discrimination and equality of impact will be considered in Chapters 10 and 11. Black prisoners constitute 11 per cent and Asian prisoners 5 per cent of the British prison population (ibid). Foreign national prisoners currently constitute over 13 per cent of the total prison population and 15 per cent of the female prison population.

9.2.2 **Prison expansion**

The most significant feature of the prison population is its massive expansion during the post-war period from 15,000 in 1945 to 88,179 on 2 December 2011. On 6 January 2012 the prison population stood at 86,638. The population has steadily increased with dramatic increases in the 1990s in both sentenced and remand prisoners.[2]

A substantial number of places are taken up by remand prisoners, large numbers of whom are remanded for non-violent offences and may be subsequently given a non-custodial sentence at trial. This is therefore one area where the population could be safely reduced and some consideration is being given to developing alternatives. The Coalition Government has said that it intends to remove the option of remanding in custody young people who are unlikely to receive a custodial sentence (Ministry of Justice 2010a: para 249).

[2] Prison statistics are published annually and updated weekly on the Ministry of Justice website.

The most important reasons for the dramatic increase in the prison population since the early 1990s are the increases in both the custody rate and sentence length. The average sentence length for those sentenced to immediate custody for indictable offences in the Crown Court increased from 22.4 months in 1996 to 25 months in 2009. There has also been an increase in the custody rate, that is the percentage of persons sentenced who receive an immediate custodial sentence, which reached 24 per cent in the Crown Court in 2009 and also increased in the magistrates' court. The use of fines has decreased since 1999. However the use of community sentences has also increased since 1999. There has also been an increase in the number of offenders coming before the courts and in the number of more serious offences being sentenced, although this is more evident in relation to male than female offenders.

Other factors contributing to the expansion in the prison population include changes in sentencing law, increased public punitiveness, and the increased importance in political agendas of punishment and of bringing offenders to justice (Piper and Easton 2006/7). The emphasis on risk management and public protection reflected in sentences of imprisonment for public protection (IPP), has added to the time spent in custody by dangerous offenders, which has added to the numbers. More prisoners are also being recalled following release on licence which is contributing to the changing demographic structure of the prison population. There has also been an increase in the number of prisoners serving life sentences and other indeterminate sentences in recent years. The implications of this for IPP prisoners were considered in Chapter 5. The amount of time served under licence and under supervision has increased under the Criminal Justice Act 2003. The reluctance to take risks with public protection is also reflected in a fall in the numbers released by the Parole Board, which has become more risk averse in the face of public concern and criticism over incidents where prisoners have been released and have gone on to commit further crimes.

As we saw in Chapter 1, there has also been an increase in the number of civil orders available to and imposed by the courts, the breach of which may incur custodial penalties and add to the burgeoning prison population. There has also been an increase in the numbers serving short sentences. Some offenders are now being sent to prison when they would not have been in the early 1990s (see Hough *et al.* 2003). Although the use of community penalties since 1995 has also increased, this has not had the effect of reducing the use of custodial sentences but in fact both have increased, while the use of fines has fallen. At present the prospects for a dramatic reduction in the prison population are unfavourable. The latest prison projections for 2017 based on current sentencing trends indicate that the highest figure will be 94,800 and the lowest 83,100 (Ministry of Justice 2011h). This is a rise from the earlier projections published in 2010, where the highest figure for 2016 was 93,600 (Ministry of Justice 2010d).

As we saw in Chapter 1, Governments are reluctant to impose penal policies which are unpopular with the public, such as sentence discounts or early release, and want to increase confidence in the criminal justice system in bringing offenders to justice and punishing them appropriately. So the use of reductionist measures will be limited by these pressures. It is also notable that the incarceration rate in England and Wales is the highest in Western Europe: at 156 per 100,000 of the population in 2011 (International Centre for Prison Studies 2011).

The Coalition Government has indicated that it wishes to reduce the population by 3,000 by a number of measures but it seems likely to remain over 80,000 for the next few years.

Both the current and the previous Governments have clearly been mindful of the financial burdens of high rates of incarceration, yet have continued to provide additional prison places.

9.2.3 **The prison estate**

The increased demand for prison places has been met by an expansion of prison building. Several new prisons opened or were commissioned in the 1970s: Long Lartin in 1972, Durham in 1978, and Channings Wood in Devon in 1982. Since the early 1980s, however, there has been a substantial building programme, with 21 new prisons opened between 1980 and 1996. A further 20,000 new prison places were provided during the period of the Labour administration, from 1997 to 2010. In the past few years the new prisons constructed have mostly been in the private sector, although a new public sector prison, HMP Kennet, opened on Merseyside in 2007. A prison ship, *HMP Weare*, was also used from 1997 to 2005. By 2011 there were 137 prisons in England and Wales, including 12 private prisons, providing over 100,000 places.[3] Usable operational capacity is calculated as the actual number of places minus 2,000 places to allow for flexibility in providing suitable accommodation and on 30 December 2011 it was 89,472.

The modern prison system is shaped by the legacy of the past, reflected in the prison infrastructure in the survival of Victorian prison buildings which make up about one-quarter of the prison estate. The prison estate includes conversions of country houses and former military camps, as well as purpose-built prisons. So while some prisoners are still housed in old Victorian buildings, these have been refurbished and now include new modern wings, whilst many prisoners are housed in prisons built since the war. The prison estate is divided into 11 geographical areas, as well as a separate division for high-security prisons. There are 13 women's prisons, including open and closed prisons and seven mother and baby units. The treatment of women prisoners will be considered in Chapter 11.[4]

However some smaller prisons have been closed. In 2011 Morton Hall was closed as a prison and is now used instead as an Immigration Removal Centre. HMP Ashwell and Lancaster Castle have closed.

Local prisons, located in towns and cities, hold remand prisoners pending and during their trials, and convicted prisoners immediately after sentence, for assessment before transferring to training prisons. They may also hold convicted prisoners serving short sentences and those nearing the end of long sentences. They often have the worst over-crowding as well as the worst conditions, and include inner-city dilapidated Victorian prisons as well as modern prisons such as Belmarsh.

Training prisons may be closed or open, and may be located further away from towns and cities. They include specialist prisons, for example the therapeutic prison Grendon in Buckinghamshire, and there are also therapeutic units inside HMP Gartree, Blundeston, and Send. Closed training prisons have varying levels of security. Prisoners in open training prisons, such as Leyhill and Ford, clearly enjoy much greater freedom. They may work in the prison or in the local community and are allowed out on shopping visits, but the rules governing prison life will be strongly enforced to compensate for the absence of external boundaries. However these regimes have been criticised because of prisoners absconding from Leyhill and rioting at Ford Open Prison. In January 2011, buildings at Ford were set alight by prisoners and criminal damage was inflicted but no one was hurt. Alcohol may have been a factor in the riot and prisoners suspected of taking alcohol

[3] Scotland and Northern Ireland have separate systems and space precludes a focus on their prison estates. However, information on prisons in Scotland and Northern Ireland can be obtained from the Scottish Prison Service on http://www.sps.gov.uk and the Northern Ireland Prison Service on http://www.niprisonservice.gov.uk. The prison population is also rising in both countries.

[4] A map of the geographical distribution of prisons can be found at: http://www.justice.gov.uk/downloads/contacts/hmps/prison-finder/prison-probation-map-2011.pdf.

refused to take breathalyser tests. The Prison Inspectorate had raised issues over the level of staffing in the period preceding the riot.

Vulnerable prisoners, such as sex offenders, are housed in special Vulnerable Prisoners' Units (VPUs) for their own safety to protect them from assaults by other prisoners. Severely disruptive or violent prisoners may be transferred to Close Supervision Centres within the High Security prison estate. There are also Protected Witness Units for those at risk.

The modern prison system is still very expensive to run despite concerted efforts to reduce costs and are much more expensive than community punishments. Cost effectiveness or value for money has become an increasingly important issue in the past 15 years as costs have risen. It constitutes a substantial claim on public spending which needs to be justified especially at a time of austerity. Additional costs may also be incurred if it is necessary to use a police cell under Operation Safeguard or, on occasions, court cells.

As well as the running costs of prison which reach over £40,000 per prison place per annum, there are also the capital costs of building and maintaining prisons. Costs of maintenance and refurbishment will be substantial in the older prisons which are not purpose-built. Older buildings may also be more expensive to staff, and staffing costs are the principal demand on the prison budget. The location of some of these prisons also means additional costs in transporting prisoners across the country and for visitors and there are currently insufficient places within the London area. If we include other ancillary costs such as prison escort services, then the cost rises substantially. Nor do these figures encompass the total public costs of imprisonment; for example, there may also be additional welfare costs for a prisoner's dependants with the loss of the prisoner's income. As is often observed, it costs more to send an offender to prison than to public school or to university, despite the increase in university fees.

9.2.4 **The categorisation and allocation of prisoners**

Decisions on the categorisation of prisoners are distinct from and precede decisions on allocation. The procedures and criteria for both processes are governed by the National Security Framework and are set out in Prison Service Instructions (PSI) 39, 40, and 41 of 2011. Adult male prisoners are divided into four categories, following the recommendations of the Mountbatten Report (Mountbatten 1966).

Decisions on category A prisoners are made by a special Category A Committee at NOMS Headquarters. Categorisation decisions for other prisoners are a matter for the Governor and are made in accordance with the National Security Framework. Prisoners should be placed in the lowest category consistent with the need for security and control. Prisons should have procedures for reviewing the categorisation of prisoners and there is now a duty to give reasons for such decisions. Categorisation should take account of the current offence and sentence, previous convictions, and previous escapes, escape attempts and absconds. Categorisation is reviewed at regular intervals and reconsidered on the basis of the risk to the public and the risk of escape. There are separate procedures for those serving life sentences and other indeterminate sentences.

Category A prisoners are those who would be highly dangerous to the public, police, or the security of the state and for whom escape must be made impossible. Category B prisoners are those who do not require the highest security conditions, but for whom escape must be made very difficult. Category C prisoners are those who cannot be trusted in open conditions, but who lack the will or resources to make a determined escape attempt, while category D prisoners can be reasonably trusted in open conditions. Remand prisoners may be categorised A or are unclassified (U). Similarly, young adult male prisoners may be categorised A, or as restricted, requiring secure accomodation, or assessed as suitable for closed or open conditions, using similar security criteria as adults. Women prisoners may be classified as category A, or as restricted, requiring designated secure accomodation or held in close conditions where the highest security conditions are not necessary but they cannot be trusted in open conditions or open conditions are not appropriate for them. Women may also be categorised as suitable for open conditions, that is, as prisoners who present a low risk to the public and can be trusted in open conditions.

Category A is further divided into three levels of risk: standard, high, and exceptional risk. High risk would include, for example, members of criminal gangs with access to sufficient resources to help them escape. Prisoners are classified as exceptional risk when they have the skills, external resources, abilities, and determination to overcome the security measures used in relation to category A prisoners, and therefore need to be contained within the most secure units available within the Prison Service. There are also special units for prisoners with dangerous and severe personality disorders within the high security prison estate.

Regimes for category A prisoners are the most stringent, for example requiring closed visits. These prisoners are more likely to be transferred to other prisons than other categories and the courts are more reluctant to interfere with transfer decisions in such cases. If they are transferred, it is difficult for them to complete educational or offending behaviour courses, which affects their chances of future classification. Prisoners may be placed on the 'escape list', that is, they are deemed to be at risk of trying to escape, for example, because they have done so in the past, and will be placed on a strict security regime and required to wear special clothes.

Prisons are becoming more secure in so far as the number of escapes has declined since the early 1980s and the risk may be highest while in transit, for example, on court visits. Prison categorisation was reviewed, however, when two category A prisoners escaped from Gartree in 1987 with the help of a helicopter which landed inside the grounds of the prison. Following this incident, exceptional risk categories are held in special security units for high-risk prisoners. In 2010–11 the target was for total escapes from prisons and prison escorts to be below 0.05 per cent of the average prison population, and the outcome was 0.002 per cent (NOMS 2011: 9).

Once sentenced, category A prisoners go to high-security prisons. These prisons will have high levels of security, including dog patrols, electronic surveillance, high walls, searching of visitors, high levels of staffing, and more searches of inmates as they move around the prison.[5] There are currently eight high-security prisons, at Belmarsh, Frankland, Full Sutton, Long Lartin, Wakefield, Whitemoor, Manchester, and Woodhill. Conditions are generally better in higher security prisons for those serving longer sentences, with more educational and work opportunities, and prisoners may be able to cook their own meals and wear their own clothes.

There are also special units to deal with difficult prisoners called Close Supervision Centres, where prisoners can be closely supervised and encouraged to address their disruptive behaviour. They have a structured regime through which prisoners must progress satisfactorily before leaving the unit. Conditions are harsher in so far as more time is spent locked up, visits are restricted, the furniture is made of cardboard, and prisoners sleep on concrete plinths rather than proper beds. There are also special cells for segregating difficult prisoners within high-security prisons and at local prisons.

[5] The factors influencing the treatment of high risk prisoners in the UK are considered by King and Resodihardjo (2010) and compared with the approach in the Netherlands and the United States.

The categorisation of prisoners was reviewed in *R (P) v Secretary of State for the Home Department* (2002). Here an elderly and ill prisoner had been placed in category A even though he would be unlikely to be able to escape, but if he did escape, he would be highly dangerous to the public, or to the police, or to the security of the state. The court held that the Prison Service was entitled to have a policy to make the escape of highly dangerous prisoners virtually impossible, but should consider prisoners' cases on an individual basis, so that if the escape risk of a particular prisoner could be managed in lower security conditions, then it would be unlawful to preclude consideration of this possibility.

Category B prisoners may stay in local prisons if serving a short sentence, or go to high-security or closed training prisons. Category C prisoners go to closed training prisons with lower security and a more relaxed regime. Category D go to open training prisons, although some may be held in category C prisons. Within some C and D prisons there are also resettlement prisons to which prisoners may be transferred shortly before release, to arrange work, and to increase contact with their families.

Decisions on allocation to particular prisons are made on the basis of the need for security and control, individual prisoner needs, and optimum use of available space, and these needs may sometimes conflict with each other. Individual needs would include age, vulnerability, any educational needs, and the prisoner's home area. Prisoners do not have a right to be allocated to any particular prison. Similar principles will apply to the allocation of young offenders although maintenance of family ties will be a key consideration, so normally young offenders are allocated to a prison as close to home as possible and when allocating women prisoners, family ties and facilitating visits from children will be a significant allocation issue.

9.3 **Prison conditions**

Bearing in mind the objectives of imprisonment (see section 9.1.2 above) we will consider the conditions in modern prisons and problems which inhibit the realisation of these objectives, as well as improvements made in recent years. If we compare the prisons of the early 1990s with those of 2012, we find considerable progress, but also clearly room for further improvement. Prison conditions have changed since the 1990s as a result of a number of factors including the Woolf Report, the rise of the New Managerialism, the increasing focus on risk-management, and the privatisation programme. The focus on risk and on transparency and measurement of prison performance has limited the autonomy and discretion of prison governors and arguably limited the scope for developing prison regimes, as has the increasing pressure on prison resources from the substantial increase in prison numbers. However, the ECHR and the HRA 1998 have had a substantial impact on prison conditions.

9.3.1 **Overview**

Prison conditions have improved considerably since the Woolf Report was published in 1991 and further improvements have been introduced following the HRA 1998. However, conditions still remain unsatisfactory in some prisons, particularly for those held on remand. Although they are entitled to wear their own clothes, have better visiting rights, and greater access to correspondence than sentenced prisoners, remand prisoners are often housed in the worst prisons with fewer facilities available for work and training. The day-to-day life inside prison is governed by the very detailed Prison Rules 1999 issued under s 47 of the Prison Act 1952. These Rules have been regularly updated and amended, most recently in 2011. The rules include provisions on a range of issues, including work, education, access to visits, offences against discipline, and the use of constraints, and they generate a substantial number of disciplinary offences each year.

A number of performance improvement strategies have been implemented, notably the introduction of prison league tables which now rank prisons on their performance in terms of 37 indicators, in four domains, Public Protection, Reducing Reoffending, Decency and Resource Management, and Operational Effectiveness. League tables were first published in July 2003 when Holloway was awarded the lowest ranking (level 1, overall performance is of serious concern) for failing to meet performance targets or providing secure, ordered, or decent regimes. Holloway is currently rated at level 3 (meeting the majority of targets) (Ministry of Justice 2011b). Pentonville was also graded level 1 in 2006–7 and is now at level 3 (ibid). The annual performance ratings for 2010/11 show that there are no prisons at level 1, four (Cookham Wood, Edmunds Hill, Isle of Wight Prison, and Forest Bank) at level 2, which means that their overall performance is of concern, with the remainder at level 3, that is, meeting the majority of targets, and level 4, rated as exceptional performance (ibid). However, while prisons in England and Wales have improved, it has been argued that prisoners in England experience worse conditions in terms of visitation rights, physical conditions, and relationships with staff than those in the Netherlands (see Kruttschnitt and Dirkzwager 2011; Easton 2011a).

The purpose of the current focus on contestability is also intended to drive up standards and penalise poor performance, through the competition between prisons for contracts.

Prison conditions are crucial to debates in penology as they have implications for human rights but also will have implications for reoffending.

9.3.2 **Overcrowding**

Overcrowding is normally measured by comparing actual numbers of inmates with Certified Normal Accommodation (CNA), that is, the uncrowded capacity calculated for each prison. Overcrowding initially declined during the 1990s as the supply of places expanded due to the prison building programme, although in some prisons overcrowding remained a problem. Overcrowding may arise not simply because of a lack of accommodation, but, in part, because of inflexibility of use because prisons may be too specialised to allow transfer of prisoners between them. Increasingly prisons have been broadening their functions with expansion and one reason behind the proposal for 'Titan' prisons in the Carter Review of Prisons (Carter 2007) was to allow for more flexibility in allocating accommodation as well as long term economies of scale, but the immediate costs of setting up these prisons made it too expensive to implement.

With the rapid expansion of the prison population, inevitably overcrowding is still a problem for the prison system. The target in 2010–11 for the number of prisoners held in accommodation units designed for fewer prisoners was no more than 26 per cent and the achieved result was 24 per cent, the same as in the previous year (NOMS 2011: 10). But given the current size of the prison population this means large numbers of prisoners are being held in cells designed for fewer prisoners.

One measure used in June 2007 to deal with the immediate problem of overcrowding was an End of Custody Licence (ECL). This permitted lower-level offenders imprisoned for no more than four years and nearing the end of their sentence to be released 18 days early, but this measure was curtailed in March 2010. Similar measures were used in 1940 to boost the number of men available for the war effort and to reduce overcrowding in 1987 (see Chapter 5, section 5.5.2). However any system of early release may be seen as politically risky for governments as it may be unpopular with the public.

Overcrowding will not be evenly distributed throughout the prison system, so there may still be unsatisfactory levels in specific institutions even if the total level of overcrowding is not substantial. Overcrowding is generally worse in local prisons, which house mostly remand prisoners and those serving short sentences or awaiting transfers. Usually training prisons and Young Offender Institutions will be protected from overcrowding at the expense of local prisons.

A statutory limit on overcrowding in the form of a new Prison Rule, under which prisons could not accommodate more prisoners than provided in its CNA, except in very limited cases, was recommended by the Woolf Report, but this recommendation was not implemented (Woolf and Tumim 1991: para 1.190). However, the level of overcrowding is used as a Key Performance Indicator Target although, as we have seen, the target is not set very high, namely that no more than 26 per cent of the prison population should be held in accommodation designed for fewer prisoners. The use of single cells for prisoners is also recommended by the European Prison Rules (EPR 18.5).

The effects of overcrowding are widespread; as well as worsening physical conditions, there may be more frequent transfers, so it is hard to implement proper training and provide educational programmes accessible to all prisoners, and to complete necessary assessments of prisoners. Overcrowding also makes prison life more impersonal, affecting the opportunity to establish good personal relationships, which may also have implications for the prevention of reoffending—moving prisons closer to a warehousing than a rehabilitative role—and for the safety of prisoners. In severe cases overcrowding may amount to inhuman and degrading treatment.

What is surprising is that the increase in numbers in custody in the 1980s and 1990s paralleled a policy that prison should be used as a last resort, and alternatives should be used where possible. In fact, the UK has more alternatives to custody than many other European states. But it would seem the alternatives available during that period, such as community service orders, probation, and fines, had the effect of net-widening rather than leading to a reduction in the prison population. Ultimately of course, it is sentencers who make the decision on whether to give a custodial sentence, but they are constrained by sentencing law and procedure when looking at the individual case. In addition, magistrates and judges will have their own views, philosophies, and traditions as well as subscribing to the principles of judicial independence and autonomy (see Chapters 2 and 3).

9.3.3 **Work, training, and offending behaviour programmes**

Prison Rule 31(1) states that 'a convicted prisoner shall be required to do useful work for not more than 10 hours per day, and arrangements shall be made to allow prisoners to work, where possible, outside the cells and in association with one another'. Exceptions are made for those who are ill or unable to work for other reasons. Otherwise, prisoners are classified into suitability for heavy, light, or medium work. Prison Rule 31 does not stipulate a minimum time spent in work.

From the prisoner's standpoint, work can provide a relief from boredom, the opportunity to acquire skills, and a limited source of income. From the standpoint of the prison it keeps prisoners in useful occupation and can prepare them for release. But in practice there is insufficient suitable work available for all prisoners able to benefit from it and increasing work opportunities is a key element of current penal policy. Preparing for work is important as there is a strong correlation between reoffending and unemployment, and whilst a correlation is not a cause, ex-offenders are more likely to reoffend if they have no legitimate source of income. The problem of providing suitable work and other purposive activities has become harder with continued expansion without corresponding increases in resources. Access to programmes varies between institutions, so access may depend on where the prisoner is allocated. Although there is no formal right to work, the European Prison Rules stipulate that prisons should attempt to provide as much work of a useful nature as is possible (EPR 26.2).

In 1991 the Woolf Report recommended that work opportunities should cater for a range of abilities and that prison regimes should try to provide constructive and purposeful employment in factories and workshops for as many prisoners as possible who could usefully be deployed. The choice of work, argued Woolf, should be influenced by the need of prisoners to find work after release. A planned programme 'should bring together work, training and education in a way that provides the most constructive mix for the prisoners who are to be involved in it' (Woolf and Tumim 1991: para 14.134). The Prison Service, he argued, should give the prisoner the opportunity to serve his or her sentence in a constructive way (ibid: para 14.9) and by making proper use of his or her time, reduce the likelihood of reoffending (ibid: para 14.10). Since the Woolf Report, there have been improvements in the provision of constructive regimes and access to basic skills education.

In the late 1990s the time spent in purposeful activity was used as a Key Performance Indicator and the target was 24 hours a week, although in practice it varied enormously. In the mid 1990s, the average time spent out of a cell in weekdays was 11.2 hours but this fell to 10 hours by 2005–6 (Hansard, House of Commons written answers, 9 January 2007). But time unlocked has not been used as a Key Performance Indicator Target since 2004. The time spent out of cell may vary between prisons but within prison it may differ, for example between prisoners, with new arrivals achieving less time out of their cells. The latest report of the Prison Inspectorate found that the majority of adult men's prisons offered prisoners between seven and nine hours out of their cells, but for some it could be as little as three hours (HM Chief Inspector of Prisons 2011a: 47). However some prisoners were locked up at 6.30 pm on weekday evenings. The failure to provide sufficient work to prisoners serving short sentences has been a particular problem (see National Audit Office 2010b). However the menial work offered to those serving longer sentences has also been highlighted by Meek (2008).

A key element of the prison regime is provision of basic skills and offending behaviour programmes. There is a duty on the Governor to ensure a safe working environment in accordance with health and safety legislation. The prisoner is entitled to be paid and, if he or she is willing to work and none is available, to receive basic pay. But rates are very low compared to the labour market outside prisons. Older prisoners beyond the state retirement age receive modest retirement pay.

Remand prisoners are permitted to work but not obliged to do so, but it is usually harder for them to obtain access to work. But most prisoners want to work to relieve the boredom and to earn money. There may be particular problems providing work for prisoners with mental health problems, older prisoners, or prisoners with learning disabilities. The minimum rate that must be paid is £4 per week but pay schemes are a matter for governors and for directors of contracted-out prisons (see PSO 4460). So each prison sets its own pay rates; the average is about £9 per week but may be as much as £30. Remand prisoners are paid the same rate as convicted prisoners.

Prisoners working for outside employers must be paid the National Minimum Wage. Prisoners are obliged to pay tax and National Insurance contributions if their earnings reach the threshold and to make contributions to maintain their dependants if their earnings are sufficient. If levels of pay were more realistic and closer to market rates, then it would be possible for prisoners to do so. At the present time board and lodging may not be deducted from this small income.

At present only 9,000 adult prisoners work in public sector prisons so the Coalition Government's plan is to expand the range of work available and to promote an ethos of work discipline among inmates (Ministry of Justice 2010a). It is envisaged that the work could be provided either by the prison or external providers or in partnership with the private sector, and it is intended to make it easier for private, voluntary, and community sectors to become involved in this enterprise. The Prisoners' Earnings Act, enacted in 1996, but not brought into force at that time, is now being implemented to facilitate reparation to victims. Under the Act deductions can be made from the wages of prisoners on enhanced wages. These funds will be used to contribute to victims' services. The Government is also considering further ways of making deductions from prisoners' wages to make reparations to victims and communities. It is intended to give eligible offenders in the community the same entitlements as other jobseekers to support and training and opportunities or to participate in the new Work Programme and to improve the resettlement of offenders by amending the Rehabilitation of Offenders Act.

Education, physical education, and offending behaviour programmes are also important elements of constructive regimes which aim to reduce reoffending, to challenge offenders' behaviour and attitudes which led to their crimes, and to provide value for money. For prisoners, constructive regimes can also make custody more tolerable (see Simon 1999; Gravett 2003; Trebilcock 2011). Constructive regimes are important precisely because so many prisoners are unemployed before beginning their sentence and because, as we have seen, there are clear correlations between reoffending and unemployment. Given the links between offending and social exclusion, both work and education programmes can offer a means of integrating prisoners into society.

Prisoners may be employed in prison workshops, in agriculture and horticulture, and in provision of services within the prison as well as providing goods and services for outside commercial enterprises. With the expansion of prison numbers there has been an increased demand for labour within the prison in providing cooking, cleaning, and other domestic services and most work will be within the internal labour market. But prison work has received less investment than other areas of prison life. Prison industries are expensive to run and it is difficult to find outside work. The prisoners who do work outside the prison are those serving in open prisons near the end of their sentence.

A great deal of work is carried out within the prison for the prison, for example, in gardens, farms, kitchens, and laundries, as well as cleaning, and making furniture. There is also some work for the clothing industry, textile weaving, and unskilled light assembly work for outside employers and apprenticeship schemes have been set up. But opportunities for industrial training work are limited. Prison workshops may be under-used because of the costs of staff supervision. However, there have been some successful collaborations with the private sector. What is needed is sufficient good quality work, training, and education for all prisoners. The European Prison Rules stipulate that sufficient work of a useful nature or other purposeful activities should be provided to keep prisoners actively employed for a normal working day. But there is no similar provision in the Prison Rules and levels of inactivity are still higher than desirable. Under the current arrangements it is estimated that one-third of prisoners are not involved in employment. The Howard League set up a very successful project, a graphic design studio at HMP Coldingley, called Barbed, which paid proper levels of pay from which workers paid tax and national insurance, as well as voluntary donations to Victim Support. The project ran from 2005 to 2008 (Green 2008, 2010).

However, prisoners who are serving short sentences or prisoners serving longer sentences, but subject to transfers, may not remain in the same institution long enough to benefit from interventions, for example, in drug treatment and education programmes. There is also the problem of following up the work when the prisoner is released.

The provision of offending behaviour programmes is an important element of rehabilitation as it gives prisoners the opportunity to change their behaviour. However, the problem in recent years has been that there are insufficient courses to meet demand, which is significant when completion of a rehabilitation programme is a key factor in parole decisions on whether to approve the release of a prisoner. This has led to a number of challenges from prisoners over this failure. In *Wells and Walker* in 2007 the High Court said this was arbitrary, unlawful, and unreasonable, while in *James* in 2007 the High Court said that if the prisoner had completed the minimum term of his sentence and he could not access the appropriate course, then he should be released. In fact his release was deferred pending an appeal by the Government to the Court of Appeal. In *Secretary of State for Justice v Walker and James* (2008) the Court of Appeal found that the Secretary of State had acted unlawfully in failing to provide appropriate access to courses to allow IPP prisoners to demonstrate to the Parole Board that their detention was no longer necessary to protect the public. There was a 'systemic' failure to put the appropriate resources in place to allow prisoners to prepare for their Parole Board assessments. The Court also said that if prisoners were detained for this reason for a long time after the minimum term had been completed it *could* breach Article 5(4) of the ECHR although it declined to uphold an order for James's release. Both parties appealed the Court's decision and the House of Lords in *Secretary of State for Justice v James (formerly Walker and another)* [2009] UKHL 11, did find that it was irrational in the public law sense to introduce the IPP sentence without adequate resources, but this did not necessarily mean that Article 5 had been infringed. For Article 5(1) to be satisfied there must be a link between the original sentence and the continued detention which was satisfied here as the prisoner's continued detention was based on risk and that detention was still subject to regular reviews. Furthermore while the number of courses was insufficient, there were still some courses available so there was no breach of Article 5(4). However, following this case IPP prisoners with short tariffs were given priority access to these courses and in the longer term, as we have noted, there are plans to replace the IPP sentence with a determinate sentence, and new provisions on dealing with dangerous offenders are included in clauses 123–127 of the Legal Aid, Sentencing and Punishment of Offenders (LAS&PO) Bill 2011. Jacobson and Hough (2010) have highlighted the problems IPP prisoners face in proving that they are no longer a risk to the public as applications to the Parole Board have been delayed because of the workload of the Board and because of these problems in obtaining access to courses. They recommend a review of the sentence and, at the least, faster procedures.

9.3.4 **Education**

Prison Rule 32(1) states that '[e]very prisoner able to profit from the educational facilities provided at a prison shall be encouraged to do so'. It also states that educational classes shall be provided at each prison and special needs should be provided for. 'Reasonable facilities shall be afforded to prisoners who wish to do so to improve their education by training, by distance learning, private study and recreational classes, in their spare time' (PR 32(2)). Library facilities should be made available at every prison and every prisoner should be allowed to have library books (PR 33).

There has been increasing awareness of the value of prison education in recent years on the part of policy makers and at the higher levels of the prison management hierarchy, especially in view of the difficulty of finding adequate work for prisoners and the value placed on the constructive use of time, as well as the perpetual problem of controlling prisoners. Clearly education, like work, is valuable in using prisoners' time effectively and preparing them for release and qualifications may be crucial for resettlement. But there is uneven provision of education between prisons, and within prisons the demand for classes may not match supply, and education programmes may be affected by staff shortages. The Woolf Report suggested using prisoners to teach other prisoners where appropriate and this has been implemented in some prisons. A system of peer mentoring has been set up by the Prisoners' Education Trust.

The range of educational opportunities has expanded considerably over the past 30 years with opportunities ranging from basic literacy and numeracy, to Open University degrees by distance learning, as well as National Vocational Qualifications since 1994. But provision of education and training varies from establishment to establishment. The provision of education in prisons and YOIs is subject to regular inspections by OFSTED which has expressed concern over the decline in the quality of learning and skills provision.

Problems still persist of ensuring regular access to classes; classes and work activities may be disrupted by other scheduled prison activities and prisoners are not always motivated to attend. Many prisoners may have a negative experience of school, often being former truants and with low levels of educational achievement. Classes need staff cover for security so educational provision may be vulnerable to cuts at times of staff shortages. Although prison education is expected to play a key role as part of a constructive prison regime, in practice it may be marginalised. There are problems of maintaining commitment to education programmes when prisoners are transferred.

We saw earlier that the poor educational background of many prisoners means that the starting point for the acquisition of skills is very low, so remedial work is needed. A priority now in prison education is to improve the basic skills of literacy and numeracy as well as providing vocational and academic qualifications, particularly for young people, and learning plans are part of the sentencing plan and offender management process. Drug education programmes are also an important element of prisoner education. In *Breaking the Cycle* it is proposed that education in prison should be geared to developing skills to enable participation in work in prison and to improve job prospects on release (Ministry of Justice 2010a).

9.4 Prison unrest

9.4.1 Prison riots

The worst riots in British penal history occurred in 1990 in Strangeways in Manchester, and this was followed by serious riots at Glen Parva, a Young Offenders Institution and remand centre, Cardiff and Bristol, both local prisons, Pucklechurch, a remand centre holding mostly young offenders, Dartmoor, a training prison, and elsewhere. These incidents of disorder led to damage to property, assaults, and loss of life. Following the riots in April 1990, an inquiry into the events leading up to the riots, headed by Lord Justice Woolf was set up, which reported in 1991 (Woolf and Tumim 1991). Its findings are considered below.

Prison riots have a long history in the UK. There were riots in the 1970s at Brixton, Hull, Gartree, and Parkhurst, and in the 1980s at Wormwood Scrubs, Albany, Haverigg, and Risley. Riots have erupted in training prisons, local and remand prisons, Young Offender Institutions and contracted-out prisons, and in prisons with a reputation for relaxed regimes. Since 1990 there have been incidents of disorder and riots, but not on the same scale as the 1990 riots. There were incidents in Portland Young Offenders Institution in 2000, a serious riot in Lincoln Prison in 2002, as well as riots at Hindley Prison in Wigan, which houses adults and young offenders, in 2005, and at Stoke Heath Young Offenders Institution in 2006. In June 2010 young offenders rioted at Cookham Wood when they were not allowed to watch the women's tennis quarter final at Wimbledon, and in January 2011 prisoners at Ford Open Prison set fire to a building. The concern is that with increased overcrowding incidents of disorder may become more frequent and more violent.

9.4.2 **Explaining prison unrest**

Various explanations for the 1990 riots have been advanced (see Woolf and Tumim 1991 and Boin and Rattray (2004). The quality of life in UK prisons in the late 1980s and early 1990s was much worse than at the present time in a number of respects. The Council of Europe's Committee for the Prevention of Torture found that conditions in Wandsworth, Brixton, and Leeds prisons in 1990 were inhuman and degrading (Council of Europe 1991). While there had been an expansion of judicial review relating to prisoners' complaints, this primarily concerned procedural problems rather than prison conditions. In the 1980s there were no national operating standards for prisons, but they were introduced in 1994, and prisons in England and Wales are now assessed on their performance in meeting targets. The UK has also adopted the European Prison Rules[6] which apply international standards to the context of imprisonment. They set out the requirements of good principle and practice in the treatment of prisoners and the management of penal institutions. These rules are not binding in law and are not legally enforceable, and have been described as 'soft law', but they do give guidelines for best practice and recommendations for States Parties who have adopted them. But they also allow for exceptions if circumstances dictate.

There were also problems of control in the 1980s and an increased focus on security because of fears of escape and because of the disorder. It was argued, at the time, that the policy of dispersing high-security prisoners throughout the prison system may have contributed to the problems, because it had an adverse impact on the receiving prisons, increasing the levels of security more than was warranted for other inmates. Volatile political prisoners, disturbed prisoners, and lifers were also blamed at the time for contributing to the problems, although, again, some of the riots occurred in prisons without such prisoners. But the Woolf Report focused on perceptions of unfairness and the sense of injustice.

9.4.3 **The Woolf Report**

Lord Woolf argued that 'the Prison Service must set security, control and justice in prisons at the right level and it must provide the right balance between them. The stability of the prison system depends on the Prison Service doing so' (Woolf and Tumim 1991: para 1.148). By security, he meant preventing prisoners escaping, by control he meant preventing prisoners causing a disturbance, while 'justice encapsulates the obligation on the Prison Service to treat prisoners with humanity and fairness' (ibid: para 1.149). Lord Woolf concluded that the riots happened because these three elements were out of balance (ibid: para 1.150). Once control is lost, then security is also at risk and 'the ability of the Prison Service to provide conditions which accord with justice will be impaired'

[6] The full text of the rules can be obtained from http://www.coe.int.

(ibid: para 10.41). Conversely, 'the achievement of justice will itself enhance security and control' (ibid: para 14.437).

The Woolf Report was critical of the poor physical conditions in English prisons but stressed that this was not the only or the key factor in the riots. While overcrowding may account for some of the unrest in English prisons, riots occurred in prisons where numbers were declining. The key issue was that the prisoners felt aggrieved that their complaints were not dealt with properly. Justice, as he points out, does not figure in PR 1 (now PR 3), although fair treatment is now emphasised in the current Statement of Purpose. At that time Boards of Visitors dealt with discipline and were able to impose punishments including loss of remission, but they were not seen as sufficiently independent. This led to a sense of injustice, and perceptions here are important, for if individuals see the world as unjust, it will influence their actions, whether or not that perception accurately reflects reality. If prisons can achieve justice and prisoners feel that they are being treated fairly, then the problems of disorder, control, and insecurity will diminish. However, if the problem is approached from the other standpoint by focusing on security, this is likely to increase the prisoners' sense of injustice. Improving standards of justice inside prisons means giving prisoners reasons for decisions which affect them, such as transfers and segregation, as well as a fair grievance and disciplinary procedure. The grievance procedure should be independent, simple, and expeditious and reasons for decisions should be given as soon as possible and in writing for matters such as transfers (ibid: para 14.308). Transfers against prisoners' wishes were a source of resentment, and a precipitating factor in the riots. If there is also a loss of legitimacy and a sense of unfairness, then relationships between staff and prisoners will be undermined and in that climate it will be easier for specific incidents to trigger disorder.

Woolf argued for improvements in both physical conditions and grievance and disciplinary procedures. Prisoners wanted more transparent decision making and openness in procedures, so the goal should be to ensure that the prison regime is seen as fair as well as humane. He advocated housing prisoners as near their homes as possible by building community prisons, with small self-contained units, near large cities, so that prisoners can stay in contact with their families, and visiting will be less onerous for families and would be easier to manage. However, many prisoners are still now housed far from their homes. Woolf also advocated improvements in home leave and frequency of visits, extending the use of phone cards to all prisons, and removals of limits on the number of letters that prisoners could post.

Prisoners, Woolf argued, should not have to share a cell (1991: para 11.81), they should have proper access to sanitation (ibid: para 11.97), and the standards of hygiene in prison should be commensurate with those in the community (ibid: para 11.113). The prison system should give all prisoners the opportunity to serve their sentence in a constructive way, making proper use of the time they spend in prison.

The Woolf Report recommended introducing a national system of accredited standards governing the treatment of prisoners and also proposed improvements in the way disciplinary offences are dealt with, recommending that the Boards of Visitors should lose their adjudicative role, and this was implemented in 1992. The Boards have now been renamed Independent Monitoring Boards.

9.4.4 **The impact of the Woolf Report**

The Woolf Report received support in principle from the Government, in its White Paper *Custody, Care and Justice* (Home Office 1991). The Report was also welcomed by prison reformers, although some felt that the Report was not critical enough. The immediate response was improved access to phones and better visiting arrangements, followed by substantial improvements in prison conditions. However, the Government said at the time that it would take 25 years to implement all the recommended improvements. Concerns are still being raised about delays in access to electronically controlled night-time sanitation at Albany and some other prisons which means effectively prisoners are still slopping out at night (HM Chief Inspector of Prisons 2011a).

National operating standards were introduced in 1994, but they are not legally enforceable and have now been overtaken by Key Performance Indicator Targets. Changes in the disciplinary system were introduced in 1992. The Prison Rules were subsequently revised in 1999 and have been subsequently amended. The consensus is that prisoners are now treated with more respect and relationships between staff and prisoners have improved.

Each prisoner is now allocated a Personal Officer although their involvement varies between prisons. Sentence planning has also been introduced, the purpose of which is to make the best use of the prisoner's time, to reduce the risk of reoffending, to prepare the prisoner for release, to co-ordinate the custodial and licence elements of the sentence, to inform the parole process, to act as a focal point for staff and prisoner relationships, and provide opportunities to review the prisoner's progress, and to assist in targeting resources. The emphasis now is on end-to-end management of the offender throughout his time in custody and on supervision, with much closer cooperation between the Prison and Probation Service.

Comparing prisons with the pre-Woolf era, we find significant improvements in the complaints and disciplinary systems. An Ombudsman was appointed in 1994 as a final means of appeal against decisions in disciplinary hearings. The Prisons and Probation Ombudsman can deal with complaints on a wide range of matters including adjudications, deaths in custody (since 2004), prison conditions, and the treatment by officers in both state and private prisons. In 2006 the remit of the Ombudsman was extended to deal with complaints from persons in immigration detention.

Following an investigation of complaints the Ombudsman issues a formal report and makes recommendations, but while these are not binding, they are usually accepted. However, for a complaint to be eligible the internal complaints procedure of the prison should be exhausted first and the matter must fall within the Ombudsman's remit, so using the Ombudsman is not an effective route for those serving short sentences and a large number of the complaints come from prisoners in high security prisons. But if the prison fails to respond to the prisoner within six weeks, then the Ombudsman may receive the complaint. Since 1999 the number of complaints received has risen every year and there has also been an increase in the number of complaints deemed eligible.

Some of the complaints are deemed ineligible as insufficiently insubstantial and because it would be a waste of public money to investigate, for example, a prisoner's complaint that the provision of mince pies at a carol concert was a bribe to convert to Christianity (Prisons and Probation Ombudsman 2011: 17). In 2010–11 the Ombudsman received 4,659 complaints about the Prison Service of which 2,416 were deemed eligible and 2,362 were completed (ibid: 48–9). The Ombudsman found in favour of the complainant in one quarter of the cases, either by mediating a settlement or upholding the complaint. Although the Ombudsman covers prisons, probation, and immigration detention, the majority (88 per cent) of complaints concerned prisons. Complaints concern a range of issues including general prison conditions, complaints about staff, lost property, and the conduct of adjudications (see Figure 9.2 below).

So compared to the early 1990s there are now considerably more safeguards for prisoners. For example, transfer should not be used as a system of punishment, reasons should be given, and inmates should be advised in writing of the reasons for transfer or segregation

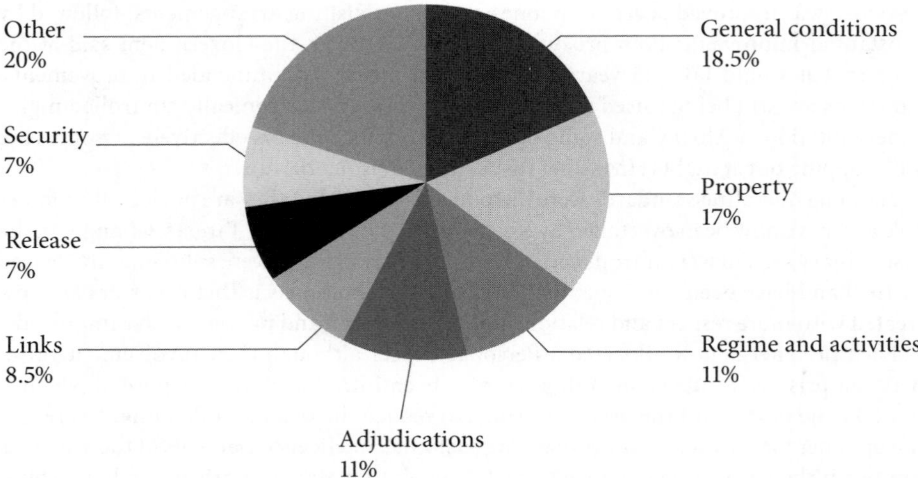

Figure 9.2 Complaints to Prison and Probation Ombudsman 2010–11
Source: Prisons and Probation Ombudsman 2011: 20.

within 24 hours. Complaints should be made within seven days to the Governor of the prison where the transfer decision was made. The prisoner may be transferred for a month and then returned, or sent to another prison. However, transfers are still used to juggle the demand for places. Decisions on transfer are reviewable, but the court is unlikely to interfere because it is open to the Governor to make the decision, if the Governor believes the prisoner's presence affects the smooth running of the prison. Prisoners' complaints can also be made to the Independent Monitoring Boards and the Boards also monitor prison disciplinary hearings and publish annual reports on individual prisons.

However, the Woolf Report's recommendation for a new Prison Rule prohibiting overcrowding was rejected and his suggestion of using smaller community prisons to allow prisoners to be held nearer their homes has not been implemented. Rather the trend has been towards larger prisons, with the closure and merger of some smaller prisons to achieve economies of scale. However, as noted earlier, the proposal for Titan prisons has been shelved.

Reports by the Prison Inspectorate on individual prisons have revealed continuing problems of poor physical conditions and poor staff relations which indicate that some of the problems still persist. The Chief Inspector has highlighted the problems facing prisons in dealing with increasing numbers of prisoners and budget cuts.

There is still insufficient work provision and there are still frequent complaints about food, particularly the timing of meals which are scheduled to fit in with staff shift changes rather than normal routines. Problems of bullying, violence, and assaults persist and may be under-reported, although reducing the number of assaults is a Key Performance Indicator Target. In 2010–11 the aim was to reduce the number of serious assaults on staff, prisoners, and others as a proportion of the average prison population to less than 1.9 per cent. The result achieved was 1.65 per cent (NOMS 2011).

All prisons now have an Incentives and Earned Privileges (IEP) Scheme, set up in 1995 under PR 8, in which privileges are earned by good behaviour or by reaching high standards in work or other activities. There are three levels: basic, standard, and enhanced. Challenging a decision to place a prisoner on a lower level may be difficult as the courts are reluctant to interfere in the way schemes are run. From the prisoners' standpoint it may be seen as an informal means of discipline without the proper safeguards of the formal disciplinary system.

So the focus is on a system of incentives and privileges earned through good behaviour, rather than on prisoners' rights or legitimate expectations. Although the IEP scheme was intended to establish a national framework, the lack of standardisation has led to complaints about the variations in schemes between prisons, which present problems for prisoners who are transferred.

It has also been argued that justice has been subordinated to security and control. The effect of the escapes in the mid-1990s was that all prisons became more security-conscious. Following the escape from Whitemoor in 1994, the Woodcock Report published in 1994 was very critical of security procedures and concern intensified after the escapes from Parkhurst in 1995. The Learmont Report (1995) was also critical of the standards of security, following which the then Director General of the Prison Service, Derek Lewis, was sacked. The effect of enhanced security measures meant cuts in home leave, restrictions on contact with the community, and extra time spent in cells which added to prisoners' sense of injustice, especially as it also affected prisoners not involved in escapes or disorder. Prisoners may still be handcuffed and chained during medical procedures on hospital visits (HM Chief Inspector of Prisons 2011a: 43).

Reports of the Prison Inspectorate have also expressed concern over the use of segregation and the continued detention of IPP prisoners beyond their tariff (HM Chief Inspector of Prisons 2010a). Some of the worst conditions in prisons may be found in segregation units (HM Chief Inspector of Prisons 2011a). Segregation may also have adverse effects on prisoners' mental health, especially if they already suffer from mental health problems (see Edgar and Rickford 2009).

The modern prison regime is much more security-aware, using technological means of surveillance, such as CCTV as well as greater staff surveillance, but escapes still occasionally occur, often while in transit. The emphasis should be on dynamic security, which means relying on good prisoner staff relations so that problems or tensions do not escalate and that prison staff are aware of developing problems and can deal with them.[7] This is more effective than relying on physical barriers or technological surveillance alone. In dealing with difficult prisoners, only the minimum amount of force necessary to prevent harm to others should be used and for the shortest possible time.

There has also been an increasing emphasis on drugs control and policing through mandatory drug testing. This is measured by the rate of positive results from random mandatory drug testing. The target in 2010–11 was 9.3 per cent and the outcome was 7.1 per cent (ibid: 10). It is estimated that over a quarter of adult and young adult males arrive at prison with drug problems, but others may start using drugs in prison. Prescription drugs may also be diverted by prisoners for recreational use.

There has also been continuing industrial unrest within the Prison Service. While prison officers are prohibited from striking by s 138 of the Criminal Justice and Immigration Act 2008, staff may 'work to rule' which will impact on prison activities and the 'no strike' rule is being challenged in the European Court of Human Rights.

9.4.5 **Suicide and self-harm**

But rioting is not the only expression of dissatisfaction or the only way prisoners deal with the pains of imprisonment. Problems with the experience of imprisonment may also

[7] See European Prison Rule 51.2.

be expressed through suicide and self-harm. Prison suicides are reviewed by the Prison Inspectorate and fatal incidents, which include suicides, deaths from natural causes, drug overdoses, accidents, homicides, or other causes, have been investigated by the Prisons Ombudsman since 2004.

There were 57 suicides in 2011 in England and Wales. Although prison suicides may be attributed to mental health problems, isolation is a contributory factor, so any policies which increase contact with home may reduce the risk. Fazel *et al.* (2005) studied suicides of male prisoners in England and Wales between 1978 and 2003 and found that the suicide rate for males in prisons was five times higher than for males outside prison and for boys aged 15–17 was 18 times higher. Being on segregation also increases the risk. In an analysis undertaken by the Ombudsman covering self-inflicted deaths from 2007–9, nearly half were in the unsentenced prison population and nearly one-third took place during the first three months in prison (PPA 2011: 37). Other risk factors include mental health or substance misuse. Several of the cases concerned offenders who had committed offences against a close relative. Precipitating factors in the period leading up to the death included breakdown of relationships, bullying or intimidation from other prisoners and upcoming court appearances (ibid: 37). Reducing suicide was part of the 'decency' agenda and proposals have been made to address this problem (see Dear 2006).

The transfer of responsibility for prison health care to the NHS has been an important factor in improvements in health care overall but clearly problems remain when dealing with the mental health problems of prisoners. Vollm (2009) found that the prevalence of self-harm in the UK female prison population was high and this confirmed the findings of earlier studies. But it has been noted that very few prisons investigate self-harming incidents which means opportunities are lost to understand the issue or develop preventive measures (HM Chief Inspector of Prisons 2011a). Health care in prisons should be provided at the same standard as health care outside on the principle of equivalence stipulated in the European Prison Rules.

9.5 Prison privatisation

9.5.1 The privatisation debate

A further significant development in the 1990s was the introduction of prison privatisation. The provisions for contracting out prisons and also escort duties were introduced in the 1991 Criminal Justice Act (ss 80–88) and for contracting-out of parts, functions, and activities of public sector prisons in the Criminal Justice and Public Order Act 1994 (ss 96–97). There are currently 12 private prisons. The Wolds and Doncaster were built and financed by the public sector but are privately managed, while the remainder were built and are also run by the private sector. They are Dovegate, Altcourse, Parc, Lowdham Grange, Forest Bank, Ashfield, Rye Hill, Bronzefield, and Peterborough. Birmingham was the first public sector prison to be transferred to the private sector in October 2011. A new private prison, Featherstone 2, will also be opened next to Featherstone in Wolverhampton in 2012. The effect of these changes will mean that the proportion of the prison population held in private prisons will increase to 14 per cent, which is higher than in the United States.

A prison previously built and run by the Prison Service may be contracted out to a private company. New prisons may also be privately designed, constructed, managed, and financed, following which the Prison Service pays a fee for each place. Privatisation may also mean privatising specific ancillary services within the prison, such as cleaning or catering, and canteens and shops have now been privatised. Moreover there are plans to increase the processes of competition and contestability by the bidding of contracts for rehabilitation services with payment by results with six pilot studies being conducted, the first of which will be at Doncaster Prison (Ministry of Justice 2010a).

When prison privatisation was proposed in the 1980s, it was purported to be a more cost-efficient way of running the prison system, as advocates argued that private companies could construct, manage, and run prisons more cheaply than the state and build them more quickly to meet the ever-increasing demand for prison places. It was thought that competition between private companies for contracts would encourage the provision of better standards at lower cost, in contrast to the monopoly position of state prisons at the time, as penalty clauses could be written into contracts to discourage breaches. It was also argued that the private prisons would be more innovative in design and management, and, particularly, to avoid the problems of industrial conflict, would recruit new staff from outside the Prison Officers' Association.

However, the case for privatisation was vigorously opposed.[8] It was argued that free competition could not be guaranteed as the firm which wins the initial contract is likely to dominate the industry; because of its experience its costs may be lower, which will give the state an interest in renewing the contract, which may deter other companies from submitting bids. Once the company is in a strong bargaining position it then may be able to negotiate higher prices for average standards as happened in the US. In the UK the market is now dominated by relatively few companies, with just three companies involved at the present time, Serco, G4S Justice Services, and Kalyx (formerly known as UKDS). There are concerns that payment by results may mean the rehabilitation market is also captured by a small group of companies (Prison Reform Trust 2011b).

The obligations of a company to its shareholders may conflict with the duty to provide the best conditions for inmates as there will be pressures to lower costs to maximise profits (see Genders and Player 2007). For example, if private companies reduce costs by recruiting fewer staff, paying lower wages, or reducing training, this may increase risks to staff and prisoners as they may be unable to manage difficult prisoners. It could also be argued that punishment should be exclusively the prerogative of the state or the integrity of the criminal justice system will be undermined (see Barak-Erez 2011). Penalty clauses may be insufficient to maintain standards if penalties are set too low. In any case, problems may persist while the contract runs its course, which could last 25 years, or before a new contract partner is found.

Critics also argue that private companies are not necessarily cheaper providers. Comparing costs accurately may be difficult as private companies are more likely to be given low-risk and therefore low-cost prisoners and, in the early stages of privatisation, the programme was focused on remand prisoners. Moreover, public sector state prisons have become more cost effective and the Prison Service has won contracts in open competition with the private sector. It has also been suggested that cost per place is actually higher in most categories of prison in the private sector than in the public sector.[9]

There are also issues regarding control and accountability as it is arguably harder to control the private sector. There is a rigorous system of auditing public bodies and Parliamentary controls over Ministers, but private contractors are more removed from

[8] For further discussion on prison privatisation, see Matthews (1989); Schichor (1995), Jago and Thompson (2001); Prison Reform Trust (2005); Genders and Player (2007); and Barak-Erez (2011). See also the July 2002 issue of *Punishment and Society* which was devoted to prison privatisation and Gaes (2008) on the problem of cost comparisons.

[9] See Hansard, House of Commons, written answer 9 January 2007.

democratic controls. All private prisons have monitors or Controllers linking them to NOMS to ensure that contracts are complied with. The overall management of the private prison is in the hands of the Director, an employee of the private company but appointed by NOMS.

There is a range of review and scrutiny mechanisms in the state sector, including Parliamentary scrutiny, Independent Monitoring Boards, the National Audit Office, the Prison Inspectorate, and the Prisons and Probation Ombudsman which also apply to the private sector. The prisoner seeking redress for grievances will have access to the courts and to the Ombudsman. Private prisons are subject to the Prison Act and Prison Rules and the European Prison Rules and their prisoners have the same legal rights as those in public sector prisons, including the protection of the HRA 1998. Prison officers, or custody officers, receive similar training to public sector prison officers. If control of a private prison was lost, during a riot, for example, the state would have the power to take it over. In this sense, the state is still responsible for punishment, even within a contracted-out prison; it has a responsibility to see that the service is provided properly. Nonetheless, there have been concerns over incidents of mistreatment in contracted-out prisons, including, for example, the case of Alton Manning who was unlawfully killed through choking from an illegal neck-lock while being restrained at Blakenhurst (Inquest 1998). There has also been overcrowding at Altcourse (HM Chief Inspector of Prisons 2011a: 30).

9.5.2 **The experience of privatisation**

Research has now been conducted to assess the relative strengths and weaknesses of public and private prisons in England and Wales. Of course in the past 10 years public sector prisons themselves have moved closer to the ethos of the private prison, under the influence of the New Managerialism. Indeed, defenders of privatisation argue that it is precisely the use of KPITs and the New Managerialism which has improved the standards in the public sector. Private prison management was endorsed as a model for public sector financial management by the Carter Review of Prisons (Carter 2007).

James *et al.* (1997) conducted fieldwork in the Wolds (the first private prison, opening in 1992) and Woodhill (a new public sector prison). They were struck by the similarities between the two prisons in terms of their 'business like approach to management' and found that the regime at the Wolds was innovative and successful. An ethos of treating prisoners with respect prevailed which allowed for a normalisation of the prison environment. There were good staff relations, more time out of cells, better access to facilities although because of prisoner apathy they were not always used, a high number of hours in purposeful activities, and good mechanisms for accountability.

However, the researchers also found similar innovations and achievements and good staff-prisoner relations in some new public sector prisons, including Woodhill, which opened in 1992. It aimed to provide a humane regime where as much time was spent out of cells as possible, the regime was relaxed and prisoners wore their own clothes. With its strong focus on financial planning, careful budgeting and devolution of budgets to units within the prison, Woodhill was similar in many ways to a private prison, although the conditions there were later criticised by the Chief Inspector of Prisons (HM Chief Inspector of Prisons 1998).

James *et al.* (1997) also examined the regimes at Blakenhurst, then a contracted-out prison, and three new public sector prisons, Belmarsh, Bullingdon and Highdown, and concluded that there was no necessary connection between innovation in regime delivery and contracted-out management status. They found that prisoners were treated with respect in both types of prison, and some public prisons had a strong value-for-money ethos with effective and high quality senior managers. Physical conditions are usually better in newer prisons than old ones, irrespective of their public or private status.

We also find disturbances and disorder in private as well as public sector prisons. Since 1996, there have been disturbances at the Wolds; drugs problems and incidents of assaults, disorder and bullying at Doncaster; and disorder, including hostage taking, at Parc Prison, where there has been high staff turnover and the contractors have been fined for failing to meet minimum standards. More recently its provision of health care has been criticised (HM Chief Inspector of Prisons 2011a: 63). There has also been overcrowding at Doncaster, Blakenhurst, and the Wolds (Park 2000; HM Chief Inspector of Prisons 2007). UKDS was fined in 1994 after losing control of Blakenhurst and it was later returned to the public sector. Rye Hill prison has also been criticised for failing to provide a safe regime (HM Chief Inspector of Prisons 2005). There is a higher turnover of staff in private prisons than public sector prisons which has been attributed to the poorer working conditions and lower pay in the private sector. The National Audit Office has expressed concern over inexperienced staff working in private prisons and over the number of assaults at Dovegate, Altcourse, Ashfield, Rye Hill, and Forest Bank. By 2001 fines imposed on private prisons amounted to almost £1 million and these related to failings including double occupancy and assaults on staff and prisoners (Jago and Thompson 2001). There is also a lower staff-to-prisoner ratio which may have safety implications.

A review of 10 private prisons by the Prison Reform Trust, in 2005, also found mixed results, with variations in performance. Although some private prisons were doing well, others were having problems. The review also raised questions regarding accountability, conflicts of interest, and profiteering from the use of private finance and the pressure for economies of scale in commercial enterprises, as well as highlighting the poorer pay and working conditions in the private sector (Prison Reform Trust 2005).

Privatisation is now deeply embedded in current penal policy, private prisons are accepted by all the main parties, and the continuing focus on contestability has spread to other areas of the criminal justice system. Despite Labour's opposition to prison privatisation expressed before coming to power, the Blair Government persisted with the privatisation programme and commitment to contestability was extended by the Brown administration to community punishment. The Carter Review of Correctional Services (Carter 2003) and the Carter Report on Prisons (Carter 2007) advocated the expanding use of competition from private and voluntary sectors in the prison and probation services to increase effectiveness and value for money. The current Coalition Government is strongly committed to the involvement of these sectors in rehabilitation services within and outside prison. So the commitment to privatisation seems likely to remain a key element of penal policy in the near future, although the gap between public and private prison costs is narrowing. But the challenge now is how to facilitate and sustain creative innovative regimes, at a time of high numbers and limited resources.

9.6 Challenging prison conditions

As well as expressing their grievances through riots, prisoners have also challenged the conditions in which they are held through the courts, using private and public law. Actions have been brought in negligence, but the court will consider the context and judge by the standards appropriate to a prison. Judicial review has been more successful in providing prisoners with an avenue to challenge administrative decisions and as a means of achieving justice. Decisions on disciplinary matters, categorisation, transfer and segregation, and mandatory life sentences have been subjected to judicial scrutiny as the disciplinary regime of the prison has been integrated into public law since the late 1970s. Generally, judges have felt more comfortable dealing with quasi-judicial matters, such as disciplinary hearings, rather than intervening in relation to prison conditions. The Prison Rules allow for considerable discretion, but this should not be exercised unreasonably. Before the HRA 1998, the criterion would have been the test in *Associated Provincial Picture Houses v Wednesbury Corporation* [1948], but now the courts will consider ECHR compliance where rights issues are raised, so the test will be that of proportionality (see *Daly* (2001); *Huang* (2007)). Human rights jurisprudence has become increasingly important in prisoners' litigation (Easton 2011a). Prisoners may also use the internal complaints procedure, make complaints to the Prisons and Probation Ombudsman, and contact their members of Parliament.

9.6.1 **Human rights, fairness, and justice**

The protections afforded prisoners both internally and through the courts have improved the safety of prisoners and raised standards in prison, but there is still some way to go. While procedural justice has improved substantially since the early 1990s, the day-to-day conditions in which prisoners are held still leave much room for improvement and there is considerable variation between prisons, as illustrated by the league tables and also supported by empirical research on prisoners' experiences, such as Meek's survey of high security prisoners (Meek 2008).

Rights are important to prisoners because they are vulnerable and dependent, as they are unable to obtain access to key goods such as work and health care by their own efforts. Strengthening rights, fairness, and justice also provides positive benefits to the Prison Service as reducing dissatisfaction would improve good order within prisons. It would also create a better climate for the rehabilitation of prisoners as it would strengthen adherence to liberal-democratic values within the regime (Easton 2008d). Respect for rights is also a key means of ensuring the legitimacy of the system. The value of a human rights-based approach is that enforceable rights offer a means of maintaining and ensuring minimum standards inside prison and arguably provide greater protection than the Key Performance Indicator Targets of New Managerialism, particularly at a time of increased pressure on resources and a strong focus on public protection and risk management. At the same time, negotiating human rights, as we saw in Chapter 5, has itself become a risk for prison governance (see Murphy and Whitty 2007).

A right to a minimum standard of living would potentially contribute to the improvement of prison conditions, provided that there are adequate enforcement mechanisms in place. An open grievance procedure enhances the legitimacy of the prison authority structure. There should be a right to the maximum autonomy compatible with the rights and freedoms of others and with the fact of imprisonment, but prison reform has not been couched in a rights framework in the UK. The Prison Service has resisted the move towards a culture of rights, preferring to use the currency of privileges and incentives which are not legally enforceable entitlements. They can be withdrawn and used as a disciplinary measure to maintain good order and discipline within the prison. Moreover, guaranteeing legally enforceable rights is much more expensive both in terms of compliance and in defending claims made in relation to alleged breaches.

Demands for rights have met with some resistance from governments and the Prison Service because of a concern with the financial costs if it opened the floodgates to litigation, but there are disincentives for prisoners to complain, such as a fear of being seen as a troublemaker, and also the need for literacy skills to bring an action. The requirement for leave for judicial review and the continuing scope for discretion have also acted as a brake on prisoners' rights litigation. Moreover, even when prisoners have succeeded in their claims, the level of damages awarded has been relatively low.

9.6.2 **Rights Conventions**

In English law the approach of the courts has been that prisoners have the same civil rights as non-prisoners except for those taken away expressly or impliedly by imprisonment.[10] But this clearly falls far short of according prisoners special rights by virtue of the fact that they are prisoners. Because of this *lacuna*, international human-rights instruments have particular significance for the prison system in the UK.

Article 5 of the Universal Declaration of Human Rights states that '[n]o one shall be subjected to torture or to cruel, inhuman or degrading treatment or punishment'. The rights in the Declaration are elaborated in rights instruments, including the International Covenant on Civil and Political Rights (ICCPR). The UK has ratified the ICCPR which includes general provisions of relevance to punishment, such as the right to life and the right not to be detained arbitrarily. Article 10 deals specifically with the penal system:

1. All persons deprived of their liberty shall be treated with humanity and with respect for the inherent dignity of the human person.
2. (a) Accused persons shall, save in exceptional circumstances, be segregated from convicted persons and shall be subject to separate treatment appropriate to their status as unconvicted persons;
   (b) Accused juvenile persons shall be separated from adults and brought as speedily as possible for adjudication.
3. The penitentiary system shall comprise the treatment of prisoners the essential aim of which shall be their reformation and rehabilitation. Juvenile offenders shall be segregated from adults and accorded treatment appropriate to their legal status.

However, the most significant rights protection in recent years has come from the ECHR, which protects a number of rights relevant to the context of imprisonment and detention (see van Zyl Smit and Snacken 2009; Easton 2011a). Even before the HRA 1998, the ECHR influenced the English courts, although the recommendations of the European Court of Human Rights were persuasive not binding. Many of the issues raised in the early Convention cases are also now covered by the European Prison Rules. However, in its jurisprudence, the European Court of Human Rights has tended to focus on the Convention rights themselves, rather than the standards in the European Prison Rules.

In addition prisons are inspected periodically, and on an ad hoc basis where there are specific concerns, by the European Committee for the Prevention of Torture. Although the recommendations of the Committee are not binding, its visits to the UK and other jurisdictions have generated a jurisprudence on the psychological impact of imprisonment. The Committee's latest UK visit has raised issues regarding the impact of overcrowding, the problems faced by IPP prisoners, and the treatment of young offenders (Council of Europe 2009).

The UK has also signed the Optional Protocol to the Convention against Torture (OPCAT) which means that the UK has to establish a National Preventive Mechanism which makes regular and independent visits to places of detention. The work of the NPM

[10] *Raymond v Honey* (1983).

is coordinated by the Inspectorate of Prisons and it published its first report in 2011 (National Preventive Mechanism 2011).

The ECHR has been extensively used by UK prisoners and has had considerable impact on prisoners' lives. Prisoners retain their rights under the ECHR notwithstanding their imprisonment and restrictions on those rights need to be justified within the criteria set out in the relevant Articles of the ECHR. Convention compliance is also considered when introducing regime changes.

Legislation has also been amended in response to decisions in the European Court of Human Rights. In some cases settlements have also been reached in anticipation of the Court's decisions. However, in other cases, notably voting rights for prisoners, the UK Government has resisted changes demanded by the Court.

The ECHR has improved the experience of punishment in a number of areas. For example, Article 2 has been used to challenge the procedures for dealing with deaths in custody, in *Edwards v UK* (2002), and in relation to the failure to prevent suicide in *Keenan v UK* (2001). Article 3 has been used to challenge inhuman and degrading prison conditions. It has also been used in relation to full body searching: while this may be legitimate under Article 8(2) it should not be used routinely. Article 5 has been used to challenge the lawfulness of continued detention by mentally disordered offenders as well as by discretionary life prisoners (see Chapter 5). Article 6 has been used to gain access to the courts, in *Golder v UK* (1975), and to challenge the conduct of disciplinary hearings. Article 8, the right to private and family life, has been used to challenge interference with prisoners' correspondence and excessive restrictions on prison visits, and to improve contact with prisoners' families. However restrictions on correspondence with prisoners' families may be permitted under Article 8(2). Article 8 has also been used to successfully challenge the denial of access to artificial insemination (AI) in *Dickson v UK* (2007). Following this case the rules relating to applications for AI have been modified. Article 8 was also successfully used by a prisoner in asserting the right to correspond freely with a medical specialist regarding his case, in *Szuluk v UK* (2009). Article 12 has been used to claim the right to temporary release from prison to marry in *Hamer v UK* (1979). If prisoners are not allowed temporary release on security grounds they may be married inside prison. These rights also extend to civil partners under the Civil Partnership Act 2004. Article 3 of Protocol No. 1 has been used to challenge the ban on convicted prisoners voting in *Hirst v UK* (2005). Article 10 has been used to protect prisoners' right to freedom of expression so prisoners may communicate with the media where they are raising matters of legitimate public interest affecting prisoners or the prison system and any restrictions on their rights must be proportionate and satisfy the requirements of Article 10(2).[11] The Court has also recognised the rights of prisoners' relatives, in the case of *Dickson* above, which concerned the reproductive and family rights of the prisoner's wife but also in the case of *Wainwright v UK* (2006) which related to the searching of prisoners' relatives on a prison visit.

From the standpoint of the Strasbourg Court, prisoners possess rights rather than expectations or privileges. However, the potential of the ECHR is limited by the fact that several of the rights protected by the ECHR may be qualified, to prevent crime, in the interests of national security and to protect the rights and freedom of others, which may be particularly appropriate to the context of imprisonment, and these qualifications have been interpreted liberally by the Court. States have in the past been accorded a wide margin of appreciation in interpreting and applying the ECHR but in recent years the Strasbourg Court has become much more assertive. It has characterised the ECHR as a

[11] See *R v SSHD ex parte Simms and O'Brien* (2000).

living instrument to be interpreted in the light of present-day conditions, that is, dynamically, and stressed the need to strike a balance between the demands of the general interests of the community and the protection of individuals' fundamental rights, using the principle of proportionality. In many of the above contested cases, the approach of the Strasbourg Court has been more favourable than the domestic courts to the rights of the prisoner.

9.6.3 **The Human Rights Act 1998**

Since the HRA 1998 came into force, reliance on Convention rights has been much enhanced. The HRA 1998 incorporates the ECHR into domestic law. Legislation must be interpreted so as to be compatible with the ECHR. If it is not possible to do so, the court should issue a declaration of incompatibility. Section 6 of the HRA 1998 makes it unlawful for public authorities to act in ways which are incompatible with the European Convention. The HRA 1998 applies to private companies if they are responsible for areas of activity which were previously in the public sector, so the Act clearly can be used against private prisons. Companies managing contracted-out prisons perform a statutory-based activity and are constrained by the same statutes as public prisons, namely the Prison Act and Prison Rules. The Act also applies to the Independent Monitoring Boards (formerly Boards of Visitors) and the Parole Board. When the HRA 1998 came into force the Prison Service took the view that its policies operating at the time were compliant with the ECHR but, since then, the application of some of these policies has been successfully challenged.

Because of the amount of time it has taken in the past for a case to be heard at Strasbourg, the ECHR was of value only to those serving longer sentences. With the HRA 1998 this problem has been substantially reduced. If a case does ultimately go to Strasbourg the procedures there have also been streamlined, with the abolition of the Commission in 1999, which came into effect in October 2000.

Before the Act, pursuing a Convention case was a burdensome and lengthy procedure. The original incident in the case of *Campbell and Fell*, for example, occurred in 1976, and the European Court's judgment was published in 1984. Those whose Convention rights are infringed can now bring proceedings and claim remedies, including damages, in the domestic courts. A Prison Service policy may be challenged under the HRA 1998, if it raises fundamental rights issues. All officers and inmates are informed of the Act and its implications and a brief Guide to the Human Rights Act, produced jointly by the Prison Service and the Prison Reform Trust, is given to all prisoners and employees.

Although in the past in the domestic courts, judges have been reluctant to acknowledge prisoners' rights, clearly since the HRA 1998 came into force they have responded more favourably to prisoners' rights claims because a rights culture is now more embedded in domestic law. Prisoners are increasingly using Convention rights to challenge prison regimes as well as securing procedural fairness.

For example, there have been several challenges by life-sentenced prisoners to delays in parole reviews for mandatory lifers following the European Court of Human Rights' decision in *Stafford v UK* (2002). However, the English courts subsequently have stressed in *R (Middleton) v Secretary of State for the Home Department* (2003) that the authorities should be allowed a reasonable time to take account of any changes. Following *Stafford* the arrangements for parole reviews have been amended so that all mandatory life prisoners who are near the end of their tariff will have a review which complies with Article 5(4). The review is conducted first on the papers and a recommendation made; then either party, if unhappy with the recommendation, can request an oral hearing.

Moreover, the House of Lords has also held that the Home Secretary's power to set minimum tariffs for mandatory-life-sentence prisoners under s 29 of the Crime (Sentences) Act 1997 breaches Article 6(1) of the ECHR, because the tariff should be set by an independent and impartial tribunal and not by the Home Secretary. The House of Lords therefore issued a declaration of incompatibility on this matter in *R (Anderson) v Secretary of the State for the Home Department* (2002) (see Chapter 5, section 5.4.4). The courts rather than the Minister now have the responsibility of determining the punitive part of the sentence.

The Criminal Justice Act 2003 subsequently set out the principles by which judges fix minimum tariffs and required judges to give reasons in court if they impose a term inconsistent with those principles. Successful challenges to delays in the parole process have been made by prisoners serving determinate sentences: these delays have been held to be unlawful and a breach of Article 5(4) (see *R (Johnson) v Secretary of State for the Home Department and Another* [2007]). In *R v Parole Board ex parte Smith; R v Parole Board ex parte West* (2005) UKHL 1, the House of Lords said that determinate prisoners on licence should have an oral hearing to consider recall to prison in order to satisfy Article 5(4).

There have also been changes in relation to disciplinary procedures. Until 2002 the power to award additional days was vested in the Governor. However, in *Ezeh and Connors v UK* (2002) the European Court of Human Rights ruled that only independent adjudicators, not Prison Governors, may impose additional days as punishment for disciplinary offences. Ezeh and Connors were charged separately with using threatening language and assault. They were found guilty at hearings before the Governor at which they were not represented. Ezeh received 40 additional days and Connors seven additional days. The European Court of Human Rights deemed that, given the charges they faced and the extent of the penalty, Article 6 was engaged, and the refusal to allow representation did violate Article 6(3)(c).

Following that decision, the Governor should decide whether a charge is so serious that it could lead to additional days if the prisoner is found guilty (PR 53A(1)). If so, the Governor must refer the case to an independent adjudicator in which case the prisoner must be offered the opportunity to seek legal representation (PR 54(3)). If the charge will not incur additional days' punishment, then the Governor can conduct the adjudication (PR 54A(2)(b)). If the Governor does proceed, but it becomes clear that additional days should be awarded, the Governor can then refer the case to an independent adjudicator, during the hearing or after the hearing, but before imposing punishment (PR 53A(3)). The independent adjudicator can award up to 42 additional days for adult prisoners and 21 additional days for young offenders. The procedures for adjudication in the *Prison Discipline Manual* were revised in January 2006 by PSO 2000.

But while more human rights cases may now be brought, this does not mean that all will succeed, as many cases taken to Strasbourg in the past by prisoners failed. While cases on access to the courts and interference with privileged correspondence have met with success, cases on conditions have been less successful. The Prison Service can defend cases under the HRA 1998 only if it can show that the decision was imposed because of necessity, rather than demonstrating its reasonableness. Prisoners are therefore more likely to succeed if they focus on areas which have previously enjoyed success at Strasbourg, such as correspondence, access to lawyers, family contact, disciplinary procedures, and treatment of life-sentence prisoners, or reviews of their detention, rather than challenging prison conditions. Even if those conditions are harsh, the nature of the prison environment means that considerable weight will be given to issues of security. In *R (G) v Home Secretary* [2005] a prisoner, who had been held in a Protected Witness Unit (PWU), committed further offences after release from prison. When he was returned to prison, he was initially detained in a PWU but was then transferred as a category A prisoner to a self-contained unit at HMP Belmarsh. A challenge to his categorisation and conditions by judicial review did not succeed.

There are also difficulties with the ECHR itself, particularly the fact that it does not include social or economic rights, reflecting the political context in which the ECHR was drafted in response to civil rights violations in Europe in the 1930s and 1940s. However, social rights are assuming more importance in international human rights law (see Búrca and de Witte 2005; Fredman, 2008). On the positive side, however, the HRA 1998 has created a rights culture and means that domestic courts are obliged to consider rights issues in all areas of law. Moreover, with increasing pressure to improve standards from international rights jurisprudence, the principle of less eligibility has become less significant in governing prison life.

A further conduit by means of which international standards enter into penal management is through the revised and updated European Prison Rules adopted by the Committee of Ministers of the Council of Europe in January 2006. Although these do not amount to enforceable rights, they do reflect the jurisprudence of the Strasbourg Court. The revised Rules take account of changes in the penal field since the 1980s, the case law and jurisprudence of the European Court of Human Rights on prison conditions, and the Reports of the European Committee for the Prevention of Torture and Inhuman or Degrading Treatment or Punishment. The changes cover a range of issues, including healthcare in prison, disciplinary measures and conditional release. The Rules cover a wide range of areas of prison life including health care, work, recreation, and procedural fairness including the opportunity to raise complaints.

9.6.4 **Prisoners and the right to vote**

An important area where a Convention challenge has succeeded in the European Court of Human Rights is in relation to prisoner disenfranchisement. However, the Court's recommendation of changes to the law has met with considerable resistance from successive UK Governments. In *Hirst v UK* in October 2005, a former prisoner argued that the provisions preventing convicted prisoners from voting in s 3 of the Representation of the People Act 1969, as amended in 1983 and 2000, violated Article 3 of Protocol No. 1 of the ECHR, which imposes on states the obligation to hold free elections under conditions which will ensure the 'free expression of the people in the choice of the legislature'.[12] The majority of the Strasbourg Court concluded that a blanket restriction which applies regardless of individual circumstances, or the gravity of the offence, falls outside the margin of appreciation. The UK Government had not considered fully whether such a ban was necessary. The impact of the ban excluded thousands of citizens from voting. Voting by convicted prisoners has been permitted in some other jurisdictions for many years, for example, in the South African constitution.

Following *Hirst* the UK Government undertook a lengthy consultation process to consider whether some categories of convicted prisoner should be permitted to vote and the possible mechanisms for voting. The first Consultation Paper sought views on the general principle of restoring the vote and possible methods of doing so and whether those convicted of electoral fraud should be permitted to vote (Department for Constitutional Affairs 2006). This paper received a mixed response, although only one quarter of

[12] Remand prisoners, and prisoners convicted for non-payment of fines and those imprisoned for contempt of court are permitted to vote.

respondents favoured the *status quo* and just under half favoured restoring the vote to all prisoners. The second Consultation Paper asked for views on the appropriate threshold for re-enfranchisement (Ministry of Justice 2009). Options considered included prisoners retaining the vote if they served less than one year, two years, or four years. The fourth option is for prisoners to retain the vote if they are sentenced to less than two years, but they would be allowed to apply to a court to retain the vote if they are sentenced to a term between two and four years so this would be subject to a judge's permission in the specific case. The Paper also invited comments on the practicalities and the best way of registering prisoners' votes. If changes are made, prisoners will be registered at their former address rather than the prison and will vote by post or proxy. The Consultation Papers made clear that the vote would at best be restored only to some convicted prisoners rather than all. Given the current size of the prison population and the numbers serving shorter sentences, the proposed changes could bring a substantial number of prisoners back into the democratic process, especially if the four-year threshold is selected.

Since *Hirst* there have been several challenges brought on the failure to allow prisoners to vote. Cases were brought by prisoners challenging the legality of the May 2007 elections in the domestic courts on the issue of Convention compliance but were unsuccessful although the amount of time taken to amend the law was criticised by the Courts (see *Traynor and Fisher* [2007], *Smith v Scott* [2007], and *Re Toner and Walsh* [2007]). In *R (Chester) v Secretary of State for Justice* [2009] the court made clear that it would not make a further declaration of incompatibility or pressurise the Government to speed up the changes as the Government was already reviewing the options.

However, as yet legislation has not been introduced despite criticism from the Committee of Ministers of the Council of Europe which has expressed its concern over the delays. Before the May 2010 General Election it strongly advised the UK Government to adopt measures to allow prisoners to vote in the forthcoming election, in anticipation of a series of applications to the Court if it failed to do so. It subsequently noted its 'profound regret' that despite its repeated calls the election was held in May with the blanket restriction still in place and 'expressed confidence that the new United Kingdom government will adopt general measures to implement the judgment ahead of elections scheduled for 2011 in Scotland, Wales and Northern Ireland, and thereby also prevent further, repetitive applications to the European Court'.[13]

In *Greens and MT v UK* (2010) the Strasbourg Court set a date for the UK Government to comply with the ruling in *Hirst*. The Court also said it would discontinue hearing these repetitive applications pending compliance by the State with the judgment. The UK Government's request for a referral to the Grand Chamber was refused in April 2011, so the *Greens* judgment became final and a new deadline for compliance was set in autumn 2011. However, a further extension was granted to the UK to await the outcome of the case of *Scoppola v Italy (No 3)* (2011) where a successful challenge to a blanket ban on prisoners' voting was referred to the Grand Chamber. The case was heard in November 2011 and the new date for the UK's compliance is six months from the date of the judgment in *Scoppola*. The UK's Attorney General addressed the court as a third party intervenor in that case and argued strongly that the question of prisoners' votes should be a matter for Parliament.

Since *Hirst* the Strasbourg Court has also considered prisoner disenfranchisement in the case of *Frodl v Austria* (2010). Here the Court was critical of the Austrian law which denied the vote to prisoners serving more than one year because the decision was not taken by a judge and because there appeared to be no link between the penalty of

[13] Decision No. 18: para 4 3 June 2010.

disenfranchisement and the offence committed, suggesting that the offence should concern issues relating to elections. So if the proposed UK legislation is enacted it is likely that there may be future Convention challenges to meet the conditions discussed in *Frodl*.

In December 2010 the Coalition Government said that some prisoners, namely those serving shorter sentences, may be given the right to vote. The Government made clear that the proposed changes were being introduced reluctantly to comply with obligations under the ECHR and to avoid making substantial compensation payments to prisoners. However, the court in the *Greens and MT* case also made it clear that, in relation to prisoners' claims concerning denial of the right to vote, a finding of a violation constitutes just satisfaction and no damages are appropriate. So the concerns over the costs of these claims have been abated.

However this prospect of prisoners voting has caused considerable disquiet and it may be difficult even for a government committed to change to enact these reforms, given substantial opposition from MPs, the press and public. There has been a strong campaign led by MPs against restoring the vote. The Government initially indicated that it might restore the vote to prisoners serving less than four years, with the courts having discretion to withhold the vote if they see this as appropriate, but it has since been reported that it is considering reducing the threshold to one year, despite the prospect of further litigation and clashes with the Strasbourg Court. The reluctance to restore the vote reflects the Government's opposition to re-enfranchisement as well as the problems of enacting change in the face of widespread Parliamentary and public opposition.

The UK Government has defended prisoner disenfranchisement on the grounds that it is an appropriate punishment and will encourage civic responsibility and respect for the law, but these arguments did not satisfy the Court in *Hirst*, and they are difficult to support, as it could be argued that including prisoners in the electoral process will encourage civic responsibility and promote social inclusion (see Easton 2006, 2009).

Defenders of prisoner disenfranchisement argue that it is a reasonable restriction and appropriate punishment for wrongdoing and that it may promote respect for the law. It is argued that prisoners do not deserve the right because of their criminal acts and also that the UK public is hostile to restoration of the vote. It is also claimed that allowing prisoners to vote may undermine the purity of the ballot box and lead to the corruption of public life if they taint the electoral process, for example by bloc voting or by electing unsuitable representatives to public office. The UK Government has also stressed the fact that many other states around the world ban prisoners from voting and compared to some other states, the UK ban is reasonable because the vote is restored as soon as prisoners return to the community. In some US states, for example, former felons may be banned for life. But all these arguments are open to challenge. While the UK position is less harsh than some other states, nonetheless the trend worldwide seems to be shifting towards re-enfranchisement and the right was given to convicted prisoners in the Republic of Ireland in 2006. Prisoners are also permitted to vote in many other states, including Spain and South Africa.

In *Hirst* the Strasbourg Court stressed that barring the vote reduces prisoners to a state of civil death which is no longer appropriate in a modern state. Moreover, the court said that the views of the public—while a factor to consider—should not be determinative when fundamental rights are at stake. Critics of disenfranchisement also argue that allowing prisoners to vote may promote civic responsibility by encouraging participation in the political life of the state and, by including them, a sense of citizenship may be promoted in prisoners, which may contribute to rehabilitation and reintegration. In those states where voting is permitted there has been no evidence of damage to the electoral process. If postal voting is used this may be more effectively monitored in the context of prison than on the outside. Giving prisoners the vote would give them a stronger voice enabling them to raise issues of concern over their treatment. The area where the European Court is willing to accept a ban is for prisoners who have committed electoral offences.

Of course prisoners themselves may not see voting rights as a key issue compared to their concerns over the physical conditions in prison or visiting rights, but this does not invalidate the point that enfranchisement acknowledges the prisoner remains a citizen. It would not be a costly measure and there are no security issues involved, as prisoners do not need to leave the prison to cast their votes.

The debate over voting rights has also highlighted the concerns over the encroachment of the Strasbourg Court on the management of the criminal justice system and social policy issues in the UK and has led to increasing calls from some politicians to repeal the HRA 1998. The Coalition Government has argued for reform of the court itself and for greater freedom for states on matters of social policy. As the UK has now taken on the role of the Chair of the Committee of Ministers of the Council of Europe, it will pursue this agenda. Questions have also been raised by some members of the judiciary over the authority and intervention of the Court.[14] A Commission to investigate the creation of a UK Bill of Rights and to consider changes to the European Court of Human Rights was established in March 2011 and is expected to publish its report at the end of 2012. Its interim advice has recommended that cases heard by the court should be limited to serious breaches of Convention rights.[15] So the future of prisoner enfranchisement remains uncertain.

9.7 Expansionist and reductionist penal policies

If we review penal policies and particularly the use of custody in recent years, we find a tension between expansionist and reductionist penal policies with a continuing expansion of prison numbers and commitment to prison building, on the one hand, and attempts to exert controls and limits on this expansion through the use of alternatives to custody and greater controls on sentencers. As governments have tried to negotiate the pressures of public opinion and anxieties over crime and punishment with spiralling costs and political crises of accountability, we find conflicting trends and conflicting messages for sentencers. Moreover, when the deeper problem of the best way to deal with offending and reoffending has been addressed, there has not been a great deal of consensus on the best way forward.

The Carter Review of Prisons published in 2007 proposed a further 6,500 places by 2012, in addition to planned increases (Carter 2007). It also proposed building three large-scale 'Titan' prisons to replace some older decrepit prisons, and recommended speeding up the existing building programme to match increased demand and this was endorsed by the Labour Government.

The rationale of the Titan prison was to concentrate facilities to achieve economies of scale and better value for money as medical and catering services, for example, could be centralised, so it was primarily cost-driven. The building costs of larger prisons would be cheaper than several smaller institutions and they would be able to offer a range of services. It was envisaged that each prison would hold up to 2,500 but juveniles and female prisoners would be held in smaller units within the perimeter. They would be built where

[14] See, for example, *R v Horncastle and another, R v Marquis and another, R v Carter* [2009] 1 EWCA Crim 964.

[15] http://www.justice.gov.uk/downloads/about/cbr/cbr-court-reform-interim-advice.pdf.

demand is highest: in London, the North-West, and the West Midlands. A Consultation Paper on Titan Prisons was published by NOMS in June 2008 to consider, inter alia, the implications of the use of such prisons for the delivery of safe and decent regimes, how the prison population should be segmented in these new prisons, and the appropriate method of commissioning for services supplied within those prisons (NOMS 2008). But the plans for Titan prisons were shelved.

The Carter Report's recommendation for large-scale prisons runs counter to the available research which suggests that smaller-scale units are more effective in providing humane regimes rather than simply 'warehousing'. Large-scale prisons may be more cost effective in the short term but raise problems of containing disorder and disruption which may be managed more easily on a smaller scale. Critics have focused on the problems of maintaining offender integration and wellbeing in a larger and more impersonal regime, and relations between staff and prisoners and prisoners themselves improve in smaller scale environments. The Chief Inspector of Prisons found a correlation between perceptions of safety, positive staff-prisoner relationships and the smaller size of prisons (HM Chief Inspector of Prisons 2011a: 20). However, the location of prison places in or near major centres of population would be better for prisoners from those areas rather than being housed in a remote rural area.

The Carter Report also proposed a permanent Sentencing Commission to ensure predictability and consistency in sentencing, arguing that a structured sentencing framework would make it easier to predict changes in the prison population. The framework would include sentence lengths, types of community sentence, levels of fines, seriousness ranking of offenders, and offender characteristics with ranges set by the Sentencing Commission which the government would be unable to change. The Sentencing Council established in 2009 has taken on these tasks.

So the acceptance of high levels of imprisonment has focused attention on cost effectiveness and efficiency in the provision of punishment and providing value for money and for improving financial controls on public sector prisons. Some of the most promising elements of the Criminal Justice Act 2003 which might have had a reductionist effect, namely custody plus and intermittent custody, have been abandoned (see Chapter 3). The proposal to reduce the prison population further by increasing the maximum sentence discount for a guilty plea from one-third to 50 per cent was jettisoned following opposition. Any changes to UK penal policy need to satisfy the public and the judiciary, and will be closely scrutinised by the media.

However, we can find some evidence of a continuing shift towards reductionism in other policy developments, as the costs of expansionist penal policies have been difficult to sustain. Furthermore there has been increasing recognition that the impact of imprisonment on crime reduction is limited. The Carter Review of Correctional Services (2003) estimated that an increased use of prison since 1997 had reduced crime by about 5 per cent and concluded that 'there is no convincing evidence that further increases in custody would significantly reduce crime' (Carter 2003: 15). The Review recommended a number of reforms which build on the sentencing framework in the Criminal Justice Act 2003 such as income-related fines for low-risk offenders, and more demanding community sentences for medium-risk offenders, with greater use of surveillance and electronic monitoring. However, at the same time, it noted that, if evidence showed that custody was effective in reducing crime, then resources should be provided to build more prisons. It argued that custody should be reserved for the most serious and dangerous and persistent offenders, but greater help should be given to persistent offenders.

The Labour Government accepted many of the recommendations in the Carter Report (Home Office 2004b). In its *Five Year Strategy for Protecting the Public and Reducing*

Re-offending (Home Office 2005b) it announced that more emphasis should be given to reparation, that greater use of fines should be considered, and that persistent offenders should be given tougher but more flexible sentences and announced its intention to introduce day fines. As we have argued, such fines would also deal with some of the problems of unequal impact referred to in Chapter 7, but in the end they were not introduced. The Labour Government also later set up the Sentencing Council and envisaged this would take account of resources. The Sentencing Council for England and Wales was established by the Coroners and Justice Act 2009 to provide greater transparency and consistency in sentencing. It replaced the Sentencing Guidelines Council and the Sentencing Advisory Panel. Its functions include preparing sentencing guidelines and publishing resource implications in respect of these guidelines, and promoting awareness of sentencing and sentencing practice.

There has also been increasing acceptance of the view that alternatives to custody should be developed for particular groups of offenders, namely women, those with mental health problems, and young offenders. This shift began under Labour but has continued with the change of government. The Coalition Government has said that there will also be more emphasis on diverting offenders with mental health problems from custody. It also proposes that there will be greater emphasis on drug recovery in prison to cut reoffending.

As we noted in chapter 1 the Coalition Government has proposed reforms to the criminal justice system, including sentencing and rehabilitation, imprisonment and community (Ministry of Justice 2010a). The emphasis will be on breaking the cycle of reoffending and reducing the financial costs of imprisonment through increased emphasis on rehabilitation and payment by results, increased competition and a greater role for private and voluntary service providers. There will also be greater provision to deal with drug and alcohol abuse and mental health provision. The Government, as we have seen, wants working prisons with prisoners working up to 40 hours per week and on prisoners using part of their earnings to provide redress to victims (see Chapter 6, section 6.2.4). The numbers in prison will also be reduced by reducing the numbers held on remand, by removing the option of remand in custody for those unlikely to receive a custodial sentence at trial, and by reducing the number of foreign national prisoners held in UK prisons. Greater use will also be made of fines, community payback, and restorative justice. There are also plans to revise the Rehabilitation of Offenders Act to facilitate resettlement of prisoners and to increase the diversion of prisoners with mental health problems away from custody, and to set up a network of mental health diversion and liaison schemes.

Many of these proposals have been welcomed by prisoner reformers, particularly the reduced use of remand, but not enough attention is given to the needs of vulnerable groups. Moreover no reference is made to voting rights for prisoners, which would increase civic responsibility. Reformers also argue for the removal of the mandatory sentence for murder and of indeterminate sentences and a return to desert-based sentencing and increased use of restorative justice for adult male offenders, as well as young offenders (Prison Reform Trust 2011b). Prisoners are already engaged in a variety of voluntary activities in prison, including peer support and community support schemes, as Edgar *et al.* have shown in their review of the activities undertaken by prisoners (Edgar *et al.* 2011). They argue that these opportunities for active citizenship should be expanded. There are also concerns over the level of resourcing needed to achieve effective rehabilitation.

Other strategies to reduce demand for prison places have been deployed, including greater use of electronic monitoring and bail hostels and encouraging foreign-national prisoners to return home by offering financial incentives. In addition, where foreign-national prisoners are awaiting deportation the process is being speeded up, and an Early Removal System releases foreign-national prisoners early for deportation.

There has also been increased emphasis on resettlement, on assisting prisoners to find work, accommodation or training on release for prison. Resettlement is included as a Key Performance Indicator Target under 'Pathways to Reducing Reoffending'. The target for the percentage of offenders in employment at the end of their sentence for 2010–11 was at least 33.7 per cent and the outcome was 37.6 per cent (NOMS 2011:10). The target for the percentage of offenders in settled or suitable accommodation at the end of their sentence for 2010–11 was at least 81.3 per cent and the outcome was 86.7 per cent (NOMS 2011: 10). The policy and practice on resettlement is reviewed by Hucklesby and Hagley-Dickinson (2007).

Proposals to reduce the size of the prison population have also been made by the House of Commons Justice Committee in its report *Cutting Crime: The Case for Justice Reinvestment*. This made suggestions to reduce the prison population including focusing resources on the prevention of criminality in high crime areas and greater use of restorative justice (House of Commons Justice Committee 2010).

When we review penal policy over the last 10 years we find elements of expansionism and reductionism. The focus on public protection, indeterminate sentences, and increased prison building have remained key elements of penal policy. But in relation to some groups of offenders, principally female offenders, there have been efforts to reduce the prison population and to consider alternatives, as we shall see in Chapter 11. The financial imperative to cut the cost of imprisonment has also focused attention again on effective rehabilitation. Prison reformers and practitioners working within the criminal justice system have argued that short prison sentences are ineffective in reforming offenders and reducing crime, and have been used excessively (see Trebilcock 2010, 2011: chapter 12.4.2).

A recent study has also indicated that some prisoners find short prison sentences less onerous than community sentences because they find it difficult to meet the demands made by the latter, including keeping appointments and the length of time involved in completing the sentence (Trebilcock 2011). Prisoners in this study referred to their boredom because of the lack of available activities and particularly the fact that there were insufficient courses available. However, for some revolving door prisoners the period inside prison in some cases gave them a better quality of life than in the community.

9.8 Conclusion

As we have seen, there have been substantial improvements in procedural justice and conditions in prisons in the past decade, so there are no public sector prisons now at the lowest level. Although the numbers in prison have continued to rise, there have been some promising developments and considerable progress. The expansion of human rights jurisprudence has had a significant effect on raising standards in prison and on recognising that prisoners remain citizens while incarcerated. Entrenched human rights provide a counterbalance to both populist punitiveness and the principle of less eligibility.

But the problems discussed in Chapter 1, of reconciling the public to prison improvements, and public punitiveness, have persisted and limited the scope for reductionist policies, and protecting the public has been reflected in the commitment to expanding prison capacity (see Roberts and Hough 2005a). Progressive developments, as we have seen, have coexisted uneasily with the managerialist focus in prisons and the quest for cost effectiveness and value for money and the increasing focus on risk management and on reliance on the private sector (see Murphy and Whitty 2007; Ministry of Justice 2010a). New developments and initiatives have come under threat with the pressure of providing for an ever-expanding prison population. There are also variations between prisons in terms of opportunities for work and training as well as accommodation. Maintaining constructive regimes during a period of expansion and pressures on accommodation and resources may be difficult. But it certainly seems likely that effective use of prisons will remain on the political agenda.

9.8.1 **Discussion questions**

In this chapter we have examined life inside modern prisons. In revising this material you may wish to reflect on the following issues:

1. Why has the prison population expanded in the last 20 years? How significant are changes in sentencing law and policy in this expansion?
2. What effect has this expansion had on prison conditions?
3. Does the treatment of prisoners in the UK comply with the European Convention on Human Rights?
4. What do you consider to be the best means of achieving the aims of imprisonment?

online resource centre

Some guidance on answering these questions is given in the Online Resource Centre.

10

Equality and difference in punishment

SUMMARY

This chapter examines in more detail the issues around the impact of punishment on various groups of offenders, depending on differential circumstances, both structural and personal. In particular we focus on the arguments against taking more account of impact mitigation at the sentencing stage (which we discussed in Chapter 7) and suggest that some disadvantages must be dealt with by social, rather than penal, policy. We then engage in a detailed discussion of gender and race differentials in crime and punishment and analyse the meaning of equality within those contexts.

10.1 Differential treatment

10.1.1 Establishing the limits of personal mitigation

> Personal mitigation casts into sharp focus some fundamental issues about sentencing principles and judicial discretion. Is justice best served by sentencing the offence or the offender? What balance ought to be struck between the two?
>
> (Jacobson and Hough 2007: 1)

As we saw in Chapter 7, it is possible but not easy to justify taking personal mitigation, especially as regards impact of sentence, into account. As Walker notes, 'Mitigation, like aggravation, is usually, though not always, based on retributive reasoning, which concludes either that the offender's culpability was not as great as the nature of the offence suggested or that... he will suffer more than most offenders from the normal penalty' (Walker 1999: 95). However, this leaves the crucial question as to when and how far mitigation should be applied. In Chapter 7 we examined the approach of the courts to illness, old age, employment, vulnerability in prison, and separation from children as factors which might increase the 'pains' of punishment and so justify a reduction in sentence. We then used fines and the law and practice in relation to mentally disordered offenders as examples of quite different ways of taking sentencing impact into account. In this chapter we widen the discussion and focus on issues stemming from socio-economic factors, race, and gender. Our aim is to analyse the appropriate division between social and penal policy and to examine the argument that equality of treatment in relation to gender and race may require differential treatment, particularly in the context of custodial punishment. In doing so, we will introduce arguments against taking punishment impact into account in sentencing.

10.1.2 **Impact of punishment on the offender's family**

Whatever the sex of the prisoners, imprisonment has a disruptive impact on the family. There are about 160,000 children who have a parent in custody each year, but the effect on children is most acute when it is their mother, rather than their father, who is imprisoned, and over 17,240 children were thought to be living apart from their mothers because of imprisonment in 2010 (Prison Reform Trust 2011a: 28). Whilst the children of fathers in prison will usually be looked after by the other parent, this is much less likely for the children of mothers in prison. The Corston Report found that only 9 per cent of children whose mothers were in prison were cared by their fathers (Corston 2007). The remainder may be looked after by friends or family but in most cases this involves leaving home and may mean being taken into local authority care. This is significant, because a predictor of future offending is previous experience of being in care. Once in prison, many prisoners lose contact with their families, because of imprisonment itself, or because they are held a long way from home. For women prisoners, the average distance from home is 55 miles and for many women the distance may be over 100 miles (Prison Reform Trust 2011a: 27).

The issue of prisoners' children has come to both public and academic attention in recent years (see Brooks-Gordon and Bainham 2004; Codd 2004; Salmon 2004: 18–20; Codd 2008; Scott and Codd 2010; Christian and Kennedy 2011; for a review of wider legal issues, see also Munro 2002) and the sentencing courts do sometimes take into account the impact on 'innocent others', particularly children.[1] However, whilst retributivist reasoning justifies the punishment only of the offender, not significant others in the offender's life, this rationale causes problems as inevitably there will be some third-party collateral costs for prisoners with families.

But giving more weight to family impact would be problematic as it would infringe the principle of equal punishment if offenders with and without families were treated differently. It might also mean that sentencers would need to judge the parenting skills of an offender to decide whether dependent children would be harmed or benefited by his or her absence, thereby introducing extrinsic factors into the sentencing process. An alternative approach might therefore be to focus on reducing the impact on third parties by giving more support to maintaining family contact during the period of imprisonment.

We noted in Chapter 7 (section 7.2.5) that the message in *Mills* (2002) was that, where possible, the court should take into account the fact that the offender is a primary carer for a child. Generally, however, the appellate court has taken a quite stringent approach which is exemplified by a series of cases involving women who took Class A drugs into prison for the person they were visiting (see Piper 2007: 147–8). Jeanne Batte, Sarah Witten, and Carmen Mackenzie[2] all had their sentences reduced but their family circumstances were horrendous. Batte, who was 60 and severely depressed, cared for a disabled brother of 69, had suffered the death of one child and cared for two others who were severely ill. Witten had three children aged six, five, and three. Mackenzie had two dependants—one child and a husband with a life-threatening illness. However, relatively minor reductions were given so that the detriment to the children was only marginally reduced; the courts

[1] There is another issue about impact which we cannot deal with here and that is whether prisoners and their partners should have access to artificial insemination (AI) facilities: see Jackson (2007). The European Court of Human Rights held in *Dickson v UK* (2007) that the refusal of a prisoner's request for AI facilities had breached Article 8.

[2] *Batte* (1999); *Witten* (2002); and *McKenzie* (2004).

made clear these were exceptional cases, and in other cases, for example, that of Angela Babington,[3] no reduction was given.

The introduction of family-impact statements to court in several areas in 2006 (see Chapter 6) suggested that impact is now taken more seriously in relation to the families of victims (see Department for Constitutional Affairs 2006; Sweeting *et al.* 2008) although these have not yet been rolled out across England and Wales (see Roberts and Manikis 2011: 7).[4] Further, the focus on the victim may increase the level of seriousness of the offending which, as we noted in Chapter 7, means the court is less likely to take personal mitigation into account.

Neither the approach of the courts nor the rationale for taking into account impact on innocent others is satisfactory. Where sentencing reductions are not adequately justified by reference to penal theory and are, instead, applied in an unprincipled and potentially discriminatory fashion, they cannot significantly address the problem of children facing trauma and disruption. It might, however, be appropriate as an explicit public policy for the courts to take into account factors which do not directly concern impact on the offender. In other words, 'mercy' could also be routinely and consistently exercised as a policy decision imposed on the courts via legislation or guidance. Whether this would be politically acceptable is another matter.

10.1.3 **Arguments against impact mitigation**

Impact mitigation raises problems for both retributivism and utilitarianism. For the former, the harm caused to the victim is not lessened by the social origins or personal problems of the offender, even though we might feel compassion or sympathy for their circumstances. Reductions in such cases would seem to strike at the principles of proportionality, equality of treatment of offenders, and the presumption of human agency at the heart of retributivist theory (see Easton 2008c). If the punishment varied according to the wider social circumstances and personal problems of the offender this would bring arbitrariness back into the punishment process. While retributivists recognise the existence and effects of social inequality, the answer to the problem of inequality is deemed to lie in social welfare rather than variations in sentencing. For Hegel (1832) the answer to problems of poverty and inequality was to use social welfare to mitigate the effects of the market, rather than to retreat from the key principles of retributivist punishment.

For modern retributivists such as von Hirsch (1993), the best way to deal with this issue is through social policy combined with a limit on overall sentencing levels for all through the setting of appropriate anchoring points. Von Hirsch and Ashworth (2005) consider the use of compassionate mitigation in Sweden and whether it could be extended to social deprivation but conclude that it would raise both practical and political problems. As we have seen, a major barrier to changes in penal policy is public opinion. The only circumstances in which culpability would be reduced would be extreme necessity. The injustice of punishing someone who steals in extreme circumstances, such as the fictional Jean Valjean,[5] would be dealt with under the criminal law of necessity.

The problem, however, is that, although poverty does exist in the UK, the levels of deprivation in the modern UK sentencing context are usually far removed from the levels of poverty and deprivation of the nineteenth century France described by Victor Hugo, so

[3] *Babington* (2005). The court distinguished *Witten* because Babington's children were older, had all been in care, and only one of her children was living with her at the time of sentence.

[4] See the Online Resource Centre for updates.

online resource centre

[5] A character in *Les Misérables*, a novel by Victor Hugo.

that the issue of necessity is less significant than relative deprivation (see Dorling *et al.* 2007). For those whose lives are adversely affected by their social circumstances the solution lies in social rather than penal policy.

For utilitarians, there would be concerns over reducing the deterrent value of penalties if sentences were reduced on the ground of deprivation. Bentham (1789) was opposed to introducing feelings into punishment, so concessions on grounds of sympathy and compassion for the accused would be difficult to justify on his theory. For Bentham, the principle of utility took precedence over principles of sympathy and antipathy which he sees as adverse to utility. Introducing feelings into punishment may lead to disproportionate punishment, both excessive and lenient.

10.2 Socio-economic factors

10.2.1 Justifications

As we saw in Chapter 3, one of the criticisms of retributivism from radical and Marxist viewpoints is that the theory allows little scope for a focus on the social disadvantage of offenders when imposing punishments, or for treating disadvantage as a mitigating factor. The rejoinder from retributivists would be that if social disadvantages are 'factored in' to sentencing decisions, these are most likely to work against offenders. If the criteria for assessment of possible completion of community punishment, or of risks of reoffending, include factors such as homelessness and unemployment, for example, the poor and unemployed will be seen as higher risks. Both these points of view need further discussion.

As noted in Chapter 7 (section 7.1.2), Bentham reviews numerous 'sensibilities' but he discusses his 32 points in the context of factors affecting the experience of pain and pleasure generally, and not specifically in relation to punishment, so it may be that some—for example climate—might not be relevant to punishment (Bentham 1789: 52). Further, even Bentham admitted that it would be impracticable to put fully into operation the aim of producing the same amount of 'pain' in a sentence for offences of equal culpability. To do so would require detailed assessments of the likelihood of greater physical, emotional, mental, economic, and social hardship and the very fluidity of the principle has been seen as a compelling reason not to attempt its general application. However, it has also been argued that, even if it is impracticable to take the principle of equal impact to its very detailed logical conclusions, it should still be influential in more *extreme* cases of possible social and economic inequality.

The utilitarian and retributivist justifications for doing so are very different. The statement by H. L. A. Hart that for 'those below a minimum level of economic prosperity... [perhaps] we should incorporate as a further excusing condition the pressure of gross forms of economic necessity' (1968: 51) is founded on a notion that the offender is fully culpable but that non-legal factors could 'excuse' or mitigate responsibility. For the retributivist, then, it may in some cases be unfair to apportion a sentence commensurate to harm and culpability without taking account of the fact that similar offenders may not have equal responsibility because of 'life' factors, but this would apply only in extreme cases of economic necessity, or because of extreme immaturity in the case of juveniles.

For the utilitarian, the issue, as noted in relation to personal mitigation in Chapter 7, is whether the sentence will be effective, and so information about the offender and his or her circumstances is needed in order to choose the sentence most likely to deter or rehabilitate.

Hudson (1998), for example, defends reduced penalties for socially deprived offenders. She recognises the value of the proportionality principle but argues that social circumstances can be considered in assessing desert. For Hudson, social and penal policy cannot be sharply distinguished and punishment has the potential to achieve justice. Individual social and economic circumstances may reduce culpability if the effect is to limit choices, and where the individual is so 'constrained by poverty or other disadvantage or situation that the "reasonable person" would have been unable to refrain from crime in similar circumstances' (ibid: 207–8). An individual's social circumstances are worthy of consideration for the purposes of a pre-sentence report, so there would be no reason to exclude them when assessing culpability.

'Selective leniency' runs the risk, as Hudson acknowledges, that the outcome will depend on how favourably or unfavourably the defendant presents himself as a specially deserving case. 'Categorical leniency' might be preferable: particular crimes which are statistically correlated with unemployment and poverty could be downgraded in terms of seriousness. However, this would not take account of differences in individual freedom of choice which should remain an important factor (ibid: 207).

The issue is again that of 'justice in an unjust society' which runs through several discussions in this book. For example, Duff, having outlined an ideal model of 'constructive punishment' in the community, acknowledges that 'the preconditions of just punishment are not met within our political societies, and are not likely to be met within the near future' (2003: 192). The issue is not the 'substantive wrongfulness' of the offender's conduct—which is accepted—but whether, given the social and economic differentials to which we have alluded, we have the 'moral standing to call them to answer... for that conduct: if we have collectively failed to treat them as our fellow citizens' (ibid).

Some of these issues are approached in an original way by Renaud (2007), a Canadian judge, who explores the principles through a fictional sentencing conference involving the major characters of *Les Misérables*—Valjean, Fantine, Javert, and the Bishop. The problems of their lives are discussed in the context of modern principles of sentencing, policing, and punishment and some of the difficulties raised in accommodating these issues within those theories are explored.

There are further critiques of sentencing theory on this issue which are external to classical or 'conventional' punishment theory (see von Hirsch and Ashworth 1998: 361–8). Norrie, for example, argues that Kant and Hegel (see Chapter 2) were (just) able to hold together retributivist theory in the light of emerging issues of social injustice but, by the nineteenth century, 'the effects of poverty and pauperism, of idleness and drunkenness, of exploitation and vice upon the criminality of the body politic could not be ignored or represented as a matter of pure individual choice' (1998: 371). He also argues that 'the radical disjuncture between the ideal and the actual is no passing feature'; rather it is 'a constant and fixed quality which necessarily undermines a principled justification of punishment in an unprincipled society' (ibid: 379). For Norrie, therefore, punishment cannot be based on individual desert, and mitigation cannot adequately encompass social and political differentials.

In section 10.4 we focus on the experience of ethnic groups in relation to compensating for disadvantage because research suggests that ethnic minorities make up a disproportionate number of prisoners, and this in part reflects problems with housing and employment.

This again raises the question of whether these factors should have been incorporated at the mitigation stage of sentencing. However, if a black unemployed offender, for example, were compensated for disadvantage by a reduction in sentence, this might appear unfair to those black offenders who are in work, as it seems to conflict with the principle of treating like cases alike. The just response might, instead, take the form of focusing on rehabilitation to deal with drug problems, or on using educational programmes to promote social inclusion.

Strict proportionality would demand punishing only those actions which are genuinely chosen by the actor, so proponents of impact mitigation would argue that taking account of adversity would be compatible with it. The approach might consider how the effects of factors such as unemployment and poor housing may be prevented from affecting outcomes, rather than how to reduce sentences for disadvantaged offenders (von Hirsch and Roberts 1997). Specifically in relation to racial or class issues, how can policies and biases be prevented from exacerbating the situation?

10.2.2 **Social exclusion as a criterion**

Using neutral criteria like social exclusion might be fairer because it would cover a wider range of offenders. Imprisonment can be seen as both a form of social exclusion and a reflection of it, if crime can be linked to social exclusion, but imprisonment may also exacerbate and perpetuate social exclusion. Although there are debates on the nature, and causes and effects, of social exclusion, the boundary between exclusion and inclusion is not fixed but fluid, and may be crossed several times. Moreover, inclusion may entail the recognition of mutual diversity (Young 1999, 2002). For example, research on the effectiveness of offending behaviour programmes should consider how useful these are to particular groups and whether men or women, or different ethnic groups, would benefit from particular programmes, or how they might be designed within and outside custody to accommodate the needs of these groups. For example, if policies are subjected to equality impact assessments, we can then consider whether they do have a disparate impact on particular groups and consider ways of avoiding this. Impact assessments have been undertaken in the Prison and the Probation Services in relation to race and gender, but if we are focusing on social exclusion, we also need to consider class.

The traditional social work ethos of the Probation Service, for example, has tended to individualise problems, focusing on the problems of clients as reflecting individual pathologies, rather than examining structural problems and the socio-economic context which may affect offending patterns, or the effects of racism (see Chapter 12, section 12.3). If the liberal ethos of social work is to treat people equally, then this might be construed as meaning no special treatment for black offenders. But if life experiences are different, punishment should take special account of this, as well as recognising the different contexts of male and female offending.

It is also important to keep in mind that the most striking feature of the prison population is its class membership. A focus on social exclusion may obscure the importance of class. Similarly the focus on cognitive behaviouralism, on individual responsibility for managing individual risks, diverts attention from the significance of class and structural causes of crime and the social reaction to crime. The term social exclusion has superseded the use of the term 'underclass' which is now seen as pejorative (see Byrne 2005).

However, while social exclusion is primarily associated with class, it may also be experienced by some ethnic groups in inner-city areas and by women, in so far as women as a group are poverty-prone, and poverty in wealthy societies is now defined in terms of social exclusion (see Pantazis *et al.* 2006). Within the prison population we also find ethnic-minority prisoners are over-represented relative to their proportions in the general population, which raises questions regarding the role of racism within the criminal justice system (see section 10.4). These issues have been explored both here and in the United States, as we saw in Chapter 5, where the war on drugs has had a disparate impact on young black male Americans in poor urban areas (see Wacquant 2007, 2008b, 2009; Curry and Corral-Camacho 2008).

In most discussions of social deprivation the focus is on poverty and class, but there are other areas of inequality we should consider which have implications for sentencing policy and treatment within prison (see Chapter 11), namely gender inequality and race inequality. We will therefore focus further on the experiences of women and ethnic minorities to explore some of these problems and conclude with a discussion of the problem of disability which may also contribute to social exclusion (see O'Grady *et al.* 2004).

10.3 Gender

10.3.1 Gender and justice

At first glance the most striking feature of the statistics for both crime and imprisonment is that women are under-represented. This has been seen by some as suggesting that women are treated more leniently than men. But it is not clear-cut. Within the prison population we find an over-representation of working-class women and a disproportionate number of ethnic-minority women, particularly foreign nationals.[6] So this suggests that a number of complex forces are operating which shape the structure of the prison population.

Research over the last 10 years does not show women *generally* are treated more harshly. The Wedderburn Report found little evidence to show that women were treated more severely than men. In fact, a lower proportion of women than men were sentenced to immediate custody for indictable offences and the average sentence length was shorter (Prison Reform Trust 2000). These patterns have persisted over the last decade. Figures published under s 95 of the Criminal Justice Act (CJA) 1991, show that a higher proportion of women defendants than men receive fines, and a lower proportion of women defendants than men receive community sentences, suspended sentences, and immediate custody. The average length of community sentences is also shorter for women than men. Women are also more likely to complete community sentences successfully (Ministry of Justice 2011c: 54).

Furthermore, for those women given an immediate custodial sentence for indictable offences, the average sentence length is 11 months compared to 17 months for men. Over 60 per cent of women in prison are serving short sentences. However, a higher proportion of women serving sentences for indictable offences have no previous convictions. So they are more likely to go to prison with fewer previous convictions than men. Data from the British Crime Survey also shows that women have higher rates of victimisation from personal crime including violence from intimates and theft from their person (Chaplin *et al.* 2011).

Women may be disadvantaged at the disposal stage because the options may be limited by restricted availability as well as by judgements about women's behaviour. Fewer hostels are available for women compared to men. Non-custodial alternatives may be seen as unsuitable for women with children, and sentencers may be reluctant to place women with dependent children on community punishment programmes if they think that it will be difficult for them to complete the programme. Some of the residential drug

[6] Information on both groups is available from Ministry of Justice statistics, *Offender Management Caseload Statistics* (Ministry of Justice 2011o) and from the publications under s 95 of the CJA 1991, namely *Women and the Criminal Justice System* and *Race and the Criminal Justice System* (Ministry of Justice 2010c and Ministry of Justice 2011c).

treatment programmes, for example, will not accept women with dependent children (Howard League for Penal Reform 2000). Moreover women who do begin community sentences, and who breach the conditions of their orders, may end up in custody and the Corston Report found that a significant number of women in prison were there because of breaches.

Whilst some women will end up with a less severe sentence than men, others will end up with a harsher sentence than men, and individual women, particularly those who do not conform to gender roles, may be treated more harshly. For example, it has been argued that women perceived as bad mothers, or who already have children in care, are more likely to be given a custodial sentence, as are younger women who are perceived to be out of control (see Worrall 1990).

The question whether sentencers are more or less indulgent to women offenders was extensively researched throughout the 1980s and 1990s. Hedderman and Gelsthorpe (1997) found that magistrates saw women as troubled rather than troublesome, more in need of help than punishment, and saw probation as appropriate for a large proportion of female offenders. They were also reluctant to fine women if it would affect children adversely.

Similar findings of differential sentencing outcomes for women were also found in Australia in a study of the Victorian courts published in 2010 (Gelb 2010). It found that women's offending tended to be less serious than men's and women were less likely to be involved in violent offences. Women were less likely to be sentenced to imprisonment and when they did, they received shorter sentences. Women prisoners had less serious criminal histories than men and fewer previous convictions, and less serious prior convictions.

A major review of the experiences of women in the UK criminal justice system as victims, offenders, and workers, was conducted by the Fawcett Commission on Women and Criminal Justice and published in 2009 (Fawcett 2009). By drawing parallels across the system, the review shows that women continue to be marginalised in a criminal justice system designed by men for men. The final report of the Commission reveals a persistent gap between strong policy development and consistent implementation. Practices and attitudes continue to discriminate against women, while women as workers are under-represented at the higher echelons of the justice system. Consequently, it is argued, the system fails to address the causes of women's offending with too many women continuing to be imprisoned on short sentences for non-violent crime. It also fails to provide female victims of violence with support, safety, or justice and also makes it difficult for women as professionals to reach higher positions in the police, prison service, legal profession and the judiciary. The Report of the All Party Parliamentary Group on Women in the Penal System (APPGW) in 2011 found that there was a higher percentage of women than men in prison for non-violent offences and an increase in the number of women in prison since 2010, including an increase in the number of women prisoners remanded in custody (APPGW 2011).

10.3.2 **Differential treatment**

There is evidence of differential treatment and differential impact at a number of levels of the criminal justice system in relation to women and ethnic minorities as offenders and as victims. It occurs at all stages of the criminal justice and penal processes: in policing; during the pre-trial process; at trial in the perceptions of juries and court officials; in the treatment of certain suspects and victims (for example, rape complainants); and post-sentence (see Hood 1992; Bowling and Phillips 2002; Carlen 2002;

Silvestri and Crowther-Dowey 2008; Singh Bhui 2009; May *et al.* 2010). A key principle of punishment is to treat like cases alike. So when we talk of discrimination, or bias, we are talking about differential treatment based not on the specific circumstances of the crime, but on arbitrary characteristics of the defendant, such as the fact that the individual is female, black, or working class. This bias can operate in an overt, direct way or unconsciously, and may operate indirectly or may be institutionalised within the system, in its procedures and practices and within formal rules of law, for example, in the criminal law relating to provocation, which has proved difficult to apply to women who kill abusive partners.

Section 95 of the CJA 1991 requires the Home Secretary to publish information considered expedient to enable those involved in the administration of criminal justice to avoid discriminating against any person on the ground of race, sex, or any other improper ground. On the basis of this information and a number of empirical studies, we can construct a picture of the population to establish whether all offenders are treated equally or whether some groups are treated differently, although evidence of difference may not itself indicate unjust or unfair treatment. Differential treatment may arise from indirect discrimination if an apparently neutral rule impacts unfairly on a particular group. There is a statutory duty on public authorities under the Equality Act 2010 to promote equality and this includes testing policies for their equality impact.

Here we focus specifically on issues of equality versus difference in relation to gender. Although the prison population is overwhelmingly male, the number and proportion of women prisoners is increasing and the treatment of women prisoners is therefore becoming more important (see section 11.2.2). More attention is also being given to developing programmes appropriate to women offenders in the community (see Worrall and Gelsthorpe 2009). We will therefore consider whether women prisoners should be treated equally, or whether and how difference should be acknowledged within the prison system. The particular problems women prisoners face during imprisonment will be considered in Chapter 11.

10.3.3 **Equality versus difference**

Gender-specific policies raise the question of reconciling differential treatment with principles of equality, as well as the risk of ascribing inherent characteristics to women, that is, the problem of essentialism. The Committee on Women's Imprisonment, chaired by Dorothy Wedderburn, which visited 14 prisons, emphasised that applying principles of punishment in an equitable and non-discriminatory way does not entail equal treatment, but rather treatment as an equal (Prison Reform Trust 2000). It should take account of the fact that women are less dangerous than men, that the social costs of women's imprisonment are higher than men's and that different treatment for men and women within the penal system is justifiable: 'Equal treatment... does not mean identical treatment, whether for women or for members of cultural or ethnic minorities' (Prison Reform Trust 2000: para 7.2). A similar approach was taken by the Corston Report (2007) and the need for gender-specific policies has been acknowledged by both Labour and Coalition Governments (see Chapter 11, section 11.5.3; see also Hedderman 2010).

If we say that women should not be incarcerated because they are not dangerous, then one could argue that this should apply to non-dangerous men. Critics might claim that a regime which is accommodating to women, which gives women differential treatment, such as extra home leave to deal with their families, would be unfair to men who may also wish to enjoy such advantages, and would be met by similar demands from men. But this argument would not defeat a claim for differential treatment as it could feasibly be extended to men and is unlikely to open the floodgates as relatively few men are primary carers. Humanising the women's prison regime may also benefit male prisoners as good practice there may provide a model for men's prisons.

However, when reforms have been introduced in other jurisdictions, they have often been challenged by men arguing denial of their right to equality. In Canada, a male prisoner argued that his rights under the equality clause (Article 15) of the Charter had been breached, because he could be searched by female as well as male officers, but women could be searched only by women officers. His claim was rejected by the Supreme Court who argued that, within wider historical, biological, and sociological contexts, the use of male officers in women's searches is potentially more threatening, so treating men and women differently in this context was not discriminatory.[7]

This issue of unfairness also arose in the South African Constitutional Court in *Hugo v President of the RSA* (1997) where, again, the Court rejected a claim of unfairness by a male prisoner. A female prisoner who had young children was released under an amnesty given by President Mandela but the amnesty was not extended to male prisoners. The majority of the court held that it was not unfair discrimination because young mothers were a vulnerable group and, even if it were seen as unfair, it could be justified because of the needs of young children.

The principle of equality is often cited as the reason for not improving the women's regime, as it would be unfair to treat men and women unequally. This rationalisation is also advantageous to the suppliers of punishment as many of the measures, such as more home leave, have cost implications.

A more controversial issue is whether a case can be made for differential sentencing of women, and particularly for using women's social and economic deprivation as grounds for mitigation of sentence (see Hudson 1998 and section 10.2). Support for the view that a woman's role as the primary carer is a factor which should be taken into account in sentencing, along with factors such as mental illness, abuse, economic position, and the effect of a custodial sentence on others in the household, is also given by the Wedderburn Report (Prison Reform Trust 2000). If women suffer disproportionately greater poverty, or abuse, or if they develop drug or alcohol addictions as a result of this abuse and exclusion, should this be reflected in the sentencing process? Such a policy is unlikely to be accepted or to be popular for the reasons we have already discussed, but Pre-Sentence Reports and Sentence Planning could take account of these problems and consider how to deal with them, for example, by setting up special programmes to deal with the effects of violence, as used in Canadian women's prisons.

Moreover, the criminal justice system still accepts that a special programme is needed to deal with young offenders (see Chapter 8) so a special programme for women's justice, which recognises that there are also special factors leading to women's crime, is feasible. However, this might militate against treating women as independent agents, rather than perpetuating ideas about the dependence and vulnerability of woman. Perhaps if such arguments were extended to male prisoners in similar circumstances, such as male carers, they would be more acceptable. So a man with dependent children should also be given consideration for additional home leave. Fair treatment would also demand a consideration of the effects of reducing a prisoner's status on the Incentives and Earned Privileges Scheme, for example, as this affects entitlement to extra visits (see Chapter 9, section 9.4.4).

[7] *Weatherall v Canada* (1993).

10.3.4 The merits and problems of a difference-based approach: empowerment in the context of coercion

Attempts were made in Canada in the 1990s to move away from a liberal feminist position of equality of provision for female offenders, which in practice usually used male standards, towards recognition of women's differences from men and the empowerment of women. A Task Force on Federally-Sentenced Women, which included feminist participants and which reported in 1990, generated the creation of five new regional facilities for women, including a Healing Lodge, replacing the former single federal penitentiary, the Prison for Women. The new regime included extended home visits, and culturally sensitive and feminist therapeutic programmes to deal with domestic violence and drugs. The effect of these changes was an overall improvement in the quality of life for women prisoners.

However, the feminist approach based on difference and applied in Canada, has been criticised on a number of grounds. The Canadian experience illustrates some of the problems with a 'difference-based' approach and highlights the problem facing feminist prison reformers, namely the conflict between feminist principles of empowerment and responsibility, on the one hand, and the reality of living in a coercive community like a prison, on the other hand, so that reforms will be neutralised. Hannah-Moffat (2002) argues that the ideas embodied in the Task Force programme in Canada have been eroded through lack of resources, and denial of basic rights. Despite the initial enthusiasm, the reforms were diluted with a move toward increased security and privatisation. Within a coercive context, the development of autonomy will inevitably be limited.

Similarly, Carlen (2002) argues that focusing on women's imprisonment, while of value and interest, can divert us from the impact of the power of the prison to punish, its retributivist function, which, she argues, has been overlooked by radical theories, including left criminology, and postmodern and feminist theories.

There is also a tendency in these reforms to see women's imprisonment as a consequence of their victimisation, treating women as passive victims, even if we call them survivors. Focusing on therapeutic programmes for individual prisoners essentially characterises the individual as an object of reform and sees the problem as the individual's maladjustment to society, rather than looking at the wider social structure.

Focusing on reform *per se* also means that less attention will be given to alternatives to prison, particularly for those serving shorter sentences, and the use of imprisonment will go unchallenged. Bringing feminism into a system of correction can have the unintended effect of legitimising incarceration and, for this reason, some feminist groups in Canada have now distanced themselves from these projects (see Hannah-Moffat 2002). But this raises difficult issues as feminist-inspired programmes have led to better conditions and improved women's lives, and feminist therapeutic programmes have assisted women on their release. There are examples of gender-sensitive regimes in the United States which have been successful in reducing reoffending and, to some extent, in empowering women (see de Cou 2002; Poteat 2002). The differences of approach and tensions in developing gendered community punishment are also considered in Haney's (2010) ethnographic study of two community-based correctional facilities in the United States. Similarly in the UK, while progressive measures are still part of a system of state incarceration and while their radical impact may be neutralised in a regressive political context, the alternative of doing nothing may be more damaging to those receiving punishment. Moreover the opportunity to participate within a therapeutic community may be empowering for women even if circumscribed by the prison context (see Parker 2006). In the light of these problems, we will consider in Chapter 11 the experience of women prisoners in England and Wales and ways in which women's imprisonment might be reformed and reduced.

10.4 A focus on race

10.4.1 Ethnic minorities and the criminal justice system

In the first part of this book, we considered the quest for justice in the context of theories of punishment and the notions of fairness in relation to proportionality, but fairness is also important in relation to the distribution of punishment. If there are racially disproportionate outcomes, then this may indicate *prima facie* unjust treatment or discrimination and this needs to be investigated and strategies developed to deal with this.

Statistical data on the criminal justice system suggests there are differentials in the experience of ethnic minorities at all stages of the criminal justice process, in rates of stop and search, arrest, remands in custody before trial, and, importantly for our purposes, in rates of imprisonment.[8] The *British Crime Survey* for 2010–11 shows that the risk of being a victim of personal crime is higher for all black and minority ethnic (BME) groups than for the white group and the highest risk was for adults from a mixed background (Chaplin *et al.* 2011).

Statistics would suggest that, in the criminal process, from a police stop to prosecution and bail decisions, members of ethnic minorities are likely to be over-represented as suspects and defendants.

Although there are wide regional variations, figures for 2009–10 suggest that, relative to their numbers in the general population, black people are 7 times more likely to be stopped and searched than white people and 3.3 times more likely to be arrested (Ministry of Justice 2011c: 13–14). Arrest rates vary between different areas and for different offences. Some differences may be due to objective factors, such as differences in offending patterns and social and economic factors which increase the risk of offending—for example, the relative youthfulness of ethnic minority populations and their concentration in inner-city

Table 10.1 Proportion of individuals at different stages of the CJS process by ethnic group compared to general population, England and Wales

	White	Black	Asian	Mixed	Chinese or Other	Unknown	Total
Population aged 10 or over 2009	88.6%	2.7%	5.6%	1.4%	1.6%	-	48,417,349
Stop and Searches (s1) 2009/10	67.2%	14.6%	9.6%	3.0%	1.2%	4.4%	1,141,839
Arrests 2009/10	79.6%	8.0%	5.6%	2.9%	1.5%	2.4%	1,386,030
Cautions 2010[(1)]	83.1%	7.1%	5.2%	-	1.8%	2.8%	230,109
Court order supervisions 2010	81.8%	6.0%	4.9%	2.8%	1.3%	3.2%	161,687
Prison population (including foreign nationals) 2010	72.0%	13.7%	7.1%	3.5%	1.4%	2.2%	85,002

Note: 1. Data based on ethnic appearance and therefore do not include the Mixed category.
Source: Ministry of Justice (2011c: 11).

[8] Statistics are published annually on *Race and the Criminal Justice System* under s 95 of the CJA 1991; see Ministry of Justice (2011c).

areas. But there are also some indications that the police may be more willing to proceed against young black suspects on weaker evidence. For example, such suspects are more likely to have cases against them terminated by the Crown Prosecution Service (Barclay and Mhlanga 2000).

Some studies show that members of ethnic-minority groups express less confidence that they will be treated fairly as defendants by the criminal justice system (Mirrlees-Black 2001). This sense of unfairness is exacerbated by the fact that within various parts of the criminal justice system ethnic minorities are over-represented as clients and under-represented as employees, relative to their numbers in the wider population. This disparity has implications for the legitimacy of the system as well as its efficiency and quality and recruitment of black and minority ethnic staff has been a key issue for the Police Force, Probation Service, and Prison Service (see Chapter 11).

It is in the composition of the prison population in England and Wales that the disproportionate presence of ethnic minorities is most striking. In 2011 black and minority ethnic prisoners constituted 26 per cent of the prison population. Black prisoners are also more likely to be serving longer sentences than white or Asian prisoners. We also find differentials in average custodial sentence length, so the figures for 2010 show that the highest average custodial sentence lengths for those given determinate sentences for indictable offences were as follows: black 20.8 months, Asian 19.9 months, other 19.7 months, and white 14.9 months (Ministry of Justice 2011c: 58).

Some of the disparity in sentence length could be accounted for by differences in offences and, among women, a high number of foreign nationals are imprisoned for drug offences, but the differences are not so marked within the indigenous population. In trying to explain this differential, particularly the issue of whether social and economic disadvantage is a significant influence, we need to consider the earlier stages of the criminal justice process. The over-representation of ethnic minorities in prison can reflect the accumulation of past decisions which draw black suspects into the criminal justice process. We need to consider the reporting of crimes, the response of the police, and the making of bail decisions by the courts. The provision in s 95 of the CJA 1991 which mandated the monitoring and publication of information about race has provided more information and this has been strengthened by the equality duty imposed by the Equality Act 2010. All agencies in the criminal justice system have a duty to promote race equality under the 2010 Act (formerly under the Race Relations (Amendment) Act 2000), and also to monitor progress towards that goal.

Official crime statistics are generally seen as giving an incomplete indication of true levels of crime, but using self-report and victim studies we can construct a picture of the experiences of ethnic groups within the criminal justice system. However, official statistics can give an indication of patterns of decision making which may be significant in explaining differentials. A variety of other sources, including the British Crime Survey, police and Ministry of Justice statistics, and research studies, can give us a picture of the ethnic minority composition and treatment of the population of suspects, offenders and victims. We also need to bear in mind that the ethnic-minority population is not homogeneous. There are different rates of incarceration for distinct subcultures, including those which are age-based, and for white ethnic minority groups. Moreover foreign-national prisoners come from a wide range of ethnic groups (see Chapter 11, section 11.7.6).

In Chapter 11 we will consider the experience of imprisonment and the way criminal justice agencies have sought to deal with racism. Reference to ethnicity/ethnicities in the following discussion is used to mean the shared history, cultural heritage, and common experiences of distinct groups. Our sense of who we are will be shaped by this awareness of difference and diversity.

10.4.2 **Racism as ideology and practice**

Racism has been seen as an ideology and set of exclusionary practices based on assumptions about racial hierarchies. Racism attributes fixed characteristics to social groups which are then used to justify denial of access to resources. Racism may be conscious, or subconscious, operate at individual, sub-cultural, or institutional levels, and lead to direct and indirect discrimination.

Racism may operate at the level of individual bias and prejudice or institutionally, being built into the culture of an organisation and embedded in its policies and practices (Macpherson 1999). The Macpherson Report highlighted the problem of institutional racism within the criminal justice system and its failure to protect ethnic minorities. By institutional racism Macpherson meant:

> the collective failure of an organization to provide an appropriate and professional service to people because of their colour, culture, or ethnic origin. It can be seen or detected in processes, attitudes and behaviour which amount to discrimination through unwitting prejudice, ignorance, thoughtlessness and racist stereotyping which disadvantage minority ethnic people.
>
> (Macpherson 1999: para 0.34)

Since that Report the Government has taken more interest in institutional racism and there has been some progress. Racial harassment is now a criminal offence and procedures dealing with racist incidents have improved. The problems of racism within the Prison Service have also been addressed by the Prison Inspectorate (HM Inspectorate of Prisons 2005), the Mubarek Report (Keith 2006; see also Chapter 11, section 11.7.5), and the Race Review (NOMS 2008). Good practice in dealing with racism is now being applied to other areas of discrimination.

10.4.3 **Research difficulties**

There are methodological problems in proving the influence of racism, in controlling for other variables, and isolating the socio-economic factors which might be the mechanisms for the production of differentials. Although there is a widely held perception in ethnic-minority communities of unfair treatment as suspects and offenders, the evidence of differential treatment is ambiguous. Higher proportions of Asian than black and white prisoners were given Home Detention Curfews in 2010–11 (Ministry of Justice 2011g: 39). The proportions given a community sentence for indictable offences in 2010 were similar for black and minority ethnic groups and white groups: 28 per cent for Asian people, 29 per cent for black, and 32 per cent for white (Ministry of Justice 2011c: 58).

However, some of the research studies have been fairly small-scale, so the numbers involved may be too small to draw firm conclusions. Although studies of particular courts during a limited time span have been conducted, there has been no systematic monitoring of sentencing outcomes for different ethnic groups so there is a lack of clear data on this issue. It is therefore difficult to draw general conclusions or to infer a racist bias on the part of sentencers, who are constrained by a number of factors in the decisions they can make (see Chapter 2 on discretion). It may be difficult to extricate the impact of specific factors (see Marsh *et al.* 2006; Spalek 2008).

Offence profiles may account to some extent for these differentials but there is also some evidence that ethnic-minority defendants value jury trial because they believe it is less biased than a summary trial and any bias on the part of individual jury members will be offset by other jurors. However, a decision to elect for jury trial will mean that if convicted they face a more severe sentence and, if they plead 'not guilty' but are then convicted, they will not receive a sentence discount and so face a longer sentence.

Some research studies suggest that black people are more likely to receive a custodial sentence even when we control for previous record, offence, and PSR recommendations. A major study of Birmingham Crown Court found that African-Caribbeans were more likely to receive a custodial sentence for offences in the middle range of seriousness (Hood 1992). Hood found that about 80 per cent of the over-representation of black men in the prison population could be accounted for by their over-representation among those convicted in the Crown Court, by the types of crime and offences with which they are charged and convicted, and by higher numbers presenting for sentencing. However, this meant that 20 per cent of the over-representation was due to differential treatment and other factors, such as not guilty pleas. Hood's study has been criticised because it fails to address the issue of why so many black defendants elect trial by jury and for assuming that factors such as previous convictions are racially neutral (see Bowling and Phillips 2002).

A later study of ethnic-minority defendants in the Crown Court by Shute, Hood, and Seemungal (2005) found that there had been improvements in attitudes towards these defendants so there was no evidence of overt racism. However, there was still a *perception* of unfairness on the part of many ethnic-minority defendants and their lawyers. A major study of the Crown Courts from 2006–8 found little evidence to support the view that juries are unfair and only small differences in verdicts based on the defendant's ethnicity (Thomas 2010). However, it did acknowledge the importance of perceptions of fairness as the proportion of BME defendants in the courts studied was greater than their proportion in the local population or BME jurors in those courts, and in some locations there were all-white juries.

10.4.4 **Racism and social deprivation**

So what can we infer from the evidence available? Factors to consider in understanding the complex relationship between race and crime include the socio-economic characteristics of ethnic-minority communities, namely deprivation and unemployment, which affect black people disproportionately. There are also demographic issues. The majority of ethnic minority communities are located in urban areas where there are higher-than-average levels of poverty, homelessness, crime, and unemployment and this will also contribute to their higher victimisation rates. Because some ethnic-minority populations are younger than the ageing white population, this will also affect the crime rate. There may also be sub-cultural differences within ethnic minorities in terms of how they deal with deprivation and racism. Ethnic groups are not homogeneous, but comprise diversities in culture, sources of identity and demographic structures whose experiences may differ substantially.

Over-representation has not only been attributed to racism at the level of individual decisions and differential treatment, but also to policies and practices which increase the speed with which black defendants move through the criminal justice system and move up the tariff. Racism may be a feature of individuals' beliefs as well as built into the policies of institutions. Some of the differentials may be due to factors such as offending patterns, whilst others reflect social and economic factors which increase the risk of offending.

If the profile of the prison population is strongly linked with social exclusion and social and economic deprivation, and if these problems are suffered by black communities and young black males are excluded from legitimate sources of status, then it may be unsurprising to find disproportionate numbers of black males in prison. Criminal activity may be an illegitimate means of social inclusion in providing the means to participate in a particular lifestyle. Criminality is strongly associated with social exclusion in so far as it links with poor social conditions. The experience of imprisonment may itself be seen as a further form of social exclusion, which reinforces housing and work problems on release.

So the marginalisation of ethnic minority communities needs to be addressed. However, others are sceptical of economic determinist and structural explanations, not least because many members of these groups may experience these problems without resorting to crime. In the current climate of increased punitiveness, these social disadvantages will be seen as less important than individual decisions to commit crimes, and it is unlikely that these disadvantages will be given serious consideration at the sentencing stage, but the implications of race and social factors for mitigation are considered by Walker (2011).

10.5 Disability

We have focused on race and gender but, of course, these are not the only grounds of discrimination. In recent years the Prison Service has become more aware of its obligations not to discriminate against staff or prisoners on the grounds of sexual orientation and has set up a network for lesbian, gay, bisexual, and transgender staff members. But the issue of disability is also important. The prison population may include a wide range of disabilities and illnesses. The ageing of the prison population will also increase the numbers of disabled prisoners (see Chapter 9, section 9.2.1).

Prisons have been prohibited from discriminating in the provision of goods, facilities and services on the basis of disability since the Disability Discrimination Act 1995 was enacted, and now have a duty to promote disability equality under the Equality Act 2010. So prisons, like other institutions, have to consider what reasonable adjustments and accommodation should be made to meet the needs of disabled prisoners as well as disabled staff, whose treatment is included in the equal opportunities regime. So as in other areas of inequality, differential treatment may be necessary to achieve equality.

New prisons have been built to comply with these legal requirements, and refurbishments of older prisons have been undertaken to ensure compliance. Particularly, prisoners must be able to understand the Prison Rules and an interpreter must be provided if necessary. Prisoners' needs should be taken account of in allocating cells and in ensuring access to work, education, and physical education. Appropriate books should be provided in the prison library. Complaints can be made through the Complaints Procedure or to the Ombudsman, or civil proceedings could be initiated.

Prisoners could also use Article 14 if issues are raised within the ambit of other Articles of the European Convention. For example, Article 8 might be breached if disabled prisoners were allowed fewer family visits than other prisoners. Prisons have Disability Liaison Officers and the Prison Service has published guidelines for dealing with disabled prisoners. It has also formulated a Disability Strategy and set up a Disability Support Network for staff.

The Prison Reform Trust study of disabled prisoners found that provision and support was variable and examples of good practice in some prisons were reported (Prison Reform Trust 2004b). As well as problems of access to facilities, because of the failure to incorporate disabled needs into prison design, there are problems of access to services, for example, for prisoners with visual and hearing impairments. But the problems may be even greater for prisoners with learning rather than physical disabilities.

A programme, *No One Knows*, to examine and publicise the experiences of people with learning difficulties and learning disabilities[9] who come into contact with the criminal justice system, was initiated by the Prison Reform Trust, in view of the increasing numbers of disabled prisoners and in response to complaints of unequal access to activities and poor treatment, including examples of prisoners confined to their cells for long periods because of inadequate facilities for their needs (Loucks 2007; Talbot 2008). It is estimated that there are about 5,000 people with learning disabilities within the prison population (see Rack 2005). Until recently this group of prisoners was under-researched but they are now receiving more attention.

The final report in the *No One Knows* series was published in 2008 and includes the results of interviews with prisoners with learning disabilities (Talbot 2008). The respondents reported problems in filling in forms and negotiating prison procedures so that they sometimes missed out on visits and had difficulty in gaining access to prison services and making themselves understood. They were also more likely than the control group to be subject to control and restraint and to be segregated and had problems gaining access to work and to offending behaviour courses. The Report makes a number of recommendations including awareness training and improved provision for these prisoners within prison education.

Moreover, if their needs are not identified as they enter the criminal justice system, this could have serious implications for outcomes during interrogation. It could also mean that they will not benefit from special measures granted by the Youth Justice and Criminal Evidence Act 1999. Prisoners with learning difficulties may also find it difficult to comply with community punishments and if in custody may find it difficult to adapt to the regimented nature of prison life resulting in disruptive behaviour and segregation. The problems of identification and assessment, as Loucks (2007) points out, will be harder at times of overcrowding when prisoners are moved around the prison estate. A review of disabled prisoners was also conducted by the Prison Inspectorate in 2009 which found that prisoners with disabilities were more negative about issues of safety and more likely to report victimisation than non-disabled prisoners (HM Inspectorate of Prisons 2009a). As we shall see in Chapter 11, greater attention is now being given to the provision for disabled prisoners in order to comply with the equality duty in the Equality Act 2010. A new Prison Service Instruction, *Ensuring Equality,* was issued in April 2011.

The problems of identifying, assessing, diverting and treating prisoners with learning disabilities were also highlighted by the Bradley Report (Department of Health (2009a). The Report recommends further research should be undertaken on this issue as well as greater coordination between agencies and continuity of care in leaving prison. The Report also addresses the problems facing prisoners with mental health issues, as we saw in Chapter 7.

10.6 Conclusion

10.6.1 The limits of penal policy?

We have identified a number of important areas where it may be difficult to achieve equality of impact and have considered some of the problems which arise in implementing

[9] Since the implementation of the recent amendments to the Mental Health Act 1983, learning difficulties are no longer part of the definition of mental disorder and so would not normally be a ground for diversion from custody: see Chapter 7, section 7.2.3.

impact mitigation. As we have seen, there are problems in compensating offenders for the personal and social problems they experience. Expecting sentencers and penal policy to solve all the problems stemming from the structural and personal factors which affect the lives and punishment of offenders is unrealistic. It may be better to address the problems we have identified and to achieve social justice through social policies aimed at rectifying inequality, promoting social inclusion, and providing support to individuals and communities. However, in relation to the specific problems experienced by particular groups within prison, improvements in prison conditions and better support for prisoners to maintain contact with their families may be the best way forward. Some of these alternative solutions will be considered in Chapter 11.

10.6.2 **Discussion question**

Amy is a mother with four children under 10 years of age. The children's father, Ben, has been in prison for two years. Amy has several convictions for theft, all preceding the period in which she went to live with Ben and had her children. Amy got into severe financial difficulties two years ago and agreed to deliver packages of drugs, on a regular basis, to distributers. By the time she was caught she had delivered a very large quantity of a Class B drug. She pleaded guilty shortly after her arrest to a charge of possession with intent to supply under the Misuse of Drugs Act 1971, s 5(3) although she insisted that she had been led to believe the drugs were only ketamine (Class C). She received a sentence of 18 months.

Ben's family have always rejected her; her own family consists of an ill and elderly mother and a sister who has two children. No one offers to look after her children and she agrees that they be voluntarily accommodated by the local authority. A recent review by the local authority noted the children's distress in their new homes (they cannot all be accommodated in the same foster family). Amy appeals her sentence.

1. How might it be possible—if at all—for the Court of Appeal to justify a decision to substitute a community order for Amy's custodial sentence?

You might wish to consult the following publications:

Jacobson, Kirby, and Hough (2011) *Public Attitudes to the Sentencing of Drug Offences.* London, Office of the Sentencing Council.

Sentencing Council (2012) *Drug Offences: Definitive Guideline.* London, Office of the Sentencing Council.[10]

2. What solutions to this type of situation—other than at the sentencing stage—can you suggest?

[10] The Sentencing Council is also issuing a guideline for magistrates in a different format: see http://sentencingcouncil.judiciary.gov.uk/guidelines/forthcoming-guidelines.htm.

11

Experiencing imprisonment

SUMMARY

In Chapter 7, we examined the issues raised in achieving justice at the point of sentencing, by considering the differential impact of the prison regime on particular groups of prisoners and highlighted the problems which arise in taking account of differences in personal circumstances at the individual level and their implications for the issue of impact mitigation. In Chapter 9 we considered the quest for justice within the prison context, while in Chapter 10 we reviewed the limits of impact mitigation in relation to class, gender, and race and argued that it was difficult to expect penal policy to solve social problems, specifically the problem of social exclusion. However, recognising this does not preclude a concern with discrimination within the criminal justice system or with differences in the experience of punishment. We will therefore consider in this Chapter the experience of imprisonment for specific groups, namely women, ethnic minorities, disabled prisoners, religious minorities, and gay prisoners. Policies which aim to reduce the risk of unfair treatment to these groups and their impact will also be discussed.

11.1 Equality, discrimination and human rights

11.1.1 UK equality law

As we shall see, there is a framework of legislation designed to promote equality and human rights. Since 2005 there have been major changes in UK equality law. The Equality Act 2006 established the new Commission for Equality and Human Rights, replacing the Commission for Racial Equality, the Equal Opportunities Commission, and the Disability Rights Commission. The role of the Commission is to enforce the equality duty under the Act and the hope was that this body would be more proactive in promoting equality and combating discrimination. The Act imposed on public authorities an 'equality duty' which means a duty to take positive action to eliminate unlawful discrimination on grounds of race, sex, disability, religion, sexual orientation, gender reassignment, or age. This was later followed by the Equality Act 2010, which has replaced the prior anti-discrimination law in the Race Relations Act 1976, Equal Pay Act 1970, the Sex Discrimination Act 1975, and the Disability Discrimination Act 1995 with a single Act, harmonised the law, and imposed a duty to promote equality. The protected characteristics under the Act include age, disability, gender reassignment, marriage and civil partnership, race, sex, sexual orientation, and religion or belief. This means that prison authorities have a duty not to discriminate against prisoners or staff on any of these grounds. In addition, the equality duty requires that prisons must develop policies to promote equality and test new policies for their equality impact. Prisoners may bring their individual complaints to the Commission.

Although equality law has been strengthened by these changes, a race equality duty had been introduced earlier by the Race Relations (Amendment) Act 2000 which imposed a statutory duty on prisons to promote race equality. The effect of this Act was to bring public services, including the Prison Service, the Probation Service, the Border Agency, and the police, within the ambit of anti-discrimination law. A disability equality duty came into force in prisons in 2006 followed by a gender equality duty in 2007.

Policies are formulated at the national level by NOMS but also by individual prison establishments. So the day-to-day life of the prison is governed by this framework of equality law.

The duty to obtain information to avoid discrimination was imposed by s 95 of the Criminal Justice Act 1991, which comprised a requirement to obtain relevant information to avoid discrimination on the grounds of race, sex, and other improper grounds. As we shall see later in this chapter, there has been a focus on race equality policies in prisons since the 1980s and some of the measures used to pursue equality are being extended to challenge discrimination in other areas.

11.1.2 **European Convention and European Union law**

There have also been advances in both European Union law and European Convention law. In European Union law, Article 13 EC enacted by the Treaty of Amsterdam, introduced a general principle of non-discrimination which prohibits discrimination on sex, racial or ethnic origin, religion, disability, age, or sexual orientation and other grounds. This came into force in May 1999. A general framework for equal treatment in employment and occupation and the prohibition of discrimination in these areas was set out in Directive 2000/78 of 27 November 2008. Article 21 of the EU Charter of Fundamental Rights and Freedoms also prohibits discrimination.

Prisoners are also protected to some extent against discrimination by the European Convention on Human Rights (ECHR). As we saw in Chapter 9, with the Human Rights Act 1998 the protection of prisoners' rights under the ECHR has been strengthened and it is possible to bring a Convention challenge in the domestic courts. Cases on racism have been brought under Article 3, the right not to be subjected to degrading treatment. In *Hilton v UK* (1976), the European Commission of Human Rights said that claims of racist abuse of a prisoner by an officer could raise an Article 3 challenge of degrading treatment.[1] An action could also be brought under Article 14, which states that the enjoyment of rights under the ECHR shall be secured without discrimination on any ground such as sex, race, colour, language, religion, political or other opinion, national or social origin, association with a national minority, property, birth, or other status. However to invoke Article 14, it is necessary to show that the discriminatory act falls within the scope of another Convention right, and that the discrimination is not justifiable. If Protocol 12 to the ECHR were to be ratified, it would be easier to bring a discrimination claim under the ECHR without engaging the other rights, but the UK Government has said that it will not ratify this Protocol. Protocol 12 states that:

1. The enjoyment of any right set forth by law shall be secured without discrimination on any ground such as sex, race, colour, language, religion, political or other opinion, national or social origin, association with a national minority, property, birth or other status.
2. No one shall be discriminated against by any public authority on any ground such as those mentioned in paragraph 1.

[1] See also *East African Asians* case (1981).

If a black prisoner could show he or she was treated less favourably than a white prisoner in relation to home visits, for example, the prisoner could invoke Articles 8 and 14. However, qualifications to Article 8 might be used in the context of the needs of the prison and the public for security. But there would have to be reasonable and objective justification for differential treatment and the measure would have to be proportionate to its aims. A case might also be brought if it could be proved that ethnic minority offenders were sentenced disproportionately compared to white offenders. For example, in *R (Clift) v Home Secretary; R (Hindawi) and another v Home Secretary* (2007) a challenge under Article 14 and Article 5 succeeded when the House of Lords held that it was discriminatory to exclude foreign-national prisoners from an early release scheme.

Women prisoners may also use Article 8 to increase access to their families and protect their right to privacy, and if women prisoners were treated differently to male prisoners in relation to other Convention rights, then they could bring a case under Article 14. To prove differential treatment, the applicant has to show that she (or he) was treated less favourably than others on the basis of a personal characteristic and that the person to whom the applicant is comparing herself is in an analogous situation. In *Lockwood v UK* (1993) it was made clear that the relevant comparator would be other prisoners within the prison population rather than an ordinary citizen in the community. For example, it could be argued that Article 8, the right to family life, is breached if women's home visits are stopped because of assumptions based on male prisoners' behaviour.

The Strasbourg Court has now recognised the existence of indirect discrimination as well as direct discrimination in a line of cases, including *Abdulaziz, Cabales and Balkandali v UK* (1985) and *Thlimmenos v Greece* (2000), and has stressed the positive duty on states to investigate discrimination in *Petropoulou-Tsakiris v Greece* (2007). The Court has also upheld complaints relating to discrimination on grounds of sexual orientation, for example in *EB v France* (2008). When the HRA 1998 came into force it was thought that more cases would be brought under Articles 8 and 14, but relatively few cases have been brought under Article 14.

11.2 Women in prison

11.2.1 The rise in the female prison population

The number of women imprisoned in England and Wales increased rapidly during the 1990s, more rapidly than the number of male prisoners, although the latter also reached record levels. The number of women prisoners was 3.5 per cent of the total prison population in 1991, increasing to 4.4 per cent in 1999, then to 6.1 per cent in 2001, and by the end of 2011 it was 5 per cent. On 24 February 2012 there were 83,376 male prisoners and 4,207 women prisoners.

Despite the dramatic percentage increase, the number of women prisoners is still relatively low compared to the number of male prisoners and relative to the number of women in the population as a whole. Women make up 51 per cent of the total population of England and Wales. Women also have a lower frequency-of-offending rate than men (Ministry of Justice 2010c: 54). The majority of women are serving short sentences of under 12 months. Approximately two-thirds of women are serving shorter sentences, that is less than one year, compared to approximately 50 per cent of men and this of course may have implications for bringing rights claims through the courts. The actual numbers cited in official statistics usually represent the count on a particular day, like a snapshot, but the number of receptions in prison throughout the year may be substantially higher. There is a substantial literature explaining women's minimal presence in the crime statistics, as well as a number of explanations for their deviance, which lie outside the scope of this book.[2]

The increase in the number of women prisoners in the 1990s was attributed to several factors, including a general increase in the use of custody, an increase in average sentence length, as well as an increase in the numbers of women appearing before the courts, and increasing numbers of women convicted for drugs offences which attract longer sentences. The change may also reflect a general increase in punitiveness and tougher sentencing of drugs-related crime. The use of suspended sentences also declined in the 1990s but has increased dramatically since the 2003 Act. The chance of receiving a custodial sentence increased for both male and female offenders in the 1990s as we saw in Chapter 9 (see Hough *et al.* 2003). So women are now more likely to receive custodial sentences for offences of theft, handling and fraud compared to the early 1990s. The numbers of women remanded in custody since the early 1990s have also increased, although over one half of women remanded in custody are not given a custodial sentence at trial.

The majority of women offenders commit fewer and less serious crimes than men. Their criminal careers are shorter and their reconviction rates are lower than men's (Ministry of Justice 2010c: 50). Although there has also been an increase in offences of violence against the person, fewer women than men are imprisoned for violence, and the majority of female prisoners do not present a danger to the public.

The differences in offending patterns for the female and male sentenced prison population are illustrated by Figure 11.1 which shows the percentage of male and female receptions into prison by offence type in 2009. The largest single offence type for women received into prison in 2009 was acquisitive crime, that is, theft and handling stolen goods.

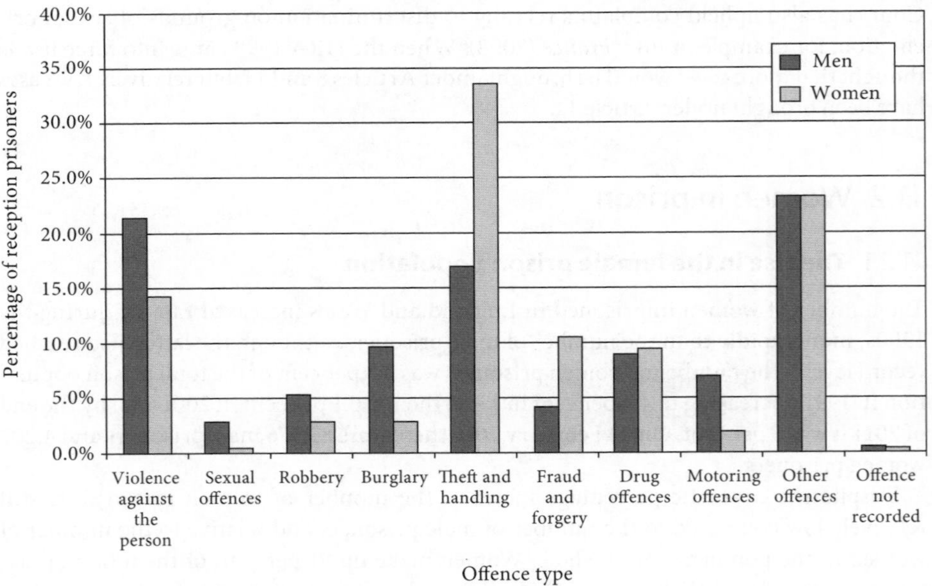

Figure 11.1 Percentage of male and female receptions (immediate custodial sentence) by offence type, 2009

Source: Ministry of Justice (2010c: 51).

[2] See, for example, the review of the literature in Howden-Windell and Clark (1999) and discussion in Silvestri and Crowther-Dowey (2008) and Renzetti (2012).

While women are becoming more involved in violent crime, and in drug crime as couriers, the attitudes of sentencers may also be changing. The most common offences for which women are imprisoned are drugs offences and property offences. The involvement of women in drugs crime has increased and these crimes attract longer sentences.

However, a larger proportion of foreign-national women prisoners are incarcerated for drugs offences (48 per cent in 2009) and fraud and forgery (24 per cent in 2009) than British national women prisoners, although the numbers of foreign-national women prisoners imprisoned for drugs offences declined from 2005–9 while the numbers imprisoned for fraud and forgery increased (Ministry of Justice 2010c: 52). But if we focus only on British male and female prisoners then violence against the person is the most prevalent offence type (ibid: 52). The decline in foreign-nationals imprisoned for drug crime may be partly accounted for by the increased use of scanning devices at airports of departure.

It was hoped that the expansion of non-custodial penalties would benefit women but the use of both community sentences and custody has increased. As Player argues: '[T]he Criminal Justice Act 2003... increases women's custodial eligibility by increasing their risk of breaching a court order, allowing their persistence to aggravate the severity of their sentence, while failing to inhibit their promotion up the sentencing tariff in pursuit of their welfare interests' (2005: 434). A wider range of options since the CJA 2003 may mean women now move up the sentencing tariff more rapidly with the unintended effects of net-widening and failure to counteract countervailing forces such as the increasing populist punitiveness and the application to women of the widely held view that 'prison works' (see Chapter 1).

The number of women supervised by the Probation Service under community orders and Suspended Sentence Orders increased from 7,146 in 2006 to 21,150 in 2009 (Ministry of Justice 2010c: 47). The average length of community sentence is longer for men than for women (ibid: 45). The greater focus on community sentences and also suspended sentence, as embodied in the CJA 2003, may have mixed effects if requirements[3] are attached to those sentences which women find difficult to meet. Women may be at greater risk of breaching conditions because of the problems of meeting both the requirements of supervision and the competing demands of child care. Some of these issues are considered by Malloch and McIvor (2011) but women's experiences of community sentences generally have been under researched. When the 2003 Act was passed, the guidance to sentencers made clear that they should take account of the offender's ability to comply with particular requirements (Sentencing Guidelines Council 2004c). Nevertheless, the Corston Report welcomed the shelving of 'custody plus' specifically because it might increase the numbers of women in prison serving short sentences and being recalled to prison for breaches (2007: para 5.17). As noted in Chapter 9, a large number of receptions into custody are for breaches and this applies to women prisoners as well. According to the Corston Report, half of new receptions into Holloway prison were for breach. In some cases the breach in question may be a failure to meet an appointment which could be because of child care or transport problems (ibid: para 5.25). The expansion of community penalties and curfews may also disadvantage women in some respects as the home becomes the focus of attention of criminal justice agencies, subject to scrutiny and surveillance, which means that, as partners of male offenders, they will also be observed. Indeed, the family is still seen as a *locus* of criminality with the emphasis on parental responsibility for young offending (see, for example, Day Sclater and Piper 2000; Reece 2005; Hollingsworth 2007; Piper 2009; Probert *et al.* 2009).

[3] See Chapter 12, section 12.2.2.

11.2.2 **The typical woman prisoner**

The experience of women as prisoners raises a number of important equality issues. The typical woman prisoner, like the typical male prisoner, is likely to have had housing problems, low educational achievement, and problems with drugs, alcohol, or mental health before entering prison. However, compared to the typical male prisoner, she is much more likely to have experienced domestic violence and sexual abuse. The Corston Report found that over one-half of women in prison reported previous domestic violence (Corston 2007: para 2.3). Two-thirds of women entering custody require drug detoxification compared to one-half of men entering prison (Corston 2007: para 2.13).

We noted in Chapter 9 the correlations between the risk of imprisonment and social class, housing problems, and poverty and unemployment, which characterise the profile of the typical prisoner, and these correlations are stronger in relation to female imprisonment (see section 9.2.1). Women are less likely than male prisoners to have been in work before imprisonment, and more likely to be unemployed after imprisonment. Women prisoners also have more experience of being in care in the past, and there is a disproportionate number of female prisoners with mental health problems compared to male prisoners (Corston 2007). A higher proportion of women in prison had housing problems prior to imprisonment compared to male prisoners. Moreover, the loss of housing while in prison does not just pose problems for the individual, but means it may be harder for women to be reunited with their families. The Wedderburn Report argued that 'women represent the extremes of social exclusion' (Prison Reform Trust 2000: xv). Many women in prison have high levels of deprivation before conviction. In some respects women are more likely to be socially excluded because they are poverty-prone, because they live longer, have higher morbidity rates, and earn less than men. Social problems which existed before entering prison may also be exacerbated by prison. Women are also less likely than men to have accommodation waiting for them on release as about one-third of women prisoners lose their homes while in prison. The Social Exclusion Unit Report (2002) found that over 40 per cent of women in prison had not worked for at least five years before entering prison and only 39 per cent had any educational qualifications.

Women in prison have higher rates of mental and physical illness than women in the general population. Of course women prisoners are not a homogeneous group; the female prison population includes black and other ethnic minority prisoners, foreign-national prisoners, women living with physical and learning disabilities, and women with a range of health problems.

11.3 Life in women's prisons

11.3.1 **The research base**

Life in women's prisons was under-researched until relatively recently. Before the 1980s there was relatively little interest in women's prisons in penal policy and few studies were conducted, but during the 1980s interest increased, especially in relation to women with mental health problems and also regarding conditions then prevailing at Holloway prison. Research showed that women prisoners had been marginalised within the penal system, in part because of their relatively low numbers compared to men. Moreover, if they fail to 'react' to poor prison conditions in terms of violence other than against themselves, this could be seen as compliance and acceptance of their conditions, instead of a reluctance to resort to male tactics. In any event, this quiescence may have contributed to their marginalisation, so the Woolf Report (1991), for example, said very little on women's prisons.

In recent years the concern has been with the expansion of the female prison population and with the development of gender-specific penal policies. The interest of the public in women's imprisonment has also increased, not least because of the salacious interest of the media which has displayed in recent years a fascination with women prisoners, portraying them as either neurotic or tough and masculine. There is also now more information available on women's imprisonment and its impact. Several major studies of women's imprisonment have been undertaken. A review of women's imprisonment was undertaken in 1997 by the then Chief Inspector of Prisons, Sir David Ramsbotham (HM Chief Inspector of Prisons 1997), with a follow up review in 2001 to assess progress (HM Chief Inspector of Prisons 2001). Problems raised in the 1997 Report included the excessive security used in women's prisons, the lack of consistency on privileges across the women's prison estate, the treatment of juveniles, the holding of young offenders in prison establishments, the training of staff, allocation procedures, the handcuffing of women during labour and on ante-natal visits, reception procedures, training for staff conducting strip searches and using control and restraint techniques, access to phones, access to translators, induction programmes, visiting arrangements, healthcare provision, particularly for women with mental health problems, and educational provision.

The Wedderburn Report on women's imprisonment, published in 2000, also argued that women serving short sentences for less serious offences and women with mental health problems should be diverted from custody, while sentences could be shortened for those in prison and greater use could be made of temporary release (Prison Reform Trust 2000). In addition, a major study of the physical and mental health of women prisoners, *The Health of Women in Prison*, was published in 2006 by researchers at Oxford University who interviewed 505 female remand prisoners over a period in 2004–5 (Plugge *et al.* 2006).

The Corston Report, published in 2007, examined women with particular vulnerabilities in the criminal justice system, arguing that custody should be used only where necessary for public protection but that there are many women in prison for non-violent offences who could be dealt with differently (Corston 2007). This research for the Review included visits to six women's prisons, three women's community centres, and a medium-secure women's hospital. In examining 'vulnerabilities' the Report focused on issues such as domestic violence, child care issues, including being a single parent, and personal issues, including mental illness, substance misuse and eating disorders, as well as socio-economic factors such as poverty and unemployment (Corston 2007: para 14).

A follow up study was undertaken in 2009 and a report published in 2011 found that progress had been made in a number of areas, including body searching, and funding for diversionary measures and one-stop centres for women (see APPGW 2011 and section 11.5). It highlighted the continuing challenges presented by women with alcohol and drug problems, and the experiences of domestic violence and sexual abuse, the need for funding for these women's centres and the problem of the rising numbers of women in custody. The Prison Inspectorate also reviewed the treatment of black and minority ethnic women prisoners in 2009 and highlighted the particular problems facing these prisoners (HM Inspectorate of Prisons 2009b; see also section 11.4.6).

Their thematic report on women prisoners in 2010 found that the majority of women's prisons were performing well with good staff-prisoner relations and that there had been improvements in health care, particularly mental health care and improvements in safety and better treatment of women with substance abuse problems (HM Inspectorate of Prisons 2010). However, the Report raised concerns over the use of segregation and incidents of bullying in some establishments, and noted the challenges in dealing with female prisoners with complex needs and particularly problems over the supply of primary health care and the treatment of women on remand.

In 2010–11 the Prison Inspectorate visited Holloway and Bronzefield, which had large numbers of women dependent on drugs, high levels of self-harm and mental health problems, and many women who were primary carers. Drake Hall was also visited and, although the performance at all three prisons was generally good, there were still concerns over health care at Bronzefield and over safety at Holloway, where some women felt unsafe when housed in dormitories. For the most part relations between staff and prisoners were good although there were some complaints about male officers at Holloway and still too high a proportion of male officers at Bronzefield (HM Chief Inspector of Prisons 2011a). In all three establishments prisoners spent a reasonable amount of time outside their cells, but too few courses were available.

We therefore have far more information on the issues involved in women's imprisonment now and both Labour and Coalition Governments have accepted that women's offending may raise different issues to men's and that women prisoners deserve separate attention so gender-specific policies are needed. The Labour Government's strategy for women prisoners was to take account of their special needs and of the specific factors which influence women's offending (Home Office 2000a, 2001b; see section 11.5.3). Some of the Corston Report's recommendations were accepted by the Labour Government (see section 11.5.3 and Ministry of Justice 2007b).

The Coalition Government in *Breaking the Cycle* has stressed that women offenders have different needs and more complex problems relating to their offending including domestic violence as well as drug and alcohol problems (Ministry of Justice 2010a, para 104). It also stated that it would apply lessons drawn from dealing with women offenders more widely, including the use of coordinated approaches to diverting women from custody, and the development of community provision.

11.3.2 **The women's prison estate**

The small size of the female prison population, and therefore the small size of the women's prison estate, means that women may be held far from home, making it difficult to organise visits or support for their families. The average distance from home is 55 miles but for many women the distance is over 100 miles (Prison Reform Trust 2011a: 32). Although the relevant Prison Service Order, PSO 4800, stipulates that women prisoners should be held as close to home as possible, in practice women are held on average further away from home than male prisoners. This also has implications for resettlement as it is harder to facilitate resettlement if they are accommodated far from their communities. There are large geographical areas, including the West Midlands and Wales, without women's prisons and these problems have increased with the closure of Brockhill Prison at Redditch to women. While a new purpose-built women's prison, Bronzefield, opened in June 2004 at Ashford, Middlesex, some women's prisons have been closed, for example the women's unit at Winchester Prison to accommodate the increase in male prisoners, and Morton Hall, to provide an Immigration Removal Centre. But any cut in the women's prison estate means that women may be held even further from home. By the end of 2011 there were 13 women's prisons.

From 1999–2004 the women's prison estate was managed separately by a special unit at Prison Service Headquarters but is now managed geographically, by Area Managers responsible for both men's and women's prisons in their areas. A Women and Young People's Group in the Prison Service gave advice and support to prisons on women's issues and it produced a Prison Service Instruction (PSI) on gender equality impact assessments (PSI 40/2007). This meant that any changes in Prison Service policy or practice needed to be assessed to consider their implications for gender equality. It formulated Gender-Specific Standards which form part of the Government's response to the Corston Report and these are intended to ensure that prison regimes are appropriate for female offenders.

Because there are fewer women's prisons, the women's prison estate is also less flexible in terms of catering for different types of prisoners with particular needs. This also means it may be harder to transfer disruptive women prisoners than male prisoners for whom more places are available. If difficult prisoners are transferred to an ordinary prison, the restrictions may mean regime changes for other prisoners and stricter control than is warranted. The small size of the estate also means less flexibility for providing appropriate accommodation for prisoners or the right level of supervision. There may be places available in closed but not open prisons and vice versa and there are no longer any semi-open prisons for women.

Women prisoners have been held in some of the worst conditions within the prison system and there has been considerable variation between prisons. When the Chief Inspector of Prisons visited Holloway in 1995 he walked out in disgust because it was so dirty with sightings of rats and cockroaches reported and, in the 2003 league table, Holloway was still rated the worst prison, at level 1, although it is now at level 3. The most recent report of the Prison Inspectorate in 2011 (HM Chief Inspector of Prisons 2011a) and the thematic report on women's prisons found that there had been improvements in most of the 14 prisons inspected, particularly in relation to safety and support for substance abuse (HM Inspectorate of Prisons 2010). However, concern was raised over the closure of some women's prisons meaning that more women are now held further from home (HM Chief Inspector of Prisons 2011a: 9).

11.3.3 **Women prisoners and male penal policies**

Until relatively recently women's imprisonment was largely subsumed within the male prison system and women were punished within a penal system designed for men, and as we saw in Chapter 10, this marginalisation of women extends across the criminal justice system (Fawcett 2009). Because women constitute a minority, they are at a disadvantage as institutions will usually favour the interests of the majority for administrative convenience. This means that women may be adversely affected by policies based on the actions of male prisoners.

If women are housed within the precincts of a men's prison, it may be difficult to guarantee their security at times of disorder and also may mean that they are subject to higher levels of security than is necessary, even in normal conditions. While the regimes for men and women will be managed separately, the ethos, procedures, and systems in core areas such as security will be those of a men's prison.

The experience of the prison riots strongly influenced penal policy in the 1990s, but these were primarily male events, so the direction of penal policy was predicated principally on male experiences, leading to a stress on the need for enhanced security and control. This has meant that women's needs have been marginalised and subsumed within a system primarily defined by men and this may make the experience of prison for women more onerous. Even where the problem was acknowledged, the focus was on accommodating women's needs within the male framework, with some minor adjustments, rather than radically rethinking the question.

While the improvements in the prison regime in the immediate post-Woolf period benefited women, women also shared in the retrenchment of these benefits. Most notably they were subject to increased security after the Whitemoor and Parkhurst escapes. In this sense they were 'punished' disproportionately as the escapes, like the earlier riots, did not involve women's prisons or women prisoners. The Learmont and Woodcock Reports also impacted disparately on women prisoners because they resulted in greater use of shackles on outside visits and, for a period, cuts in home leave. The response to the escapes also meant that there was an increase in the numbers of women held in closed prisons, even if they met the criteria for transfer to open prisons, where there would be more access to home, their families, and outside work.

During the late 1990s, security concerns and the war on drugs inside prison also disadvantaged women as they generated more intensive controls, including the use of Dedicated Search Teams, dressed in black combat clothes, to search prisoners' cells, and mandatory drug testing. In addition, visitors, including children, were subject to greater surveillance. Yet women are less likely to escape or to riot than male prisoners. If they do escape they are less likely to constitute a threat to the public, as they commit fewer offences of violence and may be easier to trace, as they are likely to contact their families. Mandatory drug-testing policies have been applied in men's and women's prisons even though there are fewer drugs-related incidents in women's prisons and the Chief Inspector of Prisons has argued that less stringent testing for drugs is appropriate in women's prisons (HM Chief Inspector of Prisons 1997, 2001). Women are generally less dangerous than men, both on official statistics and self-report studies, and are less likely to abscond, yet they have been subjected to similar levels of security. In fact, the issue during the riots was rather how best to protect women prisoners from male prisoners if a riot occurred at a shared site. Women were also subjected to full body searching, despite the fact they posed lower security risks, and, given the fact that many women prisoners have experienced sexual abuse in the past, this may be particularly stressful for them. However, routine body searching on admission to prison is no longer undertaken.

11.4 Women prisoners and the pains of imprisonment

Women prisoners deserve special attention because, it has been argued, they experience the pains of imprisonment more intensely than their male counterparts for a number of reasons, the principal one being that women are most likely to be the primary carers of children and therefore experience greater anxiety at separation from their children. In some cases, the women may not even know who is looking after their children. Disquiet has been expressed over the problems for women prisoners of maintaining contact with their children and over the presence of male officers in women's prisons. There is also concern over the large numbers of children who have a parent in custody. It is estimated that 160,000 children a year are affected (Prison Reform Trust 2011a: 28).

11.4.1 Women as carers

Women prisoners may have particular concerns about childcare, caring for elderly relatives, and anxieties about declining fertility, which will not affect men to the same extent. Women prisoners are concerned at losing contact with their children and their greatest fear is often that their children may be taken into care while they are serving their sentence. Babies are permitted to stay with their mothers for a maximum of 18 months in some units and nine months in others, and as there are only seven units, there is strong competition for places. Women are normally transferred to them in the final stages of their pregnancy and allocations will be made on the basis of the interests of mother and child, risk assessments regarding the safety and well-being of others, and the good order of the prison. Under Prison Rule 9(3) a pregnant woman can apply for transfer to a Mother and Baby Unit (MBU). Mothers' rights to retain their babies have been strengthened by the Human Rights Act as separation may breach Article 8 of the European Convention. However, if claims are raised under Article 8, the qualifications in Article 8(2) may be used to deny access. Category A prisoners are not allowed access to these units.

The blanket policy of the Prison Service to remove a child at 18 months was successfully challenged under the Human Rights Act in *R (P, Q & QB) v Secretary of the State for the Home Department* (2001). Here, the Court of Appeal said that prisoners retain the right to respect for family life while in prison. In considering whether the state's grounds for interfering with the right are justified, the court will take account of the need for security in prison, the need to avoid discrimination, and whether the rule was appropriate in the individual case, and the more serious the interference, the more compelling the justification would need to be. If the policy stemmed from the welfare of the child and if, in a particular case, the effect on the child was very adverse, the court could intervene in an exceptional case. Where challenges have been brought the courts have looked closely at the decision-making procedures and whether the risks in question can be managed.[4]

Trying to deal with family crises while inside prison is a major problem for women prisoners. Women usually remain responsible for family decisions and find it hard to co-ordinate arrangements from prison. If they are detained for a long period of time they may lose their home, which will make it harder to keep their children. While the wife of a male prisoner may struggle to keep family life going, for women who are the main carers, prison will have a more significant impact on the structure of home life. In her study of the impact on prisoners' families, Codd (2008) describes them as living in the shadow of their partners' lives as they are also affected adversely by imprisonment. But for women in prison the impact may be even greater.

Women are more likely than male prisoners to have dependent children and less likely than male prisoners to have a partner caring for their children. The Corston Report found that only 5 per cent of the children of women prisoners remained in their own home (Corston 2007: para 2.9): 12 per cent were in care or with foster or adoptive parents, 25 per cent were with grandmothers, and 29 per cent were with other family members or friends. A higher proportion of children of women prisoners end up in care compared to children of male prisoners.

So although women may have a similar social profile to men in terms of social exclusion, this may be exacerbated by the fact of being the primary carer. As women may be allocated to prisons far from their homes, there may be problems in organising regular visits from their families as children have to be escorted. While there is a means-tested allowance for close family members to visit, this is limited and long-distance visits may be very expensive. Many prisons are located in rural areas with inadequate bus services. The costs of visits may be a problem especially as it means time off work for the person escorting the children, given the distance from home for many prisoners. Provision for visits varies between prisons. Women may avoid having their children visit them because they think they would be distressed by the surroundings or being searched, although visiting facilities in women's prisons are usually superior to those in men's prisons.

The pains of imprisonment may be greater because of these anxieties regarding family obligations. Anxieties about families were a major issue for women interviewed in the Oxford study of remand prisoners. Their concerns focused on their children and the plight of elderly relatives (Plugge *et al.* 2006). Longer visits which last all day would be

[4] See for example *CF v Secretary of State for the Home Department* [2004].

better for women with children as would cheap transport to the nearest railway station. In the United States, for example, arrangements have been made in some women's prisons for children to stay with local families for the weekend to allow for longer visits.

11.4.2 **Privacy and prison conditions**

Women also may find intrusions of privacy more painful than their male counterparts, as they often have less experience of communal life, through sports activities. Because of this, open prisons, paradoxically, may seem more repressive, if it means sharing a dormitory. In addition, control in open prisons may be based more heavily on compliance with rules, rather than physical barriers, with adverse disciplinary consequences. Women may also find the physical conditions more distressing because women usually have more health awareness as the person who is most likely to take responsibility for family health. They are therefore more concerned with hygiene and may be more upset by having to eat in their cells, by the limited number of showers, and by poor hygiene standards. The Corston Report found that there were still instances of slopping out because of a failure to provide 24-hour access to facilities, or queuing to use the toilet at night, which prisoners find humiliating and degrading (Corston 2007: para 3.16).

Concerns over privacy may be exacerbated by the presence of male officers. Women prisoners do not like men entering their rooms; they do not like to be observed while washing, especially if they have previously been abused, and find providing samples for drug testing, for example, quite intrusive. Although using male officers in women's prisons was initially intended as an equal opportunities measure for staff, the policy has not been welcomed by prisoners. As large numbers of women prisoners have experienced violence from men in the past, this has made it especially difficult for them, but most women find the presence of male officers difficult to deal with. The Chief Inspector of Prisons has argued that there should be a minimum of 75 per cent female staff in women's prisons (HM Chief Inspector of Prisons 1997). However, the most recent report on women's prisons notes that some prisons still have too many male staff (HMIP 2010: para 1.13). Thirty-six per cent of NOMS staff, including Prison Service and NOMS headquarters, are female (Ministry of Justice 2011g: 9). Working at women's prisons may be unpopular because it is seen as low-status work and women officers may find it difficult to transfer because of staff shortages. Further, the prevalence of male officers may generate a masculinist occupational culture. The attitudes towards female officers in men's prisons has also been examined and found to encompass a range of responses, including chivalrous, sexualised, and ambivalent attitudes (see Crewe 2006).

11.4.3 **Expectations of women prisoners' behaviour**

Officers' expectations of women's behaviour appear to be more demanding in the sense that women are more likely than men to be reprimanded for petty offences such as swearing or other behaviour which is seen as unfeminine (Carlen 1998). Women prisoners have higher adjudication rates than male prisoners and higher rates for complaints. The punishment rate for disciplinary offences has been consistently higher for women than men. For example, in 2009 there were 150 adjudications per 100 women prisoners compared to 124 per 100 male prisoners (Ministry of Justice 2010c: 46).

Devlin (1998) argues that women are more likely to be punished for minor disciplinary matters and are subject to more intensive discipline and surveillance. Women prisoners are seen by officers as more argumentative than male prisoners and less able to accept discipline. Women may find it hard to adjust to prison for the reasons we have considered.

Because women may have had greater autonomy in running their own homes, they may also find it harder to adjust to a regime which essentially infantilises them in many ways. As women's prisons are smaller, women prisoners may be subject to greater scrutiny, so disciplinary infractions are more likely to be noticed. Women with mental health problems are more likely to be charged with disciplinary offences and may react badly to being held on a segregation unit or on cellular confinement (O'Brien *et al.* 2001). The disciplinary regime is used to control women's behaviour and to contain women with mental health problems. While women prisoners who are dissatisfied with their treatment have access to the range of remedies and the complaints procedure available to male prisoners, like them they may be reluctant to complain if they think it may cause more problems for them.

11.4.4 **Women prisoners' health needs**

Women's healthcare in prison is an important issue because women prisoners have higher rates of mental health problems and prescription drug use than male prisoners (Prison Reform Trust 2003; Social Exclusion Unit 2002). A survey of female prisoners in 1997 found that 40 per cent had received treatment for mental health problems before entering prison and about one-half of women prisoners had some drug dependency prior to prison (Singleton *et al.* 1998; O'Brien *et al.* 2001). Two-thirds of women prisoners suffer from some form of mental health problem such as depression and anxiety and about one-half are taking prescribed psychotropic drugs. A higher proportion of women than male prisoners enter prison with mental health problems which may be exacerbated in prison by worries about family and housing. The use of medicines increases in prison and many women take prescribed psychotropic drugs for the first time while in prison (see Prison Reform Trust 2003). Outside prison women have higher morbidity rates than men and this is also reflected inside prison, and these health problems may add to the stresses of imprisonment. But while many women prisoners have emotional and social problems, the number of disturbed and difficult prisoners with severe and untreatable problems is relatively small. While recognising their health problems, an over-emphasis on women's therapeutic needs runs the risk of medicalising women's deviance, which perpetuates the perception of women as unstable.

The Oxford study found that the health status of the women who entered prison was poorer than for women in the general population and problems included both physical and mental health, which meant considerable demands were made on the health services within prison (Plugge *et al.* 2006). Women prisoners were five times more likely to have a mental health problem than women in the general population; over half had used illegal drugs before going into prison. Interestingly, the research found that the health status of some women actually improved in prison, because they did *not* have access to drugs and alcohol, but they did have regular meals, healthcare, and protection from abusive relationships. However, many reported becoming unfit with lack of exercise and the researchers argue that more attention should be given to support for healthcare in prison, especially as health issues may be linked to offending behaviour, and that improving health should be a Key Performance Indicator. The prisoners interviewed emphasised that they wanted more access to exercise and healthier food rather than high-carbohydrate food. The authors' recommendations include more research on health needs of foreign-national prisoners, on measures to help women sleep to avoid the use of sleeping pills, more support for prisoners who witness suicides or self-harm, more access to cleaning materials, more help to disabled prisoners, more support for improving physical health, for example, hepatitis B vaccinations, better training for staff to improve delivery of healthcare, and access to in-cell sanitation at all times.

Many women prisoners have drug or alcohol problems which require treatment but an unintended effect of mandatory drug testing is that some prisoners are switching from cannabis to heroin, because the latter is harder to detect. In a later review of mental health in prisons, the Prison Inspectorate found that female prisoners reported the highest levels of psychological and emotional disorder and distress and were on high levels of medication when they might have benefited more from counselling (HM Inspectorate of Prisons 2007).

There are also high levels of attempted and threatened suicides and rates of self-harm in the female prison population. However, as noted in Chapter 9, the total number of suicides has fallen over the past decade and in 2010 only 1 of the 58 suicides in prison was committed by a woman. High-risk factors for suicide include neuroses, drug and alcohol misuse, and being in care as a child, all of which are present in both the female and male prison populations. Self-harming is also much higher in the female prison population and particularly amongst women under 21 and in the white prisoner group.

Women account for over half of recorded self-harming incidents but only 5 per cent of the prison population.[5] Self-harm may have been used as a way to deal with stress before imprisonment, although they may be more likely to engage in self-harm in response to poor conditions, while men may be more likely to direct violence against others or to damage property in such cases. The Chief Inspector of Prisons referred to high levels of self-harm and repeated self-harm at HMP Bronzefield where the same individual self-harmed 90 times within the space of one month (HM Chief Inspector of Prisons 2011a: 9). The failure to manage high risk women with severe personality disorders is also criticised and particularly the use of segregation for women with mental health problems (ibid: 9).

The Report by the Prison Reform Trust, *Troubled Inside* (2003), considered the mental health needs of women prisoners and raised the issue of whether prisons should be used as psychiatric hospitals and whether, given the numbers of women with mental health problems and the number of attempted suicides, it would be better to focus on the mental health needs of offenders rather than simply incarcerating them (see also Peay 2007).

Although the principle of equivalence should govern prison health care, that is standards of health care should be provided at the same level as provided by the NHS in the community, there are concerns over the standards of health care in prison, particularly for prisoners with mental health problems, in terms of the services available and quality of care (see Reed and Lyne 2000). Responsibility for healthcare has been transferred from the Prison Service to the National Health Service and responsibility for funding has moved from the Home Office to the Department of Health. This has had a beneficial effect on health service provision but there are still problems given the demand for services. Training, particularly training in mental health care, needs improving. The demands on health services in prison are greater than in the community, because of the higher rates of mental disorder, drug misuse, and self-harming in prison. The burden on prison medical staff and on officers and other prisoners would be reduced if more facilities were available to divert offenders with mental health problems from prison and if mental health care and drug treatment programmes within the community were improved. Recent policy statements suggest support for the principle of diversion for those with mental health problems but clearly this needs to be backed up by resources. Women with serious mental health problems do need access to an appropriate therapeutic regime. Until recently a proper therapeutic community for women, comparable to Grendon for male prisoners, was not available. A women's annexe at Winchester Prison, West Hill, was converted to a therapeutic centre but it closed in 2004 to make room for male prisoners. However,

[5] Hansard, House of Commons Debate 9 February 2010, col 745, cited in APPGW 2011: 9.

therapeutic units are provided for women prisoners at HMP Send, Styal, and at Eastwood Park.

The standard of care for prisoners with severe mental health problems is also dependent on facilities in the wider community. Where problems are severe and transfer to hospital is necessary, it may take several months to find a suitable hospital bed (Corston 2007: para 12). Also, because of problems within the NHS, it may take considerable time for medical staff to provide reports requested by sentencers which may delay provision of appropriate methods of disposal for women.

However, these health problems not only present huge demands on the prison, but also reflect social problems which it would be unreasonable to expect the prison system to solve. As the Corston Report concluded: 'the Prison Service cannot and should not be expected to solve social problems' (para 7.24). As we argued in Chapter 10, what are needed are social policies to address these social problems, which will include greater provision for support within the community.

11.4.5 **Constructive regimes for women**

Until the 1970s women's training was mainly domestic work servicing the prison, with limited opportunities for serious vocational or academic work. The focus was also on 'feminine' skills, such as taking pride in one's appearance, reflecting the view that adjusting to the gender role is part of the rehabilitation process. Although it has been criticised for this reason, courses such as hairdressing do at least offer a prospect of self-employment on release. Domestic work also forms a large part of male prison work, of course, as the provision of cooking and cleaning services forms a substantial proportion of prison employment.

In the 1970s vocational courses were introduced, although often in subjects like home economics. The situation now is much improved with some light industrial work for women in prison such as manufacturing clothes and furniture, printing and desktop publishing, and a wider range of educational and training courses (see Simon 1999). Improving the provision of work and training is crucial to strengthening women's position in the labour market when they return to the community. Many women prisoners, like male prisoners, have much lower literacy and numeracy skills than the wider population.

Given that most women are serving short sentences, they need intensive training for work. Although many jobs in prison are in housekeeping or cleaning, to meet the needs of the prison, this could be tied to a National Vocational Qualification, as it is crucial to improve access to the job market. A survey of women's work and training experiences in prison and on release found that while the majority of women had access to work while in custody, they also found that employment of very little value to them in finding work on release (see Hamlyn and Lewis 2000).

Because of the smaller size of women's prisons, there may be a more limited range of education and training opportunities than in men's prisons, but efforts are being made to ensure greater consistency in educational provision and greater co-ordination between different prison establishments. Prisoners are now being used to assist with the teaching of PE and other educational activities.

The provision of offending behaviour programmes in women's prisons should also take account of women's needs, and programmes specially designed for women offenders have now been developed and accredited. However, women offenders generally prefer and benefit from individual client-centred counselling and treatment approaches. Some of the issues which arise in working with women offenders as well as alternatives to imprisonment are considered by Sheehan *et al.* (2007) who draw on ideas in other jurisdictions.

The development of ideas on working with women offenders over the past 30 years, from early efforts to make women more visible towards challenging gender neutral approaches, is reviewed by Worrall and Gelsthorpe (2009).

The Corston Report (2007) has also emphasised the need to give a higher priority to training in very basic life skills, such as cooking healthy meals, and organising family life, for women whose lives have been chaotic. So a woman-centred approach should be applied to work, training, and education, but this means that issues such as life skills and building self-esteem, the Report argued, should be addressed as a priority and as a prerequisite for benefiting from vocational or educational courses. For those with more advanced skills, a course offering women help and advice in setting up small businesses, such as that offered at Holloway, is useful and could be extended further. An expansion of prison work is part of the Coalition Government's policy and it is hoped that this will also benefit female prisoners

11.4.6 **Black women prisoners**

The experiences of this group have been under-researched so relatively little information has been available until recently. Black women enmeshed in the criminal justice system have to negotiate the multiple hazards of class, gender, and ethnicity. Black women receive custodial sentences at earlier stages in their criminal careers than white women and are over-represented in prison. Some of the reasons for this were discussed in Chapter 10. Explanations have focused on the role of racism in these decisions, but the impact of poor housing and social exclusion also needs to be considered.

Black women and women from ethnic minority groups, who make up just over one quarter of the female prison population, may face additional problems within the justice system because they are subject to racist as well as patriarchal attitudes and stereotypes. Racism may shape the experience of imprisonment in a number of ways, in the allocation of resources and in treatment and attitudes, issues considered in the second part of this chapter, and for black women this will overlie and may exacerbate the problems considered earlier (see Chigwada-Bailey 2003 and also section 11.7). Although it has been noted that in the past there has been less proactive race relations work in women's than in men's prisons, with the increasing emphasis on the equality duty this has improved. Moreover, black and minority ethnic women have been found to be less negative about their treatment than black and minority ethnic men and, generally, relations between staff and prisoners seem to be better in female prisons (HM Chief Inspector of Prisons 2008). However, one group of female prisoners, foreign-national prisoners, may experience particular problems and a review of foreign-national prisoners found that family and immigration problems were major concerns for these women (HM Inspectorate of Prisons 2006, see also section 11.7.6). Support and advice for foreign-national women prisoners is given by Hibiscus, part of the Female Prisoners' Welfare Project (FPWP/Hibiscus 2010). It helps women stay in contact with their families and provides support on resettlement and has an office in Jamaica for this purpose.

The issues facing BME women prisoners were considered by the Prison Inspectorate in 2009. In *Race Relations in Prison: Responding to Adult Women from Black and Minority Ethnic Backgrounds* (HMIP 2009b) the Report noted that because black women are more likely to be single parents, they face particular problems in maintaining their households while in prison and particular problems of drug use and social disadvantage. These women also reported problems regarding health care, felt that they were disadvantaged in their access to resources within the prison and also reported higher rates of victimisation and lack of respect than non-minorities. The Report notes the need to provide a specific diversity strategy for BME women prisoners as this group has tended to be overlooked in the past in race relations work, However, relations between staff and BME prisoners were better in women's prisons overall than in men's prisons.

11.4.7 **Women's relative advantages in the prison regime**

So far the disadvantages experienced by women have been highlighted, but in some respects women would seem to benefit under the current prison regime. Generally women's prisons have better visiting facilities than men's prisons. Female prisoners also spend higher than average hours in purposeful activities than men do, longer outside their cells, and more hours in education and skills training. Moreover as noted earlier, women are also allowed to have their babies with them in a Mother and Baby Unit up to the age of 18 months (or nine months in two of the units). There are also indications that women's prisons have better relations between staff and prisoners than men's prisons.

11.5 Gender-specific policies

11.5.1 **Ameliorative justice**

As we have seen, the treatment of women prisoners has been subject to criticism on a number of grounds and a number of proposals for reform have been made by the Chief Inspector of Prisons, the Prison Reform Trust, and other campaigning groups. It has been argued that we need a *gender-specific* policy which takes account of the differing needs and circumstances of women prisoners, to achieve substantive equality rather than formal equality. This may entail providing different regimes for men and women but Carlen (1998) has argued this is justified on the principle of 'ameliorative justice'. This principle 'assumes that as women (and black women in particular), because of their different social roles and relationships and other cultural difference, are likely either to suffer more pains of imprisonment than men, or to suffer in different ways, the prison authorities are justified in running different regimes for women to make up for (or ameliorate) the differential pains of imprisonment attributable to gender or ethnic difference' (ibid: 10–11). Gender testing means 'asking whether biological or ideological differences in gender identity will require proposed regime innovations to receive differential implementation in the men's and women's prisons' (ibid: 134).

A gender-specific penal policy should, in particular, acknowledge women as primary carers and recognise that women in prison receive far less support than male prisoners from their partners. It would also demand a more sensitive drugs policy, allowing women more control over clothes and food, increasing the use of women officers in women's prisons, increasing gender awareness training for staff, meeting the needs of female offenders, and making use of women officers' experience in devising future strategies.

An increased number of assisted visits would help, as would easing restrictions imposed on mothers in their contact with their children. Temporary release, weekend leave, and weekend visits from children, perhaps lodging with local families and visiting their parents in the day, would also assist prisoners with children. Incoming calls would enable prisoners to maintain contact with their families. The resettlement of women should also take into account the need for women to move away from their home areas to escape violent relationships. Women also need more help with drug problems, and access to gender-appropriate treatment programmes inside and outside prison. A frequent criticism of the Mandatory Drug Testing programme is that it is punitive rather than constructive and does not address the source of the problem. Drug treatment and testing orders also need to be geared towards women, and improved community-based services provided for women with mental health problems who are at risk of offending. More attention should be given to improving access to health, education, and support on release into the community. Housing is also a major concern for women prisoners who want to be reunited with their families.

The Wedderburn Report (Prison Reform Trust 2000) favoured replacing existing women's prisons with geographically dispersed custodial centres, and a network of supervision, rehabilitation, and support centres. It advocated a reductionist programme on the grounds that women's patterns of offending are different and because the social costs of women's imprisonment are greater than the costs of men's imprisonment.

The Corston Report (2007) also recommended replacing women's prisons with small, multi-functional and better distributed centres and proposed a new Commission for Women who offend or are at risk of reoffending. This would be cross-departmental and incorporate the Women's Offending Reduction Programme and provide strong leadership for implementing change and addressing issues which lead to female criminality because, Corston warned, there is a danger of gender-specific agendas being diluted without a strong central structure. The Corston Report emphasised the need for a woman-centred approach which will focus on the needs of the individual women and bring together a range of services to address health, abuse, drug and alcohol misuse in community-based centres. Although this might seem expensive, by cutting the use of imprisonment this would free up prison places. Moreover, a considerable amount of expenditure has been earmarked for prison expansion and some of this could, and should, be used for reforming the facilities available for women. There are also more opportunities for commissioning innovative provision of community centres and community programmes to divert female offenders from custody. Those women who do need secure custody should be housed in small secure custodial units (Corston 2007: para 3.34).

One imaginative use of women's work on community schemes suggested by Corston is training women to renovate properties which could be used to provide accommodation for women on bail or on release (2007: 5.15). The existing women's prison estate could then be transferred to the male prison estate to reduce over-crowding there. The Report also argues for more attention to be given to gender issues within the sentencing guidelines. It also recommends that defendants who are primary carers of young children should be remanded in custody only after considering a probation report on the likely impact on the children (Corston 2007: 9).

11.5.2 **Reducing the number of women in prison**

Given that the UK has a wide range of alternatives to prison, the scope for reductionism is greater than in most other European societies. It should not be assumed by the courts that some community penalties are unsuitable for women, because of their domestic circumstances, or because they involve manual work (see Hedderman and Gelsthorpe 1997). Community punishments could be made more suitable for women offenders if childcare provision were available (Prison Reform Trust 2000: para 5.15).

An abolitionist approach for women prisoners is unlikely to be adopted given the political pressures on governments, but also because it would be seen as unfair to male prisoners. However, we can see a move towards decarceration in the recommendations of the Halliday Report and the greater emphasis on community punishment in the Criminal Justice Act 2003. There has also been a decline in the numbers being imprisoned for non-payment of fines since 1995 (see Chapter 7, section 7.3). There is now greater recognition of the need to provide differential regimes and both Labour and Coalition Governments have acknowledged this (Home Office 2001b, 2004b; Ministry of Justice 2010a, see also section 11.5.3). The Labour Government did agree with NOMS a target to reduce the number of places in the women's estate by March 2012 and there was a small decline in the number of women prisoners in 2011 (APPGW 2011).

Community sentences could be used more widely for women, as the Corston Report argued, and made more effective. One proposal is for a 'prostitution referral order' which would be delivered by a supervisor with particular expertise on working with women involved in prostitution. Using curfews and electronic monitoring more widely would also enable some women to be dealt with in the community. The Report is critical of sentencers who impose a custodial sentence for the women's own good, or own safety, or to obtain access to services like detoxification when these services would be better provided in the community.

However, if community sentences are made more demanding this also increases the risk of breach and therefore custody if fines are unpaid or conditions not met. For this reason the Corston Report recommended that we need more attention to be paid to gender-specific sanctions and disposals. A network of community centres for women could supervise community sentences and provide a range of support for offenders, including health resources, to address the underlying causes which contribute to offending behaviour. The Report made 43 recommendations on ways of improving the treatment and intervention in relation to women offenders. One proposal is that sentencers who give non-custodial community orders could review compliance (see Chapter 12, section 12.2.3), which might enhance sentencers' confidence in those sentences and would also benefit offenders themselves. Further, even more use could be made of suspended sentences. The Report also argues that the government needs to increase public awareness of the costs of women's imprisonment. It emphasises that the indications are that the public might be less punitive towards non-violent female offenders if they are made aware of the context of offending and the impact of imprisonment, and what is involved in community punishments (Corston: para 6.3.4).

The female prison population could also be reduced by cutting the number of remand prisoners through better bail provision, including hostels for women and children. A shift away from custody for women would also represent a substantial saving as community sentences are much cheaper and would not conflict with the key policy of reserving custody for dangerous and highly persistent offenders. However, as the Inspector of Prisons notes, the number of women in prison has not changed significantly (HM Chief Inspector of Prisons 2011a). Even if a fully reductionist policy is not adopted, the regime could, nevertheless, be ameliorated for those within prison, as we have previously discussed. It could also be argued that lower security in women's prisons is feasible because the women are unlikely to abscond.

11.5.3 **Government policies on female offenders**

Since 2000, the Government has affirmed the need for policies specifically geared to female offenders.

The Women's Offending Reduction Programme

In 2000 the Labour Government published its strategy for women offenders which emphasised the importance of improving women's access to health services and support for those using drugs, focusing on women's housing, education, and employment needs, and strengthening family relationships. It also acknowledged the differential impact of imprisonment on women as primary carers and because the small numbers of women prisoners may mean they are housed further from home (Home Office 2000a:1). It also recognised the links between women's offending and social exclusion and that women offenders may be victims of abuse. It engaged in a consultation process and published its Report (Home Office 2001b), following which it announced a new Women's Offending Reduction Programme (WORP) to divert women from custody. The aim was to co-ordinate efforts to deal with women's offending including efforts to deal with work, training, and healthcare and the main focus of the programme was on community provision.

WORP involved several agencies and aimed to reduce offending and promote equality of treatment and access to services drawing on the work of a range of government departments, and from the public and voluntary sectors. Its goals included increasing opportunities to deal with offending in community programmes for women, setting up links with the National Drug Strategy and focusing on women with mental health problems, and designing accredited offending behaviour programmes specifically for women. It also reviewed the accommodation of women with children in bail hostels and probation facilities. The impact of WORP meant that, in principle, more support was given to developing new initiatives to assist women, but in practice there was often insufficient funding.

The Together Women Programme

The Together Women Programme was also launched in 2005 to evaluate whether a multi-agency approach to female offenders within the community could be developed to divert women from custody, using a multi-agency and holistic approach. Five one-stop shops were set up in women's centres in the North of England, providing support and advice on life skills, parenting, mental health services, and training and counselling as well as advice on housing and employment. The women who attended included those at risk of offending as well as those already in contact with the criminal justice system (see Roberts 2010). Hedderman *et al.* (2011) interviewed women using the centres and found a positive response in terms of the good relations with key workers and the desire to desist from offending and to deal with their drug and drink issues and mental health problems. As the authors point out, studies of what works and of desistance have mostly focused on male offenders and what works for men may not work for women. Women's centres provide a range of services and support on issues including substance abuse and domestic violence and their scope could be expanded further to incorporate assistance with improving work and training skills.

The response to the Corston Report

The Labour Government accepted most of the recommendations in the Corston Report. It published a favourable response (Ministry of Justice 2007b) and set up an Inter-Ministerial Group to further the proposals. It said that its strategy would be to develop community-based services and particularly women's community centres, for women who do not need to be in custody. For those who do need a secure setting, better ways of dealing with these women would be explored. The Government accepted that custody for women should be reserved for serious and violent offenders, that community punishment should normally be used for non-violent female offenders, and that community provision should be appropriate to women's needs. But it did not accept the recommendation that women should not be remanded in custody if they were unlikely to receive a custodial sentence at trial. It also made clear that no additional resources would be made available to implement these proposals, which will affect whether these changes are introduced and how rapidly.

Progress since 2000

At a policy level, there has been considerable progress on the issue of women prisoners. There have been improvements in the management of women prisoners over the past decade with increasing recognition of their specific needs. Gender-specific standards for women in prison were introduced in 2008 and policies are assessed for their impact for gender equality. Offending behaviour programmes have been designed specifically for women. There have also been improvements in temporary release and in healthcare, for example, improved therapeutic provisions and better training for staff in mother and baby units. Provision for counselling for drug users is now in operation in all prisons and there are also intensive drug treatment programmes. New offending behaviour programmes for women have also been developed and more research is being undertaken on 'what works' for women (see Sheehan *et al.* 2007, 2010). Young women aged 15–16 have now been removed from prison accommodation and foreign-national prisoners have been allocated to specific prisons so appropriate resources can be provided for them. There have also been improvements in the provision of mental health facilities for women in the community and in prison. But prison reformers have been disappointed at the slow pace of reform in response to the Corston Report despite the acceptance of the Government of its recommendations.[6] The problem was that the policy initiatives from the Labour Government were 'too little too late' as Hedderman notes, were overtaken by changes in the criminal justice system and were not matched by sufficient funding (Hedderman 2010: 495). The expansion of community options in the 2003 Act had the effect of net widening, so women were given community sentences for less serious offences and also ran the risk of a custodial sentence for breaches. Women prisoners may still be held far from home because of the small size of the estate and there has been little progress towards smaller custodial units.

The progress made since the Corston Report was reviewed by the All Party Parliamentary Group on Women (APPGW) chaired by Baroness Corston which reported in 2011 (APPGW 2011). It drew attention to a number of changes: a new gender awareness course has been provided for staff working with women in prison; a Gender Equality Scheme has been published; and a cross-department women's unit to manage the changes recommended by Corston has been created. Conditional caution pilots have been set up to develop opportunities to divert low level female offenders if they accept a caution conditional on attendance at a women's centre. There is also now a national service framework for female offenders and gender specific standards are applied to prisons. Routine full body searching of women on reception to prison is not now undertaken unless there are grounds to justify a search. The outgoing Labour Government did allocate additional funds to develop services for women in the community, to develop alternatives to custody, and for supporting women on release into the community. But as the APPGW Report notes, we still find a higher percentage of women than men in prison for non-violent offences, and the number of women in prison has increased since 2010 with an increase in the numbers on remand.

The incoming Minister for Prisons, Crispin Blunt, has acknowledged the limitations of short sentences for both women and men (*Hansard*, 20 July 2010, col. 163). *Breaking the Cycle* also refers to the development of diversionary strategies for offenders with mental health problems which may benefit women and proposes extending some of the advances

[6] See Hansard, 31 January 2008, col. 796–825.

in the treatment of female offenders to the male prison estate (Ministry of Justice 2010a). But while the Coalition Government is strongly committed to more involvement of the voluntary sector, many of the groups currently engaged in supporting women prisoners and their families find it hard to obtain funding to support their work.

Meeting the aims of women's imprisonment

In reviewing women's imprisonment we should not lose sight of the aims of imprisonment discussed in Part A of this book. From the retributivist standpoint we should ask whether women's imprisonment in current conditions is proportionate and non-degrading. If imprisonment entails the loss of one's home and loss of contact with children as well as loss of liberty, it is arguably disproportionate and hard to justify on retributivist grounds. The loss of privacy, the use of male prison officers, and the indignities of imprisonment such as strip-searching, as we have seen, may add to the humiliation and degradation of punishment well beyond the actual loss of liberty demanded by retributivism. Given that large numbers of women entering prison have suffered physical and sexual abuse, the use of full body searching—albect now restricted—is still of concern.

It is also hard to justify the increased use of imprisonment on grounds of incapacitation or social protection, given the fact that the majority of women are not dangerous and serve short sentences and so could be incapacitated in the community by electronic monitoring and curfews. Whether prison does constitute a deterrent has been open to debate as we saw in Chapter 4.

Rethinking women's imprisonment and transferring women to community centres, for example, would also allow more prison places to be available for men's prisons and thereby reduce overcrowding. It would also cut the costs of imprisonment which are substantial, particularly when the ancillary costs of support to women's families are added to the calculation. There would also be longer-term benefits if supporting families prevented children being taken into care which, as we have seen, strongly correlates with future offending. The impact on children is now receiving more attention as we saw in Chapter 10. Providing more family-friendly opportunities to undertake community sentences within school hours and making better arrangements for paying fines would be appropriate steps in this direction.

11.6 Black and minority ethnic prisoners

The outcome of the processes discussed in Chapter 10 is that ethnic minorities are over-represented in the prison population, relative to their proportions in the population as a whole. Ethnic monitoring of the prison population began in 1984 and since then the number of ethnic minority prisoners has steadily increased, the rate of increase being faster for black and South Asian prisoners than white prisoners.

Between 2006 and 2009 the percentage of BME prisoners in the prison population fluctuated between 26 and 27 per cent. BME prisoners constituted 25 per cent of prison population in March 2011, compared to 27 per cent in April 2009 (Ministry of Justice 2011g: 30). On 30 June 2010 just under 26 per cent of the prison population, 21,878 prisoners, were from black and minority ethnic backgrounds (Ministry of Justice 2011c: 66).

If we look at the prison population as a whole in 2010 the breakdown was: 72 per cent white; 13.7 per cent black; 7.1 per cent Asian; 3.5 per cent mixed; 1.4 per cent Chinese or other; 2.2 per cent unknown. BME prisoners constituted 20 per cent of British national prisoners, compared to 18 per cent in 2006, and 63 per cent of foreign-national prisoners, defined as non-UK passport holders, compared to 70 per cent in 2006 (ibid: 67). The composition of the British national prison population in 2010 was 78 per cent white, 11 per cent black, 5 per cent Asian, and 0.3 per cent Chinese or other. The mixed ethnicity group was between 3 and 4 per cent of the British national population (ibid: 71).

We considered in Chapter 10 the problems of construing issues in terms of difference or equality and the problems of essentialism. Similar problems arise in relation to ethnic minorities as they include a wide range of groups with different issues, needs and problems, and also include white minority groups, for example, East Europeans.

11.7 The experience of imprisonment

11.7.1 Less favourable treatment?

Of course the Prison Service has no part in sentencing decisions, so it cannot control the numbers entering prison, but it has a duty to ensure that minority ethnic prisoners do not receive less favourable treatment on grounds of race or ethnic origins and to ensure justice inside prisons. The Statement of Purpose of NOMS provides a commitment to incorporate equality and diversity in all its functions and combating unlawful discrimination has been an important element of prison governance. Yet it has been argued that black and minority ethnic groups in prison have different experiences of prison compared to white prisoners. Research in the 1980s highlighted issues in relation to the allocation of work, training, and education, the promotion of inmates to positions of responsibility, and in their treatment by officers. More recent work has focused on the experience of racial abuse and harassment and issues of safety and respect. A former Director General of the Prison Service acknowledged that the Prison Service is institutionally racist and has pockets of blatant racism (HM Prison Service 2004: Appendix 5, 15). This also features in prisoners' reports of their experiences in prison (see HM Inspectorate of Prisons 2005; section 11.9.2). These issues also affect ethnic minority staff and ethnic minorities are under-represented in prison staff and on Independent Monitoring Boards.

Research on racism in prisons was undertaken in the 1980s by Genders and Player (1989) as well as by Chigwada (1989) and McDermott (1990), and in the 1990s by Fitzgerald and Marshall (1996). However, the Woolf Report said virtually nothing on racism, and referred only to the erratic compliance of establishments with the race relations policy, the need for more progress, and the failure of some prisons to monitor race relations properly. Since 2000 there have been substantial investigations by NACRO (2000a, 2003f), the former Commission for Racial Equality (2003), the Prison Inspectorate (HM Inspectorate of Prisons 2005, 2006, 2009; HM Chief Inspector of Prisons 2010b), Cheliotis and Liebling (2005), the Prison Reform Trust (2006), the Mubarek Inquiry (Keith 2006), and NOMS (2008), all of which have highlighted continuing areas of concern and made recommendations for improvement. We also now have annual reports from the Ministry of Justice detailing progress made on equality issues (see Ministry of Justice 2011g).

Racism may be direct and overt, expressed in attitudes and behaviour. Areas of discretion within the administration of the prison regime allow more opportunity for racism to be activated expressly in decisions by officers. Racism may also be indirect, in failing to take account of the social context of factors which may be relevant to offenders' behaviour in prison, and overlooking the disparate effect of apparently neutral policies. It may be institutionalised in the sense that it is embedded in the culture and practices and policies of institutions and agencies. As we shall see, direct racism may be easier to challenge than more subtle and covert, or institutional racism.

11.7.2 **Work, training, and discipline**

One of the first major studies of racism and prisons was conducted by Genders and Player (1989) who interviewed staff and prisoners and observed prison life. They found prison officers using negative racial stereotypes and expressing critical comments about race relations policies whilst the majority of ethnic-minority prisoners interviewed thought that there was a problem of racism in prison, even if they had not experienced problems themselves. The allocation of work is an area where discretion may be exercised by supervisors and the researchers highlighted various practices used by work supervisors to circumvent formal procedures and to exercise discretion and concluded that 'racial discrimination is intrinsic to the social organisation of prisons' (Genders and Player 1989: 131). For example, they found differential treatment in the allocation of work in the prison, based on racial stereotypes. White prisoners were more likely to be found in the better jobs while ethnic minorities were over-represented in the least popular jobs and more likely to be unemployed. Their research suggested a use of stereotypes, with black prisoners seen by officers as unsuitable for education and training because of a negative attitude to authority and to work.

Genders and Player (ibid) also found differences in assessment reports on those prisoners reported for disciplinary offences. They found evidence of some prison officers demonstrating high-level racist assumptions. A common assumption among white officers was that black prisoners were lazy, arrogant, hostile, and paranoid about racism, while Asian prisoners were seen as well-behaved and submissive. Genders and Player found that officers were more likely to take disciplinary action against black prisoners and that they saw black prisoners as harder to manage because they were hostile to authority. They concluded that racist attitudes were part of the occupational culture of officers, reflecting their isolation and the dangerousness of the occupation, which makes such occupations vulnerable to stereotyping. Other researchers at that time found similar problems. Chigwada (1989) interviewed black women in prison who believed that they were treated differently on account of their race in relation to the allocation of work and access to education, where priority was given to white women, and who thought that they were more likely to have their privileges withdrawn for minor matters. There was also an assumption amongst officers that black women needed more supervision, because they were trouble makers and harder to control, which had implications for their treatment.

McDermott (1990), in a study of five male adult prisons in the period 1985–9, found that black prisoners in her sample were more likely to be the subject of disciplinary charges and disciplined for the vaguer offences of disobeying orders or being disrespectful. They believed racism was a significant factor in these decisions. The perception of some officers was that black prisoners are anti-authority and disruptive.

Subsequent research undertaken by NACRO (2000a), found that black prisoners were the least satisfied regarding access to work, compared to Asian and white prisoners, but were happier than white prisoners over access to education. Black prisoners also complained that black visitors were more likely to be searched than others. A study of prisoners' perceptions of race relations in prison was also conducted by Cheliotis and Liebling (2005), using surveys of 4,860 prisoners in 49 establishments in England and Wales, and found that large proportions of the ethnic minority groups thought they were subject to unfair treatment compared to the white majority. Research by Clements of HMP Brixton also found that punishment was used disproportionately against black prisoners (Clements 2000).

Since the late 1980s, the level of awareness on the part of the prison management of the problem of racism in prison has increased with various race relations policies being formulated (see section 11.8). The ruling in the case of *Alexander v Home Office* (1988) was circulated in all prisons and the case discussed in training. The court found that Alexander had been unlawfully discriminated against when he applied for work in the prison kitchen at Parkhurst and that he was refused work on racist grounds. The decision to allocate work was based on a report containing negative and racist comments. This was the first successful reported case brought by a prisoner under the Race Relations Act 1976.

Today there is more scope to bring an action as a case can now be brought under the Human Rights Act 1998 (see Chapter 9, section 9.6.3) and, as noted earlier, the Race Relations (Amendment) Act 2000 imposed a statutory duty on prisons to promote race equality. The Equality Act 2010, has strengthened the equality duty and broadened the range of protected characteristics and means that prisons must be more pro-active in addressing equality issues (see section 11.1.2). It is also clear in Prison Service Orders and Instructions that allocation to accommodation, work, training, and education must be made on a non-discriminatory basis and all policies must be assessed for their equality implications (see PSI 32/2011).

A major review of race relations in prison was conducted by the Prison Inspectorate in 2005 using a review of survey material from 5,500 prisoners in 18 prisons (HM Inspectorate of Prisons 2005). The survey covered all ethnic groups and used consultations with white and visible-minority staff, governors, managers and prisoners, including black, Asian and mixed-race prisoners, women, young offenders and juveniles and foreign-national prisoners. The Review found that, instead of a shared understanding of race issues within prisons, there was a series of 'parallel worlds' with different groups of staff and prisoners having quite different views and experiences. Prisoners were asked about their direct experiences of racism. Visible-minority prisoners were more negative than white prisoners across the four key areas of safety, respect, purposeful activity, and resettlement. Most thought that racism existed, particularly in relation to differential access to the prison regime and treatment by staff, for example the way in which they were spoken to or searched, the way requests were dealt with, or how long they waited for things that they needed. However, young black prisoners were more positive than adult black prisoners. Moreover in one area of prison life—education and training—black and Asian prisoners were more likely than white prisoners to value education.

A later report in 2008 found prisoners continuing to refer to covert racism in the form of 'favouritism' and 'subtle prejudice' (HM Chief Inspector of Prisons 2008: 27). The NOMS *Race Review* in 2008 also reported that black prisoners reported that they felt that they were less likely to get the better quality jobs within the prison (NOMS 2008). The focus in this Review was on more subtle forms of discrimination, unconscious bias, and the exercise of discretion. Completion of Offending Behaviour Programmes was also lower than average in 2010–11 for Asian and black prisoners (Ministry of Justice 2011g). However the Prison Inspectorate suggested that BME prisoners were more likely to take part in training and education (HM Chief Inspector of Prisons 2010a).

11.7.3 **Racial harassment**

A further problem highlighted in several studies is the problem of racial harassment by both staff and other prisoners. If a prisoner wants to complain about racism, he or she can use the ordinary complaints procedure, the special local incident form, or can complain directly to the Equality and Human Rights Commission who can advise and support complainants. In addition, the prisoner can also complain to the Ombudsman. The definition of a racist incident is 'any incident which is perceived to be racist by the victim or any other person', as used in the Macpherson Report (Macpherson 1999). However, despite the formal procedures available, prisoners may be reluctant to complain for fear of being seen as trouble-makers or of causing trouble for themselves, or because they do not believe that their complaint will be taken seriously (see NACRO 2000a; HM Inspector of Prisons 2005; Keith 2006).

Clements' (2000) study of Brixton Prison in 2000 found evidence of racial harassment, abuse and racist language. In other prisons, minority ethnic prisoners have been the target of racist abuse and violence and there are some indications that these incidents of harassment have been under-reported, because of concerns that they will not be taken seriously. Racist abuse in Wormwood Scrubs was the subject of a report in 1999 and the CRE has investigated racism at Brixton, Parc, and Feltham. It conducted a full investigation into racism in the Prison Service, with reference to the need to eliminate unlawful racial discrimination and to promote equality of opportunity. The CRE examined the nature and frequency of incidents of racial discrimination, the way they are investigated and the circumstances leading to the murder of Zahid Mubarek (discussed in section 11.7.4). It examined events between mid-1991 and July 2000 in Brixton Prison, between 1998 and July 2000 in Parc Prison, and between January 1996 and November 2000 in Feltham Young Offenders Institution, in the light of reports and evidence suggesting acts of discrimination. The CRE was very critical of the Prison Service's failure to protect Mubarek and its failure to eliminate discrimination.

The CRE found the Prison Service guilty of racial discrimination at Feltham, Parc, and Brixton (Commission for Racial Equality 2003). The Report made 17 findings of unlawful racial discrimination against the Prison Service, most of which related to individual cases. Issues raised included the treatment of staff and prisoners, access to goods, services, and facilities; control of the use of discretion, disciplinary matters, and the Incentives and Earned Privileges Scheme; access to work; investigation of complaints; protection from victimisation; and management procedures. Although it had the power to issue a non-discrimination notice, instead the CRE entered into a dialogue with the Prison Service to develop an Action Plan, *Implementing Race Equality: A Shared Strategy for Change,* to deal with these problems (see section 11.8; HM Prison Service/CRE 2003). It also published a review of race relations in prison in December 2005. The CRE has now been replaced by the Equality and Human Rights Commission.

A new Prison Service Order on Race Equality (PSO 2800) was issued in 2006 to further the pursuit of race equality and to implement the race equality duty and in April 2011, it was replaced by PSI 32/2011 *Ensuring Equality* which sets out the framework for dealing with equalities issues, including harassment.

The Prison Rules include disciplinary offences of racially aggravated assault and racially aggravated damage to or destruction of any part of prison or other property, and insulting behaviour. These are directed at the behaviour of prisoners rather than staff or visitors. Racially aggravated and racist offences include assault, damage or destruction of property, threatening, abusive or insulting racist words or behaviour, and displaying any threatening, abusive, or insulting racist material. If an offence is racially aggravated, this will be reflected in increased punishment. It will be deemed to be racially aggravated if the offender expresses to the victim hostility based on the victim's membership of a racial group or is motivated by such hostility.

In addition a violence reduction strategy has been introduced by the Prison Service with all individual prisons now obliged to develop a local strategy to reduce violence and create a culture of non-violence amongst prisoners (PS0 2750). All prisons must also have, as well as an anti-bullying strategy, procedures to deal with bullying when perpetrators have been identified, although the issue in the Mubarek case was the failure to identify the risk.

Victimisation, racism, and harassment are problems which affect ethnic minority officers as well as prisoners. Because of their numbers, they may feel isolated and may be more likely to suffer victimisation and harassment (McDermott 1990). Some black staff in McDermott's sample found that the other white officers caused them more problems than the prisoners, and they found it difficult if white staff made racist comments to prisoners in front of them, making them feel both visible and invisible. A lukewarm approach to dealing with racist incidents gives a message that black officers have to learn to deal with racism rather than expecting the authorities to eliminate racism.

A support network, RESPECT, was set up in 2001 to improve the working conditions of black and minority ethnic staff and to support staff who have been victims of racism. The Prison Reform Trust (2006) surveyed and interviewed members of RESPECT in 2004–6 and found that 61 per cent of the staff interviewed believed that they had experienced racial discrimination including isolation, harassment, and verbal abuse, and had suffered this mostly from their colleagues rather than from prisoners or managers. Their respondents reported that they thought that blatant overt racism was becoming less common, but covert racism and institutional racism were more serious problems. Two-thirds of the BME staff in the PRT survey thought that institutional racism remained a problem, particularly in relation to career development and promotion and grievance procedures, with promotion hindered by subtle discrimination. There was also a lack of confidence among BME staff in procedures for dealing with complaints about racism: covert racism may be harder to prove and investigators are likely to be senior white officers. A less formal and less legalistic procedure, such as mediation, may be more effective especially as this would mean complainants take a more active role in proceedings. This study also highlighted the problem with lack of adequate training in diversity and cultural racism. Interviews with a sample of 71 prisoners undertaken by the Prison Reform Trust found that 41 prisoners had experienced racism within the previous six months, but two-thirds had not made a complaint over the incident (Edgar 2010).

11.7.4 **Deaths in custody**

Clearly a major issue of concern is where murders are committed by prisoners and there is evidence of a racist motive. Zahid Mubarek was murdered in Feltham Young Offenders Institution in March 2000. While sleeping he was clubbed into a coma by his cellmate, Robert Stewart, using part of the furniture in his cell, and died later in hospital. Prior to the murder Stewart had written racist letters and threatened to kill his cellmate. It was clear that Stewart had a personality disorder and deeply entrenched racist beliefs and had already been charged, under the Protection from Harassment Act 1997, with racially motivated malicious communications. The conditions in Feltham had also been criticised by the then Chief Inspector of Prisons, David Ramsbotham. In a similar incident, Shahid Aziz, was murdered by his white cellmate, Peter McCann, in HMP Leeds in 2004. McCann had been classified as low risk, but the inquest was critical of the failure to pass on relevant information to the prison.

Deaths in custody have also occurred following the use of excessive physical restraints, such as the Alton Manning case referred to earlier (Chapter 9, section 9.5.1).[7] There have also been cases of deaths arising from inadequate medical treatment or failure to recognise or diagnose a medical condition. Deaths in custody now fall within the remit of the

[7] See *R v DPP ex p Manning* (2001).

Prisons and Probation Ombudsman and as we saw in Chapter 9, Article 2 claims have been successfully brought against the UK which have led to changes in the way reviews are handled.

The Formal Investigation of the Commission for Racial Equality into the murder of Zahid Mubarek was highly critical of failures on the part of the prison management to spot the potential risk and to protect Mubarek from Stewart, or to follow up warnings in Stewart's file, as well as failures to follow Prison Service Orders and failures by senior managers to give priority to race issues (Commission for Racial Equality 2003). It found 20 areas of failure which, it argued, allowed Stewart to progress to murder; if any of them had been dealt with, it would have prevented Mubarek's death. A public inquiry, chaired by Mr Justice Keith, was set up to examine the measures which needed to be taken to prevent the recurrence of such a tragedy and its Report was published in 2006 (Keith 2006). It focused attention on the wider culture and practice of the Prison Service, just as the Macpherson Inquiry highlighted problems within the police.

In its submission to the second phase of the Mubarek Inquiry, the CRE reviewed the progress of the Prison Service in achieving the goals in the Action Plan. A Race and Equalities Action Group in the Prison Service was set up to oversee the implementation of the Action Plan and to ensure proactive promotion of race equality, and to take account of any possibility of discrimination in those policies. Areas for immediate attention were identified and incorporated into the Prison Service Race Equality Scheme.

The Prison Service has developed procedures for carrying out race equality impact assessments and introduced performance targets for race equality including staff recruitment. There are also training schemes for staff carrying out impact assessments, and a new system of consultation with prisoners, staff, and local communities on race equality issues.

The CRE acknowledged the efforts being made to address the problems highlighted by the death of Zahid Mubarek but found that there was still evidence of poor practice. So while the formal policies to promote race equality and challenge racism were certainly evident, they were not always being implemented (Commission for Racial Equality 2005). For example, it expressed concern about the procedures for complaints and reporting of racist incidents and noted that prisoners said they felt inhibited in making complaints because their reports were read by officers and a study by the Prison Inspectorate (2005) found this was still the case.

11.7.5 **The Report of the Mubarek Inquiry**

The Mubarek Report was published in June 2006 and reflected similar concerns to the CRE Report (Keith 2006). Although it focused on Feltham, where the murder occurred, many of the issues raised apply across the prison estate. The Inquiry investigated whether the events which led to Stewart and Mubarek sharing a cell, despite what was affected about Stewart, were attributable to a collective organisational failure which was informed by institutional racism at Feltham. The two major issues raised were the problems with enforced cell sharing and the failure to pass on information which might have prevented the attack. The Report argued for an end to enforced cell sharing to reduce the risk of prisoner-on-prisoner attacks, that a date should be set for achieving this goal, and extra funds provided from the government for this purpose. Single cells would prevent tensions escalating between prisoners as well as increasing privacy. While sharing might be desirable, for example, where there is a risk of suicide or self-harm, in most cases it should be avoided. There should also be published guidelines for officers to use in allocating prisoners to shared cells and for dealing with requests to share with particular individuals, and prisoners should be interviewed to explain any preferences for the type of prisoner with whom they would prefer to share. Moreover, the suitability of particular prisoners for sharing should be reviewed regularly in consultation with the prisoners' personal officers.

The other major issue in the failure to prevent the attack was the failure to pass on information about Stewart to Feltham, and to circulate information within Feltham, particularly about his racism, his possible involvement in a murder at another YOI, and his disruptive behaviour in other institutions. The Report recommended the importance of storing information on risk assessment on the national database for offenders in order to quickly identify prisoners who may constitute a risk to others because of their racist views or other issues. Risk assessments of prisoners should be reviewed regularly.

The emphasis in the Report was on closer scrutiny and assessment of all prisoners, using OASys. Mr Justice Keith recommended a review of training to improve and develop interpersonal skills and a review of cell-searching policy to increase the chance of finding concealed weapons in cells as it was clear that in Feltham full cell searches were not taking place on the unit. The Report also found that the care of prisoners suffering from mental health problems at the time of Mubarek's murder was poor (see Chapter 7). Diversity training for officers should also emphasise the need for staff to put themselves in the position of black and minority ethnic prisoners and give them techniques to do so. The Report also argued for the involvement of external specialists in equality and diversity in the race relations work in the prison and stressed the need for an independent element in dealing with complaints of racism.

What emerges clearly from the Report is that attacks on prisoners in their cells by other prisoners are more likely to happen in prisons which are not functioning well and the concern is, as he points out, that 'population pressures and understaffing can combine to undermine the decency agenda and compromise the Prison Service's ability to run prisons efficiently' (Keith 2006: para 63.7). These concerns are even more relevant now as the pressures on the population have further increased since 2006.

The Labour Government accepted many of the recommendations in the Mubarek Report in full or in part and they were incorporated within the Race Equality Action Plan. By the time the Report was published, many of the issues had already begun to be addressed, for example issues relating to the flow of information, and the broader issues of race equality have been moved forward by the Race Equality Plan. The Government accepted in principle that enforced cell sharing should end but has said that it will continue for some time due to population pressures and that diverting resources to this objective would have an adverse effects on other efforts to improve prison standards. Since 2006, of course, the problem of cell sharing has persisted with the prison population reaching record levels. The Government also acknowledged the need for an independent element in the investigation of complaints of racism and that Race Relations Liaison Officers (RRLOs) should be recruited from outside as well as within the Prison Service and external appointments have already been made in some prisons.

11.7.6 **Foreign-national prisoners**

As well as considering the experience of women and ethnic-minority prisoners, we also need to consider the position of foreign-national prisoners. The percentage of foreign-national prisoners in the prison population as a whole has increased from 7.8 per cent in 1993 to 14 per cent in 2007 and has fluctuated between 12 and 14 per cent over the past few years. On 30 September 2011 there were 11,076 foreign-national prisoners, which constituted at that time 13 per cent of the prison population (Ministry of Justice 2011o).

46 per cent of foreign-national women prisoners and 25 per cent of foreign-national male prisoners are serving sentences for drugs offences which attract longer sentences, even for first convictions.

The composition of the foreign-national prison population in 2010 was as follows: white 33 per cent, black 18 per cent, Asian 18 per cent and Chinese or other 9 per cent (Ministry of Justice 2011c: 71). The mixed ethnicity group made up between 3 and 4 per cent of the foreign-national population. Foreign-national prisoners come from over 156 countries but over half come from 10 countries, namely Jamaica, the Republic of Ireland, Poland, Nigeria, Romania, Vietnam, Pakistan, Lithuania, Somalia, and India (Ministry of Justice Offender Management Statistics 2011o). There has been a large increase in the number of foreign-national female prisoners from Eastern Europe and Vietnam.

The increase in the number of foreign-national prisoners is not confined to the UK, but is found throughout Western Europe, where there are increasing numbers of foreign-national prisoners sentenced for migration-related and drug-trafficking crimes (Easton 2011a). The reasons for the increase in foreign-national prisoners and the implications are considered by Banks (2011) who refers to the rise in the number of foreign-nationals receiving immediate custody and being held on remand as well as the disproportionate number convicted for drug offences, particularly within the female prison population. Changes in immigration policy, he argues, have also resulted in an increase in the numbers charged with immigration offences and fraud and forgery offences linked to attempts to enter or remain in the UK. Convicted prisoners who have ended their sentences may be held in prison rather than immigration detention centres, while they await deportation or decisions on asylum or their immigration status, with limited access to telephones and lawyers. Prison transfer agreements will be used for EU prisoners so that they can if possible serve their sentence in their country of origin. Where this is not possible prisoners will be deported on completion of their sentence.

The policy now is to concentrate foreign-national prisoners in particular prisons, principally Bullwood Hall, Canterbury, and Downview but foreign nationals also make up a large proportion of prisoners in Holloway. This is intended to provide better services by concentrating them in fewer prisons but it makes it harder to vary security levels for this group. Foreign-national prisoners can and have been allocated to Category D and sent to an open prison, but the fear of them absconding if likely to be deported will affect their allocation; however the decision should be based on individual risk, not simply on the fact that the person is a foreign national.

A thematic review of foreign-national prisoners was undertaken by the Prison Inspectorate in 2006, focusing on prisons outside London (HM Inspectorate of Prisons 2006). At the time of their research there were approximately 10,000 foreign-national prisoners, 13 per cent of the prison population as a whole, drawn from 172 different countries, but with Jamaicans and Nigerians constituting the largest groups. They found that foreign-national prisoners' key concerns related to family matters, particularly maintaining family links, language problems, and immigration issues. Although the staff they interviewed also recognised that these were problems they did not consider them as serious as the prisoners did, and they were unsure how to respond to the problems. Those prisoners who did not speak English experienced the greatest problems in access to resources. Language problems were a particular issue for prisoners from Vietnam, China, the Middle East, and Eastern Europe, while family and immigration problems were a particular issue for women prisoners. The problems often overlapped as prisoners dealing with immigration issues may lack the language skills to obtain the necessary information from appropriate sources or to use resources within the prison.

Foreign-national prisoners also experienced racism, negative stereotyping and disrespectful treatment, and resettlement problems, and had less contact with personal officers. Negative perceptions of women offenders as negligent mothers may be focused on foreign-national women who have left their children behind to carry drugs. Foreign-national prisoners receive fewer visits than other prisoners. Black and minority ethnic foreign-national prisoners reported worse experiences than white foreign-national prisoners, particularly in relation to racism and religious observance. All staff interviewed wanted more training and guidance on foreign national issues.

The Review also found low awareness of available services, for example interpreters, outside agencies, or FNP (foreign national prisoner) co-ordinators. Although Hibiscus and the Citizens Advice Bureau gave some general information to prisoners, there was insufficient independent specialist advice on individuals' immigration problems. Despite a revised PSO intended to improve liaison between the immigration authorities and the Prison Service, there was still a marked lack of co-ordination between them, which meant that some prisoners were still in prison after completing their sentence, also exacerbating overcrowding. In June 2010 over 500 foreign-national prisoners were being detained in prison at the end of their sentence under immigration powers.

There was also considerable confusion and ignorance among staff on how to support or inform prisoners awaiting deportation. There was also very little contact with home countries on resettlement issues, despite the current emphasis on end-to-end offender management. However, they did find examples of good practice in some prisons, for example the support given by the pressure group Hibiscus, part of the Female Prisoners' Welfare Project, which helps prisoners in the UK and liaises with contacts overseas, but there was no consistency or co-ordination between the Prison Service and other agencies. Resettlement support tends to focus on UK resettlement but there is little support for those being deported.

The Review therefore strongly recommended that NOMS and the Prison Service introduce national standards for treatment of foreign-national prisoners, and a national strategy and policy for their treatment and support, which prioritises the issues of family contact, immigration, and language. It argues that foreign-national strategies should be embedded within a wider diversity strategy and diversity training should include awareness of the needs of and attitudes towards foreign-national prisoners. Although they may share common problems, they are also a diverse group with important differences within the group. The Review advocated better links with the Immigration Service and better support inside prison and on departure from prison to enable speedier decision making. Each prison should have a named immigration officer to whom inquiries could be directed. In addition, prisoners could be given more practical support to maintain contact with their families.

While the larger minorities may be better provided for, there are problems for the smaller ethnic minorities. Foreign-national prisoners are not a homogeneous group as they include a diverse range of groups, including white ethnic minorities. However, they may share common problems, including family problems, immigration problems, and language problems. There are particular concerns over access to translation facilities. Insufficient information in their own language and difficulty in speaking English may affect access to work and participation in offending behaviour programmes which will also have implications for parole, and for resettlement programmes. It may also lead to problems in accessing lawyers or understanding the English legal system, or negotiating the immigration rules and procedures.

The Prison Service does provide information in 27 languages but this does not extend to minority languages within the foreign-national population. A foreign national prisoners' booklet is given to prisoners at induction. Foreign nationals may be isolated by language problems, they may also have problems arranging legal representation, and difficulties contacting home. When prison resources are stretched because of the increasing demands for prison places, their needs may be less likely to be addressed.

Foreign-national women constitute a large proportion of women prisoners in the UK, 18 per cent of the female prison population in 2010 (Ministry of Justice 2010c: 53). They experience real problems of isolation and of providing for their families. As well as difficulty in obtaining information in their own language about visiting rights, they may also have problems with the prison diet. Many of the problems faced by women prisoners, such as separation from their families, are exacerbated for foreign-national prisoners, especially for those serving long sentences, who find it difficult to keep in contact with their families and, if they do, have to deal with family problems from a distance by phone (Caddle and Crisp 1997; HM Inspectorate of Prisons 2006, HM Chief Inspector of Prisons 2011a). Many suffer from mental and physical health problems, especially as some foreign-national prisoners have experienced abuse and torture abroad, and these problems may be exacerbated by their isolation.

The issue of foreign-national prisoners has moved up the political agenda and there have been some recent changes including prison transfer agreements and some financial assistance for prisoners liable to deportation and a new scheme to deport prisoners earlier, subject to risk assessments, has been implemented. But the Prison Inspectorate found that often the best services were in smaller prisons. There were still instances of people being detained beyond their sentence and still insufficient courses on English for speakers of other languages to meet the demand. Language difficulties remains a problem particularly in relation to access to information on prison regimes and to adjudication and may also limit access to work within the prison (HM Chief Inspector of Prisons 2011a). The Prison Inspectorate found that there was insufficient provision for the needs of foreign-national prisoners at Drake Hall even though this was a centre for such prisoners (ibid). Foreign-national prisoners are more likely to report feeling unsafe. However, the number of self-inflicted deaths among foreign-national prisoners has fallen. In 2010–11 there were three compared to 23 in 2007 (Prisons and Probation Ombusdman 2011: 45).

The Coalition Government has said it will consider whether foreign-national prisoners could be removed initially instead of serving sentences in the UK and whether conditional cautions can be used to divert offenders on condition that they leave the UK, and a pilot study of this will be conducted (Ministry of Justice 2010a).

11.8 Race relations policies in the Prison Service

As we have seen, a number of problems facing black and minority ethnic prisoners and staff have been identified. Various measures designed to address some of these issues have been introduced. The Prison Service was one of the first criminal justice bodies to collect data on ethnic minorities and the first to develop a race relations policy. It was also the first public sector organisation to impose a ban on staff affiliated with known racist groups, and operates a strict policy of intolerance and dismissal for unacceptable behaviour.

The Home Office instituted a review of prison race relations work in 1981, then issued to all establishments a Circular on Race Relations which said race relations problems were rare, but this was an area of sensitivity. It gave advice on race relations work, emphasising the need to obtain more information on ethnic minorities and the importance of equal treatment. Governors were required to appoint RRLOs to provide and collect information.

A *Race Relations Manual* for the Prison Service was first published in 1991 and subsequently amended. The Manual published more detailed guidance and policies on matters including responsibility for implementing the race relations policy, measuring progress, and training. Pocket books were issued to all staff. Research carried out by the CRE and Prison Service in 1995 led to a revised Prison Service Order on race relations and a new Manual in 1997. An Advisory Group on Race was set up and met outside bodies such as the CRE and NACRO and, following their advice, strengthened the role of RRLOs and Race Relations Management Teams (RRMTs).

Research undertaken by NACRO in the late 1990s found that, although there was a commitment to race equality on the part of the Director General of the Prison Service, there was still a long way to go and a continuing perception of unfairness. Prisoners and staff in a variety of public and private prisons, including young offender institutions, were interviewed and the sample also included remand and women prisoners, white and ethnic-minority staff and prisoners. Respondents were asked how their interviewees saw race relations in prison in 1998 and 1999, following the new Race Relations Instruction to Governors from the Prison Service (NACRO 2000a). Staff were aware of the new Race Relations Instruction and white staff were more aware than black staff. Some staff were critical of 'too much political correctness' but the majority of those who had received race relations training had found it useful. The majority were in favour of ethnic monitoring, although critical of the amount of paperwork involved. Of the prisoners interviewed, about three-quarters knew that there was a Race Relations Policy, but fewer knew what the policy covered.

A higher proportion of minority ethnic prisoners thought that relations with staff were poor. Prisoners from minority ethnic groups were less likely to assess race relations as good and more likely to assess them as poor. Respondents did not think that having more black officers would help. The researchers found that verbal and racial abuse were still common, and there were still incidents of physical abuse from other prisoners, but few reported these incidents because they thought that there was no point, nothing would be done and it would just cause more trouble. The NACRO research found that racist incidents between prisoners and staff were still occurring. They found that black prisoners felt isolated if held in a prison with mostly white prisoners, especially if situated in a white rural area, and would therefore benefit from community prisons located in or near large towns. Few prisoners in the survey had contact with community groups outside.

To sum up their findings, although the Race Relations Policy had a high profile in the Prison Service, it was not working well at a day-to-day level, the policy was not fully understood, and the training was not equipping staff to deal fairly with colleagues or prisoners. The RRLOs were still overworked. Many staff were happy to leave it to the RRLOs and not to take responsibility themselves for providing regimes which do not discriminate. A follow-up study (NACRO 2003f) found that, while there had been some progress, there was still a long way to go. Later research by Spencer *et al.* (2009) who interviewed officers in four prisons in 2006 found that the respondents did take race relations work seriously but felt there was too much emphasis on statistics and insufficient time for the RRLOs to undertake their work and it was also difficult to engage the attendance of external community groups in RRMT meetings.

Other measures introduced to combat racism include RESPOND (Racial Equality for Staff and Prisoners) which was launched in 1999, following the Macpherson Report, to confront racial harassment and discrimination, support ethnic-minority staff, and ensure equal opportunities for ethnic-minority prisoners. Targets to increase the recruitment of ethnic minorities, to review complaints procedures and improve equality training and to monitor racist complaints and incidents and to monitor the career progress of BME staff, have also been introduced. A Diversity and Equality Group was established to identify policies and standards to ensure that they address the specific problems identified by the CRE and to assess the impact of policies. The CRE Report highlighted the survival of racist attitudes despite two decades of progressive legislation. Despite a well-established Race Relations Policy operating throughout the Prison Service, there were still incidents of racist abuse and harassment and a failure to protect prisoners from such incidents (Commission for Racial Equality 2003). So while there was commitment to racial equality in the Prison Service, it was still very hard to control discriminatory behaviour at a micro-level.

Action was taken to implement the CRE recommendations. An Action Plan designed by the Prison Service with the CRE identified key areas of work and relevant time scales (HM Prison Service/CRE 2003). It was designed to ensure that policies are assessed for their impact on different groups. It included the following:

- a heavier weighting for race equality within the performance management system;
- revisions to the procedures for ethnic monitoring of prisoners to include a range of factors such as privilege levels, complaints, segregation, adjudication, and access to activities;
- revisions to the Racist Incident Reporting Form;
- increased ethnic monitoring of staff to include grievances, promotion, and leavers;
- a review of intervention strategies and treatment of racial complaints;
- a review of Race and Diversity training to ensure staff met the requirements of the Race Relations (Amendment) Act 2000 and that more information was provided to staff and prisoners;
- clarification of the role of RRMTs which would include prisoner representatives and representatives from external community groups.

A new Prison Service Order in 2006 made a number of changes, including replacing the Race Relation Liaison Officers with Race Equality Officers (REOs) and RRMTS with Race Equality Action Teams (REATS), providing more support to the REO and establishing a framework for a more pro-active approach.

The Action Plan ended in 2008 and its impact was reviewed by the *Race Review: Implementing Race Equality in Prisons—Five Years On* which included a survey of 900 prisoners (NOMS 2008). It reported progress had been made in a number of key areas, including training for Race Equality Action Team members. There were also improvements in monitoring, setting, and meeting race equality targets and greater involvement of outside bodies, and improvements in dealing with racist incidents and complaints. But despite these significant changes, it reported that problems still persisted, as black prisoners still believed that they had less access to good quality work and it was also clear that BME prisoners were more likely to be segregated for disciplinary reasons and to be subjected to disciplinary charges, areas where discretion is exercised by prison officers.

The focus has now shifted from an anti-racist strategy towards a more proactive role to promote diversity and the pursuit of equality is now integrated into prison management and falls under the general equality duty in the 2010 Equality Act.

Efforts have also been made to broaden the social composition of officers with a higher number of ethnic-minority officers. Increased recruitment of ethnic-minority staff is desirable on grounds of fairness, but it may also assist in the smooth running of the prison as it legitimises the authority of prison officers and reduces tensions. BME staff account for 6 per cent of staff in NOMS as a whole and 5.7 per cent on 31 March 2011 in the Prison Service (Ministry of Justice 2011c: 80). However the Prison Inspectorate has found that in some prisons, there are still too few staff from minority ethnic groups and a lack of cultural awareness (HM Inspectorate of Prisons 2011a).

Monitoring schemes were expanded to take account of the Race Relations (Amendment) Act 2000 and the Action Plan and to cover a wider range of protected characteristics. Another positive development was the establishment of a National Body of Black Prisoner Support Groups in 1998, which supports and promotes the development of support groups for BME offenders. Since the Race Equality Review published by NOMS in 2008, there has been greater emphasis on equality with the appointment of full-time REOs and more impact assessments being undertaken.

11.9 Challenging racism

11.9.1 Policy into practice

Several initiatives would help in promoting racial equality, including greater awareness and understanding on the part of staff of the impact of institutional discrimination and the differential impact of the criminal justice system on black and minority ethnic groups and greater awareness of the race relations policy and of the value of ethnic monitoring. Staff also need more information on making outside community contacts which would help prisoners during sentence and on release. Reporting of incidents should be encouraged and prisoners should be able to feel confident that they will be dealt with properly. Ethnic monitoring of adjudications is being undertaken to examine differences in the use of disciplinary procedures. Prisoners should also be involved in discussions on how to achieve equal access to prison facilities and how to reduce racial incidents. Prisoners are now included as diversity representatives which is a positive step.

While there has been a shift in policy towards greater awareness of the problems facing minority ethnic prisoners at a managerial level, the difficulty remains of how to ensure that ameliorative measures are applied in practice especially in view of the substantial increases in the prison population. The Mubarek case brought the issue of race equality to the forefront of penal policy again and race equality is given a high priority at the formal policy level. In its response to the Carter Review, the Labour Government stressed the need to 'eliminate any aspects within the correctional services which expose offenders to danger or discrimination. In particular racism will not be tolerated' (Home Office 2004b: 23). The promotion of equal opportunity and non-discrimination is also beneficial to the good order of the prison as racial conflict is a source of tension within prisons.

11.9.2 *Parallel Worlds*

Cheliotis and Liebling (2005) found that ethnic minority prisoners rated race relations more unfavourably than white prisoners. Interestingly female prisoners and adult prisoners were more likely than males or younger prisoners to rate the quality of race relations more favourably. Perceptions of race relations correlated with other key areas of treatment including fairness, respect, humanity, relationships with staff and safety. White prisoners had a more positive view of race relations than ethnic-minority prisoners. In fact membership of an ethnic group was the main determinant of the perceived quality of race relations.

A thematic study of BME prisoners by the Prison Inspectorate, *Parallel Worlds*, published in 2008, considered the views of staff and prisoners on race relations in prison and possible problems, and examined the effectiveness of monitoring and complaints procedures. It found a gap between formal policy initiatives and the experience of different groups of staff and prisoners (HM Chief Inspector of Prisons 2008). Governors and white RRLOs were the most optimistic regarding race relations, thinking that the regime was operating fairly while acknowledging that more needed to be done. But ethnic minority staff were less likely to think that their prison was tackling race relations effectively, although they accepted some progress had been made. There were references to overt and subtle racism from colleagues, and they also felt they had insufficient support from managers in applying for promotion. White staff, however, tended to see racism as an issue between prisoners rather than an issue for staff, and did not seem aware of the extent to which their visible minority colleagues had experienced discrimination. Some minority staff felt isolated and that they were being overlooked for promotion.

Black and minority ethnic prisoners felt they received worse treatment than white prisoners. Safety was the major concern for Asian prisoners, with between one-third and one-half saying they felt unsafe, particularly women and young adults. Asian prisoners were more likely to report bullying; black prisoners were more concerned than Asian prisoners about the lack of respect they felt in their treatment from staff, but felt safer than them. However, the 2008 report of the Chief Inspector of Prisons found similar results on both safety and respect for Asian and black prisoners (HM Chief Inspector of Prisons 2008: 27). Results were also analysed by religion and Muslim prisoners gave more negative responses than non-Muslim prisoners in terms of feeling unsafe and lack of respect.

In the *Parallel Worlds* study, both black and Asian prisoners were also less positive about healthcare and the reviewers found that providers of healthcare did not recognise specific needs of ethnic-minority communities, for example in relation to sickle cell anaemia. BME prisoners are also under-represented at the therapeutic prison, HMP Grendon. the reasons for which are considered by Sullivan (2007). The outcomes of complaints of racist incidents were also examined in *Parallel Worlds*. Most of the complaints related to prisoner-on-prisoner complaints. Although investigations were undertaken properly, it was difficult for RRLOs to follow through complaints against staff as it was hard to persuade staff to report colleagues. Complaints against staff were responded to less effectively than complaints against prisoners. So minorities lacked confidence in the complaints system. Complaints about prisoners were upheld more often than complaints against staff and the outcomes were more severe for prisoners than staff.

The Report found that 'race relations management teams were operating effectively in less than half of the fieldwork establishments visited' (HM Inspectorate of Prisons 2005: para 6.37). For example, meetings were irregular and poorly attended which suggests that race relations were not a key management priority. The Report also questioned whether the race equality duty was satisfied in contracted-out prisons. The Report was critical of the quality of ethnic monitoring which was often inaccurate and not sufficiently disaggregated to show variations between experiences of different minority groups. Also, about one quarter of governors were negative about the CRE Report and seemed unsure how to progress further in the pursuit of race equality.

However, the researchers found that the prisons with the best practice were those where race and diversity was given a high priority and received sufficient support from senior managers. Examples of good practice included the establishment of the 'Parva against Racism' movement at Glen Parva YOI, which involved workshops, sport and debates, the use of mediation to deal with complaints at Huntercombe, and contact with relevant outside bodies at Styal and Forest Bank.

The Report also questioned the adequacy of training in equipping managers, governors, and officers for their responsibilities in promoting race equality. At the time of the research, in-service race awareness training was no longer given and, instead, the very limited diversity training did not focus specifically on race. The Report argued that race relations training should be both mandatory and separate from diversity training.

Most complaints of racism were about other prisoners, followed by the discriminatory impact of decisions by staff. But many prisoners would not make a complaint because they thought it would not be taken seriously or were worried about repercussions. BME prisoners were less likely than non-BME prisoners to believe that complaints would be dealt with fairly and, of course, if they feel the response will be unfair, they may be unlikely to complain at all. Furthermore, prisoners serving shorter sentences may feel it is not worth complaining.

Parallel Worlds makes depressing reading, given that it was reviewing the situation after the Mubarek and CRE Reports. Although many of the issues raised were addressed in the Action Plan, it shows that despite over 20 years of formal changes to reduce racism, problems remained.

The 2011 report from the Prison Inspectorate found that 'prisoners from a black or minority ethnic background, foreign nationals, Muslim prisoners and those under the age of 21 were more likely to report having spent time in the segregation or care and separation unit in the last six months. At both Norwich and Whatton, we reported that black and minority ethnic prisoners were disproportionately more likely to be segregated' (HM Chief Inspector of Prisons 2011a: 25). Investigations by the Prison Inspectorate indicate that 'young adult, foreign national, black and minority ethnic and Muslim respondents generally felt less well respected by staff' (ibid: 29).

On race equality there has been more rigorous monitoring and the investigation of racist incidents has improved. But problems clearly persist as the Chief Inspector of Prisons has noted. There are still inequalities in relation to segregation, the use of force, and disciplinary hearings, with black and minority ethnic prisoners over-represented in some prisons inspected (ibid: 34). However, as noted earlier, the HM Inspectorate of Prisons research suggests that black women prisoners are more positive about their treatment than black male prisoners (see section 11.4.6).

There were also differentials in perceptions of how prisons dealt with complaints, with foreign national prisoners, BME, Muslim, and disabled prisoners more negative than other prisoners. These prisoners were more likely to feel unsafe and to respond negatively to questions in surveys undertaken for the prison inspectorate. Black prisoners were particular concerned about relations with staff, while Asian prisoners were particularly worried about safety.

The latest *Equalities Report* from NOMS published in 2011 indicates that adjudication rates are still higher for black and mixed prisoners and these groups also have higher rates for complaints (Ministry of Justice 2011g). Black or black British and mixed groups also had more days on segregation and force was used more on these groups than on white prisoners. There were also higher proportions of black and mixed prisoners on the basic regime of the Incentives and Earned Privileges Scheme.

11.10 Other dimensions of inequality

The focus now is on a generic approach to equality and diversity which addresses a broader range of protected characteristics. The duty on prisons to meet the equality duty is set out by NOMS in *Promoting Equality in Prisons and Probation: the National Offender*

Management Service Single Equality Scheme 2009–2012 (NOMS 2009b). The approach taken to race equality is being extended to these other areas so annual Equalities Reports are now published reporting on progress made and on equality impact assessments and on the action taken to resolve problems. A Single Equality Scheme 2009–12 was published in March 2009, which runs until 2012.

A NOMS Independent Equalities Advisory Group has also been established. The 2011 *Equalities Annual Report* covers the period April 2010–March 2011 (Ministry of Justice 2011g). It reports that data collection has improved, with more data now available on disability and sexual orientation. All new policies are subject to equality impact assessments and are completed at both Headquarters and individual prison establishments.

Support groups have been set up for disabled staff as well as gay, lesbian, bisexual, and transgender staff and higher proportions of BME staff and gay staff have been recruited. The Prison Service Instructions on equality issues have been reviewed and revised. An Independent Equalities Advisory Group has been established to provide external scrutiny of the equalities work and this includes representatives from groups with interests in all equalities issues. More guidance has been given on monitoring and managing the welfare of gay prisoners. Diversity training materials for use with prisoners have been devised and introduced. Faith awareness courses have been conducted.

Attention is being directed towards reducing the incidence of unequal outcomes resulting from unconscious bias in the use of discretion. Research is being conducted on this and tools are being developed to address it. From 2012, instead of publishing equality schemes, the focus will be on setting out equality objectives which will include collecting accurate monitoring data, identifying disparities in outcomes, reducing disparities in race, achieving comprehensive screening for disabilities, and improving outcomes for women offenders.

Policies in prison now focus on diversity which is intended to cover a wide range of protected characteristics. However the Prison Inspectorate found that most of the policies focused on race and foreign-national prisoners, but provision for gypsy and traveller prisoners was weak. The particular areas needing further work which have been highlighted in recent reports are religion, sexual orientation, age, and disability.

Religion

As well as ethnic diversity, we find a wide range of religious beliefs held by prisoners. As well as the major religions of Christianity, Judaism, Islam, and Sikhism, prisoners may also practice Buddhism and Paganism. About 33 per cent of prisoners have no religious affiliation, 30 per cent are Anglicans, and 17 per cent are Catholic. The number of Muslim prisoners has increased in recent years, reaching over 12 per cent of the prison population in 2010, with a high concentration in high security prisons.

Prisons are obliged to allow inmates to practice their religion which means allowing them to attend services, and giving them time for worship, unless there are security problems. Freedom of religion is protected by Article 9 of the ECHR and any limits on this right have to be justified under Article 9(2). Prisoners are not required to work on special religious days and should be provided with appropriate diet as required by their religion. While the major religions are well catered for and attention to religion has improved, the Prison Inspectorate has criticised the insufficient provision for Buddhism.

Of Asian prisoners, 71 per cent are Muslim and the issues raised by their imprisonment have received more attention in the past few years. A thematic review of Muslim prisoners was undertaken by the Chief Inspector of Prisons in 2010 which involved interviews with 164 Muslim prisoners in eight prisons and with Muslim prison chaplains (HM Chief

Inspector of Prisons 2010b). Research on Muslim prisoners has also been conducted by Spalek (2002) and Beckford *et al.* (2005). Issues have been raised over their relations with prison officers, over allegations of intimidation of other prisoners and pressure on prisoners to convert to Islam, and concerns that prison is a recruiting ground for extremism. These issues were considered in the Prison Inspectorate review which found that the stress on combating extremism, and the media focus on Islam, led to some members of staff associating all Muslim prisoners with extremism, which ran the risk of alienating prisoners and undermining efforts to combat prisoner radicalisation. The review also found little evidence of forcible conversion to Islam.

Muslim prisoners reported that staff treated them all as part of a high risk group rather than treating them as individuals. These problems were worse in high security prisons. The Prison Inspectorate also found that Muslim prisoners had more negative perceptions of their treatment by staff in terms of being treated with respect than other groups and were more negative about their safety. The example is given at Full Sutton where 47 per cent of Muslim prisoners, compared to 18 per cent of non-Muslim prisoners, reported feeling unsafe at the time of the study (HM Chief Inspector of Prisons 2010b). However they were more positive than other prisoners on the question of whether their religious beliefs were respected. The Review also found that prisoners' religious needs had been met and provision was made for prayers and diet within the prison regime for these prisoners. The number of Muslim prison chaplains had increased and their role had been strengthened. Asians and white Muslims reported more positive experiences of prison life than black and mixed heritage Muslims, so race and ethnicity overlaid the religious dimension. A Muslim Prisoner Scoping study published in 2009 considered whether there should be a separate strategy for Muslim prisoners, but concluded that the emphasis should instead be on improving staff-prisoner relations generally (NOMS 2009a). Since then faith awareness training has been improved.

Sexual orientation

The Prisons and Probation Ombudsman has also raised the problem of homophobic abuse and the lack of support for gay prisoners which have been neglected in diversity policies. Because of the homophobia prevalent inside prison, prisoners may be reluctant to complain which makes it difficult to measure. In one particular prison the prisoner diversity representatives were clearly hostile to prisoners who were open about their sexuality. The Ombudsman was also concerned at the fact that staff stressed the need to respect cultural and religious objections to homosexuality in deciding whether it was safe for gay prisoners to reveal their sexuality while inside prison and emphasised that 'religious beliefs should be respected but this does not mean that discriminatory or antagonistic language or behaviour should be tolerated' (Prisons and Probation Ombudsman 2011: 23). Policies on sexual orientation should be redrafted to promote a more supportive culture. The Prison Inspectorate has found the most neglected dimension of equality is sexuality (HM Chief Inspector of Prisons 2011a: 33).

A visit by the Prison Inspectorate to Holloway, Bronzefield, and Drake Hall found that all three prisons had race equality procedures but there was little on sexuality (ibid). So this was an area where more work was needed to promote equality. However some prisons, such as Hull and Wakefield, do have support groups for gay prisoners and gay prisoner forums and efforts are made to combat homophobia. There have also been improvements in data collection on sexual orientation, developed in consultation with Stonewall, and in the recording of complaints dealing with homophobic incidents.

Transgender prisoners

Prisons now also have an equality duty to transgender prisoners under the Equality Act 2010 which means that a specific policy to deal with these prisoners is required. A Prison Service Instruction on the management of transgender prisoners has been issued. The courts have also upheld the right of a pre-operative transgender prisoner to be transferred to a women's prison in *R (on the application of AB) v (1) Secretary of State for Justice (2) Governor of Manchester Prison: QBD (Admin)* 4 September 2009.

Disability

A further area where more needs to be done to satisfy the equality duty is in relation to disabled prisoners. Prison regimes must make reasonable accommodation to address the needs of disabled prisoners and staff, under the Equality Act and formerly under the Disability Discrimination Act. A thematic review of disabled prisoners in 2009 found that they are also more likely to report feeling unsafe and more likely to experience victimisation compared to prisoners without disabilities (HM Inspectorate of Prisons 2009a). Furthermore, disabled staff, who comprise 6 per cent of staff, have also reported greater bullying and harassment over the previous 12 months than non-disabled staff (Ministry of Justice 2011g).

Surveys conducted by the Prison Inspectorate have found that disabled prisoners had more negative perceptions than other prisoners, on many issues such as safety and victimisation and respectful treatment (HM Chief Inspector of Prisons 2011a: 29). The number of complaints from disabled prisoners is increasing and these prisoners were also more negative on the issue of how complaints were treated. However, adult male prisoners were less dissatisfied than female disabled prisoners and disabled prisoners were more positive on health care than prisoners without disabilities. The emphasis in the provision for disability has been principally on the physical environment with less focus on learning disabilities. A significant issue has been the identification of disabilities as it may be harder to identify learning than physical disabilities. This was one of the problems raised by the Bradley Report, which emphasised the importance of confirming this when offenders enter prison (Department of Health 2009a). The Prison Inspectorate also gives the example of Gartree where 3 per cent of prisoners were identified as having a disability but this compared with 21 per cent in the survey who saw themselves as having a disability (HM Chief Inspector of Prisons 2011a). Disability is now being given more attention and an important advance is that all offenders undergoing learning activities are screened for learning disabilities (see Chapter 10, section 10.5).

Older prisoners

As we saw in Chapter 7, the number of older prisoners has increased and older prisoners will have higher morbidity rates and make more demands on health care within the prison, but will also face other problems including access to employment. The picture emerging is mixed, with some examples of good support, but also instances of older prisoners in the worst accommodation and problems of access to sanitation at night are worse for older prisoners. A thematic review of older prisoners in 2004 made a number of recommendations but not all had been met by the time of the follow up review in 2008. A Prison Reform Trust study of older prisoners found gaps between the health care services they received in prison and the health care they would have received in the community (Prison Reform Trust 2008). Particular problems included depression, as well as higher rates of physical illness, and problems in receiving appropriate medication. They may also be held far from home which means particular problems regarding visits from family members who may also be old. As age is a protected characteristic under the Equality

Act 2010, provision for older prisoners should now be given greater attention. NACRO has been working with older prisoners and has issued materials and a guidance toolkit to improve the their treatment.

11.11 Conclusion

11.11.1 Justice, equality, and difference?

As we have seen, there have been substantial policy changes over the last decade and the imposition of the equality duty is having an impact on the governance of prisons and the issue of diversity is receiving more attention. At a formal level, procedures and strategies are in place to prevent discrimination on grounds of race, sex, and other grounds, but perceptions of prison life on the part of BME and disabled prisoners remain more negative than those of white prisoners and prisoners without disabilities. Problems remain in relation to the exercise of discretion and the interaction of staff and prisoners.

Progressive measures have been introduced and are having an impact on penal policy. But the success of these measures depends in part on available resources which is difficult in the context of high levels of imprisonment and public spending cuts. Moreover, while progress has been made in relation to race and gender equality, there are still areas, such as homophobic behaviour, where more work needs to be done. The goal here should be equality of outcomes to ensure that policies and programmes do not disparately impact on particular groups of prisoners, in order to achieve justice in punishment.

11.11.2 Discussion questions

In revising the issues raised in Chapter 11 you may wish to reflect on the following questions:

1. Is it fair to say that the current prison regime impacts more harshly on some groups of prisoners than others? If so, consider the ways in which equality of impact might be achieved.
2. Why have gender specific policies been introduced in prisons in England and Wales?
3. Do the experiences of ethnic minorities in prison differ from those of non-minorities?
4. How will equality be achieved within prisons?

online resource centre

Guidance on dealing with these questions is given in the Online Resource Centre.

12

Just punishment in the community

SUMMARY

The focus of this chapter is the supervision and punishment of offenders who have been sentenced to a community or suspended sentence order (SSO),[1] or who have served the custodial part of a prison sentence and have been released to Probation Service supervision. The chapter examines the policy aim of reducing reoffending through specifying in orders requirements to control and rehabilitate the offender in the community, and discusses the theory and practice of rehabilitation which underpins these initiatives. Having reviewed changes in the theory and practice of probation work, the chapter reviews the debate on what counts as just punishment in the community.

12.1 **Introduction**

Two issues have again become prominent in relation to community sentences: first, concern that there is inadequate supervision of offenders released from custody to community and, secondly, that short prison sentences are both costly and lacking in utility given the lack of rehabilitation programmes and the apparent lack of any deterrent effect. The policy trend is, therefore, to encourage more use of community penalties and SSOs, and to make supervision for many offenders more intensive and controlling. This chapter will review these developments but also focus on the problems these have caused for the Probation Service and address the theoretical and practical issues raised by giving priority to rehabilitation as an aim for sentencing and punishment.

There are Council of Europe rules and recommendations relevant to this chapter: Recommendation CM/Rec (2010)1, defines the term probation as relating to 'the implementation in the community of sanctions and measures, defined by law and imposed on an offender. It includes a range of activities and interventions, which involve supervision, guidance and assistance aiming at the social inclusion of an offender, as well as at contributing to community safety' (see Aebi *et al.* 2011). This broad definition masks the conflicts of aim, method, and justification which this chapter will review; it also masks the different content and use of various orders and disposals which make comparisons

[1] In other words a suspended custody order.

between countries problematic but Table 12.1 shows the latest statistics regarding community punishments in European states.

12.1.1 **Supervision and custodial penalties**

Offenders given a suspended custodial sentence or on release from a custodial sentence (see Chapter 5, section 5.5) are an increasingly important set of 'clients' for the Probation Service. As Table 12.2 shows, in the latest figures, over 90,000 offenders were being supervised as part of suspended or other custodial orders compared with 120,000 on community orders.

Except for prisoners serving 51 or fewer weeks,[2] the second part of a custodial sentence is spent under the supervision of the Probation Service in the community. Current law on early release aims, as we noted in Chapter 5, to mandate the involvement of offenders in post-release programmes. Assessment for discretionary release and for the tailoring of post-release programmes is based on risk assessments, but for most offenders the result is a programme which addresses their persistence in reoffending. The aim is to have 'seamless' sentencing, an aim dating from the Home Office's desire for more 'flexible' sentences and the setting up of the Halliday Report (2001) to 'identify and evaluate' new frameworks 'which join up custodial and community sentences'. One of the main drivers was—and still is—frustration at the ineffectiveness of short prison sentences in reducing offending: as a former Home Secretary put it, 'it is crackers to put people in jail for a short time without any measures to change them or any plan for when they come out'.[3]

The Halliday Report (2001: Chapter 4) proposed increasing the post-release supervisory periods of all prison sentences of 12 months or more to a norm of one half, with more detailed planning by all agencies before the offender is released. Those proposals were incorporated in the Criminal Justice Act (CJA) 2003 (see Chapter 5) and implemented since April 2005. Release to Probation Service supervision is automatic at the half-way stage (s 244, but see s 247), and the courts are empowered to make a recommendation to the Home Secretary—who must consider it—of conditions to be included in the licence on release. The Home Secretary, when giving directions to the Parole Board, must have regard to the need not only to protect the public but also to rehabilitate the offender (s 239(6)). The Halliday Report had also proposed the 'custody plus' scheme for short prison sentences (2001: paras 3.10 and 3.11) but, as noted, the relevant legislation has never been implemented.[4] Intermittent custody orders have also not been implemented, as we noted in Chapter 3, because of a lack of relevant resources. This is a pity as the pilots in 2004–6 showed that the level of compliance among offenders was 'exceptionally high' (Probation Service 2006) and that 'judges ... were enthusiastic advocates of the disposal' in order to allow for employment and childcare responsibilities' (Penfold *et al.* 2006).

[2] The not implemented arrangements for prisoners given sentences of less than 51 weeks under the Criminal Justice Act (CJA) 2003, s 181 would have provided release under supervision. However, the Legal Aid, Sentencing and Punishment of Offenders Bill proposes to implement the repeal of ss 33–51 of the Criminal Justice Act (CJA) 1991 (CJA 2003, s 303) in relation to sentences of less than 12 months and bring them in line with other sentences: see the Online Resource Centre for updates.

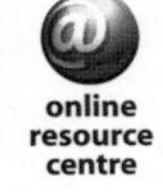

[3] David Blunkett quoted in Ellis and Winstone 2001/2: 20. *Criminal Justice: The Way Ahead* had noted that in 1999, for sentences of less than 12 months, 47 per cent of the total discharges had no opportunity of engaging in rehabilitation programmes post-release (Home Office 2001a: para 2.73).

[4] The custody plus sentence, a split custody and community sentence, modelled on the detention and training order introduced in 2000 for young offenders and also on the so-called 'weekend prison' sentences available in some other jurisdictions (for example, the Netherlands), would have entailed custody for 2–12 weeks, plus supervision in the community for six months or more (CJA 2003, ss 183–184).

Table 12.1 Breakdown (in percentages) of persons serving CSM or being under probation on 31 December 2009.

Country	Total number of persons under the supervision or care of Probation agencies per 100,000 population	Of which: Percentage of															
		Conditional suspension of the enforcement of the sentence	Fully suspended prison sentence pronounced together with probation	Partially suspended prison sentence pronounced together with probation	Conditional Pardon or conditional discharge	Community service	Electronic Monitoring	Home arrest (curfew orders)	Semi-liberty	Compensations	Ban from office, position or profession	Treatment	Conditional release / parole with probation	Conditional release / parole without probation	Mixed orders (specify)	Other (total)	Total %
	1.0	1.1	1.2	1.3	1.4	1.5	1.6	1.7	1.8	1.9	1.10	1.11	1.12	1.13	1.14	1.15	
Austria	(111.2)	---	37.6	11.0	---	---	---	---	---	---	---	---	34.0	---	---	—	83
Azerbaijan	54.7	2.0	28.7	---	---	2.5	---	---	0.3	---	0.3	---	10.3	---	---	56.0	100
Belgium	236.8	0.0		46.3	0.0	37.1	6.1	---	0.4	0.0	0.0	---	10.1	---	---	---	100
Bulgaria	(178.2)	---	---	---	0.4	38.6	---	1.0	---	---	---	---	3.1	9.1	---	---	52
Croatia	23.3	---	49.5	---	---	50.5	---	---	---	---	---	---	---	---	---	---	100
Cyprus	(95.2)	---	---	---	---	49.8	---	---	0.0	---	---	---	0.0	---	---	---	50
Denmark	153.0	---	15.5	4.3	0.2	24.6	1.5	---	---	---	---	33.7	19.3	---	---	1.0	100
Estonia	633.4	---	67.5	5.3	---	17.9	0.5	---	---	---	---	---	7.8	---	1.1	---	100
Finland	48.7	---	---	---	---	45.0	---	---	---	---	---	---	52.2	---	2.7	---	100
France	(365.0)	---		60.1	---	11.7	1.9	---	0.7	---	---	---	3.0	---	---	29.5	107
Georgia	(617.0)	---	89.4	9.1	---	0.4	---	---	---	---	4.6	---	1.5	---	---	---	105
Germany	(181.5)	---	---	---	---	---	---	---	---	---	---	---	---	---	---	---	---
Hungary	258.1	---	20.2	---	---	45.6	---	---	---	---	---	---	9.6	---	---	24.7	100

Ireland	143.5	---	---	9.4	---	20.7	---	---	---	---	---	---	---	---	---	69.9	100
Italy	(60.0)	---	9.2	---	---	---	---	14.6	2.4	---	---	6.0	5.0	---	---	---	37
Latvia	466.4	---	66.5	---	---	18.7	---	---	---	---	---	---	11.0	---	---	3.9	100
Lithuania	205.6	---	48.2	---	---	2.8	---	23.3	---	0.6	0.9	---	21.0	---	---	3.2	100
Luxembourg	215.4	---	38.2	7.1	---	32.1	1.8	---	1.8	---	---	---	13.7	---	---	5.4	100
Moldova	(188.0)	49.9	0.1	0.8	0.3	12.9	---	---	---	---	17.5	---	16.8	---	0.0	---	98
Netherlands	(241.1)	…		44.5	…	53.2	1.2	0.4	0.8	…	…	…	1.6	…	…	1.0	103
Norway	50.1	---	21.2	---	---	59.3	1.7	---	---	---	---	---	17.0	---	---	0.8	100
Poland	(1056.5)	---	68.3	---	0.9		18.5	0.0	---	---	---	---	10.7	---	---	---	98
Portugal	(152.3)	---	39.6	---	---	24.2	3.2	---	---	---	---	---	19.7	---	---	18.0	105
Romania	(35.8)	---	86.4	---	---	---	---	---	---	---	---	---	---	---	---	---	86
Serbia (Republic of)	0.1	16.7	---	---	---	16.7	---	---	---	0.0	---	66.7	---	---	---	---	100
Spain (State Admin.)	509.3	---	10.4	---	0.0	80.5	1.0	---	3.2	---	---	1.9	3.1	---	---	---	100
Spain (Catalonia)	134.1	---	16.1	---	---	49.2	0.5	---	19.2	---	---	4.7	7.6	---	1.7	1.0	100
Sweden	152.9	---	---	---	---	16.8	3.5	---	---	---	---	10.7	32.0	0.0		37.0	100
Turkey	(48.7)	11.0	3.1	0.1	0.1	1.6		---	---	---	1.8	64.0	0.6		2.8	6.9	182
UK: England and Wales	(320.8)	---	24.8	---	---	57.5	8.7	---	---	---	---	---	19.8	---	---	---	111
UK: Northern Ireland	223.8	---	---	---	---	21.7	---	---	---	---	---	---	9.2	---	30.0	42.7	104
Mean	231.0	15.9	38.8	4.3	0.3	30.0	2.4	6.5	3.2	0.2	4.2	26.8	13.1	4.5	21.4	20.1	---
Median	178.2	11.0	38.2	4.3	0.2	24.2	1.7	0.7	0.8	0.0	1.3	10.7	10.2	4.5	2.2	6.9	---
Minimum	0.1	0.0	0.1	0.0	0.0	0.4	0.0	0.0	0.0	0.0	0.0	1.9	0.0	0.0	0.0	0.8	---
Maximum	1056.5	49.9	89.4	11.0	0.9	80.5	8.7	23.3	19.2	0.6	17.5	66.7	52.2	9.1	92.8	69.9	---

Source: Aebi *et al.* (2011: Table 1.2). See Aebi *et al.* (2011: 5) for conventions used in the table.

Table 12.2 Offenders starting court order and pre and post release supervision by the Probation Service by sentence type and sex,(1) 2000 to 2010, England and Wales

Type of sentence	2000	2001	2002	2003	2004	2005	2006	2007	2008	2009	2010
Males and Females											
All court orders	**122,345**	**122.514**	**128,168**	**131,493**	**135,296**	**140,430**	**155,614**	**162,648**	**164,873**	**166,837**	**161,687**
All community sentences	**122,345**	**122,514**	**128,168**	**131.493**	**135,296**	**136.130**	**128,336**	**125,369**	**126,170**	**127,012**	**120,583**
Community order						53,248	111,752	117,860	120.743	122,796	118.696
All pre CJA orders(2)	132162	132021	138305	142623	146372	93,925	19,530	8,625	6,248	4,864	1,842
Other sentences	.					**5,952**	**33,111**	**44,991**	**46,087**	**47,430**	**48,486**
Deferred sentence	..	...	...	...	...	104	384	570	585	533	584
Suspended sentence order	...	...	...	...	...	5,848	32,727	44,421	45,502	46,897	47,902
Pre and post release supervision	52,237	49,212	51,812	50,626	48,450	46,103	43,160	43,638	47,482	45,970	46,204
Males											
All court orders	**102,790**	**102,939**	**107,594**	**111,298**	**114,415**	**119,034**	**132,363**	**138,260**	**139,340**	**140,794**	**136,562**
All community sentences	**102,790**	**102,919**	**107,594**	**111,298**	**114,415**	**115,204**	**108,595**	**106,022**	**106,392**	**106,846**	**101,302**
Community order	111,421	111,299	116,480	121.127	124,256	45,832	95,111	99,573	101,552	103.074	99,598
All pre CJA orders*						78.916	16,087	7,504	5,611	4,395	1.678
Other sentences						**5,206**	**28,752**	**38,930**	**39,499**	**40,497**	**41,683-**
Deferred sentence	...	...	...	...	...	81	306	460	473	423	475
Suspended sentence order	...	...	...	...	...	5,125	28,446	36,470	39,026	40.074	41,208
Pre and post release supervision	48,853	45,790	48,295	46,978	44,952	42.771	40,062	40,573	44.059	42,785	43,124
Females											
All court orders	**19,555**	**19,575**	**20,574**	**20,195**	**20,881**	**21,396**	**23,251**	**24,388**	**25,333**	**26,043**	**25,125**
All community sentences	**19,555**	**19,575**	**20,574**	**20,195**	**20,881**	**20,926**	**19,741**	**19,347**	**19,778**	**20,166**	**19,291**
Community order	20,741	20,722	21,825	21,496	22,116	7,416	16,641	18,287	19,191	19,722	19,098
All pre CJA orders						15,009	3,443	1,121	637	469	164
Other sentences						**746**	**4,359**	**6,061**	**6,588**	**6,933**	**6,803**
Deferred sentence	...	...	...	...	...	23	78	110	112	110	109
Suspended sentence order	...	...	...	...	...	723	4,281	5,951	6,476	6,823	6,694
Pre and post release supervision	**3,384**	**3,422**	**3.517**	**3,648**	**3,498**	**3,332**	**3,098**	**3,065**	**3,423**	**3,175**	**3,080**

1) Each person is counted only once in the total even if they started several types of supervision in the year.
2) For years prior to 2009, see Offender Management Caseload statistics 2008 for detailed breakdown of pre CJA 2003 figures.

Source: Ministry of Justice (2011o: Table A 4.1).

The policy trend, then, is that 'the boundary between custodial and community sentences is becoming more fluid', making essential more effective collaboration between the Prison and Probation Services (Raynor and Vanstone 2002: 107). To this end the Prison and Probation Services became part of the National Offender Management Service (NOMS) in 2004 with the dual aims of punishing offenders and reducing offending: see *Reducing Crime, Changing Lives* (Home Office 2004b: para 25).

The Probation Service is also increasingly concerned with supervising offenders given an SSO (see Table 12.2). This sentence has been more popular with sentencers since the CJA 2003 abolished a restrictive criterion—'exceptional circumstances'—on its use. A custodial sentence up to 12 months can be suspended and requirements must be added. However, as Ashworth notes, its status with sentencers is problematic: it is seen as 'merely' another non-custodial sentence and yet it is also a custodial sentence with serious implications if breached (2010: 302). As previously noted, the courts can recommend particular requirements for post-release supervision of immediate custody sentences but all suspended custodial sentences are subject to the requirements imposed by the sentencing court. These can be one or more of the requirements listed in s 190 of the CJA 2003, details of which can be found in ss 199–213, and are the same as those that are available for community orders (s 177).

In the last decade, there has also been a focus on the release of long-term 'dangerous' prisoners to managed rehabilitation programmes in the community. Those convicted of specified offences of sex and violence can be given 'extended sentences' where the extended part of the custodial sentence is served in the community (see Chapter 5, section 5.4.4). Offenders are assessed to determine their risk level, and the content of the community programme is tailored to addressing the offender's risk factors effectively.

The overall effect of all these new provisions is that the court has more 'say' over what happens to an offender on release from custody or during a suspended sentence order and the offender is subject to more structured programmes of rehabilitation and control in the community.

12.1.2 **The development of community penalties**

The Halliday Report asked for 'more flexible and effective community sentences' (Home Office 2001a: para 2.69) which give the courts 'a menu of options to choose from, providing elements of punishment, crime reduction and reparation, to fit both the offender and the offence' (ibid: para 2.70). The CJA 2003 did this by replacing the existing orders with a single community order, and by providing in s 177, as noted, the range of specified requirements which courts can impose (see also section 12.2.2).

Despite this high policy profile for community penalties, they are of relatively recent origin. Until the end of the nineteenth century the only non-custodial penalties were the forerunner of the conditional discharge, binding-over powers whose origins lie in the Justice of the Peace Act 1361, and fines (Worrall 1997: 7). The Probation of Offenders Act 1907, the Criminal Justice Act 1948, and the Criminal Justice Act 1972 introduced probation, attendance centre orders, and community service orders, respectively, with compensation orders becoming sentences in their own right in 1988 (ibid: 8). Before the Criminal Justice Act (CJA) 1991 the disposals with a severity level above fines and below custody were usually referred to as 'intermediate sanctions'—between fines and prison—or 'alternatives to custody' to stress the legitimacy of their use instead of prison. However, the use of such orders was varied and inconsistent and there was pressure for clarification as to when to use them rather than custody or fines. (See Table 12.3 for relative percentages before 1991.)

Table 12.3 The use of non-custodial penalties as a percentage of all sentences[a]

	1978	1983	1988
Fines	Over 50%	—	Under 40%
Community Service + Probation Orders	8	14	17
Custody	14	16	17

[a] Based on sentences given for indictable offences.
Source: Figures taken from the White Paper (Home Office 1990a: para 4.2).

There was—and still is—a need for changed attitudes to 'alternatives' to custody. As the 1990 White Paper noted, 'there seems to be an assumption that custody is the only "real" punishment' (Home Office 1990a: para 4.1). With the economic imperatives to reduce the use of custody that we discussed in Chapter 1, Government strategy by the end of the 1980s was to 'market' the top end of community penalties as sufficiently tough to be used instead of custody. A series of government policy papers—*Punishment, Custody and the Community* (Home Office 1988a), *Tackling Offending: An Action Plan* (Home Office 1988b), and *Supervision and Punishment in the Community* (Home Office 1990b)—asked for suggestions as to how to make probation more 'intensive', how to develop new forms of surveillance such as tracking, and how to transform probation.

Consequently, the 1990 White Paper gave a high profile to community penalties (itself a new term), arguing that prison was ineffective (Home Office 1990a: paras 2.6–2.9) and proposing that 'just deserts' should be the guiding principle even when punishment took place in the community (ibid: para 4.3; see also Chapter 2). The aim was that non-custodial penalties should stand in their own right, not be seen simply as (inadequate) alternatives to custody.[5] That was still the aim when the CJA 2003 was passed with plans to revitalise community punishment (see section 12.2.1).

12.1.3 **Why 'community'?**

'Community' is now a key word in policy documents and is used to describe the new penalties introduced in 1991 and in 2003. It is easy to chart its incidence and use through a series of criminal justice policy papers, including for example, *Punishment, Custody and the Community* (Home Office 1988a) and *Strengthening Punishment in the Community* (Home Office 1995a). 'Community'—'an all-pervasive rhetoric' in policy discourse (Garland 2001b: 124)—is to be found in policy documents of the 1980s and 1990s in regard, not only to criminal justice, but also to child protection, care of the old, and those with mental health problems. Some time ago Worrall referred to it as 'one of the most promiscuous words in contemporary political usage' (Worrall 1997: 46) and its use has become more widespread since then. For example, applications for many types of project funding, including those for National Lottery money, must show the potential involvement of, and use to, the community. Enhancing and strengthening 'community' is a taken-for-granted good.

[5] For a review of theories and projects around 'alternatives to custody' see Bottoms *et al.* (2004).

What the word 'community' was meant to signify in 1990, and does signify now, is not so easy to establish. It may be referring to a set of shared values or to a place and there is ambiguity in the juxtaposition of 'the community' and 'punishment'. Three possible and different relationships between the two concepts were posited by Nelken, echoing Stan Cohen's statement in relation to crime control generally: 'communities can be the agents, *locus* or beneficiaries of crime control' (Nelken 1994: 249). They still have resonance.

The community as a site

In several policy areas, notably those relating to offenders, those with mental health problems, and the old, *in* the community means the *locus* of the intervention is somewhere that is not an institution. So, for example, 'care in the community' means care in the home or family; punishment in the community means punishment imposed elsewhere than the prison setting.

The community as agent

The idea of punishment *by* the community has become increasingly important. It was evident in *Partnership in Dealing with Offenders in the Community* (Home Office 1990c) which proposed that the Probation Service provide the managers and co-ordinators for partnership with commercial and charitable projects. Likewise *Supervision and Punishment in the Community* devoted a chapter to 'The Voluntary and Private Sectors' (Home Office 1990b: Chapter 10), arguing for the greater involvement of the independent sector and, in particular, for partnership with the voluntary sector to 'involve the community at large much more in work with offenders' (ibid: para 10.4).

The community as beneficiary

Community service orders had been introduced for reasons that included the provision of reparation to the community. Punishment in the community became important symbolically as punishment *for* (the benefit of) the community. This aspect, too, has become high profile with the 'visible unpaid work initiative', rolled out across England and Wales since 2005.[6] The idea is that the community can 'see' the 'payback' to the community by offenders. At the end of 2008, 10,000 orange vests with 'Community Payback' written on the back in purple were distributed to aid such visibility.[7]

Nelken makes the point that these three possibilities reflect very different conceptions of crime; they could also reflect different conceptions of what is meant by punishment in the community. A recent research report on Community Payback schemes points to another policy motivation: 'The 2008 review by Louise Casey "Engaging Communities in Fighting Crime" suggests that public confidence in the CJS may be linked to the visibility of justice, and to how the CJS informs and engages with the public' (Moore *et al.* 2010: 1). Wasik and colleagues (1999: 69–83) argued earlier that the focus on community is part of a need to increase the legitimacy of the criminal justice system: local crime prevention schemes, such as Safer Cities and Neighbourhood Watch, are encouraged, and so provide at least the appearance of action. Daly (2003) also focuses on legitimacy, taking an analysis of the concept of governance as her starting point. She argues that because 'the state no longer occupies a privileged position of power, much of the push towards partnership can be understood as a search for legitimacy' (ibid: 123). Partnership practices and policies can be constructed as consensual and so acceptable (ibid).

[6] See Home Office Circular 66/2005 to the National Probation Service.

[7] See Bottoms (2008).

Yet, rather than diminishing social control by diverting offenders from custody, punishment in the community can increase it: discipline permeates into society's informal networks (see Brownlee 1998b: 180–2; see also Cohen 1985). Probation practice, as established at the beginning of the twentieth century, has been seen as a tool for this new form of social control, designed to inculcate specific norms and attitudes. According to Garland, 'probation, supervision, after care—all of these represent an extension and multiplication of the judicial gaze, and of the consequent range of intervention' (1985: 239). More recently, commentators have viewed the Probation Service as part of a network of preventive projects 'which dominate the law and order landscape' (Raynor and Vanstone 2002: 107; see also Crawford 1997).

The 1990 White Paper had also linked the discourse of community with that of individual and parental responsibility which underpinned several pieces of legislation at that time: 'The probation service tries to make offenders face up to what they have done to give them a greater sense of responsibility and to help them resist pressure from others to take part in crime' (Home Office 1990a: para 2.6). Lacey and Zedner focus on the idea of responsibility from a different angle. Their starting point is 'the apparent disjuncture between the demise of community and the growth of its rhetorical appeal' (1995: 301) and they point to two different histories of community as a concept. The first is the political rhetoric of welfarism after the Second World War and the development of community studies to discover the spatial entity in which these welfare interventions can be implemented.[8] The second is one where community is the site of a conservative or moral majoritarian political discourse. Lacey and Zedner argue that these appeals to community in the 1980s were used to reallocate responsibility (1995: 301) and, arguably, the strength of this discourse legitimised a diversion of responsibility for crime from the government to family and community.

This notion of 'responsibilisation' is important in current policy analysis. Kemshall examines social policies aimed at citizen 'remoralisation' (see also Chapter 8, section 8.4.2 in regard to young offenders) and argues that the Probation Service has been a key agency in the control and exclusion of the irresponsible citizen (Kemshall 2002: 41). We will return to her arguments later in this chapter: the debate on whether community punishment is a means of greater, not lesser, social control than incarceration is still very much alive.

12.2 The legal framework

12.2.1 Seriousness and liberty

As we saw in Part A of this book, seriousness and restrictions on liberty are important concepts in sentencing. The 1990 White Paper proposed that the new statutory rationale of just deserts would operate in community sentences as 'graduated restrictions on liberty, which are related to the seriousness of offending' (1990a: para 4.7). The sentencing framework introduced by the CJA 1991 incorporated these ideas and the CJA 2003 has largely repeated this approach (see Chapter 3), notwithstanding the emphasis on persistence and on risk. Just as with custodial sentences, a statutory hurdle was enacted for community sentences in s 6 of the CJA 1991 (now CJA 2003, s 148). The court may pass a community sentence only if it is of the opinion 'that the offence, or the combination of the

[8] See, for example, Hillery (1955) for a discussion of the different meanings of community in the mid-twentieth century.

offence and one or more offences associated with it' is 'serious enough to warrant such a sentence'.

The pre-2003 scheme

A just deserts rationale theoretically means that sentencers do not have the discretion to choose deterrence, rehabilitation, psychiatric treatment, or social work 'help' as the primary sentencing aim in relation to 'intermediate' sentences. The scheme proposed in the 1990 White Paper and incorporated in the CJA 1991 was that the court should make the initial sentencing decision on retributivist principles, and then consider other aims of sentencing when choosing the particular community penalty to impose. Depending on whether, for example, the offender was seen to need advice and training or be under a duty to make some reparation to the community, a probation order or community service order could be made (Home Office 1990a: para 4.8), with the 'amount' made proportionate to seriousness. In other words, desert determines the size of the penalty, and suitability dictates its form (Rex 1998: 383). The vexed question of ranking community punishments was not tackled in 1990–1.

The Criminal Justice Act 1993 made amendments to community sentencing, the Crime (Sentences) Act 1997 extended the possible use of the community service order, the attendance centre order, and curfew orders for fine default, and the resulting legislative framework was re-enacted in the Powers of Criminal Courts (Sentencing) Act (PCCSA) 2000 (ss 33–62). The Criminal Justice and Court Services Act (CJCSA) 2000 introduced new names for existing orders to stress punishment and rehabilitation as a focus for the community service order and the probation order respectively, and introduced a range of new requirements that could be added to a community rehabilitation order. In line with the continuing focus on deprivation of liberty in the community, one of the new requirements could be a curfew condition.

To summarise briefly, the scheme set up by the CJA 1991 and continued in the PCCSA 2000 had the following elements:

- 'community orders' covering a range of existing penalties which became 'sentences of the court' rather than alternatives to punishment;
- fines as the presumptive sentence with legislative hurdles to discourage inappropriate use of community (and also custodial) penalties;
- a primary sentencing decision on the basis of seriousness as to whether to impose a community penalty, plus subsequent decisions on the type of community penalty and the commensurate 'amount' of the community penalty (PCCSA 2000, ss 35(3)(a) and (b));[9]
- punishment and rehabilitation as the aims of probation supervision.

The CJA 2003

The CJA 2003 heralded, it was said, a more utilitarian approach to community sentences as indicated by the title of *Making Punishments Work* which proposed a new single community punishment order with 'ingredients' specified by the court instead of the existing community penalties (Halliday Report 2001: para 6.6). The specified elements, it proposed, would be chosen from compulsory programmes aimed at changing offending behaviour, compulsory work, restrictions and requirements such as a curfew or electronic

[9] See CJA 1991, s 8(1) (then PCCSA 2000, s 41) for probation aims, and CJA 1991, s 11 (then PCCSA 2000, s 51(3)) for combination order aims.

monitoring, reparation, and supervision to support resettlement and enforce the sentence (ibid).

The ambiguity of rationales is again evident in that para 6.6 points out that 'the punitive weight' should determine how much should be done to reduce the risks of reoffending and make reparation. There is an echo here of a much earlier consultation paper where it was stated that every penalty should have three elements: deprivation of liberty, action to reduce offending, and recompense to the victim and/or public (Home Office 1988a: para 1.5). The report pointed out that the punitive weight might be difficult to measure in some instances, but suggested an outline 'tariff' for the ingredients making up the new punishment order and set this out in relation to a bottom tier, a middle tier, and a top tier (ibid: para 6.8). The White Paper endorsed this approach (2001: para 2.70) and guidance on the CJA 2003 is framed in relation to three sentencing ranges (low, medium, and high), although flexibility is urged (Sentencing Guidelines Council 2004c). The Act has simply empowered the courts to make a community order imposing on the offender 'any one or more' of the specified requirements (s 177(1)).

The problem of choice remains.

12.2.2 Choosing the community punishment

In Part B of this book we have been looking primarily at how punishment operates in practice in the UK. In regard to community sentences, probation officers must provide—or buy in—the supervision and programmes as specified by the court, though how they do so is a matter for the Probation Service. It has been argued, however, that a clear, principled sentencing framework had not been achieved in practice, due partly to the lack of guidance, in particular as to how the court might balance proportionality with 'suitability' (Rex 1998: 384).

Writing before the 1991 Act, Wasik and Hirsch had considered various models for applying desert principles to the choice of non-custodial penalties. They argued that the key issue was how much substitution amongst such penalties was possible, arguing for a 'partial substitution' model (1988: 561) but probation, as it was then called, fits uneasily into a desert model unless conditions are added to constitute the punishment (ibid: 568–9). They concluded that the punishment component, commensurate to seriousness, must take precedence, and utilitarian aims could only determine the substitution issue. Morris and Tonry, using practice in the United States, argued for much more inter-changeability of punishment than this limited substitution model (1990: 10). When drafting what became the CJA 1991, the Government apparently took on board the suggestions of theorists such as Wasik and von Hirsch (Rex 1998: 383; Ashworth 1992: 247), rather than Morris and Tonry, although Rex would disagree (1998: 385) and these issues remain (see Harrison 2006).

There is also the difficulty of calculating the amount of deprivation of liberty, which may account for the sentencing popularity of unpaid work requirements because calculating punishment in hours is easier for sentencers (Rex 1998: 387–8). Arguably, s 166(2) of the CJA 2003, which allows the court to pass a community sentence even if the seriousness criterion for custody has been met, does remove the clear 'in/out' demarcation line which Tonry and Morris criticised. In terms of justice for offenders, both approaches are problematic. To increase the amount of rehabilitation imposed because of proportionality requirements rather than what is required to prevent reoffending might not seem sensible, but rehabilitation divorced from offence seriousness could lead to punitive levels of intervention (see section 12.4.3).

A Probation Circular (Home Office 2005c) provided guidance on the implementation and use of the new community order including a table (see Table 12.4) which gives detailed suggestions on hours and purposes for different levels of seriousness in relation to each main requirement. The Circular provided many more complicated charts and 'Model combinations of Requirements' (ibid: 12) but, as Mair *et al.* (2007) point out, 'not only are the model combination types inadequately differentiated from each other but sentencing can also take account of several purposes' (ibid: 13). They go on to say that 'in addition to the possibilities for confusion and tension between probation officers and sentencers, another key potential problem with both of the new orders is requirement overload. Sentencers, especially magistrates, tend to believe that more is almost certainly better' (ibid), although they point out that figures for the first year of use did not reveal overload, with most orders having only one or two requirements attached (ibid: 18). They found that the unpaid work requirement was becoming increasingly popular and that half of the available requirements had not been used or had been used 'very rarely' (ibid: 31).[10]

More recently, the research of Mair and Mills (2009)[11] considered the extent to which the orders have had the hoped-for impact on providing an alternative to short-term custodial sentences, as well as their impact on probation practice and the management of community-based orders. They note that '[f]or every three Community Orders started, one SSO begins' (ibid: 8)—a great increase in the use of suspended sentence orders—and summarise the trends as follows:

- Half of the Community Orders and SSOs made in the magistrates' courts are for summary offences.
- While the average number of requirements for each order has remained stable since 2005, there seems to be a slight growth in the number of single-requirement orders.
- The use of requirements continues to evolve: while unpaid work has increased, supervision has decreased (slightly more so for the SSO than the Community Order); the use of accredited programmes has dropped steadily since 2005.
- Half of the requirements that are (theoretically) available are rarely used.
- The Community Order continues to resemble the community sentences that preceded it.
- While the proportion of orders breached has recently decreased, the breach rate for both orders remains higher (at around 40 per cent) than that for CROs and CPOs in 2004.
- There is little evidence to suggest that either order is acting as an alternative to custodial sentences of 12 months or less.

(ibid: 46)

It would appear that the most recent changes have not been sufficient to make such penalties more attractive to sentencers and the public—so that they become alternatives to custody rather than to fines.

The recent requirement that community penalties must be used only if the offence is punishable by imprisonment might make a difference, and the Legal Aid, Sentencing and Punishment of Offenders (LAS&PO) Bill 2011 proposed various amendments.[12] As Worrall (1997) pointed out, there is a continuing lack of legitimacy of community

[10] For further reading on community punishment, see Lewis *et al.* (2005) (focusing on issues around race) and Worrall and Hoy (2005). See also National Offender Management Service (2006a) for policy on '*Working with Probation to Protect the Public and Reduce Re-offending*'.

[11] Accessible at www.crimeandjustice.org.uk/sentenceshreeyearson.html.

[12] See Online Resource Centre for updates.

online resource centre

Table 12.4 Criminal Justice Act 2003—requirements

Requirement	Level of Seriousness	Length	Report	Main Purpose(s)
Unpaid work	Low Medium High	40–80 hours* 80–150 hours* 150–300 hours*	'Fast Delivery' 'Fast Delivery' 'Fast Delivery'	punishment reparation rehabilitation
Supervision	Low Medium High	up to 12 months 12–18 months 12–36 months	'Fast Delivery' 'Standard' 'Standard'	rehabilitation
Programme (Accredited)	Medium High	stated number (or range) of sessions	depends on programme	rehabilitation
Drug rehabilitation Offender must consent	Low Medium High	6 months 6–12 months 12–36 months	• see footnote 'Standard' 'Standard'	rehabilitation
Alcohol treatment Offender must consent	Low Medium High	6 months 6–12 months 12–36 months	• see footnote 'Standard' 'Standard'	rehabilitation
Mental health treatment Offender must consent	Medium High	up to 36 months	'Standard'	rehabilitation
Residence	Medium High	up to 36 months	'Standard'	rehabilitation protection
(specified) Activity	Medium High	20–30 days* up to 60 days*	'Fast Delivery'	rehabilitation reparation
Prohibited Activity	Low Medium High	up to 24/36 months for SSO/CO	'Fast Delivery'	punishment protection
Exclusion	Low Medium High	up to 2 months up to 6 months* up to 12 months*	'Fast Delivery'	punishment protection
Curfew typically up to 12 hours/day	Low Medium High	up to 2 months 2–3 months* 4–6 months*	'Fast Delivery' 'Fast Delivery' 'Fast Delivery'	punishment protection
Attendance centre	Low	12–36 hours	'Fast Delivery'	punishment

Notes:
* Length= in line with Sentencing Guidelines Council Guidelines.
Report= the minimum level of Report which should be used when proposing the Requirement (but the court may be able to make the Requirement without considering such a Report [...]).
• A 'Fast Delivery' Report may be sufficient where a current treatment plan is already available.
** Purpose= indicates NPD's interpretation of the main purpose of the Requirement. All Requirements are presumed to meet the purpose of the reduction of crime, either through rehabilitation, or by deterrence through their punitive impact. [...]

Source: Home Office (2005c: 8).

punishment in the eyes of the public, due perhaps to the tenacious legacy of the Victorian principle of less eligibility, under which the offender's punishment must be seen as approximating to a poorer standard of life than that of the poorest respectable citizen (ibid: 13).

12.2.3 **Enforcement and compliance**

> Compliance is an important area of study in the probation service... as Canton highlights, 'an unenforced community penalty is indistinguishable from "getting away with it"' (2011: 123)... Offender managers described how, 'when I first started [in 2006] it was enforcement, enforcement, enforcement but now it is compliance, compliance, compliance'.
>
> (Phillips 2011: 9)

In a sense this is simply a change in words but it may also signify better relationships between offenders and their 'offender managers' or be the result of changes in practice to achieve compliance targets (ibid). Whatever the reason, non-compliance in regard to the requirements of a community or suspended sentence order is a factor which concerns governments and also the Probation Service whose credibility often rests on this (see, for example, HM Inspectorate of Probation *et al.* 2007; Mair *et al.* 2007; National Audit Office 2008). For both community and suspended sentence orders, the percentage terminated for breach is decreasing: the figure for community orders dropped from 48 per cent in 2006 to 40 per cent in the second quarter of 2008 (Mair and Mills 2009: 13) and 'More than half of our respondents thought that enforcement of Community Orders was more effective and more robust than it had been in the past' (ibid: 22).[13] However, this is still a very high figure.

There are two opposed schools of thought on how best to manage this. Eadie and Willis (1989), focusing on 'absenteeism', pointed to the different attitudes of community service supervisors and organisers with and without a social work qualification (ibid: 412) but new recruits to the Probation Service no longer need a social work qualification (see section 12.3.1) and supervisors now have much less discretion. The first draft of the new National Standards in 1988 made clear that the Probation Service must take a tougher line and subsequent versions have also taken that line (see now Ministry of Justice 2011i).

The CJCSA 2000, s 53, in effect, created a statutory warning that offenders would be issued with a maximum of one warning for an unacceptable failure to comply with a community sentence in any 12-month period. Previously there had been two possible warnings. Section 53 was never implemented but the law now in Schedule 8 to the CJA 2003 takes the same approach of only one warning before a return to court. If a breach is proved the court is no longer mandated to impose a custodial sentence, it being possible to impose more 'onerous' requirements in the order instead, but 'the wording of Schedule 8 remains severe' notwithstanding the tenor of the guidance (Ashworth 2010: 352; see also McKeever 2004).

However, it is 'one thing to promise uncompromising discipline, but another thing to deliver it': offenders who are given community orders are often the ones who require that particular disposal in order to help them become more disciplined in terms of time management (Eadie and Willis 1989: 414; see also Mair and Mills 2009: 22–4). Early return to the courts for breach then means that their treatment cannot be successful. Financial problems, drug usage and depression are often associated with the absenteeism of offenders being supervised (Farrall 2002: 267–8).

[13] See Farrall (2002) for earlier figures.

12.3 The development of probation practice

> Despite dealing with more offenders than the prison service, at lower cost and with reconviction rates that are lower than those associated with prisons, the Probation Service has been ignored, misrepresented, taken for granted and marginalized, and probation staff have been sneered at as 'do-gooders'. The service as a whole is currently under serious threat as a result of budget cuts, organizational restructuring, changes in training, and increasingly punitive policies.
>
> (Mair and Burke 2011)

This is how the authors describe the focus of their book entitled 'Redemption, Rehabilitation and Risk Management' (Mair and Burke 2011).[14] There is no question that the Probation Service has undergone several reincarnations in its history—most imposed by developments outside its control—which, it is argued, have led to the 'systematic fragmentation and demoralisation of a probation service' (Howard League 2010: 1). This section will focus on these changes and their impact.

12.3.1 The early history of the Probation Service

As a sentencing disposal, probation developed essentially as 'the practice of releasing certain people from court with some kind of condition that they behave themselves in the future' (Raynor and Vanstone 2002: 11), a practice originating in America and Britain in the nineteenth century. The first stage in the history of the Probation Service has been referred to as the 'special pleading phase'. The essential purpose was to provide information on the offender with the intention that it would mitigate the severity of the sentence imposed. In the development of probation work, the concept of the recognisance—a surety for good behaviour—was influential, as was the involvement of religious societies in what was seen as essentially 'missionary work' to the courts (Raynor and Vanstone 2002: 12–16). This practice ethos continued from the 1870s to the 1920s, beginning with the Police Court Mission and survived the establishment of a statutory Probation Service by the Probation of Offenders Act 1907.

The writings of probation officers at the beginning of the twentieth century revealed, however, an 'increasingly pseudo-psychological and eugenic tone', a 'kind of moral extemporising in the guise of theory', which prompted early pressure for their education and training (ibid: 32–5). At the same time, the development of the positivist school of criminology in the last quarter of the nineteenth century provided a theory of crime causation which focused on environmental factors and which, therefore, validated a treatment approach to dealing with offenders (see Brownlee 1998b: chapter 3; Cavadino and Dignan 2002: 49–50).

The next phase of development between the 1930s and 1970s evidenced a move towards professionalism and rehabilitative aims in probation. Social work training, based on a medical model, became a requirement and the Probation Service was heavily involved in the 'treatment ideal' based on a casework approach. This was criticised (Raynor and Vanstone 2002: 41–4) but it was the emergence of the 'nothing works' orthodoxy—the undermining of faith in rehabilitation—which seriously challenged the Probation Service. By the end of the 1970s the Probation Service was in crisis, split over ideals and aims.

[14] See http://www.routledge.com/books/details/9781843922490/.

12.3.2 **Changing the Probation Service**

A scrutiny of the articles in the *Probation Journal* at the end of the 1970s reveals quite starkly the increasing angst of the Service in relation to the aims and public expectations of its work. The loss of identity for the Service, resulting not simply from the demise of rehabilitation but also from the tension in managing the care and control aspects of their work, without an overall operational aim, led to ideological conflicts. In this period three schools of thought—the radical, the personalist, and the managerial—emerged. Although the dominant ethos of the Probation Service is now different, these various strands are still present in debate (see, for example, Mantle and Moore 2004).

The radical approach

A minority of officers criticised the traditional counselling and casework role of probation officers—based as it is on the assumption that the fault lies with an individual offender and not with society—because they held ideas about the structural rather than personalised causes of offending (Worrall 1997: 70).

The personalist approach

This paradigm—or theory of practice—was based on the belief that the treatment model contributed to injustice through coerced treatment (see Raynor and Vanstone 2002: 44–5). Bottoms and McWilliams (1979) voiced these concerns and proposed a separation of the surveillance and casework functions of probation work. They suggested that the Probation Service should concentrate on the empowerment of the offender, an approach which would enable the Probation Service to operate without the medical and discriminatory aspects of the treatment model. Harris (1980) also justified what in practice probation officers had been spending much of their time doing, notably giving practical help to offenders in arranging housing, jobs and medical care. Others emphasised the professionalism involved in this: 'to give help in a probation context requires skill of the highest order' (Celnick and McWilliams 1991: 166).

The managerialist approach

Like the radical approach, the managerialist approach is also not concerned with the individual offender *per se*. Its focus is the management of groups of offenders in cost-effective ways and in the 1980s the Probation Service was increasingly subject to what was then New Managerialist thinking. The clearest evidence of its increasing importance was the publication of the Statement of National Standards and Objectives for the Probation Service (SNOP) by the Home Office in 1984. Some probation officers viewed it as a major threat (see Mair 1997); some chief probation officers embraced it (Raynor and Vanstone 2002: 78). McLaughlin and Muncie (1994) argue that the key to this shift lay in the managerialist aims of having quantifiable outcomes for probation practice: to 'advise assist and befriend' is not readily quantifiable but is, instead, an 'expensive and unaccountable ideal' (ibid).

National Standards, revised since, prescribe a series of objectives in which the functions of the Probation Service are redefined: to divert high-risk offenders away from prison, to reduce the incidence of crime, and to deploy resources in the most cost-effective fashion. Social work-based tasks were subordinated to the role of controlling and containing offenders in the community, a focus necessary to ensure the 'loss of liberty' element of community penalties post-CJA 1991. The managerialist focus also underpinned the development of the use of commercial and voluntary providers of Probation Service projects so that the Probation Service became a manager, not only of its own work, but also of the work of providers.

The rebranding, in the CJA 1991, of probation and other community penalties as first and foremost punishments which involved control and loss of liberty also prompted a rethink. Until 1948 probation had been used instead of a conviction, and instead of a sentence until 1991, and so probation officers had conceptualised their work as an alternative to punishment. Some officers argued unsuccessfully in favour of a non-punitive paradigm in probation work.[15] Arguably, in the 1990s probation officers consequently turned into penal managers or correctional officers in the community.

12.3.3 **Penal managers**

The new requirements for probation officer training, published in *New Arrangements for the Recruitment and Qualifying Training of Probation Officers* (Home Office 1995b), were a further sign of a different government approach to the practice of probation itself: the Diploma in Social Work, or its equivalent, was no longer to be a requirement. This was fiercely opposed (see Aldridge and Eadie 1997: 111) but the issue of probation training had apparently found itself 'at the intersection of several Conservative preoccupations' (ibid: 122) and the ethos of the Service was set to change further.

The policy trend to a greater use of probation–private partnerships was also evident. Ring-fenced probation budgets—with money that could only be spent on partnership projects—meant that, with no increased resources, some forms of community penalties and rehabilitative projects could be provided only by projects part-funded and perhaps wholly run by voluntary or commercial agencies. The development necessitated the probation officer becoming a manager and fundholder with a key role in partnerships. This led Drakeford (1993) to ask 'who will do the work?', raising the issue that the statutory responsibilities placed on the probation officer are being carried out by voluntary bodies, and that professional skills are being downgraded. It also raises the issue of accountability (see the discussion in Chapter 9 in relation to prison privatisation) and the potential incompatibility of the aims and interests of the Probation Service and those voluntary or private organisations with which they are partners.[16] As we shall see, the trend towards 'out-sourcing' has now been taken much further.

12.3.4 **A National Probation Service**

Despite these concerns, and despite substantial cuts in funding in the mid-1990s, the Probation Service now has a key role in delivering criminal justice policies (Raynor and Vanstone 2002: 82). Revised approaches to rehabilitation (see, for example, Burnett and Roberts 2004; Harper and Chitty 2005; see also section 12.4.2) and, in particular, the use of cognitive behaviourism from psychology (see Home Office 2003d), together with an increasing focus on actuarial methods gave the Probation Service the resources to implement the required priority of managing risk with a dual aim of control and rehabilitation.

The Probation Service has also been subject to reorganisation into a national body. The National Probation Service (NPS) for England and Wales was set up by the CJCSA 2000, with the following aims, as set out in s 2: the protection of the public, the reduction of reoffending, the proper punishment of offenders, ensuring offenders' awareness of the

[15] Stopard (1990), for example, argued that the Probation Service has traditionally viewed control of an offender as a means to the end product of help or treatment so that the offender would learn self control (see also Singer 1991; and Home Office 1990b: para 7.3). See also, McWilliams and Pease (1990).

[16] See, for example, Smith *et al.* (1993: 33–4); see also Bretherton (1991) for the difficulties of putting partnership into practice in relation to one particular project.

effects of crime on the victims of crime and the public, and the rehabilitation of offenders. Section 1(1) sets out the tasks of the NPS as giving assistance to the courts 'in determining the appropriate sentences to pass, and making other decisions, in respect of persons charged with or convicted of offences', and as providing the supervision and rehabilitation of such persons. Section 1(2) makes clear that these functions extend in particular to giving effect to community orders, supervising persons released from prison on licence, and providing accommodation in approved premises. Section 3 makes the NPS directly accountable to the Home Secretary. Section 41 of the PCCSA 2000 re-enacted[17] the aim of probation (rehabilitation) orders as that of securing the offender's rehabilitation, or protecting the public from harm from the offender, or preventing the committing by the offender of further offences.

The CJCSA 2000 also changed the regional structure of the Service into 42 local areas, each coterminous with the local Police Service area (replacing the existing 54 Probation Services) on the basis that this would enable more efficient collaboration: see *Joining Forces to Protect the Public* (Home Office 1998a). In a parallel reorganisation of the Family Court Welfare Services, the duty of the Probation Service to provide social work reports to the courts in private law children cases was transferred to the new Children and Family Court Advisory and Support Service (CAFCASS). Revised National Standards (Home Office *et al.* 2000), analysed as 'part of a wider development that devolves to the Probation Officer increasing responsibility for punishment beyond the walls of the prison' (Sparrow *et al.* 2002: 33), nevertheless increased central control. Further revisions of National Standards were implemented in 2005, 2007, and 2011.[18]

12.3.5 **Contestability and payment by results**

Provisions in the Offender Management Act (OMA) 2007 brought to the fore issues around accountability and responsibility that, arguably, should have received earlier attention (Faulkner 2005). The Consultation Paper which preceded the OMA 2007, *A Five-Year Strategy for Protecting the Public and Reducing Re-offending*, had argued that 'we need to make sure that the way our system is designed helps us bring in the best possible people and organisations to support every offender' (Home Office 2005b: 8) and proposed a system of commissioning. The paper reasoned that if those who buy services for offenders are separated out from the providers of those services 'there is no incentive to deliver services that do not work' (ibid).[19]

Part 1 of the OMA 2007 replaced local probation boards with probation trusts and s 1(1) defines 'probation purposes', in effect the remit of the probation trusts, as:

(a) courts to be given assistance in determining the appropriate sentences to pass, and making other decisions, in respect of persons charged with or convicted of offences;

(b) authorised persons to be given assistance in determining whether conditional cautions should be given and which conditions to attach to conditional cautions;

(c) the supervision and rehabilitation of persons charged with or convicted of offences;

(d) the giving of assistance to persons remanded on bail;

(e) the supervision and rehabilitation of persons to whom conditional cautions are given;

(f) the giving of information to victims of persons charged with or convicted of offences.

[17] Section 41(1) was largely a re-enactment of the revised s 2 of the 1973 Act.

[18] Details can be found at http://www.justice.gov.uk/news/features/feature050411a.htm.

[19] See also National Offender Management Service (2006b) regarding *Public Value Partnerships*.

Section 3(2) of the Act gives the Secretary of State the power to 'make contractual or other arrangements with any other person for the making of the probation provision' and the first NOMS 'Commissioning Framework' was published in 2007 (National Offender Management Service 2007). The Foreword to this document includes the following statement:

> As we move to a needs based commissioning system, commissioners will make judgements about what type of service is needed to manage offenders effectively and to reduce reoffending. These judgements need to be based on the best available evidence about what is working and what isn't, what the priorities for improvement are, where and with whom resources should be invested.
>
> (ibid: 1)

A 'contestability prospectus'—a five-year strategy—aimed at the public, voluntary, and private sector suppliers and specifying the type, length and value of contracts available had already been published (National Offender Management Service 2006b) and received criticism as containing 'a whole range of unproven assertions' (NAPO 2006: 2). Concerns were also raised more generally about the overall impact on the Probation Service of structural organisational changes, the emphasis on contestability and the impact of penal populism on government policy (see McKnight 2009). However, further change is proposed.[20]

Breaking the Cycle (Ministry of Justice 2010a) proposes the development of Integrated Offender Management using local agencies, including police, probation, prisons, local authorities, and voluntary partners to deal with the offenders who cause most harm—prolific offenders—in local communities. This reflects the principle of de-centralisation so local areas will be responsible for identifying these offenders and developing ways of working with them, commissioning services as required. Providers of rehabilitation programmes will be given more freedom to introduce innovative programmes and more discretion in their role and, significantly, will be paid by results. It is not intended to apply the payment by results scheme to high risk offenders but the aim is to target persistent offenders as a small number of offenders are responsible for a large amount of crime. The issue of how to measure rehabilitation is subject to considerable argument but this is being explored and consideration is being given to the number of reconvictions for a given group of offenders. These changes will be accompanied by reform of NOMS and the way in which probation trusts and prisons are managed, and by enhancing the scope for flexibility and professional discretion.

Research on the voluntary sector's involvement in delivering projects has stressed the problems for that sector that are likely to be caused by increased commissioning and contestability: 'The importance of retaining the values underpinning voluntary organisations, its ethical core, will be vital in helping the sector tackle new processes and partnerships without becoming assimilated and subservient' (Silvestri 2009: 6). It also stressed the importance of upholding the voluntary sector's role in providing a voice for the needs of offenders (ibid): a voice which the NPS is, perhaps, less able to provide.

After the changes in 2007, Oldfield and Grimshaw wrote that 'our overall impression has been that a period of stability, reflection and objective analysis would be beneficial for the probation service. We are doubtful that this is likely to be the case' (2008: 5). Their doubts were well founded and, amongst all the changes, it has become increasingly imperative for the NPS, and also its partnership providers to discover 'what works', with a

[20] See the new NOMS Commissioning website for updates and links to other documents: http://www.justice.gov.uk/about/noms/commissioning.htm.

policy emphasis on evidence-based practice. The next section will, therefore, look at new theories of rehabilitation and their practical effects.

12.4 Rehabilitation: old and new

12.4.1 Introduction

The aim of rehabilitation is to reduce the crime rate by reforming and rehabilitating the individual, so he is less likely to reoffend. This approach was popular in the 1950s and early 1960s which is usually seen as the high point of the rehabilitative ideal.

As we have seen, rehabilitation is an important element of community and SSO sentences, and the licence period of custodial sentences, as well as a key factor in parole decisions. Imprisonment also offers an opportunity to reform and rehabilitate the offender, giving him skills to survive outside while also changing his attitude towards offending (see Chapter 9). Rehabilitation is utilitarian in the sense that it is forward-looking and consequentialist: its objective is for the individual to contribute to society at the end of the period of rehabilitation and thereby add to the maximisation of happiness of society as a whole as well as enhancing his own happiness. In Bentham's model prison, the individual was expected to undertake useful work and to learn how to contribute to society in future by developing his skills and rationality. Later, in the twentieth century the rehabilitative ethos focused on the individualised treatment of the offender, developing the treatment appropriate to him, rather than simply reflecting the severity of the offence. On this approach proportionality is less important than rehabilitation and treatment should be provided for as long as is necessary to rehabilitate the offender, so indeterminate sentences are favoured.

The rehabilitative ideal declined in popularity in the 1970s and 1980s, confronted by high levels of recidivism, but within the penal system there remained a commitment to it, albeit on a small scale in therapeutic programmes rather than at a macro-level. The rehabilitative approach was beneficial in so far as it encouraged the development of new programmes within the Prison and the Probation Services, stimulated the search for alternatives to incarceration, and widened the range of options. At its height the rehabilitative model was seen as much more progressive than retributivism which, as we have seen, has been (wrongly) associated with revenge and harsh punishment.

However, an attack on rehabilitation was mounted from two directions. First, it was challenged on the ground that offenders regularly reoffend despite undergoing rehabilitative programmes. Secondly, it was argued that the approach was flawed in principle because of the rights violations permitted by it. Both these criticisms will be considered.

12.4.2 Does rehabilitation 'work'?

Nothing works

A key landmark in the assault on the rehabilitative ethos was Martinson's 1974 paper 'What works?'. Martinson reviewed the results of 231 research studies of a range of programmes aimed at rehabilitation in the period 1945–67, which suggested that various therapies and regimes which had been tried at that time, as well as different types of sentence, were ineffective in preventing reoffending. At best all they could do was reduce the adverse effects of imprisonment on offenders. The programmes included counselling, individual and group work, and a range of different therapeutic environments. Martinson concluded that 'with few and isolated exceptions, the rehabilitative efforts that have been reported so far have had no appreciable effect on recidivism' (ibid: 25). Similar conclusions were drawn from other studies in that period, such as Brody's (1976) review of UK sentencing policies which found no evidence to suggest that a particular type of sentence was more effective than others in preventing reoffending. Martinson's conclusions were endorsed by a National Research Panel on Rehabilitative Techniques, set up in the United States in 1977, which commissioned papers on the issue and concluded that 'Lipton, Martinson, and Wilks were reasonably accurate in their appraisal of the rehabilitation literature' (Sechrest *et al.* 1979).

Martinson's paper was widely and mistakenly interpreted as suggesting 'nothing works', but Martinson himself was not so pessimistic (see Allen 1981). All Martinson was saying is that no one has yet proved conclusively that something works. Moreover, subsequent studies have been more promising. But the willingness to embrace a pessimistic view should also be seen in the context of the retreat from welfare in that period (see Pitts 1992b). As we noted in Chapter 1 attitudes towards welfare and penal policy are intermeshed.

In the wake of Martinson's paper, the rehabilitation movement lost support and this contributed to the loss of political will to deal with the underlying social and economic problems or to develop a socio-economic approach to crime prevention (see Allen 1981). Instead, as we saw in Chapter 1, from the mid-1980s the UK Government tried to fashion a more cost-effective justice system. In addition, the decline of the rehabilitative model undermined support for rehabilitation-oriented practices like remission for good behaviour and early release mechanisms, predicated on the presumption of rehabilitation. After Martinson there were arguments—similar to those we have already encountered in our earlier discussions of deterrence and incapacitation—over the methodologies employed to prove or disprove the value of rehabilitative programmes. Opponents claimed that contrary evidence was obscured by the way the research was conducted and, given the broad time scale of Martinson's review, many of the studies cited in his paper were out of date by the mid-1970s. Large-scale studies of reoffending do not tell us enough about *which* individuals were helped by *which* programmes, and the individual who is helped may be overlooked in data on those who were not. But it would be absurd to infer from this that nothing works; rather what evidence we now have suggests that *some* programmes are effective in reducing reoffending for *some* offenders and not others. Rehabilitative programmes are expensive so it is important to target specific programmes at those most likely to benefit.

Various approaches have been used to study the effectiveness or ineffectiveness of rehabilitation programmes, including statistical analysis, interpretive studies, and meta-analyses. Of course it is difficult when measuring reoffending to know whether offenders did reoffend but were not caught, or that they offended later, outside the period of scrutiny, or alternatively, that they would not have reoffended anyway for some other reason. It is frequently observed that juvenile offenders may mature and 'grow out of crime' and that desistance may be uneven. So it is difficult for a research study to control for all these variables. It is also difficult to draw firm conclusions because, within a group of offenders going through a programme, some may not respond to any form of corrective treatment, others might have responded better to another regime than the one tried, and there may be some who do respond positively to a particular regime but they are swamped by a large number of failures. Figures may also conceal whether the reoffending in question was committed before completing the programme. There is also the problem of the time lag for such studies. Expecting a particular programme to prevent reoffending may be unrealistic because the reasons for offending and desistance from offending are so complex, and may include a range of factors including drugs and alcohol.

As Rubin (2003) points out, in evaluating the rehabilitative ideal we should not assess it in terms of the complete reformation of the offender, but rather assess its value and effectiveness against alternatives, such as incapacitation, or warehousing, of offenders.

What works?

The major reviews of work on treatment programmes and reoffending in the 1990s were considered by McGuire and Priestley who found that the effect of treatment showed on average a reduction in recidivism rates of between 10 per cent and 12 per cent (McGuire and Priestley 1995: 9). This is the average figure but in some of the programmes the figures were much higher: for example, Lipsey's (1992) review of programmes for young offenders also found treatment had a positive effect in reducing reoffending in 64.5 per cent of the experiments he examined.

Many studies focus on whether the respondents reoffend and, if we find high numbers do reoffend, then the programme is deemed ineffective. But Wilson (1985) argues it is better to focus on the frequency of reoffending and using this we find the results are more encouraging. He refers to studies of delinquents in Chicago by Murray and Cox (1979) who found that those programmes with stronger supervision had the greatest effect on the rate of recidivism. Restrictiveness and supervision appear to be important, whether the programme is deployed in the community or custody. Wilson notes that various studies suggest that some types of offender are easier to change than others and further research on this is needed. Young, verbal, intelligent, and neurotic offenders seem to be more amenable to therapy. A programme might also be deemed a partial success if it leads to offenders committing less serious offences than the one for which they were originally convicted. The successful outcome of a particular regime may also be affected by the individuals administering it, making it more difficult to assess the results than, say, drugs trials. So to say 'nothing works' is an overstatement: some things work with some offenders but not with most or not for long and it may sometimes be difficult to identify the cases in which they do work.

Something works

Considerable research has been undertaken in recent years to establish which type of regime works best in preventing reoffending. Numerous research studies have investigated the most effective practical programmes in the United States, Canada, and Europe (see McGuire 1995). Since the late 1990s the 'nothing works' philosophy has been replaced by the view that 'something works' and some things work for some offenders. Programmes therefore need to be carefully targeted to be cost-effective. For example, evaluation of the Intensive Alternatives to Custody (IAC) pilots (using community orders with an average of 3.4 requirements) showed a compliance rate of only 56 per cent but concluded that they were likely to be more cost effective (taking account of the costs of the sentences and the costs of likely reoffending) than short custodial sentences (Hansbury 2011).[21]

Research suggests that cognitive-behavioural methods, rather than psychoanalytic or psychotherapeutic approaches or counselling which address deep-seated causes of crime, may be very effective in teaching new ways of thinking and behaving. These include teaching practical skills to cope with personal and social problems, using a range of methods of treatment, depending on participants' abilities and levels of risk, encouraging offenders to empathise with victims and to think about the effects of their actions. The aim is to enhance problem-solving skills so that individuals can control themselves

[21] See, also, Peck's research on reconviction among offenders eligible for multi-agency public protection arrangements suggesting lower rates than those before such arrangements (Peck 2011).

and their environments to avoid exposing themselves to high-risk situations. Cognitive-behavioural treatment is very popular but some programmes combine a variety of modes of treatment. A Home Office study on cognitive-behavioural programmes in England and Wales found that reconviction rates fell following the programmes (Home Office 2002a). The rates for treatment groups were up to 14 per cent lower than for control groups who did not receive treatment. If this were quantified in terms of numbers expected to complete cognitive skills programmes in 2002–3, this could potentially mean nearly 21,000 crimes prevented.

There is now more optimism regarding the value of offending-behaviour programmes and in this sense the rehabilitative ideal has gained ground. The available research on evidence-based crime prevention, including cognitive behaviour treatment (CBT) and other interventions, in a range of contexts, was reviewed by Welsh and Farrington (2006) and Sherman *et al.* (2006). Although, there have been positive results, there have also been concerns that CBT is less successful in relation to women offenders, not least because women may have different learning styles and different therapeutic needs. One theoretical perspective may not fit all groups, for example women or some minority ethnic groups, so a more flexible approach is needed. As we saw in Chapters 10 and 11, most of the findings on the rehabilitation of offenders have been drawn from research studies of male offenders.

However, more work is now being undertaken on female offenders and there is more interest in developing gender-appropriate courses. Women may benefit more from small-group therapeutic approaches, but it may be harder to 'sell' these in the prison context because of the weight given to risk-based models. 'What works' in relation to female offenders is considered by Sheehan *et al.* (2007), Blanchette and Brown (2006), and Worrall and Gelsthorpe (2009). Roberts (2010) argues for the importance of recognising women offenders' complex needs and in this context considers the role of one-stop shops dealing with low-risk offenders, focusing on the Asha Women's Centre.

Although research is now being undertaken on the effectiveness of programmes for women offenders, as Durrance *et al.* (2010) argue, there is less research on effective practice for black and minority ethnic offenders. So in considering 'what works?' they caution, we need greater sensitivity to diversity issues and a broader conceptualisation of appropriate interventions.

Because of the success of CBT in many contexts, it may be difficult for alternative approaches to rehabilitation to be given support or credence. For example, one valuable area of rehabilitative work is provision of arts programmes. Nugent and Loucks (2011) reviewed the arts programmes in Cornton Vale, a women's prison in Scotland, and the relevant international research on this topic, and argue that the arts can contribute to rehabilitation but their significance has been under rated. Similarly, Parkes and Bilby (2010) argue that artistic and spiritual activities in prison can offer a valuable contribution to rehabilitation and an alternative to traditional concepts of rehabilitation and treatment.

Research is also being undertaken on the effectiveness of short prison sentences as it has been questioned whether short prison sentences reform offenders or reduce crime and it has been argued that these sentences are used excessively. A large scale project on short sentences, surveying adult male prisoners serving sentences of up to 12 months in local prisons, was undertaken by the Howard League for Penal Reform in collaboration with the Prison Governors Association and found that many prisoners thought the prison sentence less demanding than community punishment (Trebilcock 2011). A survey of prison governors conducted as part of this study found that 81 per cent of respondents disagreed with the statement that 'short prison sentences serve to reform or rehabilitate the offender' (Trebilcock, 2010); 75 per cent of respondents thought short sentences were used excessively, and 59 per cent disagreed or strongly disagreed when asked if short sentences serve to reduce crime. Reasons given for the failure of short sentences included the difficulty of changing attitudes or behaviour within a shorter space of time, or addressing mental or physical health problems, or problems with drugs, alcohol, education, training, financial, housing, or family problems, within a short sentence. The short sentences can offer little to the individual offender or to the community which receives the individual back.

For this reason the Howard League and others favour stronger community sentences as the more cost-effective option. The Prisoner Governors' Association has argued that proposed cuts in funding will make it even harder to provide effective rehabilitation and mean that prisons simply perform a warehousing role.

Conversely for those completing longer sentences where appropriate provision is made for therapeutic programmes, the results are more promising. Greatest improvements are made by those who complete longer periods in therapy, of at least 18 months. A number of quite promising studies have been undertaken of HMP Grendon, the therapeutic category B medium-security prison which opened in 1962. Marshall's study in 1997 showed lower reconviction rates for those who went to Grendon than for those who elected for Grendon but did not go, and there were similar findings by Taylor (2000) despite that fact that there are high levels of psychopathy, dangerousness and psychological disturbances among the population there. The research of Wilson and McCabe (2002) considered how Grendon 'works' from the prisoners' perspectives[22] and found that treatment took time, new behaviours needed to be constantly strengthened by other prisoners and key staff members, and having a personal 'champion' on the staff was very important. Other prisoners played a key role in the therapy groups and the emphasis was on involving prisoners in community life so they experienced social inclusion rather than exclusion. The quality of life at Grendon was also significant, affecting how prisoners viewed the therapeutic process. Officers were polite, called prisoners by their first name, and treated them respectfully as human beings, which also assisted in this process of inclusion.

The contribution of Grendon as a therapeutic community is reviewed in the December 2010 issue of the *Howard Journal of Criminal Justice*. Genders and Player (2010) consider the problems of protecting the role of therapeutic work within prisons in the context of changes in the penal landscape in the last 20 years. Haigh (2010) explores the role of therapy within the context of a prison therapeutic community and the principles and values behind this approach.

The attack on rehabilitation from the standpoint that 'nothing works' has therefore been strongly challenged in recent years although there have been sceptical voices. For example, in relation to earlier youth justice initiatives, Pitts argued that the evidence does not suggest that we have something which works, but rather the emergence of a 'something works doctrine' which serves a useful political role in legitimising government efforts to promote an alternative non-custodial sentencing tariff (Pitts 1992b).

12.4.3 **A rights critique of rehabilitation**

A more compelling critique of the traditional rehabilitative model is from the rights-based perspective. It argues that the rehabilitative ideal, when applied in practice, may lead to rights violations, to injustice and unfairness, and to excessive punishment (see American Friends Services Committee 1971). It treats the offender as the passive recipient

[22] The researchers sat in on therapy groups (inmates met in small groups of up to eight people three to five times per week), interviewed inmates, and sought prisoners' own views and used prisoners' autobiographical materials.

of treatment, rather than as a freely consenting subject. The decline of the rehabilitative model can be attributed in part to the attack from civil libertarians and to their efforts to reassert due process rights in the late 1970s and early 1980s, particularly in response to indeterminate and individualised sentencing in the United States. It was the reaction to these concerns which stimulated the revival of retributivism.

The demands for justice and fairness, the importance of treating like cases alike, increased the pressure for determinate sentences and specific sentences for specific crimes rather than individualised sentences, in both the UK and the United States. Rehabilitation has also been strongly associated with indeterminate sentences and for allowing too much discretion to sentencers, leading to inconsistency and extended sentences. However, the attack on discretionary sentencing met with more success in the United States than the UK because attempts to curtail or limit sentencing discretion have been strongly resisted by sentencers in the UK. The revival of retributivism also occurred later in the UK, as we have seen, in the CJA 1991. Desert theory is hostile to predictive sentencing which would be acceptable on a rehabilitation model. Rehabilitative regimes may also allow the use of invasive treatments, such as drug therapies, to control behaviour.

The rehabilitative model was criticised from both left and right; from the left for failing to get to grips with the underlying social inequalities and problems which may generate crime and for treating the individual without addressing the social causes of crime. Probation practice influenced by the rehabilitative ideal has been criticised on the same grounds, that it individualises fundamental social problems which are linked to social factors such as poverty and racism. But it met with criticism from the right, because it appeared to deny individual responsibility for crime, and also for the cost of apparently wasteful programmes. The extreme form of the rehabilitative model sees the task of the criminal justice system as curing errant individuals rather than punishing them if they are not responsible, because it would be unjust to punish if the person is not responsible because of an illness which precipitates offending.

Yet at the time of its ascendancy rehabilitation was seen as a progressive theory and anti-punitive. Moreover, its fall from popularity was followed not by a rediscovery of the social context of criminality, but rather by increased punitiveness. The decline of rehabilitation created space for incapacitation and populist punitiveness to flourish. The importance of law and order as a key political issue in turn made it difficult for rehabilitation programmes to find support and funding.

Sentencing systems with judges strongly committed to the rehabilitation model, such as Canada and the United States in the 1980s, tended to generate longer and harsher sentences on average than retributivist justice, creating further problems of prisoners' institutionalisation. Such systems usually give substantial discretion to sentencers, and because protecting society from dangerous individuals is a priority, release of offenders will be undertaken cautiously. There may be problems in determining if and when someone has been rehabilitated. It may be hard for applicants to know what criteria are used which will lead to frustration. From the prisoners' standpoint, indeterminate sentences are the sentences most feared. Moreover, within a therapeutic environment, the offender feels under constant observation and strong surveillance can mean the impact of imprisonment goes deeper, affecting one's sense of self, rather than being experienced as simply 'doing time'.

12.4.4 **Modern rehabilitationism**

In response to these criticisms, rehabilitationism has adapted. Whilst this chapter has focused on punishment and rehabilitation in the community, modern rehabilitationists accept that prison can be used to reduce reoffending—and should be oriented towards this—but treatment should be non-coercive (Hudson 1993). So modern rehabilitationists demand something more positive than humane containment and minimum standards and modern rehabilitationism does not entail indeterminate sentencing: rehabilitative progress is not the criterion for sentence length (ibid). This raises issues regarding the right of the offender to refuse participation, but many would argue the offender should be obliged to take part in offending behaviour programmes.

Paradoxically, although the attack on the rehabilitative ideal was launched from a rights-based perspective, in recent years the revival of rehabilitation in the late 1990s was itself associated with a rights-based approach in the United States, particularly in the work of Rotman (1990). Rotman argued that the right of the state to punish and the right of the criminal not to be punished unduly, are best protected by rehabilitation being offered within a determinate sentence, fixed by considerations of desert and dangerousness. The obligation of the state is to provide basic physical standards in the prison and rehabilitative facilities sufficient to ensure that the offender is not damaged by the effects of incarceration. He cites the case of *Laaman v Helgemoe*, in which the court said that '[p]unishment for one crime, under conditions which spawn future crime and more punishment, serves no valid legislative purpose and is so totally without penological justification that it results in the gratuitous infliction of suffering in violation of the Eighth Amendment' (see Rotman 1990: 81–2).

In the UK the issue has arisen in relation to whether the Secretary of State is under a duty to provide sufficient offending behaviour programmes to enable prisoners to prepare themselves for consideration for release. As we saw in Chapter 9, section 9.3.3, there are still insufficient offending behaviour courses to meet the demand, so that prisoners may be detained longer than necessary after completing the minimum term of their sentence as the completion of these courses may be crucial to Parole Board decisions on release and the problems this creates for IPP (imprisonment for public protection) prisoners have been highlighted by Jacobson and Hough (2010).

The provision of constructive regimes is a key element in the prisoner's rehabilitation. Several first instance cases found that the issue was not justiciable but in *R (Cawser) v Secretary of State for the Home Department* (2003), the Court of Appeal thought it would be irrational to have a policy of making release dependent on the completion of such courses without making reasonable provision for those courses. Since then, further challenges have been brought by IPP prisoners who have argued that the failure to provide sufficient courses constitutes a breach of Article 5 of the Convention, when they are detained beyond the minimum term because of this failure. In the later case of *Secretary of State for Justice v Walker and James* (2008), the Court of Appeal found a potential breach of Article 5(4) in the failure to grant IPP prisoners access to these courses which would allow them to show to the Board their suitability for release. However, the House of Lords in *Secretary of State for Justice v James (formerly Walker and another)* [2009] UKHL 11, while critical of the inadequate resources available, did not find a breach of Article 5(1) as the prisoners' continued detention was still subject to regular reviews and was based on continuing risk and neither was Article 5(4) breached as there were some courses being offered. Following this case, IPP prisoners on shorter tariffs are now given priority and the IPP sentence is now being reviewed with new provisions on dealing with dangerous offender included in clauses 123–127 of the LAS&PO Bill 2011 and there is a shift towards determinate sentences.

Rotman (1990) distinguished the rights-based model of rehabilitation from the earlier penitentiary model, which seeks to reform through contemplation and submission to the regime, and from the therapeutic and social learning models. As we have seen the latter are problematic because it is questionable whether the individual does engage in such contemplation, or whether such regimes are effective or rather coercive. Modern rehabilitationism emphasises justice rather than treatment, so the offender's due process rights are respected and he is protected from coercive treatment. It treats the individual as possessing rights and as capable of making choices but also as having a positive right to appropriate treatment to prevent reoffending. The emphasis is on non-coercive training and treatment and on reintegrating the offender within the community. So treatment programmes may be part of restorative justice, while also respecting the human rights of both offender and victim (see Chapter 6).

At the same time, efforts have been made to 'rehabilitate' the rehabilitative ideal in the face of the extensive criticisms made during the 1970s and 1980s. Rubin (2003) rejects the association of rehabilitation with coercion, pointing out that it is absurd to dismiss this approach on the basis of its abuse by some regimes and institutions. In any event, historically rehabilitation can also be associated with progressive policies which, at the time, provided an alternative to more repressive penal practices. Moreover, within the modern American prison context, he argues, it provides the most humane way of structuring prison life: 'the rehabilitative ideal, together with the insistence on regularized, bureaucratic governance, remains the principal source of decent and humane correctional practices' (ibid: 82). He also rejects the inevitable association of rehabilitation with the use of indeterminate sentences, pointing out that such sentences can also be found in contexts where no efforts are made to rehabilitate offenders. Rehabilitation, he argues, could also impose more restraint on prison expansion, or what he describes as the 'incarcerative frenzy' in the United States, than rival theories of punishment. Given current concerns over that expansion, the political climate may now be more favourable to rehabilitation.

Modern approaches to rehabilitation therefore focus on offenders changing themselves and on active citizenship and the emphasis is on social inclusion (see Priestley and Vanstone 2010). Brayford *et al.* (2010) argue for a more open and holistic approach to intervention which considers the context of the offending and the local community and victims. What is needed, they argue, are desistance-based rehabilitative and reintegrative practices which engage with the life of the offender and treat the offender as an agent with the capacity for change, instead of the currently prevailing 'top down' model and the heavily centralised and politically driven provision of services, which is primarily focused on risk. Their preferred path is creative practice which considers the personal, social and emotional context of the offender's life:

> The context for creative practice is therefore as equally concerned with social justice and social inclusion as it is with the accountability and reform of the individual offender. It affords responsibility and social agency to offenders and other socially excluded people, offering them real opportunities to change while holding them personally accountable for the impact they have on others.
>
> (ibid: 266)

Focusing on desistance, by taking a holistic approach and using offender-focused interventions and developing the social capital of offenders, may provide an alternative to current reliance on risk based and cognitive behavioural approaches. A broader approach is also recommended by Ward and Maruna (2007) who argue for a Good Lives Model, which incorporates offenders' views of what helps them refrain from offending and a more active view of change. These ideas are explored further by Laws and Ward (2010) in relation to the rehabilitation of sex offenders.

12.5 Conclusions

12.5.1 The survival of rehabilitation

Although we find numerous references to the decline of rehabilitation in commentaries on penal policy, nonetheless the commitment to rehabilitation remains an element of UK penal policy. It survived the negative reaction to Martinson's paper, in specific programmes for offenders within prison and in work with young offenders and with specific groups such as sex offenders, rather than in mainstream penal policy. As Zimring and Hawkins (1995) have observed, rehabilitation generated far more discussion than incapacitation in penological research in the 1980s. It also remained a rationale of the work at Grendon Underwood and now underpins offending behaviour programmes in contemporary prisons (see Chapter 9). Resettlement has also been given greater priority inside prison. Robinson (2008) challenges the view that rehabilitation as a penal strategy is moribund or irrelevant and considers the way it has adapted to the modern penal context of England and Wales.

Although the CJA 1991 referred to rehabilitation only in relation to probation work, it was emphasised in the Halliday Report. It was also a feature of the White Paper, *Criminal Justice: The Way Ahead* (Home Office 2001a) which referred to reducing reoffending by improving the education and vocational qualifications of prisoners so that offenders are better prepared to re-enter society. It stressed the importance of looking at what works for which type of offender and improving the funding for prison service offending behaviour programmes as well as practical skills courses and more drug programmes, given the strong link between unemployment, homelessness, and reoffending.

Rehabilitation is clearly back on the political agenda. In *Breaking the Cycle* (Ministry of Justice 2010a), as we have seen, the need for rehabilitation is strongly emphasised with the promise of a rehabilitation revolution and payment by results for service providers who achieve this goal. The emphasis is also on practical support for drug and alcohol abuse and mental health provision and on making prisons more effective in preparing offenders for release and improving prospects for employment of ex-offenders by revising the Rehabilitation of Offenders Act. In addition there will be more use made of alternatives to custody. The implications of this for the Probation Service are considered by Ledger (2010).

Moreover, in practice there is also still a strong concern with rehabilitation amongst probation officers. The recognition of the individual's capacity to change exists alongside the obligation to manage risk and this is reflected in the conflict between care and control in the Probation Service that we have summarised. In the Prison Service too we find offending behaviour programmes which are concerned with rehabilitation and which have achieved some success. Because of the developments in penal policy considered in Chapter 1, including the focus on managerialism, risk management, cost effectiveness and increasing centralised control, however, the scope for alternative rehabilitative interventions has been limited. Moreover the greater emphasis on the voluntary sector has not been matched by sufficient funding for many of these groups, for example, in relation to implementing the recommendations of the Corston Report. One further difficulty, as we shall see in the next section, is that there is debate as to whether modern rehabilitationism is 'really' rehabilitation.

12.5.2 Rehabilitation or better risk management?

2001 saw the publication of the mission statement for the (then) new National Probation Service, *A New Choreography* (Wallis 2001). At that time Nellis asked, very aptly in relation to a policy statement so strangely entitled, whether the NPS was indeed 'dancing to a new tune' (2002: 369). The point he was making is that different interpretations can be placed on what is known about the delivery of community punishments.

That delivery can now be conceptualised in (at least) two ways. First, it could be a later version of the 'normalising' sector of the modern penal complex (Garland 1985: 238ff; see section 12.1.3), delivering a 'soft' version of discipline and rehabilitation by instilling values and helping the offender to establish a 'normal' lifestyle. Secondly, it could be perceived as an important element of a (new) late modern or postmodern penality that focuses on the actuarially-based management of risk. The first alternative implies that community punishment is still part of the penal–welfare complex originating a century ago, in which probation practice adds to social welfare rather than reduces it (ibid: 240). On the other hand, the practice of community punishment may now be a firm part of the risk management machine we discussed in Chapter 5 (see also Robinson 2002: 5).

In addition, there are the duties relating to the enhanced role of the victim which we discussed in Chapter 6, and successive revisions to National Standards have shown an increased emphasis on the rights and experiences of victims within supervision programmes as well as a greater emphasis on risk assessment at each stage of the supervision process. In the context of restorative justice ideas, Duff has asked whether 'altruism should be engaged in punishment' (2003)[23] and argues that the Probation Service should treat the offender as a member of the normative community, should include censure in supervision, but incorporate in that censure the restorative justice value of integration (ibid: 186). All this still leaves the NPS with an ambiguous role[24] in which there are role conflicts (see Howard League 2010: section 3).

Calling for 'a radical overhaul of the probation service', the Howard League made the following statement to the Parliamentary Justice Affairs Select Committee:

> Instead of being allowed to engage with vulnerable men and women in the community, the probation service and its functions have been warped by NOMS' framework of mechanistic targets. A bureaucratic managerial model averse to risk and devoid of ambition has replaced the frontline services probation formerly provided to the multi-faceted problems faced by individuals in the community.
>
> (Howard League 2010: 1)

However, in recent years there have been attempts to analyse risk management and rehabilitation in practice to determine whether they are in fact radically different or whether it is largely a question of words and methods (Robinson 1999; see also Fitz Gibbon 2007 for concerns about assessment skills). Hutchinson (2006), in an article entitled 'Countering catastrophic criminology', also analysed the continuities rather than the ruptures in modern penalty and penal practice. It could be argued, however, that the conflation of risk management with rehabilitation conceptualises modern rehabilitationism in a very narrow way. An example given of the practical integration of risk management and rehabilitation is the evolution of 'third-generation assessment instruments'. A level of service inventory, for example, measures both the likelihood of reconviction and information about the personal characteristics and the offender's social life which increase his chances of reconviction (see Robinson 1999: 429; see also Chapter 13, section 13.2.1 for information on assessment of young offenders). An inspection report also suggested an individualised risk-based approach: 'A key to effective supervision is therefore to approach each case individually and tailor supervision to its particular needs, bearing in mind the overall

[23] In fact the title reads 'Should Al Truism Be Engaged in Punishment'.

[24] See, for further earlier comment, May (1990) and Sheppard (1990).

objective of public protection' (HM Inspectorate of Probation 1997: 252–3). Robinson argues that this individualised risk-management model was given further impetus by the legislation pertaining to the registration of sex offenders (2002: 9).

In her empirical research, Robinson took traditional individual rehabilitative case work to equate to a 'modern' categorisation and practice methods based on actuarial risk assessment to equate to 'postmodern', but her findings reveal some ambivalence. At that time officers were still using clinical judgements for classification, for example, which do not fit into statistical risk assessment and other tools of the New Penology, but Robinson concluded also that normalisation—'dependent on personal interactions between the probation officer and the offender—'is no longer at the heart of probation practice' (2002: 5). A decade later that conclusion still appears to be valid as does her comment that it is now 'clear that rehabilitation is no longer understood as an all-purpose prescription, even in the relatively limited context of probation supervision' (Robinson 2002: 16).

The managers of correctional policy[25] in the community do not endorse this ambiguity about what constitutes community punishment. The view of Hopley (2002: 298), who led the team that revised the 1995 National Standards, was that opposition to their use had 'consisted—and still consists in isolated pockets of antediluvian officers—of two main strands': staff dislike of being told what to do and distrust of attempts to impose consistency. His statement clearly individualises and denigrates opposition to values underpinning the new correctional services and it ignores intense debates about the value base of probation work.[26] The new focus on value-for-money preventive programmes provided as a result of competitive tender and the closer links between the Probation Service, the Prison Service, and the police has hastened the development of a very different community corrections service. Whether the 'rehabilitation revolution' will provide sufficient resources and be regulated by sufficiently broad targets to make a significant difference is yet to be seen.

12.5.3 **Justice in community punishment**

Not surprisingly, what counts as justice in the context of community punishment is now contested and problematic. At the beginning of the twenty-first century a Chief Probation Officer argued that putting into practice the restorative concepts of penance, making amends, and the involvement of the community and victim are essential aspects of 'just' practice (Harding 2000) but Duff acknowledged that communicative community punishment could probably not be delivered within existing political societies, given that punishment is currently meted out to a group who have already suffered disadvantage and exclusion (2003: 192–4). The problem is that the risk factors which are predictive of offending are also descriptive of the caseloads of probation officers: young offenders are most likely to come from particular neighbourhoods and schools with particular factors—such as unemployment, debt, and disability—in their background (Lacey 2002: 29–30; see also Mair and May 1997). In custodial settings, too, the emphasis has moved to providing constructive regimes which try to combat social exclusion by offering education and training programmes (see Woolf and Tumim 1991; Simon 1999). This is not simply to prevent rioting and disorder in prisons but because it facilitates reintegration and rehabilitation.

[25] See, for an example of the use of this phrase, Home Office (1999b) *The Correctional Policy Framework*.

[26] See, for example, a series of articles in the *Howard Journal* in 1995 (James 1995; Nellis 1995; Masters 1997; Spencer 1995).

A further concern is that the sought-after 'flexibility' in community sentencing has 'the potential for arbitrariness and discrimination' in deciding how much 'treatment' offenders need in the community; 'flexibility' might be the opposite of justice (Raynor and Vanstone 2002: 106). Research reveals male/female variations in the use of requirements and a wide variation between probation areas with regard to the number and type of requirements used in orders (Mair *et al.* 2007: 31; see also, McIvor 1998; Bowen *et al.* 2002 for similar research results, and Chapter 11, section 11.2.1 for other gender differences) and also race discrimination (Denny 1992). Resource constraints may also affect the provision of community penalties differentially: if a particular community punishment scheme is not in operation in a particular area, it is not available to the courts. Arguably, a stronger human rights culture is needed in relation to community punishment (Hudson 2001). However, Brownlee's comment is still very pertinent:

> Given what we know (or think we know) about other advantages of punishment in the community, such as its lower costs, its general tendency to be less dehumanising than custody and to drive fewer of those who endure it to self-harm and suicide, the lack of any demonstrable superiority on the part of institutional sentencing in controlling recidivism should mean that it is the use of *custody* not community sentencing that has to be justified and defended.
>
> (Brownlee 1998b: 180)

12.5.4 **Discussion questions**

The following questions raise important issues. There is further reading, and also guidance on thinking about these issues, in the Online Resource Centre.

1. Has research and guidance on the operation of the sentencing framework established by the Criminal Justice Act 2003 for imposing those penalties which are between fines and prison shown that it is a 'better' framework than the one it replaced?
2. How does modern rehabilitationism differ from earlier forms of rehabilitation?
3. What does the Coalition Government mean by a 'Rehabilitation Revolution'? What constraints are there on the translation of this aim into practice?

13

Punishing young offenders

SUMMARY

This chapter reviews the sentencing options available to the Youth and Crown Courts in dealing with young offenders and examines the current practices and policy trends in relation to both community and custodial penalties for young offenders. It highlights the continuing deficiencies in the care of young people detained in Prison Service establishments and examines the advantages and limitations of using rights conventions to ensure more appropriate treatment of children and young people who commit offences.

13.1 Sentencing options

13.1.1 The range and use of orders

Strictly speaking it is inaccurate to speak of 'sentencing options': juveniles are not 'sentenced' after 'conviction'. Instead, since the implementation of the Children and Young Persons' Act 1933, the youth court 'makes an order upon a finding of guilt' (s 59) in relation to those minors who have been successfully prosecuted. As noted in Chapter 8, ss 65–66 of the Crime and Disorder Act (CDA) 1998 in effect introduced the presumption that children and young people under 18 will not normally be prosecuted for the first two known offences. Provided the young offender admits the offence and there would be sufficient evidence for the police to prosecute, the offender will receive a reprimand, a warning, or youth conditional caution. If the minor is prosecuted the case is normally heard in the youth court (formerly the juvenile court, the name having been changed when the upper age was raised from 17 and non-criminal cases were moved to the newly created Family Proceedings Court).[1]

However, on a first appearance at a youth court a minor is normally given a referral order which entails referral to a multi-disciplinary Youth Offender Panel (YOP). This Panel, which includes lay members and agrees a contract of activities with the young offender (ss 18, 21–27), might be seen as an attempt to include a more welfare-orientated decision-making process. On subsequent appearances at court the full range of disposals is available to the magistrates, from those available in the 'first tier' of penalties—discharges, fines, compensation orders, reparation orders—through youth rehabilitation orders[2] to a detention and training order (DTO) or other custodial orders. In England and Wales, community and custodial orders for minors, as for adults, are subject to the

[1] Criminal Justice Act 1991, s 68 and Schedule 8, Children (Allocation of Proceedings) Order 1991, SI 1991/1677.

[2] In force since April 2009. Consequently, s 177 of the Criminal Justice Act 2003 now applies only to those over 18 years of age.

same statutory seriousness hurdles that we discussed in Chapter 3. Further criteria will be discussed in this chapter.

The situation in Northern Ireland is very similar, although different legislation and terminology apply to many aspects of youth justice. In 1999, Northern Ireland also changed the name of the juvenile court to the youth court (Criminal Justice (Children) Order 1998, Article 27) and s 63 of the Justice (Northern Ireland) Act 2002 raised the upper limit from 17 to 18 years old. Sections 57–61 of the 2002 Act provide youth courts with powers to refer offenders to a 'youth conference' where an agreed plan is negotiated, somewhat similar to the referral order in England and Wales. Scotland, as we noted in Chapter 8, has a different history since the 1960s and, as Muncie points out, the more recently devolved governments of the UK have taken the opportunity to rethink youth justice policies (Muncie 2011: 42) so that Wales has, he contends, more progressive policies with an ethos of 'children first' (ibid).

Use of orders

The period 1996–2001—that is before the new orders introduced by the Criminal Justice Act (CJA) 2003 and Criminal Justice and Immigration Act (CJIA) 2008—saw a decrease in the use of lower-tariff sentencing options, such as fines, and an increase in the use of community sentences. It also saw a rise of 40 per cent in the number of young people sentenced to custody between 1992 and 1997 but this levelled off and was followed by a fall in the period 2001–3 although the period also saw an increasing number of 10–14-year olds being given custody (Audit Commission 2004: 34–6). However, as we saw in Chapter 8 (see Figure 8.2), the use of both custodial and community sentences decreased from 2007–8 to 2009–10 and the latest figures suggest a continuing decrease in the use of custody (see Allen 2011). The majority of juveniles aged 15–17 years old in prison are under sentence: 28 per cent of the those in custody have been sentenced to less than a year and 9 per cent to over four years (Berman 2011: 7; see Figure 13.1).

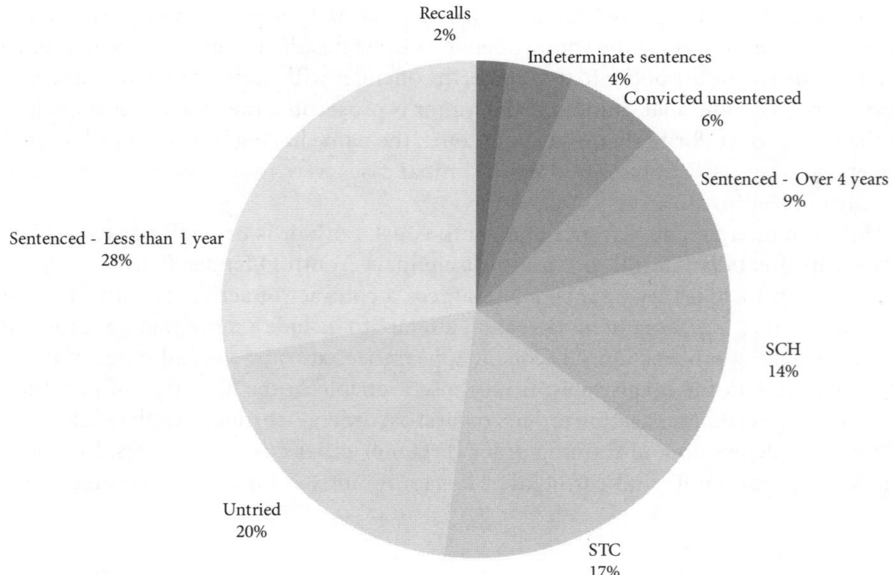

Figure 13.1 Juvenile population in custody, England and Wales, September 2011
Source: Berman (2011: chart 6).

When we wrote the second edition of this book there were 2,742 boys and girls in prison (minors on remand or sentenced) in England and Wales, compared to the 2,500 when we wrote the first edition, and double the number in 1993. However, in October 2011 the comparable figure was 2,021 (Youth Justice Board; see Table 13.1). Indeed, the number of children imprisoned in England and Wales has fallen by a third over the last three years, an unexpected fall and the largest since the 1980s (Allen 2011: 3). This is very encouraging although, as Table 13.1 shows, it is a slight increase on the previous year but that appears to be the result of the large increase of young prisoners immediately after the riots in the summer of 2011.

As Figure 13.2 shows, the fall is the result of a steep decline in the number of detention and training orders (DTOs)—37 per cent in the period 2007–8 to 2010–11 (ibid: 7).

Table 13.1 Monthly Youth Custody Report October 2011

Custody Snapshot Comparison	This Month	Previous Month		Previous Year	
	Oct-11	Sep-11	Difference†	Oct-10	Difference†
Custody Population (Under 18)	2,021	2,061	-40	1,995	+26
Custody Population (Inc 18)	2,204	2,250	-46	2,175	+29
Beds Available	2,406	2,411	-5	2,694	-288
Beds Commissioned	2,508	2,509	-1	2,805	-297
Occupancy Rate	92%	93%	-2%	81%	+11%

† The occupancy rate difference is percentage points differences.

Source: Youth Justice Board (2011d). See http://www.justice.gov.uk/publications/statistics-and-data/youth-justice/custody-data.htm.

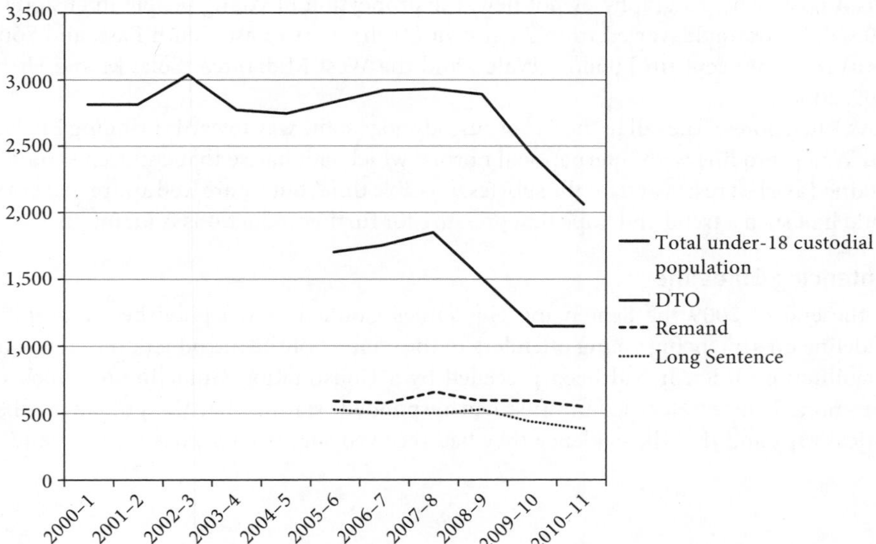

Figure 13.2 Total under 18s in custody 2000–1 to 2010–11 against DTO, remand, and long sentences 2005–6 to 2010–11

Source: Allen (2011: figure 1).

The decrease in numbers was greater for children under 15 years old and for girls. However, Allen draws attention to the fact that the percentage fall for black and minority ethnic children was only 16 per cent over the last three years. The Audit Commission noted a greater differential use of custody for certain ethnic minorities a decade ago (2004: 36–7). It is also fair to say that we still imprison more young offenders than do other countries in Europe. A Council of Europe Survey in 1996 showed that 18 per cent of the prison population in England and Wales is under 21 years of age, compared with France 10 per cent, the Netherlands 8 per cent, Portugal 6 per cent, Sweden 4 per cent, and Switzerland 4 per cent[3] and by 2008 the comparison was no more favourable: 'England and Wales, Scotland and Northern Ireland, respectively, appear as 2nd, 6th and 7th in a European table of rates of incarceration per 1,000 under-18 population' (Muncie 2011; see Muncie 2008: 116).

It is not entirely clear why this fall in the number of children imprisoned has occurred. Allen suggests that 'a range of dynamics behind the scenes have worked together', including the involvement of the former Department for Children, Schools and Families under the Labour Government, changes in police targets, and the development of more constructive responses to offending (Allen 2011: 3). 'It is worth noting that the reduction in the child custodial population appears to have been achieved without prompting any increase in youth crime' (ibid). The new Sentencing Guideline which we will go on to discuss may also now be impacting on practice but Muncie sounds a note of caution when referring to the decrease in 2009:

> Notable differences remained in the proportion of convicted under 18-year-olds sentenced to custody in different YOT areas, ranging from 20 per cent in Merthyr Tydfil... to 2 per cent in Newcastle... Such a 'postcode lottery' suggests a need to move beyond national and devolved policy discourse to learn more of the relative impact of professional decision making and practice strategies at a local level.
>
> (Muncie 2011: 52)

This 'injustice by geography' is not new: the proportion of young people in custody in 2005–6, for example, varied from 7 per cent (in the North East, South East, and South West) to 11 per cent (in London, Wales, and the West Midlands) (Solanki and Utting 2009: 20–21).

As Allen notes, 'The fall in the use of custody goes some way towards bringing England and Wales into line with international norms[4] which emphasise that children should be detained as a last resort and for the shortest possible time', but we are well aware that events could halt such a trend and hope that pressure for further reductions is maintained.

Sentencing Guideline

At the end of 2009 the Sentencing Guidelines Council (SGC) published a definitive guideline on sentencing young offenders in the context of the introduction of the youth rehabilitation order. It had been preceded by a Consultation Guideline to which the Commons Justice Select Committee had responded, stating that the guidance 'fills a critical gap', and that the evidence they had received suggested a varied understanding

[3] See House of Commons Home Affairs Select Committee Session 1997–8, Minutes of Evidence, Annex A, 5 May 1998.

[4] We will review these in section 13.4.

among sentencers of the concept that custody should only ever be 'a sentence of last resort for young people'.[5]

The Guideline included the important statement that, 'Even within the category of "youth", the response to an offence is likely to be very different depending on whether the offender is at the lower end of the age bracket, in the middle or towards the top end; in many instances, the maturity of the offender will be at least as important as the chronological age' (Sentencing Guidelines Council 2009b: para 2.2). It also drew attention to the requirement to 'have regard to' the welfare of the young offender (see Chapter 8, section 8.1.4) and spelt out in some detail, and highlighted in red, what this entailed:

> In having regard to the 'welfare' of the young person, a court should ensure that it is alert to:
>
> - the high incidence of mental health problems amongst young people in the criminal justice system;
> - the high incidence of those with learning difficulties or learning disabilities amongst young people in the criminal justice system;
> - the effect that speech and language difficulties might have on the ability of the young person (or any adult with them) to communicate with the court, to understand the sanction imposed or to fulfil the obligations resulting from that sanction;
> - the extent to which young people anticipate that they will be discriminated against by those in authority and the effect that it has on the way that they conduct themselves during court proceedings;
> - the vulnerability of young people to self harm, particularly within a custodial environment;
> - the extent to which changes taking place during adolescence can lead to experimentation;
> - the effect on young people of experiences of loss or of abuse.
>
> (Sentencing Guidelines Council 2009b: para 2.9)

The Guideline also addressed the question of the amount of impact on the sentence that the age of the offender should have:

> [T]here is an expectation that, generally, a young person will be dealt with less severely than an adult offender, although this distinction diminishes as the offender approaches age 18 (subject to an assessment of maturity and criminal sophistication). In part, this is because young people are unlikely to have the same experience and capacity as an adult to realise the effect of their actions on other people or to appreciate the pain and distress caused and because a young person is likely to be less able to resist temptation, especially where peer pressure is exerted.
>
> (Sentencing Guidelines Council 2009b: para 3.1)

Such clear statements are to be welcomed.

Before we move on to review the different orders available it might be useful to consider Figure 13.3. This shows graphically the fact that in 2009–10 theft and handling offences accounted for 21 per cent of all proven offences by young people whilst violence against the person (which includes common assault) accounted for 20 per cent, and criminal damage 12 per cent (see also Youth Justice Board/Ministry of Justice 2011b: Chart 2.2).

[5] See House of Commons Justice Committee (2009: 3), available at http://www.publications.parliament.uk/pa/cm200809/cmselect/cmjust/497/497.pdf.

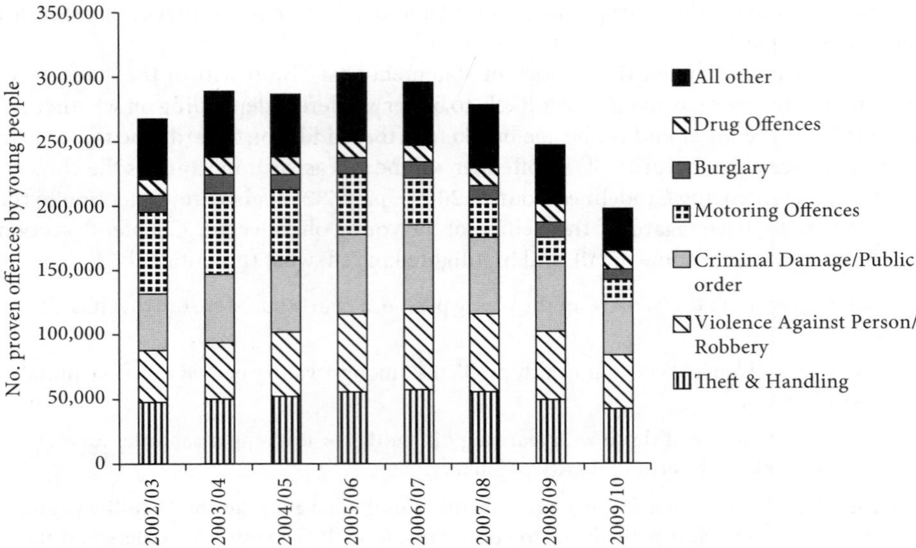

Figure 13.3 Trends in the volume of proven offences, 2002–3 to 2009–10
Source: Youth Justice Board/Ministry of Justice (2011b: Chart 2.6).

13.1.2 **Referral orders**

This order was introduced by the Youth Justice and Criminal Evidence Act 1999, re-enacted in Part III of the Powers of Criminal Courts (Sentencing) Act (PCCSA) 2000 and since amended. It has a somewhat ambivalent status in that it is a criminal order, imposed by a youth court, yet diverts the offender from the court to a Youth Offender Panel (YOP) to agree a programme of preventive or restorative activities rather than to impose punishment. It is a compromise which has its roots in the 1960s.

In 1964 a Labour policy report, *Crime: A Challenge to us All*, advocated family courts geared to achieving agreement with the offender as to what should be done to prevent his offending (see Harris and Webb 1987: 23), but, as we saw in Chapter 8, substantial legislative change was not achieved at that time in England and Wales. However, the process of dealing with first-time offenders at the youth court by the use of referral orders could be said to have established something similar to the approach envisaged 40 years ago, and implemented in Scotland in Children's Hearings.

The referral order can be for 3–12 months and amounts, then, to a new form of diversion, that of diversion from any other order that could have been imposed by the court. The YOP to which the young offender is referred includes lay members and the young offender is expected to help negotiate and agree a contract of activities—individualised preventive measures—to address his or her offending. Failure to agree or comply can mean referral back to the youth court. If the contract is successfully 'signed off' the conviction is regarded as spent. By the end of the first 18 months of operation, referral orders accounted for 30 per cent of youth court orders (Home Office 2003c: para 16); recent statistics suggest the proportion is nearer now nearer a quarter (Youth Justice Board/ Ministry of Justice 2011b: Table 4.1). As originally passed, this provision for offenders under 18, who pleaded guilty to all offences charged and who had no previous convictions or bind-overs, mandated a referral order, with two exceptions.[6] If the court considered the offence to be very serious, a custodial penalty could be imposed; if the court considered the offence to be sufficiently minor, an absolute discharge could be given. The intent was to remove the discretion of the youth court to 'punish' young offenders on a first prosecution, provided they pleaded guilty. Discretion to use the referral order or not remained where the young offender pleaded guilty to only some of the charges.

However, the referral conditions have been amended in response to several pressures. First, there was evidence of a rise in the number of apparently tactical 'guilty' pleas in order to be given a referral order rather than risk a harsher sentence. There was also a rise in the use of absolute discharges by youth courts, possibly because of concern by magistrates that the resources of the Youth Offender Panel and the preventive programmes were being 'unnecessarily' expended on referral orders for trivial offences (NACRO 2003b). Further, whilst some magistrates appeared to view referral as too heavy-handed, others were critical of the loss of their discretion to impose more punitive orders (Ball 2000). Whether the fact that, for example, not all previous convictions for very minor offences have been recorded, and so a referral order is 'wrongly' made (Newburn *et al.* 2002: 20–2), or that magistrates do not believe a three-month period of YOP supervision is necessary (see Greenhow 2003: 267), should have constituted successful pressure for change, is another question.

Since 2003, the compulsory referral conditions have the additional condition that the offence being dealt with must be an imprisonable one whilst the court has discretion to impose the order on the same conditions (in addition to the existing conditions) if the offence is not imprisonable (s 17(1A) of the PCCSA 2000).[7] The CJIA 2008 amended s 17(1A) and (2) so that the court has a discretion to make a referral order if the offender had been dealt with by a court on one previous occasion and, exceptionally, even if he had been referred to a Youth Offender Panel.[8] The Legal Aid, Sentencing and Punishment of Offenders (LAS&PO) Bill 2011, clause 80 proposes to increase discretion by allowing the use of a conditional discharge rather than a referral order.

Referral orders and (final) warnings may in practice require the young offender to engage in a form of restorative justice under which meetings are organised, with the attendance where possible of the victim and significant others in the life of the young offender. These may take the form of, for example, family group conferences, victim–offender mediation, or restorative cautioning which were discussed in Chapter 6 (section 6.3). When first implemented the scheme was criticised for assuming a young offender had sufficient maturity to engage in negotiating a package of activities or to understand fully the implications of breaking the terms of the 'contract' (see Wonnacott 1999). Using words such as contract for the outcome of this process was criticised as 'an abuse of contractual language' which hides 'too much executive discretion in respect of the contents of the order' (Ashworth 2000: 332–3).

However, early Home Office research found that some of the concerns had not materialised, with positive comments being made by parents and young offenders (Newburn *et al.* 2002). Further, the profile of the volunteer members of the youth offender panels is, encouragingly, more akin to that of the general population than to that of the lay magistracy. For example, the Audit Commission found that 37 per cent of the panel members

[6] PCCSA 2000, ss 16 and 19. The only other exception allowed by these provisions is if the Mental Health Act 1983 is applicable and a hospital order is made.

[7] Referral Orders (Amendment of Referral Conditions) Regulations SI 2003/1605.

[8] Section 35; see also ss 36–7.

were under 40 years of age, as opposed to around 4 per cent of magistrates, and 7 per cent of panel members are 'black' compared to 2 per cent of magistrates (2004: 24).[9] By 2005 the number of referral orders made accounted for almost half of all non-custodial sentences on 10–17-year-olds (Home Office 2007c: Table 3.7) and, as noted, the CJIA 2008 included amendments to increase their use further. Section 35, in force since 2009, enables the court to make a referral order where the offender has had one previous conviction but has not previously received a referral order, or the offender has previously been bound over to keep the peace, or the offender has previously received a conditional discharge. In addition the court has the power to make a second referral order, in exceptional circumstances, on the recommendation of the YOT and to revoke a referral order early for good behaviour. It can also extend the term of a referral order for up to three months on the recommendation of the youth offender panel (for example where non-compliance occurs through circumstances beyond the control of the offender, such as illness).

There would seem to be some optimism that referral orders are effective in reducing offending rates and diverting from more penal options: as Fortin notes, a former chair of the Youth Justice Board, Rod Morgan, referred to them as the 'jewel in the crown' of the youth justice system (Fortin 2009: 727).

13.2 Non-custodial options

In our review of protective sentencing in Chapter 5 we noted the importance of risk assessment (of reoffending and of harm to others) in decision making and we also referred to assessment in Chapter 12 in relation to the imposition of requirements in community sentences and SSOs, and in post-release supervision. In Chapter 6 we reviewed the development of restorative approaches and in Chapter 12 we focused on rehabilitation as an aim in community supervision, and the 'what works' approach to choice of prevention programmes to be used. Minors are not exempt from any of these trends and concerns.

13.2.1 **Assessment and information**

In Chapter 8 we referred to the importance of assessment and the use of Asset as the assessment tool used by Youth Offending Teams (YOTs) in relation to the final warning scheme.[10] Such assessments act as gatekeepers; they determine what form and quantity of intervention, if any, is to be imposed and whether the child or young person—or his/her family—is to be referred to any other agencies for more specialist help or support. Not surprisingly the importance of assessment has been flagged up in policy documents: according to *Misspent Youth* it 'allows a degree of flexibility in both sentencing and constructing the intervention plan on a [proposed] final warning' and could lead to intensive intervention to deal with family and school problems at an earlier stage (Audit Commission 1996: 69). A report in 2004 concluded that Asset is usually completed to an acceptable standard and 'is a major step forward in providing a comprehensive risk and needs assessment' (Audit Commission 2004: 73). However, the report also concluded that some YOT practitioners 'are not entirely clear about how to use the information' and that Asset is 'not always used to full effect' in identifying needs (ibid: 74–5). More recently, Wilson and Hinks found that Asset was a good predictor of proven reoffending within a

[9] This may be partly the result of a lower minimum age (18) for panel members as opposed to the 27-year-old minimum for the magistracy.

[10] See http://www.yjb.gov.uk/Publications/Resources/Downloads/Asset.pdf.

one-year period: 'Young people with higher Asset "static plus dynamic" scores were more likely to re-offend, to commit more re-offences, to commit more serious re-offences, and to receive a custodial disposal within a one-year follow-up period (compared to those with lower Asset scores)' (2011: ii). The factors which were 'highly statistically significant predictors' included 'substance use' and 'motivation to change' (ibid: iii).

Since the introduction of the 'common assessment framework' for use in relation to all children's services, the Youth Justice Board has made plain that Asset 'will continue to be used as the primary tool for assessment of young people within the youth justice system' because, inter alia, it 'is designed to focus on assessing risk of reconviction, risk of serious harm to others, and risk of vulnerability' (Youth Justice Board 2006d: 2). Asset is, then, a separate tool from that used in relation to local authority child protection duties, the *Framework for the Assessment of Children in Need and their Families* (Department of Health 2000), but the YOT can refer a young offender to the local Social Services Department if the Asset assessment reveals behaviour attributable to harm within the family. Further, according to the Ministry of Justice, 'YOTs and prevention services need to know how to access and use CAF effectively, particularly in cases where multi-agency working is required'.[11] Research has suggested, however, that few members of YOTs attend *Framework* training, which might indicate a professional approach that focuses on the risk of offending at the expense of an understanding of children's needs (Calder 2003: 29). This is particularly important in relation to 'looked-after' children[12] whose offending rate is treble the offending rate of other children (NACRO 2003c) and many of whom have been in local authority care: a decade ago it was estimated that 50 per cent of children in young offender institutions had been in care (ibid) although in a more recent study, 'Over a quarter of young men and over half of young women said they had spent some time in local authority care' (Summerfield 2011: 7). NACRO has argued that training in child development and welfare 'is vital for sharing the corporate parenting culture and associated aims and objectives', that is, necessary if effective preventive services are to be provided for looked-after children who offend. Indeed, their research suggests that access to shared training across agencies is associated with lower rates of offending by looked-after children (NACRO 2003c: 5).

A major reason for these differences is the focus on risk and on actuarial, group-based, prediction scales in relation to offenders. Assessment questionnaires and scales such as Asset, which produce a numerical score to determine outcome, are a visible indicator of 'actuarial justice' (see Chapter 1). For a child 'in need'[13] who also offends, the end product, even with the inclusion in the assessment checklists of new factors referred to as 'dynamic' factors, such as empathy with victims, might, it is argued, be an intervention which is inappropriate to the child's needs or disproportionate to the offending (Hudson 2003: 49–50). However, research completed for the YJB on the reliability and validity of Asset concluded that, whilst there was an 'acceptable' level of consistency between individual assessors (referred to as inter-rater reliability), there were significant divergences and the report suggested some YOT staff 'may be allocating ratings on the basis of perceived problems rather than the extent to which these were associated with the likelihood of further offending' (Baker *et al.* 2005: 6; see also 53).

[11] See http://www.justice.gov.uk/guidance/youth-justice/assessment/common-assessment-framework.htm.

[12] 'Looked-after children' are children voluntarily accommodated by, or in the care of, the local authority (under ss 20 and 31 respectively of the Children Act 1989).

[13] This is a term used in s 17 of the Children Act 1989 to refer to children whose health or development requires or will require the provision of services by the local authority.

For minors, as for adults, the court has required a pre-sentence report (PSR) since the Criminal Justice Act (CJA) 1991 with the purpose, according to the White Paper (Home Office 1990a), of providing the court 'with detailed information about how the offender could be punished in the community, so that option can be fully considered'. Guidance makes clear that the assessment of the young offender must be based on Asset assessment and include health, mental health—including learning disability—speech, language and communication needs, and broader welfare considerations (Youth Justice Board 2010: 49). It also notes that '[w]here a YRO is recommended, not only should the appropriate requirement(s) be identified but, in addition, the level of intervention and supervision envisaged under the Scaled Approach should be made clear' (ibid: 50) . The 'scaled approach', for use with young offenders on reparation and youth rehabilitation orders, as well as undergoing post-custody supervision, is now seen as an important risk-based assessment tool which aims to target resources more economically:

> The Scaled Approach will use quality assessment to determine the likelihood of reoffending and risk of serious harm to others. This, alongside professional judgement, will help establish which intervention level a young person needs: standard, enhanced, or intensive. The intervention level determines the minimum statutory contact a young person will have with the YOT or other assigned professionals.
>
> (Youth Justice Board: *The Scaled Approach*, undated leaflet: 2)

Research suggested that there is a correlation between the quality of PSRs and levels of custodial sentencing with, for example, more than 40 per cent of PSRs being assessed as unsatisfactory or poor in high custody areas (NACRO 2000b: 2–3). Whilst the proportion of reports recommending custody or giving no clear proposal varied, it was as high as 32 per cent in one high-custody area (ibid: 3). There is also a suggestion of racial discrimination in operation via PSRs. A review by HM Inspectorate of Probation (2000) of adult defendants found that, while 60 per cent of reports on white defendants were satisfactory, the equivalent for African or African-Caribbean defendants was 49 per cent. The quality and the type of information before the sentencing court are, then, very important.

13.2.2 **Youth rehabilitation orders**

When we wrote the second edition of this book there was a range of separate community-based orders available to the courts, a new community order for those under 16 and various provisions which had not been implemented or repealed. The sentencing situation is now much simpler.[14] At the time of the second edition, for those aged 10–15, s 147(2) of the CJA 2003 had renamed the community orders in existence as a generic new 'youth community order'. The community orders it covered included the following (the relevant sections of the PCCSA 2000 are given): a curfew order (s 163), an exclusion order (s 40A(1), introduced by the Criminal Justice and Court Services Act (CJCSA) 2000), an attendance centre order (s 163), a supervision order (s 63(1)), and an action plan order (s 69(1), introduced by the CDA 1998). *Youth Justice—Next Steps* proposed to replace all nine non-custodial sentences for 'juveniles' with one sentence, a broader Action Plan Order (Home Office 2003c: paras 7 and 17) and this proposal was endorsed in a later policy document (DfES 2004: para 4.21). What has now replaced all the previous community orders is a similar order, for all minors and with a different name—the youth rehabilitation order.

Part 1 of the CJIA 2008 introduced youth rehabilitation orders (YROs) available for all convicted offenders under 18, and in force since April 2009. Basically the order is like

[14] See pp 429–30 of the second edition of this book.

the adult ones (see Chapter 12) where the court imposes one order but can add to it any of the 15 requirements specified in s 1 (see also Schedule 1). So, for example, the youth rehabilitation order with a supervision requirement is similar in practice to the previous supervision order and, just as other requirements could be added to the supervision order, the court can now have several requirements in the one new order if it so wishes in order to get to the same outcome. The idea is to give the court more flexibility. The order can last up to three years.

In common with all the superseded orders, an attendance centre order is now only available if the young person committed an offence before 30 November 2009 but an attendance centre requirement can be added to the YRO and the main purpose is still to put a restriction on the leisure time of a young offender as the centres are usually open on Saturdays for two or three hours. The hours of attendance required depend on the age of the young offender, the maximum being 36 hours for an offender aged 16 or 17. A court can also require such attendance if a person under 21 is 'in default of payment of any sum of money': see s 60 of the Powers of Criminal Courts (Sentencing) Act 2000.

Intensive supervision and surveillance programmes (ISSPs)

Providing the offence in question is punishable by custody and the seriousness threshold for custody has been satisfied (together with a persistence criterion for those aged less than 15), the court can impose a YRO with intensive supervision and surveillance or with fostering. This possibility is part of the development of 'tougher' and more controlling forms of non-custodial punishment or 'treatment' for minors. The now-replaced supervision order was the vehicle for many of these initiatives: the CDA 1998, for example, had provided for the imposition of a reparation condition in a supervision order and widened the criteria for making a residence requirement. The ISSP was introduced by the Youth Justice Board in 2001, aimed at 15–17-year-old offenders who had been charged or warned at least four times in the previous 12 months and so were at high risk of (further) imprisonment (see Leigh 2001/2). The ISSP—which can also be a condition of post-release supervision in the second half of a detention and training order (see section 13.3.1) and as part of bail conditions—uses a combination of electronic and other forms of tracking, with staff sent to deal with non-compliance as soon as possible. In addition there can be compulsory educational or other activities, such as reparation or offending behaviour programmes. This requirement makes sense in the context of the strong link between educational attainment and offending (see Moore 2004; Waters 2007). The ISSP must last at least six months (CJIA 2008, Schedule 1, para 32).

Research on the first 41 pilot schemes concluded that, 'The frequency of offending in the ISSP sample went down by 40% over one year and by 39% over two years. The seriousness of any further offending went down by 13% in both one and two years after ISSP' (Gray *et al.* 2005: 9). Offenders who were 'persistent and serious' experienced a significant reduction in offending frequency and 'in terms of reduced offence frequency and gravity, young women performed significantly better than young men on ISSP' (ibid). An earlier study had found that reconviction rates were unaffected but that there was a 30–50 per cent reduction in the volume of crime committed by ISSP participants surveyed (Little *et al.* 2004).

In considering the use of ISSP and intensive fostering, the 'scaled approach' (discussed earlier) will be used during and after assessment of the young offender. Section 88 of the ASBA 2003 made available the fostering requirement: a child or young person can be required to live with a local authority foster parent for a period up to 12 months as part of the, then, supervision order. Section 1(3) of the CJIA 2008 now provides the power for a YRO with ISSP or with fostering. However, both of these 'extended activity'

YROs can be used only if all the relevant criteria for a custodial sentence (see section 13.3) are met.

13.2.3 **Other orders**

Reparation order

The reparation order—although carried out in the community—is not technically a community order. It was introduced by ss 67–68 of the CDA 1998, re-enacted in ss 73–75 of the Powers of Criminal Courts (Sentencing) Act 2000, and so continues as an order separate to the YRO. The distinction is of significance because, since the CJA 1991, there has been a statutory hurdle for the imposition of a community penalty on minors and adults—that the offence is 'serious enough to warrant such a sentence' (see Chapter 3). The reparation order can be imposed in relation to less serious offending. The order is available only for minors and cannot be added to a custodial or community sentence. It can involve reparation to the individual victim, if that is what the victim wants, or to the community, but the young offender cannot be required to work more than 24 hours in total over a maximum period of three months.

YROs can include curfew, exclusion, electronic monitoring, and prohibited activity requirements. These all have their origins in orders introduced since 1998 and are evidence of the more restrictive nature of requirements and orders. For example, curfew orders, introduced by the CDA 1998, were extended to children under 16 years of age by s 48 of the Criminal Justice and Police Act 2001. There are also disqualification orders, introduced by the CJCSA 2000 (ss 26–38) which can be imposed on adults and minors as an additional penalty where the offender is sentenced by the Crown Court for offences against children (as defined in Schedule 4 to the Act). The effect of the order is to prohibit the young offender from working with children in the future and a breach of the order constitutes a criminal offence. There are rights issues here, given the use of civil orders where the proceedings are not subject to the same safeguards as orders imposed in criminal proceedings.

Finally, there are of course financial penalties. The young offender can be given a fine or compensation order as can an adult (see Chapter 7). If the magistrates' court has the power to exceed a fine of £1,000 for an adult it cannot do so for an offender under 18 or exceed £250 for one under 14 (PCCSA 2000, s 135). The court can make a parent or guardian liable for the fines, victim surcharge, or compensation order of any young offender under 18 (ibid: s 137). Young offenders can also be given pre-court financial penalties—fixed penalty notices (FPNs) and penalty notices for disorder (PNDs)—and we discuss the implications of that trend in Chapter 14.

13.2.4 **Summary**

To summarise: the trend is to give courts more flexibility in constructing a programme of intervention but programmes are also becoming—at least potentially—more intensive. This approach puts a premium on there being adequate resources and training for those delivering the programmes, and for suitable 'education' of magistrates and judges. The Youth Justice Reinvestment Pathfinder Initiative is a pilot scheme which began in 2011 and through which the Youth Justice Board and the Ministry of Justice will provide extra funding to YOTs in return for their pledging to cut the use of custody over two years.[15]

[15] See http://www.justice.gov.uk/downloads/guidance/youth-justice/reducing-re-offending/YouthJusticeReinvestmentPathfinderInitiativeinformation.pdf.

Should they fail to reduce their custody levels by the agreed amount, they will have to pay a penalty. This initiative was signalled in *Breaking the Cycle* which noted that '[t]he pilots will enable us to explore how local areas can share in the financial savings and risks of custody' (Ministry of Justice 2010a: para 257).

The fear remains that negative portrayals of young offenders may undermine the push towards a reduction in punishment levels. This concern has been brought to the attention of the enquiry into press standards being conducted by Lord Justice Leveson (who is also Chair of the Sentencing Council) by the Howard League for Penal Reform. On its submission to the inquiry the Howard League noted that government initiatives around 'naming and shaming' children subject to anti-social behaviour orders (see Chapter 8, section 8.4.4) were encouraging the media 'to put potentially vulnerable children in the public eye' and referred to research in 2005 which showed that 57 per cent of media coverage of children and young people was negative.[16]

13.3 Detention

> The passing of the Children's Act, 1908, which practically forbids imprisonment before 16 years of age, marks the last stage in that slow and tedious journey which had to be undertaken by many devoted men and women who were conscious of the grave evils resulting from imprisonment, before it was generally realized that it was not by throwing children and young persons automatically and indiscriminately into gaol, that the grave problem of juvenile delinquency was going to be solved.
>
> (Sir Evelyn Ruggles-Brise K.C.B., Chairman of the Prison Commission, in *The English Prison System*, Macmillan, 1921: 101)

We draw attention to this quotation within the context of a recent decreased use of imprisonment of children and young people but in the following sections we review the range of orders available to the court to impose custody, a range which has increased in the recent past.

13.3.1 **Determinate sentences**

Detention and training order

The criteria for the imposition of a DTO, which is an option if the offence is one for which an adult could be imprisoned, are to be found in s 100 of the PCCSA 2000. Section 298 of the CJA 2003, if implemented, will amend the PCCSA 2000, s 101(2), so that six months would be the maximum term magistrates could impose on a young offender for a summary offence if the maximum for an adult is 51 weeks. Section 101(4) allows a maximum of 24 months for the detention and training order for other offences, providing it does not exceed the maximum allowed for that offence for an offender over 21 years. Before 2000, the youth court could, after trying a case, commit a 15–17-year-old to the Crown Court for sentence if it believed that its powers were insufficient.[17] Given that this power could lead to the imposition of longer custodial sentences, its repeal is to be welcomed.

The CJA 1991 repealed the relevant sections of the Criminal Justice Act 1982 so that minors and adults are now subject to the same statutory criteria for the imposition of

[16] Submitted by Frances Crook, Director, 5 December 2011: see http://www.howardleague.org/news-and-events/.

[17] The CDA 1998 repealed s 27 of the Magistrates' Courts Act 1980.

community and custodial penalties (CJA 2001, ss 148 and 152). However the research by Glover and Hibbert found that 35 per cent of their sample of 12–14 year olds on a DTO did not appear to meet the custody thresholds (2009: 4; see also NACRO 2011). Section 143(2) of the CJA 2003 also applies to minors, such that more weight is now given to previous offences in calculating seriousness.

The DTO is now, in law, available to all those over 10 years old (although there are currently no designated institutions for 10 and 11-year-olds under this order). The earlier 'normal' custodial sentence (in the CJA 1991) was detention in a youth offender institution for those aged 15–17 (only)[18] but the Criminal Justice and Public Order Act (CJPOA) 1994, ss 1–4, lowered the age at which a child could be detained by introducing secure training orders (STOs) for 12–14-year-olds. This possibility was continued in the CDA 1998 which combined the two forms of detention into 'detention and training orders' (s 73), lowered the minimum age to 10 and raised the maximum length to two years. These draconian changes were referred to as a 'legislative clampdown on children and young people' (Scraton and Haydon 2002: 314). But the provisions in s 73 were re-enacted in the PCCSA 2000.

The CDA 1998 enacted or re-enacted the criteria for imposing custody on the lower age groups—now in the PCCSA 2000 s 100(2): for those under 15 the child must be a 'persistent' offender, defined in *R v TTG* (2003) as having more than two previous convictions; in addition for those under 12 the order must be necessary to protect the public. In 2003 the Government proposed to remove the 'persistence' condition for 12–14-year-olds on the ground that it had 'proved complex in practice' (Home Office 2003c: para 21) but this has not been done. Indeed the criteria need to be more stringent: this condition is now less restrictive than the criteria for the previous STO (see Glover and Hibbert 2009: 5).

The detention and training order may be served in a variety of penal and local authority establishments—notably young offender institutions (YOIs), secure training centres, and local authority secure units—theoretically giving more flexibility to address the needs of the young offender. Since 2000, the YJB has been responsible for the allocation strategy and the presumption is that 15–17 year-olds will be placed in YOIs, whether open or closed institutions, whilst 12–14 year-olds (and 10–11 year olds under other provisions) will be accommodated outside the Prison Service, although vulnerability and gender may allow for different placements. In practice, discretionary placement outside the Prison Service is difficult because the majority of the secure juvenile estate is still to be found in Prison Service establishments (for criticism, see NACRO 2001b: 6). Barnardo's, the children's charity, has called on the Government to implement s 34 of the Offender Management Act 2007 which allows children serving a DTO to be placed elsewhere than in the secure estate. There are of course cost implications: the average cost of incarceration across different sectors is £60,000 for placement in a young offender institution, £160,000 in a secure training centre, and £215,000 in a local authority secure children's home (NACRO 2011: 6). The fact that it is cheaper to allocate to the Prison Service is of concern during a time of economic recession. However, as NACRO suggests, 'With around two thirds of the YJB budget spent on commissioning secure places, it is suggested a small reduction in the demand for places could release significant funding for community-based alternatives' (ibid).

Half the length of the order is served in an institution; the remainder is spent on supervision in the community, breaches leading to further detention. However, provided the

[18] In fact the sentence of detention in a young offender institution was also applicable to 18–20-year olds until that sentence was abolished by s 61 of the CJCSA 2000. This means that all offenders of 18 years of age and above are treated as adults for the purpose of custodial sentences.

offender has behaved and made progress in detention, the presumption since 2002 has been to release the young offender one to two months earlier than the half way stage (unless the conviction was for a serious violent or sexual offence), possibly with an electronic monitoring requirement (see NACRO 2007b).[19]

Longer sentences for 'grave' crimes

For particular offences longer sentences than the 24-month maximum available to the Youth Court can be imposed. For murder and for certain serious offences (for example, where the adult maximum penalty would be 14 years' imprisonment), the Crown Court has powers to make orders for detention at Her Majesty's Pleasure or detention for a specific period (PCCSA 2000, ss 90 and 91), and also orders for detention for life or for public protection for specified serious offences (CJA 2003, s 226). Such cases will be transferred to the Crown Court which has greater sentencing powers. The PCCSA 2000, ss 90–91, largely re-enacted legislation first passed in the Children and Young Persons Act 1933, s 53 to provide longer periods of detention to cater for what was anticipated as the exceptional circumstance of a minor committing murder (s 53(1), now PCCSA 2000, s 90) or a grave crime (s 53(2), now PCCSA 2000, s 91). Both sets of provisions now apply to all minors above the age of criminal responsibility. The murder provision had always so applied but the minimum age for the grave crimes provision was 14, until s 16 of the CJPOA 1994 lowered it to 10. There are, however, some offences which trigger s 91 only for 14–17-year olds, notably causing death by dangerous driving.

Until the Criminal Justice Act 1961, only murder, attempted murder, manslaughter, and wounding with intent to do grievous bodily harm could trigger the orders for detention at Her Majesty's pleasure (s 90) or for a specified period (s 91). In 1961 the definition of grave crimes was extended to those where the offence carried a maximum penalty of 14 years for an adult. Since then legislation has inadvertently extended the scope of the grave—now serious—crimes provision by the addition of offences with a 14-year maximum. The CJA 2003 and the Sexual Offences Act 2003 introduced further relevant maxima and the scope of s 91 was extended by the addition of specific offences for which the provision applies, for example, in relation to indecent assault since the CJPOA 1994 (see PCCSA 2000, s 91(1) and (2)).

The use of the grave/serious crimes provision has greatly increased over the years, particularly during the period 1993–97. Compared with only six sentences made under s 53(2) (or, later, s 91) in 1970, 65 were made in 1980, and 607 in 1999 (NACRO 2001b). However, there has been a decline in use since then, the total for 2010 being 250 (see Table 13.2 and Figure 13.4).

The generally upward trend over the last 80 years can only partly be explained by these factors whilst increased punitiveness on the part of youth court magistrates may also have been a factor: an increased numbers of cases, including property offences that might not have been so transferred earlier, have been sent to the Crown Court for trial (NACRO 2001/2: 8).[20] This is despite the fact that the maximum custodial sentence available to the youth court was, as we have noted, raised to two years. Further, *Mills and related appeals* (1998) had held, contrary to previous practice, that, if the maximum period for a detention and training order is deemed insufficient in relation to seriousness, the court can impose a s 91 sentence just above that maximum. A problem—in the eyes of magistrates

[19] See PCCSA 2000 s 102 and guidance issued by the Youth Justice Board in 2000 and 2002: see NACRO (2003a).

[20] Although the general power to commit 15–17-year-olds to the Crown Court for sentence was repealed by the CDA 1998, with effect from 31 May 2000.

Table 13.2 Type of custodial sentence received

Type of sentence	n	% of cases
Detention and Training Order	2,577	78%
DTO recall	384	12%
Section 91 sentence	250	8%
Section 91 recall	30	1%
Detention for public protection	17	1%
Extended sentence	16	<1%
Recall of extended sentence	2	<1%
Mandatory life sentence	7	<1%
Total	3,283	100%

Source: Jacobson *et al.* (2011: Table 2.1).

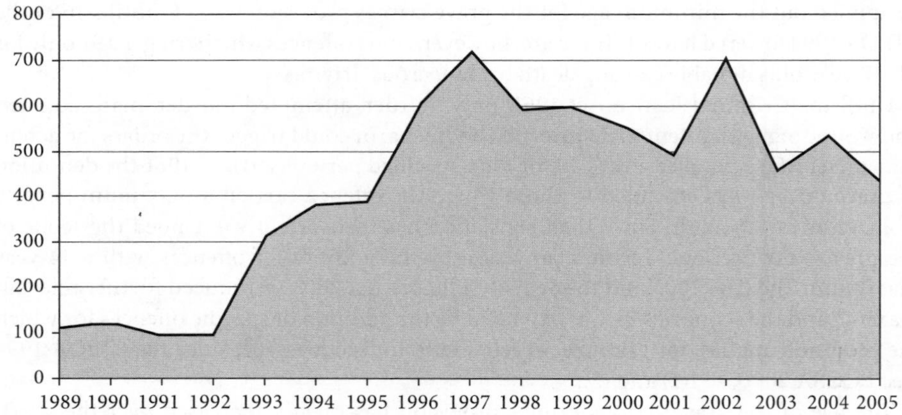

Figure 13.4 Sentences under s 91 (1980–2005)
Source: NACRO (2007d: 3).

in youth courts—has been the restrictive nature of the criteria for imposing detention and training orders on offenders under 16 years of age. Their 'solution' was to decline jurisdiction so that the Crown Court could impose detention under s 91(3) 'if the court is of the opinion that none of the other methods in which the case may legally be dealt with is suitable'. This tactic was not immediately successfully appealed but *R v Manchester City Youth Court* (2002) saw a change in thinking, and in *R (on the application of W) v Thetford Youth Court* (2002) the Divisional Court made clear that justices could not decline jurisdiction when they had no power to impose a custodial sentence simply because they felt custody was warranted. In the *Thetford* case the young offender was an 11-year-old and the circumstances of his offending could not meet the statutory criteria for a detention and training order. The Divisional Court stated that Parliament's intention to restrict the use of custody in relation to those under 14 should be upheld. In *C v Balham Youth Court* (2003) the court similarly confirmed this reasoning in relation to a 14-year-old, stating that cases which came within the s 91 provision should not be transferred to the Crown Court unless a sentence of more than two years was envisaged.

The Divisional Court has, therefore, been a useful tool to rein in the punitiveness of youth court and Crown Court sentencers.

Mandatory minimum sentences

In addition there is a new set of provisions in the CJA 2003 (ss 289–293), already in force, which import into the grave/serious crimes provision another means by which this longer sentence can be imposed on 16- and 17-year-olds at the Crown Court. The CJA 2003, s 287 provides for minimum sentences for listed firearm-related offences if the offence is committed when the offender is 18 years old or over.[21] Whilst the prescribed minimum for adults is five years, for an offender under 18 in England and Wales, or under 21 in Scotland, the minimum is three years. If the conditions are met—unless 'exceptional circumstances' apply—the courts must impose on the minor a sentence of detention 'of at least that term' (new s 91(5)). This provision automatically takes the offences beyond the sentencing powers of the youth court and so within the s 91 arrangements (NACRO 2007d: 3) but would appear to over-ride the requirement in s 91(3) that the courts must be 'of the opinion that none of the other methods in which the case may legally be dealt with is suitable'.

Extended sentences

The CJA 2003 introduced new protective sentences for both adult and juvenile 'dangerous' offenders (see Chapter 5, section 5.4) which means that, for all offences committed since April 2005, the courts have available two new sentences for offenders under 18: the sentence of detention for public protection and the extended sentence of detention. The former, which we will deal with in the following section, is an indeterminate sentence, whilst the extended sentence is a determinate prison sentence with an extended period of supervision on release. The courts now have a discretion to use this order if the offence is one of the violent or sexual offences listed in Schedule 15 to the CJA 2003, if the offender is deemed to be a risk to the public and if the court considers a proportionate custodial sentence to be at least four years (CJA 2003, s 228). For the under-18s the custodial period must be at least 12 months and the extension period cannot exceed, for adults and minors, five years for violent offences or eight years for sexual offences (ibid). This and the other provisions for 'dangerous' young offenders were more draconian before amendments made by the CJIA 2008.

13.3.2 Indeterminate sentences

For murder

The penalty for murder is mandatory—in effect a life sentence—and this has raised issues of rights in relation to the length of time spent in detention for murder before discretionary release can be considered. The most important and high-profile case was that of two boys, Robert Thompson and Jon Venables, who were given sentences of detention at Her

[21] This compares with the requirement that the offender is over 16 in relation to the mandatory minimum sentences for a third drug trafficking or domestic burglary offence (PCCSA 2000, ss 110 and 111). However, the CJA 2003, s 291 gives the Secretary of State the necessary powers to increase to 18 the minimum age for the new firearms provisions.

Majesty's pleasure for their murder of James Bulger when they were 10 years old.[22] They challenged, first by judicial review, the raising by the Home Secretary of the minimum period to be served in detention before release is considered (the tariff element of the sentence). This case went through the English appeal system and ultimately to the European Court of Human Rights where the Home Secretary's power to set a minimum detention period was deemed to be contrary to Articles 5(4) and 6(1) of the European Convention on Human Rights (ECHR) because such decisions should be made and reviewed by a judicial body (*V and T v UK* (2000)).[23] The sentencing court must now set the tariff period and *Smith* (2005) and *Dudson* (2005) concerned the proper procedure for review of the minimum period, taking into account the child's welfare. This decision is now also affected by s 269 and Schedule 21 to the CJA 2003 which require the court to have regard to a 'starting point' of 12 years in setting the tariff for a minor. This is higher than the 8 years set for Venables and Thompson by the European Court.

There has been no noticeable trend in the number of murders by 10–17 year-olds for whom a sentence under s 90 must be imposed, with total annual figures varying from 10 to 25 cases in 1989–99 (NACRO 2001b) to seven in 2010 (Jacobson *et al.* 2011:14), with figures peaking around 26 from time to time in between (NACRO 2007d: 2).

For dangerous offenders

As previously noted the CJA 2003 introduced provisions for 'dangerous' offenders, including those under 18. If the conviction of the young offender is for a 'serious' specified offence and the court believes that there is 'a significant risk to members of the public' that the young offender will cause them serious harm 'by the commission by him of further specified offences' then there are two options under s 226. For this part of the Act a 'specified offence' is one of the many sexual or violent offences listed in Schedule 15 to the Act whilst a 'serious offence' is a sub-category of specified offences for which the maximum penalty for an adult would be life or 10 years. If the young offender would otherwise have been eligible for a sentence of detention for life under the PCCSA 2000, s 91 and the offence seriousness justifies it, the court must impose that sentence. This then is not a new sentence but one with an extra set of criteria within the CJA 2003.

If the offender is not so eligible, then the court has a discretion to impose a sentence of detention for public protection (DPP)—a new sentence. This is possible only if the court assesses the seriousness of the offending as justifying a notional minimum term of at least two years (which would equate to a four-year determinate sentence in terms of seriousness). (As originally passed the court was mandated to impose a DPP order or extended sentence: see Chapter 5 for similar provisions and changes for adults.)[24] The DPP is an indeterminate sentence, with a minimum tariff period set by the court, which could last beyond the maximum which would otherwise be available.

Assessing whether the young person is 'dangerous' as required before these new sentences can be imposed (CJA 2003, s 229) is, as NACRO's first *Youth Crime Briefing* on the dangerousness provisions pointed out, crucial for the young person and yet assessment of risk is difficult and prone to inaccuracy. The Asset assessment tool, it contends, is

[22] For discussion of the moral panic which this case provoked, see Chapter 8, section 8.2.3.

[23] For a detailed discussion of the tariff element and this mandatory sentence more generally, see McDiarmid (2000).

[24] The principal difference between adults and youths is that in the case of a youth, the statutory 'exception' based on having a previous conviction for an offence listed in Schedule 15A does not apply: CJA 2003, s 225(3A).

'something of a compromise between clinical and actuarial approaches to assessment' but 'does not provide any easy answers' (NACRO 2005: 4; see also NACRO 2006).

As has also been pointed out, some of the specified offences for the purposes of these provisions would not otherwise permit a sentence of long-term detention (NACRO 2004: 7). They require the youth court to consider, when deciding on jurisdiction, whether the criteria are likely to be made out and, if so, to commit the young person for trial at the Crown Court. It may also commit to the Crown Court for sentence, having received more information in the course of the trial.

The LAS&PO Bill proposes to repeal ss 226 (the DPP sentence) and s 228 but replace the latter with a new extended sentence for young offenders. This is to be welcomed[25] although there appear to be no government plans to discontinue or amend s 91 of the PCCSA 2000 or to deal with those young offenders still imprisoned under the original DPP criteria.

13.3.3 Conditions in detention

The Howard League's participation project, U R Boss, worked with 15–17-year-old-boys in YOIs to produce *Life Inside 2010,* a report covering their day-to-day experiences. The project notes that the issue which aroused most passion in nearly all the children was in relation to the food (Howard League 2011a). The report notes that bags of fruit were in such high demand that children were bullied into buying them and handing them over. 'We were also told how fruit has become currency in one YOI because it is in such short supply' (ibid: 2).

This may seem trivial but, given the tedium of life for many young prisoners, meal times are disproportionately important as is the question of a healthy diet for all children and young people.

As we saw above, prison service establishments—rather than units run by social services—have been increasingly used for young offenders yet, as with adult prisoners, many young offenders have a history of social exclusion, including unemployment—in relation to those over 16 years to age—and also exclusion from school (see Chapter 8, section 8.1.3). In particular, young offenders are much more likely to have mental health problems than other young people: a recent report said that 43 per cent of children in contact with the youth justice system have emotional or mental health needs (Healthcare Commission 2009; see, also, Walker and Beckett 2003: 98; Lader *et al.* 2000; Lyon *et al.* 2000; Summerfield 2011: 17)—and yet those problems are often neglected, notwithstanding the potential for imprisonment to exacerbate those problems.

Safety and restraint

Conditions in YOIs have been subject to severe criticism, particularly the use of certain forms of restraint and the neglect of issues leading to the suicide or murder of young offenders in Prison Service establishments. Indeed, Goldson (2006), examining these criticisms in the context of the current United Nations concern about violence against children, concludes that what occurs is 'tantamount to institutional child abuse'.

Clearly there will be an issue of disorder and indiscipline in young offenders institutions (YOIs): young offenders were involved in prison riots and disturbances in 1990 at Glen Parva and Pucklechurch, for example, and that disorder may stem, at least in part, from frustration with poor conditions (Woolf and Tumim 1991). Inspections of youth offender institutions have, however, provided numerous examples of poor practice

online resource centre

[25] See the Online Resource Centre for updates.

in keeping good order and preventing bullying and assaults on young inmates. Group 4's privately run Medway Secure Training Centre (STC) for 12–14-year-old persistent offenders was severely criticised after an inspection in 1999 for its use of restraints and dangerous neck locks, for using unqualified staff who lacked experience of working with children, and for the absence of procedures for dealing with bullying.[26] The tragic death of Gareth Myatt in 2004, after losing consciousness whilst being restrained by staff at the Rainsbrook Secure Centre, followed four months later by that of Adam Rickwood found hanging in his cell after he had been restrained by staff at Hassockfield STC, provided a public impetus to reform.

The YJB published a draft Code of Practice in 2005 'for managing the behaviour of the troubled and troublesome young people that are cared for in secure accommodation'. It covered elements such as 'a planned approach for managing individual behaviour', 'diversion, de-escalation and diffusion processes', 'a fair system of rewards' and 'processes for consulting with children', with a final version issued in 2006 (Youth Justice Board 2006b). However, the situation proved resistant to radical change. For example, the Chief Inspector of Prisons, Anne Owers, recommended the closure of Oakhill STC, a privately run centre, because of the 'staggering levels of use of force by staff' (see HM Inspectorate of Prisons 2008).

In response to pressure, a review of restraint in juvenile secure settings was set up in 2007 but in 2008 the Justice Minister David Hanson announced that the report would be delayed to allow time for the National Children's Bureau to collect evidence on the use of restraint in secure children's homes (Children's Rights Alliance 2008: 2). The report was eventually published on 15 December 2008 (Smallridge and Williamson, 2008). It accepted that 'a degree of pain compliance may be necessary in exceptional circumstances' in secure training centres (ibid: 7) but recommended that the Prison Service should provide staff with safe restraint techniques, designed specifically for young people and which do not rely on pain compliance (ibid: para 8.33); that the Government should forbid use of the 'nose control' technique, its continued use being inconsistent with the earlier removal of the identical 'nose distraction' technique (ibid: para 8.7); and that batons should not be routinely deployed (ibid: para 8.39). Instead the Prison Service should adopt Therapeutic Crisis Intervention or a similar effective behaviour management approach in all YOIs (ibid: para 13.14), and should ensure that an enhanced Juvenile Awareness Staff Programme be mandatory for all those working with young people (ibid: para 17.11).

In its response to the Review (Ministry of Justice/DCSF, 2008), the Government accepted or partially accepted most recommendations, notably that the Government should permanently remove nose distraction and the double basket hold from the techniques currently used in Secure Training Centres but, in relation to YOIs the response was that it 'is looking to replace the nose control technique with a safer alternative within the next six months'. However, the 'exceptional circumstances' exception has been criticised and complaints about treatment have continued. A report by the Children's Commissioner (Office of the Children's Commissioner, 2011) noted that the Ministry of Justice had published in 2010 a manual created by the National Offender Management Service to train staff in safe methods of restraining young people in secure training centres and in March 2011 had published a progress report on how the Government had implemented the recommendations from the Independent Review of Restraint (ibid: 7–8) but summarised criticism of slow progress as suggesting 'distance between internationally agreed

[26] The STC received a better report in 2003 (Social Services Inspectorate 2004) though problems persisted.

standards for the use of restraint and practice in England' (ibid: 9). Having asked young offenders for their views and experiences the report expressed continuing concern about the use of pain compliant techniques in young offender institutions and secure training centres (ibid: 22) and recommended that:

1. young people with experience of the youth justice system are actively involved and engaged in reviewing and evaluating policy and practice (UNCRC, article 12);
2. the deliberate use of pain to enforce order and control is prohibited;
3. internationally agreed standards, as set out by the United Nations (including UNCRC, article 37) and European Council are used as a benchmark for how and when restraint is used on children and young people;
4. these standards are applied consistently between institutions; and
5. best practice is used across the secure estate.

(ibid: 22–3)

The report also recommended that '[i]n order to realise recommendations three, four and five we encourage the Youth Justice Board to adopt and ensure that the regulations, guidance and techniques used in secure children's homes are applied to secure training centres and young offender institutions' (ibid: 23).

A report by the Howard League has also criticised continuing methods of restraint.[27] It notes that, according to the Youth Justice Board statistics there were 6,904 incidents of (reported) restraint in 2009/2010, of which 257 resulted in injury, and that the average proportion of young people in custody who were restrained increased from 11 per cent in 08/09 to 12 per cent in 09/10, with more girls than boys restrained. (Howard League 2011: 2). Quoting examples of injuries suffered by 15-year-old boys they note that '[w]here restraints are necessary and appropriate, there are very clear authorised methods. If restraints are carried out properly these kinds of injuries should never occur. Their presence suggests that the children have been assaulted rather than restrained' (ibid: 4). Clearly, restraint is still an area where practice is not yet uniformly acceptable.

Safeguarding young people in detention has a wider remit than that of restraint techniques. A Report by HM Inspectorate of Prisons (2004) found that over one-third of those 15–18-year-olds surveyed had felt unsafe at some time whilst in custody (including all the 15-year-old girls), a quarter said they had not received any visitors, and only 30 per cent of boys said it had been easy for their parents to visit. A decade ago the Youth Justice Board had indicated that there needed to be 'a greater emphasis on safeguarding arrangements to protect children from suicide, self-harm, bullying and harm from staff and other adults' (see NACRO 2003d: 1). The propensity to suicide is higher amongst prisoners, including minors, than among the population outside: 25 boys aged 15–17 hanged themselves while in custody in the period 1990–2003 and the Prisons and Probation Ombudsman was subsequently given the responsibility for investigating all deaths in custody. Sadly, cases of death by injury or suicide involving minors hit the headlines with depressing regularity.[28] We have previously noted deaths which occurred after restraint; Liam McManus, a 15-year-old boy serving a six-week sentence for breach of a supervision order, was also found hanged in his cell in 2007 at Lancaster Farms Young Offenders' Institution making

[27] For details of the different forms of restraint allowed in various institutions see Howard League (2011: 2).

[28] For reports on suicides in US juvenile offenders institutions and also for more general information about conditions in such institutions see: Office of Juvenile Justice and Delinquency Prevention (2009) and (2010).

him the thirtieth juvenile to die in custody since 1990.[29] Sadly, the spring of 2011 saw the deaths of five teenagers in five different institutions across England in five weeks. Ryan Clark, aged 17, for example, was found hanging in his cell on 18 April at Wetherby YOI while on remand.[30]

Girls in prison

Whilst the majority of young detainees are boys and their conditions are a source of grave concern, there are also problems specific to girls. Howard League research (2004) gives a figure of 90 girls under 18 in prison on any given day and points out that, unlike the situation for boys, there are no prisons that are solely for girls. Sentenced girls are therefore held in four designated prisons where they may be placed on a separate wing for juveniles or on wings which also hold women over 18.

As we saw in Chapter 11, extensive criminological research has documented forms of disadvantage to female adult offenders on custodial regimes and community orders but there has been little on gender differences in juvenile justice until very recently (see Piper 2006, 2009). Most research stemmed from the 1970s and 1980s when a more welfare-focused system operated. However, *Girls in Prison* (Ofsted 2004) and a report by the Howard League for Penal Reform (2004), *Advice, Understanding and Underwear*, provided evidence of what amounts to discriminatory treatment of girls in custodial establishments, stemming from the much smaller numbers of young female detainees and from their different needs. There appear to be insufficient staff trained to deal with the specific problems of vulnerable (young) females and, with only four institutions, there is a greater likelihood of being placed far from home. Another report found the majority of girls on a DTO had poor educational histories and low self-esteem but appreciated the educational opportunities in custody. The comments by the girls on the community part of their sentence—which they felt was too risky for them—and on the standard of resettlement support, were more negative (Ofsted Report 2004; see also Douglas and Plugge 2007).

More recently, the report by the Children's Commissioner also found gender differences in offender responses to physical restraint:

> The use of restraint generated strong emotional responses from most of the participants, but the way girls experienced restraint varied dramatically from the boys. Many of the girls felt that the procedure impacted on them negatively in terms of their mental health and well being, and they disliked it intensely. Boys in contrast reported feelings of anger, indifference or they accepted that it was a necessary element of the custodial regime.
>
> (Office of the Children's Commissioner 2011: 21)

Young black and minority ethnic prisoners

There are also issues of racial discrimination for young offenders as for adults (see Chapter 11), with black children over-represented in custodial establishments. Wilson's ethnographic research on a small group of 16–17-year-old young black men in a young offender institution found that they 'knew nothing of the penal system's formal processes for dealing with complaints of a racial nature' and that, for this group at least, 'the Govs [the staff] were universally perceived to be able to "get away with more" than the police in the community' in regards to racist behaviour (Wilson 2003: 422–3).

[29] Reported in the *Guardian*, 30 November 2007 on p 15.

[30] Article by A. Travis in the *Guardian*, 4 May 2011.

Education

There are also problems with the provision of education and the management of the transition from custody to community. A report by Ofsted (2010) has drawn attention to the variable standards of support when children and young people move into and out of custody. The report highlights how poor initial assessment of learning needs and insufficient preparation for independent living leaves children and young people ill-equipped for outside life.

Value for money?

It would appear that the welfare of minors in custody is not yet a high enough priority, and that too many children and young people are suffering to no good purpose. Youth custody is also a waste of money: reconviction rates are very high, the Howard League giving a figure of 72 per cent within one year.[31] A small research project completed in the 1990s is instructive: a two-year follow-up of offenders who had experienced new intensive regimes at Thorn Cross YOI and Colchester Military Corrective Training Centre found that the YOI sample took longer to start reoffending and committed significantly fewer crimes (Farrington *et al.* 2002: 1). Consequently, at least £5 was saved for every £1 expended on the programme at the YOI, where the emphasis was on education and mentoring.

13.4 The role of rights for young offenders

13.4.1 The utility of rights Conventions

The Howard League has taken a policy decision in recent years to use the courts, particularly since the implementation of the Human Rights Act 1998, to challenge government policies on the treatment of young offenders (Crook 2003). We have already referred to the case which successfully challenged the interpretation in Prison Service Order (PSO) 4950 of the duty of the local authority to children in need in a custodial establishment in that area (see Chapter 8, section 8.1.4). A further case, that of *R (on the application of BP) v Secretary of State for the Home Department* (2003), concerned a 17-year-old who had been in what amounted to solitary confinement for over 23 hours a day during two periods of five and four days, in the segregation unit of a young offender institution. He claimed breaches of Articles 3 and 8 of the ECHR. The court ruled that the rules of the institution had been breached and that insufficient regard had been had to the young man's known vulnerability but did not expressly forbid the use of segregation. The Howard League brought another successful case—*R (K) v Manchester City Council* (2006)—in relation to assessing whether a child in custody would be 'in need' on release. Mr Justice Lloyd Jones decided against the argument that the YOT was the 'agency best suited to meeting the needs of K...The defendant authority is required itself to carry out an assessment. It is not entitled to delegate that function.' He further stated that YOTs can, and should, refer children to children's services, both under s 47 for a child at risk and under s 17 for child welfare.

More recently, in the case of *R (M) v The Chief Magistrate* (2010) the legal team working at the Howard League successfully argued that due process of law and good practice in any disciplinary proceeding or appeals mean that the person concerned should know what is the case against them. The child, known as M, had been awarded extra days by an

[31] See, for example, http://www.howardleague.org/francescrookblog/the-sch-debate.

independent adjudicator. He had had no legal advice and was not legally represented. The judgment highlights the need for a proactive approach to legal representation for young people facing adjudications and, as a consequence, the prison service will have to consider possible changes. In this case the judge, Collins, J, made the following significant comment: 'The welfare of the child is an important and indeed fundamental consideration in determining how a child who has committed offences should be dealt with... a young person's welfare is something that has to be properly taken into account and, indeed, that is clear from section 37 of the 1998 Act' (at para 7).

Rights-based jurisprudence can, then, be used successfully to improve the lives of young offenders. Not only are there rights applying to all age groups, notably, for the UK, the Human Rights Act 1998 and the jurisprudence of the ECHR, to which we have referred elsewhere, but there are several conventions applying exclusively to minors. The United Nations Convention on the Rights of the Child (CRC) is the best known and the most influential statement of principle on children's rights generally but there are associated conventions which focus on juvenile justice: the Beijing Rules 1985 (the UN Standard Minimum Rules for the Protection of Juvenile Liberty), the Riyadh Guidelines 1990 (UN Guidelines for the Prevention of Juvenile Delinquency), and the Tokyo Rules 1990 (UN Standard Minimum Rules for Non-Custodial Measures). The CRC has also recently published a General Comment (No. 10, 2007) on 'Children's rights in juvenile justice'.

Yet the use of rights as a tool for improving the lives of children, whether as offenders or not, can produce problems. Their employment can produce different approaches to children's welfare and their utility is sometimes questioned.[32] Further, the debates on rights do not take place in a political or social vacuum: 'they are informed, mediated and—to an extent—regulated by the historical and contemporary contexts in which they arise' (Scraton and Haydon 2002: 314; see also Chapters 9 and 11 for rights in relation to adult prisoners).

Article 40(2)(b) of the CRC enjoins governments to ensure in particular that '[e]very child alleged or accused of having infringed the penal law has at least the following guarantees' which include being presumed innocent until proven guilty, having access to information and legal advice, being dealt with 'without delay by a competent, independent and impartial authority', with access to review of a penal decision, and to having his or her privacy respected. We have already noted that Article 40 also promotes separate and different treatment and it would appear that the youth court is sufficiently separate to comply with this (Fortin 2003: 563). The CRC does not give any direct remedy for infringements, however. Those jurisdictions which have ratified the CRC are deemed to have promised to amend and operate the laws of the country to bring them in line with the CRC. The (only) sanction is the international and national censure when the Committee on the Rights of the Child publicly reports on the extent of a government's compliance with the CRC's principles. The UK Government has suffered criticism in response to its first two Reports to the Committee, particularly as we noted in Chapter 8, in regard to the age of criminal responsibility.

For individuals and for pressure groups supporting young offenders, the ECHR may provide a surer remedy. Since October 2002 children, as people, have been able to complain directly to the domestic court that their rights under the ECHR are being infringed. Several Articles, notably Article 3 (no inhuman or degrading treatment), Article 6 (the right to a fair trial), and Article 7 (no punishment without law), are of potential utility

[32] For a useful review of the different theoretical perspectives and of the sources of international rights, see Fortin (2009: Part One and also pp 714–28 in relation to issues raised in this Chapter). For a theoretical critique of reliance on rights to achieve improvements for children, see King (1997a).

for children as well as for adult defendants and offenders. The courts have ruled that the lack of legal representation for minors in Children's Hearings in Scotland, though civil proceedings, has infringed the child's rights under Article 6 (*S v Principal Reporter and the Lord Advocate* (2001)). Failing to warn a young person that an admission of guilt regarding a sexual assault—as part of the process of giving a reprimand or warning—will result in their being placed on the sex offenders' register has also been acknowledged as a breach of Article 6.[33] However, Hollingsworth (2007) argues, in the light of recent jurisprudence, that there is a lack of judicial consistency in relation to children's rights under the ECHR.

The procedures adopted by the youth courts are generally compliant with the ECHR and magistrates have recently been encouraged to make further changes to improve communication between magistrates and young offenders (Home Office 2001c). The same positive comments cannot be made about the Crown Court, the court to which, as we saw in section 13.3.2 above, minors are transferred in relation to particular crimes and outcomes. The high-profile trial of Venables and Thompson, aged 11, brought this issue to public attention. The formal setting, the relentless publicity, their relative isolation, and the length of the proceedings were at odds with the requirement under the CRC Article 40(1) that they be treated 'in a manner consistent with the promotion of the child's sense of dignity and worth', and the requirement of the Beijing Rules that the proceedings 'be conducted in an atmosphere of understanding' where the juvenile can properly participate (r 14.2). More importantly it was argued to the European Court that it infringed Articles 3 and 6 of the ECHR. Whilst the claim under Article 3 was rejected, an infringement of Article 6—the right to a fair trial—was upheld because they had been unable to participate fully in a trial pitched at the level of understanding of adult participants.

This case (*V and T v United Kingdom* (2000)) did not prohibit the use of the Crown Court for minors, although it led to a direction by the Lord Chief Justice (*Practice Note (trial of children and young people)* 2000) requiring a variety of practical changes to make the court room and process more conducive to the participation of minors. The result is, in relation to the Crown Court, that 'children are still required to sit in a dock, stared at by a jury, and cross-examined by barristers' (Fortin 2003: 565).

Of perhaps most importance, given the problems we have reviewed in the previous section, is the extensive use of detention for young offenders by the courts in England and Wales. Article 37 of the CRC states that it should be 'a measure of last resort' and the Committee on the Rights of the Child has criticised the UK for the earlier ages at which detention is now used, as well as the greater numbers being detained, the longer sentences available, and the unacceptable conditions in young offender institutions (Committee on the Rights of the Child 2002: paras 59–62).

However, as Scraton and Haydon (2002) have argued, it is too easy for the government to hide a lack of attention to the rights of minors behind a rhetoric of rights. In reference to the UK's Second Report to the Committee on the Rights of the Child (UK Government 1999), they make the following comment: 'Using a discourse of "rights" and "responsibilities", the punitive potential of the [1998] Act is reconstructed as enabling, supportive welfare intervention'. In an ironic interpretation of Article 3, the Report states: 'It is in the interests of children and young people themselves to recognise and accept responsibility, and to receive assistance in tackling criminal behaviour' (Scraton and Haydon 2002: 321). Similarly they point out that the Report justified the abolition of the presumption of *doli incapax* as a means of ensuring that the courts are able to address offending

[33] *R (U) v Comr of Metropolitan Police; R (U) v Chief Constable of Durham Constabulary* (2002): see Fortin (2003: 562–3).

behaviour by children in the 10–14 age group (UK Government 1999: 17) and the changes to the right to silence—allowing adverse inferences to be drawn—as a 'common sense' change, so that the child is not deprived of his or her responsibility to provide 'an innocent explanation' (ibid: 180).

Scraton and Haydon consequently argue for a proper rights-based approach in youth justice which they distinguish from a just deserts approach, on the basis that the former can legitimately differentiate treatment between adults and minors; it can 'mitigate' for age and maturity in a way that is currently lacking and can focus on the child's welfare without relying on an image of the child as weak and dependent (ibid: 324–5). Other commentators have suggested that the discourse has now moved away from rights. For example, Williams is concerned that the previous Labour Government's 'Every Child Matters' policies, with a focus on outcomes and the potential of children when adults, 'all suggest a deliberate decision to eschew both the language and the concept of children's rights' (Williams 2007: 263).

The 'clarification' of Articles 37 and 40 of the UN CRC in the General Comment on rights in juvenile justice (Committee on the Rights of the Child 2007) is, then, to be welcomed. It points out, for example, that Article 3 should be heeded in relation to young offenders: the best interests of the child should be a 'primary consideration' but we saw in Chapter 8 that even the weak welfare test in s 44 of the 1933 Children and Young Persons Act is being downgraded in importance. On the one hand, we have welfare being 'trumped' by the aim of preventing offending and, on the other, as we have seen, rights can become a meaningless rhetoric. So rights constitute a problematic discourse in relation to children and young people who offend but as, Kilkelly and Lundy (2006) argue, the CRC can be used as an 'auditing' tool to assess the extent of compliance or non-compliance within policy and practice. Unfortunately, as Drakeford and Butler (2007) pointed out, conditions and suicides in youth prisons do not lead to a national 'scandal' in the same way that some other child deaths do: Victoria Climbié was portrayed as a victim, Gareth Myatt was not. The pressures on politicians to 'talk tough', to respond to perceived public opinion, and not to challenge negative images of young people make it very difficult to successfully implement either the welfare or the rights of young offenders.

13.5 Conclusions

13.5.1 A critical stage?

> Devolved and local youth justice remains heavily circumscribed by central government risk-based directives and targets. Nevertheless, rather than being firmly located within any one identifiable philosophy or strategy, youth justice throughout the United Kingdom now appears ever more hybrid and contradictory.... The rationalities and technologies of risk, restoration, welfare and rights can all be brought to bear discursively in pursuit of either preventive or punitive goals.
>
> (Muncie 2011: 51)

It is very difficult to summarise trends since the second edition of this text. There have been encouraging developments in relation to preventive projects and a greater understanding on the part of some of our judiciary about both the rights and welfare of young offenders. Yet there is still a very worrying propensity on the part of the press and the government to talk tough, with resulting sentencing and penal policy which is disproportionate or unlikely to be effective. It is also, as Muncie notes above, possible to interpret policy and practice in quite different ways.

At the beginning of Chapter 8 we expressed concern that the separateness of the juvenile justice process and outcomes is under threat and that minors are increasingly being treated like adults. Arguably, adults are increasingly being treated as minors in that penal measures have often been piloted on minors. Using children and young people as a testing ground for policies is not new and not necessarily deleterious. For example, the hurdles for the imposition of custody enacted for minors in the 1980s were extended to adults in the CJA 1991 and the linked custodial punishment and community supervision in the detention and training order was, in effect, rolled out for adults with the new early release provisions. All these examples augur less punitive and more effective responses—*provided that* they are used to decrease the use of custody.

Concern stems, rather, from the fact that youth justice policies now encourage more intervention—often punitive—in the lives of young offenders, and are based on particular images of children which legitimise more punitive responses. The benefits for young offenders of experiencing 'cutting edge' and enlightened practical ideas can easily be outweighed by the drawbacks of being guinea pigs for punitive products such as curfews and intensive behaviour modification programmes.

Publicity is currently more often given by the Government to the provisions which indicate a 'tough' or 'new' approach to dealing with children who commit offences or who might progress from anti-social behaviour to criminality. For two reasons it is a pity that this more 'audible' strand of youth justice policy is punitive and underpinned by images of minors which focus on near-adult and 'dangerous' aspects. First, it obscures the fact that there are positive new approaches in juvenile justice and developments in other areas of government policy which take into account what is known about the multiple causality of offending and which aim to respond to social deprivation and need. Their lower priority precludes a wider debate about young offenders. Second, the dominant and often negative images of children and young people which underpin policy are powerful: they can legitimise practices which may not be in the child's best interest and may not even reduce offending.

Policy developments for young offenders are often presented as 'new', a break with the past, and self-evidently better than past practice. This is misleading. All is not new and commentators have pointed this out (for example, Fionda 1999). This again precludes useful debate where parallels can be drawn with past practices and their effectiveness or drawbacks used to inform present practice and policy.

So what *is* justice for 10–17-year-olds? As Weijers points out, there is a double paradox in relation to juvenile justice. There is the paradox stemming from 'the search for a compromise between deserved punishment and useful punishment' when there are 'centrifugal forces' pushing the two justifications apart (2002: 138): the theme which runs through this book. However, there is also the problem that in dealing with minors the criminal justice system 'will always have to take account of the dilemma that, while they are developing towards responsibility, they are presumed to be dependent and not yet fully responsible' (ibid: 139). Duff suggests that we should question whether the punishment meted out to minors should be different from that meted out to adults, taking account of the effect and meaning of punishment for juveniles. He concludes that 'the obvious candidate' as an inappropriate punishment for juveniles is imprisonment (2002: 132).

Developments in children's services around 'safeguarding' and the links made across youth justice, child protection and children's services by the administrative changes that have been introduced by the Children Act 2004, are, we hope, allowing more focus on the welfare of young offenders. However, we would argue that rights—as well as a greater focus on welfare—could be more important in resolving at least some of the conditions and processes identified as unacceptable. A rights approach does not mean minors are necessarily treated the same as adults. Children and young people should be treated by known procedures and by measures which are not disproportionate to what they have done but, equally, substantive and procedural law needs to be enacted and implemented on the basis of conceptions of children which acknowledge their state of both being and becoming. That would allow minors to be accorded respect for their abilities and concerns, but would acknowledge, where appropriate, their inability to be held fully responsible where their stage of maturity and life experience would make it unjust to do so. The recent Guidelines from the Sentencing Council which require an assessment of maturity or otherwise are a start—providing that assessment does not become formulaic and simplistic.

13.5.2 **Case study**

The following case study covers material in Chapter 8 as well as this chapter. There is guidance in the Online Resource Centre to help you advise these two young people.

Bilal, aged 13, and his cousin Ava, aged 17, were arrested in a video warehouse which they had entered by prising open a small window. They were taken to the local police station where, in the presence of a solicitor and an appropriate adult, Bilal confessed to burglary. Bilal had been reprimanded the previous year.

You are the solicitor:

1. Explain to Bilal what decision the police are likely to make about him.
2. Explain to Bilal what would happen if the police decided to give him a warning.

Then:
Ava was found to have stolen and hidden a quantity of videos before the arrival of the police. Ava, who had been given a warning for an offence a year previously, was prosecuted for the offence of burglary of commercial premises (Theft Act 1968, s 9) for which the maximum penalty is 10 years. She decided to plead guilty.

3. Explain to Ava what options are open to the youth court and which option they are most likely to choose.
4. Explain to Ava whether the options would be different if she had committed burglary of a residential property (for which the maximum penalty is 14 years).

Consider this alternative scenario:

Assume that Bilal and Ava confess to having jointly committed the offence of having possession of a Class B drug with intent to supply (Misuse of Drugs Act 1971, s 5(3)—for which the maximum penalty is 14 years' imprisonment). The youth court decides that a custodial sentence is the only appropriate sentence for both of them.

5. Explain to Bilal and Ava how and where might such a sentence be imposed and on what criteria. (Bilal is still 13 and Ava is still 17.)

14

Sentencing and punishment in context

SUMMARY

As in previous editions our book has reviewed a wide range of issues concerning the law, policy, and practice of sentencing and punishment and has examined the main philosophical justifications for the state's responses to those adjudged by the courts to be criminals. However, there are themes in criminology and penology, and in penal policy and practice, which cut across the chapters in this book, and which allow us to identify trends in sentencing and punishment in the late twentieth and early twenty-first centuries. In our concluding comments we will simply highlight these issues.

14.1 The role of punishment

14.1.1 Is sentencing less important?

In the second edition of this book we commented on the decreasing importance of sentencing and there is continuing evidence for this assertion in the growing recognition, in the light of socio-legal and criminological research, that the penal sanction has limited usefulness (see our discussions on deterrence, incapacitation, and rehabilitation in Chapters 4, 5, and 12 respectively). The knowledge that few crimes are reported, that even fewer are successfully prosecuted to the point of sentence, and that punishments which ensure the offender does not reoffend are rare, undermines the value of academic and professional investments in this area of public life.

In section 14.1.2 we note developments that provide a different perspective but it is fair to acknowledge that developments Crawford (2003) has referred to as the 'contractual governance' of deviant behaviour would seem to diminish further the importance of those legal provisions and punishment practices with which this book has been concerned. Crawford's argument was that 'the ultimate symbol of state sovereignty—the penal sanction—itself is in crisis' and was being supplanted as a social control mechanism by a complex mesh of localised contracts in policy areas as diverse as housing, education, and community safety (2003: 480). For Crawford, new contractual forms of government, notably crime prevention partnerships, reflect a new 'future-focused logic of crime prevention, risk minimization and insurance' which suggests 'a very different idea of justice, one that is more instrumental than moral, more consequential than symbolic and more utilitarian than retributive' (ibid: 486).

More recent analysis by O'Malley in relation to financial penalties also speaks of something akin to a brave new world in penal control:

> New forms of 'simulated' justice and policing are emerging at the convergence of telemetric regulation with two linked trends: the monetization of justice and the development

> of risk-based technologies of governance. A definitive example is the traffic fine, where, increasingly, the offence is electronically monitored, calibrated, monetized into a fine, the fine issued and expiated in simulated space—that point at which the real and the virtual converge. While all of this is very 'real' (real money is primarily electronic and digitized), binary codes rather than liberal individuals are focal.
>
> (O'Malley 2010: 795)

Another example of the declining influence of 'traditional' penal measures and the increasing use of civil or 'voluntary' measures is the repertoire of new tools for controlling anti-social behaviour. Not only do we have the anti-social behaviour order (ASBO) which we discussed in Chapter 8 (section 8.4.4), but there are also now agreements and contracts whose use has shown a huge increase since they were introduced. For example, the Respect Task Force which operated under the Blair administration, reported on the increasing use in 2003–6 of the new 'tools' of acceptable behaviour contracts (ABCs) and agreements. Guidance issued by the Home Office's Anti-Social Behaviour and Alcohol Unit noted that 'the flexible nature of ABCs means that they can be used incrementally' and provided a range of increasingly interventionist options which could be used (Home Office 2007d: 2). There developed, therefore, a whole new system of behaviour control operating outside the formal criminal justice system but making use of the shadow of the law.

There is also a trend towards the greater use of fixed penalty notices—those fines which are outside of sentencing courts and imposed administratively, not judicially, and which we discussed in Chapter 7 (section 7.3.4). Although it is difficult to calculate the full extent of this, given that different kinds of non-court penalties are recorded by various relevant bodies, it is clear that the government sees this as a way of avoiding the high cost of court processing. It does, however, raise serious questions of accountability, proportionality and impact. It is not an issue that will raise serious public concerns because generally such penalties mean that an offender is dealt with more leniently and quickly and are not, therefore, a matter for individual complaint unless the system is seen as too automatic and allowing insufficient space for putting forward a defence. It is, however a development which has implications for young offenders. Chapter 8 reviewed the developments in traditional forms of diversion from court, which originated in police cautions, and now include reprimands, warnings, and youth conditional cautions. That Chapter also dealt with civil orders to respond to anti-social behaviour and Chapter 13 with the criminal orders available or young offenders. However, those discussions obscured the fact that there are penalty notices for young people which divert from more accountable methods of responding to unacceptable behaviour. Research on the piloting of penalty notices for disorder on 10–15 year olds in 2005–6 found evidence that:

> [C]ases were diverted from prosecutions, reprimands and Final Warnings to PNDs, the most significant being the 59% fall during the pilot period in the use of Final Warnings as a form of disposal. The degree of possible diversion varied by crime type with disposals other than PNDs reducing by 63% for drunk and disorderly offences as compared with 22% for criminal damage.
>
> (Amadi 2008: iii)

They also found net-widening: in two areas 'over 2,000 individuals were brought into the Criminal Justice System that would previously not have been dealt with through a formal disposal' (ibid). Such developments, which are underpinned by less guidance and by no statutory criteria, are of concern.

In addition, with the increase in the number of civil orders for which the police can apply, the role of the police in punishing offenders has increased, with a corresponding decrease in the role of the sentencing court.

14.1.2 More emphasis on sentencing?

As we saw in Chapter 2, the Coroners and Justice Act 2009 set up a new Sentencing Council with a wider remit and greater statutory definition of its functions. That Council was established and started work immediately. It has developed publicity materials, conducted consultations, and drafted new guidelines, and has established a higher profile for sentencing in a comparatively short period of time. This development has given a higher profile to sentencing in policy and in academic literature whilst the riots in summer 2011 have brought, as we noted in the Preface to this edition, sentencing and justifications for punishment into the public arena.

There is also a greater emphasis on the sentencing stage in that the sentencer now has available a greater range of ancillary orders which can be imposed with a sentence and which we briefly reviewed in Chapter 5 (section 5.5.1), having focused on one such order—the sexual offences prevention order—at the end of Chapter 1. We now have a plethora of civil orders relating to a wider range of offences and offenders, including violent offenders, which encroach on freedom of movement. The courts are also being empowered to add more controlling types of requirements to community sentences and supervision on licence. For example, the Legal Aid, Sentencing and Punishment of Offenders Bill 2011 proposes to add a foreign travel prohibition requirement to the many options for individualised community orders.[1] The effect of these changes has also had implications for the prison population as, in some cases, breaches of those orders have led to custodial sentences. This was an issue highlighted by the Corston Report (2007) and as we saw in Chapter 11, considerable numbers of women have been imprisoned for breaches.

In policy terms, as we saw in Chapter 1, and in our review throughout this book of the major legislative innovations of 1991, 1997, 1998, 2000, 2003, 2008, and—potentially—2012, sentencing and punishment remain very high on the agenda of both the Government and the public. The law and order issue dominated elections in the 1990s, and has been an essential item on party manifestos since then. Paradoxically, the importance of the visible, sanctioning institutions of the courts and prisons increases as the state's capacity to control crime becomes more limited.

14.1.3 Greater executive control over sentencing and punishment?

We noted in the second edition that the earlier developments in regard to constraints placed on sentencers, including the establishment of the Sentencing Advisory Panel, and then the Sentencing Guidelines Council, were evidence of more control of sentencing and indeed they are: the desire on the part of the Government for efficiency and effectiveness has led to greater central control of those who deliver sentences as well as the agents of community punishment. This development also presages increasing control of sentencing guidance from outside the judiciary. The relationship between the Sentencing Guidelines Council and the Secretary of State was established in the Criminal Justice Act (CJA) 2003, s 170 and the Sentencing Guidelines Council had to appoint 'non-judicial' members with experience of policing, criminal prosecution, criminal defence, and the promotion of the

[1] See the Online Resource Centre for updates.

welfare of victims of crime, although the Lord Chief Justice was Chair (CJA 2003, s 167). The Sentencing Guidelines Council has now been replaced by the Sentencing Council, and Schedule 15 to the Coroners and Justice Act 2009 sets up a slightly different composition whereby the Lord Chancellor appoints six non-judicial members, and the Lord Chief Justice appoints eight judicial members and also appoints the Chair, albeit by agreement with each other. Whilst the judicial members are in the majority, the actions of the Council are themselves more constrained by the very detailed instructions regarding the making of guidelines set out by Parliament in the Coroners and Justice Act 2009.

The increasing centralisation of punishment in terms of fiscal controls and policies governing the day-to-day work conducted in prisons and in the Probation Service, the increasing control of discretion to implement central policies and the imposition of a 'one size fits all' approach has raised problems for delivery of services to specific groups of offenders, as we saw in Chapters 10 and 11. The current Coalition Government is strongly committed to making greater use of voluntary bodies and community involvement and devolution to the private sector, as part of its rehabilitation revolution, but the success of the proposed changes may be limited by the expanding prison population and the availability of funding to voluntary groups.

On the one hand, these developments are to be welcomed if they contribute to greater clarity of sentencing guidance and more consistency of sentencing practice, and to the reduction of injustice by geography in the provision of the best quality programmes to help and 'correct' the diverse population of offenders subject to community and custodial penalties. On the other hand, it is difficult not to feel some unease. The greater use of management tools such as monitoring, standardisation, rigid line management, and budget control are not to be welcomed if a country-wide level and form of practice is at the expense of professional expertise and a sense of doing justice on an individual basis.

14.1.4 **Reductionism**

A further example of policy conflict can be found in the goal of reducing the use of custodial penalties. This was a consistent policy imperative before the major sentencing legislation of 1991, 2003, and 2008 and yet was rarely publicised as such. But the reductionist aim will never be achieved, as many commentators have observed, whilst governments aim also to be seen as the toughest (see Hough *et al.* 2003; Sparks and Taylor 2001/2). As Sanders and Loveday pointed out following the publication of the Auld and Halliday reports, 'without identifying mass imprisonment ("punitive segregation") as the problem (rather than the solution), is not all the rest mere tinkering—just a re-arrangement of the deck-chairs on the Lab–Con's Titanic criminal justice system?' (2001–2).

However, in the face of mounting pressure on the prison system, the highest levels of the prison population on record, and the associated costs of incarceration, governments have been encouraged to explore possible reductionist policies, as we have seen, even if only in relation to specific offender groups. While some prisons have been closed, this has been primarily cost driven to save money rather than a wholesale commitment to reductionism.

This shift reflects the view that prison may not 'work' for all groups, and that, in some cases, alternatives may need to be considered for offenders convicted of non-violent offences. Ways of enhancing community punishments to make them more onerous and more acceptable to sentencers and the public have also been sought. The changes to the bail provisions to reduce the numbers remanded in custody are also primarily cost-driven.

These reductionist trends lie uneasily alongside the commitment to 'rebalance the criminal justice system' in favour of the law-abiding majority by dealing robustly with crime and anti-social behaviour, and by the restructuring of prisons to ensure efficient use of resources when dealing with high volume of offenders. So reductionism has been applied to women and plans to extend to other groups and focus on holistic programmes to deal with complex needs of women offenders.

14.2 The influence of rights jurisprudence

14.2.1 The quest for rights

In examining developments in penal policy, we have drawn attention to the influence on government policy and sentencing guidelines of judgments from the European Court of Human Rights and the domestic courts. We have noted Convention cases which have led to significant changes, for example, in the treatment of offenders in prison with increasing weight being placed on the prisoner's right to life, his right to non-degrading treatment and punishment, and on his procedural rights, and the move towards treating the prisoner as a citizen with rights and duties. The right to equality has also been given greater weight following the Equality Act 2010 imposing on custodial establishments a duty to promote equality.

Rights-driven change is also now enshrined in statute to make the sentencing decision more 'open'. For example, s 174 of the CJA 2003 imposes a duty on the sentencer to give reasons for a sentence in open court and explain 'in ordinary language' the reasons for the sentence and the effects of it. Amendments made by the Coroners and Justice Act 2009 have provided more details as to the scope of this duty. The court must, for example, now identify any relevant definitive guideline and explain how that has been applied,[2] explain—if relevant—why it is of the opinion that the criteria for a community or custodial sentence (the 'hurdles' we discussed in Chapter 3) have been met, and identify any mitigating and aggravating factors which affected the sentence. Such transparency is to be welcomed.

We have also identified a number of areas of prison life in which rights have been given effect and it seems that future litigation on prison life will continue to be framed within the rights discourse of the European Convention. As we have seen, rights have been a significant influence on both the theory and practice of punishment in recent years and continue to provide a means of raising standards in the criminal justice process, particularly within the context of custody, and to provide a counter to demands for penal austerity.

However, since the second edition of the book, we have seen more intense criticism of the Human Rights Act 1998, and clashes between the Strasbourg court and the UK Government on the questions of whether prisoners should be given the vote and on the weight given to the right to family life in deportation decisions. This has led to the establishment of an independent Commission to investigate the creation of a UK Bill of Rights and to advise on reform of the Strasbourg Court. Its report is due at the end of 2012.

14.2.2 The United Nations Convention on the Rights of the Child

Whilst these shifts in policy are to be welcomed, it is a cause for concern that rights-based change has not gone far enough in relation to children and young people who offend and that the UN Convention on the Rights of the Child has not had as much impact as many

[2] In the context of the duty in s 125 of the C&JA 2009.

commentators would wish. As Fortin notes, children and young people, particularly those in ethnic minorities, are more likely to be victims of personal crimes than adults yet:

> Despite these factors which indicate that there may be almost as many young people being sinned against as are sinners, politicians continue to curry favour with the public by playing on its fears.
>
> (Fortin 2009: 683)

Current constructions of citizenship in relation to young people are particularly problematic (see Piper 2008: Chapter 8) and, as Gray argues, the focus in social and penal policy on responsibilisation has 'done little to either boost young offenders' sense of social worth or change their material circumstances' (Gray 2007: 410). If children make 'wrong' choices or 'fail' to make any positive choices then various forms of discipline or punishment are triggered but it has been argued, whilst it 'is perfectly legitimate to promote responsibility... it is not equally legitimate to withhold rights until a young person can demonstrate that responsibility' (Childright 2005: 3). Recent emerging evidence in relation to neuroscience would suggest that early developmental influences, particularly in neglected children, have longer lasting effects than previously thought and that assumptions about the maturity of children and young people may be leading to injustice (Ross and Hilborn 2007; Walsh 2011). However, we have noted in Chapter 13 that the emphasis in sentencing guidelines on taking account of immaturity is to be welcomed although this is not yet sufficiently influential.

The sentencing framework for children and young people is also not sufficiently different from that relating to adult offenders. The CJA 2003 has continued the use of statutory criteria for all age groups for the imposition of custodial and community sentences which means that the test for custody, 'so serious that neither a fine alone nor a community sentence can be justified', therefore applies to anyone above 10 years old, the age of criminal responsibility. That the dividing line is set at 10 for the purposes of criminal proceedings is itself a cause for concern as noted in Chapter 8 (section 8.3.2). The new community rehabilitation order introduced by the Criminal Justice and Immigration Act (CJIA) 2008 is an improvement on the previous situation but whether it—and also the new conditional caution—lead to very different practice depends on how these new options are used. Further, the 18–20-year-old age group continues to be neglected and, as we saw in the last chapter, conditions in detention institutions for young people are still far from ideal.

14.2.3 **The European Union framework**

The directives and frameworks emerging from the European Union should not be classified as rights jurisprudence and placed in this section but we have done so because they are an external source of regulation of English criminal justice and sentencing which often draws its ideas from victims' rights approaches. We have mentioned in the book several measures which have been influenced by decisions of the European Union and amongst these are the Framework Decision on the Standing of Victims in Criminal Proceedings and the European Convention on the Compensation of Victims of Violent Crime. In addition, the CJIA 2008, Part 6 included new measures to implement European Framework Decision 2005/214/JHA on the mutual recognition of financial penalties, to promote 'international co-operation in relation to criminal justice matters'. The Council's Framework Decision 2008/909/JHA deals with the mutual recognition and enforcement of custodial sentences. These developments focus on the enforcement of orders, the recovery of fines and property, the making of compensation, the standing of victims, and the freezing of property. These developments can only be helpful.

14.3 The development of new approaches

14.3.1 'Community' and 'therapeutic' courts

Community courts and therapeutic courts are related developments which draw on the use of informal procedures but aim to increase the role of the court. There is an International Network on Therapeutic Jurisprudence, set up by David Wexler, who coined the phrase, whose web site explains the approach as follows:

> Therapeutic Jurisprudence concentrates on the law's impact on emotional life and psychological well-being. It is a perspective that regards the law (rules of law, legal procedures, and roles of legal actors) itself as a social force that often produces therapeutic or anti-therapeutic consequences. It does not suggest that therapeutic concerns are more important than other consequences or factors, but it does suggest that the law's role as a potential therapeutic agent should be recognized and systematically studied.[3]

Therapeutic courts are multi-disciplinary in that they draw on, or refer to, a range of associated services such as drug treatment or anger management courses, housing and welfare agencies and family support services but also use the authority of the court to ensure regular attendance at the required services. Such courts have been pioneered mainly in the United States and Australia[4] but in the UK domestic violence courts (see Burton 2006) and drug and alcohol courts have been piloted (see Harwin and Ryan 2007). The former are criminal courts, the latter have been set up either in criminal courts or in civil courts with a child protection remit. The final report of the research on the family, drug, and alcohol court in London has concluded that '[t]here are indications that FDAC may offer a better way than ordinary care proceedings of ensuring that the court system can help improve outcomes for both children and parents in cases involving parental substance misuse' (Harwin *et al.* 2011: 4).

Community courts have also been established in Liverpool and Salford, using the same multi-agency model and with a particular focus on drugs offences but with an emphasis on using a more 'user-friendly' building, for example a converted school. The North Liverpool Community Justice Centre, which opened in 2005 states that 'The three foundation stones of the Centre—a problem-solving approach, partnership working, and the unique role of the judge—are inextricably linked up with each other and cannot be disentangled' (Mair and Millings 2011: 96). The recent report also stresses the importance of the judge: 'What was the impact of the judge? Quite simply, the answer to this is—massive. While the personality of Judge Fletcher certainly played a part in his effectiveness, this was also a result of his dual role as District Judge and Crown Court Judge, and his position as the sole resident Judge at the Centre'(ibid: 97). The use, in community, drug, and violence courts, of one judge through a case and the readier access to rehabilitative and welfare services is a development to be welcomed and copied. The previous government continued to support these initiatives (see Office for Criminal Justice Reform 2009) and it is to be hoped the recession does not affect their funding.

There is some concern, nevertheless, that the pressure for encouraging change in the lives of the people before the courts—be they drug users, perpetrators of domestic abuse or minority rights violations, tax evaders, or any of the other offenders who are the focus of specialist courts worldwide—might undermine their rights to due process. Plotnikoff

[3] See http://www.law.arizona.edu/depts/upr-intj/.

[4] See, for example, the special issue, 'Therapeutic Jurisprudence', of the journal *Law in Context* (2003) Vol 20(2).

and Woolfson (2005) in their review of research on problem-solving courts in other jurisdictions, for the Department for Constitutional Affairs, pointed to the importance of involving lawyers conversant with and supportive of the new approaches. It is to be hoped, however, that they do not simply become social workers with a law degree because, as we have seen in relation to children in detention (Chapter 13, section 13.3.3), the use of courts in their traditional role can still be effective.

14.3.2 Abolitionism

A much more radical approach is abolitionism. It is difficult to define as it is not a monolithic approach, but a perspective which encompasses a range of writers from divergent periods and theoretical traditions, including the Marxian, anarchist, communitarian, and Christian traditions. However, what they share is the view that prisons are dysfunctional as they have failed to control crime, but have perpetuated the exclusion of offenders; legal institutions and criminology are also subjected to critique from this approach. Prisons simply impose pain and operate coercively on the basis of judgements by professionals. Abolitionism is part of a fundamental critique of society and argument for social change. So the criminal justice system itself is seen as part of the problem.

The philosophical foundations of penal abolitionism are discussed by Ruggiero (2010) with reference to the work of Mathiesen (2006), Christie (1977, 1982), Hulsman (1991), and Bianchi (1986). Ruggiero notes that some elements of restorative justice may incorporate elements of this approach in recognising the failing of formal systems to do justice, and the harm prison does to recipients of that punishment, as well as the way in which conflicts are stolen from participants. Both perspectives also recognise the importance of examining the relationship between victims and offenders. However, he stresses that abolitionism rejects notions of reintegrative shaming and would reconceptualise the position of victims. Abolitionism, he argues, also sees abolition as a process achieved in stages, so for example if prisons are closed, the funds saved can be used to help victims and offenders. Ruggiero focuses on European abolitionism. However, the abolitionist movement has also gathered momentum in the United States in the context of mass imprisonment, discussed in Chapter 5, and has been seen as offering a better approach to prison reform (see Davis, 2003; Piché, 2009). The *Justice Reinvestment* approach discussed in Chapter 1, section 1.2.2, also tries to develop an alternative to conventional approaches to punishment (see House of Commons Justice Committee 2010; Allen and Stern 2007). Some of these issues were also discussed at the twelfth International Conference on Penal Abolition in 2008.[5]

So while complete abolition of prisons is unlikely to be pursued in the current political climate or accepted by politicians or the public, nonetheless we find elements of abolitionism in the move towards restorative justice discussed in Chapter 6. The impact of mass imprisonment on communities is also being examined by writers such as Wacquant and a new approach within criminology, convict criminology, has allowed space for former prisoners to bring their views on these issues into the debate (see Ross *et al.* 2011).

14.4 Organisational changes in managing crime and disorder

In the criminal justice system we have seen major changes in the administration of criminal justice, with the breaking up of the Home Office, the creation of the Ministry of Justice

[5] See http://www.howardleague.org/fileadmin/howard_league/user/pdf/Icopareport.pdf.

and the transfer to it of key areas of criminal justice policy and management, including offender management, the arrival and departure of several Home Secretaries, and the election—albeit by default—of a Coalition Government, for the first time since the 1940s. Ministerial responsibility for crime and justice might now be seen as a 'poisoned chalice' for ministers given the problems we have highlighted.

A Home Secretary in the last Labour Government emphasised that the Government would be taking a 'more rounded view of tackling crime, from prevention through to rehabilitation' and that this would also mean less direct control, allowing professionals greater flexibility, and also stronger partnerships with business and industry (Home Office 2007a; see also Home Office 2007b). Certainly, we have seen the continuing rise of the market in recent years with contestability extended to a wider range of criminal justice functions including community punishment. The role and status of the Probation Service have also changed: it is now a national body, under direct central control and subject to National Standards and the detailed statutory provisions of the CJA 2003. It also became part of the larger National Offender Management Service in a merger with the Prison Service and NOMS itself has been restructured. So the criminal justice landscape is much more complex than a decade ago and this is likely to increase with proposals to make greater use of the voluntary sector in the provision of rehabilitation.

But there are also tensions between central government and corporate interests on the one hand, and local communities, the police and local government on the other, over the governance of crime in public and private space. Hadfield (2006) explores this in his study of the night-time economy in city centres and shows that, despite a commitment to rebalancing the criminal justice system in favour of the law-abiding majority, the government's relaxation of regulatory constraints on the alcohol industry has contributed to a context in which anti-social behaviour has flourished. Despite the prevalence of these problems in cities throughout the UK, the response is now to increase the price of alcohol rather than to address deeper causes of incivility and anti-social behaviour.

14.5 **Disorder and insecurity**

The first edition of this book was conceived and written after the events of 11 September 2001. In this political climate, as Zedner notes, the 'language of security is increasingly supplanting that of crime control' (2003: 151). So policing—nationally and internationally—has been dominated by terrorist threats and acts. Internationally as well as nationally, politicians perceive a need to be seen to be firm, decisive, and punitive in the 'battle' against a new and immensely more harmful form of criminality. If these attitudes and the overriding concerns with security influence attitudes to lesser forms of risk and to criminality in general, then this would reduce the chances of success of reductionist policies.

Since the first edition of this book, we have seen terrorist attacks closer to home with the 7 July 2005 bombings, and terrorism and national security have assumed further importance in the crime control agenda. This has shaped domestic criminal justice policy in so far as the fight against terrorism worldwide has become focused on threats from within, which has added to a sense of insecurity, and has been used to legitimise increases in police powers. We have seen further extensions to anti-terrorism law in the Prevention of Terrorism Act 2005 and the use of Control Orders. We have also seen increasingly a conflict between the Government and civil libertarians and professionals over this agenda, which has been framed by the UK's continued participation in major military engagements overseas.

Since the second edition of this book we have seen a further development in the war on terror, namely the focus on the prison itself, as the locus of terror, through the radicalisation of inmates, as well on universities as sources of extremism. The involvement of UK nationals, including former UK prisoners, in terrorist activities and organizations overseas has drawn attention to the prison as a possible source of radicalism. This issue has been raised in Europe and is also being investigated in the United States, particularly the activities and effects of the prison organization Jam'iyyat Ul-Islam Is-Saheeh (JIS) (see Neumann and Rogers 2008; Neumann 2010; US Department of Justice 2008). Prison officers in the UK have been receiving training to identify extremism and the implications of this were considered in Chapter 11. This focus on extremism has also raised issues regarding the treatment of whole communities as 'suspect', as generators of terrorism. This issue has been debated by Greer (2010) and Pantazis and Pemberton (2009, 2011).

Conversely, concern over the incarceration of terror suspects here and the United States has increased scrutiny of the criminal justice process and the institutions of punishment. This has led to questions over the maintenance of rights during the interrogation process and the treatment of prisoners convicted of terrorist related offences, both in Europe and in the United States. The European Court has made clear in *A and others v UK* (2009) the importance of maintaining non-degrading treatment even in the most extreme circumstances.

We have also witnessed the urban riots in the UK in the summer of 2011. The experience of the riots, and particularly the sentencing of those convicted for riot-related offences, highlighted the issues we have addressed in this book. Following the riots, some first time offenders were convicted and given relatively severe custodial sentences for thefts of small value items and despite guilty pleas. Although some of these sentences were reduced subsequently on appeal, they raised questions about the purposes of sentencing and the problems of exemplary sentencing, not least the inconsistency between the treatment of offenders in the riots and those committing similar crimes in other contexts. The punishment of rioters also reflected political pressures on sentencers from the government and the media to deal firmly with the perpetrators. It seemed that desert principles were being sacrificed on the altar of public opinion for benefits which were difficult to identify. It also meant that the prison population was swollen further, reaching record levels in the autumn of 2011.[6]

14.6 The quest for justice

The subtitle of this book is 'The Quest for Justice' and this has been a recurring theme throughout our review of sentencing and penal policy. Justice appears as a neutral word—the 'pure' end product of a positive moral process. The even-handed figure with the scales, the 'avenging angel' of Miss Marple in Agatha Christie's *Nemesis*, the wise Judge Solomon: all are symbols of justice dealt out above the everyday ambiguities and complexities of life.

Yet in practice justice is inextricably linked with money and more so now when we are writing this third edition in a period of continued recession. According to retributivist principles, justice is done only if punishment is seen by all concerned as commensurate with seriousness. When the public's and sentencers' perception of seriousness is heightened then, without restraint, the system will lead to harsher sentences. More intensive

[6] See http://blog.oup.com/2011/08/sentencing-the-rioters/ and http://blog.oup.com/2011/09/tough-sentencing/.

supervision or (longer) prison sentences mean that the cost rises and even restorative justice is not immune from the link between money and justice, despite the principle that it pays back and restores. If what has been damaged, be it property or person, is seen by those at a restorative conference as a great harm, the procedures to ensure adequate reparation may themselves be costly and reflected in governmental efforts to shift the burden to private and voluntary organisations. Utilitarian principles are seemingly more economic in so far as the principle of parsimony demands that intervention should be the minimum necessary to achieve the outcome. But implementing 'what works', although cheaper than 'blanket' solutions, is still expensive and success is not guaranteed. Incapacitation is clearly expensive and deterrence requires a high level of publicity and education to be effective.

The variables which influence what counts as justice are not independent and can all be manipulated:

- the selection of agreed justifying principles and an agreed notion of the inalienable components of justice;
- the selection of concepts of what counts as serious and dangerous and the different levels of seriousness and dangerousness;
- the amount of money the electorate is prepared to spend on achieving justice in sentencing and punishment.

If these variables, and their operation in the dispensing of justice in sentencing and punishment, could be more openly debated, some progress might be made.

We set out these variables for debate, and our hope for honest, public debate in the previous editions of this text but the need, regrettably, still exists. The climate of populist punitiveness, the sense of international, national and personal insecurity—albeit with changing components—and the lack of an ethical consensus on dealing with 'evil' and 'deviance' continue to preclude proper debate. In addition the desire to cut costs is seen as even more imperative in a time of recession. Despite this pessimism we continue to hope that this book might encourage debate and change.

Bibliography

Abel, R. (1982) *The Politics of Informal Justice*. New York, Academic Press.

Adler, R. (1985) *Taking Juvenile Justice Seriously*. Edinburgh, Scottish Academic Press.

Advisory Council on the Penal System (1977) *The Length of Prison Sentences*, Interim Report. London, HMSO.

Advisory Council on the Penal System (1978) *The Review of Maximum Sentences*, Final Report. London, HMSO.

Aebi, M., Delgrande, N., and Marguet, Y. (2011) *Annual Penal Statistics, SPACE II 2009, Survey on Non-Custodial Sanctions and Measures in the Council of Europe Member Countries*, PC-CP (2011) 4, Council of Europe.

Aertsen, I., Daems, T., and Robert, L. (eds) (2006) *Institutionalizing Restorative Justice*. Cullompton, Willan.

Aldridge, M. and Eadie, T. (1997) 'Manufacturing an Issue: The Case of Probation Officer Training' *Critical Social Policy* Vol 17(1), 111–24.

All Party Parliamentary Group on Women in the Penal System (2011) *Women in the penal system, Second report on women with particular vulnerabilities in the criminal justice system*. London, Howard League.

Alldridge, P. and Mumford, A. (2005) 'Tax Evasion and the Proceeds of Crime Act 2002' *Legal Studies* Vol 25(3), 353–73.

Allen, F. (1981) *The Decline of the Rehabilitative Ideal*. New Haven, CT, Yale University Press.

Allen, R. (1996) *Children and Crime*. London, Institute for Public Policy Research.

Allen, R. (2011) *Last Resort? Exploring the reduction in child imprisonment 2008–11*. London, Prison Reform Trust.

Allen, R. and Stern, V. (eds) (2007) *Justice Reinvestment, A New Approach to Crime and Justice*. London, ICPS.

Althusser, L. (1971) *Lenin and Philosophy*. London, New Left Books.

Amadi, J. (2008) *Piloting Penalty Notices for Disorder on 10- to 15-year-olds, results from a one year pilot*, Ministry of Justice Research Series 19/08. London, Ministry of Justice.

American Friends Services Committee (1971) *Struggle for Justice: A Report on Crime and Punishment in America*. New York, Hill and Wang.

Amos, M. (2004) '*R v Secretary of State for the Home Department ex parte Anderson*—Ending the Home Secretary's Sentencing Role' MLR Vol 67, 108–23.

Andenaes, J. (1974) *Punishment and Deterrence*. Ann Arbor, University of Michigan Press.

Archard, D. (1993) *Children, Rights and Childhood*. London, Routledge.

Ashworth, A. (1983) *Sentencing and Penal Policy*. London, Weidenfeld and Nicolson.

Ashworth, A. (1984) 'Techniques of Guidance on Sentencing' *Criminal Law Review*, 519–30.

Ashworth, A. (1987) 'Disentangling Disparity' in C. Pennington and S. Lloyd-Bostock (eds) *The Psychology of Sentencing*. Oxford, Oxford Centre for Socio-legal Studies, Wolfson College, Oxford University, 24–7.

Ashworth, A. (1992) 'Non-Custodial Sentences' *Criminal Law Review*, 242–51.

ASHWORTH, A. (1993) 'Victim Impact Statements and Sentencing' Crim LR, 498–509.

ASHWORTH, A. (1998a) 'Structuring Sentencing Discretion' and 'Four techniques for reducing sentencing disparity' in A. von Hirsch and A. Ashworth (eds) *Principled Sentencing: Readings on Theory and Practice* (2nd edn). Oxford, Hart Publishing, 212–19, 227–39.

ASHWORTH, A. (1998b) *The Criminal Process* (2nd edn). Oxford, Clarendon Press.

ASHWORTH, A. (2000) *Sentencing and Criminal Justice* (3rd edn). London, Butterworths.

ASHWORTH, A. (2002) 'Responsibilities, Rights and Restorative Justice' *British Journal of Criminology* Vol 42, 578–95.

ASHWORTH, A. (2003) 'New Sentencing Proposals for England and Wales' *Sentencing Observer*, No 2, 9.

ASHWORTH, A. (2004) 'Criminal Justice Act 2003: Part 2: Criminal Justice Reform—Principle, Human Rights and Public Protection' *Criminal Law Review*, 516–32.

ASHWORTH, A. (2005) *Sentencing and Criminal Justice* (4th edn). Cambridge, Cambridge University Press.

ASHWORTH, A. (2008) 'English sentencing guidelines in their public and political context' in Freiberg, A. and Gelb, K. (eds) (2008) *Penal Populism, Sentencing Councils and Sentencing Policy*, Willan Publishing.

ASHWORTH, A. (2010) *Sentencing and Criminal Justice* (4th edn). Cambridge, Cambridge University Press.

ASHWORTH, A. AND PLAYER, E. (1998) 'Sentencing, Equal Treatment and the Impact of Sanctions' in A. Ashworth and M. Wasik (eds) *Fundamentals of Sentencing Theory*. Oxford, Clarendon Press.

ASHWORTH, A. AND PLAYER, E. (2005) 'The Criminal Justice Act 2003: The Sentencing Provisions' *Modern Law Review* Vol 68(5), 822–38.

ASHWORTH, A. AND VON HIRSCH, A. (1997) 'Recognising Elephants: The Problem of the Custody Threshold' *Criminal Law Review*, 187–200.

ASP, P. (2010) 'Previous convictions and proportionate punishment under Swedish law' in J. V. Roberts and A. von Hirsch (eds) *Previous Convictions at Sentencing, Theoretical and Applied Perspectives*. Oxford, Hart, 207–26.

ASQUITH, S. (2002) 'Justice, Retribution and Children' in J. Muncie, G. Hughes and E. McLaughlin (eds) *Youth Justice, Critical Readings*. London, Sage, 275–83.

AUDIT COMMISSION (1996) *Misspent Youth: Young People and Crime*. London, Audit Commission.

AUDIT COMMISSION (1998) *Misspent Youth, '98: The Challenge for Youth Justice*. London, Audit Commission.

AUDIT COMMISSION (2004) *Youth Justice 2004*. London, Audit Commission.

AULD, LORD JUSTICE (2001) *Review of the Criminal Courts of England and Wales*. London, The Stationery Office.

BAGARIC, M. (2001) *Punishment and Sentencing: A Rational Approach*. London, Cavendish.

BAILEY, W. C. (1980) 'Deterrence and the Celerity of the Death Penalty: A Neglected Question in Deterrence Research' *Social Forces* Vol 58, 1308–33.

BAILEY, W. C. AND PETERSON, R. D. (1997) 'Murder, Capital Punishment and Deterrence: A Review of the Literature' in H. Bedau (ed) *The Death Penalty in America: Current Controversies*. New York, Oxford University Press, 135–61.

BAILIN, A. (2002) 'The Inhumanity of Mandatory Sentences' *Criminal Law Review*, 641–45.

BAKER, E. (1993) 'Dangerousness, Rights and Criminal Justice' *Modern Law Review* Vol 56, 528–47.

Baker, E. and Clarkson, C. M. V. (2002) 'Making Punishments Work? An Evaluation of the Halliday Report on Sentencing in England and Wales' *Criminal Law Review*, 81–97.

Baker, K. (2010) 'More Harm Than Good? The Language of Public Protection' *Howard Journal* Vol 49(1), 42–53.

Baker, K., Jones, S., Merrington, S., and Roberts, C. (2005) *Further Development of Asset*. London, Youth Justice Board.

Ball, C. (1995) 'Youth Justice and the Youth Court—The End of a Separate System?' *Child and Family Law Quarterly* Vol 7(4), 196–208.

Ball, C. (2000) 'The Youth Justice and Criminal Evidence Act 1999 Part I: A Significant Move towards Restorative Justice or a Recipe for Unintended Consequences?' *Criminal Law Review*, 211–22.

Ball, C. (2004) 'Youth Justice? Half a Century of Responses to Youth Offending' *Criminal Law Review*, 167–80.

Bandalli, S. (1998) 'Abolition of the Presumption of *Doli Incapax* and the Criminalisation of Children' *Howard Journal* Vol 37(2), 114–23.

Banks, J. (2011) 'Foreign National Prisoners in the UK, Explanations and Implications' *Howard Journal* Vol 50(2), 184–98.

Bar Council, The (2006) *Guide to Sentences for Serious Crimes*. http://www.criminalbar.com/210/redirect/SentencingNov06.pdf.

Barak-Erez, D. (2011) 'The Private Prison Controversy and the Privatization Continuum' *The Law & Ethics of Human Rights* Vol 5(1), Article 4. Available at http.//www.bepress.com/lehr/vol5/iss1/art4.

Barclay, G. and Mhlanga, B. (2000) *Ethnic differences in Decisions on Young Defendants Dealt With by the Crown Prosecution Service*, Home Office Section 95 Findings 1. London, Home Office.

Barker, V. (2009) *The Politics of Imprisonment, How the Democratic Process Shapes the Way America Punishes Offenders*. New York, Oxford University Press.

Barry, M. (2005) *Youth Policy and Social Inclusion*. London, Routledge.

Bateman, T. (2007) 'Ignoring Necessity: The Court's Decision to Impose an ASBO on a Child' *Child and Family Law Quarterly* Vol 19(3), 304–21.

Beccaria, C. (1767) *On Crimes and Punishments and Other Writings*, ed. R. Bellemy (1995). Cambridge, Cambridge University Press.

Beck, U. (1992) *Risk Society, Towards a New Modernity*, London, Sage.

Beckett, K. and Western, B. (2001) 'Governing Social Marginality: Welfare, Incarceration and the Transformation of State Policy' in D. Garland (ed) *Mass Imprisonment*. London, Sage, 35–50.

Beckford, J. A., Joly, D. and Khosrokhavar, F. (2005) *Muslims in Prison: Challenge and Change in Britain and France*. London, Palgrave.

Bedau, H. (1997) 'Prison Homicides, Recividist Murder and Life Imprisonment' in H. Bedau (ed) *The Death Penalty in America: Current Controversies*. New York, Oxford University Press, 176–82.

Beinart, S., Anderson, B., Lee, S., and Utting, D. (2002) *Youth at Risk? A National Survey of Risk Factors and Problem Behaviour among Young People in England, Scotland and Wales*. London, Communities that Care.

Bentham, J. (1789) *Introduction to the Principles of Morals and Legislation*, ed J. L. Burns and H. L. A. Hart (1996). Oxford, Clarendon.

Bentham, J. (1830) *The Rationale of Punishment* ed J. McHugh (2009). Amherst, New York, Prometheus Books.

Bentham, J. (1843) 'Anarchical Fallacies' in J. Bowring (ed) *The Works of Jeremy Bentham*. Edinburgh, William Tait.

Benton D. (2007) 'The Impact of Diet on Anti-Social, Violent and Criminal Behaviour' *Neuroscience & Biobehavioral Reviews* Vol 31(5), 752–74.

Berman, G. (2011) *Prison Population Statistics, SN/SG/4334*. London, House of Commons Library.

Besemer, S., van der Geest, V., Murray, J., Bijleveld, C., and Farrington, D. (2011) 'The Relationship Between Parental Imprisonment and Offspring Offending in England and The Netherlands' *British Journal of Criminology* Vol 51, 413–37.

Beyleveld, D. (1980) *A Bibliography on General Deterrence*. Farnborough, Saxon House.

Bianchi, H. (1986) 'Abolitionism, Assensus and Sanctuary' in H. Bianchi and R. van Swaaningen (eds) *Abolitionism, Towards a Non Repressive Approach to Crime*. Amsterdam, Free Press.

Black Committee (1979) *Report of the Children and Young Persons' Review Group*. Belfast, HMSO.

Blad, J., Cornwell, D., and Wright, M. (eds) (2012) *Civilising Criminal Justice*. Winchester, Waterside Press (forthcoming).

Blagg, H. (1985) 'Reparation and Justice for Juveniles' *British Journal of Criminology* Vol 25(7), 267–79.

Blanchette, K. and Brown, S. L. (2006) *The Assessment and Treatment of Women Offenders: An Integrative Perspective*. Chichester, John Wiley.

Block, B. (1993) 'A Fine Mess' *Justice of the Peace*, 16 May, 308.

Blumstein, A., Cohen, J., and Nagin, D. (1978) (eds) *Deterrence and Incapacitation*. Washington, DC, National Academy of Sciences.

Bohm, R. (2008) 'Karl Marx and the Death Penalty' *Critical Criminology* Vol 16(4), 285–91.

Boin, A. and Rattray, W. A. (2004) 'Understanding Prison Riots: Towards a Threshold Theory' *Punishment and Society* Vol 6(1), 47–66.

Bonger, W. (1916) *Criminality and Economic Conditions*. Boston, Little, Brown.

Boone, M. and Moerings, M. (eds) (2007) *Dutch Prisons*. The Hague, BJu Legal Publishers.

Boswell, G. (1991) *Section 53 Offenders: An Exploration of Experience and Needs*. London, The Prince's Trust.

Bottoms, A. (1985) 'Justice for Juveniles 75 years on' in D. Hoath (ed) *75 Years of Law at Sheffield 1909–84*. Sheffield, University Printing Unit.

Bottoms, A. (1995) 'The Philosophy and Politics of Sentencing' in C. M. V. Clarkson and R. Morgan (eds) *The Politics of Sentencing Reform*. Oxford, Clarendon.

Bottoms, A. (2002) 'On the Decriminalisation of English Juvenile Courts' in J. Muncie, G. Hughes, and E. McLaughlin (eds) *Youth Justice, Critical Readings*. London, Sage, 216–27.

Bottoms, A. (2008) 'The Community Dimension of Community Penalties' *Howard Journal* Vol 47(2), 146–69.

Bottoms, A. and McWilliams, W. (1979) 'A Non-Treatment Paradigm for Probation Practice' *British Journal of Social Work* Vol 9(2), 159–202.

Bottoms, A. and Roberts, J. (eds) (2010) *Hearing the Victim, Adversarial Justice, Crime Victims and the State*. Cullompton, Willan.

Bottoms, A., Rex, S., and Robinson, G. (eds) (2004) *Alternatives to Prison, Options for an Insecure Society*. Cullompton, Willan.

Bowcott, O. (2011) 'Appeal court criticises judge's approach to riot sentencing' *The Guardian* 27 September.

Bowden, P. (1996) 'Violence and Mental Disorder' in N. Walker (ed) *Dangerous People*. London, Blackstone, 13–27.

Bowen, E., Brown, L., and Gilchrist, E. (2002) 'Evaluating Probation-based

Offender Programmes for Domestic Violence Perpetrators: A Pro-feminist Approach' *Howard Journal* Vol 41(3), 221–36.

Bowen, E., El Komy., M., and Heron, J. (2008a) *Anti-social and other problem behaviours among young children, patterns and associated child characteristics* Findings 282. London, Home Office.

Bowen, E., El Komy, M., and Steer, C. (2008b) *Characteristics associated with resilience in children at high risk of involvement in anti-social and other problem behaviour,* Findings 283. London, Home Office.

Bowles, R., Faure, M., and Garoupa, N. (2008) 'The Scope of Criminal Law and Criminal Sanctions: An Economic View and Policy Implications' *Journal of Law and Society* Vol 25(3), 389–416.

Bowling, B. and Phillips, C. (2002) *Racism, Crime and Justice.* London, Longman.

Boyd, C. M. J. (2009) 'Can a Marxist believe in Human Rights?' *Critique* Vol 37(4), 579–600.

Boyle, M. H. and Lipman, E. (2002) 'Do Places Matter? Socioeconomic Disadvantage and Behavioral Problems of Children in Canada' *Journal of Consulting and Clinical Psychology* Vol 70(2), 378–89.

Braithwaite, J. (1989) *Crime, Shame and Reintegration.* Cambridge, Cambridge University Press.

Braithwaite, J. (2000) *Regulation, Crime, Freedom.* Aldershot, Ashgate.

Braithwaite, J. (2002) *Restorative Justice and Responsive Regulation.* Oxford, Oxford University Press.

Braithwaite, J. (2003) 'Principles of Restorative Justice' in A. von Hirsch, J. Roberts, A. Bottoms, K. Roach, and M. Schiff (eds) *Restorative Justice and Criminal Justice, Competing or Reconcilable Paradigms?* Oxford, Hart Publishing, 1–20.

Braithwaite, J. and Pettit, P. (1990) *Not Just Deserts: A Republican Theory of Criminal Justice.* Oxford, Clarendon Press.

Brasse, G. (2003) 'Money Laundering—Who's Been Taken to the Cleaners?' *Family Law,* 492–6.

Brayford, J., Cowe, F., and Deering J. (eds) (2010) *What Else Works? Creative work with offenders.* Cullompton, Willan.

Bretherton, H. (1991) 'Partnership in Practice' *Probation Journal,* 132–5.

Britton, B., Hope, B., Locke, T., and Wainman, L. (1988) *Policy and Information in Juvenile Justice Systems.* London, NACRO/Save the Children Fund.

Brody, S. (1976) *The Effectiveness of Sentencing,* Home Office Research Study No 35. London, HMSO.

Brooks, L. (2011) 'An Ugly Totem for the Abject Failure of Our Criminal Justice System' *The Guardian,* 18 March.

Brooks-Gordon, B. and Bainham, A. (2004) 'Prisoners' Families and the Regulation of Contact' *Journal of Social Welfare and Family Law* Vol 26, 263.

Brown, M. (2002) 'The Politics of Penal Excess and the Echo of Colonial Penality' *Punishment and Society* Vol 4(4), 403–23.

Brownlee, I. (1998a) 'New Labour—New Penology? Punitive Rhetoric and the Limits of Managerialism in Criminal Justice Policy' *Journal of Law and Society* Vol 25(3), 313–35.

Brownlee, I. (1998b) *Community Punishment.* London, Longman.

Bui, H.S. (2004) 'Criminal Justice and Mental Health' *Probation Journal* Vol 51(3), 260–1.

Bullock, K. (2010) 'Enforcing financial penalties—the case of confiscation orders' *Howard Journal* Vol 49(4), 328–39.

Bullock, K., Mann, D., Street, R. and Coxon, C. (2009) *Examining attrition in confiscating the proceeds of crime,* Home Office Research Report No 17. London, Home Office.

Búrca, G. and de Witte, B. (2005) (eds) *Social Rights in Europe*. Oxford, Oxford University Press.

Burnett, R. and Roberts, G. (eds) (2004) *What Works in Probation and Youth Justice: Developing Evidence-Based Practice*. Cullompton, Willan.

Burney, E. (1985) 'All Things to All Men: Justifying Custody under the 1982 Act' *Criminal Law Review*, 284–93.

Burney, E. (2002) 'Talking Tough, Acting Coy: What Happened to the Anti-Social Behaviour Order?' *Howard Journal* Vol 41(5), 469–84.

Burney, E. (2003) Book review. *Howard Journal* Vol 42(4), 405–6.

Burney, E. (2005) *Making People Behave: Anti-social Behaviour, Politics and Policy*. Cullompton, Willan.

Burney, E. and Pearson, G. (1995) 'Mentally Disordered Offenders: Finding a Focus for Diversion' *Howard Journal* Vol 34, 291–313.

Burton, M. (2006) 'Judicial Monitoring of Compliance: Introducing "Problem Solving" Approaches into Domestic Violence Courts in England and Wales' *International Journal of Law, Policy and Family* Vol 20(3), 366–78.

Byrne, D. (2005) *Social Exclusion* (2nd edn). London, Sage.

Caddle, D. and Crisp, D. (1997) *Imprisoned Women and Mothers*, Home Office Research Study No 162. London, Home Office.

Calder, M. (2003) 'The Assessment Framework: A Critique and Reformulation' in C. Calder and S. Hackett (eds) *Assessment in Child Care: Using and Developing Frameworks for Practice*. Lyme Regis, Russell House Publishing, 3–60.

Campbell, S. (2002) *A Review of Anti-Social Behaviour Orders*, Home Office Research Study No 236. London, Home Office.

Campbell, T. (1983) *The Left and Rights: A Conceptual Analysis of the Idea of Socialist Rights*. London, Routledge & Kegan Paul.

Campbell, T. (2010) *Justice* (3rd edn). Basingstoke, Palgrave Macmillan.

Canton, R. (2011) *Probation, Working with Offenders*. Abingdon, Routledge.

Carlen, P. (1989) 'Crime, Inequality and Sentencing' in P. Carlen and D. Cook (eds) *Paying for Crime*. Milton Keynes, Open University Press, 8–28.

Carlen, P. (1998) *Sledgehammer: Women's Imprisonment at the Millennium*. London, Macmillan.

Carlen, P. (ed) (2002) *Women and Punishment: The Struggle for Justice*. Cullompton, Willan.

Carlisle, Lord (1988) *The Parole System in England and Wales*, Report of the Review Committee. London, HMSO.

Carrabine, E. (2010) 'Youth Justice in the United Kingdom' *Essex Human Rights Review* Vol 7(1), 12–24. Available at http. ehrr.org.

Carter, Lord (2007) *Securing the Future: Proposals for the Efficient and Sustainable Use of Custody in England and Wales*. London, Ministry of Justice.

Carter, P. (2003) *Managing Offenders, Reducing Crime: A New Approach* (The Carter Report). London, The Stationery Office.

Cavadino, M. and Dignan, J. (2002) *The Penal System* (3rd edn). London, Sage.

Cavadino, M. and Dignan, J. (2006) *Penal Systems, A Comparative Approach*. London, Sage.

Cavadino, M. and Wiles, P. (1994) 'Seriousness of Offences: The Perceptions of Practitioners' *Criminal Law Review*, 489–98.

Celnick A. and McWilliams W. (1991) 'Helping, Treating and Doing Good' *Probation Journal* Vol 39, 164–70.

Centre for Reviews and Dissemination (1999) *Systematic Review of the International Literature on the Epidemiology of Mentally Disordered Offenders*, CRD Report 15. York, York University.

Chaplin, R., Flatley, J., and Smith, K. (2011) *Crime in England and Wales 2010/11 Findings from the British Crime Survey and police recorded crime*, Home Office Statistical Bulletin 10/11. London, Home Office.

Cheliotis, L. K. and Liebling, A. (2005) 'Race Matters in British Prisons: Towards a Research Agenda' *British Journal of Criminology* Vol 46, 286–317.

Chigwada, R. (1989) 'The Criminalisation and Imprisonment of Black Women' *Probation Journal* Vol 37, 100–5.

Chigwada-Bailey, R. (2003) *Black Women's Experience of Criminal Justice: A Discourse on Disadvantage* (2nd edn). Winchester, Waterside.

Children's Rights Alliance (2008) *Children's Rights Bulletin for children and young people* Issue 27 May. London, CRAE.

Childright (2005) 'Which Youth Matters? Comments on the Government Green Paper' *Agenda*. Colchester, Children's Legal Centre, University of Essex.

Christian, J. and Kennedy, L.W. (2011) 'Secondary narratives in the aftermath of crime, Defining family members' relationships with prisoners' *Punishment and Society* Vol 13(4), 379–402.

Christie, N. (1977) 'Conflicts as Property' *British Journal of Criminology* Vol 23, 289, reprinted in E. McLaughlin, R. Ferguson, G. Hughes, and L. Westmarland (2003) *Restorative Justice, Critical Issues*. Milton Keynes, Open University Press and London, Sage. Chapter 1.

Christie, N. (1982) *Limits to Pain*. Oxford, Martin Robertson.

Christie, N. (2007) 'Restorative Justice: Answers to Deficits in Modernity' in D. Downes, P. Rock, C. Chinkin, and C. Gearty (eds) *Crime, Social Control and Human Rights*. Cullompton, Willan.

Christie, N. (2010) 'Victim movements at a crossroad' *Punishment and Society* Vol 12(2), 115–22.

Clarke, K. (2010) *Speech for the Judges*, Mansion House, 13 July 2010. London, Ministry of Justice.

Clarke, K. (2011) Comment, *Guardian online* 5 September 2011.

Clarkson, C. (1997) 'Beyond Just Deserts: Sentencing Violent and Sexual Offenders' *Howard Journal* Vol 36(3), 284–92.

Clear, T. (2007) *Imprisoning Communities*. New York, Oxford University Press.

Cleland, A. and Tisdall, K. (2005) 'The Challenge of Anti-social Behaviour: New Relationships between the State, Children and Parents' *International Journal of Law, Policy and the Family* Vol 19(3), 395–420.

Clements, J. (2000) *Assessment of Race Relations at HMP Brixton*. London, Prison Service.

Clemmer, D. (1940) *The Prison Community*. New York, Holt, Rhinehart, and Winston.

Cobb, N. (2007) 'Governance through Publicity: Anti-social Behaviour Orders, Young People, and the Problematization of the Right to Anonymity' *Journal of Law and Society* Vol 34(3), 342–73.

Codd, H. (2004) 'Prisoners' Families: Issues in Law and Policy' *Amicus Curiae* Vol 55, 2.

Codd, H. (2008) *In the Shadow of Prison, Families, Imprisonment and Criminal Justice*. Cullompton, Willan.

Cohen, J. (1978) 'The Incapacitative Effect of Imprisonment' in A. Blumstein, J. Cohen, and D. Nagin *et al.* (eds) *Deterrence and Incapacitation: Estimating the Effects on Crime Rates*. Washington, National Academy of Sciences, 187–243.

Cohen, S. (1985) *Visions of Social Control*. Cambridge, Polity Press.

Coleman, R. and McCahill, M. (2010) *Surveillance and Crime*. London, Sage.

Commission for Racial Equality (2003) *A Formal Investigation by the CRE into HM Prison Service, England and Wales, Part I, The Murder of Zahid Mubarek; Part II, Racial Equality in Prisons*. London, CRE.

Commission for Racial Equality (2005) *Submission to the Zahid Mubarek Inquiry*. London, CRE.

Committee of Public Accounts (2002) *Collection of Fines and Other Financial Penalties in the Criminal Justice System*, HC999, Sixty-eighth Report of Session 2001–02, London: The Stationery Office.

Commission on English Prisons Today (2009) *Do Better Do Less, The Report of the Commission on English Prisons Today*. London, Howard League.

Committee on the Rights of the Child (1995) *Concluding Observations of the Committee on the Rights of the Child: United Kingdom of Great Britain and Northern Ireland*. CRC/C/15/Add 34. Geneva, Centre for Human Rights.

Committee on the Rights of the Child (2002) *Concluding Observations of the Committee on the Rights of the Child: United Kingdom of Great Britain and Northern Ireland*. CRC/C/15/Add 188. Geneva, Centre for Human Rights.

Committee on the Rights of the Child (2007) *General Comment No. 10 (2007), Children's Rights in Juvenile Justice*. CRC/C/GC/10. Geneva, Centre for Human Rights.

Committee on the Rights of the Child (2007) *Children's Rights in Juvenile Justice* General Comment No. 10, CRC/C/GC/10.

Committee on the Rights of the Child (2008) *Consideration of Reports Submitted by States Parties Under Article 44 of the Convention, Concluding Observations, United Kingdom of Great Britain and Northern Ireland*, CRC/C/GBR/CO/4.

Cook, D. (1989) 'Fiddling Tax and Benefits' in P. Carlen and D. Cook (eds) *Paying for Crime*. Milton Keynes, Open University Press, 109–27.

Cope, N. (2003) 'It's No Time or High Time: Young Offenders' Experience of Time and Drug Use in Prison' *Howard Journal* Vol 42(2), 158–75.

Corbett, C. (2000) 'The Social Construction of Speeding as Not "Real Crime"' *Crime Prevention and Community Safety* Vol 2(4), 33–46.

Corbett, C. and Caramlau, I. (2006) 'Gender Differences in Responses to Speed Cameras: Typology Findings and Implications for Road Safety'. *Criminology and Criminal Justice* Issue 4, 411–33.

Corston, J. (2007) *The Corston Report: A Report by Baroness Jean Corston of a Review of Women with Particular Vulnerabilities in the Criminal Justice System*. London, Home Office.

Council of Europe (1987) European Prison Rules, adopted 12 February 1987. Strasbourg, Council of Europe.

Council of Europe (1991) *Report to the United Kingdom Government on the Visit to the United Kingdom Carried out by the European Committee for the Prevention of Torture and Inhuman or Degrading Treatment or Punishment from 29 June 1990 to 10 August 1990*. Strasbourg: Council of Europe.

Council of Europe (2009) *Report to the United Kingdom Government on the visit to the United Kingdom carried out by the European Committee for the Prevention of Torture and Inhuman or Degrading Treatment or Punishment (CPT) from 18 November to 1 December 2008*, CPT/Inf (91) 30. Strasbourg, Council of Europe.

Council of Europe Parliamentary Assembly (2011) *The death penalty in Council of Europe member and observer states, a violation of human rights*, Doc. 12456, Strasbourg, Council of Europe.

CPS (1988) *Annual Report 1987–8*. London, HMSO.

CPS (1991) *Annual Report 1990–91*. London, HMSO.

CPS (1994) *The Code for Crown Prosecutors* (3rd edn). London, Director of Public Prosecutions.

CPS (2000) *The Code for Crown Prosecutors* (4th edn). London, Director of Public Prosecutions.

Cracknell, S. (2000) 'Anti-Social Behaviour Orders' *Journal of Social Welfare and Family Law* Vol 22(1), 108–15.

Crawford, A. (1997) *The Local Governance of Crime*. Oxford, Oxford University Press.

Crawford, A. (2000) 'Justice de Proximité—The Growth of "Houses of Justice" and Victim/Offender mediation in France: A Very UnFrench Legal Response?' *Social & Legal Studies* Vol 9(1), 29–53.

Crawford, A. (2003) 'Contractual Governance of Deviant Behaviour' *Journal of Law and Society* Vol 30(4), 479–505.

Crawford, A. (2009) 'Governing Through Anti-social Behaviour, Regulatory Challenges to Criminal Justice' *British Journal of Criminology* Vol 49, 810–31.

Crawford, A. and Enterkin, J. (2001) 'Victim Contact Work in the Probation Service: Paradigm Shift or Pandora's Box?' *British Journal of Criminology* Vol 41, 705–25.

Crawley, E. and Sparks, R. (2005) 'Hidden Injuries: Researching the Experience of Older Men in English Prisons' *Howard Journal* Vol 44(4), 345–6.

Crawley, E. and Sparks, R. (2008) *Age of Imprisonment*. Cullompton, Willan.

Cretney, S. (1998) 'The State as a Parent, the Children Act 1948 in Retrospect' *Law Quarterly Review* Vol 114, 419–59.

Crewe, B. (2006) 'Male Prisoners, Orientation Towards Female Officers in an English Prison' *Punishment and Society* Vol 8(4), 395–421.

Croall, H. (1992) *White Collar Crime*. Milton Keynes, Open University Press.

Crofts, T. (2002) *The Criminal Responsibility of Children and Young Persons: A Comparison of English and German Law*. Aldershot, Ashgate.

Crook, F. (2003) 'Children in Prison: Advocating for the Human Rights of Young Offenders' *Criminal Justice Matters* No 54, 24–5.

Cross, R. (and Ashworth, A.) (1981) *The English Sentencing System*. London, Butterworths.

Crossman, G. (2007) *Overlooked, Surveillance and Personal Privacy in Modern Britain*. London, Liberty.

Crow, I. and Simon, F. (1987) *Unemployment and Magistrates' Courts*. London, NACRO.

Crowley, A. (1998) *A Criminal Waste: A Study of Child Offenders Eligible for Secure Training Centres*. London, The Children's Society.

Cummins, I. (2006) 'A Path Not Taken? Mentally Disordered Offenders and the Criminal Justice System' *Journal of Social Welfare and Family Law* Vol 28 (3–4), 267–81.

Cunliffe, J. and Shepherd, A. (2007) *Re-offending of Adults: Results from the 2004 Cohort*. London, Home Office.

Cuppleditch, L. and Evans, W. (2005) *Re-offending of Adults: Results from the 2002 Cohort*, Home Office Statistical Bulletin. London, Home Office.

Curry, T. R. and Corral-Camacho, G. (2008) 'Sentencing Young Minority Males for Drug Offenses, Testing for Conditional Effects Between Race/Ethnicity, Gender and Age During the US War on Drugs' *Punishment and Society* Vol 10(3), 253–76.

Da Silva, N., Cowell, P., Chinegwundoh, V., Mason, T., Maresh, J., and Williamson, K. (2007) *Prison Population Projections 2007–2014, England and Wales*. London, Ministry of Justice.

Daly, M. (2003) 'Governance and Social Policy' *Journal of Social Policy* Vol 32(1), 113–28.

Darbyshire, P. (2011) *Sitting in Judgment, The Working Lives of Judges.* Oxford, Hart.

Davies, A. (2010) 'Dangerous Offenders Scheme to be Axed?' *Channel 4 News*, 15 February Available at http://www.channel4.com/news/dangerous-offenders-scheme-to-be-axed.

Davies, P. Francis, P., and Jupp, V. (2003) *Victimisation, Theory, Research and Practice.* Basingstoke, Palgrave Macmillan.

Davis, A. Y. (2003) *Are Prisons Obsolete?* New York, Seven Sisters Press.

Davis, G. (1992) *Making Amends: Mediation and Reparation in Criminal Justice.* London, Routledge.

Davis, G., Boucherat, J., and Watson, D. (1988) 'Reparation in the Service of Diversion: The Subordination of a Good Idea' *Howard Journal* Vol 27(2), 127–33.

Davis, K. C. (1969) *Discretionary Justice: A Preliminary Inquiry.* Baton Rouge, Louisiana State University Press.

Davis, M., Takal, J-P., and Tyrer, J. (2004) 'Sentencing Burglars and Explaining the Differences between Jurisdictions' *British Journal of Criminology* Vol 44, 741–58.

Davis, R., Lurigio, A., and Skogan, W. (eds) (1997) *Victims of Crime* (2nd edn). Thousand Oaks, CA, Sage.

Dawes, W., Harvey, P., McIntosh, B., Nunney, F., and Phillips A. (2011) *Attitudes to Guilty Plea Sentence Reductions*, Sentencing Council Research Series 02/11. London, Sentencing Council.

Day Sclater, S. and Piper, C. (1999) 'The Family Law Act 1996 in Context' in S. Day Sclater and C. Piper (eds) *Undercurrents of Divorce.* Ashgate, Aldershot.

Day Sclater, S. and Piper, C. (2000) 'Re-moralising the Family? Family Policy, Family Law and Youth Justice' *Child and Family Law Quarterly* Vol 12(2), 135–51.

DCSF (Department for Children, Schools and Families) (2007) *The Children's Plan: Building Brighter Futures* Cm 7280. London, The Stationery Office.

de Cou, K. (2002) 'A Gender-wise Prison: Opportunities for, and Limits to, Reform' in P. Carlen (ed) *Women and Punishment: The Struggle for Justice*, Cullompton, Willan, 97–109.

De Giorgi, A. (2010) 'Immigration Control, PostFordism and Less Eligibility. A Materialist Critique of the Criminalization of Immigration Across Europe' *Punishment and Society* Vol 12(2), 147–67.

de Koster, W., van der Waal, J., Achterberg, P., and Houtman, D. (2008) 'The Rise of the Penal State, New-Liberalization or New Political Culture?' *British Journal of Criminology* Vol 48(6), 720–34.

Dear, G. E. (2006) *Preventing Suicide and Other Self-Harm in Prison.* London, Palgrave.

Deering, J. (2011) *Probation Practice and the New Penology.* Aldershot, Ashgate.

Demker, A., Towns, A., Duus-Otterström, G., and Sebring, J. (2008) 'Fear and punishment in Sweden, Exploring penal attitudes' *Punishment and Society* Vol 10(3), 319–32.

Denny, D. (1992) *Racism and Anti-Racism in Probation.* London, Routledge.

Denver, M., Best, J., and Haas, K. C. (2008) 'Methods of execution as institutional fads' *Punishment and Society* Vol 10(3), 227–52.

Department for Constitutional Affairs (2006) *Your Choice to Have a Voice in Court.* London, Office for Criminal Justice Reform.

Department of Health (1999) *Review of the Mental Health Act 1983.* London, Department of Health.

Department of Health (2000) *Framework for the Assessment of Children in Need and their Families*. London, HMSO.

Department of Health (2009a) *The Bradley Report: Lord Bradley's review of people with mental health problems or learning disabilities in the criminal justice system*. London, Department of Health.

Department of Health (2009b) *A Resource Pack for Working with Older Prisoners*. London, Department of Health/ NACRO.

Department of Health (2011) *No Health Without Mental Health*. London, Department of Health.

Department of Health/Home Office (1992) *Review of Mental Health and Social Services for Mentally Disordered Offenders and Others Requiring Similar Services* Vol 1: Final Summary Report, Cm 2088. London, HMSO.

Department of Health/Home Office (2000) *Reforming the Mental Health Act: Part II High Risk Patients*. Cm 5016-II. London, The Stationery Office.

Devlin, A. (1998) *Invisible Women*. Winchester, Waterside Press.

DfES (Department for Education and Skills) (2003) *Every Child Matters* Cm 5860. London, The Stationery Office.

DfES (Department for Education and Skills) (2004) *Every Child Matters: Next Steps*. London, The Stationery Office.

DfES (Department for Education and Skills) (2005) *Youth Matters* Cm 6629. London, The Stationery Office.

DfES (Department for Education and Skills) (2007) *Every Parent Matters*. London, DfES.

Dicey, A. V. (1885) *Introduction to the Study of the Law of the Constitution*. London, Macmillan.

Diduck, A. (1999) 'Justice and Childhood: Reflections on Refashioned Boundaries' in M. King (ed) *Moral Agendas for Children's Welfare*. London, Routledge.

Dignan, J. (1999) 'The Crime and Disorder Act and the Prospects for Restorative Justice' *Criminal Law Review*, 48–60.

Dignan, J. and Lowey, K. (2000) *Restorative Justice Options for Northern Ireland: A Comparative Review*. Belfast, Criminal Justice Review Group.

Dignan, J. and Marsh, P. (2001) 'Restorative Justice and Family Group Conferences in England: Current State and Future Prospects' in A. Morris and G. Maxwell (eds) *Restorative Justice for Juveniles: Conferencing, Mediation and Circles* Oxford, Hart Publishing, 85–101.

Dingwall, G. (1998) 'Selective Incapacitation after the Criminal Justice Act 1991: A Proportional Response to Protecting the Public?' *Howard Journal* Vol 37(2), 177–87.

Dingwall, G. (2008) 'Deserting Desert? Locating the Present Role of Retributivism in the Sentencing of Adult Offenders' *Howard Journal* Vol 47(4), 400–10.

Ditchfield, J. (1976) *Police Cautioning in England and Wales*, Home Office Research Study No 37. London, HMSO.

Dobson, G. (2010) 'New Labour's Prison Legacy' *Probation Journal* Vol 57(3), 322–8.

Domanick, J. (2004) *Cruel Justice: Three Strikes and the Politics of Crime in America's Golden State*. Berkeley, University of California Press.

Donoghue, J. (2007) 'The Judiciary as a Primary Definer on Anti-Social Behaviour Orders' *Howard Journal* Vol 46(4), 417–30.

Donoghue, J. (2010) *Anti-Social Behaviour Orders, A Culture of Control?* London, Macmillan.

Donohue, J. J. and Wolfers, J. (2006) 'Uses and Abuses of Empirical Evidence in the Death Penalty Debate' *Stanford Law Review* Vol 58, 791–846.

Donzelot, J. (1980) *The Policing of Families*. London, Hutchinson.

Dorling, D., Rigby, J., Wheeler, B., Ballas, D., Thomas, B., Fahmy, E., Gordon, D., and Lupton, R. (2007) *Poverty, Wealth and Place in Britain, 1968 to 2005*. Bristol, Policy Press.

DOUGLAS, N. AND PLUGGE, E. (2007) 'The Health of Young Women in Custody: Emerging Concerns and a Case for Advocacy' *Childright* CR 238, 14–17.

DOWNES, D. (2001/2) 'Four Years Hard: New Labour and Crime Control' *Criminal Justice Matters* Vol 46, 8–9.

DRAKEFORD, M. (1993) 'But Who Will Do the Work?' *Critical Social Policy* Vol 3(2), 64–76.

DRAKEFORD, M. AND BUTLER, I. (2007) 'Everyday Tragedies: Justice, Scandal and Young People in Contemporary Britain' *Howard Journal* Vol 46(3), 219–35.

DUDECK, M., DRENKHAHN, KIRSTIN., SPITZER, C., BARNOW, S., KOPP, D., KUWERT, P., FREYBERGER, H., AND DÜNKEL, F. (2011) 'Traumatization and mental distress in long-term prisoners in Europe' *Punishment and Society* Vol 13(4), 403–23.

DUFF, A. (2002) 'Punishing the Young' in I. Weijers and A. Duff (eds) *Punishing Juveniles, Principle and Critique*. Oxford, Hart Publishing, 115–34.

DUFF, A. (2003) 'Probation, Punishment and Restorative Justice: Should Al Truism be Engaged in Punishment?' *Howard Journal* Vol 42(2), 181–97.

DUNBAR, I. AND LANGTON, A. (1998) *Tough Justice, Sentencing and Penal Policies in the 1990s*. London, Blackstone Press.

DUPONT, C. AND ZAKKOUR, P. (2003) *Trends in Environmental Sentencing in England and Wales*. London, Department for Environment, Food and Rural Affairs.

DURRANCE, P., DIXON, L., AND SINGH BHUI, H. (2010) 'Creative working with minority ethnic offenders' in J. Brayford, F. Cowe, and J. Deering (eds) *What Else Works? Creative work with offenders*. Cullompton, Willan, 138–154.

DWORKIN, R. (1977) *Taking Rights Seriously*, London, Duckworth.

DWORKIN, R. (1986) *A Matter of Principle*. Oxford, Oxford University Press.

DWORKIN, R. (2011) *Justice for Hedgehogs*, Cambridge, Mass., Harvard University Press.

DYSON, S. AND BOSWELL, G. (2006) 'Sickle Cell Anaemia and Deaths in Custody in the UK and USA' *Howard Journal* Vol 45(1), 14–28.

EADIE, T. AND WILLIS, A. (1989) 'National Standards for Discipline and Breach Proceedings in Community Service: An Exercise in Penal Rhetoric?' *Criminal Law Review*, 412–19.

EASTON, S. (ed) (2008a) *Marx and Law*. Aldershot, Ashgate.

EASTON, S. (2008b) 'Marx's Legacy' in S. Easton (ed) *Marx and Law*. Aldershot, Ashgate, xi–xxix.

EASTON, S. (2008c) 'Dangerous Waters: Taking Account of Impact in Sentencing' *Criminal Law Review*, 2, 105–20.

EASTON, S. (2008d) 'Constructing Citizenship, Making Room for Prisoners' Rights' *Journal of Social Welfare and Family Law* Vol 30(2), 127–46.

EASTON, S. (2009) 'The Prisoner's Right to Vote and Civic Responsibility: Reaffirming the Social Contract' *Probation Journal* Vol 56(3), 224–37.

EASTON, S. (2011a) *Prisoners' Rights, Principles and Practice*. London, Routledge.

EASTON, S. (2011b) 'Possession of Extreme Pornography, Sword or Shield?' *Journal of Criminal Law*, 75, 391–413.

EDGAR, K. (2010) *A Fair Response, developing responses to racist incidents that earn the confidence of black and minority ethnic prisoners*. London, Prison Reform Trust.

EDGAR, K. AND RICKFORD, D. (2009) 'Neglecting the mental health of prisoners' *International Journal of Prisoner Health* Vol 5(3), 166–70.

EDGAR, K., JACOBSON, J., AND BIGGAR, K. (2011) *Time Well Spent, A Practical Guide to Active Citizenship and Volunteering in Prison*. London, Prison Reform Trust.

Edwards, I. (2001) 'Victim Participation in Sentencing: The Problems of Incoherence' *Howard Journal* Vol 40(1), 39–54.

Edwards, I. (2002) 'The Place of Victims' Preferences in the Sentencing of "Their" Offenders' *Criminal Law Review,* 689–702.

Edwards, I. (2006) 'Restorative Justice, Sentencing and the Court of Appeal' *Criminal Law Review,* 110–23.

Ehrlich, I. (1975) 'The Deterrent Effects of Capital Punishment: A Question of Life or Death' *American Economic Review* Vol 65, 397–417.

Einat, T. (2004) 'Criminal Fine Enforcement in Israel' *Punishment and Society* Vol 6(2), 175–94.

Ellis, T. and Winstone, J. (2001–2) 'Halliday, Sentencers and the National Probation Service' *Criminal Justice Matters* No 46 Winter, 20.

Engels, F. (1843) 'Outline of a Critique of Political Economy'. *Marx and Engels: Collected Works* Vol 3, London, Lawrence & Wishart (1975), 418–43.

Erez, E. (1999) 'Who's Afraid of the Big Bad Victim? Victim Impact Statements as Victim Empowerment and Enhancement of Justice' Crim L R, 545–56.

Etzioni, A. (1993) *The Spirit of Community: Rights, Responsibilities and the Communitarian Agenda*. New York, Crown Publishers.

Etzioni, A. (2003) *The Monochrome Society.* Princeton, New Jersey, Princeton University Press.

Evans, R. (1994) 'Cautioning: Counting the Cost of Retrenchment' *Criminal Law Review,* 566–75.

Exworthy, T. and Gunn, J. (2003) 'Taking Another Tilt at High Secure Hospitals' *British Journal of Psychiatry* Vol 182, 469–71.

Farrall, S. (2002) 'Long Term Absences from Probation: Officers' and Probationers' Accounts' *Howard Journal* Vol 41(3), 263–78.

Farrall, S. and Maltby, S. (2003) 'The Victimisation of Probationers' *Howard Journal* Vol 42, 32–54.

Farrall, S., Bottoms, A., and Shapland, J. (2010) 'Social Structures and Desistance from Crime' *European Journal of Criminology* Vol 7(6), 546–70.

Farrington, D. (1997) 'Human Development and Criminal Careers' in M. Maguire *et al.* (eds) *The Oxford Handbook of Criminology* (2nd edn). Oxford, Oxford University Press, 361–408.

Farrington, D. (2002) 'Understanding and Preventing Crime' in J. Muncie, G. Hughes and E. McLaughlin (eds) *Youth Justice, Critical Readings.* London, Sage, 425–30.

Farrington, D. (2007) 'Childhood Risk Factors and Risk-focused Prevention' in M. Maguire, R. Morgan and R. Reiner (Eds) *The Oxford Handbook of Criminology* (4th edn). Oxford, Oxford University Press, 602–40.

Farrington, D. and Bennett, T. (1981) 'Police Cautioning of Juveniles in London' *British Journal of Criminology* Vol 21(1), 123–35.

Farrington, D., Ditchfield, J., Howard, P., and Jolliffe, D. (2002) *Two Intensive Regimes for Young Offenders: A Follow-up Evaluation*, RDSD Findings 163. London, Home Office.

Faulkner, D. (2005) 'Relationships, Accountability and Responsibility in the National Offender Management Service' *Public Money and Management* Vol 25(5), 299.

Fawcett Commission on Women and the Criminal Justice System (2009) *Engendering Justice, From Policy to Practice, Final Report on Women and the Criminal Justice System.* London, Fawcett Society.

Fazel, S., Benning, R., and Danesh, J. (2005) 'Suicides in Male Prisoners in England and Wales, 1978–2003, *The Lancet* Vol 366(9493), 1301–2.

FEELEY, M. AND SIMON, J. (1992) 'The New Penology: Notes on the Emerging Strategy of Corrections and its Implications' *Criminology* Vol 30 (4), 449–74.

FEINBERG, J. (1994) 'The Expressive Function of Punishment' in A. Duff and D. Garland (eds) *A Reader on Punishment*. Oxford, Oxford University Press, 71–91.

FELDMAN, M. (1992) 'Social Limits to Discretion' in K. Hawkins (ed) *The Uses of Discretion*. Oxford, Clarendon, 164–83.

FEMALE PRISONERS' WELFARE PROJECT/ HIBISCUS (2010) *Annual Report* 2009/10. London, FPWP.

FENWICK, H. (1997) 'Procedural "Rights" of Victims of Crime: Public or Private Ordering of the Criminal Justice Process?' *Modern Law Review* Vol 60(3), 317–33.

FIELD, S. (2007) 'Practice Cultures and the "New" Youth Justice in (England and) Wales' *British Journal of Criminology* Vol 47, 311–30.

FIONDA, J. (1999) 'New Labour, Old Hat: Youth Justice and the Crime and Disorder Act' *Criminal Law Review*, 36–47.

FISH, M. J. (2008) 'An Eye for an Eye, Proportionality as a Moral Principle of Punishment' *Oxford Journal of Legal Studies* Vol 28(1), 57–71.

FITZGERALD, M. AND MARSHALL, P. (1996) 'Ethnic Minorities in British Prisons: Some Research Implications' in R. Matthews and P. Francis (eds) *Prisons 2000: An International Perspective on the Current State and Future of Imprisonment*. London, Macmillan, 139–62.

FITZGIBBON, D. (2007) 'Risk Analysis and the New Practitioner' *Punishment and Society* Vol 9(1), 87–97.

FLAHERTY, P. (2006/7) 'Sentencing the Recidivist: Reconciling Harsher Treatment for Repeat Offenders with Modern Retributivist Theory' *Contemporary Issues in Law* Vol 8(4), 319–36.

FLETCHER, G. (1982) 'The Recidivist Premium' *Criminal Justice Ethics* Vol 1(2), 54–9.

FLOOD-PAGE, C. AND MACKIE, A. (1998) *Sentencing Practice: An Examination of Decisions in Magistrates' Courts and the Crown Court in the mid-1990s*, Home Office Research Study No 180. London: Home Office.

FLOOD-PAGE, C. *ET AL.* (2000) *Youth Crime: Findings from the 1998/99 Youth Lifestyles Survey*, Home Office Research Study No 209. London, Home Office.

FLOUD, J. (1982) 'Dangerousness and Criminal Justice' *British Journal of Criminology* Vol 22(3), 213–28.

FORTIN, J. (2003) *Children's Rights and the Developing Law* (2nd edn). London, Lexis Nexis.

FORTIN, J. (2009) *Children's Rights and the Developing Law* (3rd edn). Cambridge, Cambridge University Press.

FOUCAULT, M. (1977) *Discipline and Punish: The Birth of the Prison*. London, Allen Lane.

FOX, C. AND ALBERTSON, A. (2010) 'Could Economics Solve the Prison Crisis?' *Probation Journal* Vol 57(3), 263–80.

FOX, D., DHAMI, M., AND MANTLE, G. (2006) 'Restorative Final Warnings: Policy and Practice' *Howard Journal* Vol 45(2), 129–40.

FREDMAN, S. (2008) *Human Rights Transformed, Positive Rights and Positive Duties*. Oxford, Oxford University Press.

FREIBERG, A. (2000) 'Guerillas in our Midst? Judicial Responses to Governing the Dangerous' in M. Brown and J. Pratt (eds) *Dangerous Offenders*. London, Routledge, 51–69.

FROST, N. A. (2008) 'The mismeasure of punishment, Alternatives measures of punitiveness and their substantial consequences' *Punishment and Society* Vol 10(3), 277–300.

GAES, G. (2008) 'Cost, Performance Studies Look at Prison Privatization' *National Institute of Justice Journal*, Issue No 259, 32–6.

Garland, D. (1985) *Punishment and Welfare: A History of Penal Strategies*. Aldershot, Gower.

Garland, D. (1991) 'Sociological Perspectives on Punishment' in N. Morris and M. Tonry (eds) *Crime and Justice* Vol 14. Chicago, University of Chicago Press.

Garland, D. (ed) (2001a) *Mass Imprisonment*. London, Sage.

Garland, D. (2001b) *The Culture of Control*. Oxford, Oxford University Press.

Garland, D. (2010) *Peculiar Institution, America's Death Penalty in an Age of Abolition*. Oxford, Oxford University Press.

Gelb, K. (2008) *More Myths and Misconceptions*. State of Victoria, Sentencing Advisory Council.

Gelb, K. (2010) *Gender Differences in Sentencing Outcome*. Melbourne, Sentencing Advisory Panel.

Gelsthorpe, L. (2002) 'Recent Changes in Youth Justice Policy in England and Wales' in I. Weijers and A. Duff (eds) *Punishing Juveniles: Principle and Critique*. Oxford, Hart Publishing, 45–66.

Gelsthorpe, L. and Morris, A. (1999) 'Much Ado About Nothing—A Critical Comment on Key Provisions Relating to Children in the Crime and Disorder Act 1998' *Child and Family Law Quarterly* Vol 11(3), 209–21.

Gelsthorpe, L. and Morris, A. (2002) 'Restorative Youth Justice: The Last Vestiges of Welfare?' in J. Muncie, G. Hughes, and E. McLaughlin (eds) *Youth Justice: Critical Readings*. London/Milton Keynes, Sage/Open University Press, 238–54.

Gelsthorpe, L. and Padfield, N. (eds) (2003) *Exercising Discretion, Decision-making in the Criminal Justice System and Beyond*. Cullompton, Willan.

Genders, E. (2003) 'Privatisation and Innovation—Rhetoric and Reality: The Development of a Therapeutic Community Prison' *Howard Journal* Vol 42(2), 137–57.

Genders, E. and Player, E. (1989) *Race Relations in Prison*. Oxford, Clarendon Press.

Genders, E. and Player, E. (2007) 'The Commercial Context of Criminal Justice: Prison Privatisation and the Perversion of Purpose' *Criminal Law Review*, 513–29.

Genders, E. and Player, E. (2010) 'Therapy in Prison, Revisiting Grendon 20 Years On' *Howard Journal* Vol 49, 431–50.

Genn, H. (1988) *Hard Bargaining: Out of Court Settlement in Personal Injury Actions*. Oxford, Clarendon Press.

Genn, H. (1999) *Paths to Justice: What People Do and Think about Going to Law*. Oxford, Hart Publishing.

Gesch, C. B., Hammond, S. M., Hampson, S. E., Eves, A. and Chowder, M. J. (2002) 'Influence of Supplementary Vitamins, Minerals and Essential Fatty Acids on the Antisocial Behaviour of Adult Prisoners: Randomised, Placebo-controlled Trial' *British Journal of Psychiatry* Vol 181, 22–8.

Gibson, B. (1990) *Unit Fines*. Winchester, Waterside Press.

Giddens, A. (1990) *The Consequences of Modernity*. Cambridge, Polity Press.

Giddens, A. (1998) *The Third Way*, Cambridge. Cambridge, Polity Press.

Giddens, A. (1999) 'Risk and Responsibility' MLR Vol 62(1), 1–10.

Giddens, A. (2000) *The Third Way and its Critics*. Cambridge, Polity Press.

Gill, M. and Spriggs, A. (2005) *Assessing the Impact of CCTV*, Home Office Research Study No 292. London, Home Office.

Giller, H. (2000) *Final Warning Interventions*. London, Youth Justice Board.

Gil-Robles, A. (2005) *Report by the Commissioner for Human Rights on his Visit to the UK*. Strasbourg, Council of Europe.

Glover, J. and Hibbert, P. (2009) *Locking Up or Giving Up? Why custody thresholds for teenagers aged 12, 13 and 14 need to be raised*. Essex, Barnardo's.

Goldson, B. (1999) 'Youth (In)Justice: Contemporary Developments in Policy and Practice' in B. Goldson (ed) *Youth Justice: Contemporary Policy and Practice*. Aldershot, Ashgate, 1–27.

Goldson, B. (2000a) 'Wither Diversion? Interventionism and the New Youth Justice' in B. Goldson (ed) *The New Youth Justice*. Lyme Regis, Russell House Publishing, 35–7.

Goldson, B. (2000b) 'Children "in Need" or "Young Offenders"? Hardening Ideology, Organisational Change and New Challenges for Social Work with Children in Trouble' *Child and Family Social Work* Issue 5, 255–65.

Goldson, B. (2006) 'Damage, Harm and Death in Child Prisons in England and Wales: Questions of Abuse and Accountability' *Howard Journal* Vol 45(5), 449–67.

Graham, J. and Bowling, B. (1995) *Young People and Crime*, Home Office Research Study No 145. London, Home Office.

Gravett, S. (2003) *Coping with Prison*. London, Sage.

Gray, P. (2007) 'Youth Justice, Social Exclusion and the Demise of Social Justice' *Howard Journal* Vol 46(4), 401–16.

Gray, E., Taylor, E., Roberts, C., Merrington, S., Fernandez, R., and Moore, R. (2005) *Intensive Supervision and Surveillance Programme: The Final Report*. London, Youth Justice Board.

Green, P. (2008) *Prison Work and Social Enterprise: the Story of Barbed*. London, Howard League.

Green, P. (2010) *Barbed, What Happened Next? Follow up story of employees of a prison social enterprise*. London, Howard League.

Greenhow, J. (2003) 'Referral Orders: Problems in Practice' *Criminal Law Review*, 266–8.

Greer, S. (2010) 'Anti-terrorist Laws and the United Kingdom's "Suspect Muslim Community": A Reply to Pantazis and Pemberton' *British Journal of Criminology* Vol 50, 1171–90.

Greig, D. (2002*) Neither Bad nor Mad: The Competing Discourses of Psychiatry, Law and Politics*. London, Jessica Kingsley.

Grimshaw, R., Mills, H., Silvestri, A., and Silberhorn-Armantrading, F. (2010a) *Prison and probation expenditure, 1999–2009*. London, Centre for Crime and Justice Studies.

Grimshaw, R., Mills, H., Silvestri, A., and Silberhorn-Armantrading, F. (2010b) *Magistrates' Courts and Crown Court Expenditure, 1999–2009*. London, Centre for Crime and Justice Studies.

Grosman, B. (ed) (1980) *New Directions in Sentencing*. Toronto, Butterworths.

Gullick, M. (2004) 'Sentencing and Early Release of Fixed Term Prisoners' *Criminal Law Review*, 653–62.

Haas, H., Farrington, D., Killias, M., and Sattar, G. (2004) 'The Impact of Different Configurations on Delinquency' *British Journal of Criminology* Vol 44, 520–32.

Hackler, J. and Garapon, A. (1986) *Stealing Conflicts in Juvenile Justice: Contrasting France and Canada*, Discussion Paper 8, Centre for Criminological Research, Edmonton, Alberta, University of Alberta.

Hadfield, P. (2006) *Bar Wars*. Oxford, Oxford University Press.

Hagell, A. and Newburn, T. (1994) *Persistent Young Offenders*. London, Policy Studies Institute.

Haigh, R. (2010), 'Grendon's Contribution to Therapeutic Communities and Personality Disorder' *Howard Journal* Vol 49(5), 503–12.

Hall, M. (2010) *Victims and Policy-Making: A Comparative Perspective*. Cullompton, Willan.

Halliday Report (2001) *Making Punishments Work: Review of the Sentencing Framework for England and Wales*. London, Home Office.

Hamilton, J. and Wisniewski, M. (1996) *The Use of the Compensation Order in Scotland*, Crime and Criminal Justice Research Findings No 14. Edinburgh, The Scottish Office.

Hamlyn, B. and Lewis, D. (2000) *Women Prisoners: A Survey of their Work and Training Experiences in Custody and on Release*, Home Office Research Study No 208, London, Home Office.

Haney, L.A. (2010) *Offending Women: Power, Punishment and the Regulation of Desire*. Berkeley, University of California Press.

Hanmer, J., Griffiths, S., and Jerwood, D. (1999) 'Arresting Evidence, Domestic Violence and Repeat Victimisation' *Police Research Series, Paper 104*. London, Home Office Policing and Reduce Crime Unit, Research and Statistics Directorate.

Hannah-Moffat, K. (2002) 'Creating Choices: Reflecting on Choices' in P. Carlen (ed) *Women in Punishment: The Struggle for Justice*. Cullompton, Willan, 199–219.

Hannah-Moffat, K. and O'Malley, P. (eds) (2007) *Gendered Risks*. London, Routledge-Cavendish.

Hansbury, S (ed) (2011) *Evaluation of the Intensive Alternatives to Custody Pilots*, Research Summary 3/11. London, Ministry of Justice.

Harding, J. (2000) 'A Community Justice Dimension to Effective Probation Practice' *Howard Journal* Vol 39(2), 132–49.

Harper, G. and Chitty, C. (eds) (2005) *The Impact of Corrections on Re-offending: A Review of 'What Works'* (3rd edn), Home Office Research Study No 291. London, HORDSD.

Harris, M. K. (1998) 'Reflections of a Skeptical Dreamer: Some Dilemmas in Restorative Justice Theory and Practice' *Contemporary Justice Review* Vol 1, 57–69.

Harris, R. (1980) 'A Changing Service—The Case for Separating Care and Control in Probation Practice' *British Journal of Social Work* Vol 10(3), 163–84.

Harris, R. (1992) *Crime, Criminal Justice and the Probation Service*. London, Routledge.

Harris, R. and Webb, D. (1987) *Welfare, Power and Juvenile Justice*. London, Tavistock.

Harrison, K. (2006) 'Community Punishment or Community Rehabilitation: Which is the Highest in the Sentencing Tariff?' *Howard Journal* Vol 45(2), 141–58.

Harrison, K. (2011) *Dangerousness, Risk and the Governance of Serious Violent and Sexual Offenders*, London, Routledge.

Hart, H. L. A. (1968) *Punishment and Responsibility: Essays in the Philosophy of Law*. Oxford, Oxford University Press.

Harvey, C. W. (1984) 'Hegel's Theory of Punishment Reconsidered' *Dialogos* Vol 43, 71–80.

Harwin, J. and Ryan, M. (2007) 'The Role of the Court in Cases Concerning Parental Substance Misuse and Children at Risk of Harm' *Journal of Social Welfare and Family Law* Vol 29 (3 and 4), 277–92.

Harwin, J., Ryan, R., Tunnard, J., Pokhrel, S., Alrouh, B., Matias, C., and Momenian-Schneid, Dr. (2011) *The Family Drug & Alcohol Court (FDAC) Evaluation Project Final Report*. Brunel University, Uxbridge.

Hawkins, K. (2002) *Law as Last Resort*. Oxford, Oxford University Press.

Hawkins, K. (ed) (1992) *The Uses of Discretion*. Oxford, Clarendon.

Hay, C. (1995) 'Mobilisation through Interpellation—James Bulger, Juvenile Crime and the Construction of a Moral Panic' *Social and Legal Studies* Vol 4(2), 197–223.

Hay, D., Linebaugh, P., and Thompson, E. P. (1975) *Albion's Fatal Tree*. London, Allen Lane.

Hayes, M. and Williams, C. (1999) '"Offending" Behaviour and Children under 10' *Family Law*, 317–20.

Hazell, N. (2008) *Cross-national Comparison of Youth Justice*. London, YJB.

Health and Safety Executive (2011) *Statistics 2010–11*, London, HSE.

Healthcare Commission (2009) *Actions speak louder, a second review of healthcare in the community for young people who offend*. London, Commission for Healthcare Audit and Inspection and HM Inspectorate of Probation.

Hebenton, B. and Seddon, T. (2009) 'From Dangerousness to Precaution, Managing Sexual and Violent Offenders in an Insecure and Uncertain Age' *British Journal of Criminology*. Vol 49, 343–62.

Hedderman, C. (1990) *The Effect of Defendants' Demeanour on Sentencing in the Magistrates' Courts*, Home Office Research and Development Research Bulletin No 29, 32–6.

Hedderman, C. (2010) 'Government Policy on Women Offenders, Labour's Legacy and the Coalition's Challenge' *Punishment and Society* Vol 12(4), 485–500.

Hedderman, C. and Gelsthorpe, L. (1997) *Understanding the Sentencing of Women*, Home Office Research Study No 170. London, HMSO.

Hedderman, C., Gunby, C., and Shelton, N. (2011) 'What women want, the importance of qualitative approaches in evaluating work with women offenders' *Criminology and Criminal Justice* Vol 11(1), 3–19.

Hegel, G. W. (1832) *Hegel's Philosophy of Right*, trans. T. M. Knox, 1952. Oxford, Clarendon Press.

Heidensohn, F. (ed) (2006) *Gender and Justice: New Concepts and Approaches*. Cullompton, Willan.

Henham, R. (1995) 'Sentencing Policy and the Role of the Court of Appeal' *Howard Journal* Vol 34(3), 218–27.

Henham, R. (1999) 'Bargain Justice or Justice Denied? Sentence Discounts and the Criminal Process' *Modern Law Review* Vol 62(4), 515–38.

Henham, R. (1997) 'Anglo-American Approaches to Cumulative Sentencing and the Implications for UK Sentencing Policy' *Howard Journal* Vol 36(3), 263–83.

Henham, R. (2001) 'Sentencing Dangerous Offenders: Policy and Practice in the Crown Court' *Criminal Law Review*, 693–711.

Hetherington, A. (1996) 'The Legitimacy of Capital Punishment in Hegel's' *Philosophy of Right' Owl of Minerva* Vol 27, 167–74.

Heyman, S. J. (1996) 'The Legitimacy of Capital Punishment in Hegel's *Philosophy of Right*: A Comment' *Owl of Minerva* Vol 27, 175–80.

Hillery, G. (1955) 'Definitions of Community: Areas of Agreement' *Rural Sociology* Vol 20(2), 111–23.

Hinchman, L. P. (1991) 'On Reconciling Happiness and Autonomy: An Interpretation of Hegel's Moral Philosophy' *Owl of Minerva* Vol 23, 29–48.

Hine, J. (2007) 'Young People's Perspectives on Final Warnings' *Web JCLI* Vol 2 (available at http://webjcli.ncl.ac.uk/2007/issue2/hine2.html).

HM Chief Inspector of Prisons (1997) *Women in Prison: A Thematic Review*. London, Home Office.

HM Chief Inspector of Prisons (1998) *Report on an Unannounced Short Inspection of HMP Woodhill 14–16 July 1998*. London, HMCIP.

HM Chief Inspector of Prisons (2001) *Follow up to Women in Prison: A Thematic Review*. London, Home Office.

HM Chief Inspector of Prisons (2005) *Report on an Unannounced*

Inspection of HMP Rye Hill, 11–15 April 2005. London, HMIP.

HM Chief Inspector of Prisons (2007) *Annual Report England and Wales 2005–06*. London, Stationery Office.

HM Chief Inspector of Prisons (2008) *Annual Report England and Wales 2006–07*. London, The Stationery Office.

HM Chief Inspector of Prisons for England and Wales (2008) *Older Prisoners in England and Wales: a follow-up to the 2004 thematic review by HM Chief Inspector of Prisons*. London, HMIP.

HM Chief Inspector of Prisons (2010a) *Annual Report 2008–09*. London, HMIP.

HM Chief Inspector of Prisons (2010b) *Muslim Prisoners' Experiences: A Thematic Review*. London, HMIP.

HM Chief Inspector of Prisons (2011a) *Annual Report 2010–11*. London, HMIP.

HM Chief Inspector of Prisons (2011b) *Report on a full unannounced inspection of HMP & YOI Parc*, 15–24 September 2010. London, HMIP.

HM Government (2005) *Statutory Guidance on Inter-agency Co-operation to Improve the Wellbeing of Children: Children's Trusts*. London, DfES.

HM Inspectorate of Prisons (2004) *Juveniles in Custody*. London, HMIP.

HM Inspectorate of Prisons (2005) *Parallel Worlds: A Thematic Review of Race Relations in Prison*. London, HMIP.

HM Inspectorate of Prisons (2006) *Foreign National Prisoners: A Thematic Review*. London, HMIP.

HM Inspectorate of Prisons (2007) *The Mental Health of Prisoners: A Thematic Review of the Care and Support of Prisoners with Mental Health Needs*. London, HMIP.

HM Inspectorate of Prisons (2008) *Report on an Announced Inspection of the Management, Care and Control of Young People at Oakhill Secure Training Centre*. London, HMIP.

HM Inspectorate of Prisons (2009a) *Disabled Prisoners: A Short Thematic Review on the Care and Support of Prisoners with a Disability*. London, HMIP.

HM Inspectorate of Prisons (2009b) *Race Relations in Prison: Responding to Adult Women from Black and Minority Ethnic Backgrounds*. London, HMIP.

HM Inspectorate of Prisons (2010) *Women in Prison: A Short Thematic Review*. London, HMIP.

HM Inspectorate of Probation (1997) 'Risk Management Guidance' in *Management and Assessment of Risk in the Probation Service*. London, Home Office.

HM Inspectorate of Probation (2000) *Towards Race Equality: A Thematic Inspection*. London, HMSO.

HM Inspectorate of Probation (2006a) *An Independent Review of a Serious Further Offence Case: Anthony Rice*. London, Home Office.

HM Inspectorate of Probation (2006b) *Working to Make Amends*. London, HMIP.

HM Inspectorate of Probation, HM Inspectorate of Courts Administration, HM Inspectorate of Constabulary (2007) *A Summary of Findings on the Enforcement of Community Penalties from Three Joint Area Inspections*, Thematic Inspections Report. London, Home Office.

HM Prison Service (2004) *Annual Report 2003–4*. London, HM Prison Service.

HM Prison Service (2007) *Business Plan 2006–2007*. London, NOMS.

HM Prison Service/CRE (2003) *Implementing Race Equality in Prisons: A Shared Agenda for Change*. London, HM Prison Service.

Hobbes, T. (1651) *Leviathan*, ed. J. Plamenatz (1962). Glasgow, Collins.

Hodgson Committee (1984) *The Profits of Crime and Their Recovery*. Aldershot, Gower.

HOLDAWAY, S. AND DESBOROUGH, S. (2004) *The National Evaluation of the Youth Justice Board's Final Warning Projects*. London: YJB.

HOLDAWAY, S., DAVIDSON, N., DIGNAN, J., HAMMERSLEY, R., HINE, J., AND MARSH, P. (2001) *New Strategies to Address Youth Offending—The National Evaluation of the Pilot Youth Offending Teams*, RDS Occasional Paper 69. London, Home Office.

HOLLINGSWORTH, K. (2006) '*R(W) v Commissioner of Police for the Metropolis and Another*—Interpreting Child Curfews: A Question of Rights?' *Child and Family Law Quarterly* Vol 18(2), 253–68.

HOLLINGSWORTH, K. (2007) 'Responsibility and Rights: Children and their Parents in the Youth Justice System' *International Journal of Law, Policy and the Family* Vol 21(2), 190–219.

HOME OFFICE (1951) *Sixth Report on the Work of the Children's Department*. London, HMSO.

HOME OFFICE (1968) *Children in Trouble*, Cmnd 3601. London, HMSO.

HOME OFFICE (1984) *Statement of National Standards and Objectives for the Probation Service*. London, Home Office.

HOME OFFICE (1988a) *Punishment, Custody and the Community* Consultation Paper, Cm 424. London: HMSO.

HOME OFFICE (1988b) *Tackling Offending: An Action Plan*. London, HMSO.

HOME OFFICE (1990a) *Crime, Justice and Protecting the Public: The Government's Proposals for Legislation*, Cm 965. London, HMSO.

HOME OFFICE (1990b) *Supervision and Punishment in the Community*, Cm 966. London, HMSO.

HOME OFFICE (1990c) *Partnership in Dealing with Offenders in the Community*, London, HMSO.

HOME OFFICE (1990d) *Provision for Mentally Disordered Offenders*. Circular 66/1990. London, HMSO.

HOME OFFICE (1991) *Custody, Care and Justice: The Way Ahead for the Prison Service in England and Wales*, Cm 1647. London, HMSO.

HOME OFFICE (1994a) *Monitoring of the Criminal Justice Acts 1991 and 1993—Results from a Special Data Collection Exercise*, Home Office Statistical Bulletin Issue 20/94. London, Home Office.

HOME OFFICE (1994b) *Revised Standards: The Cautioning of Offenders*. London, Home Office.

HOME OFFICE (1995a) *Strengthening Punishment in the Community*, Cmnd 2780. London, HMSO.

HOME OFFICE (1995b) *New Arrangements for the Recruitment and Qualifying Training of Probation Officers*. London, Home Office.

HOME OFFICE (1996a) *Protecting the Public: The Government's Strategy on Crime in England and Wales*, Cm 3190. London, HMSO.

HOME OFFICE (1996b) *The Prison Population in 1995*, Home Office Statistical Bulletin Issue 14/96. London, Home Office.

HOME OFFICE (1997a) *No More Excuses: A New Approach to Tackling Youth Crime in England and Wales*, Cm 3809. London, The Stationery Office.

HOME OFFICE (1998a) *Joining Forces to Protect the Public: Prisons–probation*. London, Home Office.

HOME OFFICE (1998b) *Bind Overs: A Power for the 21st Century*, Cm 3908. London, Home Office.

HOME OFFICE (1999a) *Managing Dangerous People with Severe Personality Disorder. Proposals for Policy Development*. London, Home Office.

HOME OFFICE (1999b) *The Correctional Policy Framework*. London, Home Office.

HOME OFFICE (2000a) *The Government's Strategy for Women Offenders*. London, Home Office.

Home Office (2000b) *The Victim Perspective: Ensuring the Victim Matters.* Thematic Inspection Report, HM Inspectorate of Probation. London, Home Office.

Home Office (2001a) *Criminal Justice: The Way Ahead.* Cm 5074. London, HMSO.

Home Office (2001b) *The Government's Strategy for Women Offenders: Consultation Report.* London, Home Office.

Home Office (2001c) *Victim Personal Statements*, Circular 35/2001. London, Justice and Victims' Unit, Home Office.

Home Office (2002a) *An Evaluation of Cognitive Behavioural Treatment for Prisoners.* London, Home Office.

Home Office (2002b) 'Falconer—Clear and Effective Sentencing Policy' Press Release: 257/2002. London, Home Office.

Home Office (2002c) *Justice for All*, Cm 5563. London, The Stationery Office.

Home Office (2002d) *Press Release 274/2002.* London, Home Office.

Home Office (2003a) *Restorative Justice: The Government's Strategy*, Consultation Paper. London, Home Office.

Home Office (2003b) *Respect and Responsibility—Taking a Stand against Anti-social Behaviour,* Cm 5778. London, Stationery Office.

Home Office (2003c) *Youth Justice—The Next Steps.* London, Home Office.

Home Office (2003d) *A New Deal for Victims and Witnesses.* London, Home Office.

Home Office (2003e) *Valuing the Victim—An Inspection into National Victim Contact Arrangements*, Thematic Inspection Report, HM Inspectorate of Probation. London, Home Office.

Home Office (2003f) *Prison Statistics: England and Wales 2002*, Cm 5996. London, The Stationery Office.

Home Office (2003g) *Criminal Statistics, England and Wales 2002*, Cm 6054. London, The Stationery Office.

Home Office (2004a) *Compensation and Support for Victims of Crime*, A Consultation Paper. London, Home Office.

Home Office (2004b) *Reducing Crime—Changing Lives.* London, The Stationery Office.

Home Office (2005a) *OASys Implementation and its Development*, Probation Circular 14/2005. London, Home Office.

Home Office (2005b) *A Five Year Strategy for Protecting the Public and Reducing Re-offending*, Cm 6717. London, The Stationery Office.

Home Office (2005c) *Probation Circular 25/2005: Criminal Justice Act 2003: Implementation on 4 April.* London, Home Office.

Home Office (2006a) *Rebalancing the Criminal Justice System in Favour of the Law Abiding Majority: Reducing Reoffending and Protecting the Public.* London, Home Office.

Home Office (2006b) *Improving Prison and Probation Services: Public Value Partnerships.* London, Home Office.

Home Office (2006c) *Tackling Anti-Social Behaviour,* National Audit Office 'Value for Money' Report by the Comptroller and Auditor General, HC 99 2006–7.

Home Office (2007a) *Cutting Crime: A New Partnership.* London, Home Office.

Home Office (2007b) *Bringing Offenders to Justice: Criminal Justice Penalties and Sentencing.* London, Home Office.

Home Office (2007c) *Sentencing Statistics 2005 England and Wales,* Home Office Statistical Bulletin 03/07. London, Home Office.

Home Office (2007d) *Guidance on the Use of Acceptable Behaviour Contracts and Agreements.* London: Home Office.

Home Office (2008) *Working Together to Protect the Public: The Home Office Strategy 2008–11.* London, Home Office.

Home Office (2010) *Prolific and Other Priority Offenders, Results from the 2009 cohort for England and Wales. Available at* http://rds.homeoffice.gov.uk/rds/stats-release.html.

Home Office (2011a) *An Overview of Recorded Crimes and Arrests Resulting from Disorder Events in August 2011.* London, Home Office.

Home Office (2011b) *More Effective Responses to Anti-Social Behaviour.* London, Home Office.

Home Office, Department of Health and Welsh Office (2000) *National Standards for the Supervision of Offenders in the Community.* London, The Stationery Office.

Home Office, Ministry of Justice, Cabinet Office, Department for Children, Schools and Families (2008) *Youth Crime Action Plan 2008.* London, HM Government.

Home Office/Youth Justice Board (2002) *Final Warning Scheme, Guidance to the Police and Youth Offending Teams.* London, Home Office.

Home Secretary, Lord Chancellor and Attorney General (2006) *Making Sentencing Clearer: A Consultation and Report of a Review.* London, Home Office.

Hood, R. (1962) *Sentencing in Magistrates' Courts.* London, Tavistock.

Hood, R. (1992) *Race and Sentencing.* Oxford, Clarendon Press.

Hood, R. and Hoyle, C. (2008) *The Death Penalty: A World-wide Perspective* (4th edn). Oxford, Clarendon.

Hood, R., Shute, S., Feilzer, M., and Wilcox, M. (2002) *Reconviction Rates of Serious Sex Offenders and Assessments of their Risk* HORS 164. London, Home Office.

Hopley, K. (2002) 'National Standards: Defining Service' in D. Ward, J. Scott and M. Lacey (eds) *Probation: Working for Justice* (2nd edn). Oxford, Oxford University Press.

Hough, M. and Jacobson, J. (2008) *Creating a Sentencing Commission for England and Wales: An opportunity to address the prison crisis.* London, Prison Reform Trust.

Hough, M. and Roberts, J. (1998) *Attitudes to Punishment: Findings from the British Crime Survey*, Home Office Research Study No 179. London, HMSO.

Hough, M. and Roberts, J. (2005) 'Sentencing Young Offenders: Public Opinion in England and Wales' *Criminal Justice* Vol 5(3), 12–32.

Hough, M., Jacobson, J., and Millie, A. (2003) *The Decision to Imprison: Sentencing and the Prison Population.* London, Prison Reform Trust.

Hough, M., Roberts, J. V., Jacobson, J., Moon, N., and Steel, N. (2009) *Public Attitudes to the Principles of Sentencing*, Sentencing Advisory Panel Report No. 6. London, Sentencing Advisory Panel.

House of Commons Justice Committee (2009) *Draft Sentencing Guideline: Overarching Principles–Sentencing Youths*, Tenth Report of Session 2008–9, HC 497. London, The Stationery Office.

House of Commons Justice Committee (2010) *Cutting crime, the case for justice reinvestment, First Report of Session 2009–10* Vol 1, HC 94–1. London, The Stationery Office.

Howard League for Penal Reform (2000) *A Chance to Break the Cycle, Women and the Drug Treatment and Testing Order*, Briefing Paper. London, Howard League for Penal Reform.

Howard League for Penal Reform (2004) *Advice, Understanding and Underwear: Working with Girls in Prison.* London, Howard League for Penal Reform.

Howard League for Penal Reform (2007) *Children in Prison: An Independent Submission to the United Nations Committee on the Rights of the Child.*

London, Howard League for Penal Reform.

Howard League (2008) *Punishing Children: A Survey of Criminal Responsibility and Approaches Across Europe*. London, Howard League

Howard League for Penal Reform (2010) *Submission to the Justice Affairs Select Committee Inquiry on the Role of the Probation Service*, 16 September. London, Howard League.

Howard League for Penal Reform (2011) *Twisted, The Use of Force on Children in Custody*. London, Howard League.

Howard, D. and Christophersen, O. (2003) *Statistics of Mentally Disordered Offenders 2002*. RDS 14/03. London, Home Office.

Howden-Windell, J. and Clark, D. (1999) *Criminogenic Needs of Female Offenders: A Literature Review, Report to Women's Policy Group*. London, Home Office.

Howse, K. (2003) *Growing Old in Prison—A Scoping Study of Older Prisoners*. London, Prison Reform Trust.

Hoyle, C. (2008) *Restorative Justice Working Group Discussion Paper*. London, Commission on English Prisons Today.

Hoyle, C., Young, R., and Hill, R. (2002) *Proceed with Caution: An Evaluation of the Thames Valley Police Initiative in Restorative Cautioning*. York, Joseph Rowntree Foundation.

Hucklesby, A. and Hagley-Dickinson, L. (eds) (2007) *Prisoner Resettlement: Current Policy and Practice*. Cullompton, Willan.

Hudson, B. (1993) *Penal Policy and Social Justice*. London, Macmillan.

Hudson, B. (1998) 'Mitigation for Socially Deprived Offenders' in A. von Hirsch and A. Ashworth (eds) *Principled Sentencing: Readings on Theory and Policy*. Oxford, Hart, 205–8.

Hudson, B. (2001) 'Human Rights, Public Safety and the Probation Service: Defending Justice in the Risk Society' *Howard Journal* Vol 40(2), 103–13.

Hudson, B. (2001/2) 'The Halliday Report: Opening or Closing the Revolving Door?' *Criminal Justice Matters* No 46, 7–8.

Hudson, B. (2003) *Justice in the Risk Society*. London, Sage.

Hulsman, L. (1991) 'Alternatives to Criminal Justice, Decriminalization and Depenalization' in Z. Lazocik, M. Platek, and I. Rzeplinska (eds) *Abolitionism in History, On Another Way of Thinking*. Warsaw, Institute of Social Prevention and Resocialization.

Human Rights Joint Committee (2011) Twenty-Second Report, *Legislative Scrutiny, Legal Aid, Sentencing and Punishment of Offenders Bill*, Houses of Parliament, London.

Hutchinson, S. (2006) 'Countering Catastrophic Criminology' *Punishment and Society* Vol 8(4), 443–67.

Hutton, N. (2005) 'Beyond Popular Punitiveness?' *Punishment and Society* Vol 73(3), 243–58.

Impalox Group (2007) *Evaluation of the Assessment Procedure at Two Pilot Sites in the DSPD Programme*. London, Home Office.

Ingleby Report (1960) *Report of the Committee on Children and Young Persons* Cmnd 1190. London, HMSO.

Inquest (1998) *Report on the Death in Prison Custody of Alton Manning*. London, Inquest.

International Centre for Prison Studies (2011) *World Prison Brief*, Colchester, University of Essex.

Jackson, E. (2007) 'Prisoners, their Partners and the Right to Family Life' *Child and Family Law Quarterly* Vol 19(2), 239–46.

Jackson, J. (2003) 'Justice for All: Putting Victims at the Heart of Criminal Justice' *Journal of Law and Society* Vol 30(2), 309–26.

Jackson, S. (1999) Family Group Conferences and Youth Justice' in

B. Goldson (ed) *Youth Justice: Contemporary Policy and Practice*. Aldershot, Ashgate.

Jacobson, J. and Hough, M. (2007) *Mitigation: The Role of Personal Factors in Sentencing*. London, Prison Reform Trust.

Jacobson, J. and Hough, M. (2010) *Unjust Deserts, Imprisonment for Public Protection*. London, Prison Reform Trust.

Jacobson, J., Bhardwa, B., Gyateng, T., Hunter, G., and Hough, M. (2011) *Punishing disadvantage, a profile of children in custody*. London, Prison Reform Trust.

Jacobson, J., Kirby, A., and Hough, M. (2011), *Public Attitudes to the Sentencing of Drug Offences* Sentencing Council Research Series 01/11. London, Office of the Sentencing Council.

Jago, R. and Thompson, E. (2001) 'Private Prison Contractors' *The Prisons Handbook*. Winchester, Waterside Press, 253–6.

James, A. (1995) 'Probation Values for the 1990s—and Beyond?' *Howard Journal* Vol 34(4), 326–43.

James, A. and James, A. L. (2008) 'Changing Childhood in England: Reconstructing Discourse of "Risk" and "Protection" in Children's Best Interests' in A. James and A. L. James (eds) *European Childhoods: Culture, Politics and Participation*. Basingstoke, Palgrave Macmillan.

James, A. L., Bottomley, A. K., Liebling, A., and Clare, E. (1997) *Privatizing Prisons: Rhetoric and Reality*. London, Sage.

Jeffrey, C. R. (1965) 'Criminal Behaviour and Learning Theory' *Journal of Criminal Law, Criminology and Police Science* Vol 56, 294–300.

Jenks, C. (1996) *Childhood*. London, Routledge.

Johnson, D. (2009) 'Anger about crime and support for punitive criminal justice policies' *Punishment and Society* Vol 11(1), 51–66.

Johnstone, G. (ed) (2011) *Restorative Justice* (2nd edn). London, Routledge.

Jones, A. and Singer, L. (2007) *Statistics on Race and the Criminal Justice System—2006*. London, Ministry of Justice.

Jones, D. (2001) '"Misjudged Youth": A Critique of the Audit Commission's Reports on Youth Justice' *British Journal of Criminology* Vol 41, 362–80.

Jones, K. (2003) 'Coping with Complexity' *Mediation Matters* Issue 75, 8.

Judicial Studies Board (undated) Reporting Restrictions: Magistrates' Courts http://www.jsboard.co.uk/publications/rrmc/index.htm (accessed 12 September 2007).

Junger-Tas J. (2002) 'The Juvenile System: Past and Present Trends in Western Society' in I. Weijers and A. Duff (eds) *Punishing Juveniles, Principle and Critique*. Oxford, Hart, 23–44.

Junger-Tas, J. (1994) 'The Changing Family and its Relationship with Delinquent Behaviour' in C. Henricson (ed) *Crime and the Family*, Family Policy Studies Centre Occasional Paper 20. London, Family Policy Studies Centre, 18–25.

JUSTICE (1998) *Victims in Criminal Justice*, Report of the JUSTICE Committee on the Role of the Victim in Criminal Justice. London, JUSTICE.

Justice Committee (2009) *Sentencing Guidelines and Parliament: Building a Bridge*, Sixth Report of the House of Commons Justice Committee Session 2008–9. Available at http://www.publications.parliament.uk/pa/cm200809/cmselect/cmjust/715/71502.htm.

Kant, I. (1796–7) *The Metaphysics of Morals*, trans. Mary Gregor (1991). Cambridge, Cambridge University Press.

Kazemian, L. (2010) 'Assessing the Impact of a Recidivist Sentencing Premium' in J. V. Roberts and A. von Hirsch (eds) *Previous Convictions at Sentencing*,

Theoretical and Applied Perspectives. Oxford, Hart Publishing, 227–50.

Kazemian, L., Farrington, D. P., and LeBlanc, M. (2009) 'Can we make accurate predictions about patterns of de-escalation in offending behaviour?' *Journal of Youth and Adolescence* Vol 38, 384–400.

Keating, H. (2007) 'The "responsibility" of children in criminal law' *Child and Family Law Quarterly* Vol 19(2), 183–203.

Keith, B. (2006) *Report of the Zahid Mubarek Inquiry,* HC 1082. London, The Stationery Office.

Kelly, D. P. and Erez, E. (1997) 'Victim Participation in the Criminal Justice System' in R. C. Davis, A. J. Lurigio and W. G. Skogan (eds) *Victims of Crime* (2nd edn). Thousand Oaks, Sage, 211–30.

Kempf-Leonard, K. and Peterson, E. (2000) 'Expanding the Realms of the New Penology' *Punishment and Society* Vol 2(1), 66–97.

Kemshall, H. (2002) 'Effective Practice in Probation: An Example of "Advanced Liberal" Responsibilisation?' *Howard Journal* Vol 31(1), 41–58.

Kemshall, H. and Wood, J. (2010) *Child Sex Offender Review (CSOR) Public Disclosure Pilots, A Process Evaluation* (2nd edn), Home Office Research Report No 32. London, Home Office.

Kennedy, D. M. (2009) *Deterrence and Crime Prevention: Reconsidering the prospect of sanction.* London, Routledge.

Kennedy, L. (1990) *On the Borders of Crime, Conflict Management and Criminology.* New York, Longmans.

Kershaw, C., Goodman, J., and White, S. (1999) *Reconvictions of Offenders Sentenced or Discharged from Prison in 1995 in England and Wales,* Home Office Statistical Bulletin 19/99. London, Home Office.

Kilbrandon, Lord (1964) *Children and Young Persons, Scotland.* Edinburgh, Scottish Home and Health Department.

Kilkelly, U. and Lundy, L. (2006) 'Children's Rights in Action in Using the UN Convention on the Rights of the Child as an Auditing Tool' *Child and Family Law Quarterly* Vol 18(3), 331–50.

King, A. and Maruna, S. (2009) 'Is a conservative just a liberal who has been mugged? Exploring the origins of punitive views' *Punishment and Society* Vol 11(2), 147–69.

King, M. (1997a) *A Better World for Children? Explorations in Morality and Authority.* London, Routledge.

King, M. (1997b) 'The James Bulger Trial: Good or Bad for Guilty or Innocent Children?' in M. King, *A Better World for Children.* London, Routledge.

King, M. and Piper, C. (1995) *How the Law Thinks about Children* (2nd edn). Aldershot, Arena.

King, R. and Resodihardjo, S. (2010) 'To Max or not to Max. Dealing with High Risk Prisoners in the Netherlands and England and Wales' *Punishment and Society* Vol 12(1), 65–84.

King, R. S., Mauer, M., and Young, M. C. (2005) *Incarceration and Crime, A Complex Relationship.* Washington, D.C., The Sentencing Project.

Koffman, L. (2006) 'The Rise and Fall of Proportionality: The Failure of the Criminal Justice Act 1991' *Criminal Law Review,* 281–99.

Koffman, L. (2008) 'Holding Parents to Account: Tough on Children, Tough on the Causes of Children?' *Journal of Law and Society* Vol 35(1), 113–30.

Koffman, L. and Dingwall, G. (2007) 'The Diversion of Young Offenders: A Proportionate Response?' *Web JCL,* 2, I.

Kruttshnitt, C. and Dirkzwager (2011) 'Are there still Contrasts in Tolerance? Imprisonment in the Netherlands and England 20 years later' *Punishment and Society* Vol 13(3), 283–306.

Labour Party (1964) *Crime: A Challenge to Us All.* London, Labour Party.

Lacey, M. (2002) 'Justice, Humanity and Mercy' in D. Ward, J. Scott, and M. Lacey *Probation, Working for Justice* (2nd edn). Oxford, Oxford University Press, 25–38.

Lacey, N. (1988) *State Punishment.* London, Routledge.

Lacey, N. (1998) 'Punishment and Community' in A. von Hirsch and A. Ashworth (eds) *Principled Sentencing: Readings on Theory and Policy.* Oxford, Hart, 394–408.

Lacey, N. (2003) 'Penal theory and penal practice, a communitarian approach' in S. McConville (ed) *The Use of Punishment.* Cullompton, Willan, 175–98.

Lacey, N. (2008) 'The Prisoner's Dilemma' *Political Economy and Punishment in Contemporary Democracies.* Cambridge, Cambridge University Press.

Lacey, N. and Zedner, L. (1995) 'Discourses of Community in Criminal Justice' *Journal of Law and Society* Vol 22(3), 301–25.

Lader, D., Singleton, N., and Meltzer, H. (2000) *Psychiatric Morbidity among Young Offenders in England and Wales,* Report by the ONS (Office for National Statistics) for the Department of Health. London, ONS.

Laing, J. (1999) 'Diversion of Mentally Disordered Offenders: Victim and Offender Perspectives' *Criminal Law Review,* 805–19.

Landau, S. (1981) 'Juveniles and the Police—Who Is Charged Immediately and Who Is Referred to the Juvenile Bureau?' *British Journal of Criminology* Vol 21(1), 27.

Laws, R. and Ward, T. (2010) *Desistance from Sex Offending: Alternatives to Throwing Away the Keys.* London, Routledge.

Le Grand, J. (1998) 'The Third Way Begins with CORA' *New Statesman* 6 March.

Lea, J. and Young, J. (1984) *What Is to Be Done about Law and Order?* Harmondsworth, Penguin.

Learmont, J. (1995) *Review of Prison Service Security in England and Wales and the Escape from Parkhurst Prison on Tuesday 3rd January 1995,* Cm 3020. London, HMSO.

Ledger, J. (2010) 'Rehabilitation Revolution, Will Probation Pay the Price?' *Probation Journal* Vol 57(4), 415–22.

Leigh, A. (2001/2) 'Keeping on the Right Track' *Safer Society* Winter, 25–6.

Lemert, E. (1967) *Human Deviance, Social Problems and Social Control.* Englewood Cliffs, NJ, Prentice Hall.

Levi, M. (1989) 'Suite Justice: Sentencing for Fraud' *Criminal Law Review,* 420–34.

Levi, M. and Pithouse, A. (2000) *White Collar Crime and its Victims.* Oxford, Clarendon.

Lewis, S., Raynor, P., Smith, D., and Wardack, A. (eds) (2005) *Race and Probation Alternatives to Prison, Alternatives to Prison.* Cullompton, Willan.

Liberty (2006) *Renewing the Prevention of Terrorism Act 2005: Submission to the Joint Committee on Human Rights.* London, Liberty.

Liberty (2007) *Briefing on the Criminal Justice and Immigration Bill.* London, Liberty.

Liebmann, M. (2000) 'A Survey of RJ in Custodial Settings' *RJ* Issue 3, 1.

Lippke, R. L. (2007) *Rethinking Imprisonment.* Oxford, Oxford University Press.

Lipsey, M. W. (1992) 'The Effect of Treatment on Juvenile Delinquents: Results from Meta-analysis' in F. Losel, T. Bliesener, and D. Bender (eds) *Psychology and Law: International Perspectives.* Berlin, de Gruyter.

Little, M., Kogan, J., Bullock, R., and van der Laan, P. (2004) 'An Experiment in Multi-Systemic Responses to Persistent Young Offenders Known to Children's Services' *British Journal of Criminology* Vol 44, 225–40.

Littlechild, B. (1997) 'Young Offenders, Punitive Policy and the Rights of Children' *Critical Social Policy* Vol 17(3), 73–91.

Locke, T. (1988) 'Policy, Information and Monitoring Juvenile Crime and Justice' in B. Britton, B. Hope, T. Locke, and L. Wainman (eds) *Policy and Information in Juvenile Justice Systems*. London, NACRO/ Save the Children.

Loucks, N. (2007) *No One Knows: The Prevalence and Associated Needs of Offenders with Learning Difficulties and Learning Disabilities*. London, PRT.

Lovegrove, A. (2011) 'Putting the Offender Back into Sentencing: An Empirical Study of the Public's Understanding of Personal Mitigation' *Criminology and Criminal Justice* Vol 11(1), 37–57.

Lyon, D. (ed) (2006) *Theorizing Surveillance: The Panopticon and Beyond*. Cullompton, Willan.

Lyon, J. (2003) 'The Cost of a Broken Promise' *Criminal Justice Matters* Vol 54, 28–9.

Lyon, J., Dennison, C. and Wilson, A. (2000) *Tell Them so They Listen: Messages from Young People in Custody*, Home Office Research Study No 201. London, HMSO.

MacDonald, S. and Telford, M. (2007) 'The Use of ASBOs against Young People in England and Wales: Lessons from Scotland' *Legal Studies* Vol 27(4), 604–29.

Mackenzie, S., Bannister, J., Flint, J., Parr, S., Millie A., and Fleetwood, J. (2010) *The drivers of perceptions of anti-social behaviour*, Research Report 34. London, Home Office.

Mackie, A., Raine, J. W., Burrows, J., Hopkins, M. and Dunstan, E. (2003) *Clearing the Debts: The Enforcement of Financial Penalties in Magistrates' Courts*, Home Office On-Line Report 09/03. London, Home Office.

Macpherson, W. (1999) *The Stephen Lawrence Inquiry, Report of an Inquiry by Sir William Macpherson of Cluny, Advised by Tom Cook, The Right Revd. Dr John Sentamu and Dr Richard Stone*, Cm 4262–1. London, Home Office.

Magistrates' Association (1997, 2003) *Magistrates' Court Guidelines*. London, The Magistrates' Association.

Maguire, M. (2002) 'Crime Statistics' in M. Maguire, R. Morgan, and R. Reiner (eds) *The Oxford Handbook of Criminology* (3rd edn). Oxford, Oxford University Press, 322–75.

Maguire, M. and Shapland, J. (1997) 'Provision for Victims in an International Context' in R. Davis, A. Lurigio, and W. Skogan (eds) *Victims of Crime* (2nd edn). Thousand Oaks, CA, Sage, 211–28.

Mair, G. (1997) 'Community Penalties and Probation' in M. Maguire, R. Morgan, and R. Reiner (eds) *The Oxford Handbook of Criminology* (2nd edn). Oxford, Clarendon Press, 1195–232.

Mair, G. and Burke, L. (2011) *Redemption Rehabilitation and Risk Management*. London, Routledge.

Mair, G. and May, C. (1997) *Offenders on Probation*, HORS 167. London, Home Office.

Mair, G. and Millings, M. (2011) *Doing Justice Locally, The North Liverpool Community Justice Centre*. London, Centre for Crime and Justice Studies.

Mair, G. and Mills, H. (2009) *Three Years On: The Community Order and Suspended Sentence Order—the views and experiences of probation officers and offenders. London, Centre for Crime and Justice Studies.*

Mair, G., Cross, N., and Taylor, S. (2007) *The Use and Impact of the Community Order and the Suspended Sentence Order*. London, Centre for Criminal Justice Studies.

Malloch, M. and McIvor, G. (2011) 'Women and Community Sentences'

Criminology and Criminal Justice, 11,4, 325–44.

Mantle, G. and Moore, S. (2004) 'On Probation: Pickled and Nothing to Say' *Howard Journal* Vol 43(3), 299–316.

Marcuse, H. (2002) *One-Dimensional Man*. London, Routledge.

Markel, D. (2005) 'State Be Not Proud, A Retributivist Defence of the Commutation of Death Row and the Abolition of the Death Penalty' *Harvard Civil Rights—Civil Liberties Law Review* Vol 40, 407–80.

Marquart, J. W., Ekland-Olsen, S., and Sorensen, J. R. (1989) 'A National Study of *Furman*-Commuted Inmates: Assessing the Threat to Society from Capital Offenders' *Loyola of Los Angeles Law Review* Vol 23(1), November 5–28.

Marsh, I., Melville, G., Morgan, K., and Norris, G. (2006) 'Explaining the Criminal Behaviour of Ethnic Minorities' in I. Marsh (ed) *Theories of Crime*. London, Routledge.

Marshall, P. (1997) *A Reconviction Study of HMP Grendon Therapeutic Community*. London, Home Office.

Marshall, T. (1985) *Alternatives to Criminal Courts*. Aldershot, Gower.

Marshall, T. (1992) Seminar, 21 January, Law Department, Brunel University.

Marshall, T. (1997) 'Seeking the Whole Justice' in S. Hayman and M. Wright (eds) *Repairing the Damage: Restorative Justice in Action*. London, ISTD.

Marshall, T. H. (1950) *Citizenship and Social Rights*. Cambridge, Cambridge University Press.

Martin, J. and Webster, D. (1971) *The Social Consequences of Conviction*. London, Heinemann.

Martinson, R. (1974) 'What Works? Questions and Answers about Prison Reform' *The Public Interest* (Spring), 22–54.

Marx, K. (1853) 'Capital Punishment' first published in *New York Daily Tribune*, February 17 and 18, reprinted in *Marx and Engels: Collected Works* Vol 11. London, Lawrence and Wishart (1979), 495–501.

Marx, K. and Engels, F. (1845) 'The Holy Family' in *Marx and Engels: Collected Works* Vol 4 (1975), London, Lawrence and Wishart (1975), 5–211.

Mason, T. and Mercer, D. (1999) A *Sociology of the Mentally Disordered Offender*. London, Longman.

Mason, T., de Silva, N., Sharma, N., Brown, D., and Harper, G. (2007) *Local Variation in Sentencing in England and Wales*. London, Ministry of Justice.

Masters, G. (1997) 'Values for Probation, Society and Beyond' *Howard Journal* Vol 36(3), 237–47.

Mathews, J. (2010) 'The Management of Sex Offenders in the Community' *Probation Journal* Vol 57(4), 423–4.

Mathiesen, T. (2006) *Prison on Trial* (3rd edn). Winchester, Waterside Press.

Matthews, R. (1988) *Informal Justice*. London, Sage.

Matthews, R. (ed) (1989) *Privatising Criminal Justice*. London, Sage.

Mattinson, J. and Mirrlees-Black, C. (2000) *Attitudes to Crime and Criminal Justice: Findings from the 1998 British Crime Survey*, Home Office Research Study No 200. London, Home Office.

Mauer, M. (2001) 'The Causes and Consequences of Prison Growth in the United States' in D. Garland (ed) *Mass Imprisonment*. London, Sage, 4–14.

Mauer, M. (2011) 'Addressing racial disparities in incarceration' *Prison Journal Supplement* Vol 91(3) 87S-101S.

May, M. (2002) 'Innocence and Experience: The Evolution of the Concept of Juvenile Delinquency in the Mid-nineteenth Century' in J. Muncie, G. Hughes, and E. McLaughlin (eds) (2002) *Youth Justice, Critical Readings*. London, Sage, 98–114.

May, T. (1990) *Probation: Politics, Policy and Practice*. Milton Keynes, Open University Press.

May, T., Gyateng, T., and Hough, M. (2010) *Differential Treatment in the Youth Justice System*, EHRC Report 50. London, ICPR.

McBride, W. L. (1975) 'The Concept of Justice in Marx, Engels and Others' *Ethics* Vol 85, 204–18.

McDermott, K. (1990), 'We Have No Problem: The Experience of Racism in Prison' *New Community*, 213–28.

McDiarmid, C. (2000) 'Children Who Murder: What Is Her Majesty's Pleasure?' *Criminal Law Review*, 547–63.

McDonald, I. (2006) 'The "Respect Action Plan": Something New or More of the Same?' *Journal of Social Welfare and Family Law* Vol 28(2), 191–200.

McEvoy, K., Mika, H., and Hudson, B. (2002) 'Practice, Performance and Prospects for Restorative Justice' *British Journal of Criminology* Vol 42, 469–75.

McGuire, J. (ed) (1995) *What Works? Reducing Reoffending*. Chichester, John Wiley.

McGuire, J. and Priestley, P. (1995) 'Reviewing "What Works": Past, Present and Future' in J. McGuire (ed) *What Works? Reducing Reoffending*. Chichester, John Wiley, 3–34.

McIvor, G. (1998) 'Jobs for the Boys? Gender Differences in Referral to Community Service' *Howard Journal* Vol 37(3), 280–90.

McKeever, G. (2004) 'Social Security as a Criminal Sanction' *Journal of Social and Welfare Law* Vol 26(1), 1–16.

McKnight, J. (2009) 'Speaking up for Probation' *Howard Journal* Vol 48, 327–43.

McLaughlin, E. and Muncie, J. (1994) 'Managing the Criminal Justice System' in J. Clarke, A. Cochrane, E. McLaughlin (eds) *Managing Social Policy*. London: Sage.

McLaughlin, E., Ferguson, R., Hughes, G., and Westmarland, L. (2003) *Restorative Justice, Critical Issues*. Milton Keynes, Open University Press and London, Sage.

McLaughlin, E., Muncie, J., and Hughes, G. (2001) 'The Permanent Revolution: New Labour, New Public Management and the Modernization of Criminal Justice' *Criminal Justice* Vol 1(3), 301–18.

McRobbie, A. and Thornton, S. (2002) 'Rethinking "Moral Panic" for Multi-mediated Social Worlds' in J. Muncie, G. Hughes, and E. McLaughlin (eds) *Youth Justice: Critical Readings*. London, Sage, 68–79.

McWilliams, W. and Pease, K. (1990) 'Probation Practice and an End to Punishment' *Howard Journal* Vol 29(1), 14–24.

Meek, R. (2008) *High Security Prisons, Prisoner Perspectives*. London, Howard League.

Miers, D. (1990) *Compensation for Criminal Injuries*. London, Butterworths.

Miers, D. (2004) 'Situating and Researching Restorative Justice in Great Britain' *Punishment and Society* Vol 6(1), 23–46.

Miers, D., Maguire, M., Goldie, S., Sharpe, K., Hale, C., Netton, K., Doolin, S., Uglow, S., Enterkin, J., and Newburn, T. (2001) *An Exploratory Evaluation of Restorative Justice Schemes*. Crime Reduction Research Series Paper 9. London, Home Office.

Mill, J. S. (1859) *On Liberty and Other Essays*, ed J. Gray (2008). Oxford, Oxford University Press.

Mill, J. S. (1861) *Utilitarianism*. Oxford, Oxford University Press, 1998.

Mills, M. (2009) 'Cruel and Unusual, *State v Mata*, the Electric Chair and the Nebraska Supreme Court's Rejection of a Subjective Intent Requirement in Death Penalty Jurisprudence' *Nebraska Law Review* Vol 88, 235–260.

Ministry of Justice (2007a) *Offender Management Caseload Statistics 2006*. London, Ministry of Justice.

Ministry of Justice (2007b) *The Government's Response to the Report by Baroness Corston of a Review of Women with Particular Vulnerabilities in the Criminal Justice System*, Cm 7261. London, The Stationery Office.

Ministry of Justice (2007c) *Statistics of Mentally Disordered Offenders 2006, England and Wales*, Statistical Bulletin. London, Ministry of Justice.

Ministry of Justice (2007d) *Sentencing Statistics 2006 England and Wales*, Statistical Bulletin. London, Ministry of Justice.

Ministry of Justice (2009) *Voting Rights of Convicted Prisoners Detained within the United Kingdom, Second Stage Consultation*. London, Ministry of Justice.

Ministry of Justice (2010a) *Breaking the Cycle, Effective Punishment, Rehabilitation and Sentencing of Offenders*. London, Ministry of Justice.

Ministry of Justice (2010b) *Compendium of Reoffending Statistics and Analysis, Ministry of Justice Statistics Bulletin*. London, Ministry of Justice.

Ministry of Justice (2010c) *Statistics on Women and the Criminal Justice System*. London, Ministry of Justice.

Ministry of Justice (2010d) *Prison Population Projections 2010–2016*, Ministry of Justice Statistics Bulletin, London, Ministry of Justice.

Ministry of Justice (2010e) *Statistics of Mentally Disordered Offenders 2008 England and Wales*. London, Ministry of Justice.

Ministry of Justice (2010f) *Multi Agency Public Protection Arrangements Annual Report 2009/10*. London, Ministry of Justice Statistics Bulletin.

Ministry of Justice (2011a) *Breaking the Cycle, Government Response*, Cm 8070, London, Ministry of Justice.

Ministry of Justice (2011b) *Prison Annual Performance Ratings*. London, Ministry of Justice/NOMS.

Ministry of Justice (2011c) *Statistics on Race and the Criminal Justice System*. London, Ministry of Justice.

Ministry of Justice (2011d) *National Offender Management Service Annual Report 2009/10 Management Information Addendum*. London, Ministry of Justice.

Ministry of Justice (2011e) *Competition Strategy for Offender Services*. London, Ministry of Justice.

Ministry of Justice (2011f) *IPP Factsheet*, Ministry of Justice, London.

Ministry of Justice (2011g) *Equalities Annual Report 2010–2011*. London Ministry of Justice.

Ministry of Justice (2011h) *Prison Population Projections 2011–2017 England and Wales*. London, Ministry of Justice.

Ministry of Justice (2011i) *National Standards for the Management of Offenders*. London, Ministry of Justice.

Ministry of Justice (2011j) *Increasing the Magistrates' Court fine limit—Equality Impact Assessment*. Tabled at Commons Report Stage, Legal Aid Sentencing and Punishment of Offenders Bill.

Ministry of Justice (2011k) *Criminal Justice Statistics Quarterly Update to December 2010*, Ministry of Justice Statistics Bulletin. London. Ministry of Justice.

Ministry of Justice (2011m) *Criminal Justice Statistics Quarterly Update to March 2011*, Ministry of Justice Statistics bulletin. London, Ministry of Justice.

Ministry of Justice (2011n) *Criminal Justice Statistics, England and Wales—12 months ending June 2011*. London, Ministry of Justice.

Ministry of Justice (2011o) *Offender Management Caseload Statistics* 2010, London Ministry of Justice.

Ministry of Justice/DCSF (2008) *The Government's Response to the Report by Peter Smallridge and Andrew Williamson of a Review of the Use of Restraint in Juvenile Secure Settings*, Cm 7501. London, The Stationery Office.

Mirrlees-Black, C. (2001) *Confidence in the Criminal Justice System: Findings from the 2000 British Crime Survey*, Home Office Research Findings No 137. London, Home Office.

Mitchell, B. and Mackay, R. D. (2011) 'Investigating Involuntary Manslaughter: An Empirical Study of 127 Cases' *Oxford Journal of Legal Studies* Vol 31(1), 165–91.

Mitchell, B. and Roberts, J. V. (2010) *Public Opinion and Sentencing For Murder. An empirical investigation of public knowledge and attitudes in England and Wales*. Available online at http://www.nuffieldfoundation.org.

Mitchell, B. and Roberts, J. V. (2012) 'Sentencing for Murder, Exploring Public Knowledge and Public Opinion in England and Wales' *British Journal of Criminology* Vol 52(1), 141–58.

Moloney Report (1927) *Report of the Departmental Committee on the Treatment of Offenders*. Cmnd 2381. London, HMSO.

Monaghan, G., Moore, S., and Hibbert, P. (2003) *Children in Trouble: Time for Change*. Barkingside, Barnardo's.

Moore, L., Phillips, A., and Kostadintcheva, K. (2010) *Community Payback and local criminal justice engagement initiatives, public perceptions and awareness, Research Summary 3/10*. Ministry of Justice, London.

Moore, R. (2003a) 'The Use of Financial Penalties and the Amounts Imposed: the Need for a New Approach' *Criminal Law Review*, 13–27.

Moore, R. (2003b) 'Executing Warrants against Fine defaulters: The Continuing Search for Effectiveness and Efficiency' *Criminal Law Review*, 595–606.

Moore, R. (2004) 'Intensive Supervision and Surveillance Programmes for Young Offenders: The Evidence Base so Far' in R. Burnett and C. Roberts (eds) *What Works in Probation and Youth Justice: Developing Evidence-based Practice*. Cullompton, Willan.

Morgan, R. (2000) *The Judiciary in the Magistrates' Courts*, Home Office RDS Occasional Paper No 66. London, Home Office.

Morgan, R. (2008) *Summary Justice, Fast—but Fair?* London, Centre for Crime and Justice Studies, Kings College.

Morrell, G., Scott, S., McNeish, D., and Webster, S. (2011) *The August Riots in England, Understanding the Involvement of Young People*. London, National Centre for Social Research.

Morris, A. and Gelsthorpe, L. (1990) 'Not Paying for Crime: Issues in Fine Enforcement' *Criminal Law Review*, 839–51.

Morris, A. and Giller, H. (1987) *Understanding Juvenile Justice*. Beckenham, Croom Helm.

Morris, A. and Maxwell, G. (2001) 'Implementing Restorative Justice: What Works?' in A. Morris and G. Maxwell (eds) *Restorative Justice for Juveniles: Conferencing, Mediation and Circles*. Oxford, Hart, 267–81.

Morris, N. (1974) *The Future of Imprisonment*. Chicago, University of Chicago Press.

Morris, N. and Miller, M. (1985) 'Predictions of Dangerousness' in M. Tonry and N. Morris (eds) *Crime and Justice: An Annual Review of Research* Vol 6. Chicago, University of Chicago Press, 1–50.

Morris, N. and Tonry, M. (1990) *Between Prison and Probation*. Oxford, Oxford University Press.

Moster, A., Wnuk, D. W., and Jeglic, E. J. (2008) 'Cognitive behavioural therapy interventions with sex offenders' *Journal of Correctional Health Care* Vol 14(2), 109–21.

Mountbatten, Lord (1966) *Report of the Inquiry into Prison Escapes and Security*, Cm 3175. London, HMSO.

Moxon, D., Corkery, J. M., and Hedderman, C. (1992) *Some Developments in the Use of Compensation Orders in Magistrates' Courts since 1988*, Home Office Research Study 126. London, HMSO.

Mulcahy, L. (2000) 'The Devil and the Deep Blue Sea? A Critique of the Ability of Community Mediation to Suppress and Facilitate Participation in Civil Life' *Journal of Law and Society* Vol 27(1), 133–50.

Muncie, J. (1999) 'Institutionalised Intolerance: Youth Justice and the 1998 Crime and Disorder Act' *Critical Social Policy* Vol 19(2), 147–75.

Muncie, J. (2000) 'Pragmatic Realism? Searching for Criminology in the New Youth Justice' in B. Goldson (ed) *The New Youth Justice*. Lyme Regis, Russell House Publishing, 14–34.

Muncie, J. (2004) *Youth and Crime: A Critical Introduction* (2nd edn). London, Sage.

Muncie, J. (2006) 'Repenalisation and Rights: Explorations in Comparative Youth Criminology' *Howard Journal* Vol 45(1), 42–70.

Muncie, J. (2008) 'The Punitive Turn in Juvenile Justice, Cultures of Control and Rights Compliance in Western Europe and the USA' *Youth Justice, An International Journal* Vol 8, 107–21.

Muncie, J. (2011) 'Illusions of Difference, Comparative Youth Justice in the Devolved United Kingdom' *British Journal of Criminology* Vol 51, 40–57.

Muncie, J. and Hughes, E. (2002) 'Modes of Youth Governance: Political Rationalities, Criminalization and Resistance' in J. Muncie, G. Hughes, and E. McLaughlin (eds) *Youth Justice: Critical Readings*. London, Sage, 1–18.

Munro, V. (2002) 'The Emerging Rights of Imprisoned Mothers and their Children' *Child and Family Law Quarterly* Vol 14, 303.

Murphy, J. G. (1973) 'Marxism and Retribution' *Philosophy and Public Affairs* Vol 2, 217–43.

Murphy, K. and Harris, N. (2007) 'Shaming, Shame and Recidivism' *British Journal of Criminology* Vol 47(6), 900–17.

Murphy, T. and Whitty, N. (2007) 'Risk and Human Rights in UK Prison Governance' *British Journal of Criminology* Vol 47(5), 798–816.

Murray, C. and Cox, L. (1979) *Beyond Probation: Juvenile Corrections and Chronic Delinquent*. Beverly Hills, CA, Sage.

NACRO (1985) *Juvenile Crime*, Juvenile Crime Briefing. London, NACRO.

NACRO (1986) *Cautioning and Diversion of Juvenile Offenders*, Juvenile Crime Briefing. London, NACRO.

NACRO (1989) *Diverting Juvenile Offenders from Prosecution*, Juvenile Crime Policy Paper 2. London, NACRO.

NACRO (1993) 'Supplementary Guidance on Cautioning' NACRO Briefing, December. London, NACRO.

NACRO (2000a) *Race & Prisons*. London, NACRO.

NACRO (2000b) *Pre-Sentence Reports and Custodial Sentencing*. NACRO Briefing, December. London, NACRO.

NACRO (2000c) *Some Facts about Young Offenders*. NACRO Briefing. London, NACRO.

NACRO (2001/2) 'Children Who Commit Grave Crimes' *Safer Society* Winter, 8–9.

NACRO (2001a) *Public Opinion and Youth Justice*. Youth Crime Briefing. 12/01. London.

NACRO (2001b) *The Grave Crimes Provision*. Youth Justice Briefing. London, NACRO.

NACRO (2003a) *Detention and Training Order Early Release—The Revised Guidance and Use of Electronic Monitoring*, Youth Crime Briefing, March. London, NACRO.

NACRO (2003b) *Youth Crime, Section Update, September 2003*. London, NACRO.

NACRO (2003c) *Looked After Children Who Offend: The Quality Protects Programme and YOTS*, Youth Crime Briefing. London, NACRO.

NACRO (2003d) *Youth Crime, Section Update, December*. London, NACRO.

NACRO (2003e) *Family Group Conferencing and Youth Justice*, Youth Crime Briefing. London, NACRO.

NACRO (2003f) *Race and Prisons: Where Are We Now?* London, NACRO.

NACRO (2004) *New Legislation—Impact on Sentencing*, Youth Crime Briefing. London, NACRO.

NACRO (2005) *Dangerousness and the Criminal Justice Act 2003*, Youth Crime Briefing, June. London, NACRO.

NACRO (2006) *Managing Risk in the Community in the Youth Justice System*, Youth Crime Briefing, September. London, NACRO.

NACRO (2007a) *Further Developments in Measures Related to Anti-social Behaviour*, Youth Crime Briefing, March. London, NACRO.

NACRO (2007b) *The Detention and Training Order*, Youth Crime Briefing, June. London, NACRO.

NACRO (2007c) *Some Facts about Children and Young People Who Offend—2005*, Youth Crime Briefing. London, NACRO.

NACRO (2007d) *'Grave Crimes' Mode of Trial and Long Term Detention*, Youth Crime Briefing. London, NACRO.

NACRO (2008) *Some Facts about Children and Young People Who Offend—2006*, Youth Crime Briefing. London, NACRO.

NACRO (2010) Some Facts about Children and Young People Who Offend—2008, Youth Crime Briefing. London, NACRO.

NACRO (2011) *Reducing the Number of Children and Young People in Custody*. London, NACRO.

NAPO (2006) *News*, Issue 182, 15 September.

Nash, M. and Williams, A. (2008) *The Anatomy of Serous Further Offending*. Oxford, Oxford University Press.

National Audit Office (2008), *National Probation Service: The Supervision of Community Orders in England and Wales*. London, The Stationery Office.

National Audit Office (2010a) *The Youth Justice System in England and Wales: Reducing Offending by Young People*, Report by the Comptroller and Auditor General, HC 663 Session 2010–2011. London, The Stationery Office.

National Audit Office (2010b) *Managing Offenders on Short Custodial Sentences*. London, The Stationery Office.

National Offender Management Service (NOMS) (2006a) *Working with Probation to Protect the Public and Reduce Re-offending*. London, Home Office.

National Offender Management Service (NOMS) (2006b) *Improving Prison and Probation Services: Public Value Partnerships*. London, Home Office.

National Offender Management Service (NOMS) (2007) *Commissioning Framework, National Commissioning Plan 2007–8*. London, Home Office.

National Offender Mangement Service (NOMS) (2008) *Race Review Implementing Race Equality in Prisons—Five Years On*. London, Ministry of Justice.

National Offender Management Service (NOMS) (2009a) *Muslim Prisoners Scoping Study*. London, NOMS.

National Offender Management Service (NOMS 2009b) *Promoting Equality in Prisons and Probation: the National Offender Management Service Single Equality Scheme 2009–2012*. London, NOMS.

National Offender Management Service (NOMS) (2011) *Annual Report and Accounts 2010–2011*. London, The Stationery Office, HC 1345.

National Preventive Mechanism (NPM) (2011) *Monitoring Places of Detention, First Annual Report of the United Kingdom's National Preventive Mechanism, 1 April 2009—31 March 2010*, Cm 8010. London, The Stationery Office.

National Probation Service (NPS) (2003) *OASys: The New Offender Assessment System: Important information for Sentencers*, Briefing note Issue 3. London, National Probation Service.

Nelken, D. (1994) 'Community Involvement in Crime Control' in N. Lacey (ed) *A Reader in Criminal Justice*. Oxford, Oxford University Press, 247–77.

Nellis, M. (1995) 'Probation Values for the 1990s' *Howard Journal* Vol 34, 19–44.

Nellis, M. (2002) 'Probation Partnership and Civil Society' in D. Ward, J. Scott, and M. Lacey (eds) *Probation, Working for Justice* (2nd edn). Oxford, Oxford University Press, 356–74.

Neumann P. (2010) *Prisons and Terrorism, Radicalisation and De-Radicalisation in 15 Countries*. London, ICSR.

Neumann, P. and Rogers, B. (2008) *Recruitment and Mobilisation for the Islamic Militant Movement in Europe*. London, Kings College, ICSR.

Newburn, T. (1988) *The Use and Enforcement of Compensation Orders in Magistrates Courts*, Home Office Research Study No 102. London, HMSO.

Newburn, T. (1995) *Crime and Criminal Justice Policy*. London, Longmans.

Newburn, T. (1996) 'Back to the Future? Youth Crime, Youth Justice and the Rediscovery of "Authoritarian Populism"' in J. Pilcher and S. Wagg (eds) *Thatcher's Children, Politics, Childhood and Society in the 1980s and 1990s*. London, Falmer Press, 61–76.

Newburn, T., Crawford, A., Earle, R., Goldie, S., Hale, C., Hallam, A., Masters, G., Netten, A., Saunders, R., Sharpe, K., and Uglow, S. (2002) *The Introduction of Referral Orders into the Youth Justice System: Final Report*. Home Office Research Study No 242. London, Home Office.

Newbury, A. (2011) '"I would have been able to hear what they think", Tensions in achieving restorative outcomes in the English Youth Justice System' *Youth Justice* Vol 11(3), 250–65.

Nicholson, P. (1982) 'Hegel on Crime' *History of Political Thought* Vol 3, 103–21.

Norrie, A. (1998) 'The Limits of Legal Ideology' in A. von Hirsch and A. Ashworth (eds) *Principled Sentencing: Readings on Theory and Policy*. Oxford, Hart, 369–80.

Northern Ireland Office (2007) *A Protocol for Community-Based Restorative Justice Schemes*. Belfast, Northern Ireland Office.

Nozick, R. (1974) *Anarchy, State and Utopia*, Oxford: Blackwell.

Nugent, B. and Loucks, N. (2011) 'The Arts and Prisoners, Experiences of Creative Rehabilitation' *Howard Journal* Vol 50, 356–370.

O'Brien, M., Mortimer, L., Singleton, N., and Meltzer, H. (2001) *Psychiatric Morbidity among Women Prisoners in England and Wales*, London, Office for National Statistics.

O'Grady, A., Pleasance, P., Balmer, N. J., Buck, A., and Genn, H. (2004) 'Disability, Social Exclusion and the Consequential Experience of Justiciable Problems' *Disability and Society* Vol 19(3), 259–72.

O'Mahoney, D. (2004) 'Restorative Justice and Youth Conferencing—Transforming Youth Justice in Northern Ireland'. Paper presented at the SLSA Annual Conference April, Glasgow University.

O'Mahoney, D. and Deazley, R. (2000) *Juvenile Crime and Justice*, Review of Criminal Justice in Northern Ireland,

Research Report 17. Belfast, Northern Ireland Office.

O'Malley, P. (2000) 'Risk Societies and the Government of Crime' in M. Brown and J. Pratt (eds) *Dangerous Offenders*. London and New York, Routledge, 17–33.

O'Malley, P. (2009) *The Currency of Justice, Fines and Damages in Consumer Societies*. Abingdon, Routledge.

O'Malley, P. (2010) 'Simulated Justice, Risk, Money and Telemetric Policing' *British Journal of Criminology* Vol 50(5), 795–807.

O'Shea, N., Moran, I., and Bergin, S. (2003) *Snakes and Ladders: Mental Health and Criminal Justice*. London, Revolving Doors Agency.

Office for Criminal Justice Reform (2009), *Engaging Communities in Criminal Justice*. London, Ministry of Justice.

Office for Criminal Justice Reform (2010) *Initial Findings from a Review of the Use of Out-of-court Disposals*. London, Ministry of Justice.

Office of Juvenile Justice and Delinquency Prevention (2009) *Characteristics of Juvenile Suicide in Confinement*. Washington, US Department of Justice.

Office of Juvenile Justice and Delinquency Prevention (2010) *Youth's Needs and Services, Findings from the Survey of Youth in Residential Placement*. Washington, US Department of Justice.

Office of the Children's Commissioner (with User Voice) (2011) *Young People's Views on Restraint in the Secure Estate*. London, Office of the Children's Commissioner.

Ofsted (2010) *Transition through Detention and Custody: Arrangements for Learning and Skills for Young People in Custodial or Secure Settings*. London, Ofsted.

Ofsted (Office of Standards in Education in consultation with HM Chief Inspector of Prisons) (2004) *Girls in Prison: The Education and Training of Under-18s Serving Detention and Training Orders*. London, HM Inspectorate of Prisons.

Oldfield, M. and Grimshaw, R. (2008) *Probation Resources, Staffing and Workloads 2001–2008*. London, Centre for Crime and Justice Studies, King's College, in association with NAPO.

Olson, S. and Dzur, W. (2004) 'Revising Informal Justice: Restorative Justice and Democratic Professionalism' *Law and Society Review* Vol 38(1), 139–76.

Orton, S. and Vennard, J. (1988) 'Minor Offences and the Fixed Penalty: A Survey in England and Wales' in N. Walker and M. Hough (eds) *Public Attitudes to Sentencing*. Aldershot, Gower, 160–77.

Osborne, S. (ed) (2009) *The New Public Governance?* London, Routledge.

Owen, T. (2007) 'Culture of Crime Control: Through a Post-Foucauldian Lens' *Internet Journal of Criminology*. Available at http://www.internetjournalofcriminology.com.

Padfield, N. (2002) 'Tariffs in Murder Cases' *Criminal Law Review*, 192–204.

Padfield, N. (2007) 'Distinguishing the Unlawful from the Unjustifiable in the Rules on Early Release from Prison' *Cambridge Law Joural* Vol 66(2), 255–8.

Pantazis, C. and Pemberton, S. (2009) 'From the "Old" to the "New" Suspect Community, Examining the Impacts of Recent UK Counter-Terrorist Legislation' *British Journal of Criminology* Vol 49(5), 646–66.

Pantazis, C. and Pemberton, S. (2011) 'Restating the Case for the "Suspect" Community, A Reply to Greer' *British Journal of Criminology* Vol 51(6), 1054–62.

Pantazis, C., Gordon, D., and Levitas, R. (2006) *Poverty and Social Exclusion: The Millennium Survey*. Bristol, Policy Press.

Parfrement-Hopkins, J. and Hall, P. (2009) 'Perceptions of anti-social behaviour' in Moon, D. and Walker, A. (eds) *Perceptions of crime and anti-social behaviour, Findings from the 2008/09 British Crime Survey Supplementary Volume 1 to Crime in England and Wales 2008/09*, 17/09. London, Home Office.

Park, I. (2000) *Review of Comparative Costs and Performance of Privately and Publicly Operated Prisons 1998–9*, Home Office Statistical Bulletin, 6/00. London, Home Office.

Parker, M. (2006) (ed) *Dynamic Security: The Democratic Therapeutic Community in Prison*. London, Jessica Kingsley.

Parkes, R. and Bilby, C. (2010) 'The Courage to Create, The Role of Artistic and Spiritual Activities in Prisons' *Howard Journal* Vol 49, 97–110.

Patterson, A. and Thorpe, K. (2006) 'Public Perceptions' in A. Walker, C. Kershaw and S. Nicholas (eds) *Crime in England and Wales 2005/2006*, Home Office Statistical Bulletin 12/06. London, Home Office.

Payne, S. (2009) *Redefining Justice, Addressing the individual needs of victims and witnesses*. Available at http://www.justice.gov.uk/publications/docs/sara-payne-redefining-justice.pdf.

Pearson, G. (2002) 'Youth Crime and Moral Decline: Permissiveness and Tradition' in J. Muncie, G. Hughes, and E. McLaughlin (eds) *Youth Justice, Critical Readings*. London, Sage, 45–9.

Peay, J. (2002) 'Mentally Disordered Offenders, Mental Health and Crime' in M. Maguire, R. Morgan, and R. Reiner (eds) *The Oxford Handbook of Criminology* (3rd edn). Oxford, Oxford University Press, 746–91.

Peay, J. (2007) 'Mentally Disordered Offenders, Mental Health and Crime' in M. Maguire, R. Morgan, and R. Reiner (eds) *The Oxford Handbook of Criminology* (4th edn). Oxford, Oxford University Press, 496–527.

Peck, M. (2011) *Patterns of Reconviction Among Offenders Eligible for Multi-Agency Public Protection Arrangements*, Ministry of Justice Research Series 6/1. London, Ministry of Justice.

Penfold, C., Hunter, G., and Hough, M. (2006) *The Intermittent Custody Pilot: A Descriptive Study*, Home Office Findings No 280. London, Home Office.

Peterson, R. and Bailey, W. (2003) 'Is the Death Penalty an Effective Deterrent for Murder? An examination of Social Science Research' in J. Acker, R. Bohm, and C. Lanier (eds) *America's Experiment with Capital Punishment*. Durham, Carolina Academic Press, pp 251–82.

Pettit, P. with Braithwaite, J. (1998) 'Republicanism in Sentencing: Recognition, Recompense and Reassurance' in A. von Hirsch and A. Ashworth (eds) *Principled Sentencing: Readings on Theory and Policy*. Oxford, Hart, 317–30.

Phillips, J. (2011) 'The Exercise of Discretion in the Probation Service and Bottoms' Model of Compliance' in *ECAN Bulletin* 11 (Oct) 9–12. London, Howard League for Penal Reform.

Phillips, Lord (2007) 'Issues in Criminal Justice—Murder' Speech, University of Birmingham, March 8.

Piché, J. (2009) 'Penal Abolitionism, a Different Kind of Reform' *Criminal Justice Matters* Vol 77(1), 30–1.

Pinchbeck, I. and Hewitt, M. (1973) *Children in English Society: From the 18th Century to the Children Act 1948* Vol 2. London, Routledge & Kegan Paul.

Piper, C. (1999) 'The Crime and Disorder Act—Child or Community Safety?' *Modern Law Review* Vol 62, 397–408.

Piper, C. (2001) 'Who Are These Youths? Language in the Service of Policy' *Youth Justice* Vol 1(2), 30–9.

Piper, C. (2006b) 'Feminist Perspectives on Youth Justice' in A. Diduck and K. O'Donovan, *Feminist Perspectives on Family Law*. London, Routledge Cavendish.

Piper, C. (2007) 'Should Impact Constitute Mitigation? Structured Discretion versus Mercy' *Criminal Law Review*, 141–55.

Piper, C. (2008) *Investing in Children: Policy, Law and Practice in Context*. Cullompton, Willan.

Piper, C. (2009) 'Rights and Responsibility: Girls And Boys Who Behave Badly' in J. Wallbank, S. Choudhry, and J. Herring (eds) *Rights, Gender and Family Law*. London, Routledge.

Piper, C. (2011) 'The English Riots and Tough Sentencing'. Available online at http://blog.oup.com/2011/09/tough-sentencing.

Piper, C. and Easton, S. (2006/7) 'What's Sentencing Got to Do with It?' *Contemporary Issues in Law* Special Issue: Current Issues in Sentencing Policy Vol 8(4), 356–76.

Piper, C. and Easton, S. (2012) 'Seriousness, limiting a disproportionate construction' in Blad, J., Cornwell, D., and Wright, M. (eds) *Civilising Criminal Justice*. Winchester, Waterside Press (forthcoming).

Pitts, J. (1988) *The Politics of Juvenile Justice*. London, Sage.

Pitts, J. (1992a) 'Juvenile Justice Policy in England and Wales' in J. Coleman and C. Warren-Adamson (eds) *Youth Policy in the 1990s*. London, Routledge, 172–88.

Pitts, J. (1992b) 'The End of an Era' *Howard Journal* Vol 31(2), 133–49.

Player, E. (2005) 'The Reduction of Women's Imprisonment in England and Wales' *Punishment and Society* Vol 7(4), 419–39.

Plotnikoff, J. and Woolfson, R. (2005) *Review of the Effectiveness of Specialist Courts in Other Jurisdictions*, DCA Research Series 3/05. London, Department for Constitutional Affairs.

Plugge, E., Douglas, N., and Fitzpatrick, R. (2006) *The Health of Women in Prison*. Oxford, Department of Public Health, University of Oxford.

PMSU (Prime Minister's Strategy Unit) (2007) *Building on Progress: Families*. London, Cabinet Office.

Poteat, S. (2002) 'The Women at Risk Programme' in P. Carlen (ed) *Women and Punishment: The Struggle for Justice*. Cullompton, Willan, 125–37.

Povey, D. (ed), Mulchandani, R., Hand, T. and Panesar, L. K. (2011) *Police Powers and Procedures 2009–10* (2nd edn), Home Office Statistical Bulletin 7/11. London, Home Office.

Pratt, J. (1986) 'Diversion from the Juvenile Court' *British Journal of Criminology* Vol 26(3), 212–33.

Pratt, J. (1996) 'Governing the Dangerous: An Historical Overview of Dangerous Offender Legislation' *Social and Legal Studies* Vol 5(1), 21–36.

Pratt, J. (1998) 'Towards the "Decivilizing" of Punishment?' *Social and Legal Studies* Vol 7(4), 487–515.

Pratt, J. (2000) 'Dangerousness and Modern Society' in M. Brown and J. Pratt (eds) *Dangerous Offenders*. London, Routledge, 35–48.

Priestley, P. and Vanstone, M. (eds) (2010) *Offenders or Citizens, Readings in Rehabilitation*. Cullompton, Willan.

Prins, H. (2005) *Offenders, Deviants and Patients*. London, Routledge.

Prison Reform Trust (2000) *Justice for Women: The Need for Reform*. London, Prison Reform Trust.

Prison Reform Trust (2003) *Troubled Inside: Responding to the Mental Health Needs of Women in Prison*. London, Prison Reform Trust.

Prison Reform Trust (2004a) *Briefing Paper*. London, Prison Reform Trust.

Prison Reform Trust (2004b) *Disabled Prisoners*. London, Prison Reform Trust.

Prison Reform Trust (2005) *Private Punishment: Who Profits?* London, Prison Reform Trust.

Prison Reform Trust (2006) *Experiences of Minority Ethnic Employees in Prisons*. London, Prison Reform Trust.

Prison Reform Trust (2007a) *Bromley Briefings Prison Factfile*. London, Prison Reform Trust, December.

Prison Reform Trust (2008) *Doing Time: the Experiences and Needs of Older People in Prison*. London, Prison Reform Trust.

Prison Reform Trust (2010) *Bromley Briefings Prison Factfile. December.* London, Prison Reform Trust.

Prison Reform Trust (2011a) *Bromley Briefings Prison Factfile*. London, Prison Reform Trust.

Prison Reform Trust (2011b) Prison Reform trust submission to the Ministry of Justice, *Breaking the Cycle, Effective Punishment, Rehabilitation and Sentencing of Offenders*. London, Prison Reform Trust.

Prisons and Probation Ombudsman for England and Wales (2011) *Annual Report 2010– 2011*, CM 8105. London, Office of the PPO.

Probation Service (2006): *Intermittent Custody: Withdrawal of Authority to Supervise Offenders*. National Probation Service Bulletin Issue 41, 084/06.

Probert, R., Gilmore, S., and Herring, J. (Eds) (2009) *Responsible Parents and Parental Responsibility.* Oxford, Hart Publishing.

Rack, J. (2005) *The Incidence of Hidden Disabilities in the Prison Population*. Egham, The Dyslexia Institute.

Raine, J. and Dunstan, E. (2009) 'How well do sentencing guidelines work? Equity, proportionality and consistency in the determination of fine levels in the magistrates' courts of England and Wales' *Howard Journal* Vol 48(1), 13–36.

Raine, J., Dunstan, E. and Mackie, A. (2004) 'Financial Penalties: Who Pays, Who Doesn't and Why Not?' *Howard Journal* Vol 43(5), 518–38.

Ramsay, M. (2011) *The Early Years of the DSPD (Dangerous and Severe Personality Disorder) Programme: Results of Two Process Studies*, Research Summary 4/11. Ministry of Justice, London.

Rawls, J. (1971) *A Theory of Justice*. Cambridge, MA, Harvard University Press.

Raynor, P. and Vanstone, M. (2002) *Understanding Community Penalties, Probation Policy and Social Change*. Buckingham, Open University Press.

Reece, H. (2005) 'From Parental Responsibility to Parenting Responsibly' *Current Legal Issues* Vol 8, 459–83.

Reed, J. L. and Lyne, M. (2000) 'In-patient Care of Mentally Ill Prisoners; Results of a Year's Programme of Semi-structured Inspections' *British Medical Journal* Vol 320, 1031–4.

Reeves, H. and Dunn, P. (2010) 'The Status of Crime Victims and Witnesses in the 21st Century' in A Bottoms and J Roberts (eds) *Hearing the Victim, Adversarial Justice, Crime Victims and the State*. Cullompton, Willan Publishing.

Renaud, G. (2007) *Les Misérables on Sentencing, Valjean, Fantine, Javert and the Bishop Debate the Principles*, Melbourne, Sandstone Press.

Renzetti, C. M. (2012) *Feminist Criminology*. London, Routledge.

Respect Task Force (2006) *Respect Action Plan*. London, Home Office.

Respect Task Force (2007) *Tools and Powers to Tackle Anti-social Behaviour.* London, Home Office.

Rex, S. (1998) 'Applying Desert Principles to Community Sentences: Lessons from Two Criminal Justice Acts' *Criminal Law Review*, 381–91.

Reynolds, F. (1985) 'Magistrates' Justifications for Making Custodial Orders on Juvenile Offenders' *Criminal Law Review*, 294–98.

Rhode, D. (1989) *Gender and Justice*. Cambridge, MA, Harvard University Press.

RICHARDS, K. (2010) 'Police-referred restorative justice for juveniles in Australia' *Trends & Issues in Crime and Criminal Justice* No 398. Canberra: Australian Institute of Criminology.

RICHARDS, M. (1998) *Censure without Sanctions*. Winchester, Waterside Press.

RICKFORD, D. AND EDGAR, K. (2005) *Troubled Inside: Responding to the Mental Health Needs of Men in Prison*. London, Prison Reform Trust/King's Fund.

RINGLAND, C. AND FITZGERALD, J. (2010) *Factors which influence the sentencing of domestic violence offenders*, Crime and Justice Statistics Issue paper no. 48, NSW Bureau of Crime, Statistics and Research.

RIVERA BEIRAS, I. (2005) 'State Form, Labour Market and Penal System: The New Punitive Rationality in Context' *Punishment and Society* Vol 7(2), 167–82.

RIX, A., SKIDMORE, K, MAGUIRE, M., AND PIERPOINT, H. (2010) *Fine Payment Work Process Study*, Research Summary 8/10. London, Ministry of Justice.

ROBERTS, J. (2002) 'Alchemy in Sentencing: An Analysis of Sentencing Reform Proposals in England and Wales' *Punishment and Society* Vol 4(4), 425–42.

ROBERTS, J. (2008a) 'Aggravating and Mitigating Factors at Sentencing, Towards Greater Consistency of Application. *Criminal Law Review*, 264–76.

ROBERTS J. (2008b) *Punishing Persistent Offenders*, Oxford University Press

ROBERTS, J. (2010) 'Women Offenders, More Troubled Than Troublesome?' in Brayford, J., Cowe, F., and Deering J. (eds) *What Else Works? Creative work with offenders*. Cullompton, Willan, 91–116.

ROBERTS, J. AND HOUGH, M. (2005a) 'The State of the Prisons: Exploring Public Knowledge and Opinion' *Howard Journal* Vol 44(3), 286–306.

ROBERTS, J. AND HOUGH, M. (2005b) *Understanding Public Attitudes to Criminal Justice*. Milton Keynes, Open University Press.

ROBERTS, J. AND MANIKIS, M. (2011) *Victim Personal Statements: A Review of Empirical Research*, Report for the Commissioner for Victims and Witnesses in England and Wales. London, Ministry of Justice.

ROBERTS, J., HOUGH, M., JACOBSON, J., AND MOON, N. (2009) 'Public Attitudes to Sentencing Purposes and Sentencing Factors, An Empirical Analysis' *Criminal Law Review* 11, 771–82.

ROBERTS, J., HOUGH, M., JACOBSON, J., BREDEE, A., AND MOON, N. (2008) 'Public Attitudes to Sentencing Offences Involving Death by Driving' *Criminal Law Review* 7, 525–38.

ROBERTS, S. (1979) *Order and Dispute*. Harmondsworth, Penguin.

ROBINSON, G. (1999) 'Risk Management and Rehabilitation in the Probation Service: Collision and Collusion' *Howard Journal* Vol 38(4), 421–33.

ROBINSON, G. (2002) 'Exploring Risk Management in Probation Practice' *Punishment and Society* Vol 4(1), 5–25.

ROBINSON, G. (2008) 'Late-modern Rehabilitation: The Evolution of a Penal Strategy' *Punishment and Society* Vol 10(4), 429–46.

ROBINSON, P. (2008) 'Competing Conceptions of Modern Desert: Vengeful, Deontological, and Empirical' *Cambridge Law Journal* Vol 67(1), 145–75.

ROBINSON, P. AND DARLEY, J. M. (2004) 'Does Criminal Law Deter? A Behavioural Science Investigation' *Oxford Journal of Legal Studies* Vol 23(2), 173–206.

ROCHE, D. (2003) *Accountability in Restorative Justice*. Oxford, Oxford University Press.

ROCK, P. (2002) 'On Becoming a Victim' in C. Hoyle and R. Young (eds) *New Visions of Crime Victims*. Oxford, Hart, 1–11.

ROSE, N. (1987) 'Beyond the Public/Private Division: Law, Power and the Family'

Journal of Law and Society Vol 14, 61–76.

Rose, N. (1990) *Governing the Soul: The Shaping of the Private Self.* London, Routledge.

Ross, H. L. (1973) 'Deterrence Regained: The Cheshire Constabulary's Breathalyzer Blitz' *Journal of Legal Studies* Vol 2, 1–78.

Ross, H. L. (1992) *Confronting Drunk Driving.* New Haven, CT, Yale University Press.

Ross, J., Richards, S., Newbold, G., Lenza, M., and Grigsby, R. (2011) 'Convict criminology' in W. S. DeKeseredy, and M. Dragiewicz (eds) *Routledge Handbook of Critical Criminology.* London, Routledge.

Ross, R. and Hilborn, J. (2007) *Rehabilitating Rehabilitation, Neurocriminology for Treatment of AntiSocial Behaviour.* Ottawa, Cognitive Centre of Canada.

Rossi, P., Waite, E., Bose, C. E., and Berk, R. E. (1974) 'The Seriousness of Crime: Normative Structure and Individual Differences' *American Sociological Review* Vol 39, 224–37.

Rotman, E. (1990) *Beyond Punishment: A New View of the Rehabilitation of Offenders.* Connecticut, Greenwood Press.

Rousseau, J. -J. (1743) *The Social Contract* ed M. Cranston (1968). Harmondsworth, Penguin.

Royal Commission on Capital Punishment (1953) *Report* Cmnd 8932. London, HMSO.

Royal Commission on Criminal Justice (1993) *Report* (Chair: Lord Runciman) Cm 2263. London, HMSO.

Royal Commission on Criminal Procedure (1981) *Report*, Cm 8092. London, HMSO.

Rubin, A. (2011) 'Punitive Penal Preferences and Support for Welfare: Applying the Governance of Social Marginality Thesis on the Individual Level' *Punishment and Society* Vol 13(2), 198–229.

Rubin, E. (2003) 'Just Say No to Retribution' *Buffalo Criminal Law Review* Vol 7(1), 17–83.

Ruggiero, V. (2010) *Penal Abolitionism.* Oxford, Oxford University Press.

Rusche, G. and Kirchheimer, O. (1939) *Punishment and Social Structure.* New York, Russell and Russell.

Rutter, M. and Giller, H. (1983) *Juvenile Delinquency: Trends and Perspectives.* Harmondsworth, Penguin.

Ryberg, J (2005) 'Retributivism and Multiple Offending' *Res Publica* Vol 11(3), 213–33.

Salmon, S. (2004) 'Children with a Prisoner in the Family' *Childright,* 203.

Salter, M. and Twist, S. (2007) 'The Micro-Sovereignty of Discretion in Legal Decision-Making: Carl Schmitt's Critique of Liberal Principles of Legality' *Web Journal of Current Legal Issues* Vol 3.

Sanders, A. (1985) 'Class Bias in Prosecutions' *Howard Journal* Vol 24(3), 176–99.

Sanders, A. (2001) *Community Justice: Modernising the Magistracy in England and Wales.* London, IPPR.

Sanders, A. (2002) 'Victim Participation in an Exclusionary Criminal Justice System' in C. Hoyle and R. Young (eds) *New Visions of Crime Victims.* Oxford, Hart.

Sanders, A. (2003) Book Review, *Modern Law Review* Vol 66(1), 160–7.

Sanders, A. and Loveday, B. (2001–2) Editorial, CJM No 46 Winter. London, Centre for Crime and Justice Studies, Kings College.

Sanders, A., Hoyle, C., Morgan, R., and Cape, E. (2001) 'Victim Impact Statements: Don't Work, Can't Work' *Criminal Law Review,* 447–58.

Sanders, A., Young, R. and Burton, M. (2010) *Criminal Justice* (4th edn). Oxford, Oxford University Press.

SARAT, A. (1976) 'Public Opinion, the Death Penalty and the Eighth Amendment' *Wisconsin Law Review* Vol 17, 171–206.

SATZ, D. AND REICH, R. (eds) (2009) *Toward a Humanist Justice: The Political Philosophy of Susan Moller Okin*. Oxford, Oxford University Press.

SAYLES, G. (1950) *The Medieval Foundations of England* (2nd edn). London, Methuen.

SCHICHOR, D. (1995) *Punishment for Profit: Private Prisons, Public Concerns*. Thousand Oaks, CA, Sage.

SCHOFIELD, P. (2007) 'Jeremy Bentham. The French Revolution and Political Radicalization' in F. Rosen (ed) *Jeremy Bentham*. Aldershot, Ashgate, 535–8.

SCOTT, D. AND CODD, H. (2010) *Controversial Issues in Prisons*. Maidenhead, McGraw Hill/Open University Press.

SCOTTISH EXECUTIVE (1999) *A Review of the Research Literature on Serious Violent and Sexual Offenders*. Edinburgh, Scottish Executive.

SCOTTISH EXECUTIVE (2001) *Scottish Strategy for Victims*. Edinburgh, Scottish Executive.

SCOTTISH EXECUTIVE (2002a) *Victims in the Scottish Criminal Justice System. The EU Framework Decision on the Standing of Victims in Criminal Procedure*. Edinburgh, Scottish Executive.

SCOTTISH EXECUTIVE (2002b) *Youth Justice in Scotland: A Progress Report for All those Working for Young People*. Edinburgh, Scottish Executive.

SCRATON, P. AND HAYDON, D. (2002) 'Challenging the Criminalization of Children and Young People' in J. Muncie, G. Hughes, and E. McLaughlin (eds) *Youth Justice: Critical Readings*. London, Sage, 311–28.

SECHREST, L. B., WHITE, S. O., AND BROWN, E. D. (1979) *The Rehabilitation of Criminal Offenders*. Washington DC, National Academy of Sciences.

SEDDON, T. (2006) *Punishment and Madness*. London, Routledge.

SEDDON, T. (2008) 'Dangerous Liaisons, Personality Disorder and the Politics of Risk' *Punishment and Society* Vol 10(3), 301–17.

SENTENCING ADVISORY PANEL (2000) *Advice to the Court of Appeal—4. Racially Aggravated Offences*. London, Home Office.

SENTENCING ADVISORY PANEL (2002) *Minimum Terms in Murder Cases: The Panel's Advice to the Court of Appeal*. London, Home Office.

SENTENCING ADVISORY PANEL (2003) *Driving Offences—Causing Death by Driving: The Panel's Advice to the Sentencing Guidelines Council*. London, SAP.

SENTENCING ADVISORY PANEL (2007) *Consultation Paper on Breach of an Anti-Social Behaviour Order*. London, SAP.

SENTENCING COMMISSION WORKING GROUP (2008a) *A Structured Sentencing Framework and Sentencing Commission: A consultation*.

SENTENCING COMMISSION WORKING GROUP (2008b) *A Summary of Responses to the Sentencing Commission Working Group's Consultation Paper*.

SENTENCING COMMISSION WORKING GROUP (2008c) *Sentencing Guidelines in England and Wales, An Evolutionary Approach*, The Gage Report, London, Sentencing Commission Working Group.

SENTENCING COUNCIL (2010) *Breaking the Cycle, Effective Punishment, Rehabilitation and Sentencing of Offenders, Response from the Sentencing Council*. London, Sentencing Council.

SENTENCING COUNCIL (2011a) *Assault: Definitive Guideline*. London, Sentencing Council.

SENTENCING COUNCIL (2011b) *Burglary Offences: Definitive Guideline*. London, Sentencing Council.

SENTENCING COUNCIL (2011c) *Consultation Stage Resource Assessment: Guidelines on Totality, TICs and Allocation*, London, Sentencing Council.

SENTENCING COUNCIL (2011d) *Crown Court Sentencing Survey, October 2010 to March 2011 results*. London, Sentencing Council.

SENTENCING COUNCIL (2012) *Drug Offences: Definitive Guideline*. London, Office of the Sentencing Council.

SENTENCING GUIDELINES COUNCIL (2004a) *Overarching Principles: Seriousness*. London, SGC.

SENTENCING GUIDELINES COUNCIL (2004b) *Reduction in Sentence for a Guilty Plea*. London, SGC.

SENTENCING GUIDELINES COUNCIL (2004c) *New Sentences: Criminal Justice Act 2003*. London, SGC.

SENTENCING GUIDELINES COUNCIL (2005) *Guideline Judgments Case Compendium*. London, SGC.

SENTENCING GUIDELINES COUNCIL (2006) *Overarching Principles: Domestic Violence*. London, SGC.

SENTENCING GUIDELINES COUNCIL (2007a) *Definitive Guideline on the Reduction in Sentence for a Guilty Plea*. London, SGC.

SENTENCING GUIDELINES COUNCIL (2007b) *Dangerous Offenders: Guide for Sentencers and Practitioners*. London, SGC.

SENTENCING GUIDELINES COUNCIL (2007c) *Sexual Offences Act 2003: Definitive Guideline*. London, SGC.

SENTENCING GUIDELINES COUNCIL (2008a) *Assault and Other Offences against the Person. Definitive Guideline*. London, SGC.

SENTENCING GUIDELINES COUNCIL (2008b) *Overarching Principles: Assaults on Children and Cruelty to a Child*. London, SGC.

SENTENCING GUIDELINES COUNCIL (2008c) *Causing Death by Driving: Consultation Guideline*. London, SGC.

SENTENCING GUIDELINES COUNCIL (2008d) *Theft and Burglary in a Building other than a Dwelling: Definitive Guideline*. London, SGC.

SENTENCING GUIDELINES COUNCIL (2008e) *Causing Death by Driving: Definitive Guideline*. London, SGC.

SENTENCING GUIDELINES COUNCIL (2008f) *Overarching Principles, Assaults on Children and Cruelty to a Child: Definitive Guideline*, London, SGC.

SENTENCING GUIDELINES COUNCIL (2008g) *Dangerousness: Guide for Sentencers and Practitioners* (Supplement to the Compendium). London, SGC.

SENTENCING GUIDELINES COUNCIL (2008h) *Magistrates' Court Sentencing Guidelines: Definitive Guideline*. London, SGC.

SENTENCING GUIDELINES COUNCIL (2009a) *Sentencing for Fraud: Statutory Offences*. London, SGC.

SENTENCING GUIDELINES COUNCIL (2009b) *Overarching Principles: Sentencing Youths, Definitive Guideline*. London, SGC.

SENTENCING GUIDELINES COUNCIL (2010) *Corporate Manslaughter & Health and Safety Offences Causing Death, Definitive Guideline*, SGC.

SHAPLAND, J. (1981) *Between Conviction and Sentence: The Process of Mitigation*. London, Routledge & Kegan Paul.

SHAPLAND, J. (2003) 'Restorative Justice and Criminal Justice: Just Reponses to Crime?' in A. von Hirsch, J. Roberts, A. Bottoms, K. Roach and M. Schiff (eds) *Restorative Justice and Criminal Justice: Competing or Reconcilable Paradigms?* Oxford, Hart, 195–218.

SHAPLAND, J. AND BOTTOMS, A. (2011) 'Reflections on social values, offending and desistance among young adult recidivists' *Punishment and Society* Vol 13(3), 256–82.

Shapland, J., Atkinson, A., Atkinson, H., Chapman, B., Dignan, J., Howes, M., Johnstone, J., Robinson, G., and Scorsby, A. (2007a) *Restorative Justice: The Views of Victims and Offenders—The Third Report from the Evaluation of Three Schemes.* Ministry of Justice Research Series 3/07. London, Ministry of Justice.

Shapland, J., Atkinson, A., Atkinson, H., Colledge, E., Dignan, J. Howes, M., Johnstone, J., Robinson, G. and Scorsby, A. (2007b) 'Situating Restorative Justice within Criminal Justice' *Theoretical Criminology* Vol 10(4), 505–32.

Shapland, J., Atkinson, A., Atkinson, H., Dignan, J., Edwards, L., Hibbert, J., Howes, M., Johnstone, J., Robinson, G. and Sorsby, A. (2008) *Does restorative justice affect reconviction? The fourth report from the evaluation of three schemes,* Ministry of Justice Research Series 10/8. London, Ministry of Justice.

Shapland, J., Robinson, G., and Soresby, A. (2011) *Restorative Justice in Practice.* London, Willan/Routledge.

Sheehan, R., McIvor, G., and Trotter, G. (eds) (2007) *What Works with Women Offenders*. Cullompton, Willan.

Sheehan, R., McIvor, G., and Trotter, C. (eds) (2010) *Working with Women Offenders in the Community.* London, Routledge.

Sheppard, G. (1990) 'Management: Short of Ideals?' *Probation Journal* Vol 37(4), 176–9.

Sherman, L. W. and Berk, R. A. (1983) 'The Specific Deterrent Effects of Arrest for Domestic Assault: Preliminary Findings' Unpublished Paper, Police Foundation, Washington.

Sherman, L. W., Strang H., and Woods, D. (2010) *Recidivism patterns in the Canberra Reintegrative Shaming Experiments (RISE).* Canberra. Available at http://www.aic.gov.au/criminal_justice_system/rjustice/rise/recidivism.aspx.

Sherman, L. W., Strang, H., Newbury-Birch, D., and Bennett, S. (2007a) *Key Indicators of Effective Practice in Restorative Justice (KEEP).* London, Youth Justice Board.

Sherman, L. W. and Strang, H., with Barnes, G., Bennett, S., Angel, C. M., Newbury-Birch, D., Woods, D. J., and Gill, C. E. (2007b) *Restorative Justice: The Evidence.* London, Smith Institute.

Sherman, L. W., Farrington, D. P., Leyton MacKenzie, D., and Welsh, B. C. (eds) (2006) *Evidence-Based Crime Prevention.* London, Routledge.

Shute, S. (2004a) 'The Sexual Offences Act 2003 (4) New Civil Preventative Orders: Sexual Offences Prevention Orders, Foreign Travel Orders; Risk of Sexual Harm Orders' *Criminal Law Review,* 417–40.

Shute, S. (2004b) 'Punishing Murderers: Release Procedures and the "Tariff", 1953–2004' *Criminal Law Review,* 873–95.

Shute, S., Hood, R., and Seemungal, F. (2005) *A Fair Hearing? Ethnic Minorities in the Criminal Courts.* Cullompton, Willan.

Silvestri, A. (2009) *Partners or Prisoners?* London, Centre for Crime and Justice Studies.

Silvestri, A. (ed) (2011) *Lessons for the Coalition, an End of Term Report on New Labour and Criminal Justice.* London, Centre for Crime and Justice Studies.

Silvestri, M. and Crowther-Dowey, C. (2008) *Gender and Crime.* London, Sage.

Simon, F. (1999) *Prisoners' Work and Vocational Training.* London, Routledge.

Simon, J. (1995) 'The Boot Camp and the Limits of Modern Penality' *Social Justice* Vol 22(2), 25–48.

Simon, J. (1998) 'Managing the Monstrous: Sex Offenders and the New Penology' *Psychology, Public Policy and the Law* Vol 4(1), 1–16.

SIMON, J. (2007) *Governing Through Crime: How the War on Crime Transformed American Democracy and Created a Culture of Fear.* New York, Oxford University Press.

SIMON, J. (2011) 'Mass Incarceration on Trial' *Punishment and Society* Vol 13(3), 251–5.

SINGER, L. (1991) 'A Non-punitive Paradigm of Probation Practice: Some Sobering Thoughts' *British Journal of Social Work* Vol 21, 611–26.

SINGH BHUI, H. (ed) (2009) *Race and Criminal Justice.* London, Sage.

SINGLETON, N., MELTZER, H., GATWARD, R., COID, J., AND DEASY, D. (1998) *Psychiatric Morbidity among Prisoners.* London, HMSO.

SMALLRIDGE, P. AND WILLIAMSON, A. (2008) *Independent Review of Restraint in Juvenile Secure Settings.* London, Ministry of Justice/Department for Children, Schools and Families.

SMART, J. J. C. AND WILLIAMS, B. (1973) *Utilitarianism: For and Against.* Cambridge, Cambridge University Press.

SMITH, A. (1998) 'Psychiatric Evidence and Discretionary Life Sentences' *Journal of Forensic Psychiatry* Vol 9(1), 17–38.

SMITH, B. AND HILLENBRAND, S. (1997) 'Making Victims Whole Again' in R. Davis, A. Lurigio, and W. Skogan (eds) (1997) *Victims of Crime* (2nd edn). Thousand Oaks, CA, Sage, 245–56.

SMITH, D. (2010) *Public Confidence in the Criminal Justice System: Findings from the British Crime Survey 2002/03 to 2007/08.* London, Ministry of Justice.

SMITH, D., BLAGG, H., AND DERRICOURT, N. (1988) 'Mediation in South Yorkshire' *British Journal of Criminology* Vol 28(3), 378–95.

SMITH, D., PALER, I., AND MITCHELL, P. (1993) 'Partnerships between the Independent Sector and the Probation Service' *Howard Journal* Vol 32(1), 25–39.

SOCIAL EXCLUSION UNIT (2002) *Reducing Re-Offending by Ex-Prisoners.* London, Social Exclusion Unit.

SOCIAL SERVICES INSPECTORATE (2004) *Inspection of Medway Secure Training Centre, Kent.* London, Department of Health.

SOLANKI, A. AND UTTING, D. (2009) *Fine Art or Science Sentencers? Deciding between community penalties and custody.* London: Youth Justice Board

SOLOMON, E. AND GARSIDE, R. (2008) *Ten years of Labour's Youth Justice Reforms, an Independent Audit.* London, Centre for Crime and Justice, Kings College.

SPALEK, B. (ed) (2002) *Islam, Crime and Criminal Justice.* Cullompton, Willan.

SPALEK, B. (ed) (2008) *Ethnicity and Crime: A Reader.* Milton Keynes, Open University Press.

SPARKS, C. AND TAYLOR, M. (2001/2: 6) 'Challenging Times' CJM No 46, Winter, 6–7. London, Centre for Crime and Justice Studies, Kings College.

SPARROW, P., BROOKS, G., AND WEBB, D. (2002) 'National Standards for the Probation Service: Managing Post-Fordist Penality' *Howard Journal* Vol 41(1), 27–40.

SPELMAN, W. (2000) 'The Limited Importance o100f Prison Expansion' in A. Blumstein and J. Wallman (eds) *The Crime Drop in America.* Cambridge, Cambridge University Press, 97–129.

SPENCER, J. (1995) 'A Response to Mike Nellis: Probation Values for the 1990s' *Howard Journal* Vol 34(4), 344–9.

SPENCER, J., HASLEWOOD-POCSIK, I., AND SMITH, E. (2009) '"Trying to get it right": What Prison Staff Say About Implementing Race Relations Policy' *Criminology and Criminal Justice* Vol 9(2) 187–206.

STANTON, J. M. (1969) 'Murderers on Parole' *Crime and Delinquency* Vol 15, 149–55.

STEEN, S. AND BANDY, R. (2007) 'When the Policy Becomes the Problem: Criminal Justice in the New Millennium' *Punishment and Society* Vol 9(1), 5–26.

STEIN, P. (1984) *Legal Institutions: The Development of Dispute Settlement*. London, Butterworths.

STEINER, E. (2003) 'Early Release for Seriously Ill and Elderly Prisoners: Should French Practice Be Followed?' *Probation Journal* Vol 50(3), 267–76.

STEWART, S. (1998) *Conflict Resolution: A Foundation Guide*. Winchester, Waterside Press.

STOCKDALE, E. AND DEVLIN, K. (1987) *Sentencing* (1st edn). London, Waterlow Publishers.

STOPARD, P. (1990) 'Punishment and Probation: The Rhetoric and Reality of the White Paper' *Probation Journal* Vol 3(3), 123–6.

STRANG, H. (2003) *Repair or Revenge*. Oxford, Oxford University Press.

STRANG, H. (2007) 'Institutionalizing Restorative Justice' *British Journal of Criminology* Vol 47(4), 704–6.

STRAW, J. (1996) *Tackling Disorder, Insecurity and Crime*. London, Labour Party.

SULLIVAN, E. (2007) 'Straight from the Horse's Mouth' *Prison Service Journal* September Vol 173, 9–14.

SUMMERFIELD, A. (2011) *Children and Young People in Custody 2010–11: An Analysis of the Experiences of 15–18-year-olds in Prison*. HM Inspectorate of Prisons/Youth Justice Board. London, The Stationery Office.

SWEETING, A., OWEN, R. AND TURLEY, C. (2008) *Evaluation of the Victims' Advocate Scheme Pilots*. London, Ministry of Justice.

TAKET, A., CRISP, B., NEVILL, A., LAMARO, G., GRAHAM, M., AND BARTER-GODFREY, S. (2009) *Theorising Social Exclusion*. London, Routledge.

TALBOT, J. (2007) *No One Knows: Identifying and Supporting Prisoners with Learning Difficulties and Learning Disabilities: The Views of Prison Staff*. London, Prison Reform Trust.

TALBOT, J. (2008) *No One Knows, Report and Final Recommendations: Prisoners' Voices, The Experience of the Criminal Justice System by Prisoners with learning disabilities and difficulties*. London, The Prisoner Reform Trust.

TALBOT, J. AND RILEY, C. (2007) 'No One Knows: Offenders with Learning Difficulties and Learning Disabilities' *British Journal of Learning Disabilities* Vol 35 (3), 154–61.

TARLING, R. (1979) *The 'Incapacitation' Effects of Imprisonment*, Home Office Research Bulletin No 7, 6–8. London, Home Office.

TARLING, R. (1993) *Analysing Offending: Data, Models and Interpretations*. London, HMSO.

TARLING, R. (2006) 'Sentencing Practice in Magistrates' Courts Revisited' *Howard Journal* Vol 45(1), 29–41.

TAURI, J. AND MORRIS, A. (2003) 'Reforming Justice: The Potential of Maori Processes' in E. McLaughlin, R. Ferguson, G. Hughes, and L. Westmarland (eds) *Restorative Justice, Critical Issues*. Milton Keynes, Open University Press and London, Sage, 44–53.

TAYLOR, R. (2000) *A Seven Year Reconviction Study of HMP Grendon Therapeutic Community*, London, Home Office.

TAYLOR, R. (2006) '*Re S (A Child) (Identification: Restrictions on Publication)* and *A Local Authority v W*: Children's Privacy and Press Freedom in Criminal Cases' *Child and Family Law Quarterly* Vol 18(2), 269–86.

TEUBNER, G. (1989) 'How the Law Thinks: Towards a Constructive Epistemology of Law' *Law and Society Review* Vol 23(5), 727–56.

The Sentencing Commission for Scotland (2006) *The Basis on which Fines are Determined*. Available at http://www.scotland.gov.uk/Resource/Doc/925/0116782.pdf.

Thomas, C. (2010) *Are Juries Fair?* Ministry of Justice Research Series 1/10. London, Ministry of Justice.

Thomas, D. (1995) 'Sentencing Reform in England and Wales' in C. Clarkson and R. Morgan (eds) *The Politics of Sentencing Reform*. Oxford, Clarendon Press.

Thomas, D. (2002) 'The Sentencing Process' in M. McConville and G. Wilson (eds) *The Handbook of the Criminal Process*. Oxford, Oxford University Press, 473–86.

Thomas, D. (2007) 'Case Commentary: *Thomas* [2006] EWCA Crim 2036' *Criminal Law Review*, 171–2.

Thompson, E. P. (1977) *Whigs and Hunters: The Origin of the Black Act*. Harmondsworth, Penguin.

Tickell, S. and Akester, K. (2004) *Restorative Justice: The Way Ahead*. London, JUSTICE.

Tilt, R., Perry, B., Martin, C., et al. (2000) *Report of the Review of Security at the High Security Hospitals*. London, Department of Health.

Titmuss, R. (1968) *Commitment to Welfare*. London, Allen and Unwin.

Toch, H. (ed) (1976) *Living in Prison: The Ecology of Survival*. Maryland, American Psychological Association.

Tombs, J. (2004) *A Unique Punishment: Sentencing and the Prison Population in Scotland*. Edinburgh, Scottish Consortium on Crime and Criminal Justice.

Tombs, J. and Jagger, E. (2006) 'Denying Responsibility: Sentencers' Accounts of their Decision to Imprison' *British Journal of Criminology* Vol 46, 803.

Tonry, M. (1993) 'Proportionality, Interchangeability and Intermediate Punishments' in R. Dobash, A. Duff, and D. Marshall (eds) *Penal Theory and Penal Practice*. Manchester, Manchester University Press.

Tonry, M. (1996) *Sentencing Matters*. Oxford and New York, Oxford University Press.

Tonry, M. (2009) 'Explanations of American Punishment Policies, A National History' *Punishment and Society* Vol 11(3), 377–94.

Tonry, M. (2010) 'The Costly Consequences of Populist Posturing, ASBOs, Victims, "Rebalancing"; and Diminution in Support for Civil Liberties' *Punishment and Society* Vol 12(4), 387–413.

Travis, A. (2011) 'Teenage Deaths in Prison Cause Mounting Concern' *Guardian* 4 May.

Trebilcock, J. (2011) *No Winners—the Reality of Short Term Prison Sentences*. London, Howard League.

Trebilcock, J. and Weaver, T. (2011a) *Multi-method Evaluation of the Management, Organisation and Staffing (MEMOS) in High Security Services for People with Dangerous and Severe Personality Disorder (DSPD)*. London, Ministry of Justice.

Trebilcock, J. and Weaver, T. (2011b) *Study of the Legal Status of Dangerous and Severe Personality Disorder (DSPD) Patients and Prisoners, and the Impact of DSPD Status on Parole Board and Mental Health Review Tribunal Decision-Making*. London, Ministry of Justice.

UK Government (1999) *Second Periodic Report to the United Nations Committee on Rights of the Child* (CRC/C/83/Add.3).

US Department of Justice, Office of Justice Programs, National Institute of Justice (2008) *Prisoner Radicalization, Assessing the Threat in U.S. Correctional Institutions*. Washington, DC.

Umbreit, M (1994) *Victim Meets Offender: The Impact of Restorative Justice and*

Mediation. Monsey, NY, Criminal Justice Press.

Unnever, J. (2010) 'Global Support for the Death Penalty' *Punishment and Society* Vol 12(4), 463–84.

Vail, J., Wheelock, J., and Hill, M. (eds) (1999) *Insecure Times*. London and New York, Routledge.

Valier, C. (2003) 'Minimum Terms of Imprisonment in Murder, Just Deserts and the Sentencing Guidelines' *Criminal Law Review*, 326–35.

van Marle, F. and Maruna, S. (2010) '"Ontological insecurity" and "terror management", Linking two free-floating anxieties' *Punishment and Society* Vol 12(1), 7–26.

van den Haag, E. (1981) 'Punishment as a Device for Controlling the Crime Rate' *Rutgers Law Journal* Vol 33, 706.

van den Haag, E. (1985) 'The Death Penalty Once More' *University of California Davis Law Review* Vol 18, Summer, 957–72.

van Zyl Smit, D. (2000) 'Mandatory Sentences—A Conundrum for the New South Africa?' *Punishment and Society* Vol 2(2), 197–212.

van Zyl Smit, D. and Ashworth, A. (2004) 'Disproportionate Sentences and Human Rights Violations' MLR Vol 67(4), 541–60.

van Zyl Smit, D. and Snacken, S. (2009) *Principles of European Prison law and Policy, Penology and Human Rights*. Oxford, Oxford University Press.

Vaughan, B. (2000) 'The Government of Youth: Disorder *and* Dependence?' *Social and Legal Studies* Vol 9(3), 347–66.

Vollm, B. A. (2009) 'Self-harm among UK female prisoners, a cross-sectional study' *Journal of Forensic Psychiatry and Psychology* Vol 20(4), 741–51.

von Hirsch, A. (1976) *Doing Justice: The Choice of Punishments*. New York, Hill and Wang.

von Hirsch, A. (1986) *Past or Future Crimes: Deservedness and Dangerousness in the Sentencing of Criminals*. Manchester, Manchester University Press.

von Hirsch, A. (1993) *Censure and Sanctions*. Oxford, Clarendon.

von Hirsch, A. (1998) 'Selective Incapacitation: Some Doubts' in A. von Hirsch and A. Ashworth (eds) *Principled Sentencing: Readings on Theory and Practice*. Oxford, Hart, 121–6.

von Hirsch, A. (1999) *Criminal Deterrence and Sentence Severity*. Oxford, Hart.

von Hirsch, A. and Ashworth, A. (1996) 'Protective Sentencing under Section 2(2)(b): The Criteria for Dangerousness' *Criminal Law Review*, 175–83.

von Hirsch, A. and Ashworth, A. (2005) *Proportionate Sentencing: Exploring the Principles*. Oxford, Oxford University Press.

von Hirsch, A. and Ashworth, A. (eds) (1998) *Principled Sentencing: Readings on Theory and Practice* (2nd edn). Oxford, Hart.

von Hirsch, A. and Roberts, J. (1997) 'Racial Disparity in Sentencing: Reflections on the Hood Study' *Howard Journal* Vol 36(3), 227–36.

von Hirsch, A. and Roberts, J. (2004) 'Legislating Sentencing Principles: The Provisions of the Criminal Justice Act 2003 Relating to Sentencing Purposes and the Role of Previous Convictions' *Criminal Law Review*, 639–52.

von Hirsch, A., Ashworth, A., and Shearing, C. (2005) 'Restorative Justice: A "Making Amends" Model?' in A. von Hirsch and A. Ashworth, *Proportionate Sentencing*. Oxford, Oxford University Press, 110–30.

von Hirsch, A., Bottoms, A. E., Burney, E., and Wikstrom, P.-O. (1999) *Criminal Deterrence and Sentence Severity*. Oxford, Hart.

von Hirsch, A., Roberts, J., Bottoms, A., Roach, K., and Schiff, M. (eds) (2003) *Restorative Justice and Criminal Justice: Competing or Reconcilable Paradigms?* Oxford, Hart.

Wacquant, L. (2001a) *Prisons of Poverty.* Minneapolis, University of Minnesota Press.

Wacquant, L. (2001b) 'Deadly Symbiosis: When Ghetto and Prison Meet and Mesh' *Punishment and Society* Vol 3(1), 95–133.

Wacquant, L. (2007) *Urban Outcasts: A Comparative Study of Advanced Marginality.* Cambridge, Polity Press.

Wacquant, L. (2008a) 'Ghettos and Anti-Ghettos: An Anatomy of the New Urban Poverty' *Thesis Eleven* Vol 94, 113–18.

Wacquant, L. (2008b) *Urban Outcasts.* Cambridge, Polity Press.

Wacquant, L. (2009) *Prisons of Poverty.* Minneapolis, University of Minnesota Press.

Wahidin, A. (2004), *Older Women in the Criminal Justice System.* London, Jessica Kingsley.

Waiton, S. (2008) *The Politics of Antisocial Behaviour: Amoral Panics.* London, Routledge.

Walker, K. (2011) 'Equality before the law: Race and social factors as sources of mitigation in sentencing' in J. Roberts (ed) *Mitigation and Aggravation at Sentencing.* Cambridge, Cambridge University Press, 124–45.

Walker, N. (1985) *Sentencing: Theory, Law and Practice.* Oxford, Oxford University Press.

Walker, N. (1991) *Why Punish?* Oxford, Oxford University Press.

Walker, N. (1999) *Aggravation, Mitigation and Mercy in English Criminal Justice,* Oxford, Blackstone.

Walker, S. and Beckett, C. (2003) *Social Work Assessment and Intervention.* Lyme Regis, Russell House.

Walklate, S. (2004) 'Justice for All in the 21st Century: The Political Context of the Policy Focus on Victims' in E. Cape (ed) *Reconcilable Rights?* London, Legal Action Group, 27–36.

Walklate, S. (2011) 'Review' *New Criminal Law Review Vol 14(2), 330.*

Wallis, E. (2001) 'A New Choreography—An Integrated Strategy for the National Probation Service for England and Wales' *Strategic Framework 2001–2004.* London, Home Office.

Walsh, C. (2011) 'Youth Justice and Neuroscience, a dual-use dilemma' *British Journal of Criminology* Vol 51(1), 21–39.

Walton, A. S. (1983) 'Hegel, Utilitarianism and the Common Good' *Ethics* Vol 93, 753–71.

Ward, T. and Maruna, S. (2007) *Rehabilitation, Beyond the Risk Paradigm.* London, Routledge.

Wargent, M. (2002) 'The New Governance of Probation' *Howard Journal* Vol 41(2), 182–200.

Warner, K. and Davis, J. (2012) 'Using Jurors to explore public attitudes to sentencing' *British Journal of Criminology* Vol 52(1), 93–112.

Warr, M. (1989) 'What Is the Perceived Seriousness of Crimes?' *Criminology* Vol 27(4), 795–821.

Wasik, M. (1983) 'Excuses at the Sentencing Stage' *Criminal Law Review,* 450–65.

Wasik, M. (2001) 'The Vital Importance of Certain Previous Convictions' *Criminal Law Review,* 363–73.

Wasik, M. and Turner, A. (1992) 'Sentencing Guidelines for the Magistrates Courts' *Criminal Law Review,* 345–56.

Wasik, M. and von Hirsch, A. (1988) 'Non-Custodial Penalties and the Principles of Desert' *Criminal Law Review,* 555–71.

Wasik, M. and von Hirsch, A. (1994) 'Section 29 Revisited: Previous Convictions in Sentencing' *Criminal Law Review,* 409–18.

WASIK, M., GIBBONS, T., AND REDMAYNE, M. (1999) *Criminal Justice, Text and Materials*. London, Longman.

WATERS, I. (2007) 'The Policing of Young Offenders' *British Journal of Criminology* Vol 47(4), 635–54.

WATSON, S. AND RICE, S. (with prisoners at HMP Wolds) (2004) *Daddy's Working Away*. London, Care for the Family.

WEATHERBURN, D. AND MOFFATT, S. (2011) 'The Specific Deterrent Effect of Higher Fines on Drink-Driving Offenders' *British Journal of Criminology* Vol 5(5), 789–803.

WEIJERS, I. (2002) 'The Moral Dialogue: A Pedagogical Perspective on Juvenile Justice' in I. Weijers and A. Duff (eds) *Punishing Juveniles: Principles and Critique*. Oxford, Hart, 135–54.

WEIJERS, I. AND DUFF, A. (2002) 'Introduction: Themes in Juvenile Justice' in I. Weijers and A. Duff (eds) *Punishing Juveniles: Principles and Critique*. Oxford, Hart, 1–21.

WEITEKAMP, E. AND KERNER, H. -J. (eds) (2002) *Restorative Justice: Theoretical Foundations*. Cullompton, Willan.

WELSH, B. C. AND FARRINGTON, D. P. (2002) *Crime Prevention Effects of Closed Circuit Television: A Systematic Review*, Home Office Research Study No 252. London, Home Office.

WELSH, B. C. AND FARRINGTON, D. P. (eds) (2006) *Preventing Crime: What Works for Chidren, Offenders, Victims and Places*. New York, Springer.

WELSHMAN, J. (2007) *From Transmitted Deprivation to Social Exclusion: Policy, Poverty and Parenting*. Bristol, Policy Press.

WHITTACKER, C. AND MACKIE, A. (1997) *Enforcing Financial Penalties*, Home Office Research Study No 165. London, Home Office.

WHITTY, N. (2011) 'Human Rights as Risk, UK Prisons and the Management of Right and Risks' *Punishment and Society* Vol 13(2), 123–48.

WILCOX, A., YOUNG, R., AND HOYLE, C. (2004) *An Evaluation of the Impact of Restorative Cautioning: Findings from a Reconviction Study*, Home Office Findings 255. London, Home Office.

WILKINSON, C. AND EVANS, R. (1990) 'Police Cautioning of Juveniles—The Impact of Circular 14/1985' *Criminal Law Review*, 165–76.

WILLIAMS, B. (1999) 'The Victims Charter: Citizens as Consumers of the Criminal Justice Service' *Howard Journal* Vol 38(4), 384–96.

WILLIAMS, J. (2007) 'Incorporating Children's Rights: The Divergence in Law and Policy' *Legal Studies* Vol 27(2), 261–87.

WILSON, D. (2003) '"Keeping Quiet" or "Going Nuts": Some Emerging Strategies Used by Young Black People in Custody at a Time of Childhood Being Re-constructed' *Howard Journal* Vol 42(5), 411–25.

WILSON, D. AND MCCABE, S. (2002) 'How HMP Grendon Works in the Words of Those Undergoing Therapy' *Howard Journal* Vol 41(3), 279–91.

WILSON, E. AND HINKS, S. (2011) *Assessing the Predictive Validity of the Asset Youth Risk Assessment Tool using the Juvenile Cohort Study* (JCS), Ministry of Justice Research Series 10/11. London, Ministry of Justice.

WILSON, J. Q. (1985) *Thinking about Crime* (2nd edn). New York, Vintage Books.

WINDZIO, M. (2006) 'Is There a Deterrent Effect of Pains of Imprisonment? The Impact of "Social Costs" of First Incarceration on the Hazard Rate of Recidivism' *Punishment and Society* Vol 8(3), 341–64.

WINTERDYK, J. A. (2002) *Juvenile Justice Systems, International Perspectives*. Toronto, Canadian Scholars Press.

WINTERDYK, J. A. (2005) 'Juvenile Justice in the International era' in P. Reichel (ed) *Handbook of Transnational Crime and Justice*. Thousand Oaks: Sage.

Wolpin, K. I. (1978) 'An Economic Analysis of Crime and Punishment in England and Wales, 1894–1967' *Journal of Political Economy* Vol 86, 815–40.

Wonnacott, C. (1999) 'The Counterfeit Contract—Reform, Pretence and Muddled Principles in the New Referral Order' *Child and Family Law Quarterly* 271.

Wood, A. (1972) 'The Marxian Critique of Justice' *Philosophy and Public Affairs* Vol 1(3) 244–82.

Wood, A. (2004) *Karl Marx* (2nd edn). London, Routledge.

Wood, J. and Kemshall, H. (2007) *The Operation and Experience of Multi-Agency Public Protection Arrangements*, Home Office Findings 285. London, Home Office.

Woodcock, J. (1994) *The Escape from Whitemoor Prison on Friday 9th September 1994*, the *Woodcock Enquiry*, Cm 2741. London, HMSO.

Woolf, H. and Tumim, S. (1991) *Prison Disturbances April 1990*. Report of an Inquiry, Cm 1456. London, HMSO.

Woolf, Lord (2003) Speech, Perrie Lecture Awards, 6 June.

Woolford, A. and Ratner, R. S. (2007) *Informal Reckonings: Conflict Resolution in Mediation, Restorative Justice and Reparations*. London, Routledge-Cavendish.

Worrall, A. (1990) *Offending Women: Female Law-breakers and the Criminal Justice System*. London, Routledge.

Worrall, A. (1997) *Punishment in the Community*. London, Addison Wesley Longman.

Worrall, A. and Gelsthorpe (2009) 'What Works with Women Offenders, the Past 30 Years' *Probation Journal* Vol 56(4), 329–45.

Worrall, A. and Hoy, C. (2005) *Punishment in the Community* (2nd edn). Cullompton, Willan.

Wright, M. (1996) *Justice for Victims and Offenders* (2nd edn). Winchester, Waterside Press.

Young, J. (2002) 'Crime and Social Exclusion' in M. Maguire, R. Morgan, and R. Reiner (eds) *The Oxford Handbook of Criminology* (3rd edn). Oxford, Oxford University Press, 457–90.

Young , J. (1999) *The Exclusive Society*. London, Sage.

Young, P. (1989) 'Punishment, Money and a Sense of Justice' in P. Carlen and D. Cook (eds) *Paying for Crime*. Milton Keynes, Open University Press, 46–65.

Young, P. (1997) *Crime and Criminal Justice in Scotland*. Edinburgh, Stationery Office.

Youth Justice Board (2001) *Youth at Risk? A national survey of risk factors, protective factors and problem behaviour among young people in England, Scotland and Wales*, London, YJB.

Youth Justice Board (2004a) *MORI Youth Survey*. London, YJB.

Youth Justice Board (2004b) *Restorative Justice in the Juvenile Secure Estate*. London, YJB.

Youth Justice Board (2006a) *Anti-social Behaviour Orders (Summary)*. London, YJB.

Youth Justice Board (2006b) *Managing Children and Young People's Behaviour in the Secure Estate: A Code of Practice*. London, YJB.

Youth Justice Board (2006c) *Dangerousness and the New Sentences for Public Protection: Guidance for Youth Offending Teams*. London, YJB.

Youth Justice Board (2006d) *Common Assessment Framework, Draft Guidance for Youth Offending Teams*. London, YJB.

Youth Justice Board (2008) *Referral Order Action Plan 2009–10*. London, YJB.

Youth Justice Board (2009a) *Youth Survey 2008: Young people in mainstream education*. London, YJB

Youth Justice Board (2009b) *Girls and Offending—Patterns, Perceptions and Interventions*. London, YJB.

Youth Justice Board (2010) *National Standards for Youth Justice Services*, B420. London, YJB.

Youth Justice Board (2011a) *Monthly Data and Analysis Custody Report—April 2011*. London, YJB.

Youth Justice Board/Ministry of Justice (2011b) *Youth Justice Statistics 2009/10 England and Wales Statistics Bulletin*. London, YJB.

Youth Justice Board (2011c) *Youth Restorative Disposal Process Evaluation*, London, Ministry of Justice.

Youth Justice Board (2011d) *Monthly Youth Custody Report October 2011*. London, YJB.

Zedner, L. (2003) 'The Concept of Security: An Agenda for Comparative Analysis' *Legal Studies* Vol 23(1), 151–76.

Zehr, H. (1985) 'Retributive Justice, Restorative Justice' *New Perspectives in Crime and Justice* Vol 4. Akron, PA: MCC Office of Crime and Justice.

Zimring, F. (2001) 'Imprisonment Rates and the New Politics of Criminal Punishment' in D. Garland (ed) *Mass Imprisonment*. London, Sage, 145–9.

Zimring, F. (2005) *American Juvenile Justice*. New York, Oxford University Press.

Zimring, F. and Hawkins, G. (1986) *Capital Punishment and the American Agenda*. New York, Cambridge University Press.

Zimring, F. and Hawkins, G. (1995) *Incapacitation: Penal Confinement and the Restraint of Crime*. New York, Oxford University Press.

Index